CATHERINE
THE GREAT

CATHERINE THE GREAT

Life and Legend

John T. Alexander

OXFORD UNIVERSITY PRESS
New York   Oxford

Oxford University Press

Oxford   New York   Toronto
Delhi   Bombay   Calcutta   Madras   Karachi
Petaling Jaya   Singapore   Hong Kong   Tokyo
Nairobi   Dar es Salaam   Cape Town
Melbourne   Auckland

and associated companies in
Berlin   Ibadan

Copyright © 1989 by Oxford University Press, Inc.

Published by Oxford University Press, Inc.,
200 Madison Avenue, New York, New York 10016
Oxford is a registered trademark of Oxford University Press

Library of Congress Cataloging-in-Publication Data

Alexander, John T.
Catherine the Great : life and legend / John T. Alexander.
p.   cm.
Bibliography: p.
Includes index.

1. Catherine II, Empress of Russia, 1729-1796.   2. Soviet Union—
Kings and rulers—Biography.   3. Soviet Union—History—Catherine II,
1762-1796.   I. Title.
DK170.A58 1989
947'.063'0924—dc19
[B]   88-10122

Credits for illustrations following page 178 (in order)
Sochineniia Imperatritsy Ekateriny II, vol. 12, ed. A. N. Pypin (Spb., 1907)/Giacomo Casanova, *History of My Life,* vol. 10, tr. Willard Trask (N.Y., 1970)/*Iz proshlogo: istoricheskie materialy leib-gvardii Semenovskago polka* (Spb., 1911)/*Sochineniia Imperatritsy Ekateriny II,* vol. 12, ed. A. N. Pypin (Spb., 1970/*Starye gody* (July–September 1911)/*Iz proshlogo: istoricheskie materialy leib-gvardii Semenovskago polka* (Spb., 1911)/The Rosenbach Museum and Library, Philadelphia/*Starye gody* February 1911)/Heinz Müller-Dietz and Eduard D. Gribanov, *Medizin und Ärzte auf russischen Medaillen* (Berlin, 1984), reproduced with the permission of Professor-Dr. Müller-Dietz/L. Ia. Skorokhodov, *Materialy po istorii meditsinskoi mikrobiologii v dorevoliutsionnoi Rossii* (M., 1948)/Photograph by John T. Alexander, 1971/Graphics Department, State Historical Museum in Moscow/*Literaturnoe nasledstvo,* vols. 9 and 10 (M., 1933)/A. K. Lebedev, *Russkaia istoricheskaia zhivopis' do oktiabria 1917 goda* (M., 1962)/*Starye gody* (June 1913)/*Starye gody* (July–September 1911)/K. V. Mikhailova and G. V. Smirnov, *Portretnaia miniatiura iz sobraniia gosudarstvennogo Russkogo muzeia,* vol. 1 (L., 1974)/*Starye gody* (July–September 1910)/I. N. Bozherianov, "Nevskii prospekt," vol. 2 (Spb., 1902)/*Kamerfur'erskii zhurnal,* 1787 (Spb., 1886)/Reproduced by courtesy of the Trustees of the British Museum/*The Satirical Etchings of James Gillray,* ed. Draper Hill (N.Y., 1976), reproduced with the permission of Dover Publications, Inc./Peter Cowie, ed., *World Filmography, 1968* (London, 1968), reproduced with the permission of Tantivy Press, Ltd./Copyright by Universal Pictures, a division of Universal City Studios, Inc. Courtesy of MCA Publicity Rights, a division of MCA, Inc./Jon Tuska, *The Films of Mae West* (Secaucus, N.J.: Citadel Press, 1973), reproduced with the permission of Lyle Stuart, Inc./Reproduced from photographs supplied by Steve Allen.

Printed in the United States of America

To Maria, the other empress in my life,
with love and heartfelt gratitude

Preface

The woman who became known as Catherine the Great led a life so full of varied activities in such exotic settings, amid so many dramatic events and memorable personalities, that it took on all the trappings of legend. Throughout her lengthy, turbulent career (1729–1796) she confronted multiple crises—personal and political, physical and psychological. She seemed to surmount them all so successfully that her long reign (from 1762 to 1796) ranks among the most celebrated in Russian, European, and world history. Almost two centuries after her death, she still enjoys immense recognition as celebrity, superstar, and sex symbol—reputations that show no sign of flagging. Both the culturally literate and the ordinary public know her name and sense her fame or notoriety.

The many books about Catherine the Great may be divided into two main types: broad popular treatments that are long on gossip and drama but short on facts and context, and specialized scholarly studies that are often inaccessible to general readers. This book aspires to bridge the chasm between the two. It aims to utilize both specialized literature and popular accounts, together with a broad cross section of published and unpublished sources, for the purpose of presenting a balanced biography accessible to the average educated reader. In contrast to most popular biographies, which follow Catherine's autobiographical writings in their disproportionate focus on her life before she seized the throne, my attention will concentrate on her long reign: the personality, actions, policies, and events that made her career memorable for millions of people over many generations. Relatively less space will be apportioned to Catherine's early life, not because it was unimportant for her later years, but because that period is better known through her own so-called memoirs and, more particularly, because her primary claim to fame rests on her multiple roles as sovereign ruler of the emergent political colossus of Europe and Asia—the multinational Russian Empire.

Some of the attractions of Catherine's life are the controversies that she stirred in contemporaries and posterity alike. Nobody reacts neutrally to her. You are infatuated and intrigued by her charm immediately, or dismayed and disgusted by her supposed hypocrisy, vanity, conceit, brazen ambition, manipulation, and exploitation of others. Her career raises fundamental issues between the sexes. Is it any surprise that women writers have generally treated her more sympathetically than their male counterparts? Or that the scandalous, pornographic tales about her private life are overwhelmingly the product of male imaginations? Indeed, the images of Catherine that have spanned three centuries testify to the strong emotions her life aroused at the time and long afterwards. On the one hand, the title and surtitle added to her Russian name—*Empress* Catherine *the Great*—conjure up notions of imperial splendor, military glory, political genius, territorial advance, and intellectual brilliance. Challenging such praise, on the other hand, are the attacks of an army of critics and moralists who brand her an adultress, usurper, murderess, tyrant, conqueror, oppressor, hypocrite, egotist, bad mother, nymphomaniac, and worse. One favorite label, applied by friend and foe, is "the Semiramis of the North"—after the mythical Queen of Babylonia who used charm and religion to usurp the throne and rule over her contentious subjects. Another comparison was with Messalina, the lustful third wife of the Roman Emperor Claudius who was executed by her enemies in A.D. 48.

This biography will look into the basis of such adulation and condemnation. It evinces neither prudish disdain for the charges of sexual license, nor prurient preoccupation with their significance. The main effort will be to present Catherine as ruler of the largest territorial political unit in modern history. That she was a fascinating woman with wide interests will also be explored. And her own endeavors to influence posterity's opinion of her reign will be explicated, for she was always concerned about her image.

Anyone who ruled such a large state for more than three decades would rank as a significant historical personage. It is doubly odd, therefore, that such a figure should go unheralded (or be spurned) in the USSR today. No Soviet author has yet published a biography of Catherine, in sharp contrast to the continual praise heaped on her illustrious predecessor, Peter the Great. Several reasons may be suggested for such neglect. For one, Catherine's foreign origins may challenge Russian national self-esteem. For another, her sex and her checkered reputation may not help her cause with the overwhelmingly male, officially Victorian historical establishment in the Soviet Union, where a nationalistic brand of Marxism-Leninism finds little justification for the study of a great, female, foreign-born, pre-revolutionary sovereign. Such attitudes have caused most Soviet writers to shy away from Catherine and her era in general, except for the study of rebels and critics of various sorts. Fortunately, much basic research was accomplished and published in Russia before 1917, and British, European, and North American scholars have extended this tradition during the last few decades, tapping Soviet archives in the process. The moment seems ripe for a fresh look at Catherine that will synthesize Russian and foreign scholarship.

The present study differs from others, most of all, in its concept of Catherine's life as a series of crises and conquests, psychological and political. Despite her own efforts to celebrate will power and wit in explanation of her triumphant life against unfavorable odds, her own voluminous writings and the testimony of contemporaries convey abundant hints of doubts, uncertainties, anxieties, frustrations, and fears, all of which depict her development in terms at once more human and more conventional than the encomia or slander of her own and later generations. In reconstructing her life I have given greater attention than usual to questions of health, mental and physical alike, and have attempted to address soberly the issue of her sexuality. This presentation taps graphic as well as written sources. It uses several little known caches of Catherine's letters: her love notes to Peter Zavadovskii, her informal notes to Procurator-General Viazemskii, and her letters to Governor-General Saltykov. This presentation draws extensively on the officially published court ceremonial journals, a rich source (perhaps 20,000 pages for Catherine's reign) strangely neglected by previous scholars. It also cites some manuscript sources and many unpublished dissertations. These pages seek to convey an intimate appraisal of Catherine's career in the context of her time and in the light of recent scholarship on Russian and European history.

Lawrence, Kansas   J. T. A.
March 1988

Acknowledgments

As a work of synthesis this book has drawn on more than twenty years of research at home and abroad that involved scores of institutions and individuals. For purposes of brevity, however, I will here enumerate only those institutions and individuals that contributed directly to my work on this manuscript over the past seven years. Financial support and release time were provided by a semester-long sabbatical grant from the University of Kansas in the spring of 1981 and by summer grants from its General Research Fund: no. 3708 for 1979–80, no. 3680 for 1981–82, no. 3308 for 1982–83, no. 3748 for 1984–85, no. 3453 for 1986–87, and no. 3528 for 1987–88. Outside assistance was received from the Kennan Institute for Advanced Russian Studies, which supported a month's research in Washington, D.C., in January 1981 and again in June 1987; from the Penrose Fund of the American Philosophical Society (no. 9216 in 1982); and from the National Endowment for the Humanities travel to collections program (RY-20639-84) in 1984. Research was conducted at the following libraries: the Watson, Kenneth E. Spencer Research, and Helen F. Spencer Art Libraries of the University of Kansas; the Library of Congress, the Indiana University Library, and the Library of the University of Illinois at Champaign-Urbana. At the last named institution three sojourns at the summer research laboratory on Russia and East Europe, in 1979, 1982, and 1984, resulted in much intellectual stimulation from a variety of scholars, especially Marianna Choldin, Ralph Fisher, Maurice Friedberg, David Ransel, and Benjamin Uroff among the local staff, and from fellow participants Kenneth Craven, James Duran, Karen Rasmussen, Mary Hrabik-Samal, and Mary Zirin. Portions of this study were inflicted on conference or public audiences at San Antonio in 1982, Albuquerque and Vancouver in 1983, Urbana, Bloomington, Columbia, and Hays in 1984, London, Aberystwyth, and Leeds in 1985, Reno and New Orleans in 1986, Washington, Chapel Hill, and Wichita in 1987, and Long Beach in 1988.

Specific materials and information were obtained from the Department of Prints and Drawings of the British Museum in London, The Rosenbach Museum and Library, Philadelphia, from Steve Allen and Jayne Meadows Allen, and from Norman Saul, Max Okenfuss, Jerry Stannard, Vernon Chamberlin, Heinz Müller-Dietz, Lynn Nelson, Bob Hudson, and Susan Meyer-Strom. Herbert Galton kindly helped with some problems of translation. Isabel de Madariaga, the recognized senior specialist in this field, gave me the benefit of her immense knowledge and insight in an extensive critique that corrected many errors and imperfections. Gary Marker also suggested several improvements. The Kansas University Cartographic Service prepared the maps and graphics. The manuscript was processed and reprocessed with accuracy, patience, and good cheer by Sandee Kennedy, Pam LeRow, Beth Ridenour, and Denisa Brown of the Word Processing Center in Wescoe Hall. Nancy Lane and Rosemary Wellner provided expert editorial guidance. I thank all these individuals and institutions; none of them is responsible, of course, for the use I have made of their assistance.

Contents

I

Catherine's Youth and Her Accession to the Throne

1

Catherine's Coup d'état

By five A.M. on 28 June 1762 dawn would have dispersed the last vestiges of the "white nights" that illuminate the brief St. Petersburg summer. Catherine, the estranged wife of Emperor Peter III of Russia, was awakened that Friday morning in the small palace of Mon Plaisir built for Peter the Great in his favorite summer residence of Peterhof twenty-nine kilometers from the new imperial capital. A chambermaid announced her visitor, Aleksei Orlov, the ferocious scar-faced brother of her current lover and one of the principal backers of her bid for the throne. "Time to rise," he advised; "everything is prepared to proclaim you." When Catherine inquired about specifics, Orlov replied that their fellow conspirator Captain Passek had been arrested. That meant they must act at once, before the Emperor heard the news at his nearby estate of Oranienbaum. Catherine dressed quickly, followed Orlov through the gardens to his coach, and sat tensely as the vehicle hurtled toward Petersburg.[1]

If one cannot reconstruct Catherine's thoughts as she hurried to claim her great destiny, the circumstances that inspired them can be briefly sketched. The threat of death, physical or political, animated her conspiracy. At a formal dinner three weeks earlier the erratic Emperor had publicly humiliated her by shrieking that she was a fool (*dura!*) in declining to rise for a toast. Moreover, it was widely believed that he had ordered her arrest that same evening in preparation for incarcerating her in a convent, disinheriting their son Grand Duke Paul Petrovich, and marrying his fat, ugly mistress, Elizaveta Vorontsova. But her uncle from Holstein, Prince Georg, had supposedly talked Peter out of such rash measures. Nevertheless, rumors were rife that the Emperor wished to rid himself of his troublesome spouse, by prison or by poison.[2]

This drama involved issues far weightier than an eighteenth-century court

3

soap opera. The future of the mighty Russian Empire and its ruling dynasty was at stake. In less than six months of rule Peter III had managed to offend important segments of the narrow elite that administered the Empire's central institutions. His piercing voice, foreign accent, contempt for things Russian, and drunken antics irritated the Russian courtiers who could not understand why his aunt, the childless Empress Elizabeth, had brought the sickly simpleton from his native Holstein to become heir presumptive to the all-Russian throne. Many suspected that only Elizabeth's death on 25 December 1761 had foiled a plan to set aside her bumptious nephew in favor of his son with Catherine as regent. Peter's outspoken Prussophile sentiments, his public avowal that he would gladly serve under his idol Frederick the Great, outraged Russian patriotism inflamed by six years of bloody warfare against Prussia. Insult superseded injury when Peter III abruptly pulled Russia out of the conflict, thereby extricating "Old Fritz" from a critical position, and then allied with him to declare war on Denmark for the purpose of recovering Holstein territory. Furthermore, his Lutheran proclivities combined with his scorn for Russian Orthodox ritual to incite anxiety among the Russian clergy. That anxiety took on sharper tones when the Emperor ordered church estates, and the peasants bound to them, to be secularized under direct state control. He even halted persecution of the schismatic Old Believers and offered those who had fled abroad incentives to return. The Orthodox hierarchy was not pleased.[3]

Even more blatantly provocative were steps that seemed to challenge the Empire's political bases. Enraptured with military drill as only an armchair commander can be, Peter III strove to upgrade Russia's army after the Prussian pattern. He scorned the elite Guards regiments as "janissaries"—a military liability and a political menace—ordered expensive new uniforms in the Prussian style, disbanded one unit, and constantly drilled the others. Meanwhile, the stature of the Holstein regiment climbed higher and higher, to the deepening jealousy of other units. Some Guardsmen surmised that the ultimate aim was to abolish the Guards altogether, a move fraught with political implications because of their noble composition and their strategic location in the capital. Prominent aristocrats such as Count Kirill Razumovskii and Prince Nikita Trubetskoi were promoted to high military rank and required to drill their units in person, discomfiting them and their troops alike.[4] Even the celebrated emancipation of the nobility from compulsory state service in peacetime, an enactment warmly received in most quarters, contained the troubling implication that the nobility might forfeit its traditional role in society and find its functions taken over by pen-pushing bureaucrats, commoners, and foreign favorites. Finally, in regard to civil administration, the new Emperor reorganized procedures in a way that undermined the status of the Governing Senate, an executive and judicial council comprising a cross section of the Russian power elite.[5]

Abolition of the dreaded political police, the so-called Secret Chancery, together with the return of several prominent personages from exile, could not compensate for the Emperor's affronts to Russian national sentiments. There was nothing to prevent the restoration of the political police whenever the sovereign needed it, as time would show, although the temporary eclipse of that venerable Russian institution may have weakened Peter's regime in the crucial months ahead. Thus Peter III appeared to be aiming for a more centralized, bureaucratic regime than his indolent aunt had favored. It seemed certain that foreigners would play key roles under the foreign-born Emperor.[6]

All these policy changes left influential groups and individuals threatened, disgruntled, anxious. Catherine headed the list of those aggrieved. She enjoyed widespread sympathy and valuable personal contacts, beginning with her lover Grigorii Orlov, whose towering physique, courage in battle, free-spending manner, and amorous exploits had all secured a spirited following among his fellow Guardsmen. He worked closely with his four brothers. As the mother of Grand Duke Paul Petrovich, age seven, Catherine also cultivated the goodwill of Nikita Panin, an experienced diplomat who supervised her son's education as his "governor." Panin had suffered personal insult at the Emperor's hands, feared for his own and his pupil's future, and detested the arbitrary, capricious policies of the new regime. In Catherine he saw a promising alternative and hoped that she might agree to take the throne as regent until Paul attained his majority. A third kind of support accrued to Catherine from persons such as Princess Ekaterina Dashkova, born Vorontsova, the nineteen-year-old sister of Peter III's mistress. Eager for fame and fortune, Dashkova was as enthralled by Catherine's charm and shrewdness as she was appalled by her sister's taste in lovers. Her family's eminence facilitated extensive acquaintanceships within the governmental elite.[7]

These three different factions—the Orlovs, Panin, and Dashkova—all wanted Catherine to reign for different reasons. Of course, Catherine had her own reasons, and she kept the three factions largely unaware of each other's efforts. The role of coordinator she reserved for herself, making liberal use of money secretly advanced by the anti-Prussian governments of Denmark, Austria, and France.[8] Since arriving in Russia in 1744, she had sensed a great future. Bitter experience and self-education had prepared her to make the future her own, which she did on 28 June 1762 when she "fled" from Peterhof back to St. Petersburg.

At the time that Catherine's flight turned into triumph she was thirty-three years old. If the first flush of youth had faded, her appearance and manner captivated all who saw her. "Nature seemed to have formed this Princess for the highest state of human elevation," remarked Claude Carloman de Rulhière, an employee of the French embassy in Petersburg, who left this portrait of Catherine:

> Her figure is noble and agreeably impressive; her gait majestic; her person and deportment graceful in the highest degree. Her air is that of a sovereign. Every feature proclaims a superior character. Her neck is lofty, and the head finely detached. The union of these two parts, especially in profile, possesses wonderful beauty; and this beauty, in the movements of her head, she has the art of setting off to wonderful advantage. Her forehead is large and open; the nose borders on the aquiline; her mouth is sweetly fresh, and embellished by a singularly regular and beautiful set of teeth, the chin somewhat plump, and rather inclin-

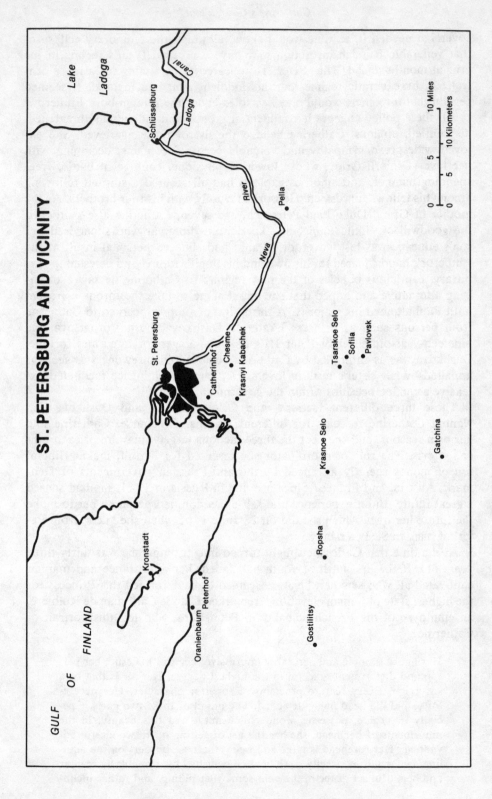

ST. PETERSBURG AND VICINITY

Lake Ladoga

Schlüsselburg

Ladoga Canal

Neva River

Pella

St. Petersburg

Catherinhof

Chesme

Krasnyi Kabachek

Tsarskoe Selo

Sofiia

Pavlovsk

Krasnoe Selo

Gatchina

Kronstadt

GULF OF FINLAND

Ropsha

Peterhof

Oranienbaum

Gostilitsy

10 Miles

10 Kilometers

5

5

0

0

ing to double, but without the smallest tendency to fatness. Her hair is chestnut-coloured, and uncommonly fine; the eyebrows are dark brown; the eyes hazel, and extremely fascinating. The reflexes of light give them a bluish tint; and her complexion is dazzlingly clear. Loftiness is the true character of her physiognomy, taken as a whole. The softer characters of gentleness and goodness, which are there likewise depicted, appear, to a penetrating observer, only as the effort of an ardent desire to please; and those seductive expressions discover but too plainly an intention to seduce.[9]

Five kilometers outside Petersburg, after Catherine's exhausted horses had pulled up lame, Grigorii Orlov whisked her into his small coach and conducted his mistress to the suburban quarters of the Izmailovskii Guards. The bleary-eyed Guardsmen, roused by Orlov, streamed out to receive their "Little Mother" (*matiushka*) as their new sovereign, and to repudiate Peter III by swearing allegiance to Catherine. Hurrahs punctuated the morning quiet. Some soldiers kissed her hand or the hem of her dress. Others wept with joy. Several assisted the regiment's venerable priest, Father Aleksei, as he approached, cross in hand, to administer the new oath of allegiance. Count Kirill Razumovskii, colonel of the regiment and longtime admirer of Catherine, hurried forward to kiss her hand on bended knee.[10] Whether choreographed or improvised on the spot, the first phase of the coup had proceeded without a hitch. It was planned to be a bloodless palace revolution—swift and safe and lucrative for those who backed the winner. All assumed the common people would applaud the revolt.

Toward eight o'clock the excited crowd formed a column behind Father Aleksei and Count Razumovskii and then convoyed Catherine's carriage through town toward the quarters of the Semenovskii Guards. The news had preceded them, however, so that crowds of *Semenovtsy* rushed out to greet their new sovereign. The multiplying crowd diverted the procession from visiting the other Guards quarters and led it onto Nevskii Prospekt, the capital's central avenue. Meanwhile, companies from Peter III's favorite Guards regiment, the Preobrazhenskii, ignored attempts by some officers to restrain them from joining the crowds then streaming toward the center of town. When some *Preobrazhentsy* overtook the procession on Nevskii Prospekt they apologized for their lateness and loudly declared: "We want the same thing our brethren do!"[11]

Growing by the minute, the dense crowd filled the broad avenue as it slowly moved toward the Church of Our Lady of Kazan. Catherine entered the packed church in the company of the Orlovs, Count Razumovskii, Prince Volkonskii, Count Bruce, Count Stroganov, and a throng of Guards officers. Priests greeted her with icons, offered prayers for the long life of "autocratrix Catherine the Second" and of her heir Tsarevich Paul Petrovich, and rang the church bells as the procession resumed its progress toward the Winter Palace. Surrounded by grandees on horseback, with Grigorii Orlov on the running board of her two-seat carriage, Catherine waved and smiled to the crowd as she arrived at the Winter Palace about ten A.M.[12]

On the squares before and beside the palace, regiments of regular troops

stood guard and quickly swore the oath of allegiance read by Veniamin, archbishop of Petersburg. Inside the palace the same oath was administered to
everybody there including many high court, military, and ecclesiastical officials. For several hours the palace was open to anyone who wished to see the
Empress. As a further gesture to the crowds, Nikita Panin hustled young Paul
Petrovich, still clad in night clothes, from the Summer Palace to the Winter
Palace, where Catherine displayed her son from the balcony to joyous exclamations. There was no talk of a regency, however, since neither Catherine
nor the Orlovs favored any such arrangement.[13]

That morning the Empress's first manifesto—composed by Grigorii Teplov
and Kirill Razumovskii, printed a few days earlier, and concealed by the
Piedmontese Odart—announced her assumption of the throne but made no
mention of Paul.[14] Her accession was justified by claims that Orthodoxy had
been endangered, Russia's military glory sullied and enslaved by the alliance
with Prussia, and the Empire's institutions "completely undermined." "Therefore, being convinced of such danger to all our loyal subjects, We were compelled, accepting God and His justice as assistance, and especially seeing the
clear and unfeigned desire of all our loyal subjects, to mount our all-Russian
sovereign throne, wherein all our loyal subjects have solemnly given us the
oath." Assuredly, it was no oversight that the manifesto ignored Peter III's
person altogether. The absolutist political tradition of Russia held no place
for an ex-emperor who, once he lost the throne, was presumed to be politically
dead. An ambiguous phrase blamed the rapprochement with Prussia on "its
very miscreant," evidently meaning Peter III, but some thought the reference
was to Frederick II.[15]

Catherine and the conspirators spent the rest of the day consolidating their
coup. Troops were assigned to guard every approach to the capital with orders to prevent departures and detain anybody who arrived from Oranienbaum or Peterhof. Scant resistance occurred. The Life Cuirassiers Regiment,
one of Peter III's favorites, vacillated at news of the coup and could only be
brought to the oath after the arrest of its German officers. Prince Georg of
Holstein, whom many soldiers hated because of the favor he enjoyed with
Peter III, was arrested along with Policemaster-General Korf. The German
Korf, whom Catherine had carefully cultivated some months before, was
taken to swear his loyalty to the Empress, who named him to the Senate that
very evening; but Prince Georg was confined to his house, which the soldiers
vengefully looted. Within a few weeks, however, Prince Georg was awarded
100,000 rubles for his losses and allowed to return to Holstein with sixty-two
others. He died a year later. These incidents were exceptional, for the general
spirit in town was happy yet orderly, though the people and soldiers took
vodka and beer from the taverns for free. (Tavernkeepers and spirits merchants later submitted claims for about 105,000 rubles worth of drink lost
during Catherine's accession.) Some foreigners were rumored to have bought
barrels of vodka for distribution, to advertise their approval of the coup and
cushion themselves against popular animosity, especially anti-Prussian feeling. Perhaps for some of the same reasons, after noon the Empress left the
newly finished Winter Palace for the old wooden one where Elizabeth had

died. She was greeted enthusiastically by the troops still surrounding the palace and was surprised to notice that they had changed to the old uniforms of Elizabeth's time. The men gladly doffed the despised Prussian-style uniforms prescribed by the former Emperor.[16]

By two o'clock in the afternoon the initial excitement had waned. Petersburg was secure and Catherine was officially Empress. But what should she do about her husband and his courtiers at Oranienbaum? Obviously, he would try to rally support from troops outside the capital who had not yet acknowledged the new government. The Empress and her advisers therefore dispatched couriers to army and naval units with her manifesto and sheets for signatures to the oath of allegiance. They worried about the forces at Kronstadt in particular, for that island-fortress lay within sight of Oranienbaum. Peter III would find naval forces, infantry, and munitions there with which he might mount an attack on Petersburg or escape by sea. Since the conspirators were unsure how much of the day's events had become known in Kronstadt, they sent Admiral Talyzin with a note from Catherine empowering him to do whatever he thought fit. They also ordered Rear-Admiral Miloslavskii to administer the oath to naval units in the Gulf of Finland and guard against any seaborne assault from that direction. And they resolved the issue of Peter III's fate. On capture, he would be taken to the fortress-prison of Schlüsselburg, situated on an island at the source of the Neva River some forty kilometers upstream from the capital.[17]

Later in the afternoon several members of Peter III's entourage arrived from Peterhof, ostensibly to remonstrate with Catherine or, more likely, to switch allegiance while propriety still permitted. Chancellor Mikhail Vorontsov, for example, upbraided the Empress for her impetuosity. She led him to the window, gestured to the massed troops on the square below, and exclaimed: "You see—it's not I who is acting; I only obey the people's wish." Vorontsov submitted, soon followed by Prince Nikita Trubetskoi and Count Alexander Shuvalov. The most prominent officials of the old government had recognized the new regime.[18]

Catherine's confidence rose even higher at the news, relayed from spies at Peterhof, that Peter III had not yet concerted any countermeasures. Firmly in control of the capital, she resolved on an immediate offensive against her deposed consort. The Senate, to which she had just appointed four new members, received responsibility for Petersburg and for Grand Duke Paul Petrovich. As the Empress explained to the senators before she mounted her steed Brilliant about ten o'clock that evening: "I go now with the army to reinforce and to secure the throne, leaving to you, as my supreme government, with complete confidence, to guard the fatherland, the people, and my son."[19]

The "campaign" against Peterhof cast Catherine in a new role with scant precedent in Russia: a woman sovereign as commander-in-chief. It also challenged Peter III in the most direct fashion. A lifelong drillmaster imbued with "military mania," he never saw action until confronted by his wife at the head of overwhelming forces. Catherine reveled in her military role. An expert horsewoman, she bestrode the white stallion, saber in hand, dressed in the green uniform of a colonel of the Preobrazhenskii Guards—the same rank

Peter the Great had taken. As the platoons of Guards filed past in the twilight of the white night, they lustily cheered their new sovereign, who personally commanded the rearguard. Accompanying Catherine on horseback was Princess Dashkova, also dressed in a Guards uniform, and a convoy of high officials: Prince Trubetskoi, Count Buturlin, Count Razumovskii, Prince Volkonskii, Quartermaster-General Villebois, and Count Shuvalov. Aleksei Orlov led the advanceguard of cavalry and mounted hussars, which had left several hours earlier, followed by artillery units. All three detachments took the road along the Gulf of Finland toward Peterhof, confident that their advance would encounter little resistance. Indeed, fatigued by the day's tensions, excitement, and revelry, Catherine's army dawdled along the road. The rearguard only reached Krasnyi Kabachek, a tavern five kilometers outside Petersburg, at two A.M. There they stopped for a rest.[20]

The End of a Reign

The morning of 28 June, while Catherine was being enthroned in Petersburg, Peter III arose late at Oranienbaum with a throbbing headache. But his mood brightened after he watched his Holsteiners drill smartly. At one P.M. the Emperor, his mistress Vorontsova, the Prussian envoy Baron Goltz, and a score of courtiers climbed into conveyances for the short drive over to Peterhof, where they expected to dine with Catherine on the eve of Peter's and Paul's nameday. Imagine their astonishment when they found the Empress's palace empty! Peter scoured the premises, even looked under the bed, all the while complaining to his mistress: "I told you she was capable of anything!"[21]

Everybody sensed something awry. Soon three senior officials—Prince Trubetskoi, Count Shuvalov, and Count Vorontsov—proposed going to Petersburg to find Catherine and dissuade her from whatever folly had possessed her. Peter agreed. Trubetskoi and Shuvalov returned, but only the next day and as members of Catherine's triumphant troupe. In preparation for flight, the courtiers followed the Emperor down to the seashore, where several boats rocked at the wharf. A longboat pulled up with a Guards officer and fireworks for the celebration. On leaving Petersburg at nine o'clock that morning, the officer admitted, he had heard a tumult among the Preobrazhenskii Regiment and had seen soldiers running about with bared sabers proclaiming Catherine as their sovereign. This news demolished all doubts and hopes. Sobbing and moaning seized the stunned courtiers.[22]

Yet Peter and his aides quickly dispatched officers to Petersburg and Kronstadt to reconnoiter and rally troops for the Emperor. After this flurry of activity Peter spent the rest of the afternoon awaiting the return of his couriers and considering his options. He and his advisers decided that, for his safety, they should sail over to nearby Kronstadt, but Peter first wished to wait until they learned more exactly what had happened in Petersburg. Field Marshal Münnich, the eighty-year-old veteran of three previous coups whom Peter had brought back from exile, urged him to imitate Peter the Great by dashing into the capital with a select band of supporters to confront the conspirators

before they could get their footing. His bold plan was rejected as too hazard-
ous. Obviously, Peter III was not like his celebrated grandfather. Baron Goltz,
the Prussian envoy, suggested fleeing westward to Holstein, Finland, or the
Ukraine. Although none of these plans was adopted, General Count Peter
Devier was dispatched to Kronstadt at four P.M. with orders to prepare the
3,000-man garrison for the Emperor's arrival.[23]

General Gustav Nummers, the commandant of Kronstadt, found himself in
a quandary when Devier arrived at five o'clock with news of Peter's impending visit and, two hours later, a courier from Admiral Talyzin in Petersburg
brought a sealed order directing Nummers to isolate the island. Unsure what
to do, the commandant took no chances; he hid the secret order from General
Devier but allowed his aide, Prince Bariatinskii, to report back to Peterhof.
Nummers' uncertainty was soon resolved by the arrival of Admiral Talyzin
himself, who showed him Catherine's authorization. With Nummers' assistance, he promptly administered the oath of allegiance to the garrison and
the army and naval forces. General Devier was arrested. Then Talyzin put the
island-fortress on alert and sounded the alarm after eleven P.M. to make certain the troops were awake.[24]

Of all Peter's efforts, only the move to Kronstadt seemed ready by the
early evening. His other couriers had failed to return. Tired and tipsy, the
Emperor ordered the embarkation to Kronstadt. Forty-seven courtiers and
officials clambered aboard a galley and a yacht, which cast off at midnight
and caught the breeze toward the island-fortress. Within an hour the flotilla approached the Kronstadt harbor, where access was blocked by a boom.
The Emperor's galley dropped anchor and sent a boat to request removal of the
boom. But the sentry on the bastion refused with threats. Thinking that the
sentry was merely following General Devier's orders not to admit anybody,
Peter III identified himself, displayed his ribbon of St. Andrew, and loudly
demanded entry. The sentry yelled back that Peter III no longer existed, only
Catherine II. He was told to depart or he would be fired on, as the alarm
sounded inside Kronstadt.[25]

Since an armed vessel blocked the channel westward to the open sea, the
galley headed for Oranienbaum while the yacht returned to Peterhof. Utterly
unstrung, Peter descended into the cabin and fainted away. As Frederick the
Great remarked at the news of his disciple's overthrow, Peter III "let himself
be driven from the throne as a child is sent to bed."[26] His confused efforts to
mobilize support simply revealed his own ineptitude. Absolutism is an effective form of government only insofar as the sovereign can inspire loyalty or
fear. Peter III inspired neither and Catherine filled the political void.

After five o'clock in the morning of Saturday, 29 June, the Empress's army
resumed its march on Peterhof. Along the road they met deserters from the
Emperor's suite and arrested several Holsteiner hussars sent to reconnoiter.
At the Trinity Monastery appeared Vice-Chancellor Alexander Golitsyn with
a letter from Peter to Catherine in which he acknowledged his injustice to her,
promised to reform, and asked for reconciliation. The Empress declined to
reply, but she relaxed somewhat at the news that Aleksei Orlov's vanguard
had already occupied Peterhof and Oranienbaum without resistance or blood-

shed. Loud hurrahs and cannon salutes welcomed Catherine to Peterhof after ten A.M. A second letter, handwritten in pencil, arrived from Peter imploring forgiveness, renouncing the throne, and requesting permission to leave for Holstein with Vorontsova and General Gudovich. This time Catherine must have smiled, all the more so when the messenger, General Izmailov, offered to deliver Peter to her after he freely signed a formal abdication. The document was drafted on the spot and dispatched at once with General Izmailov, accompanied by Vice-Chancellor Golitsyn and Grigorii Orlov. Peter signed immediately. Shortly afterwards he entered his carriage, with Vorontsova, Gudovich, and Izmailov, and rode glumly over to Peterhof with a convoy of jubilant hussars and horse-guards. Throngs of troops greeted the ex-emperor with shouts of "Long Live Catherine the Second!"[27]

In a virtual trance Peter stepped out of the carriage and handed over his sword and his ribbon of St. Andrew. Vorontsova and Gudovich were led away under arrest. Taken to the room where he had frequently resided while visiting Peterhof, the ex-Emperor had to surrender his Preobrazhenskii Guards uniform. Nikita Panin visited Peter there and long remembered the pathetic sight, "the greatest misfortune of my life." So disoriented was Peter that he begged only not to be separated from his "Fräulein," Vorontsova. He did not even request a meeting with Catherine, who discreetly avoided witnessing her husband's humiliation.[28]

Later that afternoon a select guard led by Aleksei Orlov, Captain Passek, whose arrest had triggered the start of the coup, Prince Fedor Bariatinskii, and Lieutenant Baskakov supervised Peter's transfer to Ropsha, an estate some thirty kilometers inland that Empress Elizabeth had granted him as grand duke. A large coach pulled by more than six horses, the side curtains drawn shut and with armed guards on the running boards, spirited the former sovereign into temporary captivity at Ropsha, until permanent accommodations could be readied at Schlüsselburg.[29] There could be no thought of allowing him to leave the country.

Peter's abdication completed the coup's formalities, so Catherine left Peterhof that evening in a carriage convoyed by horse-guards. Halfway back to Petersburg, the Empress halted at Prince Kurakin's dacha where she crumpled into bed completely exhausted—the first sleep she had savored in more than forty hours. In barely two days her prospects had completely changed. From a threatened, neglected, and powerless consort, Catherine had abruptly wrested command of the entire political arena and re-entered St. Petersburg in triumph on the morning of Sunday, 30 June. On horseback once again, the Empress rode into the capital at the head of the Preobrazhenskii Regiment along with the other Guards regiments, artillery, and three line regiments. The city turned out to see her grand entry, so unlike the one she had made two days before, as the clergy blessed her with holy water, churchbells pealed, and martial music rippled the summer air. Crowds lined the streets and speckled the rooftops. At noon Catherine pulled up before the Summer Palace, where Grand Duke Paul welcomed his mother amid rank upon rank of government and church officials. Constantly solicitous of Russian religious sentiments, the Empress proceeded directly to the court chapel for prayers.[30]

Sunday in Russia is also the traditional time for tippling. The raucous drinking, which began the day of the coup and resulted in some looting while Catherine was away at Peterhof, now redoubled in volume, led by delirious Guardsmen and abetted by police inaction or complicity. Shouting, singing, fighting resounded through the city far into the luminous night. Suddenly some drunken hussar started bellowing about a threat to Catherine's safety—30,000 Prussians were allegedly coming "to kidnap our Little Mother!" Others joined the tumult and refused to calm down even at the urging of Aleksei and Grigorii Orlov. Though the exhausted Empress had already retired for the night, Captain Passek awakened her in alarm and accompanied her carriage on a visit to the Izmailovskii Guards past midnight. "I told them that I was completely healthy," the Empress later recalled, "that they should go to sleep and leave me in peace, that I had not slept for three nights and had just fallen asleep; I expressed my desire that henceforth they obey their officers. They replied that the damned Prussians had alarmed them but that they were ready to die for me. I told them: 'Well, fine, thanks; but now go to sleep.' They wished me a good night, good health, and dispersed like lambs, all looking back at my carriage."[31] The role of mediator and peacemaker appealed to the new autocratrix.

Early the next morning all drinking establishments were ordered to close. Pickets of troops with loaded cannon and lighted linstocks were arrayed along all bridges, public squares, and street crossings. In the face of such measures and in the natural course of things the celebration/agitation quickly subsided. Within a week the taverns could reopen. The troops ringing the capital were withdrawn; commercial and postal communications were restored. On Sunday, 7 July, the public parks were reopened to persons of all classes and both sexes, clean and neatly dressed, except for those wearing bast footwear (i.e., peasants) or Prussian clothes. That same day, with life in the capital having returned to normal, Catherine's government issued a lengthy "detailed" manifesto justifying her accession. Presumably Catherine herself dictated the basic ideas, which her state secretaries then carefully reworked and rephrased into the slightly archaic Russian used in official pronouncements.[32]

Addressed to "All Our loyal subjects ecclesiastical, military, and civil," Catherine's manifesto amounted to a full-scale indictment of Peter III, who was charged with manifold crimes and criminal designs against Catherine and Paul, church and state, the army and the Guards in particular. Indeed, the manifesto maintained that the Emperor, after provoking universal discontent, had blamed it on Catherine and planned "to destroy Us completely and to deprive Us of life." He was also branded as unfit to rule, tyrannical, and ungrateful; for he had supposedly planned to exclude Paul from the succession instituted by Empress Elizabeth, whose pious memory he had repeatedly insulted. It was the threat to Catherine and the country, the manifesto insisted, that had caused "loyal subjects selected from the people" to rush to her defense and save the Empire from enslavement or bloody rebellion. The coup was itself depicted as simply a matter of Catherine, "armed with the might of the Lord," agreeing with the wishes of those "selected from the people" (who selected them and who they were, of course, went unsaid) and accepting the allegiance willingly tendered by church, military, and civil officials. Peter's abdication, quoted in full, was described as having been arranged only after he had ordered Catherine to be killed.[33]

"By this action, thanks be to God, We accepted the Sovereign throne of Our beloved fatherland upon Ourselves without any bloodshed, but God alone and Our beloved fatherland helped Us through those they selected." Then the manifesto outlined the new regime's aspirations. In sharp contrast to Peter III, Catherine promised to preserve and to protect "Our Orthodox Faith," to strengthen and to defend the Empire, to uphold justice, and to extirpate "evil and all sorts of injustices and oppressions." The Empress professed notions sometimes termed "democratic autocracy," in her desire "to be worthy of the love of Our people," to prescribe limits for all offices and laws so as to facilitate "good order in everything," all of which would "preserve the integrity of the Empire and Our Sovereign authority, somewhat undermined by the recent adversity, and deliver from despondency and insult those truly loyal and zealous for their fatherland."[34] In short, Catherine envisioned a government in the tradition of Russian absolutism, unlimited in law but prescribed by religious precepts, custom, and national sentiments. Autocratrix meant simply "independent ruler" or "sovereign mistress," according to English commentators of the time, who saw in Catherine's "revolution" momentous constitutional change: "the most absolute power on earth is now held by an elective monarch."[35]

Not everybody believed the account of Peter III purveyed in this manifesto. Some thirty-five years later, a few months after Catherine's death, Emperor Paul ordered the document stricken from the published laws of the Empire. Yet the same day Catherine's manifesto appeared the government issued a traditional boon to the populace by lowering the price of state-sold salt by ten copecks per *pud* (36 lbs.). This gesture provoked one historian to sarcasm: "The people, like the nightingale, could not live on fables: one would have to eat a whole *pud* of salt in order to experience 10 copecks' worth of the Empress's thanks."[36]

Other events of these days signified the completion of Catherine's coup in a practical as well as a formal sense. Peter abruptly perished at Ropsha on 6 July. Catherine received the news that very evening and issued an announcement the next day attributing his demise to a "hemorrhoidal colic." (A French wit, the philosophe D'Alembert, would later comment that hemorrhoids are very dangerous in Russia!)[37] It was a surprise that was no surprise. Peter was an embarrassment to Catherine and her cronies so long as he lived. Although locked away from the world, he would have attracted constant attention and awkward questions. He might have escaped. Followers might try to free him or act in his name. The logic of the situation demanded his extinction. Otherwise Catherine could never sit securely on the Russian throne. The examples of Ivan the Terrible and Peter the Great, both of whom had killed their own heirs, evoked no protest when mentioned in Catherine's presence. Apparently her intimates, the Orlov brothers in particular, silently drew the conclusion that she wished the prisoner eliminated but could not explicitly order it. Their position was fragile as long as hers was. Moreover, Grigorii Orlov could not marry her as long as Peter was alive. Whatever Catherine thought of such a marriage in principle, she would not subject herself to the indignity of a public divorce to marry Orlov.[38]

For more than a century, only hearsay contradicted the official version of Peter's death. In 1881, however, was published the letter of Aleksei Orlov to Catherine that informed her of the violent deed, took full responsibility for it, and begged her forgiveness. To this day many circumstances of the death remain murky—one in the long dark line of disputed deaths in Russian history. This much is certain: Peter was murdered—probably strangled or smothered in much the same fashion that his son, Emperor Paul, would be four decades later. The act occurred with the direct complicity of Aleksei Orlov and Fedor Bariatinskii, as Orlov's letter admitted, and in the presence of several other persons—perhaps as many as fourteen. Evidently drink inflamed the scene; some later suspected poison. In fact, Catherine demanded a postmortem, which revealed nothing.[39] Thirty years later the following version was still being whispered about in Petersburg:

> Two Corporals were employed to put him between two feather beds and in which they succeeded and Baratinski and another person were actually upon the bed for the purpose of smothering him. But being though not a strong man very active he disengaged himself. Alexi Orloff then went in, seized him exhausted as he was by the throat, squeezed it with all his extraordinary force, and the unhappy Prince dropped down dead as if he had been shot. The two Corporals did not survive that day. For Poison had been administered to them before they undertook the business.[40]

Although the news stunned the Empress momentarily (the allegation that some conspirators were poisoned was probably a later invention), she recovered quickly and moved swiftly to cope with the consequences. The new reign could not be allowed to begin with a murder, Catherine and her advisers resolved; hence her manifesto announcing Peter's death and calling on the people to pay their last respects at the Alexander Nevskii Monastery, where the body lay in state. Orlov's letter she locked in her study, where it lay in oblivion thirty-four years until Emperor Paul unsealed it the day of her death and, relieved that it exonerated his mother of direct complicity, burned it. (Fortunately for history, one of Paul's friends had made a copy.)

Peter's corpse, dressed in a light blue Holstein uniform with an ample cravat covering his throat and a large hat concealing much of his darkened face (as if victimized by apoplexy, some thought), lay on public display for two days. Crowds of common folk filed past the bier in perplexity, urged on by insistent guards. It was hoped that such publicity would squelch any doubts that the ex-Emperor was actually dead, and forestall the possibility that pretenders might fasten on the imperial persona. Catherine made motions as if to attend the burial on 10 July, but the Senate dissuaded her, supposedly out of concern for her health. In a further effort to play down Peter III's political significance and separate him from the ruling dynasty, his body was interred at the same monastery instead of being placed with his imperial fore-bears in the Peter and Paul Cathedral in central Petersburg.[41]

Despite all these efforts to justify Catherine's accession, cloak the true nature of Peter's death, and distance the Empress from her spouse's demise, doubts surfaced at once about the legitimacy of it all. In refusing the oath of allegiance, for instance, one Elychin confided to a priest in the town of Odoev on 8 July: "Be there anywhere in the world that a wife might take liberty from a husband? Alas, there's nobody for me to ask, and then I won't have to go all around the city for the oath!" When chided for not swearing allegiance and told "it's an important matter," Elychin retorted: "What's it to me? Will copecks be given out? Let them announce a decree, to swear by what power and is the former sovereign alive or not?"[42]

Catherine's coup had dethroned Peter in two days and compassed his death a week later, but his ghost could not be exorcised so easily. In various guises he would stalk her until death. Neither promises nor processions, oaths of allegiance or copecks however liberally disbursed or insistently re-peated, could camouflage the fact that Catherine had usurped the throne from a legitimate monarch by force and deceit. That she had overthrown her own husband only complicated the crime in the minds of many.

2

The Education of a
Russian Empress (1729-1762)

Empress Catherine the Great, born an obscure German princess, could never have become sovereign of all the Russias without the political and dynastic transformations wrought by Peter the Great (1672–1725). His imperious image dominated her life. Before her birth he had made Muscovy into the Russian Empire, named himself emperor, and pushed the western border of his giant domain hundreds of leagues closer to the north European nations he sought to emulate. To cement Russia's commitment to the new, avowedly European orientation, the tsar-emperor abolished the traditional order of dynastic succession by seniority through the male line. As absolute ruler he proclaimed his right to select whomever he deemed fit for the throne—a sure formula for dynastic chaos, intrafamily competition, and political instability.

Having already murdered one son (Aleksei, 1690–1718) and heir by his first wife, Peter compounded the confusion by elevating his plebeian second wife Catherine to the status of empress (officially crowned in 1724), marrying off one daughter and one niece to German princes, and then failing to specify a successor. His cronies and the Guards regiments therefore declared his wife Empress Catherine I the first female ruler in modern Russian history. Illiterate and sottish, she functioned mainly as a figurehead for her brief reign (1725–1727); but she strove to resolve the dynastic muddle by decreeing that, if Grand Duke Peter should die without children, the succession should then pass to her daughters Anna and Elizabeth and their descendants but with the male heirs to be favored over the females whenever possible.[1] Nature and human frailty allowed that possibility but rarely. Besides, aspirants with another crown or those who did not accept Russian Orthodoxy were explicitly excluded. The late tsarevich Aleksei's son (Peter the Great's grandson by his first marriage) succeeded Catherine I as Peter II, but he spent all of his short reign in Moscow under a regency and died from smallpox without issue—and without naming a successor—in 1730.

17

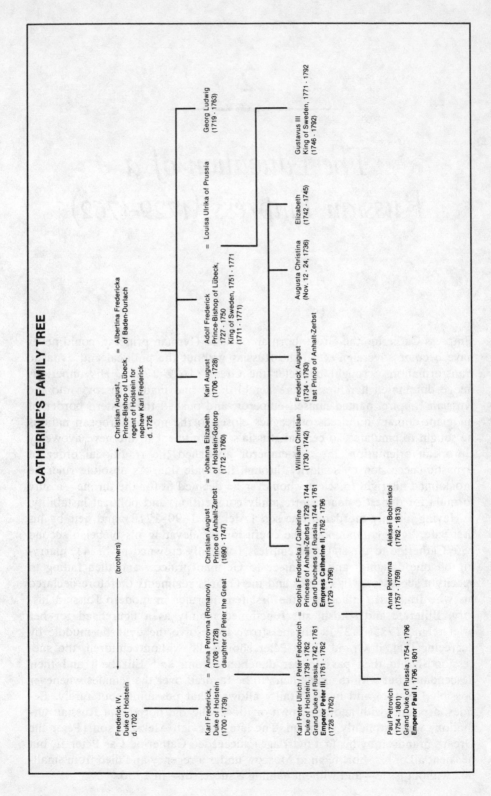

CATHERINE'S FAMILY TREE

Frederick IV,
Duke of Holstein
d. 1702

Christian August,
Prince-Bishop of Lübeck,
regent of Holstein for
nephew Karl Frederick
d. 1726

= Albertina Fredericka
of Baden-Durlach

Karl Frederick,
Duke of Holstein
(1700 - 1739)

= Anna Petrovna (Romanov)
(1708 - 1728)
daughter of Peter the Great

Christian August
Prince of Anhalt-Zerbst
(1690 - 1747)

Johanna Elizabeth
of Holstein-Gottorp
(1712 - 1760)

Adolf Frederick
Prince-Bishop of Lübeck,
1727 - 1750
King of Sweden, 1751- 1771
(1711 - 1771)

Karl August
(1706 - 1728)

(brothers)

Georg Ludwig
(1719 - 1763)

= Louisa Ulrika of Prussia

Karl Peter Ulrich / Peter Fedorovich
Duke of Holstein, 1739 - 1762
Grand Duke of Russia, 1742 - 1761
Emperor Peter III, 1761 - 1762
(1728 - 1762)

= Sophia Fredericka / Catherine
Princess of Anhalt-Zerbst, 1729 - 1744
Grand Duchess of Russia, 1744 - 1761
Empress Catherine II, 1762 - 1796
(1729 - 1796)

William Christian
(1730 - 1742)

Frederick August
(1734 - 1793)
last Prince of Anhalt-Zerbst

Augusta Christina
(Nov. 12 - 24, 1736)

Elizabeth
(1742 - 1745)

Gustavus III
King of Sweden, 1771 - 1792
(1746 - 1792)

Paul Petrovich
(1754 - 1801)
Grand Duke of Russia, 1754 - 1796
Emperor Paul I, 1796 - 1801

Anna Petrovna
(1757 - 1759)

Aleksei Bobrinskoi
(1762 - 1813)

18

The implications of the Petrine transformation of the order of succession now became manifest, with no adult male heir available and with multiple female candidates at home and abroad and from different family branches. The Supreme Privy Council, a small conclave of aristocrats who had administered the empire under Catherine I and Peter II, attempted to halt such dynastic drift and overthrow the principle of absolute rule by imposing restrictive conditions on Peter the Great's niece Anna Ivanovna, the widowed duchess of Kurland. The council offered the crown to Anna Ivanovna in preference to any Petrine descendant because she had neither children nor spouse to complicate the chaos of conflicting dynastic claims and because, moreover, as a solitary middle-aged woman she could be expected to abide by the prescribed conditions. Anna Ivanovna accepted the crown and the council's conditions, but tore up the latter when she discovered that few noblemen supported the oligarchs' pretensions. Thus she became Russia's first female sovereign to rule in fact. She abolished the Supreme Privy Council and exiled several of its members, although she also adopted some of the reforms it had proposed to conciliate the noble elite. Furthermore, she reaffirmed her fidelity to the Petrine legacy by returning the court to St. Petersburg.[2] Since she was childless, however, she faced the same problems of succession as her immediate predecessors had. Although Russian tradition sanctioned the preference for male succession, there were still no adult male heirs available, and the political crisis of 1730 had dramatized the dangers of a regency. At the same time the claims of a female successor loomed ever larger in the person of Peter the Great's daughter Elizabeth, whose engagement to Prince Karl August of Holstein-Gottorp had ended with his death from smallpox in 1727. Born in 1709 (before her parents officially married), the vivacious Elizabeth combined the robust vigor and commanding presence of her parents in a way that promised wide popularity. Princely suitors coveted her hand and, although she stayed away from the imperial court, her amorous affairs sparked constant gossip.

The intrafamily competition took on greater complexity when Anna Ivanovna invited her niece Anna Leopol'dovna, daughter of Catherine Duchess of Mecklenburg, to come to Russia with her husband, Prince Anton Ulrich of Brunswick-Luneberg, as heirs presumptive to the throne. Shortly before the Empress's death on 17 October 1740, she appointed their baby son, Prince Ivan Antonovich, her successor under the regency of her German favorite, Ernst Johann Biron, Duke of Kurland. Biron's regency lasted barely three weeks. On 9 November 1740 Field Marshal Münnich led the Guards regiments against him and proclaimed Anna Leopol'dovna as the new regent for Ivan Antonovich (Ivan VI). One year later, on the night of 24/25 November 1741, Grand Duchess Elizabeth seized power with the backing of the Guards, the connivance of the French envoy, and the assistance of adventurers such as the court surgeon Armand Lestocq.[3]

The latest coup proved as bloodless as the others. Elizabeth arrested and imprisoned the infant tsar, his parents, and family, but she also declared that her actions had been in the interest of Peter the Great's grandson, her nephew Duke Peter Karl Ulrich of Holstein. Thus Elizabeth restored the rights of her branch of the family—the direct line from Peter the Great—and followed her mother's succession rule in choosing an heir from the male offspring of her deceased elder sister. To guarantee the succession against the claims of Ivan VI, Elizabeth hastily brought her teenage nephew from Holstein to Russia, had him renounce his claim to the Swedish crown and convert to Orthodoxy, and then proclaimed him heir presumptive. The next step was to find a suitable bride for the newly renamed Grand Duke Peter Fedorovich. The Empress looked abroad again and promptly found a promising candidate in the niece of her late fiancé from Holstein.[4]

It was through these dynastic machinations, political overturns, and genealogical calculations that a young German princess arrived in Russia to marry the sole surviving grandson of Peter the Great. Through further twists and turns of fate and nature this young woman made herself into Catherine the Great, Empress and autocratrix of all the Russias.

Youth and Girlhood

The future empress of Russia was born Sophia Augusta Fredericka, Princess of Anhalt-Zerbst, on 21 April/2 May 1729 in the Pomeranian seaport of Stettin (part of Poland since World War II). Pomerania was a Baltic borderland between Poland and Prussia that had been under Swedish control throughout the seventeenth century until the western part was ceded to Prussia in 1720. Indeed, Sophia's father, Prince Christian August, served in the Prussian army as a major-general in command of the Anhalt-Zerbst infantry regiment no. 8. His was an obscure and penurious German princely family, its ancestral lands so paltry that Christian August entered Prussian service in his youth and spent the flower of his manhood fighting the French and the Swedes all over Europe. Born in 1690, he married at age thirty-seven the sixteen-year-old Princess Johanna Elizabeth of Holstein-Gottorp, the younger sister of Prince Karl August who had been engaged to Grand Duchess Elizabeth of Russia before his sudden death in Petersburg in 1727. If the bride's family ties overshadowed the groom's, her immediate prospects were dim. Her father was already dead and her marriage to a Prussian general hardly promised repute or riches.[5] Yet she was ambitious for her family, which was closely linked to the royal houses of Denmark and Sweden (her brother Adolf Frederick became the constitutional monarch of Sweden in 1751); and she may have persuaded her stolid spouse to inform the Russian court of their marriage, mentioning the bride's close relation to Elizabeth's unfortunate fiancé and the groom's distant relation to Peter II through the tsar's mother.[6] Johanna Elizabeth seized on Russia's ties with Holstein; for Duke Karl Frederick, whose marriage to Peter the Great's daughter Anna had produced the future Grand Duke Peter Fedorovich, was her first cousin. Of course, many German princely families recognized the bright dynastic prospects opened by the Romanovs' new respectability in the European monarchical marriage mart. Like many other German princesses, Johanna Elizabeth's allotted role in life was to produce marriageable children, preferably males so as to ensure family continuity and preservation of ancestral lands. She must have been slightly disappointed when her first-born was a girl. Despite a difficult delivery, mother and daughter displayed excellent health. Indeed, Johanna Elizabeth gave birth to four more children in short order. Since all were sickly and two were male, she devoted most of her attention to them. Both girls died young; only one son survived to adulthood. Meanwhile, her daughter, nicknamed Fike or the dimunitive Figchen, grew up quite independently. Little is known about her youth except what she chose to record several decades later when she had already gained the Russian throne. She wrote at least seven different versions of her reminiscences over a period of some forty years and, not surprisingly, changed many details from one draft to another. Although some specifics are questionable or incomplete and the chronology is occasionally awry, these memoirs offer much insight into Catherine's attitudes and her psychosocial development, particularly when one compares different versions of the same events. It then becomes evident that Catherine artfully selected facts and deduced motives in fashioning a dramatic account of her brilliant career.[7]

Young Fike showed early signs of precocity and stubbornness. Her French Huguenot governess, Elizabeth Cardel, remarked on her independence of mind or "esprit gauche."[8] She loved playing with other children, especially at rough and tumble boys' games, and being the center of attention. But she also soon learned to hide her feelings and cultivate others—to please and be pleasing. Her relationship with her mother seems to have been cool and sporadic. She felt unwanted, unattractive, unloved. Serious illness at age seven resulted in a curvature of the spine that eventually straightened out in a few years, thanks in part to folk remedies—rubdowns with a maid's spittle and wearing a corrective harness. Supervised by the local hangman, these treatments may have contributed to Catherine's lifelong suspicion of medical practitioners, whether professionals or quacks. Even so, she developed both splendid posture and periodic backaches. Highspirited and energetic, she chaffed at "tedious lessons" from tutors in German, French, religion, and music, but loved dancing and reading. Apparently she never attended a school or group lessons. One of her disputes with her tutor in religion, a Lutheran pastor, revealed an early interest in sexuality. She wished to know the meaning of circumcision, but neither pastor nor governess would explain.[9]

By age ten or a bit later Fike's interest in matters sensual became more persistent and pronounced. Evidently she began masturbating frequently. "I was very boisterous in those days," she admitted later, feigning sleep when put to bed early; "but as soon as I was alone I climbed astride my pillows and galloped in my bed until I was quite worn out. . . . I was never caught in the act, nor did anyone ever know that I travelled post-haste in my bed on my pillows."[10]

Princess Fike learned a great deal by accompanying her mother, whom she remembered as "beautiful, gay, and frivolous," as well as "extravagant and exceedingly generous" and "fond of entertainment and social life," on frequent trips to other courts. The "truly regal" court of Brunswick captivated the young princess with its constant round of "balls, operas, concerts, hunts, excursions, dinners, gossip, and matchmaking." By contrast, the court of

Berlin seemed less civilized and not as splendid.[11] During a visit in 1739 to her mother's brother Adolf Frederick, the Prince-Bishop of Lübeck and future king of Sweden, Catherine first laid eyes on her cousin, Duke Peter Karl Ulrich of Holstein, whom she would follow to Russia and to the throne. The eleven-year-old boy, though pale and delicate, struck her as "goodlooking, well-mannered, and courteous"—praise that she carefully tempered by noting his hot temper, rebelliousness, and proclivity for drink.[12] But it is hard to know what ten-year-old Sophia actually thought of her cousin at the time. In some reminiscences she professes indifference but notes her mother's interest; in others she describes his appearance and the rumors about him, blaming his defects of character on parental neglect and excessive discipline by his guardians, officials, and tutors.[13]

By her teenage years Princess Sophia began to perceive that she was not an ugly duckling after all. At age thirteen, on a visit to Varel in the Duchy of Oldenburg, she met an impressively liberated woman, Countess Bentinck, who fascinated her by riding a horse astride, flaunting a child out of wedlock, and behaving as she pleased: "danced when the whim took her to do so, sang and laughed and pranced about like a child, though she was well into her thirties at the time—she was already separated from her husband."[14] Riding horses like a man later became one of Catherine's "dominant passions" in Russia. The psychosexual implications of such passion are apparent: the desire for mastery, personal autonomy, sensual gratification, and power. Countess Bentinck, who may have been Voltaire's mistress while he was in Prussia and later corresponded with him after 1750, captivated the young princess despite her parents' disapproval of such dissolute "manners." These multiple challenges to social conventions could only give the youngster strange ideas about marriage, love, and happiness. If Bentinck did not become a role model for Sophia, she certainly made a strong impression.[15]

Another relationship recollected by the adult Catherine reveals her deepening awareness of male/female and mother/daughter tensions. Prince Georg Ludwig, Sophia's uncle and senior by ten years, began frequenting his sister's household and spending hours with his teenaged niece. Babette Cardel protested at this interference with her charge's studies, but Sophia considered his attentions thoughtful and affectionate, and innocently led him on. Complaining of gossip and constraints, he finally declared his passion and begged her to marry him. She thought he was joking at first. "I knew nothing about love and never associated him with it." She scoffed at the idea, felt embarrassed around him, and avoided his company. Even so, he pressed his suit and her defenses crumbled. "He was very good-looking at the time, had beautiful eyes, and knew my disposition. I was accustomed to him, I began to feel attracted by him and did not avoid him." She even promised to marry him if her parents approved; years later she concluded that her mother must have known what was going on. Evidently she enjoyed teasing her "bashful lover, very repressed" and making him jealous, "but, except for a few kisses, our relationship remained very innocent." She concealed the affair from Babette Cardel and her mother. But when her journey to Russia was arranged, her mother suddenly voiced misgivings over Prince Georg's reception of the news.[16] It is difficult to discern the meaning of these Lolita-like episodes and whether Catherine remembered them accurately. At the very least, the story highlights an awakening sexuality, a latent desire for adult experience, and ambivalent feelings toward her mother—accusatory hints of connivance mixed with barely concealed boasts of sexual rivalry. Told that she was mature beyond her years, Sophia may have started believing it.

Matchmaking and the Journey to Russia

There was much talk about Sophia's marital prospects as she entered her teens in the 1740s. But the invitation to come to Russia still triggered tremendous excitement in Zerbst when it arrived via Berlin on 1 January 1744. Actually the matter had been painstakingly arranged by the two determined women, Empress Elizabeth and Princess Johanna Elizabeth, working independently and with different motives. Certainly neither conceived of the political career that they were launching.

Although Princess Johanna and Empress Elizabeth had never met, they had known about each other, through mutual friends and relations in Holstein, for many years. So, when Elizabeth seized power on 25 November 1741, Johanna immediately wrote to congratulate the new empress, wishing her a long reign and praising the portrait of the young Elizabeth with her late sister, Duchess Anna of Holstein. This portrait piqued Elizabeth's sentimental memories, and "cousin" Johanna speedily honored her request for it. The Empress reciprocated by sending Johanna her own portrait encrusted with diamonds (18,000 rubles worth), the most fabulous gift ever seen in Zerbst! And even King Frederick hastened to cultivate Petersburg's goodwill toward the Zerbst family, promoting his general Prince Christian August to the rank of field marshal. Meanwhile, Elizabeth summoned to Petersburg her Holstein nephew, "the infant of Kiel" and "little devil" as he had been unceremoniously called by the nervous government of Anna Ivanovna. On 7 November 1742 he was proclaimed heir to the Russian throne. His renunciation of his rights to the Swedish throne also benefited Johanna's family, for at Russian insistence her brother was chosen crown-prince of Sweden. Alive to further possibilities and encouraged by King Frederick, Johanna also sent her daughter's portrait to Petersburg, personally delivered by her brother Prince Augustus of Holstein in March 1743. The young princess's "expressive physiognomy" delighted the Empress and the Grand Duke[17]

The childless Elizabeth had spent many months reviewing possible brides for her nephew and heir. A foreign princess was preferred as a symbol of prestige and to avoid domestic complications, but French, British, Prussian, and Saxon candidates were all rejected in the brisk competition. Several considerations recommended Princess Sophia. She was the right age, Elizabeth knew her family, and she came from the same cultural background as Grand Duke Peter. Her selection would conciliate Prussia, a rising power on the European stage. Indeed, Elizabeth included King Frederick in the arrangements to invite Princess Johanna and her daughter to Russia. Money for travel expenses was channeled through Berlin, which mother and daughter visited before setting out on their winter journey. Both Frederick and Elizabeth took pains to conceal the purpose of the invitation. In retrospect, their attempts at secrecy and speed look ridiculously amateurish. Using the alias of Countess Rheinbeck, Johanna was to accompany her daughter alone with only a small suite; her husband was not invited. So the travellers took "only" four coaches when they left Berlin on 16 January 1744. Their convoy lumbered across the frozen plains of Pomerania and East Prussia in three weeks, dodging highwaymen, enduring provincial inns, and swilling beer.[18]

At Riga, on 6 February 1744, the world majestically brightened for the two German princesses. They entered the Russian Empire in a special coach, conducted into the city by troops and officials amid cannon salutes, trumpets, and kettledrums. This reception was intended to awe the newcomers with the splendor and grandeur of Elizabeth's mighty realm. A letter from Brümmer, the Grand Duke's Holsteiner governor, urged the newcomers to hasten onward to Moscow via St. Petersburg and advised them how to greet the Empress at first, namely, to show "extraordinary respect, kissing her hand, according to the custom of this country." From Riga on 29 January/9 February—the Julian calendar of Russia was now adopted, eleven days behind Europe's Gregorian calendar—the guests left in special imperial sleighs fitted with carriage bodies, swathed in sables and cushioned by silk mattresses, each vehicle pulled swiftly by ten horses. At noon of 3 February when the imperial train stopped in front of St. Petersburg's Winter Palace, the guns of the Peter and Paul Fortress thundered a welcome across the ice-clad Neva.[19]

St. Petersburg, Peter the Great's northern "paradise" founded in 1703 astride the marshy delta of the Neva's multiple arms debouching into the Gulf of Finland, epitomized the new Russia forcibly wrenched westward to meet maritime Europe. European in layout and architecture, the new capital glistened half-finished and, with the court away at Moscow, half-deserted. Still, it was the largest, most magnificent city the princesses of Anhalt-Zerbst had ever seen. All visitors agreed that St. Petersburg, already a busy port with a population approaching 100,000, would soon rank among the great cosmopolitan capitals of Europe.

The Zerbst princesses spent the next three days meeting whole battalions of officials, aristocrats, generals, ambassadors, and clergymen. Even elephants were brought to edify the German guests. They toured the city, heard elderly generals recount the deeds of their "creator" Peter the Great, and inspected the barracks of the Preobrazhenskii Guards from where Elizabeth had initiated her coup. Baron Mardefeld, the Prussian envoy, and the Marquis de la Chétardie, the French minister, bent Johanna's ear with tales of the political situation at the Russian court, execrating the malevolent intrigues of Vice-Chancellor Aleksei Petrovich Bestuzhev-Riumin to block her daughter's candidacy. They advised her to work with Brümmer, the Grand Duke's governor, and with Lestocq, the wily confidant of the Empress, against Bestuzhev's overweening influence. The flighty Johanna, certain that she understood Russian court politics, left for Moscow on the night of 5/6 February 1744 determined to secure Sophia's future by dislodging the odious Bestuzhev.[20]

Eager to reach Moscow by 9 February, the eve of the Grand Duke's birthday, the guests sped through the snow in a caravan of twenty or thirty sleighs travelling day and night, only pausing at roadside palaces for meals. Courtiers met them several times to report their progress and urge them onward; the Empress and the Grand Duke were counting the seconds till their arrival. Seventy kilometers from Moscow on the afternoon of 9 February, they were told what to wear at supper with the Empress that evening and sixteen horses were hitched to the sleigh for the final dash, which they covered in four hours, driving up to the Golovin Palace in Moscow's Foreign Suburb after seven P.M. Brümmer and Lestocq met the guests in the entryway and ushered them into their rooms, where Grand Duke Peter tenderly greeted them. Soon they were taken to the main reception hall to meet the Empress, who embraced and kissed mother and daughter in the warmly vigorous Russian manner. As instructed beforehand, Princess Johanna kissed Elizabeth's hand and effusively acknowledged her favor, generosity, and hospitality.[21]

Elizabeth cut an impressive figure before her would-be relatives. At thirty-five, Peter the Great's daughter carried her hefty torso majestically, her bulk enveloped in a huge hooped dress of silvery moire with gold braid; a black feather and diamonds in her hair set off her noble head and beautiful complexion. Goodnatured and highly emotional, she radiated maternal affection as she gazed intently at the young princess in whom she hoped to find a dynastic helpmate. Did she ever guess that this slim fourteen-year-old would surpass her own daring and vivacity in pursuit of power, pomp, and popularity in Russia and the world? Probably not, though they liked each other at once. Indeed, Princess Sophia had been advised by her father on leaving Zerbst that she must exert herself to please the Empress and the Grand Duke while adapting to the culture of her new homeland. For her part, Elizabeth was enraptured by daughter and mother alike. The day after their arrival she awarded them both the Order of St. Catherine, established in memory of her mother, in a splendid ceremony.[22]

At Moscow the two princesses received their own court: two gentlemen of the chamber, two officers of the chamber, four chamber pages, and a multitude of servants. "We are living like queens," Johanna crowed to her husband. "Everything is in lace, faced with gold, magnificent. When we go out, our going out is splendid." She decided that the Empress was on her side and plunged into intrigues aimed at undermining the Prussophobe Bestuzhev-Riumin. Meanwhile, her daughter charmed all and sundry, beginning with the Empress and the Grand Duke, and within ten days Johanna wrote her husband that their main purpose had been achieved. Sophia had won the Empress's enthusiastic approval and was already being prepared for her role as grand duchess; "c'est une affaire faite."[23]

Princess Sophia pleased the Grand Duke most of all, he confided to her right away, because she was his relative and someone with whom he could freely converse—in French, apparently, for he knew little more Russian than she did, which was none. At one of their first meetings he confessed his love for a lady-in-waiting who had been banished from court the previous year when her mother, Madame Lopukhina, suffered torture and exile for involvement in a plot against the Empress. Since the lady in question could not be his bride now, he was resigned to pleasing his aunt by marrying Princess Sophia, who blushed at this "premature confidence." Nevertheless, she acknowledged Peter's assiduous attentions and his concern to help her gain her bearings in the unfamiliar environment. She quickly won his trust by listening attentively to his self-absorbed discourses without interruption.[24]

In fact, Peter and Sophia shared many of the same problems. The need to adapt rapidly to a strange country and culture, to cultivate the favor of an uncertain autocratrix who felt constantly threatened; the lack of parental guidance and emotional support, the intellectual deficiencies left by sporadic, solitary educational experiences, the passions and frivolities of the teenage years—all these difficulties bound the two cousins together. Besides, he loved to talk and to joke; she was willing to listen and laugh. They became good friends for a time.

Illness, Conversion, and Engagement

Soon they had another experience in common: life-threatening illness. Peter Fedorovich, born on 10/21 February 1728, did not inherit his grandfather's robust physique; he remained pale, thin, and sickly throughout his life. Almost as soon as he came to Russia he endured a serious bout with measles. Three months before Princess Sophia's arrival Peter fainted with a fever and spent five weeks in bed; the doctors despaired that he would ever recover and confined him to his room for two months. During this period his sporadic lessons were discontinued. He lost interest in everything, even music, one of his lifelong amusements.[25]

By contrast, Princess Sophia had rarely been ill, never seriously. Consequently she vividly remembered the sickness she contracted in Moscow barely a month after her arrival in Russia. It was one of the reasons she disliked Moscow ever after. A pneumonic infection seized her on 6 March 1744 while the Empress was away on a pilgrimage. The high fever, delirium, and pain in the side persuaded her mother it was smallpox; so she vetoed blood-letting, which the doctors recommended, contending that her brother had died of smallpox in Russia only because he had been bled. While Princess Johanna argued with the physicians, her daughter moaned in pain. The Empress rushed back to Moscow at the news, found Sophia delirious, then cradled her head while a surgeon opened a vein. Over the next four weeks the Princess was bled frequently, sometimes four times a day, despite her mother's loud and tearful protests. An official announcement reported the malady as a "fever from flux," which had then turned into a "dangerous rheumatism with asthma."[26] Whatever the affliction was, young Sophia's strong constitution brought her through the ordeal, which did nothing to raise the low opinion of medical practitioners that she had imbibed from her childhood governess.

Her behavior during the crisis, however, only reinforced Elizabeth's admiration for the young Princess at the same time that it injured her mother's standing. Johanna was accused of neglecting her daughter, who later maintained that she had caught cold from rising early to study her Russian lessons. She also requested visits from Simon Todorskii, her instructor in Russian Orthodoxy, thereby reiterating her determination to become a Russian in speech and religion. Subsequently she claimed to have used the occasion for purposes of gathering information about the doings at court, as she pretended to doze while monitoring the conversations of the ladies assigned to her care. Considering that she had only just begun learning Russian, however, this seems an unlikely tale, although it may be psychologically and politically revealing: an outsider feeling her way in a new milieu. At any rate, the sickness brought her redoubled attention from the Empress and the Grand Duke, who gave her presents of jewelry—a monogram with diamonds and brooches worth 20,000 rubles (her calculating mother's estimate) and a watch studded with diamonds and rubies valued at 4,000 rubles.[27] These were not trifles for a penurious princess from Pomerania.

By April she began to walk around her bedchamber, but did not venture out until 20 April, when a dinner was served in her quarters for a company of courtiers. The next evening, her fifteenth birthday, she received congratulations in her quarters, attended a supper for forty persons, and appeared at her first ball, where the foreign ministers were also present. Though fast regaining her strength, she felt extremely sensitive about her appearance, wryly commenting decades later that "I suppose the company was not very taken with me. I had become thin as a skeleton; I had grown taller, but my face and all its features were drawn, my hair had fallen out, and on my face there was a mortal pallor. I myself saw that I could frighten people with my ugliness; I didn't even recognize myself. The Empress sent me a pot of rouge that day and ordered me to use it."[28]

On the mend as spring opened, Princess Sophia resumed her study of Russian with Vasilii Adodurov, a writer who also tutored the Grand Duke, her religious instruction with Simon Todorskii, and dancing lessons with the balletmaster Jean-Baptiste Lande. Presumably the latter included general instruction in poise and body movement, two of the Princess's skills that later elicited much favorable comment. Her excellent memory and eager application facilitated rapid progress in speaking Russian, a skill in which she soon surpassed the Grand Duke. Meanwhile, the Empress wrote Sophia's father requesting his blessing for his daughter's conversion and betrothal. To the teenaged couple, these were mere formalities; they already considered themselves engaged and looked ahead to the marriage ceremony.[29]

But Sophia's flighty mother nearly botched everything. Her intrigues against Bestuzhev-Riumin on behalf of France and Prussia came to light in intercepted dispatches from the Marquis de la Chétardie, dispatches that railed at Elizabeth for indolence and ignorance while revealing Princess Johanna as a veritable Prussian agent. The Empress, already cooling toward Sophia's mother because of the latter's lack of tenderness during her daughter's illness, flew into a rage at such crude political meddling, which Bestuzhev artfully exposed in decoded messages. As a result, on 6 June 1744 the Marquis de la Chétardie was ordered out of the country forthwith; he was escorted to the frontier. Elizabeth reduced Johanna to tears with a tongue-lashing that also threatened her expulsion. On 13 June, the Empress promoted Bestuzhev-Riumin to grand chancellor and signed a treaty with Saxony that reinforced the Austro-Russian alliance, implicitly directed against Prussia. Thenceforth the Prussian ambassador's position became untenable. Even so, none of these changes reflected on Princess Sophia personally. When her father's blessing arrived on 12 June, Grand Duke Peter jumped for joy and Elizabeth set the ceremonies for 28 and 29 June, the eve and day of her nephew's nameday. These particular dates would become memorable for the consorts in ways none could have foreseen.[30]

Princess Sophia's conversion to Orthodoxy took place on Wednesday, 28 June 1744, at the chapel of the Golovin Palace. Though weak from fasting in preparation, nervous and excited, she made the occasion a personal triumph. Her simple attire and unpowdered hair, adorned only with a white ribbon, contrasted strikingly with the splendid gowns, dress uniforms, and decorations of the courtiers. Before the bearded Archbishop of Novgorod, she repeated the profession of faith with a clear, confident voice in almost flawless Russian. The Empress and many others wept with joy. Elizabeth also chose the Princess's new Russian name, Catherine (Ekaterina Alekseevna), in honor of her own mother, Catherine I. To russify the name Sophia would have recalled the disgraceful memory of Peter the Great's half-sister who had conspired against his succession and died in prison. Perhaps the patronymic Alekseevna was selected simply because it sounded more Russian, for Elizabeth aspired to restore the Russian nationalism of Petrine times. In reward for Catherine's impressive performance, the Empress awarded her a diamond necklace and bodice ornament worth some 150,000 rubles. So exhausted was Catherine after the ceremony that she was excused from dinner that day. In the evening, however, she accompanied her ladies to the Grand Duke's apartments to congratulate him on his upcoming nameday with a gift of a hunting kit studded with diamonds and emeralds (undoubtedly provided by the Empress). To prepare for the next day's ceremonies, the consorts were driven incognito to the Kremlin, the spiritual and governmental center of the old capital and the historical center of the Great Russian nationality.[31]

Converting to Orthodoxy and assuming a Russian name signified Catherine's official membership in Russian society. Her public engagement the next day, solemnized in the Kremlin's Assumption Cathedral, confirmed her new political significance as the chosen vessel to continue the main branch of the Romanov dynasty. Princess Sophia of Anhalt-Zerbst had become Her Imperial Highness Grand Duchess Catherine of Russia. Her mother even believed, or affected to believe, that her daughter had officially entered the succession at the time of her betrothal, a curious claim later repeated by contemporaries and historians alike. Their contention held that Catherine enjoyed the right of succession in the event that Peter died without issue. The claim is false, albeit significant. Catherine later remembered that her mother's proposal that she be titled heiress as well as grand duchess had been curtly rejected.[32]

There was no need for such a provision so long as Elizabeth followed her mother's rules of succession, which she had already done by proclaiming Grand Duke Peter as her successor. If Peter died without children during Elizabeth's lifetime, then the Empress could designate whomever she wished to succeed her, as her father's rule of succession had specified. In that situation, she could choose Catherine, it is true, but that would have contradicted the customary preference for blood relations, even if they were females. Besides, there was the remote possibility that Elizabeth might have children of her own from her secret, morganatic marriage to Aleksei Razumovskii, or she might legitimize the supposed offspring of some earlier liaison. In theory, Catherine's own legal claim to the Russian throne was extremely remote. In practice, however, all the rules of succession depended on the wish of the reigning sovereign, the ultimate source of all state law. The Empress could disinherit the Grand Duke, for example, if she decided he was unfit to rule. So, Princess Johanna's frivolous claim for her daughter's right of succession masked a larger truth: Catherine's future depended on winning Elizabeth's confidence and respect, independently of Grand Duke Peter, whose succession could not be assumed if only because of his uncertain health.

Catherine's new status entitled her to a small court of her own including 30,000 rubles annual allowance. The dutiful Grand Duchess immediately wrote her father offering to pay for her sick brother's treatments in Hamburg.[33] She also made gifts to the many new persons she met almost daily in the whirl of receptions, parties, balls, and celebrations of the peace with Sweden. This gift-giving soon put her in debt at the same time it raised her personal and political credit. Since Russian aristocrats did not worry about repaying their debts, neither did she. A grand duchess was expected to live opulently. The personnel of her court, handpicked by the Empress without consulting Catherine's mother, consisted of three gentlemen of the chamber and three young officers of the chamber: Count Zakhar Chernyshev, Count Peter Bestuzhev-Riumin, and Prince Alexander Golitsyn—all Russians who knew French and German—in addition to Countess Maria Rumiantseva, a lady-in-waiting and head mistress of the new court, and three maids of honor: two princesses Golitsyna and a mademoiselle Kosheleva. Countess Rumiantseva's high status, visits to the courts of Versailles and St. James, and long experience at court from Petrine times (she enjoyed hinting that her soldier son Peter was the product of Peter the Great's seed), offered many opportunities for the newcomer to learn Russian court lore and make new acquaintances. The Grand Duchess became especially close to Rumiantseva's daughters Praskov'ia and Anna, the future Countess Bruce and Madame Naryshkina. Within a year in age, the three became lifelong confidantes. At Catherine's behest Praskov'ia "often slept in my room and even in my bed and then the whole night went in romping, dancing, and absurdities; sometimes we only went to bed toward morning, we carried on such terrible pranks." They resembled a small sorority engaged in a perpetual pajama party.[34]

The new court facilitated Catherine's progress in adopting the culture and

customs of her new homeland. Furthermore, it reinforced her independence
from her meddling mother, who persisted in petty intrigues that further compromised her unenviable reputation. During the Empress's pilgrimage to Kiev
in August 1744, Peter and Catherine preceded the main party in two coaches
with their courtiers and Princess Johanna, who complained incessantly about
the youngsters' pranks and merriment. The Grand Duke's dislike for his prospective mother-in-law flared into hatred in consequence of her outburst when
he accidentally upset her writing box. Catherine's own attempt to intercede
only redirected Johanna's wrath to herself and reduced her to tears. Never
very close, mother and daughter grew increasingly alienated.[35]

The journey to Kiev, a distance of some 750 kilometers by coach from
Moscow, gave Catherine her first extended look at the country outside the
two capitals. Although the roads were specially prepared for Elizabeth's huge
entourage of 230 courtiers, Catherine could not help noticing the enormous
expanses of the Russian Empire, the sparse settlement of the southern provinces, and the stark contrast between the humble peasants and the occasionally palatial estates of great aristocrats such as the Razumovskii brothers,
whom Elizabeth had plucked from provincial obscurity to install in courtly
splendor.[36]

On returning to Moscow, the young consorts plunged into another round
of entertainments. A series of transvestite balls intrigued Catherine especially,
for she shared Elizabeth's love of male attire, in which both looked dashing
in comparison with the "comical" men: "these monstrous colossi who were
very clumsy in handling their immense crinolines and kept butting into us."
At one comedy, however, Count Lestocq approached Catherine after he had
engaged in a heated discussion with the Empress who, he reported, was furious at the Grand Duchess's debts. Peter unctuously seconded his aunt's sentiments, and Princess Johanna declared acidly that she was washing her hands
of her wilful, spendthrift daughter. These debts, Catherine explained in retrospect, stemmed from the paltry wardrobe she had brought to Russia—hence
her constant need for luxurious clothes at the fashion-crazy Russian court—
from her practice of cultivating friendships by presents (particularly gifts to
the Grand Duke and her mother), and from Countess Rumiantseva's extrava-
gance. "These presents were the result of a fixed principle," she declared
later, "of a natural prodigality and of a contempt for riches upon which I
have always looked only as a means to procure for myself anything I liked."
They were all part of her campaign to please the Grand Duke, the Empress,
and the nation—that is, those persons with influence at court.[37]

Catherine's first aim appeared to be succeeding reasonably well, although
her relationship with Peter apparently included neither political conversations—they were forbidden to discuss state affairs—nor any physical intimacy.
Indeed, she became incensed at her mother's accusation that she had once
visited the Grand Duke's apartments on the pretext of taking a stroll in the
garden.[38] One wonders whether she resented this "calumny" more because
it was not true than because she wished it had been, if only to show her prying parent that she was a young woman who could act as she chose. Apparently she and Peter amused each other at first, but had few interests in

common except for a desire to gain some independence from the tiresome tutelage of boring adults. There must have been some mutual affection between the cousins, both struggling to find their way to adulthood in a strange society. Both gradually recognized that their individual difficulties could affect their common destiny.

Peter's poor health obviously threatened them both. On the trip to Kiev he suffered from an upset stomach, and after returning to Moscow a siege of pleurisy in October confined him to bed for several weeks. His fiancée attempted to lighten his boredom with notes in French.[39]

In November the Grand Duke came down with chickenpox, but his physician isolated him for fear that it was smallpox, measles, or spotted fever. Frightening precautions were taken, and only in mid-November did the Empress inform Catherine that he was recovering. On 26 November, at prayers of thanksgiving in the chapel of the Golovin Palace, the Grand Duchess wept with joy on catching sight of her consort. Two days later they danced together at a court masquerade. "The Grand Duke loved me passionately," Catherine recalled a decade later, "and everything taken together helped make me hope for a happy future." He was still quite weak in mid-December when the court left Moscow for Petersburg. Halfway there Peter became nauseated and feverish. Dr. Kau-Boerhaave thought he had overeaten, so the travellers pushed on. But at Khotilovo, 400 kilometers from Moscow, the fever prostrated the Grand Duke. The doctors kept Catherine away for fear it was smallpox, which appeared that very evening. Despite her protests, her mother took her away to Petersburg, where they arrived on 24 December. Elizabeth, whom they overtook near Novgorod, rushed back to nurse her nephew in person. This illness, if not his earlier bout with measles, may well have left young Peter permanently sterile, a condition pregnant with political complications for himself, his future wife, and Russia.[40]

In Petersburg, Catherine and Johanna received separate apartments near the Winter Palace, an arrangement that Elizabeth had dictated with a view toward separating daughter and mother. Catherine had been advised beforehand and was given her choice of accommodations. Johanna felt insulted, however, groused that her rooms were inferior, and upbraided Catherine for concealing her knowledge of the arrangement. Mother and daughter drifted further apart. Catherine subsequently blamed her mother for their estrangement, implying that Johanna's "great intimacy" with Ivan Betskoi displeased the Empress. Meanwhile, Elizabeth kept Catherine informed of the Grand Duke's condition via frequent letters. The Grand Duchess answered these with letters in Russian which captivated the Empress, who did not know that they were drafted in French, translated into Russian by her teacher Adodurov, and then recopied by Catherine. Only on 26 January 1745 did she see Peter again. She scarcely recognized his swollen, pockmarked features. "I stammered the customary good wishes on account of his recovery, but in fact he had become horribly ugly." Elizabeth tried to lift Catherine's spirits by showing her special solicitude. On 10 February, Peter's seventeenth birthday, the Empress dined alone with Catherine while seated on the throne, lauding both her youthful beauty and her Russian accent. She also appointed four Russian ladies as companions to the Grand Duchess, who delighted in their high spirits and silly games such as blindman's bluff. "In this way I made swift progress in the Russian language."[41]

Wedding Preparations

Concern about the Grand Duke's precarious health resurged at the start of March, when a fever and cold put him to bed again for more than a week. Despite the doctors' advice that Peter was not ready for marriage because of his frailty and youth—he had yet to reach puberty, Catherine later asserted on grounds unknown—Elizabeth could wait no longer. On 16 March 1745 her personal decree announced the wedding for the first days of July. Elaborate preparations were already underway to ensure that the festivities would eclipse anything ever seen in Russia. The noble elite, the top four classes of the fourteen official gradations of rank, were authorized a year's salary in advance for the purchase of rich clothes, carriages, and uniforms for their attendants, whose numbers were specified for each class. As soon as navigation opened through the Baltic that spring, dozens of ships began delivering cloth, carriages, and costumes from European dealers. Silken cloth from Zerbst yielded in popularity only to "English stuffs, particularly white and other light colors with large flowers of gold and silver." Catherine's father also sent a shipment of Zerbst beer, but it found little favor in Petersburg, where governmental activity virtually ceased as the Empress personally supervised the myriad details. In fact, the preparations consumed so much time that the wedding date was postponed twice, finally being set for 21 August with the festivities to conclude ten days later on the holiday of the knightly Order of St. Alexander Nevskii.[42]

As the wedding day approached, Catherine felt expectant and excited, confused and constrained, sad and solitary. Her consort's behavior puzzled her as he seemed to avoid her company, to prefer playing with dolls or playing soldiers. Nevertheless, while inwardly resenting his lack of eagerness and affection, she outwardly humored his caprices. She even boasted that his military instruction taught her how "to shoulder arms today as well as the best-drilled grenadier." A mixture of pride and exasperation informed her later recollections of these diversions. "For hours at a time I had to stand guard with a musket on my shoulder at the door of the room which lay between his room and mine." As the dutiful daughter of a Prussian general, Catherine was accustomed to the military life and shrewdly pandered to Peter's passion for the parade ground. In similar fashion, she began learning to ride horses, a recreation which, along with dancing, she knew Elizabeth (and Russians generally) passionately admired. Later she added hunting to her recreational pursuits, all of which had their political uses.[43]

Thoughts of marriage naturally led to questions about sex. One night in June the Grand Duchess staged an impromptu slumber party for her ladies and maids, "but before we went to sleep we had a prolonged discussion on the difference between the sexes." None had any clear ideas. "Next day I put the question to my mother and was severely scolded." Mother and daughter got along fitfully. Both were much affected by news of the death of Catherine's sister Elizabeth, a sorrow that may have drawn them closer for a time. At any rate, on the eve of the wedding, "we had a long and friendly talk, she exhorted me concerning my future duties, we cried a little together and parted very tenderly." Apparently Johanna was herself already pregnant at this time by Ivan Betskoi, the bastard son of Prince Trubetskoi by a Swedish woman. Still she persisted in political intrigues with her German friends Brümmer, Mardefeld, and Lestocq, and secretly corresponded with Frederick II, unaware that the Russian authorities were reading her letters. Indeed, the Empress wished the marriage celebrated as soon as possible, among other reasons, so that the obnoxious Johanna would go home.[44]

On Friday, 21 August 1745, crowds flocked around Admiralty Square in central Petersburg where fountains had been erected which would flow with wine, banquet tables set up for the public feast, and scaffolding built for spectators and hung with velvet and cloth. A squadron of galleys and yachts lay in the river in front of the Winter Palace and the Admiralty. Troops lined the way from the palace along Nevskii Prospekt to the Church of Our Lady of Kazan. At seven o'clock in the morning Catherine entered the Empress's dressing room, where she was dressed, made up, and loaded with jewelry topped by a small crown with diamonds. "This decoration, the precious stones with which she was covered, gave her a bewitching appearance," her mother commented. "She was lightly rouged, and the color of her face never looked so pretty as at this time. Her light brown hair, sleekly glowing, set off her youthful appearance even more and lent the charms of a brunette to the tenderness of a blonde." Her wedding dress of silver silk brocade, with elaborate embroidery, is now preserved in the Kremlin Armory. Heavy and uncomfortable, the gown accented her eighteen-inch waist.[45]

At ten o'clock trumpets and kettledrums signaled the start of the procession. Detachments of cuirassiers, horse-guards, dragoons, and hussars separated the immense line of 120 coaches, each accompanied by flocks of retainers. Catherine and Peter rode in Elizabeth's coach, "truly a little castle" drawn by eight horses, each ridden by a groom. So long was the cavalcade that the consorts needed three hours to ride the few blocks to the church. The Orthodox service lasted another three hours, with Simon Todorskii, now the Bishop of Pskov, officiating for his former pupils. They all returned to the palace for supper and a ball, which ended past midnight. Elizabeth led the newlyweds away earlier, however, and Catherine was put to bed by her ladies. She remained alone several hours before Peter joined her, giggling at the novelty. Nothing happened that night, or so Catherine remembered. Hers was not a marriage made in Heaven.[46]

Married Life and Court Life

One consequence of the wedding was Princess Johanna's departure from Petersburg on 28 September 1745. Though Elizabeth loaded her with presents including 50,000 rubles in cash, Johanna's debts greatly exceeded that amount and burdened her daughter long afterwards. Before leaving, Johanna tearfully implored Elizabeth's forgiveness, but she was coldly dismissed and told that she had mended her ways too late. She received another chastening slap in the face at Riga in the form of a letter from the Empress requesting that when Johanna passed through Berlin she should tell King Frederick of the need to recall his ambassador Mardefeld. This gesture was calculated to offend both Johanna and Frederick, who reluctantly withdrew Mardefeld a year later. Russo-Prussian relations rapidly deteriorated, as Frederick had a Russian spy beheaded and Elizabeth banished a Prussian agent to Siberia. The arrest and disgrace of Count Lestocq in 1748 carried the estrangement still further and all official ties lapsed after 1750 for more than a decade during this eighteenth-century "cold war." Such hostility hurt Catherine's position in Russia, for she was constantly suspected of Prussian sympathies and clandestine contacts with her mother and other Prussophiles. She was therefore forbidden to correspond with her relatives except through the Collegium of Foreign Affairs, which the Prussophobe Bestuzhev-Riumin imperiously administered.[47]

Before Princess Johanna left her daughter alone in Russia she did her one last nasty favor, or so Catherine perceived the action in subsequent bewildered ruminations. Her mother had the Empress dismiss the Grand Duchess's favorite Russian maid of honor, Maria Zhukova. Although the two young women could barely converse because they did not yet share a common language, they appreciated each other's lively personality, spent much time together, and developed mutual trust; Catherine entrusted Zhukova with the key to her jewelry box. The day of Princess Johanna's departure Zhukova left court, supposedly to rejoin her parents in Moscow. Two days later the Empress informed Catherine of her mother's request for Zhukova's dismissal on grounds that it was dangerous to allow favorites close to the Grand Duchess. It was a great shock to lose such a friend at such a traumatic time and in such an abrupt, insulting way. Long afterwards Catherine professed her own innocent ignorance in the episode; she could not divine whether the motive for dismissal had been mostly personal/sexual—from her mother's jealousy of Zhukova and concern for propriety—or more political, as a demonstration of Elizabeth's power over her new daughter-in-law. In fact, the Grand Duchess wondered whether the whole thing might have been the Empress's doing. The bare hint of a lesbian relationship prompted an outraged denial: "For at that time I had never had a thought of evil; on the contrary if I had died I should have gone straight to Paradise; I was so innocent in heart and mind." Furthermore, she congratulated herself on helping to arrange Zhukova's marriage, supporting her surreptitiously, and even buying her a country estate. Catherine stuck by her friends.[48]

Marriage and her mother's departure resulted in somewhat greater freedom for the Grand Duchess in her daily life. Obviously Elizabeth wished the young newlyweds to have some time alone together, but in fact they seldom saw each other in privacy. Peter's military exercises, childish games, and preference for the company of lackeys held no appeal for his wife, who "yawned and yawned with boredom having no one to amuse me, but only my social duties to perform." They both attended the biweekly balls of the winter social season and enjoyed entertaining guests. Indeed, in contradiction to Catherine's later condemnation of Peter's character, tastes, and attitudes, she admitted that "on the whole we lived happily, the Grand Duke and I." She became extremely upset when, at the end of the social season in early March 1746, the Grand Duke caught cold and woke up the next morning with a bad headache and a violent fever. All the old fears for his life revived. He was bled frequently, and the Empress visited him several times a day. Noticing Catherine's faithful attendance at bedside, worried countenance, and tearful eyes, Elizabeth sent word that she should trust in God's aid and reassured her that in no circumstances would she be abandoned. Nevertheless, that spring several circumstances incited the Empress's wrath toward the Young Court, as the consorts' household was known.[49]

Elizabeth became nervous, first of all, at the news of the death of Princess Anna Leopol'dovna in exile at the northern town of Kholmogory on 7 March 1746, a week after she had given birth to another son, her third child since her loss of the throne. All five of her children held rights of succession in the event that Elizabeth's line died out, and since her eldest son had reigned briefly as Ivan VI, he was confined separately from the rest of the family. The Brunswick family weighed on Elizabeth's conscience. At one time she had considered expelling them all from Russia, but then decided on their permanent imprisonment at the remote Solovetskii Monastery on an island in the White Sea. Bad weather and bad roads, the arbiters of life in rural Russia, stopped the prisoners short in the backwater of Kholmogory, where the birth of two more children multiplied their political threat to Elizabeth. So worried was the Empress on this account, she had secretly ordered that in case Anna Leopol'dovna or her husband died in confinement, their bodies should be dissected, preserved in alcohol, and sent immediately to Petersburg for public burial. Furthermore, when she learned of Anna Leopol'dovna's death she wrote her husband Anton Ulrich demanding that he explain the cause of her death—apparently childbed fever—but without any mention of the birth of a prince. The Empress did not want people to know how many children were in the Brunswick family. Although none dared speak of Prince Ivan openly, rumor ran amuck. The body of Anna Leopol'dovna was buried on 21 March at the Alexander Nevskii Monastery in Petersburg next to the coffin of her mother, Princess Catherine of Mecklenburg. Grand Duchess Catherine attended the funeral with Elizabeth, who wept throughout.[50]

These tears probably flowed from sorrow and regret, fear and frustration. Elizabeth's emotional temperament felt the shadow of mortality, darkened by the spectacle of her late cousin's healthy brood in contrast to her own lack of offspring and her nephew's incessant illnesses. Catherine's virginal condition mocked the Empress's effort to procure the necessary male heir. After seven months of marriage why had she not conceived a child? The Empress evidently had no idea of the couple's estrangement until the Grand Duke's infantile audacity accidentally caught her eye.

Toward the end of his most recent illness Peter organized a puppet theater

in a room that opened into one of the Empress's apartments, the door between the two having been nailed shut. His theater attracted claques of courtiers. One evening, while preparing a performance, he heard voices through
the sealed door and decided to investigate, using a brace and bit to bore
peepholes. In the other room he could observe Elizabeth, her favorite Razumovskii, and some of their intimates supping and conversing without ceremony. This spectacle so amused the Grand Duke that he invited Catherine
and his guests to witness the proceedings, setting up chairs, benches, and
stools for their convenience. Catherine was scandalized as well as frightened.
In separate recollections penned decades after the fact, she claimed that she
looked only once in one instance, not at all in another. The peepshow quickly
ended, it seems, but within days Elizabeth found out and exploded in wrath.
She raged at Peter like a Fury, threatening him with the same treatment that
Peter the Great had visited on his ungrateful son Aleksei. When the Grand
Duke retorted insolently, the Empress lost control; "she showered furious
condemnations and gross words upon him, betraying as much contempt for
him as anger," Catherine remembered. Noticing Catherine's agitation, Elizabeth calmed down enough to assure her that she was deemed innocent in the
whole affair. After Elizabeth stormed out, the consorts discussed the outburst in mixed tones of bewilderment, terror, and contrition. A maid rational-
ized the incident as a mother's momentary anger and advised mollifying the
Empress with a magic phrase—"vinovaty, Matushka" (we beg your pardon,
Mama). Catherine later used this formula with some success in future altercations.[51]

This silly incident entailed serious consequences for the consorts within
a few weeks. Elizabeth dictated a complete reorganization of the Young
Court, commissioning Bestuzhev-Riumin to draft detailed instructions for
the supervision of the conduct of each spouse. For the Grand Duchess, these
instructions called for zealous adherence to Russian Orthodoxy, close surveillance of all contacts with others, noninterference in all matters of state including those of Holstein, and free access to the Empress at all times for the
oral communication of her needs. But Catherine's marital obligations received the most elaborate explication. Her whole purpose and position in
Russia, she was bluntly informed, were predicated on her producing a male
successor as a matter of urgent state necessity. This responsibility was presented as hers alone. Peter's problems, by contrast, were seen to be of another order. As the reigning Duke of Holstein who had reached his majority
and could now administer his own domain, he was tacitly conceded full authority in Holstein affairs. As heir to the Russian throne, however, he must
be reformed and disciplined. Specifically, the person entrusted with overseeing Peter's conduct was charged to change his scornful attitude and dis-
respectful behavior toward the dogmas and the clergy of the established
Church, "whereby all those in church have been publicly outraged." The
Grand Duke was also criticized for his childish games, such as drilling lackeys in military uniform and thus converting military art into jokes, his preference for vulgar companions, even his lack of table manners—harassing servants, spilling wine, joking indecently, and making faces. In short, Peter's

supervisor was to take the eighteen-year-old in hand, but not to interfere in Holstein affairs. Nothing was said about the Grand Duke's marital obligations.[52]

The contrast between these two sets of instructions nicely delineates the different roles expected of Peter and Catherine. He should prepare himself to rule the Russian Empire; she should concern herself solely with producing a male heir as soon as possible. No other activities, interests, or contacts were to be encouraged, not even correspondence with her parents. Procreation was her *raison d'être*. Of course, it is one thing to prescribe behavior, especially biological behavior; quite another to dictate it. By crudely challenging the consorts' personal autonomy and dignity, these instructions provoked more of the behavior they sought to scotch. Peter began lavishing attention on Holstein affairs, for example, to the neglect of matters Russian; whereas Catherine in her isolated boredom entered into petty intrigues and began secretly corresponding with her mother. Between the spouses, though, nothing changed.

Elizabeth's instructions were accompanied by a purge of the Young Court. Brümmer was dismissed and returned to Holstein, replaced as Peter's principal supervisor by a Russian, Prince Vasilii Repnin. Three Chernyshev brothers, chamberlains to the Grand Duke, were sent away and even arrested for a time because of their intimacy with both consorts. Another Chernyshev chamberlain, Count Zakhar Grigor'evich, had earlier been sent abroad at the request of Catherine's mother for fear that he had fallen in love with the Grand Duchess. Several of Catherine's attendants were also removed and a new personage assigned as her chief supervisor—Maria Semenovna Choglokova, a distant relative and favorite of the Empress. As a young woman of station, married only a few years, fervently in love with her spouse, and already the mother of several children, Choglokova's example was supposed to inspire Catherine in the fulfillment of her marital duties. Naturally the Grand Duchess disliked her at once; "I cried a great deal when I saw her arrive and went on crying for the rest of the day." Elizabeth reacted to this display of emotion by storming into Catherine's apartment the next day and raining accusations and reproaches on her head. Only the magic phrase "Vinovaty, Matushka" saved the Grand Duchess from a slap or worse.[53]

The purge of the Young Court resulted in much stricter surveillance over Catherine, which tested her powers of dissimulation and deception. She lightened her boredom and cultivated the hated Choglokova, for instance, by pandering to the latter's passion for gambling although that practice, along with the gifts she lavished on this "Argus," put the Grand Duchess further in debt. The constant changes of faces among the consorts' servants and attendants—it seemed that everyone they took a liking to was quickly removed—had the effect of widening Catherine's circle of acquaintances. Thus she discovered a "living archive" in Praskov'ia Vladislavova, a new lady of the chamber who, though reputed to be a tool of Bestuzhev-Riumin's, served Catherine loyally and furnished much useful information about Russian politics and personalities in the years prior to Elizabeth's reign. Timofei Evreinov, a valet, also proved his loyalty to the Grand Duchess and became a trusted adviser, a veritable "oracle."[54] Then too, the reorganization of the administration of Holstein affairs deprived Peter of several intimates and forced him to turn to Catherine for consultation. Although she never admitted the fact, she obviously picked up information and insights from her unloved spouse, in whom she found "a certain perspicacity, but no judgment," little discretion, and less tact.[55]

Another consequence of Catherine's boredom and isolation was that she took up reading, or rather rediscovered a previous pastime. The different versions of her memoirs give different accounts of how this phase of her self-education began. In one, at her grandmother's house in Hamburg she responded to the urgings of a special Swedish emissary, Count Adolf Gyllenborg, who had chided Princess Johanna's negligent attitude toward her daughter's higher education. She and Gyllenborg corresponded briefly in 1743 about their common interest in the works of Voltaire. At age fifteen she encountered Gyllenborg again, this time in St. Petersburg, where he remonstrated with her for wallowing in mindless pleasures. She should develop her mind and fortify her spirit, he insisted, by reading serious books such as Plutarch and Montesquieu. The difficulty of obtaining foreign authors in Petersburg gave Catherine a good excuse for not following this advice, but she did compose for Gyllenborg a self-appraisal entitled "Portrait of a Fifteen-Year-Old Philosopher," evidently her first autobiographical work, which she later destroyed in connection with Bestuzhev-Riumin's disgrace. Gyllenborg returned it with extensive comments that aimed, she recalled years later, "to inculcate in me greatness of soul and determination besides the other qualities of heart and spirit. I read and re-read many times what he had written. I allowed it to sink into my consciousness and intended to follow his advice very seriously." Yet she did not start reading the books he recommended.[56]

The first book to come to hand, and the first she remembered reading from start to finish, was a French (actually Catalan) picaresque romance, *Tiran le Blanc:* "I was delighted with the Princess who had so fine skin that when she drank the red wine could be seen flowing down her throat." No doubt she also noticed the work's ribald streak. After the marriage Catherine soon tired of social functions and gossip and travels from one imperial estate to another. "My partiality for romances disappeared; accidentally the letters of Madame Sévigné fell into my hands and gave me much pleasure. After I had devoured them, I read the works of Voltaire and never again got loose from them. When I had finished this reading I looked for something similar, but since I could find nothing like it, I read in the meantime whatever fell into my hands." The wit of Madame Sévigné in particular furnished a model for Catherine's own writings. Later on she enjoyed the scandalous, amoral memoirs of Brantome (1540–1614) and Péréfixe's life of Henry IV of France, who became her favorite hero. In any event, reading became a favorite diversion.[57]

Gradually Catherine tried more difficult works. In 1751 she started reading four huge folio volumes of Bayle's *Historical and Critical Dictionary*. It took her almost three years to plough through this classic of the early European

Enlightenment, which may have begun undermining her childhood belief in political and moral absolutes. As Catherine later remarked, it was very unusual for anybody, still less for a woman, to take an interest in books at the Russian court, where half could barely read and scarcely one-third could write. Starting as an avid reader, she later became an ardent pen-pusher, rarely passing a day in which she did not write something. Graphomania became one of her most persistent and most politically potent pastimes. By contrast, the Grand Duke also liked to read, but his tastes were limited to adventure stories and novels.[58]

If Catherine's intellectual development blossomed after marriage, her emotional and physical capacities underwent periodic crises as she grew into womanhood. Loneliness tormented her incessantly. Her mother's departure from Russia and her father's death in 1747 removed two emotional pillars of her girlhood. She fell prey to depression, especially at the time of her monthly period. On one occasion she may have half-heartedly attempted suicide. Her melancholia was sometimes treated by blood-letting. Her sexual frustration steadily intensified and undoubtedly contributed to severe headaches and insomnia. Episodes of disease and debility also disturbed the routine of her life. Twice she was thought to have contracted smallpox, for which she maintained a vivid horror, but it turned out to be measles in both instances. Long afer her severe illness in Moscow in 1744 the court doctor feared that frequent chest pains and coughing up blood meant that she would develop consumption. "It is astonishing that I did not," commented Catherine more than forty years later, "for I lived a life for eighteen years from which ten others would have gone crazy and twenty in my place would have died of melancholy." Slowly she grew taller and, though thin by the standard of the time, developed "a fine figure, except that it was a little lacking in fullness." She also learned how to dress with taste and originality, a practice that usually won the heart of the jealous Elizabeth, especially when both wore male attire.[59]

Travels with Elizabeth's peripatetic court introduced Catherine to the Empire's immensity and the diversity of its peoples and regions. Only once did she visit non-Russian areas: in Estland in July 1746 at Reval (present-day Tallin), nearby Catherinental (a Petrine estate named for Catherine I), and the port of Rogervik. A peculiar scare disrupted this sojourn. The Empress, who had planned to proceed westward to Riga, abruptly abandoned the journey after a warning from a "fanatical and crazy Lutheran pastor" that a murderer lay in wait at Riga. Elizabeth's unexplained return perplexed everybody. Two decades later Catherine was appalled, in retrospect, by the flimsiness of the evidence and her predecessor's timidity. A second scare affected Catherine much more directly two years later at Gostilitsy, Andrei Razumovskii's estate west of Petersburg. At eight o'clock in the morning of 25 May 1748, after an all-night revel in special clothes ordered by the Empress, the Young Court were all asleep in a small wooden palace that suddenly slipped off its foundations with a crash like an earthquake. Catherine barely escaped with bruises all over her arms, legs, and right side. Whereas Peter jumped out before the collapse, a score of their courtiers including

Princess Anna Gagarina were maimed or killed. To calm Catherine's shattered nerves, she was bled at once, but the terror haunted her long afterwards. Elizabeth, lodged elsewhere, seemed more upset at the embarrassment of Razumovskii, who threatened suicide as a result. All the same, she ordered other palaces checked for similar hazards.[60]

For exercise the Grand Duchess enjoyed and excelled at dancing, riding, and shooting. Riding, particularly riding astride, relieved some of her sexual tension and lessened her monthly hypochondria. Since the Empress disapproved of her riding astride for fear it would impair fecundity, she devised a convertible saddle that could be ridden either way. Hunting offered an exciting escape from the dull confines of court life; "the more violent the exercise the more I enjoyed it, so that if a horse ever broke away I galloped after it and brought it back." Sometimes she spent as many as thirteen hours in the saddle. She was a tireless dancer and crack shot, often rising early to shoot fowl in the woods or along the seashore. Usually a lone huntsman accompanied her; Peter joined in but rarely. All this exercise facilitated Catherine's physical development, cultivated such "masculine" virtues as boldness, courage, and agility, and fostered independence and individual autonomy. Such outdoor activities also allowed her to outfox the ubiquitous surveillance at court in town, by exploiting "the laziness of my guardians." She gradually asserted control over larger areas of her life and future.[61]

Relations with her husband remained tense and complex, however, all the more so because he manifested signs of assertiveness, too, while enduring some of the same sexual frustration and political repression, loneliness and boredom. Peter handled these problems somewhat differently than Catherine did. After all, because he was male, different things were expected of him, and he lacked her will power and gift for manipulation. Like his wife, he tried to please his formidable aunt, although often ineptly, and sought diversion in sodden frolics with friends and flirtations with various women at court. Both these amusements held the added psychological advantage that they irritated his resentful spouse. Indeed, he delighted in boasting to Catherine of his gallantries with other women. It took her several years to recognize that his affairs never went "beyond languishing glances." Apparently young Peter, without sisters or brothers or experience with other children, was extremely self-conscious about his body and quite timid in the presence of females. The fact that the Empress had as much as ordered him to beget children, and that everyone at court knew her expectations for him, merely deepened his embarrassment about matters sexual. What Catherine saw as cool indifference and insulting disdain was probably more a case of innocent ignorance and adolescent ambivalence. As a timorous and frustrated male, Peter found psychic release in military games, training hounds, playing the violin, and carousing with subordinates; these preoccupations gave him illusions of mastery and competence. Drink in particular conquered his timidity with women, so he began drinking regularly and heavily, though mostly in private. All these new interests of Peter's annoyed Catherine, who spurned him more than ever.[62]

One of his few attempts to establish intimacy with her occurred, not surprisingly, under the influence of drink. One evening at supper he provoked Catherine by flirting with the hunchbacked Princess of Kurland. Complaining of a bad headache, the Grand Duchess left the table to retire early. Her lady-in-waiting Vladislavova tried to soothe her outrage, which she saw as caused by jealousy of the Princess of Kurland and by Peter's abusive treatment. But this well-meant tirade only made Catherine cry all the harder; "I could not endure the thought that I had aroused anybody's pity and she had let me see that she sympathized with my position." After the Grand Duchess finally fell asleep alone, Peter joined her in bed and, tipsy, endeavored to rouse his spouse by loudly "enumerating all the eminent qualities of his lady love." Though awakened, Catherine "pretended to be fast asleep to stop him talking, but after talking more and more loudly to wake me up and seeing that I gave no sign of awakening, he gave me two or three rather violent punches to the side, grumbling about my sleeping so soundly, and then turned over and went off to sleep himself." She cried much of the night from shame and frustration. The next morning neither spouse mentioned the incident. The consorts revenged themselves on each other, and both lost.[63]

The longer that Peter and Catherine lived in Russia without producing an heir, the shakier their position appeared. Elizabeth might act on her threat to disinherit the Grand Duke. If she did, it would surely undercut Catherine's position. Equally menacing was the question of their fate if Elizabeth should die before they begot the desired heir. This was not a matter of idle speculation, for the Empress's health started to show danger signs as early as the winter of 1748–49 in Moscow, where she suffered a serious bout of what was politely termed constipation. Although Elizabeth's condition was kept secret, it lasted several weeks and provoked great anxiety and frequent clandestine consultations among her top advisers, Bestuzhev-Riumin and General Stepan Apraksin. Peter and Catherine heard about these comings and goings despite efforts to keep them in the dark and in virtual political imprisonment. Both sensed the dangers of the situation and plotted together to defend their position in case of Elizabeth's sudden demise. Catherine proved especially adept at collecting intelligence about the Empress's condition, tapping Vladislavova's intimate contacts with the priests and cantors assigned to the court. She told Peter that in case of need they could escape from their rooms by jumping out of the ground floor windows. Furthermore, she reassured him that their friend Zakhar Chernyshev and several other Guards officers would support their claims to the throne. Since Elizabeth recovered shortly thereafter, no action was taken. But the incident revealed not only the consorts' fear for their future, but their readiness to conspire with others in pursuit of the throne—in short, a valuable exercise in Russian court politics.[64]

Later in 1749 another incident dramatized anew the Grand Duke's political prospects and his wife's role in protecting those prospects. A conspiracy came to light involving Ioasaf Baturin, a debt-ridden lieutenant stationed in Moscow, who wanted to place Peter on the throne by violent means. Peter's passion for training a pack of hunting dogs had led him to make the acquaintance of several huntsmen, who first told him about Baturin's extraordinary admiration for the Grand Duke and ardent desire to "serve" him.

Through the huntsmen Baturin asked to be presented to Peter, who consented more or less reluctantly. At any rate, one day when Peter was out hunting in the environs of Moscow, Baturin suddenly accosted him, dropped to his knees before the Grand Duke, swore passionately that he would serve no other master, and vowed to follow his "orders." Peter panicked. He spurred his steed and left Baturin alone on his knees in the wood. Nothing further happened that day, but the Grand Duke soon quaked in his boots at the huntsmen's report that Baturin had been arrested and taken for interrogation to the dread Secret Chancery in the Moscow suburb of Preobrazhenskoe.

What terrified Peter above all, as he confided "reluctantly and incoherently" to Catherine, was the possibility of his being implicated in Baturin's desperate venture. Although Catherine suspected more than he told her, she reassured him that Baturin's folly need not compromise the Grand Duke. In fact, the huntsmen were quickly released and, before they were expelled from Russia, they contrived to inform Peter that his name had not been mentioned during the interrogations. Peter rejoiced, all the more so because it transpired that Baturin and several confederates had confessed under torture to a whole catalogue of heinous intentions: to murder Elizabeth and her favorite Aleksei Razumovskii, to torch the Golovin Palace as a diversion while rallying 50,000 soldiers and clothworkers for the Grand Duke, who was expected to purge the government of corrupt officials and to institute conservative, nationalistic, and strictly religious policies. Baturin's main confederates were beaten with the knout and banished; he himself was locked in the dungeon of the fortress of Schlüsselburg, where he still languished when Peter succeeded to the throne and when Catherine seized power. Since he continued plotting even in prison, she deported him to Siberia, where he participated in one final plot.[65]

For Catherine, the lessons to be drawn from Baturin's conspiracy were several. First, it hinted at how unsure Elizabeth's hold on the throne might appear to bold soldiers bent on installing another claimant. Second, it indicated that the Grand Duke enjoyed some popularity outside court circles, an anti-government popularity that he did nothing to foster and which he did not know how to use. And third, it revealed both Peter's ineptitude in a crisis and his newly urgent desire for power. "After this time I observed that the wish to rule grew stronger in the Grand Duke's heart," Catherine would later recall; "it nearly killed him yet he did nothing to make himself worthy of it." By contrast, the Grand Duchess quietly prepared herself to rule with or without Peter.[66]

Some days after the resolution of Baturin's conspiracy, Peter had an altercation with Choglokova in which Catherine detected an echo of the incident that constituted a threat from the Empress to both consorts. It was the start of Lent, a season when it was Russian custom to take a steambath as part of the preparation for Easter. Choglokova transmitted the Empress's order that both consorts should go for their baths. Peter, who hated the custom, flatly refused, arguing with the obstinate Choglokova that steambaths were harmful to his constitution. The Empress would not force something so repugnant on him, he tartly told Choglokova, whose threats to report his disobedience he

defiantly dismissed with the remark: "After all, I am not a child any more."
Choglokova exploded with rage and threatened, among other things, that the
Empress would imprison him. "He then began to cry bitterly and they said
all the outrageous things to one another that anger can inspire; they had
both literally taken leave of their senses." Choglokova left to report the incident and shortly returned with the news that "the Empress was very angry
that we had no children and wanted to know whose fault it was; she was
going to send me a midwife, and the Grand Duke a doctor." She never did
either, according to Catherine, but she excused Peter from the steambath. In
pondering the motives behind this altercation, the Grand Duchess decided
the threat of imprisonment must have come directly from Elizabeth, who also
conveyed her hostility toward Peter by ceasing to kiss his hand when he
came to kiss hers. Catherine had stayed out of the argument, she maintained
later, because the protagonists' vehemence left no chance to intervene and
because she considered it "completely absurd on both sides." Subsequently,
the link to Baturin's conspiracy having occurred to her, she understood more
clearly the grave political threat to her husband and herself.[67]

Their personal and political salvation depended more urgently than ever
on the birth of an heir, preferably male; yet five years of wedlock had passed
without a single pregnancy. No wonder Elizabeth was worried. Catherine
had to worry, too, since "everybody knew" her marriage had not been consummated. Alternative solutions were suggested to the consorts, almost certainly with Elizabeth's blessing. Thus, Choglokova arranged with Peter's
French valet to have an experienced woman, the pretty widow Groot, initiate
the Grand Duke into the mysteries of sexual love—with unknown results.
There is a story that Peter could not function sexually because of a minor
physical handicap: some kind of stricture of the foreskin. Others suspect he
was impotent and sterile. Perhaps the truth will never be known. Of course,
Catherine in her reminiscences asserted that their marriage had not been
consummated after five years, blaming the fact on her hapless husband.
Though candid on many other physical facts, she never mentioned any particular disability, never admitted having intercourse with Peter, and strongly
implied that others were responsible for her pregnancies.[68] Doubts must
surround these matters until such time as historical bloodtests will be per-
fected.

Passion and Procreation

If Peter would not or could not father an heir, state necessity demanded that
Catherine should bear the needed child by somebody else. Political and personal imperatives overrode any moral scruples. Actually, she had none. Since
the early days of her marriage she had been searching for the affection that
her husband rarely provided. As she blossomed into a pretty young woman
of charm and grace and spirit, her need for male attention and approval grew
commensurately. Furthermore, her personal isolation, boredom, and frustration with the constraints of court life were all conducive to petty romantic

intrigues. Probably most of these were quite innocent, as for example her relations with Andrei Chernyshev in 1746–47. But Elizabeth took that flirtation so seriously that she had Catherine's confessor inquire about it after Chernyshev had been interrogated by the Secret Chancery and sent away under house arrest. Nevertheless, the Grand Duchess discovered Chernyshev's place of temporary detention on the edge of Petersburg through her valet Evreinov, secretly corresponded with him, and sent him "some money and other trifles." Others pined for the young Catherine, too, including the Swedish envoy, Count Kirill Razumovskii, and especially Count Zakhar Chernyshev.[69]

Smitten with her charm at first sight, Zakhar Chernyshev had been sent abroad to cool his ardor (or so Catherine asserted), but on returning to Petersburg in 1751 he laid siege to the Grand Duchess. "He started by saying that he found me much more beautiful. This was the first time that anyone had said anything of the kind to me. I found it quite pleasing. I did more, I naively believed he spoke the truth." They began secretly exchanging love notes. He proposed a visit to her room in disguise, but she refused and their affair went no further. Or so she maintained in later remembrances. If she retained her virginity, however, her heart was obviously slipping away. A few days before he left to rejoin his regiment, Catherine asked for a bloodletting—usually a sign of emotional frustration—and later went sledding and dancing with him and others, from which she "came home very late, without anyone knowing what had happened to me." This tale may conceal more than meets the eye. Their love notes certainly exhibit some affection, and Zakhar Chernyshev apparently entered Catherine's political calculations as early as 1749 in connection with the consorts' fright over Elizabeth's "constipation" in Moscow. Whatever the physical facts behind these episodes, they reveal Catherine's growing confidence and boldness in relations with other men. "To tell the truth, I never believed myself to be very beautiful," she recorded many years later, "but I was pleasant and that, I suppose, was my strength."[70] Understatement, indeed.

Her charm also attracted two aristocratic chamberlains of the Young Court, Lev Naryshkin and Sergei Saltykov. The former diverted the Grand Duchess with his comic absurdities and ready wit; the latter, though recently married, danced attendance on the Choglokovs first and then boldly accosted Catherine, who thought him "handsome as the dawn." It is hard to decide whose was the initiative in their affair. Catherine's recollections offer both romantic and mundane versions, implying that his ardor overwhelmed her reluctance or, alternatively, that she and Peter answered Elizabeth's summons to procreate by coolly selecting Saltykov. In any event, the deed was done. The Grand Duchess left for Moscow in mid-December 1752 "with a few slight symptoms of pregnancy," but these disappeared with "violent hemorrhages" just before her arrival. This first miscarriage heralded a troubled sojourn in Moscow, the old capital for which Catherine's initial dislike gradually festered into deep disgust. She was lodged with sixteen other court ladies in cramped rooms of the Golovin Palace "filled with every kind of insect." Later in this sojourn her disgust with Moscow's pathetic palaces was reinforced by the sight of a huge rat, which the Grand Duke had caught in his room and then tortured and hanged with mock military ceremony. He was offended, however, when she laughed at "the madness of the whole thing." Additional evidence of Moscow's perils came in November 1753 when the Golovin Palace suddenly burned to the ground. As Catherine and her attendants rushed out of the wooden firetrap, she looked back at a "remarkable spectacle: a prodigious number of rats and mice were filing down the stairs, not even hurrying much." Elizabeth lost 4,000 dresses in the blaze, but she had an army of carpenters rebuild the palace in six weeks. This was only one of many fires that Catherine witnessed there in 1753–54. "It often happened that I saw from the windows of the Summer Palace two, three, four, sometimes five fires at the same time in different parts of Moscow." Her own quarters caught fire two or three more times.[71]

While the court was in Moscow none other than the Grand Chancellor Bestuzhev-Riumin made overtures to Saltykov and Catherine, artfully encouraging them to resume their liaison. Choglokova did the same with Catherine in private, perhaps impelled by Elizabeth's obvious disappointment with both consorts. By May 1753 the Grand Duchess was pregnant again. Within another month, however, she miscarried for the second time, on 30 June 1753, and fell dangerously ill for two weeks. Catherine convalesced slowly, felt depressed, and asked for Saltykov's visits to be renewed—"all this made me feel like a bear with a sore head." She also professed to be worried about her husband's jealousy of Saltykov. Still, she became pregnant for the third time by February 1754.[72]

Great efforts were made to protect this pregnancy. A midwife constantly attended the Grand Duchess, and both Saltykov and Naryshkin accompanied her on the slow journey back to Petersburg in May 1754. That spring she renewed her clandestine correspondence with her mother, whom she informed of the pregnancy on 7/18 April. Yet Catherine's spirits fell into depression because Saltykov was not allowed close to her, and because she loathed the new official assigned to the Young Court, Count Alexander Shuvalov, whose duties included supervision of the notorious Secret Chancery. "These functions, so it was said, had given him a sort of convulsion that affected the entire right side of his face, from the eye to the chin, whenever he was overcome with joy, anger, fear, or anxiety." He was a member of the new "party" dominant at court, and Catherine held Elizabeth responsible for his unfortunate appointment. "It was astonishing that a man with such a hideous facial affliction should have been chosen to be continuously with a young pregnant woman," for folk wisdom suspected that such circumstances might taint a birth. On returning in August from the fresh air of Peterhof to await the delivery, Catherine received a "deadly shock": her labor room adjoined Elizabeth's apartments in the decrepit Summer Palace. Indeed, as these accommodations foretold, when she gave birth to a son on 20 September 1754 after a difficult delivery, the Empress immediately took charge of the baby, whom she named Paul. Catherine's duty done, she was left alone in great discomfort for several hours and not allowed to see her son for more than a week. "The Grand Duke in his rooms did nothing but drink with whomever came to see him, while the Empress was busy with the child." When Paul was christened a week later, Elizabeth rewarded his mother with some second-rate jewelry and 100,000 rubles. Catherine appreciated the money, for she was crippled with debts; but a few days later she had to loan it back to the Empress, who used it to satisfy Peter's importunities. Having provided the needed heir, the Grand Duchess concluded that her period of relative favor and influence was over. Saltykov's dispatch abroad left her feeling deserted and depressed, exploited and excluded. Even the joys of motherhood were denied her; she was rarely allowed to see her own son.[73]

Whose son was he anyway? In all versions of her memoirs Catherine leads us to think Paul's father was Sergei Saltykov. Many contemporaries thought the same. But others point to the contrast between Saltykov's handsome features and Paul's plain visage, arguing against any blood relationship while drawing parallels in personality between Paul and Peter. To be sure, arguments about genealogy are notoriously uncertain. The handsome Saltykov had a very ugly brother, and the close blood relationship between Peter and Catherine should not be forgotten, either. Presumably the consorts would have had trouble producing a normal child. It is often asserted that the question holds significance because if Peter was not Paul's father, then the direct line of succession of the Romanov dynasty ceased with Peter. Elizabeth thought otherwise. According to a story repeated by foreign envoys in Russia in 1755, when a lady at court remarked on the contrast in complexion between Peter and Paul, the baby being "very brown," the Empress erupted: "Hold your tongue you B____ I know what you mean, you want to insinuate He is a Bastard, but if He is, He is not the first that has been in my Family."[74]

Conspiracy Thwarted and Renewed

The year 1754 signified a great divide in Catherine's life. She had fulfilled at last the primary reason for coming to Russia and marrying the heir to the throne. Nothing more was expected of her. She could determine the rest of her life herself. The irksome surveillance over her largely ceased, and she enjoyed much greater freedom of movement, association, and correspondence. While recovering from childbirth, the Grand Duchess resumed her education by reading more serious books than before, many with a political orientation: historical works by Voltaire, the *Annals* of Tacitus, which made her search for motivations behind political events, and Montesquieu's great *Spirit of the Laws*. For the first time she also read books in Russian, starting with two hefty volumes of Baronius's ecclesiastical annals in translation. These works initiated the Grand Duchess into the theory of statecraft and offered many contrasts to what she knew and would personally witness of Russia's political history.[75]

The practice of statecraft she learned by observation, reflection, discussion, and personal involvement in the administration of Holstein affairs. Though Peter professed "an extraordinary passion for the corner of the world where he was born," the details of routine administration bewildered and bored him. Hence he occasionally consulted his wife about issues related to Holstein, despite the Empress's ban on political activity by the Grand Duchess. In 1750–51, for example, when the Danish envoy Count Lynar visited Petersburg with a proposal that Peter renounce his claims to Sleswig in favor of Denmark and exchange Holstein for the Duchy of Oldenburg, the Grand Duke could not decide how to handle the negotiations. He asked Catherine's opinion and accepted her view that the proposed exchange represented a diplomatic maneuver by Bestuzhev-Riumin which, though it might forward some of Russia's interests, might also compromise the Grand Duke's own prestige. Soon the issue was dropped. All the same, from the mid-1750s Peter periodically consulted Catherine about Holstein affairs and even delegated some authority to her in that regard. "His confidence in the Great Dutchess is so great," reported the British ambassador in October 1755, "that sometimes he tells people, that tho' he does not understand things himself, yet His wife understands everything." He rightly dubbed her "Madame la Ressource."[76]

Unlike Peter, however, Catherine made no emotional investment in Holstein. She noticed Elizabeth's hostility toward her husband's preoccupation with Holstein and his indifference toward Russia. Indeed, when Peter contrived to bring a whole detachment of Holsteiners to Russia and, wearing a Holstein uniform himself, drilled them at Oranienbaum in the summer of 1755, Catherine shunned the spectacle and "trembled to think what a disastrous effect it would have on the Grand Duke's prestige from the Russians' point of view, let alone from that of the Empress whose feelings on the subject were known to me." The Grand Duchess also reacted against Peter's new Holsteiner chamberlain, Brockdorff, whose influence she thought pandered to the Grand Duke's taste for "drink and dissoluteness," his dinner parties at Oranienbaum often turning into "real orgies." Therefore, when Denmark in 1756 proposed anew the exchange of Holstein for Oldenburg and Delmenhorst, and Brockdorff opposed the deal, Catherine dropped her previous opposition and favored the exchange as a means of conciliating Denmark. Nothing happened as a result, but Bestuzhev-Riumin had warned the Danish envoy years earlier that Peter's first priority on taking power would be war with Denmark to recover Sleswig. That foolish war led directly to Peter's overthrow and Catherine's accession.[77]

By the spring of 1755 Catherine re-entered the whirl of Russian court politics with new resolution and confidence, qualities that she also employed in her search for male affection. She did not pine very long over Saltykov, although reports of his amorous indiscretions abroad irritated her. A worthy successor soon appeared. At Oranienbaum on 29 June 1755, the feast day of Saints Peter and Paul, the Young Court first received the new English envoy, Sir Charles Hanbury-Williams, whose numerous and luxurious entourage included a young Polish aristocrat—Count Stanislas August Poniatowski. Catherine, radiant at age twenty-six in the ripe fullness of recent motherhood, mesmerized the cultivated young Pole, fresh from the salons of Paris. He was enthralled by her eyes, "the bluest and merriest in the world, subjugating all who came within her orbit," and remembered her appearance long afterwards.

> With her dark hair she had a complexion of dazzling whiteness, the most lively coloring, large expressive blooming blue eyes, eye lashes that were dark and very long, a pointed nose, a mouth that seemed to invite kisses, perfect hands and arms, a shapely figure rather big than small, a bearing entirely nimble and yet of the greatest nobility, a pleasant-sounding voice and a laugh as merry as her mood, which she could transpose with equal facility from the silliest, most childish games to matters of business, the physical work of which bothered her no more than the text howsoever important or even perilous the matter might be.[78]

Her sexuality fully awakened by Saltykov if not before, she dextrously seduced the handsome, virginal Pole. By late fall, she thought herself pregnant again, perhaps anticipating the prospect, but it proved to be a false alarm. With the help of Lev Naryshkin and his sister-in-law, Catherine took to slipping out of the palace at night, disguised in men's clothing, to join them and Poniatowski in clandestine revelry almost weekly. Later Poniatowski contrived to visit his mistress so often that her pet dog once divulged the nature of their relationship to a perceptive outsider by welcoming the Count with obvious affection. The Grand Duke put no obstacles in their way. When not smoking, drinking, or drilling his Holsteiners, Peter pursued amorous conquests of his own, particularly Elizaveta Vorontsova, daughter of Vice-Chancellor Mikhail Vorontsov. The Grand Duke could compete with his wife no more successfully in love affairs than in political intrigue. A small measure of her emerging self-confidence was her resumption of riding lessons in the spring and summer of 1756, every morning at six except on Sundays. She made such rapid progress that her riding teacher awarded her silver spurs and urged her to try a steeplechase, an experiment that had to be postponed.[79]

The passionate, prolonged affair with Poniatowski certainly compensated completely for Catherine's pitifully naive, painfully concluded liaison with Saltykov. Psychologically, the Pole's passion showed her that she could inspire adoration and devotion. Culturally, his cosmopolitan manner helped to expand her outlook and experience, while shielding her from Peter's coarse ways. Politically, Poniatowski joined Hanbury-Williams in introducing Catherine to the vagaries of European diplomacy as they impinged on Russian court politics. Passion and politics conjoined to animate the Grand Duchess's expanding ambitions.

The pace of Russian political affairs quickened in 1756 with the frenetic diplomacy centering on the outbreak of the Seven Years' War, the establishment of a new supreme council—the Conference at the Imperial Court, which was charged to oversee mobilization for the Russian attack on Prussia—and Elizabeth's obviously failing health. Because of the deepening international and domestic crisis, Elizabeth vainly attempted to conceal the state of her health from friend and foe alike. Even so, by the late summer of 1756

Catherine and Bestuzhev-Riumin both began actively planning for the transition of power after Elizabeth's death. The Empress's deterioration raised constant alarms. Indeed, she collapsed on 26 October, and Catherine confided to Hanbury-Williams two days later that "my surgeon, a man of great experience and good sense, expects an apoplectic seizure, which would certainly carry her off."[80]

The Grand Duchess had made Hanbury-Williams her confidant, with whom she discussed Russian political affairs and from whom she borrowed substantial sums. She treated him like a favorite uncle; he reciprocated with adoration and sage advice. His kindly patronage and courtly attention inspired an intense outpouring of graphomania. They clandestinely corresponded almost daily for a year, and Catherine composed the first, hasty draft of her autobiography for him in 1756–57. As early as 18 August 1756 she asked his opinion of her "dream" for guaranteeing the succession to her husband and son. She foresaw a need for quick action in concert with Bestuzhev-Riumin, Apraksin, and loyal officers of the Guards. The entire enterprise should encounter no difficulties, as Catherine naively concluded: "Much will depend on the general aspect, or on the view which I shall take of things. Pray Heaven to give me a clear head. The extreme hatred for the Schuvalov [party], which all those who do not belong to them feel, the justice of my cause, as well as the easy sequence of everything which runs its natural course, make me hope for a happy issue." This plan was never acted on, for Elizabeth rallied temporarily from her disabilities; but it reveals Catherine's intensifying political involvement, her search for allies, and her own soaring ambitions. Apparently she first thought to gain power through her husband, confident that she could control him and succeed him should his health fail; "for I am resolved, as you know, to perish or to reign." So she encouraged Peter to participate in the Conference at the Imperial Court, which he did but rarely and even then reluctantly, since he idolized King Frederick and the Prussian army. In private Catherine also admired Frederick's shrewd determination and his cultured wit, welcoming his secret assurances of support for the Young Court.[81]

Friendship with Hanbury-Williams buoyed Catherine's spirits in the months that Poniatowski was away in Poland, from July to December 1756, and provided her a sounding board for her doubts and hopes and fears. "I would like to feel fear, but I cannot," she confessed on 27 August 1756; "the invisible hand which has led me for thirteen years along a very rough road will never allow me to give way, of that I am firmly and perhaps foolishly convinced. If you knew all the precipices and misfortunes which have threatened me, and which I have overcome, you would place more confidence in conclusions which are too hollow for those who think as deeply as you." As Catherine and Hanbury-Williams feverishly pressed Bestuzhev-Riumin to block the imminent Franco-Russian alliance and to bring Poniatowski back to Petersburg, they lent each other continual encouragement amid a virtual seminar of advanced court politics. Her political confidence grew in concert with her ambitions. "Since seven in the morning until this moment, seven in the evening, omitting the hours for dinner, I have done nothing but write and read documents," she noted. "Might it not be said of me that I am a Minister of State?"

She began to think of herself as one, following "in the footprints of Peter the Great," and under her mentor's guidance she even started studying English (three hours a day, she boasted). But when he outlined the necessary actions to secure the succession on 16 October 1756, she suddenly bridled before the prospect. "I only hope that your vision of happiness [i.e., her reign] may come true, but I will tell you in confidence that I am afraid of not being able to live up to a name which has too soon become famous. If I dare to use such an expression, I have within myself great enemies to my success, which you may well know nothing about; how shall I avoid being led, how shall I act to escape being blinded? . . . my vanity and my ambition tremble at the thought that I may yet have to complain of some unknown enemy." Some days after Hanbury-Williams left Russia in June 1757 she blessed him with a final confidence: "Two things I know well: one is, that my ambition is as great as is humanly possible; the other, that I shall do some good for your country." He died two years later, before his pupil achieved her ambition.[82]

The international situation changed drastically with the Prussian invasion of Saxony in August 1756, igniting what soon escalated into a wider war, eventually global in scope. That costly and complex conflict saw Russian armies invading East Prussia in 1757, in alliance with Austria and France, whereas British subsidies supported Frederick II against the three powers and their allies. The war embittered Russian court politics. Frederick II hoped for Elizabeth's imminent death and Peter's accession, which he assumed would remove Russia from the hostile alliance. He also counted on Catherine's support through her opposition to French influence and its minions in Petersburg such as the Shuvalovs. Though Hanbury-Williams soon left Russia on 28 June 1757 because of the hostilities with Prussia, he had rendered Catherine valuable personal and financial assistance. His loans helped her extend her political credit by entertaining on a lavish scale.

Bestuzhev-Riumin drew closer and closer to Catherine as the tensions at court wound tighter in 1756–57. Decades of foreign and state service since Petrine times made the sixty-three-year-old Grand Chancellor a walking library of practical political expertise. His network of patronage extended far and wide among the Russian elite. Three relatives—his nephews General Prince Mikhail Volkonskii and chamberlain Alexander Talyzin, and his cousin Admiral Ivan Talyzin—all played prominent parts in Catherine's coup. Although he had originally opposed the selection of Catherine to marry the heir to the throne, he gradually recognized her abilities and came to see in her a useful counterweight to the Grand Duke, whose pro-Prussian and anti-Russian sentiments he abhorred. He had helped arrange Catherine's affair with Saltykov and encouraged her relationship with Poniatowski. Through her, he kept informed of Holstein affairs too, and when the Grand Duke's minister of administration died, Bestuzhev-Riumin had Catherine persuade Peter to appoint a certain von Stambke to the post with authority to work with the Grand Duchess. Stambke served her as a loyal conduit to the Grand Chancellor, who feared that Elizabeth's death and Peter's accession would spell his own downfall, since the Grand Duke hated him and his Prussophobia. Hence Bestuzhev advised Catherine about potential supporters in the Conference at the Imperial Court and put her in touch with Field Marshal Apraksin, head of the War Collegium and commander-in-chief of the Russian forces being mobilized to attack Prussia.

He also drew up his own plan of action in the event of Elizabeth's sudden demise, proposing that Peter be declared emperor with Catherine as a participant in the imperial administration, with all the main branches under his own overlordship. This plan probably took shape in reaction to the stroke that struck down Elizabeth in public on 8 September 1757 and to the storm of recriminations in Petersburg against Apraksin for retreating instead of exploiting his victory over the Prussians at Grossjägerndorf in July. Catherine studied Bestuzhev's plan. If she later professed to find its timing inopportune and its pretensions excessive, she must have been flattered at the central role allotted her: Bestuzhev-Riumin "looked upon me personally as perhaps the only individual upon whom at that time the hopes of the public could be based when the Empress was no more." She "corrected" the draft, which Bestuzhev-Riumin rewrote several times, and kept a copy of the proposed manifesto and detailed instructions to the Grand Duke on how to act when the Empress died.[83]

As before, Catherine took great care with the two persons who held the greatest power over her future—the Grand Duke and the Empress. With her husband, she maintained some semblance of propriety, gave him occasional advice (especially concerning Holstein), and alternately catered to his whims, scoffed at his caprices, and intimated to others his shameful treatment of herself. The consorts' personal relations remained distant, for the most part, and were subjected to greater stress from the late spring of 1757 onward, as Catherine showed new signs of pregnancy. Morning sickness tormented her occasionally. But her condition did not show although she dreaded a miscarriage, especially when she fell getting out of a carriage. At first, Peter had not objected to Poniatowski's visiting his wife and, after accidentally intercepting him one night at Oranienbaum in late June, the Grand Duke blithely condoned the liaison; he and his mistress Vorontsova even entertained the Count on his subsequent visits to the Grand Duchess. Yet Catherine found that Peter "was almost always ill-tempered with me," which she attributed to her coolness toward Brockdorff and especially Vorontsova, "who was again becoming the head of the harem." To assuage the bad mood of her spouse and advertise her own liberality and rising stature at court, the Grand Duchess staged a magnificent feast and entertainment in her new garden at Oranienbaum on 17 June 1757. An orchestra of sixty provided music for singers and dancers who performed with special props for the numerous guests, many of whom never appeared at court and who were invited to a lottery that dispensed gifts freely. Copious wine enlivened the proceedings, which concluded with a "superlative" supper and dancing until six o'clock in the morning. This extravaganza cost Catherine close to 15,000 rubles, or half her annual income, but she considered it a worthwhile triumph that "disarmed all my enemies"—for a time. A month later she gave a big dinner for the Grand Duke and all the Oranienbaum courtiers on the occasion of the public prayers of thanksgiving for Apraksin's victory at Grossjägerndorf. Determined to cultivate popularity outside the court, Catherine donated on the same day a roasted ox for the laborers and masons of Oranienbaum. A few days later, with the summer social season considered over, both consorts returned to the Summer Palace in Petersburg.[84]

For Catherine, relations with Peter and Elizabeth began to sour early in the fall of 1757. Immediately on returning to Petersburg, the Grand Duchess was summoned by Elizabeth for an interview that proved to be "more like an inquisition." The Empress asked about the Grand Duke's private life and entourage, and listened coldly to Catherine's account of Holstein affairs. The Grand Duchess was charged by Alexander Shuvalov, the "inquisitor-general," to keep this meeting very secret. One wonders whether the encounter played any part in the stroke that caused Elizabeth's collapse on 8 September 1757 while attending church at Tsarskoe Selo.

Peter and Catherine only heard about this episode the next morning from a note that Poniatowski sent to Oranienbaum. Simultaneously they learned of Apraksin's retreat from East Prussia and the ugly rumors that his conduct had provoked in Petersburg. At Bestuzhev-Riumin's behest, Catherine wrote Apraksin urging him to reverse the retreat. On 7 October, however, Bestuzhev joined four other members of the Conference at the Imperial Court in recommending to the Empress, in response to her demand, that Apraksin be relieved of his command and summoned to Riga, where a court-martial should investigate his actions. Bestuzhev acknowledged his friendship with Apraksin and defended the Field Marshal only by opposing his immediate arrest, an action that he thought would besmirch Elizabeth's government with the stain of Asiatic despotism.[85]

Bestuzhev-Riumin's apprehensions of a full-scale political crisis worsened from mid-October onward, as he began to fear that the Shuvalovs would control the succession by persuading the Empress to leave her throne to three-year-old Grand Duke Paul under a regency council headed by Peter Shuvalov, who was thought to control the army and the treasury. That contingency threatened disaster to the Young Court and its adherents. Indeed, nobody at court expected anything from the widely detested Grand Duke, and the Empress was believed to know of Catherine's intrigues and "amourettes" with Poniatowski, and to be planning a showdown with them all in the near future.[86]

Catherine in her recollections later recorded her belief that Apraksin had acted on the basis of reports about Elizabeth's deteriorating health; supposedly his concern was not to be caught outside Russian borders when her death seemed imminent. Actually the retreat had been decided not by Apraksin alone but by general councils of war on 27 August, 13 and 28 September, mainly because of failing supplies. Apraksin was not court-martialled, after all, but he lost his command and was brought back to Narva under house arrest—a scapegoat for the indignant protests of Austria and France. In mid-January 1758 Count Shuvalov, the "inquisitor-general," left for Narva to interrogate Apraksin, returning at the start of February with the Field Marshal's sworn denial that he had received any directions from the Grand Duchess. Nevertheless, he admitted corresponding with Catherine and gave

Shuvalov copies of her letters. This was the evidence that resulted in Bestuzhev-Riumin's arrest at the conference session of 14 February 1758.[87]

During the same period of tension and confusion, Catherine's pregnancy had ended on 9 December 1757 with the birth of a daughter, whom Elizabeth named Anna Petrovna after her sister, the late Duchess of Holstein. This was something of a slap at Catherine, who had proposed to name the new princess after the Empress. Although Peter merrily celebrated the occasion, to friends he had expressed doubts about the child's paternity. Catherine countered his doubts by demanding that he substantiate them in the form of an oath, performed before the baleful Alexander Shuvalov, that he had never slept with her. He declined. All the same, Peter's imprudence inspired Catherine to reconsider her prospects. Ahead she discerned "three equally difficult paths": (1) to share the fate of her spouse, (2) to accept passively either his support or his rejection, or (3) to make her own way. "But, speaking more plainly, it was a matter of either perishing with (or because of) him, or else of saving myself, the children, and perhaps the State from the perdition which the moral and physical qualities of this sovereign compelled one to foresee. This last choice seemed to me the safest."[88]

Catherine's resolve soon faced a severe test as a result of Bestuzhev's arrest, which she knew might implicate her in treasonous activities. She learned of his arrest the very next morning; a note from Poniatowski via Lev Naryshkin simply recorded the fact and mentioned the arrests of three others—the court jeweler Bernardi, Ivan Elagin, and Vasilii Adodurov. All three men were associates of Bestuzhev and Catherine, and many courtiers used Bernardi as a go-between. Their arrests must inevitably cast suspicion on the Grand Duchess, who felt as if a dagger had been plunged into her heart. Her worst apprehensions were partially allayed, however, when Stambke delivered a note from Bestuzhev reassuring the Grand Duchess that he had succeeded in burning everything that might incriminate them. Nevertheless, within a few days Stambke was dismissed and ordered expelled from the country and Poniatowski's recall was requested, both moves having resulted from the discovery of their secret correspondence with Bestuzhev. Seeing in these events a cue, Catherine immediately burned all her papers and accounts.[89]

On Friday of Shrovetide, 27 February 1758, an imperial manifesto announced the arrest of Bestuzhev on charges of offending the Empress. Already stripped of his offices and decorations, he was remanded to a special commission for investigation. The inquiry meandered along more than a year without discovering anything of great moment, before the former grand chancellor was banished to his estates. Meanwhile, Bernardi was exiled to Kazan, Elagin to his estate in Kazan guberniia, and Adodurov to Orenburg. Catherine's favorite attendant Vladislavova was also removed. Field Marshal Apraksin died of a stroke on 6 August 1758, the same week that Count Poniatowski left Petersburg for Poland.[90]

Catherine survived her friends' debacle by shrewdly playing on Elizabeth's manifest disappointment with Peter as heir presumptive. At an after-midnight interview with the Empress on 13 April 1758, the Grand Duchess put Elizabeth on the defensive by tearfully begging to be sent back to her mother. She protested Peter's neglect and denied any involvement in treasonous activities. Asked about her letters to Apraksin, she avowed that she had taken an interest in him as a friend and had urged him to follow his orders. To Elizabeth's objection that she could not desert her children, the Grand Duchess praised the Empress's tender care of them while lamenting that she herself hardly ever saw her own offspring. She also used the occasion to rebut her husband's charges of vanity and arrogance, verbally flaying Peter, who was present throughout these conversations that lasted an hour and a half. Indeed, Catherine later admitted that she could not remember all that was said, but she was sure the confrontation had ended in her favor.[91]

Perhaps it did. Ivan Shuvalov, the reigning favorite, later assured her that everything would be done according to her wish, and Vice-Chancellor Vorontsov urged her in Elizabeth's name not to abandon Russia. She was heartened, moreover, by her maid's relay of a priest's report that the Empress privately termed Peter a monster and a fool. On 23 May, Elizabeth recalled her for a second interview, this time alone. According to Catherine, the Empress asked her again about Apraksin's letters, accepted her assurance that she had written only three, and then inquired about Peter's mode of life. Although Catherine's account breaks off abruptly at this point, she obviously made peace with Elizabeth. Indeed, the two women became so completely reconciled that Poniatowski believed the Empress "inwardly" approved of their liaison, while her (unspecified) assurances to the Grand Duchess gave grounds "to expect the most serious consequences for the internal relations of the court and, consequently, for all of the state." Did Elizabeth tell Catherine in so many words that she intended to disinherit Peter in favor of his progeny? Between themselves Peter and Catherine had agreed, by 10 July 1758, not to interfere with their respective relationships with Vorontsova and Poniatowski.[92]

Though Catherine depicted her meetings with Elizabeth as dramatic triumphs of mind and will, she knew all along, as she admits, that Elizabeth could not send her away. A twofold calculus forbade such action. First, it would have been painfully awkward to explain and, second, it would have imperiled the succession in view of Elizabeth's declining health, her doubts about Peter's capacities and his uncertain health, and the infancy and fragile health of Paul. Possibly from this time onward, the Empress began to consider seriously the possibility of disinheriting Peter in favor of Paul, with Catherine as regent.

That possibility gained strength when the baby Princess Anna Petrovna suddenly died on 8 March 1759. Over the next week Catherine attended the funeral ceremonies and the burial on 15 March at the Alexander Nevskii Monastery. If grief gripped her firmly as she went through the Orthodox ritual that included kissing the corpse before the coffin was closed, she could only share her grief with Poniatowski from a distance. Afterwards she never referred to her dead daughter, not once in any of the several versions of her autobiographical sketches. For political purposes if no other, she always preferred male offspring. Even so, this loss may have assisted her reconciliation with the tender-hearted Empress. Elizabeth could not bring herself to contemplate her own death, much less events after her demise; and though increasingly concerned over Peter's blatantly pro-Prussian sympathies while Russian armies battled his hero Frederick II and even occupied Berlin briefly, she took no action against her wayward nephew.[93]

If Catherine survived the crisis of Bestuzhev's fall with few scars, she still found herself dangerously isolated amid the conflicting currents of Russian court politics in the last years of Elizabeth's reign. With Bestuzhev's disgrace and exile, publicly announced on 8 April 1759, all hope of securing Poniatowski's return vanished. The entire ordeal impressed on the Grand Duchess several stern lessons: the need for greater caution and better preparation in making arrangements for her political future, the necessity of cultivating the Empress, and the need to neutralize the Grand Duke. As before, she found solace in reading—a five-volume history of voyages and the first volumes of Diderot's famous *Encyclopedia*. She also continued to correspond secretly with Poniatowski and with her mother, who had fled from Prussian-occupied Zerbst in 1758 to Paris, where she accumulated huge debts before her death on 19 May 1760. Johanna Elizabeth's death frightened her daughter as much as it saddened her. Indeed, Catherine trembled at the thought of her letters to her mother falling into the hands of the Russian envoy in Paris, only to learn with great relief that the wily Johanna had destroyed them. Despite Elizabeth's suspicions of Johanna, she agreed to cover her debts of more than 400,000 livres in order "to avoid the shame" of having her effects sold at public auction.[94]

Passion and Politics Pursued

The Grand Duchess gradually re-entered political life after the crisis of 1758 and her prominence rose as Elizabeth's health declined and fears of Peter mounted. In fact, the longer the war with Prussia lasted the clearer the Grand Duke's Prussian sympathies shone forth. He would not compromise his Holstein interests to conciliate Denmark, bluntly refusing in February 1759 to waive his claims to Sleswig or to exchange Holstein for another territory. A year later he boasted of leading the army against Denmark in defense of Holstein. Futhermore, Peter supplied Frederick II with news of Russian troop movements, smiled at Prussian successes, and frowned at their reverses. And when Count Schwerin, an adjutant of Frederick's captured at the battle Zorndorf in August 1758, arrived in Petersburg on 12 April 1759, the Grand Duke hobnobbed with him about town and assured him that "if I were sovereign you would not be a prisoner of war." Catherine, by contrast, censured Peter's absurdities and confided to the Danish ambassador, who spread the word, her hopes that the Empress would alter the succession in favor of Paul, thereby conferring a greater role on herself. Yet when Poniatowski suggested she work for a regency she dismissed the notion as impolitic. She cultivated the new British envoy Robert Keith and even borrowed money from him, but his friendship with Peter soon cooled her interest.[95]

Stung by the sudden loss of her friends and her lover Poniatowski, Catherine looked anew for male companionship in quarters with political potential. Count Schwerin had been accompanied to Petersburg by a young Guardsman already renowned for his bravery on the fields of Mars and Venus—Lieutenant Grigorii Orlov, the best looking and most popular of five brothers. The son of a provincial governor, Grigorii had received little formal education before enrolling in the Izmailovskii Guards Regiment in Petersburg at the age of eighteen. At the battle of Zorndorf, "one of the bloodiest routs of the century," three wounds failed to deter Lieutenant Orlov. His heroic disdain for death, gigantic physique, handsome features, devil-may-care audacity, and affable manner won him wide repute in the army, providing a perfect entree to Petersburg high society when he returned from Prussia in March 1759. He was quickly made adjutant to Count Peter Shuvalov, grand master of ordnance and cousin of Elizabeth's favorite, and set tongues wagging by his affair with Shuvalov's beautiful mistress, Princess Elena Kurakina (daughter of the late Field Marshal Apraksin). Gossip had it that only Shuvalov's death in January 1762 saved Orlov from death or disgrace for this deed.[96]

Naturally Catherine noticed Orlov at once. Legend contends that she caught sight of his bearlike bulk from her palace window, but they probably met while he was attending Count Schwerin, possibly in her husband's presence. Their attraction was both physical and political. Orlov's commanding physique and dashing reputation seized Catherine's imagination. Better looking than either Saltykov or Poniatowski, he was reputed to be a sexual athlete endowed with exceptional genital development. Or so a ribald poet recorded at the time. In sexual terms, Grigorii Orlov epitomized the masterful male in the same way that Catherine personified the insatiable, penis-conquering female. These depictions are largely myths, of course, but there is some factual basis to them. Catherine and Orlov became lovers sometime in 1761; by August she felt the pangs of pregnancy. Only a few close friends such as Countess Praskov'ia Bruce knew about this new affair.[97]

Orlov's political potential, in Catherine's eyes, almost equalled his sexual prowess. He was 100 percent Russian and a military hero. He and his four brothers, the energetic and resourceful Aleksei above all, were the darlings of the capital's four elite Guards regiments, which comprised the flower of the Russian nobility. They were young, patriotic, and politically malleable, with loyalties to persons more than to theoretical principles or particular court parties. They were ambitious for prestige and creature comforts, and thus welcomed the flattering attentions and monetary incentives dispensed by the charmingly cultivated Grand Duchess. In short, Orlov provided Catherine with a perfect bridge to strategically placed military-political muscle.

Just as the Grand Duchess pursued romance and popularity in the Guards regiments through the Orlov brothers, she cultivated a replacement for Bestuzhev in the person of her son's newly designated *Oberhofmeister,* Nikita Panin. The son of a newly risen Petrine general and senator, Panin had enjoyed a long friendship with Elizabeth and, through Bestuzhev's patronage, had served as Russian ambassador to Sweden in 1748–1760. He was born in Danzig, and received an excellent education in Estland and Russia, supplemented by extensive experience abroad. His family was connected by marriage to such eminent noble clans as the Kurakins, Nepliuevs, and Tatishchevs. His brother Peter was a rising army officer recently promoted to general for his exploits against the Prussians. As early as October 1756 Catherine intimated to Hanbury-Williams, on the basis of some letters from Nikita: "I have for some time past seen a future vice-chancellor in Panin; and I am delighted that you should think so." Nikita returned to Petersburg from Stockholm in the spring of 1760; his appointment was engineered by Chancellor Vorontsov as a means to prevent his rivals the Shuvalovs from occupying such a sensitive court office. Panin's cosmopolitan culture, varied political experience, and valuable family ties all interested Catherine in securing his confidence and cooperation. Both shared intellectual interests in European political theory, especially the teachings of Montesquieu. Both also disliked the disarray of Elizabeth's government and the overweening influence of the Shuvalovs and the Vorontsovs.[98]

Another sign of Catherine's search for political supporters was her patronage of Princess Ekaterina Dashkova, the married younger sister of Peter's mistress. In the summer of 1761 while the Empress stayed at Peterhof and the Grand Duchess at Oranienbaum, Princess Dashkova lived between them at the dacha of her uncle, Chancellor Vorontsov. Catherine encouraged young Dashkova's love for reading and occasionally invited her to share the evening's company at Oranienbaum. Disgusted with her sister's pandering to the coarse Grand Duke, Dashkova sympathized with the refined Grand Duchess and saw in her a worthy model of cultured decorum. She was completely unaware of Orlov's place in her heroine's life and plans for the future. Dashkova could provide valuable intelligence about the machinations of her sister and the entire Vorontsov "party."[99]

Some six months' pregnant, Catherine could scarcely attempt any desperate action when Elizabeth finally died on 25 December 1761. Her debts amounted to the stupendous sum of 675,000 rubles, and she had no more credit—"not even enough to order a dress made at Christmas." She still owned a small fortune in diamonds, "but I did not dare to sell them or to pawn them." Though everybody except King Frederick II feared what would happen when Peter took the throne, nobody dared thwart his succession. He was proclaimed Emperor Peter III that very day without any official mention of his wife or son. Led by Dashkova's husband, a captain of the Guards, some of Catherine's adherents supposedly resolved on immediate action on her behalf, but she dissuaded them. A disorganized, premature bid for power risked bloodshed and civil war. Her refusal to rush, or to force events, confirmed Catherine's political maturity. After seventeen years in Russia, years in which she witnessed some harrowing events and heard about many others, she had finally learned the prudence of patience. That day she donned a commodious black dress of mourning that she wore throughout her husband's six-month reign. Her swollen shape thus concealed, she began an assiduous vigil at Elizabeth's bier (despite the strench of the corpse) and after the funeral largely withdrew from everyday court life.[100]

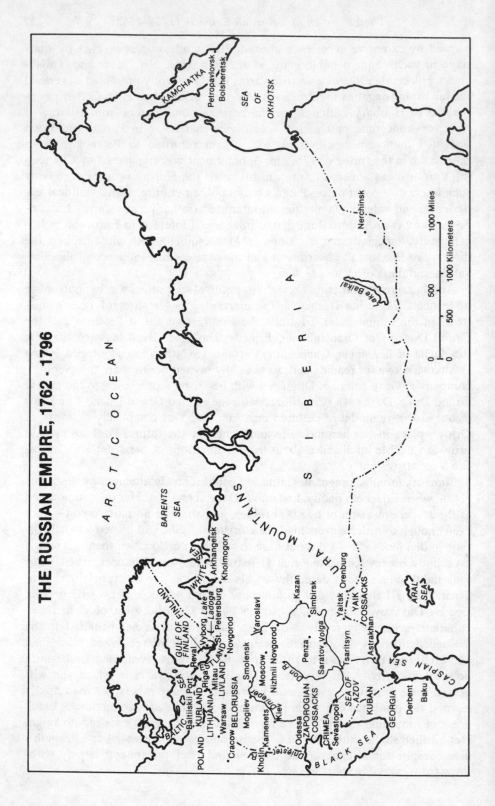

THE RUSSIAN EMPIRE, 1762 - 1796

KAMCHATKA

Petropavlovsk
Bolsheretsk

SEA
OF
OKHOTSK

Nerchinsk

S I B E R I A

Lake Baikal

1000 Miles

1000 Kilometers

500

500

0

0

ARCTIC OCEAN

BARENTS
SEA

URAL MOUNTAINS

ARAL
SEA

WHITE SEA

GULF OF FINLAND

Arkhangelsk
Kholmogory

BALTIC SEA

Baltiiskii Port
Reval
Riga
Mitau
Vyborg
Lake
Ladoga
St. Petersburg
Novgorod
Yaroslavl
Kazan
Simbirsk
Orenburg
Yaitsk
YAIK
COSSACKS

KURLAND
LIVLAND
LITHUANIA

POLAND
Warsaw

Smolensk
Moscow
Moscow
Nizhnii Novgorod
Penza
Saratov
Volga

BELORUSSIA
Mogilev
Dnieper R.

Cracow

Kholtin
Kamenets
Dniester R.

Kiev
Odessa
ZAPOROGIAN
COSSACKS
Sevastopol
CRIMEA
Tsaritsyn
Don R.
SEA OF
AZOV
KUBAN

Astrakhan

Derbent
Baku

CASPIAN SEA

GEORGIA

BLACK SEA

Saratov

Catherine's position and prospects in early 1762 were summarized soberly by Jean Louis Favier, a French secret agent recently returned from several years in Petersburg:

> The personality of the grand duchess has already been the subject of much unfounded or exaggerated praise. But much about her may be valued by its merit. We shall begin with her beauty, about which it could least of all be said that she is dazzling: her waist is rather long and thin, but not supple; her carriage is noble, but her walk is not graceful and is affected; her bosom is narrow, her face long, especially the chin; her mouth smiles, but is flat and as if indented; her nose has a tiny little hump; her eyes are not large, but her glance is lively and pleasant; on her face are slight traces of small pocks. This is the actual portrait of a woman who is pretty rather than ugly, but about whom there is nothing special to be lauded.
>
> Her inclination to coquetry has also been exaggerated. The two romances that she has had, have made people look upon her as a woman with a tempestuous character and with fantasies. On the contrary, being a woman of feeling, quite passionate, tender yet romantic, she yielded only to the inclination of the heart and, perhaps, the quite natural desire to have children.
>
> The mind of the grand duchess, equally as glorified as her beauty, is likewise as romantic as her heart. The almost hermit-like mode of life that she leads, spending the seven winter months without leaving her rooms, the sparse society that she sees there and which presents no interest for her, all this has forced her to occupy herself with reading.
>
> Moreover, she has never ceased to be reminded that the grand duke himself will never rule, that he will busy himself with inspections and military matters, and that the administration of internal and external affairs will inexorably fall upon a chief minister, whose first concern will be to remove from the grand duchess any trust, and consequently any respect, and that the sole means to ward off such a misfortune is to prepare herself so as to have the possibility of exercising the duties of the chief minister herself.
>
> These assurances, which were quite credible, inspired her with the commendable urge to take up her own self-education. Reading and reflection were for her the sole means to that end. But, instead of acquiring theoretical and practical knowledge of state administration, she threw herself into the metaphysics and moral theories of our most recent philosophers. From them she learned that one ought not divorce the art of educating people from the art of ruling them. And from all these rules, as vague as they are dazzling, she, like these philosophers, has compiled for herself a code of political convictions, quite elevated ones, but which are not applicable to actual affairs.
>
> The implementation into practice of such an administration would be the more difficult and even dangerous, inasmuch as one would have to deal with a coarse people which, instead of ideas, possesses only superstitious traditions, and instead of manners—slavish fear and stupid sub-

mission. These forces are quite alive, and it would be irrational to endeavor to replace them with others.[101]

This evaluation, the more truthful and insightful because it stemmed from an obviously hostile outside observer, attests to the ambivalent reputation that Catherine enjoyed at home and abroad at the end of Elizabeth's reign. Her ambition to rule with or without Peter, and her competence to do so, were widely assumed. His deficiencies became more manifest by the day. He was his own worst enemy, and Catherine knew it.

Meanwhile she patiently knitted together the separate strands of conspiracy. Hardly anyone noticed the change in her shape after 11 April 1762 when her son by Orlov, christened Aleksei Grigor'evich (no surname), was secretly delivered and spirited away by courtiers. She recovered quickly and on her birthday, 21 April, received the Austrian envoy with a cordiality for his government that contrasted sharply with her husband's Prussophilia. Ten weeks later her well-coached partisans put her on the throne without protest or bloodshed.

The coup of 28 June 1762 combined elements that Catherine had slowly learned to assemble and deploy during eighteen years in her adopted country. Above all, she presented herself—and was seen by others—as thoroughly russified, completely at home in the huge empire. She had adopted the religion, learned the language, mastered the customs, enlisted support from many of the politically powerful. From a mere slip of a girl brought to Russia at age fourteen, the Grand Duchess had blossomed into a full-bodied woman of majestic, dynamic presence and smoldering sensuality—qualities captured in Rotari's portrait of about 1760. But could a middle-aged female not born in Russia and soon to be a widow, without a legal claim to the crown and with scant administrative experience, actually rule such a large and troubled realm? Many observers wondered.

3

Coronation, Consolidation, Challenges

It is a truism that governments brought to power by revolution encounter immediate difficulties. For everyday public administration requires skills other than conspiratorial manipulation and demagogic exhortation (although both may have their uses). Two sources of difficulty typically predominate: the abnormal circumstances that gave rise to the revolution in the first place, and the new authorities' own insecurity and lack of practical governmental experience. Both sorts of problems may be complicated by the atmosphere of crisis and heightened expectations that usually accompanies any abrupt change of political authority. Although the coup d'état of 28 June 1762 was a palace revolution confined to the upper echelons of Russian society in the environs of St. Petersburg, Catherine faced the same challenges as any other revolutionary ruler the day after the revolution.

The most immediate task—to establish her own legitimacy—was encumbered by her lack of legal claim to the succession and by the existence of three competing claimants: Peter III and Ivan VI (both in prison) and her son Paul (only seven years old). Within days of the coup a soldier was arrested for babbling that Peter was dead and that Paul soon would be.[1] Peter's sudden death removed one claimant. That left the other two in addition to the general handicaps of Catherine's foreign background, her sex—female sovereigns had been an ill-starred rarity in Russia—her administrative inexperience and ignorance of the vast domain that she hoped to rule. Besides, both Elizabeth and Peter III had left the realm in disarray while offering egregious examples of rulership.

Three decades later, Catherine would paint in somber hues the critical situation she inherited after her coup: an empty treasury, the army in Prussia unpaid for months, no credit abroad, huge state debts, thousands of peasants and workers on strike or in revolt, rampant ignorance and incompetence among officialdom—in short, utter chaos and near paralysis of government. Against this forbidding backdrop, of course, Catherine's political genius and glorious reign both stood out in brilliant relief, just as she intended. In reality, the start of her reign was at once more prosaic and confused than her remembrance admitted.[2]

Though inexperienced in the practice of ruling, the new Empress brought to the task great talents. She was highly intelligent, quick to grasp central issues, widely read, eager to learn and to teach others, a shrewd judge of character, determined yet flexible, and incredibly industrious. The indolent, erratic statecraft of Elizabeth and Peter III appalled her; she aspired to be a female Peter the Great, but without his despotic, militaristic tendencies. At thirty-three she felt at the height of personal and political power, eager to show her mettle.

To the new regime's advantage, Catherine's accession had been accomplished so quickly and so easily that merely minimal force sufficed to overawe public opposition. Her coup created few enemies. To capitalize on the antiwar and antiforeign sentiments behind her conspiracy, the Empress immediately ordered the Russian commanders in Prussia to withdraw their troops to Russian territory. The war with Denmark and the alliance with Prussia were thus cancelled, but she assured the Prussians that she had no notion of fighting them or anyone else. This policy of peace aimed to calm tensions at home and promised an easing of economic burdens. The government could begin to repair the damage wrought by the Seven Years' War.[3]

Since few officials had stayed with Peter III till the end, few were compromised in Catherine's eyes. Some who were suspect, such as Chancellor Vorontsov and Ivan Shuvalov, kept out of sight and soon left on prudently extended tours abroad. She took over the bureaucratic machine of government, however poorly manned and badly organized, virtually intact. This was important in view of her own limited experience in government. It also explains why many of her first initiatives in internal affairs silently imitated those of her maligned predecessors. Acutely conscious of her inexperience in matters of high policy, Catherine on the day of the coup sent for Bestuzhev-Riumin, the exiled senior statesman and exemplar of the Petrine heritage, obviously planning to pick his brain in the course of organizing her new regime. (Peter III had distrusted the former chancellor and had refused to pardon him.) He received an extraordinary reception on his arrival on 12 July. Met by Grigorii Orlov thirty kilometers outside Petersburg, he rode in an imperial coach to the Summer Palace, where Catherine embraced her venerable friend and mentor, announced the restoration of all of his ranks and titles, and awarded him a splendid house with court-furnished table, wine cellar, and carriage. Soon she sought his advice on all kinds of matters: border fortresses, Church estates, Kurland and Poland, Siberia, and so on. At his behest, moreover, she published a manifesto on 31 August proclaiming his innocence of the charges made in 1758 and naming him the first imperial councilor (a new title), with an annual pension of 20,000 rubles, and the first member of the new imperial council to be established at court. The other courtiers exiled in connection with Bestuzhev's fall were also reinstated with great honor. General Ivan Weimarn was transferred from Siberia to St. Petersburg. Ivan Elagin was named to her personal cabinet with the rank of actual state councilor at a salary of 1,000 rubles per year. Vasilii Adodurov was appointed president of the Collegium of Manufactures, granted the salary withheld during his arrest, and promoted to privy councilor with an annual salary of 2,000 rubles. Registrar Karl Kantsler was returned from exile in Astrakhan. Catherine did not forget her friends.[4]

Naturally she richly rewarded those who had put her on the throne. Promotions, titles, decorations, money, serfs, and estates were liberally distributed from the day of the coup onward. On 4 July the sum of 50,000 rubles was "set aside" for Grigorii Orlov, of which he was given 3,000 the next day. On 9 July the soldiers of the Petersburg garrison were all granted a half year's salary—a total sum of 225,890 rubles. The next day Grand Duke Paul was awarded 120,000 rubles annual allowance. Some 454 persons were rewarded for participation in the coup, 330 of them Guardsmen. Smaller sums were disbursed in the next few weeks, and on 9 August the *Sanktpeterburgskie vedomosti,* the capital's official gazette, announced awards of 18,000 "souls" (male serfs) and 526,000 rubles to forty stalwarts—the principal leaders of the coup. Kirill Razumovskii, Nikita Panin, and Mikhail Volkonskii all received perpetual pensions of 5,000 rubles annually. Seventeen others, including Grigorii and Aleksei Orlov, Peter Passek and Ekaterina Dashkova, received 800 souls or 24,000 rubles each. Eleven persons—Second Lieutenant Grigorii Potemkin was one—obtained 600 souls or 18,000 rubles each, and nine got from 300 to 500 souls. Catherine awarded Grigorii Teplov 20,000 rubles and granted 1,000 souls to Vasilii Shkurin and his wife, the foster parents of her son Aleksei Grigor'evich; she also awarded them noble status. On this occasion alone the Empress rewarded these forty conspirators with more than a million rubles' worth of serfs and cash—an astonishing sum in a state with a total annual budget of roughly 16 million rubles.[5]

Despite the treasury's depleted condition, Catherine spent lavishly on her political future. The carefree spending of her days as grand duchess now became state policy. To her former lover Sergei Saltykov, newly appointed envoy to France, she forwarded 20,000 rubles for the journey and, two years later, loaned him 20,000 more to cover his debts, which were so great that he had pawned his cross of St. Catherine. Although the Empress approved his transfer to Saxony in 1764, she frowned at his "mischief" and ineptitude: "everywhere he will be a fifth wheel on the carriage." He tumbled into obscurity although he lived until 1813, presumably abroad and without further contact with Catherine. She even took care of poor Elizaveta Vorontsova, Peter III's mistress. Warning her relatives not to let her "traipse into the palace," Catherine ordered her father to provide room and board for his daughter to live "quietly" in Moscow and later bought her a house there.[6]

Plans for a splendid coronation in Moscow preoccupied the Empress almost as soon as she seized the throne. Prince Nikita Trubetskoi was put in charge of the preparations on 1 July with an initial budget of 50,000 rubles. Fireworks were ordered and on 7 July the ceremony was announced for sometime in September. Vasilii Shkurin, supervising Catherine's wardrobe, received

20,000 rubles to meet the occasion. Like a polite guest, the Empress did not
intend to visit Moscow empty-handed, ordering 120 oak barrels of silver coins
for distribution to the populace that she planned to impress to the tune of
600,000 rubles.[7]

Catherine hastened to be formally crowned in Moscow, the old capital and
the traditional place of coronation, eager as she was to advertise her Russian-
ness and respect for tradition in contrast to Peter III's foreign outlook and
alien actions. Even though she loathed Moscow, she perceived its potency
in Russian political-religious symbolism and its importance as the Empire's
largest city and "first-crowned capital." St. Petersburg was not Russia, everyone admitted. Whoever wished to become the recognized sovereign of Russia
must receive the crown in Moscow. Peter III had considered being crowned
in St. Petersburg, and had died uncrowned—a fate that the prescient Catherine vowed to avoid.[8]

Elements of the Petersburg administrative departments began leaving for
Moscow in late July, and the migration intensified throughout August. To
guarantee security in the half-empty city, Catherine appointed five senators
in charge, with the venerable Ivan Nepliuev, brother-in-law to Nikita Panin,
residing in the old wooden Winter Palace as temporary chief commander.
Grand Duke Paul left on 27 August in the company of Nikita Panin with 27
carriages and 257 horses. Five days later the Empress's suite—23 persons
with 63 coaches and wagons pulled by 395 horses—lumbered off toward
Moscow, preceded by Grigorii Orlov. Although Catherine's convoy travelled
slowly, she overtook Paul's party, which had stopped at a waystation when
the Grand Duke became feverish. He seemed to feel better on seeing his
mother, however, so she pressed onward and reached Petrovskoe, Kirill Razumovskii's estate outside Moscow, by 10 September, only to learn that Paul
had suffered a relapse. Nevertheless, the Grand Duke rejoined her the day before their triumphal entry into Moscow on Friday, 13 September.[9]

The old capital swarmed with crowds of every rank, age, and occupation.
Decorations shielded the thousands of shabby wooden houses, huddled around
hundreds of picturesque churches with gilded or painted tops amid the huge
city's forested hills, ravines, and winding riverbanks. So great was the influx
of people, the local authorities feared that food and fodder prices would sky-
rocket. The contrast between courtly splendor and popular poverty was so
striking that, on 17 September, the Collegium of Commerce publicly announced a ban on the import of gold- and silver-worked fabrics because of
the government's plan to prohibit the wearing of such clothes one year after
the coronation.[10]

Catherine was crowned on Sunday, 22 September 1762, in the Kremlin's
Assumption Cathedral, the site of her formal engagement eighteen years earlier. All the resources of Church and state lent pomp and splendor to the
ceremonies. Catherine donned the imperial purple and the ribbon of St. Andrew, then placed the crown on her head herself (just as Elizabeth had done
twenty years earlier), and stood before the throne with scepter in one hand
and imperial globe in the other while cannon salutes thundered across the
square outside. Anointed by the Archbishop of Novgorod, she took commu-

nion and then walked outside to pay her respects to the icons in the nearby cathedrals of the Archangel and the Annunciation. Music, drums, salutes, and hurrahs rippled the air as the procession crossed the Ivanov Square flinging coins to the crowd. The religious part of the ceremony over, the newly crowned Empress returned to the Great Kremlin Palace to receive her court and to reward her stalwarts with another shower of decorations, courtly ranks, and bejewelled swords. Grigorii Orlov, her favorite subject, was named adjutant-general and all five brothers were elevated to the dignity of count. That evening the crowds tarried around the illuminated buildings of the Kremlin, and when Catherine ventured out on the historic Red Staircase at midnight to view the spectacle, she was met by loud hurrahs.[11]

So began a week of celebrations with public feasts and a whole series of receptions that culminated on the evening of 29 September with a "splendid firework" on Tsaritsyn Meadow across the Moskva River from the Kremlin. Weeks of private festivities commenced the usual winter social season—a constant round of balls and masquerades, operas and plays, festivals and feasts, weddings, games, and excursions, all of which climaxed on 30 January 1763 with a giant public masquerade entitled "Minerva Triumphant." This three-day spectacle involved a procession two kilometers long of 4,000 actors and musicians who depicted forty scenes lampooning "the preoccupations of narrow minds": mockery, drunkenness, ignorance, disagreement, deceit, bribery, life's vicissitudes, pride, and prodigality, ending with portrayals of the golden age, peace, and virtue. "Minerva" referred to Catherine, of course, who fondly desired that her reign be seen as a golden age of peace and virtue. On the coronation proper she spent a total of 32,585 rubles.[12]

The Empress attended many of these entertainments, at which Grigorii Orlov also cut a "very striking" figure and excited much envy. As in her youth, Catherine delighted especially in transvestite balls and later recounted how, masked and dressed in an officer's uniform, she flirted avidly with Princess Dolgorukova, to the young lady's intense consternation. "A man's dress is what suits her best," agreed Lord Buckingham, the British envoy; "she wears it always when she rides on horseback." And he marvelled at her equestrian skill. "It is scarce credible what she does in that way, managing horses, even fiery horses, with all the skill and courage of a groom." She meant to manage Russia the same way.[13]

Plots and Political Police

Two shocks interrupted Catherine's enjoyment of the coronation festivities, both providing unwelcome reminders of her still precarious political position. First, her son suffered a serious relapse the day after the fireworks display and spent the first two weeks of October bedridden with a fever. Since this marked his third attack within one month, his mother and physicians showed extraordinary concern. In fact, Catherine was so upset that she vowed to endow a public hospital in Moscow in the Grand Duke's name. Apparently Paul's fever led to delirium, which caused him to forget his lessons. A year later his tutor remembered the experience as a time of frequent "anguish and numbness" for all who loved "this Seigneur full of expectations." On 10 October the British ambassador reported that "the Grand Duke is in a very bad state of health, and the empress is said to be greatly altered by the care and constant anxiety of mind She has lately laboured under."[14]

Though Catherine now wore the crown and sat on the throne, she had not forgotten Paul's superior rights to both. Indeed, she had partly justified her seizure of power by condemning Peter III's neglect of Paul's rights of succession, tacitly implying that she would defend those very rights. From the day of the coup, she made much of Paul in public and noticed the warm reception he received from the crowds in Moscow. His popularity did not threaten her so long as he remained a minor. On the contrary, his life was widely considered to be her "greatest security." Thus Catherine felt enormous relief on 13 October when Paul first left his sickbed. Four days later she left on a pilgrimage to the nearby Trinity-St. Sergius Monastery. Thenceforward, whenever she was separated from her son, she regularly wrote Nikita Panin, constantly inquiring about Paul's health. Maternal, dynastic, and political instincts all fused in Catherine's solicitude for her son and sole legitimate heir. Her invitation to the philosophe and mathematician D'Alembert to be Paul's tutor was politely declined.[15]

The second shock proved equally unnerving. A "horrid conspiracy" against Catherine was detected among some Guardsmen in Moscow. Catherine's coup had infected others with the same contagious idea, just as her lavish largesse had flaunted the gains that boldness might reap. On 3 October her long-time chamberlain, Vasilii Shkurin, tearfully reported a conspiracy among the Izmailovskii Guards led by one Peter Khrushchev. Thunderstruck, the Empress immediately ordered Kirill Razumovskii to head a secret investigation. Fifteen persons were arrested within forty-eight hours. Interrogations, exhortations, and confrontations revealed that Captain Ivan Gur'ev had mentioned a conspiracy of great lords to install Ivan VI as emperor. His brother Semen had supposedly spoken of an opposition party in the making and of rampant disaffection among several regiments. Someone had been sent to fetch "Prince Ivan," he claimed. When asked about these allegations, however, Semen blamed most of them on Peter Khrushchev, but he admitted inventing the tale of sending for Ivan VI. His motive, he confessed, was jealous anger. Although he had stood watch at Peterhof during Catherine's coup, he had received none of the rewards tendered to others. Captain Mikhail Shipov assured the investigators that Semen Gur'ev had also championed the rights of Grand Duke Paul. Much of this loose talk had occurred at a drunken dinner given by Lieutenant Khrushchev on 29 September, the last day of the coronation festivities. Ten officers had attended. Several testified that their host had boasted of "doing things" to enthrone Ivan VI, lamented Catherine's accession and toasted "the last day of joy," cursed the Empress and claimed to have one thousand "in our party." On 6 October, at Catherine's order, Peter Khrushchev and Semen Gur'ev were beaten with sticks (*batogi*) to see if they would confess anything more. Neither did. So the investigators concluded that the whole business involved merely drunken posturing. They recommended transferring eleven men to other regiments, distant garrisons, or back to their estates without the right of appearing wherever the Empress might be. Four others were found completely innocent.

Incensed by these tepid conclusions, Catherine rejected the proposed sentences and called for harsher punishments as a deterrent. The investigators responded by proposing death sentences for five suspects. The Empress passed these findings on to the Senate, which as the Empire's highest court she empowered to try the accused and submit their sentences for her final review. As expected, the Senate softened the punishments somewhat, condemning only Peter Khrushchev and Semen Gur'ev to death by decapitation, sentencing Ivan and Peter Gur'ev to "political death"—that is, mock execution, eternal exile at hard labor, and the transfer of all moveable property to their heirs—and consigning Aleksei Khrushchev to settlement in Siberia. Four others were to lose all ranks and noble status.

In reviewing these sentences Catherine altered them further before she issued an empire-wide manifesto about the affair on 24 October, her first public announcement since the coronation. She briefly recounted the case without mentioning Ivan VI, Paul, or any other specifics. Indignant that seditious designs should have been bruited amid the coronation celebrations, she condemned Peter Khrushchev and Semen Gur'ev to lose their ranks, noble status, and surnames, to have their swords broken over their heads, and to be sent forever to Fort Bol'sheretsk on the Kamchatka Peninsula of eastern Siberia. Ivan and Peter Gur'ev were to lose their ranks and to be exiled forever to Yakutsk, whereas Aleksei Khrushchev was to lose all ranks and live on his estates without the right of entering either capital. The sentences were executed on Red Square on 28 October. Immediately afterward Khrushchev and the three Gur'evs began the long trek to Siberia. None of the four died there, however, although Aleksei Khrushchev perished in government service after losing his estate. Peter Khrushchev escaped in 1772 with other rebel convicts and entered French service. All three Gur'evs were pardoned—for not joining the escapees—and allowed to return to their estates in European Russia.[16]

The entire episode struck Catherine where she was most vulnerable. Linking the claims of Ivan VI and Paul to dissaffection among the Guards fused a political powderkeg, which any drunken soldier might put a match to. Worse still, the example of the Khrushchevs and the Gur'evs might inspire other desperate enterprises; hence the Empress's efforts to conceal the aims of the conspiracy. "My position is such that I have to observe the greatest caution," she admitted to Poniatowski on the heels of these alarms. "The least soldier of the Guard thinks when he sees me: 'That is the work of my hands.'" She liberally (albeit secretly) rewarded the Guards officers who denounced the conspirators. A few months later, however, Major Vasilii Passek of the Preobrazhenskii Guards was banished to Kazan, accused of uttering "important unseemly words, about which it is known to Her Imperial Majesty," but he was released in May 1763 on condition that he refrain from drunkenness and from "unseemly loose talk." The Empress showed the same nervous concern in the case of soldier Mikhail Kruglikov, accused in 1763 of saying that 500 men were assembling to help Ivan VI's father. She ordered the interrogators to ask the accused where the 500 men were, had he seen them, or only heard about them. Whatever his answers, he was beaten with sticks and exiled to a Siberian garrison.[17]

Another measure of Catherine's fright was her order of 2 October that cases related to the "two points"—designs against the sovereign and treason against the state—be handled by Procurator-General Alexander Glebov and Nikita Panin with her knowledge. This seemingly innocent directive signified the formal reconstitution of the Secret Chancery, the fearsome political police abolished by Peter III. Catherine's decree of 19 October reiterated its abolition and prohibited anonymous denunciations but referred such matters to the Senate, which soon sprouted the Secret Branch—a lineal descendant of the Secret Chancery that lasted throughout Catherine's reign. Its most notorious operative, "Senate Secretary" Stepan Sheshkovskii, signed the instructions to the Guards conveying Khrushchev and the Gur'evs to Siberia. He began working in the Secret Branch in December 1763. Yet the nature of his duties was carefully concealed from the public, as when the announcement of his promotion to senior secretary in 1767 spoke vaguely of service with the Senate. Barely three months into Catherine's reign, she felt compelled to revive the traditional defense of Russian absolutism. The Secret Branch showed great zeal in protecting the Empress. At the start of the reign two maids of the bedchamber were interrogated for disparaging remarks about Catherine's femininity; both were exiled to their estates.[18]

The honeymoon was over, as the "settled melancholy" on Catherine's countenance attested. Amid the investigation of the Khrushchevs and the Gur'evs she confessed to the British envoy a sense of detachment and alienation: "the habit of it imperceptibly grew upon Her, She knew not why."[19] She had begun to experience the burdens and the loneliness of great power.

The Politics of Absolutism

On seizing power, Catherine soon plunged into every sphere of governmental activity. It was as if she felt a compulsion to justify her rule by frenetic efforts to reform Russia overnight. From Montesquieu she had some vague general ideas of what to do and how to do it. For one thing, she would be an active sovereign after the style of Peter the Great: involved in all facets of governmental policies and societal development, a mover and shaker often seen in public, not a recluse in the palace. For another, she would lead the Russian Empire by persuasion, not coerce it as Peter the Great had done, into closer relationships with the progressive states and cultures of western Europe and Great Britain. She would help Russia regain the momentum of Petrine times, with greater attention to consensus and peaceful development.

Like Elizabeth at the start of her reign, Catherine called for the restoration of Petrine institutions and attitudes. She moved immediately to reclaim the Senate's formerly paramount position in central policymaking and execution, and frequently attended its sessions. She appointed new senators and a few retired, but no general purge occurred and she worked closely with some of Peter III's ministers, such as Procurator-General Glebov. If attending sessions of the Senate gave Catherine a crash course in policymaking, she was appalled by the senators' laggardness, pettifoggery, and factionalism. On 16 September 1762 she issued this obviously irritated order: "Messieurs Senators are to be in the Senate from half-past eight until twelve-thirty, and in nowise pronounce irrelevant speeches."[20]

Very quickly a personal cabinet evolved to transmit Catherine's energy to the Empire's cumbersome bureaucracy. Adam Olsuf'ev headed the cabinet, received petitions, and disbursed monies. Ivan Elagin and Grigorii Teplov assisted the Empress in composing decrees. By September 1763, Catherine assigned them regular days to meet her at eight o'clock in the morning: Teplov on Mondays and Wednesdays, Olsuf'ev on Tuesdays and Thursdays, Elagin on Fridays and Saturdays. All three were well educated and widely acquainted with Russian politics and administration. Soon they were joined by three other state secretaries: Sergei Koz'min, Grigorii Kozitskii, and Stepan Strekalov.[21]

Catherine listened patiently at first to innumerable discussions and reports. After a year on the throne, however, she demanded more action. "The awful delay in the Senate of all affairs forces me to order you," she sternly informed Procurator-General Glebov on 12 November 1763, "that on Friday, that is the day after tomorrow, the project about the Little Russian census of Mr. Teplov be presented in the Senate; and he should be there." With her cabinet secretaries she could be equally insistent. "Listen, Perfil'evich," she scolded Elagin in the spring of 1764, "if by the end of this week you do not bring me the instructions for the governors' duties, the manifesto against extortionists and Beket'ev's affairs completely finished, then I shall say there is no lazybones in the world like you, and that nobody with so many matters entrusted to him drags them out, as you do." Demanding of her cabinet secretaries, the Empress also showed solicitude for their personal problems. She advised Elagin, for example, against coming to work on crutches because of the difficulty of negotiating the palace steps with his injured foot.[22]

In the narrow sense, Catherine and her cabinet were the Russian government, but they worked closely with the Senate and a host of other central administrative bodies. The greatest problem for the sovereign since Petrine times was how to coordinate the workings of all the different bureaucratic structures. In theory, the sovereign provided such coordination. In practice, that proved humanly impossible, so some sort of council usually appeared in times of crisis. Such was the Conference under Elizabeth, which Peter III abolished.

Since Catherine faced a crisis on assuming control of the Russian government, it was natural to think of a council to help. With Nikita Panin, who abhorred the irregularity and favoritism of the two previous regimes, she began planning such a body in the very first weeks after the coup, and even appointed Bestuzhev-Riumin to it at the end of August. Panin drew up a lengthy project for the council complete with an imperial manifesto proclaiming its establishment in conjunction with a basic reorganization of the Senate. The plan envisaged a small body of six to eight members, prominent officials from the central administration who would be appointed by the sovereign for life. They would advise the sovereign on all matters put before them, but could issue no decisions without the sovereign's approval. Proposals approved by the sovereign, however, would only become law when countersigned by the responsible councilor. In support of the council, Panin proposed expanding the Senate's membership and its division into six departments along functional lines. The Senate's functions would thus be restricted mainly to the judicial sphere. In motivation, Panin's proposals aimed to regularize government procedures, to guarantee legality and security for the aristocratic elite represented in the council and the Senate, and to guard against the influence of "accidental persons" (favorites) and, tacitly, caprices of the sovereign.

If Panin's proposals represented an abstract constitutional reform with an aristocratic or oligarchic orientation, they assumed a more immediate import in the struggle for influence among court factions or parties then forming within Catherine's government. These parties were based on familial or clientele groupings. Loosely defined, they usually focused on some individual become powerful through official position and, ultimately, the sovereign's favor. Catherine had become familiar with such parties during Elizabeth's reign with the Vorontsov, Shuvalov, and Razumovskii factions. After her own accession to the throne, a realignment of court parties ensued. Nikita Panin headed a grouping of senior officials and dignitaries who, imbued with Petrine values, aspired to institute order, legality, and security into Russian politics. Panin himself enjoyed repute in the diplomatic corps in addition to Catherine's confidence through his guardianship of Grand Duke Paul. His brother, General Peter Panin, wielded influence in the army, and Catherine made them both senators. They were connected to many other noble clans by marriage and patronage.

By contrast, the five Orlov brothers were younger, less experienced, and less well connected, but they presumably had the Empress's ear through Grigorii's ministrations and their role in her coup. In September 1763 she appointed Fedor Orlov to observe the Senate's sessions and everyday affairs from the procurator-general's desk—a kind of administrative apprenticeship in preparation for new appointments. Soon the Orlovs found an important new ally in Bestuzhev-Riumin, whom Catherine respectfully addressed as "Little Father" (*Batiushka*) and continually consulted during the first year of her reign. He reciprocated in kind, suggesting on the eve of the coronation that the Senate cap the ceremony by naming the Empress "Mother of the Fatherland" in recognition of her role in saving the Empire from catastrophe. That title woulld recall the honors given Peter the Great when, having concluded the victorious peace with Sweden, he had been named "Emperor, the Great, and Father of the Fatherland." But Catherine politely declined the honor. "It seems to me that it is still early to present this proposal," she informed Bestuzhev, "because it will be interpreted by the public as boasting, but I thank you for your zeal." Twice within the next twelve months Bestuzhev retrieved the plan, but with the same result.[23]

In this situation, Panin's council proposal threatened the Orlov-Bestuzhev combination, aimed as it was against parvenus without connections. The council seemed intended to constrain Catherine's choice of advisers. The Orlovs insinuated that Panin aimed at nothing less than an aristocratic constitution that would curb Catherine's absolutism and, perhaps, prepare the way for Paul's eventual succession. Their warning worked. At the end of December 1762, just when Panin presented the plan for final adoption, Catherine abruptly postponed its consideration. Nevertheless, she established a special commission to review the question of the nobility's freedom from compulsory state service, and she implemented the reform of the Senate.

The Commission on Noble Freedom was composed of the very same individuals Panin had recommended for appointment to the council. Catherine's instructions to it called for a review of Peter III's liberation of the nobility from compulsory state service in peacetime, evidently with a view toward creating incentives to keep noblemen in service. But the Panin-led majority proposed broadening the nobility's privileges and restricting entry into the nobility through the Table of Ranks—notions attractive to the aristocratic elite. By contrast, Bestuzhev-Riumin strongly opposed any state interference in noble-serf relations and advocated noble participation in local government—ideas likely to attract the bulk of the nobility. When Catherine received these proposals in October 1763 she put them aside, apparently dissatisfied with their thrust and leery of the party conflict behind them. The issues looked too ticklish to tackle head-on; hence she delayed further action, though she had the Senate reconfirm Peter III's liberation decree several times by way of forestalling any fears of its reversal.[24]

The same commission took up the issue of Senate reform. By December 1763 Catherine acted on its recommendations for division into six functional departments. A few months before, she cemented a new alignment of court parties by endorsing Nikita Panin's proposed alliance with Prussia for cooperation in the upcoming election for a new king of Poland and by placing Panin himself in charge of the Collegium of Foreign Affairs. Both moves resulted in Bestuzhev's sudden loss of favor and retirement to his estates, where he died in April 1766 at the age of seventy-six. Yet Panin's triumph was incomplete; he was not named chancellor—nobody was—and he had evidently hoped for greater say in domestic affairs, which his new diplomatic responsibilities would largely preclude. Moreover, Catherine arranged two months later for the replacement of Procurator-General Glebov, in whom she had lost confidence owing to accusations of corruption, by a completely new face in high court politics—Prince Alexander Viazemskii. This was the post Nikita Panin might have wished for himself or his clients.[25]

In appointing Prince Viazemskii, the Empress drafted for his guidance a candid account of her political principles, her analysis of the current domestic situation, and her plans for the future. This document revealed a new clarity and breadth of political conceptions on Catherine's part, evidence of her rapid maturity in the field of imperial politics. The Empress's "most secret instructions" to Viazemskii first explained her reasons for firing Glebov: his shady dealings, bad associations, and lack of candor had sapped her trust, essential to the effective operation of that powerful office. She promised

Viazemskii full support in return for loyalty, application, and candor. In the Senate, which the procurator-general was obliged to oversee, Catherine discerned two competing parties. "In the one you will find persons of honest manners although shortsighted minds; in the other I think the views extend further, but it is unclear whether they are always practicable"—obviously allusions to a conservative or traditionalist group and to the Panin party. Viazemskii was told to ignore their rivalry, to treat both equally, and to rely on Catherine's support in case of controversy. She stressed the necessity of confining the Senate to implementation of the law and of preventing it from dominating the other branches of government, as had happened under weak sovereigns and their favorites (read: Elizabeth and Peter III).[26]

All these considerations prompted Catherine's formulation of a political credo based on Montesquieu: "The Russian Empire is so extensive that except for a sovereign master every other form of administration is harmful to it, for all the rest is slower in implementation and contains a great multitude of various passions which all tend to the fragmentation of central authority and power, than does a single sovereign who possesses all means for the curtailment of every kind of harm and considers the common good his own." In other words, centralized absolute rule was the government best suited to Russian circumstances. Catherine also advised Viazemskii to look into monetary matters, for Russia badly needed more money and a stable coinage; she urged him to run his own office firmly and dispense with unworthy subordinates. The Empire's laws needed reform and reordering—urgent tasks for the future—and both the salt and the spirits monopolies required reorganization to lessen the burden on the people and to discourage bootlegging and other abuses. Finally, because Little Russia (i.e., the Ukraine), Livland, and Finland all lived on legal bases different from the rest of the Empire, prudence dictated that they gradually be brought into conformity with the whole, primarily by appointing sensible governors who would expedite the process of integration. These instructions to Viazemskii were all the more significant in that Catherine immediately authorized him to appoint procurators at the middle or province level of territorial administration, thereby increasing their numbers by fifty and reinforcing their functions as an independent chain of command from the center to the guberniias and provinces. By early 1764, Catherine's own brand of bureaucratic absolutism was rapidly emerging. Particularly revealing was her decision to rule without a chancellor, in silent imitation of Peter III and Peter the Great.[27]

True to her promise, she gave Viazemskii wholehearted support and began entrusting him with a great variety of assignments (including supervision of the Secret Branch, which supposedly held some sessions in his house). They worked hand-in-glove for twenty-seven years until a stroke forced his retirement. Indeed, under Viazemskii the office of procurator-general swiftly expanded beyond the confines of the Senate to become a virtual ministry of internal affairs, justice, and finance. With Viazemskii the Empress patiently worked to bring the central bureaucracy under central direction and to inculcate respect for regular procedures. An example of her operational style may be seen in a letter of 9 December 1764.

Prince Alexander Alekseevich.

Order summoned to you the procurator of the War Collegium—it will be remembered, that he is called Verigin—and tell him that it has been noticed that the War Collegium has been acting against the instruction to the governors, it sends to the governors decrees, and not communications, and ask him for what reason does he allow them to act in contradiction to a Personal decree, and remind him of his duty; yet if you notice in him needless timidity vis-a-vis Zakhar [Chernyshev, head of the War Collegium], then give him to understand that you are speaking for me.

[P.S.] And in everything, please acquaint yourself with all the procurators, so that they gradually learn from you how to fulfill their duties and are in your hands and rely upon you, consequently, and upon Me too; otherwise cowardice toward the chiefs of the collegia will lead them into the omission of duty to the detriment of My political and civic Interest.[28]

Catherine's informal, often ungrammatical and misspelled working notes to Viazemskii disclose a practical administrator immersed in a multitude of state affairs, and also a human being subject to human frailties, yet able to joke wryly about them and herself. For example, she complained in one undated note: "Prince Alexander Alekseevich, it is impossible for me to be with you; I arose with an aching head; I fear it will hurt more from the usual Senate racket." Or in another: "Prince Alexander Alekseevich, because of a second attack of colic, which all night and even now still afflicts me, I cannot come to the Senate today, but shall tomorrow, so therefore take your measures." Sometimes Catherine injected sarcastic references to other government offices, as when Governor Chicherin of Siberia guberniia proposed some unbudgeted staff changes: "But I am not sending this report to the Senate for review, in order that they not get angry with Chicherin that, past their illustrious highnesses and excellencies, he writes directly to me for effect." Or again: "The Kamer Collegium itself does not know how much and where its monies are." The Empress even asked Viazemskii to intervene for her in purely personal affairs such as the impending marriage of Princess Trubetskaia: "please, if you could, have a word with Prince Peter Nikitich [Trubetskoi]: really, people will say that his daughter is pregnant, so therefore make haste . . . ; you may say that I said so, if you wish." In this instance Catherine may have called on Viazemskii because he had married into the Trubetskoi clan.[29]

The Marriage Issue

Amid the institutional changes of Catherine's first months of rule, her relationship with Grigorii Orlov aroused widespread apprehension. Indeed, the day after the coup Princess Dashkova was outraged to find Orlov at Peterhof pawing through official papers. What if Catherine should decide to marry the handsome stud? Everybody wondered. "She is certainly no perfect Character," commented Lord Buckingham, "& perhaps the best Description of Her is, that she is a Woman as well as an Empress. For the present perhaps the Woman may have as much to say as the Empress, but if She lives and reigns a few years the Empress will get the better of the Woman." Prophetic words, however male chauvinist in inspiration! The same observer remarked on Catherine's admiration for the reign of Queen Elizabeth of England, whose wily management of the marriage issue she may have taken to heart.[30]

Evidently the Orlovs hoped Catherine would marry Grigorii, if only to ensure their newly won eminence. Since the Empress owed them so much, and since she was also bound to Grigorii by bonds of affection or sexual infatuation, she had to consider the proposal quite seriously. Besides, Orlov was not the only suitor. On hearing of the coup, Stanislas Poniatowski wrote his former mistress in hopes of a reunion. Catherine gently dissuaded him, mentioning the antiforeign ferment in Petersburg and delicately alluding to her "great obligations" to the Orlovs and to Grigorii's "passion" and "innumerable follies" on her behalf. Poniatowski stayed home, but she remembered him a year later in resurrecting Hanbury-Williams' old dream to see him on the elective throne of Poland. Although Orlov enjoyed Catherine's affection, his political innocence and obscure origins amused, amazed, and antagonized other courtiers. His familiar manner with Catherine excited jealous resentment. Once, when he tactlessly boasted at a small gathering that he could overthrow her in a month if he chose, Kirill Razumovskii acidly retorted: "Could be; but, my friend, instead of waiting a month, we would have hanged you in two weeks."[31]

The marriage issue put Catherine in a quandary. She could not afford to alienate the Orlovs with an outright refusal. They had already unlimbered their political muscle once. All the same, she could guess the outrage such a match would incite, particularly among the Panin party—a group she saw as essential to her reform program. Any marriage would obviously be seen as jeopardizing Paul's rights of succession. If other courtiers already envied the Orlovs' eminence, how much more would they resent her marrying such an uncultured upstart? Indeed, Nikita Panin reportedly reacted to the plan by angrily advising that "a madame Orlova could never be Empress of All the Russias."[32] Catherine judiciously delayed. She persisted in her public patronage of the Orlovs while discreetly sounding opinion on the subject. Her subterfuges confused the situation and produced some shocking revelations. She learned more than she wished to know.

In May 1763, while Catherine was on another pilgrimage from Moscow to Rostov the Great, she had Bestuzhev circulate a paper seeking signatures of prominent officials in support of her marrying again. The reason advanced was the fragility of the succession in view of Paul's frailty. The project (no copy is known) may not have specified the intended spouse, but doubtless many assumed it would be Grigorii Orlov. Some signed, others balked. Rumors flew around Moscow, a city renowned for avid gossipmongering. These rumors triggered a fervently patriotic outburst from one of the young Guardsmen most prominent in the coup—Captain of the cavalry and gentleman of the chamber Fedor Khitrovo. He condemned the marriage, in which he discerned a plot by "the old devil" Bestuzhev, "stupid" Grigorii Orlov, and "the great rogue" Aleksei Orlov. Nikita Panin suspected that Catherine condoned the venture and was assembling a conclave of aristocrats against it, Khitrovo alleged, adding that the Orlovs should be seized. If Catherine would marry again, he remarked, better she should wed a brother of "Ivanushka" (Ivan VI). Arrested quietly on 27 May 1763, Khitrovo admitted under interrogation his opposition to Catherine's marriage, and when Aleksei Orlov entered the room he apologized for planning to kill him and his brothers in the event that they pursued the marriage.[33]

This confession infuriated the Empress. Her ire turned into alarm over Khitrovo's claim that, on the eve of the coup, she had promised Panin to become regent and had only accepted autocratic power at the Orlovs' insistence. On cross-examination, Khitrovo maintained that Aleksei Orlov had given him this information. Catherine demanded to know who had joined the conspiracy, who had conceived it, what they had intended to do with her if she refused their "help," and where Khitrovo had heard about her alleged agreement with Panin. Furthermore, she asked whether Khitrovo's arrest had caused alarm in Moscow. No firm answers to any of her questions were found. Most of the persons implicated in the affair said their knowledge came from "the echo" on the street—that is, hearsay. All Moscow seemed to be discussing the matter in a manner that recalled the conspiracy of the Khrushchevs and the Gur'evs. Accordingly, Catherine decided against a public inquiry and trial, the results of which might be embarrassingly unpredictable. The case was resolved "administratively." All the papers were sealed in a special packet not to be opened without Catherine's express order. Khitrovo was banished to his estates where he died in 1774; one supposed officer-accomplice was exiled with his wife to a southern fortress, another to the Ukraine. Perhaps the lenity of these sentences reflected some feeling of complicity on Catherine's part. After all, her sounding of public opinion had set the whole charade in motion.[34]

The Khitrovo affair finally settled one problem: there would be no more talk of marriage, to Orlov or anyone else. In this sense, Catherine benefited. One wonders how she explained it all to Grigorii. Yet the affair obviously shook the Empress, revived old fears, and conjured up new ones. She sensed a wider conspiracy involving Guardsmen and grandees, the prime movers behind her coup. The alleged move against the Orlovs showed her how hated they had become to their former fellows. Evidently she suspected that murdering them implied the same fate for herself. The allusions to Ivan VI and to the circumstances of her accession were doubly mortifying; both betrayed doubts about her legitimacy and her methods of political manipulation, doubts the more painful for being voiced almost a year after the coup by its principals. Moreover, Catherine felt hurt by the mere thought that people were casually discussing such sensitive matters. So a special manifesto was announced in Moscow on 4 June 1763, with copies sent to all government offices throughout the Empire, forbidding "all impudent and unseemly loose talk," which was repeatedly branded as "infectious" and dangerous to public tranquility. Catherine privately called this measure "the manifesto about silence." At the same time, in preparation for the court's return to Petersburg, she entrusted direction of a local section of the Secret Branch to the newly appointed governor-general of Moscow, Field Marshal and Senator Count Peter Saltykov, an old friend and military hero. She wished to leave a firm hand in control of the unruly metropolis.[35]

In fact, despite these precautions, animosity toward the Orlovs simmered in various subterranean forms. In October 1763 Grigorii himself received a present from Moscow containing a hollowed out cheese filled with horse dung and pierced with a truncheon, obviously a hostile gift. Later in the year an anonymous proclamation in Catherine's name appeared in multiple copies. This handwritten diatribe assailed the nobility for corruption and indolence, indifference and injustice. Petrine times were fondly recalled,

> But now they have undermined all justice and driven it out of Russia, and they do not even wish to hear about it, that the Russian people has been orphaned, the small children without their mothers have been orphaned. Either these noblemen do not die, or there is no judgment of them before God, but they will have the very same judgment, and you also will be measured by its measure.

The government ordered these sheets to be burned by the public executioner, and proclaimed on 17 March 1764 that only printed government decrees should be considered genuine—a pronouncement that would be repeated more than once in subsequent decades.[36]

Curbing the Church

Besides the question of the succession and Catherine's marital status, one of the most delicate issues confronting her government in the first months of power revolved around the estates and serfs held by the Orthodox Church. Peter III's attempt to secularize ecclesiastical estates had provoked vociferous opposition, which Catherine's coup deftly exploited. To sustain the support of clerical opinion, she abolished on 12 August the Collegium of Economy, the state agency that administered ecclesiastical properties, and established a commission to investigate the issue. On 27 November, however, she reinstituted the same agency with a slightly different name as part of a general reform designed to specify budgets and staffing for all Church institutions. This move aroused clerical ire by raising again the specter of secularization. Many clerics grumbled, but only one protested openly. Metropolitan Arsenii Matsievich, a sixty-five-year-old hierarch of Polish extraction and a member of the Holy Synod, had long opposed state interference in Church affairs, particularly the seizure of Church lands. So well known were Arsenii's views that Catherine deliberately excluded him from the coronation festivities in Moscow. Nevertheless, she was scheduled to make a pilgrimage to Rostov, Arsenii's see, early in 1763 for the purpose of celebrating the newly established shrine of St. Dmitrii Rostovskii. A confrontation with Arsenii thus seemed imminent. But when Catherine postponed her visit, Arsenii took the initiative by dispatching a vehement denunciation of secularization to the Holy Synod on 6 March 1763. If secularization were pursued, Arsenii contended, its injustice would cause calamity to Church and Empire alike. After hearing his protest on 13 March, the members of the Holy Synod decided it contained insults to the Empress that required condemnation. When Catherine's opinion was solicited, she found Arsenii's arguments "perverse and inflammatory distortions." A Guards officer galloped off to Rostov to bring the Metropolitan back for trial. In the meantime Arsenii wrote another report denouncing the transfer of estates and peasants from the Church's hands, sarcastically remarking that "with us it is not like in England, that one is to live and make one's way by money alone." He also asked to retire.[37]

Metropolitan Arsenii was brought to Moscow under arrest on 17 March. Despite a plea by Bestuzhev for mercy, Catherine insisted that "the liar and humbug" be punished as an example to others. Starting on 1 April, the Holy Synod grilled its former member in extraordinary nocturnal sessions so as to conceal the proceedings. They brushed aside Arsenii's explanation that he had intended no offense to the sovereign. Indeed, they scented a conspiracy and pressed the old man for news of accomplices and followers before sentencing him, on 7 April, to lose his office and rank. He was incarcerated in a northern monastery under guard and forbidden access to pen and ink. When he persisted in protesting Catherine's highhanded ways and was accused of a new conspiracy in 1767, he was transferred to a casemate at Reval and ended his days there in 1772 in solitary confinement, known to the guards only as "Andrei the Liar."[38]

Catherine soon exploited the aftermath of this extraordinary affair to humble the Holy Synod with a speech bluntly calling for the divestiture of Church lands, which she branded as illegally gained and improperly held. The Collegium of Economy was reestablished on 12 May 1763 and final secularization was announced on 26 February 1764. As a result, about one million male peasants—or two million persons in all—came under direct state control. Classified as a special category of state peasants, these so-called economic peasants paid taxes and dues to the state via the Collegium of Economy. For Catherine, these events signalled a triumph of state over Church, the former gaining one million new taxpayers and large expanses of land. The Church, by contrast, lost a chief economic support and forfeited whatever administrative autonomy it had left; many monasteries closed as a consequence. The Empress had used the Church in her quest for political power, only to subordinate the institution to that power once the clergy's assistance was no longer crucial. Like Peter the Great, she wished the Orthodox Church to assume a more active role in social welfare and education, under state guidance, but she was loath to provide adequate funds for those purposes.

The commission on Church estates was only one of several that Catherine established in the first two years of her reign. The commission form allowed her to work outside the regular institutions of government, which she was not yet accustomed to managing. Besides, each commission involved several officials and thus gave her the opportunity to place her friends and supporters in positions of influence, without directly threatening the regular administrative bodies. She could likewise ensure representation of the various court parties in each commission, thereby reserving the balance of power to herself. Instinctively, she adopted a policy of divide and rule, as she frankly admitted to Lord Buckingham in 1763.[39] Creating commissions also had the virtue of delaying consideration of sensitive issues, such as Church estates and noble rights, until the Empress gained a better feel for the practical possibilities in each instance. Still, her system of delegating authority ran the risk of undue delay and confusion through lack of coordination, fostering the impression that nobody was in charge and that the Empress lacked a consistent policy. As the British envoy saw it, Catherine tried to do too much too quickly:

> Those who are most in her society assure me that her application to business is incredible. The welfare and prosperity of her subjects, the glory of her empire, are always present to her; and to all appearance her care will raise the reputation and power of Russia to a point which, at present, they have never reached, if she does not indulge too much in far-fetched and impractical theories, which interested or ignorant people are too ready to suggest to her. Her foible is to be too systematic, and that may be the rock on which she may, perhaps, split. She embraces too many objects at once; she likes to begin, regulate, and correct projects all in a moment.[40]

But this judgment missed Catherine's belief in the urgent necessity to nudge Russia along the Petrine path. She calculated that prudently progressive policies would reinforce her hold on the throne, and she was eager to involve the Russian power elite in the process. Indeed, she saw in Bestuzhev's proposal a challenge—to earn the title of Mother of the Fatherland. Such a mother needed active sons. Her own example, coupled with promises of glory and reward, offered potent incentives to action. Consequently, in addition to impressive ceremonies and extended visits to the Russian heartland, the first year and half of her reign witnessed a flurry of governmental activity in diverse spheres.

One of her first pronouncements, on 18 July 1762, set the tone of her first year of rule by loudly proclaiming her selfless dedication to the Empire's best interests in the style of "Our Grandfather Emperor Peter the Great" before she denounced the "plague" of corruption that had "infected" all levels of government. What elicited her rage was a report of a minor official extorting a ruble from each person to whom he administered the oath of loyalty to the Empress. This case and others heard by the Senate convinced Catherine that she must remove unworthy officials in the interests of administrative efficiency and the restoration of public respect for the government. All this revealed some measure of her ignorance of Russian administrative practice, where extortion and bribery were a way of life.[41]

Another measure of her administrative naivete was her willingness to receive petitioners in person. As early as 3 July she complained in the Senate about petitions submitted outside the established channels, forbidding the practice on the basis of previous legislation and on practical grounds. Nevertheless, she was inundated with all manner of requests—her three cabinet secretaries received 300 each in Moscow—and the Senate protested this irregular procedure; so she ordered petitions to be submitted only through proper channels, though she still accepted them directly on occasion.[42] She was eager to govern in person and impatient to see results, virtues that, in a huge empire run by a huge bureaucracy, could cause as much harm as good.

Economics and Immigration

Even before leaving Petersburg for her coronation Catherine took several steps aimed at relaxing the war-strained economy. Food prices in Petersburg were checked twice a week. Most state monopolies were abolished. Grain magazines were promised for each town to control bread prices, the main indicator of the cost of living. Thirty thousand rubles were advanced to rebuild in masonry the hemp warehouses in Petersburg destroyed by fire in 1761. Visiting Moscow gave Catherine additional ideas about regulating both capitals and court-residences. On 23 October 1762 she banned construction of new manufactories and workshops in the dual capitals, overcrowded and unsanitary as they already were. Industrial expansion should proceed in provincial towns instead, as the German cameralists Bielfeld and Justi advised. To monitor the growth of Moscow, the Empress requested weekly reports of food prices and monthly tabulations of population. She fused these initiatives together in November and December 1762 by creating the Commission for the Reconstruction in Masonry of Moscow and St. Petersburg, a high-level urban planning agency headed by Count Zakhar Chernyshev, Prince Mikhail Dashkov, and Ivan Betskoi.[43]

The commission soon began surveying both capitals with a view toward compiling new plans for each, plans that would make maximum use of existing buildings. Moreover, when fire devastated the town of Tver in May 1763, Catherine had the commission plan its reconstruction as well, granting large sums for the purpose. Consequently the commission's jurisdiction expanded to include the compilation of new plans for all towns. The ubiquity of fires in Russia's largely wooden towns guaranteed ample occasion for the implementation of such plans. By 22 June 1763 the Empress asked the Senate to review the plan for Tver. Thus Catherine moved swiftly from particular urban problems to general solutions. In a broad sense she aimed to remold Russia's cities and towns in the Europeanized image of St. Petersburg—planned, prosperous, beautiful, fireproof, orderly, clean, and tranquil. Her vision would require decades and millions of rubles to achieve even partially: all the more reason for an early start.[44]

A dual concern to conserve and increase population spurred Catherine's support for public health facilities in Moscow and for immigration. Before returning to Petersburg in June 1763 she proclaimed the establishment of Paul's Hospital on the outskirts of Moscow. Financed completely from her purse, this small institution was the old capital's first public hospital offering free professional treatment to the curable poor of both sexes. It opened on 14 September 1763 in a wooden house formerly owned by Procurator-General Glebov which the Senate provided in remission for 15,000 rubles of his debts. In 1766, when the hospital transferred to a new building, it expanded from twenty-five to fifty beds. Statistics on admissions and releases (but not mortality) were published monthly in the local gazette. Also in June 1763 the Empress approved Ivan Betskoi's plan for a foundling home and lying-in hospital in Moscow, which opened on her birthday a year later, 21 April 1764. Inspired by British and European prototypes, the Moscow Foundling Home was intended to discourage infanticide by unmarried or indigent mothers. It received babies without any questions asked and strove to train children in useful arts and trades. Catherine granted large sums for its foundation and for building a huge masonry complex to house it in central Moscow, encouraging prominent Muscovites in similar patronage. Unfortunately, despite these efforts the Moscow Foundling Home and its branch in St. Petersburg, which opened in 1770, suffered the same awesome mortality rates as their European predecessors and therefore earned the derisive title of "angel factories."[45]

On 14 October 1762 the Empress directed the Senate to facilitate foreign immigration and the return of Russian refugees for the settlement of the Empire's unpopulated expanses. Economic and political calculations animated this new policy. Current populationist theories hailed the growth of population as an essential element of national power in the form of military recruits and taxpayers, artisans and husbandrymen. Foreign immigrants, it was hoped, could stimulate the economy with new skills and capital while settling empty lands. Furthermore, such immigrants posed no obvious threat to serfdom in Russia, inasmuch as foreign farmers would not be seen as the traditional kind of peasants. Some noble landowners were even eager to invite foreign farmers to demonstrate advanced methods of agriculture to their tradition-bound serfs. For prospective immigrants Catherine looked westward, hoping to take advantage of the chaotic conditions in central Europe left by the Seven Years' War. She also sought the return of Russian deserters and other refugees, mainly schismatic Old Believers, as she repeated Peter III's efforts to lure such people back to Russia with promises of pardon and freedom to settle wherever they wished on state lands. Not that she was above sending army units across the Polish border to round up runaways who proved reluctant to return. Foreign immigrants were promised religious toleration. Only Jews were excluded—a continuation of Elizabeth's policy that Catherine was afraid to change publicly for fear of inciting Russian religious prejudice but which she soon found means to circumvent.[46]

The Empress gradually committed substantial resources to this settlement program, which she publicized in foreign languages and countries. She advertised its high priority by establishing on 22 July 1763 a special administration, the Chancery of Guardianship for Foreigners, equal in status to the regular collegiia. Indeed, she took the occasion to name Grigorii Orlov president of the new agency, his first civilian administrative appointment in her government, with an initial budget of 200,000 rubles per annum. Though Orlov had no experience in such matters, neither did anyone else in Russia; so his appointment reflected a shrewd move by Catherine to mollify her favorite without antagonizing other dignitaries. Orlov displayed great interest in this office, which was directly and solely responsible to Catherine and which he kept for ten years. His responsibility was to oversee the wave of immigration that brought more than 30,000 immigrants, mainly Germans, to settle the Empire's southern territories by 1775. Yet the cost to the state proved considerable: more than five and a half million rubles by 1770.[47]

Public Health, State Finance, and Commerce

Linked in a general way with these concerns were Catherine's early reforms in the sphere of medical administration and public health. She evinced a healthy skepticism toward medical practitioners in general as a result of their horrific ministrations during her youth. Still, she remembered Dr. Antonio Sanchez's efforts to save her life in 1744 so vividly that she awarded him an annual pension of 1,000 rubles for life soon after her accession. Count Lestocq, the exiled former court physician, she pardoned, awarded an estate, and restored his annual salary of 7,000 rubles in place of a pension. Moreover, she believed in principle in the benefits of professional medical care and felt confident with the German cameralists that its extension to the population at large would improve health and conserve population. On her accession, Dr. James ("Rhubarb") Mounsey resigned for reasons of health as chief imperial physician (archiater) and head of the Medical Chancery. The Empress awarded him 1,500 rubles but left the office vacant, perhaps to avoid appointing another foreigner in the chauvinistic atmosphere of mid-1762. While in Moscow, however, she suggested the urgent need for improvements in medical care for the army, which employed the great majority of all practitioners, and then solicited proposals for reform of the Medical Chancery itself. Meanwhile, she called on the Medical Chancery to institute a network of secret hospitals or clinics for the treatment of venereal disease. In the fall of 1763 she delegated Grigorii Teplov and Baron Alexander Cherkassov, an enlightened aristocrat who was an old friend, to fashion the various proposals into a comprehensive overhaul of the state's medical administration. This resulted in the formation of the Medical Collegium on 12 November 1763.[48]

Catherine's new Medical Collegium abolished the Petrine office of archiater, invariably occupied by a foreign M.D., in favor of a bifurcated administration comprising a Collegium of Medical and Surgical Arts, which supervised professional affairs and set general policy, and a business office. Court practitioners were removed from the jurisdiction of the Medical Collegium, perhaps to insulate them from political pressures. Instead of the Medical Chancery's single physician head, the Medical Collegium was jointly administered by a board of seven practitioners and a nonprofessional president. Baron Cherkassov served as the first president until 1775, working closely with Catherine throughout that period. He chose the professional members, all of them practitioners of foreign extraction and training. Catherine justified the reform as an application of Petrine collegial principles (although Peter the Great had never applied them to medical matters), and she charged the Medical Collegium to expand professional health care by assigning a doctor to each province, to increase the numbers of Russian (or Slavic) medical professionals in cooperation with Moscow University, and to regulate apothecary shops. In June 1764 she even authorized the Collegium to grant the M.D. degree to worthy candidates after examination, whereas the newly established medical faculty of Moscow University only received that authority in 1791.

In fact, the Medical Collegium rarely awarded degrees and only reluctantly conferred its first in 1768 after intense pressure from Catherine and Cherkassov. The professional members argued that Russian physicians ought to undergo advanced training at foreign universities rather than receive second-rate degrees in Russia. Catherine deplored such attitudes, but she recognized they could not be changed overnight. More important, she and Cherkassov strove to increase the number of Slavs in the surgical schools, and to employ Slavic M.D.'s as instructors in those schools. Though the Medical Collegium commanded larger resources than its predecessor, the number of practitioners continued to grow at a modest rate, and they remained very scarce in civilian service in general and in rural areas in particular. Like urban planning, public health was a field in which Catherine's reform initiatives needed many years to yield results. That she hoped the Medical Collegium would foster further expansion of medical care is manifest in a notation she appended to the instructions to the new institution: "Do not forget to make institutions about hospitals in the provinces as well, and submit them to Us."[49]

Questions of economic policy preoccupied Catherine from the very start of her reign. This was only natural because of the difficult situation she inherited, a situation that had haunted the reigns of Elizabeth and Peter III, under both of whom significant changes had been introduced. Finances were a prime concern, for the Empress had to reward her supporters and introduce order into the chaos bequeathed by her predecessors. As empress, Catherine spent freely, yet she constantly worried about state revenues. Lack of information crippled any calculations. As she complained to Procurator-General Glebov on 16 August 1762: "Concerning the soul [capitation] tax I have information, but concerning the other revenues I still know nothing, likewise concerning expenditures—please make for me a clear and brief extract." Glebov could not fulfill this request, to Catherine's chagrin, but then neither could his successor for many years. Nobody compiled a comprehensive state financial statement in Russia between 1724 and 1781! Finances were something that Catherine never grasped in detail. In fact, she admitted to Adam Olsuf'ev in 1767: "I confess I do not understand anything about great accounts and therefore I request you to note again, how much do I have at my disposal [to spend], without halting any allocated expenditures."[50]

As examples of the financial and economic issues that Catherine confronted, she questioned the Senate on 30 October 1762 about the retirement from circulation of lightweight coins and its likely effect on exchange rates. Under Peter III a plethora of copper money had been coined and plans made to print five million rubles worth of paper money, both steps fueling severe inflation. Catherine had immediately banned such tampering with the coinage, and her government gradually withdrew the lightweight coins by 1767. This success proved to be merely temporary, however, for the outbreak of war in 1768 brought a massive emission of paper money.[51]

Foreign observers were constantly perplexed over Russia's finances. Thus Lord Buckingham in late October 1764 relayed Nikita Panin's "insinuations" about Catherine's being short of money "and was not a little surprised, some days ago, when She was pleased to take notice to me of the present affluent state of Her finances, and of the great increase Her arrangements had made in the public revenue." Four months later his successor, Sir George Macartney, estimated Catherine's "private treasure" at seven million rubles, "and such is Her economy, that it augments considerably every day; but, notwithstanding She is so very rich, the country seems poor, and in the hands of the merchants and at the gaming tables there is no such thing to be seen as gold or silver." The favorable balance of trade that Russia enjoyed with England in particular, some £600,000 per year, puzzled Macartney in view of the high prices and scarce specie in Petersburg; "but there are many paradoxes here that would demand uncommon ingenuity to reconcile."[52]

Many years later Catherine claimed that state revenues had soared from 16 million rubles in 1762 to 28 million in 1764, with a surplus of 5.5 million rubles a year later and three-quarters of the debts from Elizabeth's reign paid. These claims appear to be considerably exaggerated. Revenues in 1767 barely exceeded 25 million rubles without any adjustment for the steady inflation of those years. Besides, the advent of peace in 1762 could account for much of the budgetary improvement regardless of state policies. Yet her administration did balance the budget every year but one before 1769, a war year.[53]

In basic economic outlook the Empress soon showed herself to be an advocate of growth and expansion, and an opponent of restrictions. Thus she abolished most state monopolies, authorized grain exports, and reconfirmed Peter III's ban on the purchase of serfs by non-nobles for factory labor. Her prohibition on establishing new manufactories in Moscow and St. Petersburg aimed to protect both capitals from such perils as pollution, overpopulation, inflation, and deforestation of the hinterland; but it also envisioned a redistribution of industry to provincial towns as a measure of general economic stimulation. Nationalist sentiments also received recognition when she renamed the newly founded harbor of Rogervik on the Estonian coast Baltiiskii Port.[54]

Meeting with the Senate in Moscow on 9 December 1762, Catherine reviewed commercial policy, asking whether consuls should be stationed in Spain, England, Holland, and elsewhere to promote Russian maritime trade. She also voiced a desire for a revision of the tariff in the near future. Russia's trade policy should discourage the import of luxurious novelities, she urged, and encourage the production of native goods for the domestic market and for export. Relieved of senseless burdens, merchants and manufacturers should be assisted in their pursuits by means that did not injure others. Her ideal was the best possible balance of trade in favor of Russia. If the Senate was too busy to consider these matters fully, she suggested the formation of a commission on commerce for that purpose. This matter hung in limbo nearly a year, evidently pushed aside by more pressing concerns. But on 20 October 1763 Catherine inquired whether the Senate had yet authorized Governor-General Brown of Livland to establish a commission for the review of trade at the port of Riga. Sometime thereafter she confided to Nikita Panin her intention to found a commission on commerce with the additional responsibility of reviewing state finances, for which she asked his advice in framing the instruction.[55]

The Commission on Commerce was officially announced on 8 December 1763. Its membership included Senator Ivan Nepliuev, Prince Yakov Shakhovskoi, Count Ioann Ernst Münnich, and Grigorii Teplov, assisted by three well-informed officials: state councilor Timofei von Klingshtet, procurator Mikhail Pushkin of the Commerce Collegium, and court councilor Mikhail Odart. Catherine's instruction empowered the commission to study the Empire's "commerce," understood in a very broad sense, with a view toward removing obstacles and stimulating mercantile activity by helpful legislation. Specifically, the commissioners should seek to expand exports of natural and finished products, and to secure reliable credit for Russian merchants at home and abroad. The Empress transmitted a body of projects and observations for consultation by the commission, which she authorized to meet together or to study problems individually at home. The commission could obtain money and staff support from the Senate and solicit information from it and other government offices, yet it remained independent and directly subordinate to Catherine, who promised to attend its sessions on occasion. Although it is uncertain whether the Empress ever attended the commission, she kept in close touch with its proceedings, and to speed its progress she soon authorized a smaller group—Münnich, Teplov, Klingshtet, Pushkin, and Odart—to examine projects and proposed legislation prior to their consideration by the full commission. In fact, the Commission on Commerce provided a forum for wide-ranging debates about the nature of the Russian economy, its social bases, and the government's role in the evolving economic policies and realities. An early product was the new, more liberalized tariff of 1766. These discussions and the commission both lasted throughout Catherine's reign.[56]

Issues of industry and finance, labor policy and state security, were all involved in the unrest gripping peasant-workers at the mines and metalworks of the Ural Mountains. This unrest had begun under Peter III, and one of Catherine's first decrees reiterated his call for submission. On 6 December 1762 the Empress dispatched Quartermaster-General Prince Alexander Viazemskii to Kazan posthaste with special instructions and a manifesto exhorting submission from rebellious peasants assigned to factory labor in the Urals.

This mission signified the start of Viazemskii's long career as a trouble-shooter for Catherine. It also marked her first encounter with the restive, volatile population on the southeastern frontier and with the special problems of the Urals metallurgical industry, the Empire's largest and the principal source of its armaments and coinage.[57]

Catherine instructed Viazemskii first to obtain submission, by persuasion or by force, before he considered the workers' grievances. After restoring order at the metalworks, Viazemskii was to investigate the industry's use of bondaged labor with an eye toward employing freely hired workers instead. This directive reflected Catherine's firm belief in the superiority of free labor, a belief already implied in her reconfirmation of Peter III's ban on the purchase of peasants by non-nobles for industrial labor. Even so, the labor agitation in the Urals proved extremely complex because the rebellious workers were mostly state peasants assigned to work seasonally at the metalworks, many of which were owned by noblemen.[58]

Catherine's manifesto, which Viazemskii was to announce only in rebellious areas, blamed the unrest not on the workers themselves but on "several impudent idlers," whom she advised Viazemskii to single out for arrest. He was also to confiscate any written materials or phoney manifestoes found among the strikers, for a fraudulent announcement of her accession had promised liberation to the peasants assigned to labor at the mines and metalworks. Redress of grievances could begin only after the strikers resumed work; "for our just and merciful intention is to correct the simple and the errant, to defend the insulted, and to deflect direct attacks and oppressions on those peasants by means of the good arrangement of their work with beneficial pay, in proportion to their labors, or by their recall from those manufactories, as we shall find useful for their own prosperity and for the preservation of the manufactories." Inserted by Nikita Panin, these words appeared inflammatory in the conditions that Prince Viazemskii discovered on the spot. He achieved enough success, however, that Catherine was impressed and recalled him at the end of 1763 to become procurator-general, sending as his replacement Major-General Alexander Bibikov, a confidant of the Panins who continued the pacification. In support of this campaign Catherine replaced the governor of Orenburg guberniia with Dmitrii Volkov, whom she commissioned to inspect the region and to suggest reforms; she also took under state control the metalworks of Count Andrei Shuvalov, hard hit by peasant unrest, in return for writing off his debts to the state of 686,000 rubles.[59]

The investigations by Viazemskii and Bibikov brought to Catherine's attention the great complexities confronting state administration of the Urals mines and metalworks. On 18 July 1765 she therefore appointed a five-man commission to review the findings of the previous investigators with a view toward easing the burdens of the assigned peasants, preserving labor peace, and safeguarding the state's profit. For fear of provoking renewed disorders, the entire inquiry was to proceed in strict secrecy. Catherine's directions for this new inquiry reveal her improved grasp of state economic policies, which she was determined to rationalize in the interests of greater productivity, social tranquility, and orderly administration. Thus she asked the commissioners to consider whether the metalworks should be state owned or left in private hands, owned by nobles or non-nobles, why the disorders had occurred and how others could be avoided, and whether the metalworks could be expanded without devastating the forests for their charcoal fuel. At the very least, the Empress hoped to defuse this social and economic tinderbox in the Urals, where production rose rapidly throughout the 1760s and into the early 1770s, boosting economic advance while stoking the fuel of future rebellion. The commission met irregularly until January 1767, when its final report was submitted to Catherine. Although some reforms were made, tensions persisted.[60]

The Armed Forces and the Ukraine

The armed forces constituted a crucial political factor in eighteenth-century Russia, as re-emphasized by their role in Catherine's coup. Within days of the coup the Empress countermanded Peter III's reorganization of the Guards and other units, except for pay raises, and called for a special military commission to review the armed forces' budget, manpower, and leadership. Her decree of 4 July appointed Paul colonel of the Life Cuirassiers regiment, renamed the Imperial Heir's Cuirassiers. He also received the rank of General-Admiral by a decree of 20 December 1762, which drew explicit parallels between Paul's appointment and the early naval exploits of Peter the Great. Just before Catherine's coronation she received a proposal from General Peter Panin for issuance of an imperial manifesto lauding the army's victories in the Prussian campaign and awarding the combat forces an extra half-year's pay. She issued it on her coronation day, mentioning in addition the establishment of a military commission to review grievances and suggest reforms. Proclaimed on 11 November 1762, this temporary Military Commission comprised ten prominent commanders, most of them longtime friends of the Empress: field marshals Kirill Razumovskii and Peter Saltykov, generals Alexander Golitsyn, Zakhar Chernyshev, Peter Panin, Mikhail Volkonskii, Vasilii Dolgorukii, grand master or ordnance Alexander Villebois, and lieutenant-generals Vasilii Suvorov, Vladimir Lopukhin, and Gustav von Berg. The first seven all played leading political and military roles during long periods of Catherine's reign. At least three—Razumovskii, Chernyshev, and Villebois—had been in love with her when she was grand duchess. Catherine's initial military reforms simply restored Elizabethan norms in place of Peter III's much resented innovations (although, oddly enough, the Prussian-style uniforms were retained). Meanwhile she solicited suggestions from the army leadership. It was Peter Saltykov's idea to have a military commission review the army in light of its performance in the Seven Years' War. A similar commission looked into the fleet.[61]

The main reforms that resulted from the Military Commission's review in 1764–65 involved a clearer determination of numbers, revised recruiting procedures, exclusion of field and Guards units from internal police duties and tax collection, quartering units in barracks instead of private houses, decorations and promotions to worthy veteran officers to retain them in view of the cessation of compulsory state service for the nobility in peacetime, and formation of a General Staff. In its reform proposals the Military Commission insisted that the army's strength lay not in numbers alone, but in discipline, training, maintenance, and loyalty—all based on a common language, faith, customs, and ethnic origin. To improve mobility, one cavalry unit was to support every two infantry regiments, the number of heavy cavalry units (cuirassiers, carabineers, dragoons, and hussars) was increased, and field artillery was concentrated into units. A special commission inspected the border forts and standardized their garrisons; indeed, the size of the garrison forces was substantially expanded. By 1765, the army numbered approximately 303,000 men, the largest force in eastern Europe by far, and it slowly expanded to 413,000 by the end of Catherine's reign. At the same time, the Baltic fleet grew rapidly, with many officers being sent abroad for training, and many foreign officers, mainly British, hired. Soon the Russian fleet outnumbered both the Swedish and the Danish.[62]

Whom to place in charge of the War Collegium, the central administration of the army, posed a ticklish problem for the Empress, considering the great authority and influence inherent in that post. At first she left it vacant while the Military Commission introduced its reforms. Her former admirer Count Zakhar Chernyshev forced the issue early in 1764, however, by suddenly retiring, allegedly for reasons of weak health and straitened finances. Catherine let him know her displeasure. "Full leisure was given him to repent," commented the British envoy; "at last he was obliged to humble himself before the man (Gregor Gregorievitch Orlow) whom most he hates, and was only through his intercession restored to his former situation." The Empress appointed Chernyshev vice-president of the War Collegium—there was no president—on 4 March 1764. His younger brother Ivan headed the Admiralty. Thus Catherine entrusted management of the newly reformed armed forces to two aristocrat friends of long standing.

Besides reorganizing the army and the navy, the Empress devoted constant attention to them both in person. She and Paul attended church at Petersburg's Peter and Paul fortress on the Grand Duke's nameday—29 June 1763—and reviewed the fleet at Kronstadt in mid-July. The next summer she inspected the troops and fleet at Reval, and sailed to Baltiiskii Port to observe mock sea battles. In June 1765 she and Paul both attended the army's summer camp maneuvers at Krasnoe Selo. Yet Catherine's solicitude for the armed forces had its limits; at one point she angrily threatened to disband the Military Commission for insubordination and fiscal malfeasance. On another occasion she asked Elagin to inform his brother-in-law, Field Marshal Buturlin, in her name that he should play less at cards and attend more to military affairs—"really I have no need for idlers."[63]

Another major problem Catherine felt compelled to resolve early in her reign was the status of the Ukraine and its elected chief, Hetman Kirill Razumovskii. Here, too, she acted cautiously because of the obligations incurred by his prominence in her coup, as well as his wealth and eminence.

Her attention was attracted to issues of frontier security and colonization on the southwest border by an investigation of General Khorvat, leader of the military colony of New Serbia established in the 1750s. His reckless administration provoked a storm of complaints that brought his deposition and exile in 1763. The colony was abolished and reorganized into the guberniia of Novorossiia—New Russia—an expanse stretching from the domains of the Don cossacks in the east to the Polish border on the west and jutting southward into the autonomous territory of the Zaporozhian cossacks. In late May 1763 Catherine became furious at a report of a Zaporozhian officer having burned two settlements along the lower Dnieper. She even had the Senate consider transfer of the Zaporozhians' stronghold, but deferred to its advice that such action should be postponed until Polish affairs improved and Turkish reactions could be gauged.[64]

About Hetman Razumovskii and his administration the Empress soon developed doubts, evidently incited by Grigorii Teplov, who had long assisted the Hetman before joining Catherine's cabinet. Although she liked Razumovskii, she thought him easily influenced by craven cronies, naive, self-indulgent, and inept. Even before her coronation some kind of commission was investigating the Hetman's affairs, an inquiry that continued in Moscow during Catherine's sojourn there. When she returned to Petersburg in June 1763 Razumovskii went back to his residence in Glukhov, though he had spent little time there since being chosen Hetman in 1750. All the same, he suddenly began lobbying the Ukrainian nobility and officials to make the office of hetman hereditary in his family. This notion angered Catherine, who suspected Razumovskii of wishing to carve out a satrapy in his native region. Indeed, the very word hetman became anathema to the Empress. She had several senators intimate her ire to Razumovskii with the suggestion that he resign. Rumors blaming Grigorii Orlov for "persecution" of the Hetman outraged Catherine so much that she directed Adam Olsuf'ev to counteract such talk by showing pertinent documents to prominent courtiers. Razumovskii was "very coolly received" at Petersburg in late January 1764 and then kept in the dark about his fate until November, when he was induced to retire as hetman and the hetmanate itself was abolished. In recompense for this humiliation, Razumovskii received 60,000 rubles in annual pension and subsistence in addition to huge landholdings in the Ukraine. He quickly regained Catherine's trust and retained prominence as a senator and wealthy host and patron.[65]

On 10 November 1764 the Empress established a collegium to administer the Ukraine under the supervision of Governor-General Peter Rumiantsev, whom she provided with detailed secret instructions that stressed the necessity of reforming the region's administration in a bureaucratic, centralizing, and russifying manner so as to promote order and security, prosperity and economic exchange, population growth and settlement.[66] Though German-born, Catherine had identified herself so completely with Russia that she wished the border regions of the Empire to develop gradually according to the institutional pattern of its Great Russian core.

The Demise of Ivan VI

Amid the controversy over Hetman Razumovskii and Ukrainian autonomy, Catherine completed preparations for her second major journey outside Petersburg. Ambitiously conceived in August 1763 as a sea and land tour through the Baltic Provinces and return via Smolensk and Pskov, this excursion may have been intended to fulfill Elizabeth's cancelled Riga trip of 1746 and to impress Polish and European opinion with her support for Johann Biron, the newly installed Duke of Kurland. Assuredly, it would advertise Catherine's venturesome vigor. Some speculated that she might meet or even marry Stanislas Poniatowski en route. Others warned her against such follies, talked her out of taking Paul along, and had her shorten the itinerary. She would be away only three weeks and go no farther than Mitau in Kurland.[67]

Well before her departure on 20 June 1764, however, persistent rumors and anonymous letters threatened imminent disaster and bandied about the name of Ivan VI. Thus one missive forecast a riot that would dismember Zakhar Chernyshev, Aleksei Razumovskii, and Grigorii Orlov before Catherine was dispatched "to her own land" and the "viceless and guiltless" Ivan enthroned. Scorning such threats, the Empress departed on schedule, confident of her crown since Ivan VI was locked in a cell of the Schlüsselburg Fortress. She had already reached Riga on 9 July when word arrived of Ivan's death during an attempt to free him. Her initial reaction mixed amazement with relief: "God's guidance is miraculous and unfathomable!"[68]

This incident contained the weirdest challenge yet to Catherine's position, and it marked the end of the period of prolonged crisis that she had faced on achieving power. The roots of the plot extended back to the Ukraine of Petrine times. Lieutenant Vasilii Mirovich, the self-appointed champion of Ivan VI, had been born in Siberia, the son of an exiled Ukrainian nobleman and the grandson of a cossack officer who had supported Hetman Mazepa, Sweden, and Turkey against Peter the Great. Imbued with Ukrainian patriotism, Mirovich sought to recover his family's fortune and position. Without money or connections or education, he entered the army and, while stationed in Petersburg, witnessed Catherine's coup. Nevertheless, when he approached Hetman Razumovskii for help in reclaiming his forebears' confiscated lands, he was told that such claims were hopeless and advised to find another way "to grab fortune by the forelock."

Age twenty-two when Catherine mounted the throne, Mirovich reminds one of a latter-day Raskol'nikov or Lee Harvey Oswald. Tormented by restless ambition and feelings of guilt and grudge, in penury and isolation, he vainly pursued his family's lands before the Senate while making spartan pledges not to smoke, play cards, or do "devilish dances." Since his regiment was stationed at Schlüsselburg, it was only natural for him to wonder about the "nameless prisoner no. 1" held in the casemate under constant guard. In time he learned that it was the pathetic "Ivanushka."[69]

What Mirovich did not know—what only Catherine and Nikita Panin and two guards, Captain Danilo Vlas'ev and Lieutenant Luka Chekin, did know—was that any effort to free the prisoner would seal his doom. After inspecting Ivan in the summer of 1762 the Empress had reconfirmed Peter III's secret orders to kill the ex-emperor rather than let him leave confinement alive. Actually she hoped Vlas'ev and Chekin could persuade the prisoner to embrace political death—tonsure as a monk—or that he would die of natural causes. Ivan did neither. Furthermore, despite the physical and psychological pressures on him, he retained a lively sense of who he was and what his rights to the throne were. He argued with his guards, who reported bimonthly to Nikita Panin importuning for relief from their onerous confinement with the refractory prisoner-prince. On 28 December 1763 Panin sent them each 1,000 rubles with the assurance that they would be transferred no later than early summer. Did Panin foresee the denouement of 5 July 1764, or was he simply placating the bored guards? Perhaps both. A little foresight could envision the end of Ivan's legal claims by tonsure or by sickness (medical attention was expressly denied him), and Panin obviously wished to encourage Vlas'ev and Chekin. After Ivan's death Panin continued his faithful service to Catherine in this respect by assuring the British envoy of the late prince's insanity: "his understanding absolutely confused, and his ideas blended together, without the least rational distinction." These false assurances were part of a carefully orchestrated effort to discredit posthumously Ivan's rights to the throne.[70]

With a fellow officer, Appolon Ushakov, Mirovich concerted plans in early May 1764 to free Ivan and proclaim him emperor in Petersburg a few days after the Empress had left on her Baltic journey. According to their plan, Ushakov would come to Schlüsselburg by boat at night when Mirovich was on sentry duty there. Ushakov would pretend to be a courier from the Empress, and Mirovich would pretend to recognize him, accepting a decree in her name that ordered Ivan's release. Mirovich would then announce this decree to his troops, arrest the commandant, and release the prisoner. Once in command of the fortress and in possession of Ivan, the conspirators would commandeer a cutter to transport the ex-emperor and his supporters down the Neva to Petersburg, where they would proclaim him to the troops and the people, announcing his accession and instituting the oath of submission.

To be sure, this "desperate and foolish coup," as Catherine scornfully termed it later, did not happen according to plan. Ushakov was unexpectedly dispatched to convoy army funds to Smolensk. After leaving Petersburg on 23 May, he took sick or feigned sickness on the road, headed back toward the capital, and drowned in a river by accident (or was it suicide?). His death stunned Mirovich, who ineptly pursued new accomplices among lackeys at court and drunken soldiers before deciding to act alone. Undeterred by this failure and determined to exploit Catherine's absence from the capital, Mirovich drafted the necessary documents—a manifesto announcing Ivan's accession and the oath of submission to him—and on 4 July exhorted his subordinate troops to support the plan. Some agreed on condition that others would join in.[71]

Mirovich could not sleep that night and, fearful lest the commandant discover his plot, called his men to arms about two A.M. Under cover of dense fog they seized control of the main gates. When the commandant rushed out to see what was happening, Mirovich clubbed him unconscious with a musket butt and then marched his men toward the casemate. Firing erupted between the attackers and the casemate guards. To inspire his men, Mirovich loudly read the manifesto proclaiming Ivan's enthronement and hurriedly searched for powder and shot to use in a cannon, with which he planned to overawe the remaining guards at the casemate. In fact, the guards agreed to cease fire, and Mirovich collared Lieutenant Chekin demanding to know where the sovereign was. "Where is the sovereign?" Chekin blankly replied: "We have only a lady sovereign." Inside the casemate Mirovich found Ivan's still warm body in a pool of blood. Chekin and Vlas'ev had executed their secret orders. "The first stab awaked the unfortunate youth, who was asleep in bed," the British envoy reported; "He made so stout a resistance, as to break one of their swords, and received eight wounds before he expired." After reverently kissing the corpse Mirovich meekly surrendered.[72]

The Petersburg authorities—Ivan Nepliuev in town, Nikita Panin with Grand Duke Paul at Tsarskoe Selo twenty kilometers away—suspected a wider plot. So did Catherine when she heard the news. Lord Buckingham expected that "much more will come out hereafter; printed declarations have been seized which justify this intended revolution, as the natural consequence of the Empress's having abandoned Her dominions, with an intention to marry one of Her subjects." Catherine herself wished the matter investigated without publicity and without concealment "inasmuch as the affair itself cannot remain secret, more than two hundred persons having a part in it." The body was to be buried at Schlüsselburg, and General Weimarn was to oversee the investigation. "It seems they had a plan," Catherine concluded. Two days later, having read the first interrogations of "the miscreant Mirovich (the son and grandson of rebels)," she ordered all leads pursued and discerned three different hands in the written materials captured. She approved the precautions taken in Petersburg after "the Schlüsselburg folly," announced her intention to return soon to witness "the speedy end of this insane affair," and lamented the drowning of Ushakov, Mirovich's principal accomplice.[73]

In the next few days the Empress expressed great concern over reports of masked persons seen arriving at Schlüsselburg by water from Petersburg. From General Weimarn's interrogations of Mirovich and his personal papers she saw no sign of accomplices, but coldly remarked on his intention to kill her. The manifesto announcing Ivan's accession enraged her by its indictment of her reign. That the conspirators had propagated their plot around Petersburg could not be denied, she observed, "inasmuch as, from Holy Week onward, there were many almost exact denunciations about this happening, scorned by my disdain." Her eagerness to return to Petersburg permitted only a short day in Mitau on 13 July 1764, the single occasion she left the Empire. Already approaching Petersburg on 22 July, the Empress hoped that Weimarn's interrogations would soon put a stop to idle talk. So fatigued was she from the tremulous journey, she could not face Petersburg, "where everything will pile on me," before resting two days at Peterhof. Only on Sunday evening, 25 July, did Catherine return to the new Summer Palace in Petersburg "in perfect health, but a little fatigued with her journey." The worries of the past two weeks told in her gentle rebuke to Nikita Panin for not reporting on Paul's health: "I imagine the churlish Schlüsselburg affair is the cause for that."[74]

Catherine consulted with General Weimarn the day of her return, urging him to finish the investigation. A week later she received his final report. She was "indisposed" for two or three days. Her manifesto of 17 August gave the official version of the tragic events, alleged that Ivan had been insane, and announced Mirovich's trial by a special court composed of the Senate, the Holy Synod, the heads of state collegia, and members of the top three ranks of nobility—forty-eight dignitaries in all. The court was empowered to review Weimarn's findings and to pass sentence according to the laws and subject to Catherine's confirmation. Sessions began on 19 August, the day after Catherine went to Tsarskoe Selo, but the proceedings moved so slowly that a delegation asked the Empress on 25 August to authorize the court to reach decisions by majority vote, evidently despairing of achieving unanimity. She acceded to this request, waiving any vengeful punishment for Mirovich's offense to her person. Through Procurator-General Viazemskii she closely monitored the trial, eager as she was to end the nerve-wracking embarrassment.[75]

Mirovich, though brought before the court three times and exhorted by a select delegation to confess everything, doggedly reaffirmed his previous testimony. Still doubtful that he had bared all, some members of the court advocated torture. Indeed, Baron Cherkassov loudly protested that if torture were omitted, they would all be branded "machines moved from outside or even comedians." The outcry that greeted this allegation was quieted only by Catherine's insistence, relayed by Viazemskii, that they proceed with the sentence after accepting Cherkassov's apology for excessive zeal. On 3 September, when Mirovich was clapped in irons he broke into tears, but after renewed exhortation to confess all, he still refused to incriminate anybody else. The court signed the sentence on 9 September. Mirovich was condemned to death by beheading, six soldiers were sentenced to beating (*Spitsruten*) by passage through a gauntlet of 1,000 men ten or twelve times and then exile at hard labor, thirty-eight soldiers to run the gauntlet ten times for four selected by lot and five times for the others before exile to distant garrisons, six others to remote garrisons, and eighteen released without corporal punishment. These sentences were executed on 15 September.[76]

So serenely did Mirovich face death on the block that some bystanders even expected he might be pardoned at the very last moment. When the executioner displayed his severed head, the huge crowd gasped in amazement. His remains were left on public display till evening when they were burned along with the gallows. Catherine, who only returned to town two days later, congratulated Nikita Panin on the election to the Polish throne of Stanislas

Poniatowski, "the king which we have made," but she also complained of backpains, perhaps testimony to psychic distress.[77]

As with the death of Peter III, the conspiracy of the Gur'evs and the Khrushchevs, and the Khitrovo affair, great efforts were made to paint out the events and whitewash awkward details. Catherine's instructions to Vlas'ev and Chekin were never mentioned, for example, and there was no inquiry into their role in Ivan's death, which was attributed by implication to Mirovich alone. In fact, both officers were promoted in rank and granted 7,000 rubles reward for their solicitude, about which they were sternly sworn to silence on three separate occasions. The sixteen soldiers under their command, after receiving 100 rubles each, likewise pledged eternal secrecy and silence about everything they had seen and heard.[78] For Catherine the main benefit was the removal of another claimant to the throne. Until Paul attained his majority she would enjoy a firm monopoly of power, or so court opinion believed. Foreign and popular opinion speculated in perplexity over these odd Russian happenings. As the British envoy concluded even before the trial and execution:

> I must rather think Her Imperial Majesty's situation strengthened than shaken, by what happened lately, and that there is no immediate reason to fear any revolution, though, from that characteristical credulity of every imposture, and of every idle report, which the history of this country so strongly exemplifies, and the constant dissatisfaction with the present, and hourly wish to change, which it is impossible to frequent the Russian Ministers, and not discover, events of that nature will ever be less surprising here, than in other Kingdoms, where the individuals are less oppressed, more informed, and more employed.[79]

Popular sympathy for the dead Ivan gradually seeped through the wall of official silence. Though Voltaire dismissed it as a mere trifle, other foreign commentators pounced on "the new Scene of Horror in Russia," pondered the event's "extraordinary circumstances . . . so extremely mysterious and unaccountable in many particulars," and pronounced it a disgrace to the Russian throne, "that *immaculate* throne, the steps to which have so often been washed in the blood of its own Princes!"[80] And when a publication appeared in Hamburg entitled "Innocence Oppressed, or the Death of Ivan, Emperor of Russia," the local Russian consul vainly strove to identify the author and publishers. Inside Russia the Secret Branch investigated six cases in 1766 in which Ivan's name was cited, two more the next year. As late as 1788 the merchant Kurdilov claimed to be Ivan. Moreover, Ivan's death animated folk images of Peter III, already rumored to be alive. In 1764 the first of many impostors appeared to proclaim the late tsar's return. If Catherine felt relieved by Ivan's death, she was affronted at suspicions of her connivance, as she tearfully admitted to Lord Buckingham. Like him, she apprehended exploitation of the tragedy by foreign powers and foreign critics. She would have agreed with Sir Joseph Yorke's appraisal: "My blood runs cold at the tragical fate of the ill-starred Prince Ivan, and I fancy I am reading history three hundred years ago. . . . This story will adorn the stage in future ages, but it makes one blush for this."[81]

Catherine had easily triumphed over the claims of Peter III and Ivan VI. To vanquish the claims of their ghosts would test her more severely, for the Empire's internal affairs in late 1764 struck Lord Buckingham as "one great mass of combustibles with incendiaries placed in every corner."[82] By 1765, however, Catherine had weathered the multiple crises surrounding her seizure and consolidation of power. Despite numerous challenges, she had shown herself capable of governing the Russian Empire: flexible and innovative in her policies, generous to her friends and charitable to many of her foes, tenacious in defense of her absolute authority. She had superintended a considerable reorganization of the central administration based on a new constellation of court parties, factions, and individuals. She had withdrawn Russia from an unpopular war and maintained peace while securing political advantage abroad. Her regime began to look stable and progressive. She had begun busily appropriating the symbols and rhetoric of the Petrine legacy. Could she sustain her auspicious start?

II

The Crises of Mid-Life

4

Crisis Renewed:
The Volga Voyage and
the Legislative Commission

By the mid-1760s Catherine felt more securely in power than during the nervous first years of her reign. She obviously loved ruling, reveled in being the center of attention, and showed ever greater confidence in her political abilities and prospects. Some of this confidence was bluster. To Madame Geoffrin, an old Parisian friend of her mother's and patroness of a leading intellectual salon, she confided her sense of inadequacy as compared to Frederick the Great, thinking he would have achieved much more in her place. Others privately doubted her abilities. Thus Lord Buckingham, frustrated at his failure to sign a new trade treaty with Russia, bristled at "the meanness with which she submits to the ill-bred inattention of Orlow, and the little affection she shows to the Grand Duke," but his indictment ignored her need to share time and attention with her son, her lover, and her constantly multiplying duties.[1]

As before, Catherine evinced worrisome concern for Paul's health. In April 1765 another minor illness of the Grand Duke roused his mother's fears such that she warned Nikita Panin not to bring him to Tsarskoe Selo because of the "extremely cold weather, and most of all, in this palace it is so cold in all the rooms that sometimes we do not know where to sit or to eat." And on 1 May, when Panin proposed to accompany Paul on horseback to a public promenade at suburban Catherinhof, the Empress anxiously objected. "I am amazed that you are taking my son to such a place, where there is a countless multitude of people and, consequently, not without those who have smallpox in the house. I recall that more than once you yourself cautioned me against this, when I wished to take him with me in such cases; now nothing remains for me except only to wish the continuation of his health." Panin took the hint and the Tsarevich stayed home that evening. In mid-June, however, Paul went with his mother to observe the army camp and maneuvers at Krasnoe Selo (she merrily termed these constant travels "the life of a Kalmyk"); but she left him behind a month later while on a hunting excursion and inspection tour of Peter the Great's Ladoga Canal, which she ordered to be lengthened and repaired. Although Catherine could spend little time with Paul, she watched over his intellectual and social growth, allowed him to amuse himself with the members of her entourage, and frequently asked him to confer awards on worthy officials. His excellent French and lively wit delighted her in person and by letter. She encouraged him to assist Panin in correspondence and applauded his useful, self-motivated preparations for an active, though yet undefined, role in state affairs.[2]

With Grigorii Orlov the Empress managed a relationship of a different order. He and his brothers provided important political support, frequented her company, and offered advice when asked. In Grigorii she discerned "the mind of an eagle," admiring his honesty, candor, quick perception, and "the extreme strength of his body and temperament," while lamenting his lack of education and polish, both of which she strove to inculcate. Once the fears of his marrying the Empress had subsided, he settled into a comfortable life at court that antagonized few and patronized many. As Sir George Macartney, the new young British special envoy and diplomatic dandy, described Orlov in 1767:

> His figure is rather colossal, his countenance open, his understanding tho' by no means despicable yet totally unimproved by reading, reflection, or experience. He is good natur'd, indolent, unaffected, and unassuming. His sudden elevation has neither made him giddy nor ungrateful; and his present friends are the same satellites which attended his course whilst he moved in a humbler sphere. He hates business and never intermeddles in foreign affairs. In domestic concerns, when ever he exerts his influence, he is rather driven to it by importunity than led to it by inclination.[3]

Perhaps this portrait unjustly undervalued Orlov's contribution to Catherine's well-being. At this early stage of her imperial career, still learning the rudiments of practical statecraft, she needed constant psychological support without the threat of political domination. Orlov's passion and modesty may have satisfied the woman and fortified the sovereign. Considering the continual political pressure on the Empress and the huge volume of work that she transacted, she must have valued Orlov's uncomplicated character, easygoing manner, and avowed lack of political ambition. Besides, she entrusted him with several important offices, frequently asked his advice, and, on at least one occasion, let him explain her ideas to the Senate. Later on, probably sensing his restless eagerness for action, Catherine would employ him on extraordinary commissions. Apparently she trusted him and his brothers absolutely. As she later confided to Potemkin, his successor in her affections, Orlov "would have remained for ever had he not been the first to tire." Throughout the 1760s, however, neither the Empress nor her robust favorite had yet tired. An Englishman who met them around 1766 long remembered their "fine figures" and mutual affection; "they did not forbear their Caresses for his presence."[4] She pretended to be unmoved by his "romps" with other women, although Lord Buckingham believed that she minded and that she herself "has at times eyes for others, and particularly for an amiable and accomplished man who is not undeserving of her affection; he has good advisers and is not without some chance of success." Perhaps he meant Potemkin.[5]

Orlov must have gradually recognized that Catherine's primary passion was politics. With golden plums of patronage she periodically reaffirmed her regard for those who had put her on the throne and rewarded those who kept her there by making her government work. In March 1765, for instance, she distributed 175,000 rubles to eight "big gentlemen"—her sarcastic epithet underlined the *quid pro quo* nature of the awards—including senators Yakov Shakhovskoi, Nikita and Peter Panin, and Zakhar Chernyshev (30,000 each), Procurator-General Viazemskii and Master of Requests Ivan Kozlov (10,000 each), General Evdokim Shcherbinin (15,000) and Admiral Ivan Talyzin (20,000). Kozlov and Talyzin, who were evidently planning to retire from service, received their awards secretly so as to avoid exciting undue expectations in other prospective retirees. At the same time, with the retirement of Grand Master of Ordnance Villebois, the Empress appointed Grigorii Orlov to that powerful and lucrative post after subordinating it to the Senate's jurisdiction. On the third anniversary of her coup she presented silver dinner services to thirty-three stalwarts, among them (in rough order of their prominence in the conspiracy) Kirill Razumovskii, Nikita Panin, Princess Dashkova, three Orlovs, and—toward the end of the list—Grigorii Potemkin.[6]

Catherine consciously set the tone for her court. She dressed modestly while working, but like Elizabeth she habitually changed outfits several times a day. On public, ceremonial, and festive occasions she wore elegant clothes and copious jewels. Indeed, the opulence of her court and the affable dignity of her demeanor bewitched newcomers to Russia such as the amorous Sir George Macartney, who recorded this rapturous portrait in 1766:

> Of all the sovereigns of Europe I believe the Empress of Russia is the richest in diamonds. She has a kind of passion for them; perhaps she has no other weaknesses. . . . She has shewn infinite taste in the manner of setting them, nothing being more advantageous to their lustre. The star of her order is one of the finest pieces of workmanship in the world. Her dress is never gaudy, always rich and yet still more elegant than rich. She appears to her great advantage in regimentals and is fond of appearing in them. During the whole time of the encampment last summer [at Krasnoe Selo] she wore no other habit. Her air is commanding and full of dignity. Her eye might be called fierce and tyrannical, if not softened by the other features of her face, which tho' not regular are eminently pleasing. I never saw in my life a person whose port, manner, and behavior answered so strongly to the idea I had formed to myself of her. Tho' in the thirty seventh year of her age she may still be called beautiful. Those who knew her younger say they never remembered her so lovely as at present, and *I very readily believe it.* . . . It is inconceivable with what address she mingles the ease of behavior with the dignity of her rank, with what facility she familiarizes herself with the meanest of her subjects, without losing a point of her authority and with what astonishing magic she inspires at once both re-

spect and affection. Her conversation is brilliant, perhaps too brilliant
for she loves to shine in conversation. She does so to an uncommon degree, and 'tis almost impossible to follow her, her sallies are so quick,
so full of fire, spirit, and vivacity.[7]

During these peaceful years Catherine undertook initiatives that attested to
her expanding ambitions for domestic reform. In 1765 she sponsored establishment of the Free Economic Society for the Encouragement of Agriculture
and Husbandry, a study group of officials, aristocrats (such as Grigorii Orlov), and noble landowners that was supposed to publicize advanced methods of farming and estate management as practiced in foreign countries. Endowed by the Empress with funds for a building and library, the Free Economic
Society worked to propagate Physiocratic ideas of fostering progress in agriculture, the mainstay of the Empire's economy. Like Frederick the Great,
Catherine and the Free Economic Society strongly endorsed the introduction
of potatoes, "ground apples" the Russians called them, which were believed
to have both medicinal and nutritional benefits. This society also attracted international attention by sponsoring an essay competition (secretly suggested
and financed by Catherine) on the subject of property rights for peasants—a
most provocative topic in the Russia of serfdom. No less a figure than Voltaire, with whom Catherine had begun a regular correspondence in 1763, contributed an entry. The two winners, a Frenchman and a Russian, both favored property rights for peasants, as did Catherine herself.[8]

Far more ambitious was Catherine's desire to codify Russia's chaotic laws
on the basis of recent European social philosophy as applied to Russian conditions. Two primary motivations drew her to the legislative enterprise: her
Montesquieuian concept of the good sovereign's duty to foster enlightenment
and gradual social change by molding "the climate of opinion," and her urge
to succeed in a sphere in which her predecessors, notably Peter the Great, had
failed. She undertook this project as early as February 1764 when she penned
her secret instructions to Viazemskii. By early 1765 she boasted to Madame
Geoffrin of spending three hours each morning on the laws—"this is an immense work." She laughed at Grigorii Orlov and her physicians for advising
against too much sedentary labor. By September she started showing drafts of
her proposed guidelines for codification to selected officials. Grigorii Orlov
and Count Münnich praised her efforts to the skies, but Nikita Panin apprehended a threat to the entire social order: "These are axioms to break down
walls." Vasilii Baskakov, a veteran judicial official, and Alexander Sumaro-
kov, a conservative playwright and poet, offered detailed critiques in May
1766, as did Alexander Bibikov somewhat later. The Empress hearkened to
their criticism, crossed out some passages, and rewrote others before settling
on a final text of 22 chapters comprising 655 articles. Entitled the *Great Instruction* (*Bol'shoi nakaz*), her compilation "pillaged" Montesquieu's *Spirit
of the Laws* in particular, borrowing some 294 articles from that source. In
addition, she drew many articles from the Italian legal theorist Cesare Bec-
caria, the German cameralist writers Jacob Bielfeld and Johann Justi, and
Diderot's famous *Encyclopedia*. Far from concealing her sources, Catherine

didactically celebrated them in her search for "universally accepted principles," as she informed Voltaire, to guide the reform of her Empire's laws. Neither did she neglect Russian tradition, referring to the revised code as "the new *Ulozhenie*" and placing a copy of Tsar Aleksei's *Ulozhenie* of 1649 on public display in a gilded silver shrine.[9]

In this eclectic collection of enlightened maxims and sentiments the Empress addressed the educated public at home and abroad. Often reissued in Russian, her *Great Instruction* was eventually translated into all the main European languages including English, Italian, Greek, Swedish, Dutch, Polish, and Rumanian. In 1770 the Russian Academy of Sciences issued a sumptuous quadrilingual edition in Russian, French, German, and Latin (but it was overpriced at two rubles and sold poorly). It signified her first bid for the title of philosopher-sovereign, her boldest venture yet in search of international celebrity and immortality. Voltaire labelled it "the finest monument of the age" and mocked the French censors for banning the work, a compliment that would guarantee its popularity. Frederick the Great played on the theme of sexual politics: "a masculine, nervous Performance, and worthy of a great man." Comparing Catherine to Semiramis, Elizabeth of England, and Maria Theresa, he concluded that "we have never heard of any Female being a Lawgiver. This Glory was reserved for the Empress of Russia." In a purely political sense the document was a masterpiece; it appeared to promise much without obligation. It became the centerpiece in a rapidly emerging Catherinian cult of rulership that gradually displaced the Petrine model.[10]

The *Great Instruction* adumbrated the political credo that Catherine had first formulated for Viazemskii. The Russian Empire, she proclaimed, had become a European state since the time of Peter the Great. So much for barbarian "manners" and Oriental tyranny. Russia was a monarchy according to Montesquieu's definition, with fundamental laws and religious restraints on arbitrary rule. The sheer size of the Empire, in conjunction with the diversity of its inhabitants and their varied historical evolution, dictated absolute monarchy—"autocratic rulership," not to be confused with despotism—as the form of government best suited to Russia's current circumstances and its subjects' manners. Centralized administration was more efficient in governing such a huge political unit, Catherine affirmed in agreement with Montesquieu; any other form of government risked disunity and weakness. To dampen fears of aristocratic oligarchy—possibly a caution to the Panin party—she forthrightly declared that "it is better to be subject to the Laws under one Master, than to be subservient to many." Her government considered itself the servant of the people, whose "natural liberty" it strove to protect and enhance by wise laws, rational policies, and religious solicitude. Its immediate aims were security, peace, and prosperity for all subjects, who were to be treated equally before the law. Torture in judicial proceedings was denounced, and capital punishment, which Elizabeth had abolished, was shunned in all but exceptional circumstances such as sedition or civil war. Concerning serfdom, that pillar and blight of Russian society, nothing was said directly except to censure the enslavement of free persons and to caution against the sudden emancipation of many bondmen. In economic policies Catherine praised agriculture and trade, especially exports, while she berated blind money-grubbing as well as artificial constraints such as monopolies. All in all, her *Great Instruction* offered ambiguous, benevolent sounding advice on a vast array of subjects, all the while conveying the message that she would be an enlightened, sensible, moderate, and solicitous sovereign dedicated to the greater glory and betterment of Russia as a new European nation.[11]

At some point in the process of compiling the *Great Instruction* Catherine linked it to the convocation of a codificatory commission. Such commissions were nothing new in Russia; one convened by Elizabeth had lasted into the first years of Catherine's reign seeking to sort out the heap of legislation accumulated since the issuance of the code of 1649. But she disregarded precedent in three bold innovations. First, the new code was to be formulated in consultation with representatives selected from all free "estates" (i.e., legal categories or classes), ethnic groups, territorial subdivisions, and main central government offices meeting together in public. Second, the *Great Instruction* would furnish general guidelines to assist the deputies in devising new laws and codifying old ones. Third, all deputies were to bring with them lists (*nakazy*) of proposals, grievances, and needs that their electors considered deserving of legislative attention. On 14 December 1766 the Empress issued her call for the selection of deputies, compilation of *nakazy,* and their assembly in Moscow within six months. One deputy was to be chosen for each government office designated by the Senate, each district with resident nobility, each town, each province with petty freeholders (*odnodvortsy* or single homesteaders), state peasants, and non-nomadic nations of non-Christian religion, and from the various cossack hosts as decided by their supreme commanders. The deputies received a distinctive badge, lifelong immunity from torture, corporal or capital punishment, and were granted salaries of 400 rubles per year for noblemen, 122 for townsmen, 37 for peasants and others. The Empress hoped that these privileges would overcome the traditional Russian tendency to disparage service in elective office as an onerous burden. "By this institution," her manifesto concluded, "We give to Our people an example of our sincerity, of our great belief in them, and of our true Maternal love." Even so, she took some care to organize the selection of deputies so as to avoid unseemly altercations, secretly ordering the Petersburg postmaster to copy the letters of some Livland noblemen suspected of harboring separatist sentiments.[12]

Return to Moscow

Catherine soon let it be known that she intended to open the Legislative Commission in Moscow in person. Practical political calculations underlay her convocation of the commission and her choice of venue for its opening. By summoning the newfangled assembly to Moscow, the traditional capital and administrative center of Great Russia, she could advertise her program of enlightened reforms before a large audience, mobilizing public opinion on her own behalf while flaunting her political self-confidence. She would challenge Muscovite lethargy and rumor-mongering with a display of vigorous action in pursuit of the public good, dispensing a golden shower of patronage wherever she went. Furthermore, to dramatize her pilgrimage from "European" Petersburg to "Oriental" Moscow and to publicize her venturesome spirit, she resolved on a preliminary grand voyage down the Volga, visiting towns and provinces that no Russian sovereign had seen since Petrine times. In theory, such a tour would inspire provincial officialdom and society with her personal presence, and she would learn more about her vast realm by firsthand observation. The new knowledge thus gained of persons, problems, and conditions would enable her to rule more effectively. Besides, the journey would tap a bonanza of publicity at home and abroad. As she wrote Voltaire from Moscow on 26 March 1767, "perhaps at the moment when you least expect it, you will receive a letter from some corner of Asia."[13]

Preceded by Grand Duke Paul and Nikita Panin (and delayed several days by a bad cold), Catherine left for Moscow on 7 February 1767. Months before departure she had ordered the Golovin Palace repaired and a new palace built at suburban Kolomenskoe to replace the gigantic wooden relic of the seventeenth century. In charge of Petersburg she left General Ivan Glebov, the senior senator of those departments remaining, with special instructions to combat thieves and brigands in the city and its environs, using Guards or field troops in addition to the police. The Empress felt slightly apprehensive about the climate of opinion in Moscow, for she suggested that Governor-General Saltykov delay selection of the city's deputy to the Legislative Commission until after her arrival, in view of possible "difficulties and doubts." As usual, she kept an ear cocked for "unseemly talk" in the rumor-hungry metropolis. In 1766 she had secretly ordered Saltykov to call in Prince Alexander Khovanskii, warning him to rein in his "abominable tongue"; otherwise "he will lead himself to a land where a crow will not even find his bones." The Empress had not forgotten this incident a year later when, at the selection meeting of the Moscow district nobility, somebody put straw in the ballot box instead of a ball. "This impertinence" revived her suspicions of Prince Khovanskii, and it inflamed her scornful perception of the Moscow nobility as spoiled, malicious idlers.[14]

In fact, Catherine's second visit to Moscow as empress exacerbated her animus against the old capital. From Moscow she confided to Frau Bielcke, an old Hamburg friend of her mother's, that "I prefer Petersburg, which is improving from day to day and in which I make everything work; whereas this city always seems to me to have the false look of Ispahan, which it loses, however, if I become angry." (Calling Moscow "Ispahan" was a sarcastic reference to Montesquieu's *Persian Letters*.) Only a few days earlier she had ordered Governor-General Saltykov to have a team of local architects carefully inspect the Kremlin's three main cathedrals for the purpose of determining what repairs were needed for stability and safety. Her accommodations in Moscow left a bad impression, too, as she complained to Nikita Panin on returning to Petersburg's suburban palaces: "You cannot believe how nice Tsarskoe Selo is, having passed twenty-nine shabby post-stations and palaces, from which I do not exclude the palace of the first-crowned capital, where we endured anxieties of various kinds for a whole year." Plans for rebuilding central Moscow were already maturing in her mind.[15]

Issues of police administration, industrial policy, and location of enterprises troubled Catherine even before she revisited the Empire's industrial capital. On 15 March 1766 she had dispatched Policemaster-General Nikolai Chicherin to Moscow "for the better observation of police deficiencies in that spacious city," in preparation for proposing reforms. Rising grain prices and fears of dearth in Moscow prompted the Empress to have Chicherin and Saltykov institute the emergency measures adopted in Petersburg: namely, suspension of unauthorized shipments out of the city, and a house-by-house inventory of local supplies. Two weeks later, she reacted furiously to news of a violent clash in the Moscow suburb of Pokrovskoe, a village belonging to the crown, where the peasant inhabitants had forcibly expelled a police search for an allegedly illegal textile manufactory not authorized by the Collegium of Manufactures.

This incident, as the investigation disclosed, dramatized the ambiguities and anomalous effects of the government's own economic policies. The enterprise in question proved to be a peasant-operated workshop that had been functioning with the approval of the Moscow Municipal Administration; in addition, further inquiries uncovered scores of similar enterprises in Pokrovskoe and adjacent suburbs. An obvious question arose: why should some government agencies suppress one form of industry—small textile workshops run by peasants and small merchants—on behalf of the large manufactories operated by privileged entrepreneurs and employing bondaged workers? To Catherine, who strongly believed in the superiority of freely hired labor over bondage, this matter manifested economic irrationality in conjunction with social injustice and an affront to public order. Apparently her orders to punish the residents of Pokrovskoe were laid aside while she pondered these issues. In Petersburg, which she saw more and more as the model for reforming Moscow, she had inquired in September 1766 about the impact of leatherworking and linen weaving in the Moscow region on the new tariff prohibitions against the export of undressed skins and linen thread. Indeed, on revisiting Moscow in 1767 the Empress initiated a reversal of state economic policy toward industry.[16]

The reversal of industrial policy built on the liberalizing trend of economic policy fitfully followed since Catherine's accession, now given sharper definition by consideration of local conditions, such as the Pokrovskoe violence of 1766, and the ripening influence of cameralist theory on the Empress— Bielfeld's formulations in particular. Catherine was conversant with Bielfeld's political-administrative theories, published in French in 1760, from the start of her reign. She consulted them extensively in preparing her *Great Instruction,* especially in Chapter 21 on police which was only published in February 1768, the same year that the first volume of an official Russian translation of Bielfeld's treatise appeared. Concerning industry in capital cities he offered cogent advice that Catherine found directly applicable to Moscow and its problems.[17]

Large manufactories that produce cheap wares and employ many workers should be banned from capitals, Bielfeld insisted; better they should be located in provincial towns or villages. Only small enterprises that produce high-value goods, hire few workers, and cater to changing fashion should be allowed in the capital. "The reasons for this maxim are so clear, so palpable, that I believe I may be excused from reciting them," Bielfeld concluded, but he explicated the evil his maxim was designed to avoid. "The excessive aggrandizement of a capital, which is made at the expense of provincial towns, can never be a sign of a state's prosperity, which then presents the image of a monster in which the head is of an excessive enormity, and the body is small and withered, and all the limbs are weak." These images seemed literal descriptions of Moscow and its position in central Russia as Catherine perceived them. Besides, in the more than twenty years that she had witnessed the old capital's fitful growth, it appeared to be decaying as fast as it grew. When the Empress left the city in late April 1767 to embark on her Volga voyage, so many onlookers and carriages escorted her departure that she sourly remarked to Nikita Panin: "Moscow is populous to the point of tedium." A principal culprit in such overpopulation could be seen in the city's large textile manufactories.[18]

Before leaving on her Volga tour, therefore, Catherine undertook a secret step toward resolving the clash between large, privileged manufactories and small, prohibited workshops. On 17 April 1767 she personally directed the Collegium of Manufactures to cease its harassment of unregistered enterprises, "handicrafts and handiwork whereby urban residents can earn their subsistence without sin," and to return anything confiscated from unregistered enterprises to their owners.[19] This abrupt reversal of policy was instituted surreptitiously, without any public announcement, because the Empress wished to forestall any immediate outcry from privileged entrepreneurs, on the one side, and to avoid any appearance of sanctioning violence in defense of economic interests, on the other. Yet she took this step partly in response to the Pokrovskoe incident of 1766 and also in reaction to an anonymous evaluation of Russian industry, largely drawn from Diderot's *Encyclopedia* and evidently prepared by somebody (perhaps Dmitrii Volkov) familiar with the operations of the Collegium of Manufactures and conversant with the tenets of cameralist political economy.

This adviser condemned Russia's large manufactories and bondaged labor, á la Bielfeld's prescriptions, as dens of iniquity and depravity, inhibitors of normal population growth, impediments to the development of crafts and agriculture, and incubators of social distress and disturbance. All these abuses were sharply contrasted to the advantages of smaller enterprises based on freely hired workers and located in the provinces. So impressed was Catherine with these views, she transmitted them to the Collegium of Manufactures for consultation in drafting its own instruction to the forthcoming Legislative Commission, and she brushed aside any effort at defending the large manufactories.[20] Since Moscow and its environs housed a large portion of the Empire's industry, the new policy immediately took on national significance and held weighty implications for the evolution of its largest city. Without fanfare, Catherine was proceeding seriously to stimulate social and economic change in Russia on the basis of recent European social theory, notably cameralist precepts, and with a view toward boosting productivity and efficiency in a framework of stability and progress.

Beyond instituting new policies for the amelioration of conditions in Moscow, the Empress took the occasion to cheer up her venerable friend Governor-General Saltykov, bereaved by the recent death of his wife and bent by the burdens of administering the unruly metropolis. She assured him of her sympathy and trust, excused herself for pestering him with "my scribbling," and invited him to converse with her at any time of his choice. At some point she decided on a more direct approach, revealing some of her political philosophy in the bargain.

> Count Peter Semenovich,
>
> I have heard from Count Grigorii Orlov that you harbor much dissatisfaction from your commission and sometimes approve, against your will, that to which your sentiments are not inclined, yet you are doubtful of explaining yourself to me, which I never expected: inasmuch as it is not unknown to you, that not favor and chance put matters into motion with me, but since the sole subject with me is the general felicity, consequently each possesses unhindered access to me to express his thoughts, the more so for such a person as you, according to rank and your merits, I do not find the least hindrance. And so, if you have something to say to me, I beg you to come on Thursday at 11 o'clock, without apprehending any person, inasmuch as I am master; yet my thought is explained above, wherein you can be quite certain.
>
> Catherine
>
> [P.S.] On Monday at Chistoi. I congratulate those who fast on horse-radish and on radish and on white cabbage.[21]

Here Catherine showed her tact toward a friend and senior official as well as her very personal style of rule. Her little lecture to Saltykov also offered a concise formulation of the practical conflict between personal government and bureaucratic administration, in her denial of the role of "favor and chance" as mainsprings of governmental action and her recognition of service rank and personal merit instead. Yet her mention of Grigorii Orlov as an unofficial conduit of inside information about the process of government belied her professed reliance on the established channels of communication. Catherine constantly harped on the importance of following the rules and regulations of government, but she could not long deny herself the traditional privilege of Russian sovereigns to waive the rules in any particular instance. Some might term such action prudent flexibility and wise administration. Others might call it arbitrary government and inefficient inconsistency. More often than not, it worked—in the short run at least.

Cruising down the Volga

With a suite of nearly 2,000 persons including the diplomatic corps, the Empress left Moscow on 28 April 1767, arriving that evening at Tver, where they boarded a flotilla of eleven specially equipped galleys and started downstream on 2 May. Accommodated on the Empress's galley, *Tver,* were Grigorii and Vladimir Orlov, Zakhar and Ivan Chernyshev, Alexander Bibikov, Dmitrii Volkov, Sergei Meshcherskii, Alexander Naryshkin, and her state secretaries— Ivan Elagin, Sergei Koz'min, and Grigorii Kozitskii. Nikita Panin stayed behind with Paul in Moscow, as did Aleksei Orlov, gravely ill with an "impostume" (ulcer?) of the stomach. His condition perturbed the Empress, who anxiously read the reports of his progress relayed by Nikita Panin. Late in 1767 Catherine awarded Orlov an engraved gold cube and promoted him to lieuteant-colonel of the Preobrazhenskii Guards. Concurrently, ever conscious of balancing favors and court factions, she conferred the title of count on Nikita and Peter Panin.[22]

Catherine boasted to Frau Bielcke of pursuing the Volga voyage "despite the cowards" who opposed it. After five days on the water she proudly wrote the French novelist Marmontel whose novel *Belisarius* she had just read (and which the voyagers translated into Russian): "I do not know where to mark my letter from, as I am on a vessel in the middle of the Volga with weather bad enough that many ladies would call it a terrible storm." All the same, the Empress kept in constant communication by courier with her ministers in Moscow. On 8 May she informed Nikita Panin of her progress toward Yaroslavl, despite cold weather and contrary winds, anticipating that the Volga would widen and the winds abate once they passed its confluence with the Mologa. "We are all healthy and in the hospital there are only 5 persons sick, though in my suite there are close to two thousand persons of every calling." Because of her slower than expected progress she asked Panin not to send his couriers ahead; "for yesterday and the day before we were without news from Moscow, having expected it at any hour, which added no little tedium to that which occurred from the loss of a day standing at anchor." At Rybinsk the next day, however, she admitted miscalculating the time needed for the journey: "truth to tell, into my calculation did not enter the various maritime adventures that have contradicted our intentions." From Yaroslavl on 10 May she asked Panin to send her more state papers—"I live idly in the extreme." She could not shuck the habit of administration even for a few days.[23]

Yaroslavl was her first significant stop. At this historic town and bustling commercial center Catherine spent several days touring the local sights, visiting the large textile mills, greeting the officials and the nobility assembled from several districts in the archbishop's refectory—a building commissioned by Patriarch Filaret, father of the first Romanov tsar, in imitation of the Kremlin's Faceted Palace. Yaroslavl "pleases everybody extremely," Catherine informed Prince Mikhail Vorontsov: "its situation could not be better, and the Volga is incomparably better than the Neva." Not everything impressed the Empress. After the journey she ordered the voevoda of Yaroslavl to be replaced, criticizing his weakness and ineptitude. And she dispatched a Guards officer to investigate disorders among the Yaroslavl merchantry within whose ranks he was to restore "peace, tranquility, and order."[24]

At Kostroma on 14–15 May the voyagers became tearfully ecstatic over the magnificent reception staged for them by the local nobility. Catherine inspected the picturesque Ipatiev Monastery outside town from where Tsar Mikhail Romanov had left to receive the crown in 1613. Before leaving Kostroma she bade farewell to the diplomatic corps, whose representatives returned to Moscow by land. She delighted in the Volga settlements and crowds that greeted her warmly all along the way; "yet I know the proverb: one hand washes the other," she confided to Paul, "and myself have the same manners with them."[25]

Less happy was her stay at Nizhnii Novgorod on 20–22 May. "This town is beautiful in its situation, but abominable in construction"; thus she ordered reconstruction or construction of the governor's house, the guberniia chancery, the archive, salt and spirits warehouses. To spur the local economy and merchantry, she sponsored the organization of a Nizhnii Novgorod trading company open to anyone with at least 25 rubles to invest, promising interest-free loans of 20,000 rubles for five years in return for the company's pledge to ship grain to Petersburg and build its warehouses in brick eventually. In this instance Catherine attempted to combine notions of economic stimulation with her hopes for town planning and reconstruction, both in the service of stronger commercial ties between the capitals, provincial towns, and the agrarian countryside.[26]

On a different plane she frowned over complaints of persecution by the Church hierarchy and the Orthodox clergy against the numerous Old Believers, Muslims, and pagans of the Nizhnii Novgorod bishopric. Writing secretly to Archbishop Dimitrii Sechenov, prominent member of the Holy Synod, Catherine described how a group of clergy in the village of Gorodets had petitioned her in person, blaming their poverty on the loss of parishioners to the Old Belief—an allegation that a check of the census records seemed to confirm. She was equally upset by a delegation of Old Believers from that same village who informed Elagin that the local clergy treated them like Muslims, refusing to christen the newborn. Although the Empress had little sympathy for the schismatics, she abhorred religious persecution on principle; hence her outrage at the local "spirit of persecution" and her recommendation that the Synod appoint worthy candidates when vacancies occurred in that bishopric. Such episodes betokened her growing appreciation of the many complex problems and tensions that beset rural Russia.[27]

As the flotilla sailed southeastward in late May, Catherine's spirits brightened at the faster progress and the prospect that the trip would soon be over. Indeed, she had decided to disembark at Simbirsk for the return to Moscow by road, instead of venturing farther south as originally planned. "There can be nothing more pleasant than voyaging as an entire house without fatigue," she crowed to Nikita Panin and, fifty kilometers away from Kazan, she rejoiced that the voyage had taken only 7 days 9½ hours traveling time as compared to 15 days 15½ hours on visits or at anchor. (She was one of those travellers who must account for every moment away from the office.)[28]

Her entry into Kazan on Saturday afternoon, 25 May, proved the grandest of all. The welcoming crowds were so numerous that they would have formed a human carpet if permitted, but when a throng of muzhiks met her on the road with candles to light her way, they were driven off by the nervous guards. "Excluding this excess, everything is proceeding extremely respectfully everywhere," Catherine enthusiastically remarked; "here the triumphal gates are such that I have not seen better." Kazan impressed her most favorably. "This town is indisputably the first in Russia after Moscow, while Tver is the best after Petersburg; in everything one sees that Kazan is the capital of a large realm."[29]

Kazan's size and regional significance caused Catherine to spend a whole week there visiting all the local sights and dignitaries, receiving endless deputations of well-wishers with gifts from local officialdom, clergymen, noblemen, seminarians, merchants, and their wives from Kazan, the local Tatar and other non-Russian communities, and from many lesser provincial towns. All this hospitality culminated on 31 May with a grand entertainment at the governor's suburban house. As she described the scene for Paul, "there was a ball in the yard for the Mordvins, Chuvash, Cheremis, Votiaks and Tatars, who all danced according to their custom; then the Kazan nobility assembled in the rooms of the house in masquerade dress and danced; after this followed supper and a firework, and it was very merry and there were many people, well dressed, and they dance as if they had studied with Granzhe, only you were absent." Ever the gracious guest, Catherine stayed past midnight.[30]

The Empress felt herself in a different world and, struck by the ethnic and cultural diversity she had recently observed, began ruminating about its implications for her style of rule. As she wrote Voltaire from Kazan on 29 May:

> These laws about which so much has been said are in the first analysis not yet enacted, and who can answer for their usefulness? It is posterity, and not we, who will have to decide that question. Consider, if you will, that they must be applied to Asia as well as Europe, and what difference of climate, peoples, customs, and even ideas! Here I am in Asia: I wished to see it all with my own eyes. There are in this city twenty different peoples, which in no way resemble one another. We have nevertheless to design a garment to fit them all. They can agree on general principles well enough, but what about the details? And what details! I have come to realize that we have to create a world, unify and conserve it, etc. I shall not finish and here there are too many of all the patterns.

Two days later she expressed the same ideas even more forcefully: "There are so many objects worthy of a glance, one could collect enough ideas here for ten years. This is an Empire to itself and only here can one see what an immense enterprise it is as concerns our laws, and how little these conform at present to the situation of the Empire in general."[31] To rule the Russian Empire rationally, with full cognizance of the diversity of local peoples and circumstances, customs and traditions, involved much more than she had ever dreamed about in Petersburg and Moscow.

Complicating this awesome task, moreover, was disarray among the Russian administrators of these "Asiatic" frontiers. Catherine was appalled to discover rampant feuding between the governor of Kazan and most of the nobility, egged on by guberniia procurator Esipov. Beginning with the governor's wife, whom she exhorted to be "more polite and affable to the people," the Empress admonished all and sundry to cease their bickering and cajoled Esipov into initiating a general reconciliation. Even so, she reported the situation to Procurator-General Viazemskii, Esipov's direct superior, obviously fearful that the settlement would not last.[32]

While in Kazan the Empress met Peter Panin's "immortal grandfather," Nefed Nikitich Kudriavtsev, a retired general and veteran of Peter the Great's Persian campaign. She conversed with the old man, then in his late eighties, almost blind, and unable to care for himself. He presented her with a fine team of black horses for her return to Moscow, and she sent him a gold snuffbox in thanks for his hospitality. This meeting illustrated Catherine's respect for her friends' relatives and her cultivation of the living representatives of the Petrine legacy. Seven years later she was shocked and saddened by the news of Kudriavtsev's violent death at the hands of Pugachev's rebels.[33]

En route from Kazan to Simbirsk the Empress visited the famous ruins of Bolgary, ancient city of the Volga Bulgars and a Muslim holy place rebuilt by Tamerlane. Two lofty minarets impressed her, but she censured the Russian church buildings erected there under Elizabeth; they struck her as evidence of the persecution of Islam and a violation of Peter the Great's order to preserve the site. The local standard of living left a favorable impression. "Here the people all along the Volga are rich and extremely well fed," she informed Nikita Panin, "and although prices are high everywhere, yet everybody eats grain and nobody complains or suffers want." After spending the night of 3/4 June at a village of Ivan Orlov's on the eastern or meadow side of the Volga, she waxed lyrical in praise of the region's riches. "The grain of every kind is so good here, as we have never seen before; in the woods there are wild cherries and roses everywhere, and the wood is nothing other than oak and linden; the earth is such dark stuff as is not seen elsewhere in garden beds. In a word, these people are spoiled by God; since birth, I have not eaten such tasty fish as here, and everything is in such abundance that you cannot imagine, and I do not know anything they might need; everything is here, and everything is cheap."[34]

Such pastoral pleasures contrasted all the more glaringly in the heat of late spring with the shabby houses of Simbirsk (now named Ul'ianovsk, the birthplace of Lenin a century later), where the flotilla unloaded the voyagers, their baggage, carriages, and horses for the return to Moscow by road. Lodged in the mansion of merchant and Urals metallurgical tycoon Ivan Tverdyshev, Catherine bemoaned the fact that most of the other houses in town had been confiscated by the state for arrears in the salt and spirits duties, "and so my town is in my hands," she remarked bitingly. To Nikita Panin she wondered aloud about the value of such confiscatory policies, pondering whether state interests would be better served by returning "these splinters" to their owners and looking for means to repay their debts of "only" 107,000 rubles—a paltry amount for the state, but a prodigious sum for penurious provincial merchants. It remains unclear what, if anything, the Empress did about this situation.[35]

Departing Simbirsk on 8 June, her entourage raced through the districts of Alatyr, Arzamas, Murom, and Vladimir before reaching Kolomenskoe a week later, "tired to death and worn out." The heat of summer compelled them to travel at night and rest during the day. As Catherine whirled through these agricultural areas she noticed the discrepancies in soil quality, extent of cultivation, and degree of settlement between the fertile yet sparsely worked and settled regions of the southeast and the less fertile, albeit intensively tilled, heavily populated lands to the northwest. Concerned about supplying grain to Petersburg and Moscow, she puzzled over the profusion of grain in the rural districts along the middle Volga, the high prices in towns, and the fear of dearth in both capitals.[36]

These observations convinced Catherine that Russian agriculture was sufficiently productive to feed the country and supply grain for export. Moreover, she doubted that the steady rise of grain prices could be blamed on harvest failure, "which has not been noticed by me in the 2300 versts that I have covered this spring." Hence she approved further grain exports from Arkhangel'sk so long as twenty percent of the rye and wheat delivered there was purchased for the state granary as insurance against dearth. Yet she also took steps to ensure grain shipments from Reval to Petersburg, and on 22 June 1767 ordered the Senate to make secret inquiries of all governors and voevodas concerning the causes of the inflation of grain prices.[37]

Agricultural economics perplexed Catherine, who obviously suspected that with proper management Russia could become a much richer country than it looked in the 1760s. As Physiocratic and cameralist theory postulated, promotion of internal trade in agricultural products and their export could increase agrarian productivity and rural prosperity while providing cheap food to the towns and cities, thereby restraining price inflation from population influx, and earning much needed foreign specie. Awaiting an explanation for the rise in grain prices, Catherine felt encouraged about the prospects for economic advance via agricultural expansion. Of more than six hundred petitions submitted to her during the Volga tour, she noted with satisfaction that few complained about the government and that, except for some serfs protesting their lords' exactions (petitions she had refused to accept), most contained pleas for more land. This indicated the great need for a general survey of landholding. Even so, private information persuaded her there was no actual shortage of land, "for almost everywhere there is three times as much as they can work." Such a survey would encourage greater settlement in the fertile southeastern provinces, augmenting grain output and restraining the current price rise. Despite hail damage in July 1767 and drought later on, Russian grain exports to Europe jumped five- to sevenfold by 1770. Whether along the Volga or in the Ukraine, Catherine's eyes looked southward for the Empire's agricultural future. Her Volga voyage dramatized the new orientation. And in her capacity as manager of palace estates, the administration of which might set a good example for other landowners, she recommended that the peasants of two palace estates in the Kostroma district be persuaded to build their wooden houses on brick foundations, using abundant clay deposits along the banks of the Volga. The Empress's maternal solicitude, her urge to instruct and improve, extended even to the housing conditions of her humblest subjects.[38]

The Commission Convenes

As soon as Catherine returned to Moscow in mid-June 1767 she plunged into preparations for the opening of the Legislative Commission. The deputies were already arriving, and the Empress wished to impress them and the public at large with the grandeur of the undertaking. She personally attended to a multitude of details. At ten A.M. on Sunday, 30 July 1767, the Empress left the Golovin Palace for the Kremlin in a magnificent coach drawn by eight horses, preceded by her courtiers in sixteen carriages and followed by Grigorii Orlov with a detachment of horse-guards. After them came Grand Duke Paul in his own ceremonial coach. At the Cathedral of the Assumption, where Catherine stepped down from her coach, she was joined by the deputies, who marched across the square in specified order two by two behind Procurator-General Viazemskii. After the church service, during which the non-Christian deputies remained outside, the Empress proceeded to the Great Kremlin Palace while the deputies signed the oath of office. Catherine then received them in the reception hall.[39]

Wearing the imperial mantle and a small crown, she stood on the top stair before the raised throne. On her right stood a table draped in red velvet displaying copies of her *Great Instruction,* the rules of procedure for the commission, and her instructions to the procurator-general. On her left stood Paul with the governmental elite, the officers of the court, and the foreign ambassadors. Farther to her right stood the most prominent ladies. Metropolitan Dimitrii of Novgorod, deputy from the Holy Synod, opened the ceremony with a flowery oration likening Catherine to Justinian and other great Christian codifiers of the law. In response, Vice Chancellor Golitsyn read Catherine's greeting, which reiterated her confidence in the deputies' zeal and her hopes for their assistance in "this great cause" for "the common good, the felicity of mankind, and the introduction of good manners and humanity, tranquility, security, and felicity to your dear fatherland." The deputies enjoyed a unique occasion, the Empress announced, "to glorify yourselves and your century, to acquire for yourselves the respect and gratitude of future centuries; from you all the peoples under the sun await an example; your glory is in your own hands and the path to it is open for you; upon your agreement in all matters useful to the fatherland will depend its completion as well." So ended the opening ceremonies.[40]

The next morning the commission began its first working session in the

Kremlin's Faceted Palace. As temporary convenor, Procurator-General Viazemskii asked the 428 deputies to nominate three candidates for marshal.
Ivan and Grigorii Orlov led in the balloting, but the favorite asked to be
excused because of other duties, so the meeting nominated Ivan Orlov, Zakhar Chernyshev, and Alexander Bibikov. Catherine endorsed Bibikov, whose
selection (apparently prearranged) was announced to the second session on
3 August. He immediately received the marshal's baton from Viazemskii,
and the deputies sat back to listen to Catherine's *Great Instruction*, the reading of which was only completed at the fifth session on 9 August to general
acclamation. Indeed, Marshal Bibikov and the deputies obtained an audience
with the Empress after the Sunday service on 12 August, at which time they
urged her to accept their thanks for her inspirational work by assuming the
title of "The Great, Most Wise, and Mother of the Fatherland." Catherine
regally declined the honor, explaining that only posterity could impartially
judge her achievements as great, that God alone could be most wise, and
that she considered it her duty to love the subjects entrusted by God to her
care, whereas it was her desire to be loved by them. The marshal and deputies bowed in response and lined up to kiss her hand before filing out quietly.
Six weeks later they all signed two copies of their request, kept one with the
commission and sent the other to the Senate, which on 10 December 1767
thanked the deputies for their zeal, accepted the document for safekeeping, and promised to publish it in the newspapers in Russian, French, and
German.[41]

This occasion displayed Catherine's political artistry in full flower: florid
plaudits spontaneously delivered by fervent subjects in a splendid public setting. Her tactful refusal merely added modesty to her virtues. Who could
doubt the stability and broad support of such an able, enlightened sovereign?
And there was no mention of Paul in the titles offered her. If one British observer sourly pronounced the Legislative Commission a "farce," two others
proclaimed it "a most noble undertaking" and "a voluntary transfer of do-
minion . . . by an absolute Prince in favour of the People."[42]

The Empress watched some of the commission's plenary sessions from a
closed gallery and followed its tortuous, confused progress. It was organized
into three supervisory commissions, occasional plenary sessions, a codification committee, and nineteen subcommittees to draft legislation in specific
spheres. Besides, the number of deputies ebbed and flowed over time. They
could transmit their authority to others without reference to those who selected them, and governors visiting the capital could participate in the sessions if they desired. By the standards of the time, representation was fairly
broad. Of some 564 deputies, 38 came from government offices, 162 from
assemblies of nobles, 206 from town corporations, 58 from state peasant
meetings, 56 from non-Christian peoples, and 54 from cossack communities.
Serfs, although constituting more than half the total population, could not
send deputies because they did not belong to a free estate and were not, therefore, considered subjects in the eyes of the law. Their owners were presumed
to represent their interests. Anyway, given the widespread illiteracy among
the lower social strata, they could scarcely be expected to articulate their

interests in any constructive fashion. By contrast, the nobility dominated the proceedings not simply because of their numbers—besides the deputies chosen by noble assemblies, deputies who were noblemen were chosen by both capitals, several other towns, and all the government offices—but also because of their superior education, higher rate of literacy, governmental experience, and social self-confidence.[43]

In Catherine's view, one of the Legislative Commission's most important functions was to extract and digest the proposals and grievances expressed in the *nakazy* that the deputies delivered to Moscow. Since, according to the selection procedure, each deputy was to bring one *nakaz,* hundreds were compiled. Some groups of electors submitted more than one because of disagreements, and the six state peasant deputies from Arkhangel'sk guberniia brought with them a mass of 730 petitions. In size and form the *nakazy* varied from bare lists of jumbled, sometimes unrelated or contradictory concerns to fairly polished programs of reform, such as the virtual treatise of 403 articles submitted by the Chief Police Administration, which applied to Russian conditions many of the cameralist prescriptions of Bielfeld and Justi. This mass of material was transmitted to the Commission for the Analysis of Nakazy, to be digested and then routed to the appropriate subcommittees. It was not intended that any *nakazy* be presented *in toto* to plenary sessions. Nevertheless, in the first weeks several from the state peasantry were read to occupy the deputies, who had nothing to discuss because the codification commission had not finished its compilation of previous legislation and none of the subcommittees had yet drafted any proposals for new laws.[44]

The commission's dawdling pace irritated Catherine, impatient as she was by nature and inexperienced in public legislative politics, the novelty of which palled on her within a few months. Though unhappy with her accommodations at the new Kolomenskoe Palace, she boasted to Frau Bielcke of her busy work schedule amid Muscovite lassitude.

> I arise at six o'clock and until half past eight I read or write all alone in my study. Toward nine my secretaries arrive and I am with them until eleven. Then I dress [in day clothes] and meanwhile chat with whomever is in my room. My toilet does not always last an hour, then I enter my reception room, I dine between one and two; after dinner I sew and have a book read to me until four, then those arrive who could not speak about business with me in the morning and I am with them until six when I either go out for a walk, or to play, or to chat, or to a play. I sup between nine and ten, after supper I go to bed.[45]

In hopes of facilitating the commission's work, she approved the employment of foreign legal experts: the French jurist Mercier de la Rivière and a German named Willebrad who had written a book about police. Apparently the latter declined her invitation, and when she met the Frenchman on her return to Petersburg in January 1768 his arrogant loquacity earned a stinging indictment: "he is similar to a doctor." His stay in Russia proved to be brief and barren. Long afterwards Catherine denounced "Solon-La-Rivière" and chortled about him for supposedly rearranging his apartment into different departments and bureaux on the assumption that he had been summoned to administer the entire Empire! To improve the records kept of the commission's proceedings, she sent Bibikov copies of the British parliament's journals on 27 October, but later remarked in exasperation: "I ordered them to make laws for the Russian Empire, and they make apologies for my qualities." On another occasion, however, she warned Bibikov against alienating the assembly by hasty consideration of some issue.[46]

Not only the plenary sessions disappointed the impatient Empress; some of the subcommittees incited her ire by their bumbling. She exploded, for example, on learning that the subcommittee on towns had adjourned while her *Great Instruction* was being bound. "Have they really lost those copies which they already received as deputies in Moscow?" she raged to Prince Viazemskii. "From this act is evident laziness, and in actual fact a violation of the Procedures: for it was ordered to spend the first days in formalities, whereas now they are using for that those days in which they could have already begun to work. About this it is necessary that the Directing Commission respectfully inform them."[47] Catherine's irritation in this instance sprang from two considerations: her belief in following prescribed procedures and her eagerness for tangible results.

The Empress carefully followed the commission's proceedings, which she strove to keep free of passion and undue controversy. Her intervention was kept out of sight, for the most part, and exercised through Procurator-General Viazemskii. Concerning one unspecified issue she gave him the following instructions: "If possible, keep them from moving to a vote today, especially if it will be evident to you amid the reading that the matter is going awry." Furthermore, the subject of noble rights involved such disruptive implications that the Empress advised Viazemskii to read aloud only those points of the Heraldmaster's *nakaz* that commanded common assent; "for the rest, as for example the one about how an officer enters the list of nobility, will cause great anxieties and will prolong the matter." Yet the British ambassador was impressed by the freedom and vigor of the debates, and marveled at the absence of lawyers in the assembly. He relayed to his government an assessment of the Legislative Commission that reflected Catherine's own Montesquieuian views: "This institution appears to me in the light of a scaffolding to be removed of course when the Empress has completed the noble edifice She has planned, a code of laws upon her own principles, but in the manner the most consistent with the true interest and the inclination of all her subjects."[48]

The matter of serfdom involved such explosive complexities that the Empress risked much in allowing it to be broached at all. Vehement reactions by noble spokesmen made her even more apprehensive, fearful that noble intransigence might excite peasant militance. She was appalled in more than one respect by Count Stroganov's public condemnation of the murder of a lord and his wife by their serfs, and by the Senate's proposal to punish an entire village for failure to defend its lord against murderers. Such incidents testified to acute noble-serf tensions that threatened a downward spiral of noble-instigated government repression that might undermine all possibility of peaceful, gradual, and legal change. To Viazemskii she confided her thinking about government action in such a sensitive issue:

1. The Senate cannot issue laws.
2. The old ones it can confirm.
3. The Senate ought to uphold, in a word, the laws. Consequently
4. To explain the laws it cannot, and still less give them a meaning that is nowhere to be found in the words of the law.
5. I endeavor in all ways to distinguish crimes and punishments, yet
6. The Senate confounds murder with non-defense of a lord and wishes that the murderers be equated with the non-defenders; but there is a great difference between murder, knowledge of murder, and obstruction or non-obstruction to murder.
7. One can prophesy that, if in response to and in punishment for the life of one lord whole hamlets will be destroyed, a riot of all bond-aged hamlets will ensue and that
8. The position of the lords' serfs is so critical, that except for tranquility and humane institutions it can nowise be avoided.
9. A general emancipation from the unbearable and cruel yoke will not ensue, for not having defense either in the laws nor in any place else, every trifle may consequently bring them to desperation; all the more so such a vengeful law as the Senate has thought to issue without rhyme or reason. And so
10. I ask you to be extremely cautious in similar cases, so as not to speed up the already threatening calamity, if in the new legislation measures not be taken for the curtailment of these dangerous consequences.
11. For if we do not agree to the diminution of cruelty and the amelioration of the intolerable position for the human species, then
12. Even against our will they themselves will seize it sooner or later. Your Excellency may make such use of these lines as you yourself judge best for the good of the Empire. For it is not necessary that I alone not only feel this, but that others also consider their own prejudices.

It is not known what happened in the particular case mentioned, but the episode certainly revealed Catherine's clear recognition of the dangers inherent in serfdom.[49]

Tired of Moscow's laggardly atmosphere and perhaps hopeful that a change of venue would revitalize the commission's progress, Catherine decided to halt the sessions on 14 December and reopen them in Petersburg on 18 February 1768. This step changed the composition of the commission, for thirty-five deputies employed in Moscow or the provinces ceased to attend. Despite "terrible cold," the Empress raced back from Moscow by sledge over the frozen highway—"the noses and ears of my suite remained whole"— arriving at Tsarskoe Selo on 22 January after only four days on the road and a mere fifty-three hours in actual travel, as she boasted to Frau Bielcke. She was glad to be home. "Petersburg seems paradise in comparison to Ispahan, and especially the palace," she told Nikita Panin and after her first *Kur-*

Tag (literally "court-day," a public evening party at court) since returning, she rejoiced at the unexpectedly large turnout.[50]

Hardly had Catherine returned to friendly Petersburg than disquieting news arrived from restive Moscow. An anonymous letter postmarked in Moscow was delivered to Grigorii Orlov warning of a plot headed by one Ivan Eropkin to seize the favorite, force him to divulge the whereabouts of Ivan VI's brother and sister, and then kill him. The plotters were allegedly recruiting others by charging that Orlov had strangled eight persons. Governor-General Saltykov had informed the Empress by special courier on 29 January that the denunciation was the work of retired Lieutenant-Colonel Nikolai Kolyshkin, formerly in service at the imperial court. Catherine recognized the name: "an extremely unpropertied person, a drunkard, cardplayer and spendthrift never satisfied with anything; his acquaintance is usually with people like himself." All the same, she ordered Saltykov to haul in Eropkin for questioning and, if no witnesses could be found, to confine him for forty-eight hours without food or drink to see whether he would stick by his story. Although the Empress doubted Kolyshkin's veracity because of earlier denunciations, she wanted the affair checked out thoroughly, albeit surreptitiously, so as to avoid rumors and loose talk. Eropkin was a retired Guards lieutenant, she noted, notorious for drunkenness, free-spending, and complicity in "all sorts of pranks and outrage." Furthermore, she was incensed by the fact that Kolyshkin had withheld his denunciation until her departure from Moscow, thereby violating the law that required the submission of such information within three days of its discovery.

On interrogation, Kolyshkin supplemented his story with claims of thirty retired men planning to rejoin the state service in pursuit of the plot; he also implicated a Vologda landowner named Berdiaev, whom Catherine characterized as "filled with chicanery and impudence mixed with stupidity." She wanted Saltykov to find out from Eropkin who the eight persons were that the Orlovs had supposedly killed, how, and when; who the thirty men were in their "party"; and, if Berdiaev were implicated, to interrogate him as well. When Eropkin was questioned, however, he denied the accusation. Kolyshkin could produce neither witnesses nor other proof, contradicted his own earlier testimony and what he had told others, and infuriated the Empress by claiming to be her secret agent in Moscow. "I have never from birth used him or anybody else for the like perdition," she protested to Saltykov: "for I hate every sort of slander and braggadocio that come from them." Even so, she suspected that Eropkin had indulged in drunken boasts and asked that Saltykov employ his relative, collegiate councilor Khrushchov, to coax a confession from the accused, whose friends should be watched too. If any evidence emerged against Berdiaev, she authorized Saltykov to pressure him for revelations by intimating that Eropkin and others had confessed to Kolyshkin's accusations, implicating him as well. Kolyshkin should also be pressed to find out with whom exactly he had discussed the affair; "for it is known that many were informed from him, including Master of Requests Kozlov." Urging Saltykov to avoid provoking rumors, the Empress asked him to report frequently and reassured him of her *direct* good wishes (meaning money or some other special favor?).

The upshot, after a month of interrogations and confrontations, was nothing solid—only lingering suspicions. Since the case did not involve actual blood-shed or authenticated action, and since Catherine's celebrated *Great Instruction* had roundly condemned the use of torture in judicial investigations, Kolyshkin was sentenced to be confined to his estates forever, without the right to appear wherever the Empress was or to submit denunciations. Erop-kin, though he never admitted anything, was still considered doubtful and was therefore forbidden to be in the same place as the Empress, and his rela-tive Khrushchov was charged to observe his behavior secretly. These pro-hibitions were repeated for both men by Procurator-General Viazemskii seven years later when the court returned to Petersburg after nearly a year's sojourn in Moscow. In retrospect a tempest in a teapot, this incident rekindled old fears in Catherine, who reacted nervously to all talk of plots involving sol-diers and who saw all threats to the Orlovs as threats to herself. Such fears darkened her already somber view of Moscow.[51]

Another incident late in 1767 also made Catherine anxious. Samoilo Chog-lokov, youngest of three sons of her former Russian governess, was interro-gated by the Secret Branch and found guilty of "insolent slanderous words" as well as "malevolent intention" against her person. Ostensibly enraged at being passed over for promotion, the fourteen-year-old Guardsman had al-legedly sworn to shoot or stab the Empress. Catherine forgave the insult, but after an ignominious beating with rods—a punishment usually reserved for the young or low-born—Choglokov was banished in December 1767 to a Siberian garrison with the right of earning promotion for meritorious service. He languished in Siberian service more than twenty years, once earning pro-motion only to be demoted for new "disorderly deeds," before his death in 1793.[52]

Transfer of the Legislative Commission to Petersburg resulted in no great improvement in that body's progress. Indeed, the longer the deputies met, the more they disputed. Catherine watched in helpless frustration and growing vexation as they wrangled over the rights of the nobility, criticized the slight-est amelioration of the rigors of serfdom, even rejected her repudiation of torture as a means of judicial investigation and called for the reintroduction of capital punishment. If the nobility, the best educated and most civilized estate in the Empire, could not agree on the basis of its status and privileges, how could the principles of her *Great Instruction* inspire beneficial change in other estates for the Empire's greater glory?

The nobility's nervous intransigence on the subject of serfdom, the blind refusal to see serfs as human beings, grated on Catherine morally and intel-lectually. Politically, however, such views showed her the limits she must honor to preserve the support necessary for survival in power. It was a chas-tening experience for her to perceive the inevitable and dangerous clash of lofty, enlightened ideals with the resistant realities of Russian society. She recorded the shock of this recognition in private comments penned more than twenty years after the adjournment of the Legislative Commission's plenary sessions in December 1768. Ruminating on the nobility's disdainful attitude toward their serfs, she sorrowfully recalled:

> You hardly dare say that they are just the same people as we; and even when I myself say this I risk having stones hurled at me; what indeed did I not have to endure from such an unreasonable and cruel public when in the Legislative Commission they started discussing some questions related to this subject, and when ignorant noblemen, whose number was immeasurably greater than I could ever have supposed (for I esteemed too highly those who surrounded me daily), started to apprehend that these questions might lead to some improvement in the current position of the husbandmen, did we not see that even Count Alexander Sergeevich Stroganov, a person very gentle and essentially very humane, the kindness of whose heart borders on weakness, how even this man with indignation and passion defended the cause of slavery, which ought to have betrayed the entire structure of his soul. It is not for me, however, to determine whether this role was suggested to him, or whether it stemmed from baseness, but I introduce this example as one of those which seemed to me the most astonishing. All one can say is that, if he sinned, then at least it was done with full consciousness, and yet how many there were who were guided by prejudice or poorly understood advantage! I think there were not even twenty persons who would have thought about this subject humanely and as human beings.[53]

The Legislative Commission and Catherine's Volga voyage opened her eyes as never before to the immensity, the stupendous variety and diversity, of the Empire that she had planned to reform so rapidly and so fully. Her attempt at codification and reform of the laws proved to be far more complicated than she had imagined while composing the *Great Instruction* in the privacy of her study. Her enlightened sentiments, which had evoked joyful tears in the grateful deputies on first reading, seemed forgotten when they collided with fundamental issues of the multinational, hierarchical society of her giant realm. The problems turned out to be larger than the Empress had anticipated. Although she enjoyed greater support than ever, she knew her writ was little known and less understood outside Petersburg. From the Legislative Commission she reaped abundant publicity at home and abroad, presenting herself as an enlightened, practical philosopher-sovereign seated firmly on a brilliant throne. Yet its leisurely progress tried her patience, just as its sporadically acrimonious debates tested her nerves. Her interest in the plenary sessions may already have been waning when the Ottoman Empire declared war in October 1768, necessitating the departure of many deputies for military service and compelling most officials, and the Empress herself, to devote primary attention to military mobilization. Plenary sessions of the Legislative Commission were postponed as a result, but the Empress hoped they would reconvene after the war, widely expected to yield victory in short order. In the meantime, the nineteen subcommittees continued their practical substantive work, preparing draft legislation for the Empress's future consideration.

Although the commission never reconvened in plenary session, and although codification of the laws was not accomplished until forty years after Catherine's death, the *Great Instruction* left a living testimony of her youthful ideals—and an early example of the policy of *glasnost* (openness) celebrated in later centuries. Furthermore, the hundreds of *nakazy* brought to the Legislative Commission gave voice to a breadth of public opinion unprecedented in Russian history. If the Legislative Commission disappointed Catherine, who must bear some responsibility for its inadequate preparation and confused proceedings, it also enriched her political experience and knowledge. Toward the end of her reign, in 1794, she praised the commission as a venture that "brought me light and knowledge from the whole empire, with which we had to deal and which we had to care for."[54] In the short run, however, it seemed to merge personal triumph confusingly with political fiasco. From this resurgent domestic crisis Catherine temporarily turned her attention to a larger, more immediately menacing international crisis.

5

Foreign Policy and War, Poland and Turkey

Even before Catherine saw Russia she sensed its emergent power and prestige in European international politics. The arrangements for her marriage reinforced notions of hitching her destiny to a European power on the rise, or so she could deduce from the excitement of her ambitious mother and the eager assistance of Frederick II, the youthful mastermind in charge of the other new power in northeastern Europe—the kingdom of Brandenburg-Prussia. In an era of ubiquitous international rivalries, conflicts, and dynastic matchmaking, the conduct of foreign policy ranked first among a sovereign's concerns. Even the indolent Empress Elizabeth showed a sporadic interest in directing Russian foreign policy. And Catherine's background and political instincts made her keenly receptive to the heroic examples of Peter the Great and Frederick the Great, both of whom had earned immortality in their lifetime by shrewd personal management of foreign policy. By contrast, the mismanagement of Russian diplomacy under Elizabeth and Peter III offered an object lesson in how *not* to conduct foreign relations. This was the sphere of politics, moreover, in which the Grand Duchess had considerable direct experience owing to her mother's intrigues, her own involvement in the administration of Holstein, and her machinations with Bestuzhev-Riumin, Hanbury-Williams, and Poniatowski—all of which may account for her immediate assumption of primacy in the direction of Russian foreign policy and her obvious confidence in its success. Although she recalled Bestuzhev from exile the day of the coup, she declined to name him or anyone else chancellor—the office traditionally entrusted with the supervision of foreign relations. Furthermore, her appointment of Nikita Panin as senior member of the Collegium of Foreign Affairs in the fall of 1763 was motivated more by a desire to inhibit his influence in domestic policymaking, and to employ safely his knowledge and experience, than by any urge to spare herself the final responsibility. From the start of her reign she made all the main decisions in foreign affairs. Asked whether she would review ambassadorial reports in full or, like previous sovereigns, only in extracts, she demanded the complete dispatches.[1]

Catherine moved quickly after the coup to assert herself in this crucial political pastime. She proclaimed a policy of peace by canceling Peter III's war with Denmark and denouncing his alliance with Prussia, although she assured Frederick II of her intention to honor the peace. Russian troops were hastily withdrawn from Prussian territory and negotiations opened with Denmark, a traditional ally of Russia, concerning the status of Holstein. The governmental paralysis and near bankruptcy that Catherine inherited on her accession both dictated a peaceful policy; but within a few months she adopted a more activist orientation to her western neighbors, Poland and Kurland. To her intimate friend Stanislas Poniatowski she wrote on 2 August 1762 promising to support his candidacy for Poland's elective kingship, which was expected to become vacant in the near future with the death of Augustus III, Elector of Saxony. At the same time she moved to restore Ernst Johann Biron, the seventy-two-year-old former favorite of Empress Anna Ivanovna, to the duchy of Kurland, a fief of the Polish crown that had long been a virtual Russian satellite. Both maneuvers aimed at strengthening Russian preponderance over the ramshackle Polish-Lithuanian Commonwealth, a multinational aristocratic republic headed by an elected monarch.[2]

In plunging into the morass of Polish politics, Catherine loosely followed Petrine precedent. Peter the Great had defeated Sweden for hegemony in the northeastern Baltic, but despite great efforts had failed to establish stability in Poland and suffered humiliating defeat, after initial victories, against the Ottoman Turks and their Crimean Tatar vassals. These two foreign policy problems, the Polish-Lithuanian Commonwealth and the Ottoman Empire, tended to become linked in strategic and political calculations of the time because they shared long, unstable borders that were considered vulnerable to attack by ambitious, militarily stronger powers. Russia had exercised a thinly veiled protectorate over Poland for decades, routinely marching troops through its territory en route to campaigns farther west or south and in search of runaway peasants. Since the late seventeenth century the Commonwealth had lurched into continuous political decay, with the body politic consumed by internal strife generated by the clash of three conflicting principles—extreme democracy in the need for unanimity in decisions of the Diet (any deputy could nullify decisions and dissolve the Diet by invoking the *Liberum veto*), elective monarchy, and the right of confederation (i.e., organized resistance to royal despotism or external threats). All these conflicts both invited and aggravated religious dissension and foreign intervention. Since Poland itself was so unstable, the Russian grip on the Commonwealth was likewise shaky.

The idea of partition, of seizing portions of Poland's exposed frontiers, periodically intrigued her neighbors, the three emergent eastern empires—Russia, Prussia, and Austria. Yet the Russian government usually rejected the idea, preferring its vague protectorate, however unstable, to the diplomatic gamble of partition. As Catherine saw the situation at the time of her accession, the "fortunate anarchy" in Poland played into Russia's hands, and her backing of Poniatowski's election bespoke not respect but contempt for him and his chaotic realm. She thought the Poles arrogant and quixotic, fanatical and corruptible. Her contemptuous attitude toward Poland combined elements of German-Lutheran scorn and Russian Orthodox disdain for militant Catholicism with a touch of Enlightenment condescension for organized religion and a full measure of cynical opportunism. Weaker than ever following the ravages of the Seven Years' War, Poland looked temptingly vulnerable as the king's health rapidly declined and the turmoil of a new election loomed imminent.[3]

Beyond Catherine's personal friendship with Poniatowski, who was related through his mother to the wealthy, powerful, pro-Russian family of the Czartoryskis, her interest in Poland was piqued by impassioned appeals for support from Orthodox "dissidents," as the non-Catholic minorities in Poland were officially termed. Since the late seventeenth century the dissidents had been denied political rights in the Commonwealth and, though they were guaranteed freedom of religious practice, they endured periodic harassment and persecution at the hands of the Catholic majority. Naturally some dissident leaders looked abroad for political support: the Protestants to Prussia, the Orthodox to Russia. Both powers gave them occasional diplomatic support and won promises from the Polish royal authorities to protect minority religious rights and restore their political representation, but such outside pressure could not avert recurrent troubles on the local level—troubles that sparked increasingly militant appeals for foreign support. The question of dissident rights thus gave Russia and Prussia a common interest in Poland and a constant pretext for interference in the Commonwealth's internal affairs.[4]

Catherine looked into the dissident issue from the start of her reign. The very day of her coup, in fact, the Holy Synod received an appeal from a dissident primate, Bishop Georgii Konisskii (or Jerzy Koniski) of Polish Belorussia, bewailing his flock's urgent need for Russian protection. Eager to champion Orthodoxy in the chauvinistic atmosphere surrounding her coup, the Empress invited Bishop Georgii to her coronation in Moscow, where she listened to his account of Catholic- and Uniat-instigated abuses and attacks on the Orthodox population in Belorussia. Among other horrors, Konisskii recounted how Uniat missionaries, in concert with Polish noblemen, had assaulted him and his flock in the middle of a service in the town of Orsha, forcibly ejecting them from the church and the town. He petitioned the Empress to protect the Orthodox by a dramatic act to intimidate the Polish persecutors—seizure and internment in Russia of several instigators, priests in particular. At the same time another Orthodox militant, Abbot Feofan Leontovich-Dorumin of the Holy Spirit Monastery in Vilna, bent Catherine's ear about Catholic outrages committed there in 1756. Amid his litany of woe the Empress coolly inquired what political profit could be expected from Russian support for the dissidents. To which Leontovich replied: "For our Russian state it will be possible to take from the Poles 600 versts of the very best and most fertile land, with countless Orthodox folk, justly and justifiably before all the world."[5]

What could be a better enticement for a sovereign intent on demonstrating her devotion to Russian Orthodoxy in the furtherance of Russia's greater power and glory in the world of European politics? In the dissidents' cause Catherine discerned a powerful lever to turn Polish politics into an eastward orientation and to insinuate Russian influence all the more deeply and strongly. She could use the dissidents to subordinate Poland to her wishes in the same way that she had used Arsenii Matsievich's protest to pressure the Holy Synod into accepting her sequestration of Church properties and reorganization of the structure of clerical service. If this was Catherine's thinking about Poland, it betrayed a strange concatenation of foresight and naivete, cold calculation and impatient glory-seeking, unconcealed avarice and callous disregard for national tradition. Above all, she displayed no sense of the likely complications and implications for Russia itself and its other foreign policy problems. But then, too much foresight may hamstring all action, and Catherine was eager to act.[6]

Money and troops were the Empress's favored springs of action in Polish affairs. After appointing Count Herman Keyserling her minister in Warsaw, she instructed him to reactivate the pro-Russian party centered around the Czartoryski family and sound their opinions as to candidates for the throne. So Keyserling was "courted to an inconceivable degree" after he reached Warsaw in December 1762. Indeed, the Czartoryskis were so hostile to the ruling Saxon dynasty that they requested Russian support for the formation of a confederation against the king. Their proposal intrigued Catherine, but before she could decide anything she was startled by news of Augustus III's imminent demise. To prepare for the anticipated interregnum, she and her top advisers resolved to back Poniatowski for the throne or, failing that, to support Prince Adam Czartoryski. These preferences were to be kept secret, of course, and a force of 30,000 men held in readiness on the Polish border with 50,000 more in reserve. Although the king recovered, his days were obviously numbered; so Catherine and the Czartoryskis pursued their preparations. In early April 1763 she sent Keyserling 50,000 ducats to finance the pro-Russian party, and by mid-summer the Czartoryskis were asking for 200,000 more for the final organization of their confederation, which they planned to declare in conjunction with the arrival of Russian troops from Smolensk and Kiev. Even so, the Empress hesitated to sanction a confederation during the king's lifetime. By way of supporting the Czartoryskis' plans, however, she allowed a Russian force to march from Kurland to Kiev through Polish territory in the summer of 1763, but she hastily curtailed this politico-military demonstration when Keyserling warned that it might trigger civil war. Her freedom of action was also hobbled by scant finances, the ongoing reform of the armed forces, and her desire to coordinate policy with Prussia. For she foresaw the folly of attempting to dictate the election without assistance from other interested powers. And she knew Frederick II preferred a Piast candidate, that is, a native Pole as opposed to the Saxon dynasty, because his unratified alliance with Peter III had stipulated joint Russo-Prussian support for a Piast.[7]

Prussia was the logical power for Russia to approach about concerted action in Poland because of its geographical propinquity, previous interest in the dissidents, and hostility to Saxony, Austria, and France, all of which could be assumed to favor a Saxon candidate. Besides, since the conclusion of the Seven Years' War by the peace of Hubertusburg in February 1763, Prussia shared with Russia a dangerous isolation in European international affairs. That nearly fatal war for Prussia had impressed on Frederick II his need for military support on land and Russia's formidable capability in that regard. Moreover, although Catherine did not know it at the time, the King had since 1752 coveted Polish Prussia and Danzig, separating as they did his Brandenburg and East Prussian possessions. An alliance of Prussia and Russia was thus in prospect from the spring of 1763, and the two powers began coordinating policy in Poland even before Augustus III died on 25 September 1763. "Do not laugh at me for jumping off my chair when I received the news of the death of the Polish king," Catherine merrily informed Nikita Panin on 6 October: "the King of Prussia jumped out from behind his desk when he heard it."[8] Both knew a golden political opportunity when they saw one.

That same morning the Empress convened a special "conference" of top advisers to concert policy during the Polish interregnum. All except Bestuzhev-Riumin, who declined to attend but sent his objections in writing, endorsed a Piast for the vacant throne and advised alerting Russian troops in preparation for imminent intervention. Zakhar Chernyshev, head of the War Collegium, adopted an even more hawkish stance calling for the immediate occupation and annexation of the Commonwealth's northeastern frontiers. But the rest of the conferees demurred from this bold proposal, arguing that it could not be achieved in the current circumstances. On this question Catherine kept silent, concerned not to provoke opposition by precipitous action, yet thrilled by Chernyshev's daring and the glorious vistas his plan might open. For the time being, the Empress preferred to pursue diplomatic means. To Count Keyserling she allocated up to 100,000 rubles to purchase the goodwill of Count Lubienski, temporarily in charge of the Polish government as Interrex and the man responsible for arranging a new election. To reinforce her venerable envoy in Warsaw, she consolidated the Panin party's newly dominant position at court by dispatching Prince Nikolai Repnin, Nikita Panin's nephew by marriage, with her endorsement of Poniatowski. Repnin and Keyserling were to push Poniatowski's candidacy by threatening force against any opposition and even forcible annexation of Polish territory if Russian troops had to be called in. Once Poniatowski was elected, the Empress expected him to repay his political debts by establishing a commission to restore the dissidents their rights. But she did not intend for her puppet to show any other initiative. Poland must not be allowed to reform itself. Thus, she insisted that the kingship not become hereditary, that the *Liberum veto* not be abolished, and that the army not be increased—

all of which undercut the Czartoryskis' plans to revive the Commonwealth's power through constitutional reform. Wary of Bestuzhev's clandestine machinations with the Austrian envoy to undermine rapprochement with Prussia, the Empress ordered any secret correspondence intercepted and angrily threatened the envoy's recall.[9]

Publicly, however, both Catherine and Frederick denounced all talk of dismembering Poland. They finally formalized their cooperation in the treaty of 31 March/11 April 1764, whereby they pledged to aid each other, in case of attack in Poland, with 10,000 infantry and 2,000 cavalry, or with an annual subsidy of 400,000 rubles if they were attacked in some other theater. Ostensibly a defensive alliance (like the Nazi-Soviet Pact of 1939), their treaty secretly presumed intervention in Poland, where Russia's senior position was frankly recognized: a Prussian force of 20,000 would police Poland's western frontier, entering the Commonwealth only in the event of an attack by a third outside power. The allies were to coordinate troop movements on the frontiers while their ministers in Warsaw arranged Poniatowski's election. If some Poles opposed the new "lawfully elected king" by proclaiming a confederation, then Catherine and Frederick would employ "military severity" against them and their lands "without the slightest mercy." Later on, they would work to restore the dissidents' rights. The alliance was for eight years. But if the new allies accurately calculated the time needed to cage the Polish eagle, Catherine in particular did not envisage the costs and damages its talons could inflict nor the complications its struggles could incite.[10]

Meanwhile, intensive, sometimes violent electioneering, which threatened to erupt into outright civil war, convulsed the Commonwealth as the Convocation Diet drew near in May 1764. The main opposition to the Czartoryskis, with their Russo-Prussian backing, rallied around the grand hetman of the crown, Jan Branicki, who enjoyed support from several prominent families (the Radziwills, the Potockis) and bishops. Yet Branicki and his adherents could not match the forces or the speed of the Czartoryskis' coalition. By April, Russian troops entered Poland on the pretext of protecting the Commonwealth from the violent acts of Branicki's partisans. Simultaneously, a Russian-approved confederation was declared in Lithuania with the same avowed purposes, and Russian troops surrounded Warsaw. Amid these tensions the Convocation Diet opened on 7 May 1764. Despite an attempt by Branicki's party to dissolve the Diet for meeting under duress, the Czartoryskis took control of the Diet and the city, and they replaced the grand hetman with August Czartoryski. These actions could not be blocked by use of the *Liberum veto;* the Convocation Diet was by definition a general confederation of the estates, and confederations were ruled by plurality voting. Furthermore, the Czartoryskis quickly strengthened their position by formally uniting the confederation of the crown forces with that of Lithuania. Concerning the explosive issue of the dissidents, however, the Diet simply reaffirmed their current status without change.[11]

Branicki, supported by Bishop Soltyk of Cracow and other magnates and primates who opposed the Czartoryskis and their Russian-dominated Diet, tried to rally armed resistance and appeal for foreign assistance. In both quests they failed. They could not agree on a program for a confederation of their own, and their paltry forces were routed by Russian regulars and the Polish crown troops. Branicki fled to Hungary, Karol Radziwill to Moldavia. Delighted with these successes, Catherine congratulated General Prince Mikhail Volkonskii on 30 June 1764 for his defeat of Radziwill's forces.[12]

Still, the Empress kept pressure on the Poles to convoke in orderly fashion the Election Diet, scheduled to open outside Warsaw on 16/27 August. The interested concern of other powers in the forthcoming election was impressed on her by a declaration of the Ottoman Porte welcoming the Russo-Prussian alliance and support for a Piast candidate but declining to accept Poniatowski because of his youth, inexperience, and bachelor status. This Ottoman declaration, in which Catherine detected a French intrigue, publicized a rumor discussed in private for the past two years: namely, that Poniatowski would repay his benefactress by marrying her, thereby uniting the two realms. Poniatowski would have gladly embraced the proposal. But Catherine and the Czartoryskis knew it would mean political suicide for the myopic Poniatowski and a blatant affront to neighboring powers, as the Turkish note attested. Already sobered by the domestic fiasco attendant on the plan to marry Grigorii Orlov, the Empress would not hazard such a provocative maneuver on an international stage. Both she and the Czartoryskis understood that such a marriage would touch off an explosion in Poland, if not a religious war as well as foreign intervention. They therefore pressured Poniatowski into election promises that he would marry only with the approval of the Diet or the Senate, and that he would select a Catholic bride, preferably of Polish origin. As a result, the Election Diet proceeded without incident, protected by Russian and Polish troops, unanimously electing Poniatowski on 26 August/6 September 1764. The new king accepted the election stipulations a week later and was crowned in Warsaw on 14/25 November. The Election Diet also abolished the *Liberum veto* by proclaiming the General Confederation to be permanent.[13]

While the Election Diet began its deliberations on the Wola Field outside Warsaw, Catherine was busy arranging for the trial of Mirovich and keeping an eye on the Turks. To General Volkonskii, commander of Russian troops in Poland, she stressed the need for firmness and maximum visibility to intimidate any would-be rebels, politely postponing his request for leave as inopportune. Although there was no special cause for apprehension about Turkish intentions, the Empress lamented the Seraglio's susceptibility to foreign blandishments and asked Volkonskii to detach several regiments in support of the Ukrainian division. Should the Turks attack Russian forces in Poland or the Ukraine, she confidently remarked, Prussia was obligated to commit 20,000 troops in support of the Russian occupation of Poland. Catherine thought she had all bets covered. So when the news of Poniatowski's election reached Petersburg in mid-September, she congratulated Nikita Panin "with the king we have made," lauding his (and her own) artful conduct of the affair.[14]

Catherine and Nikita Panin rejoiced in their victory in Poland because it was their first big triumph in foreign affairs, it seemed an easy and un-sullied success, and it marked their first step along the road to a grandiose system of alliances in northern Europe that might counterbalance the Haps-burg-Bourbon combination in the west and south. Building on the Russo-Prussian alliance and their success in Poland, the Empress and her leading minister negotiated an alliance with Denmark in March 1765 that guaran-teed Holstein to Grand Duke Paul during his minority, and they spent large sums in concert with Prussia to ensure the parliamentary success of the anti-French Cap Party in Sweden in 1765–66. Negotiations with Britain failed to result in alliance because of Whitehall's refusal to accept the "Turkish clause," that is, Russian insistence on military aid in case of war with the Ottoman Empire; but the two nations did agree on a new commercial treaty in 1766 and remained on cordial terms.[15] Russian exports carried in British bottoms went all over Europe and to the British colonies in distant North America. Newly powerful in northern Europe, the Russian government be-gan entertaining some global aspirations.

Catherine's triumph in Poland coincided with the end of the first period of crisis she faced since gaining the throne. Certainly it gave her new pres-tige at home and abroad, bolstering her confidence and feeding her ambition. Her ministers were equally jubilant. At dinner with Nikita Panin and Grand Duke Paul on 4 October 1764, Zakhar Chernyshev recited a panegyric to the Russian army. He was delighted at their ability to move 36,000 troops into Poland quickly and smoothly in contrast to the army's previous reputa-tion for irresolute sloth. Indeed, the triumph had come with such ease that the Empress began to overestimate her ability to control Polish affairs and underestimate the Commonwealth's political decay. She thought Poniatow-ski and the Czartoryskis could govern the country the way she wanted it governed. But she did not understand what a fateful genie of destruction had been uncorked in the dissident issue, nor what compensation King Fred-erick would expect for his assistance. Even before the election Catherine began to incite the dissidents by receiving one of their representatives at Mitau during her Baltic tour. In the summer of 1765 she sent Bishop Konis-skii back to Poland with a long list of the dissidents' grievances, which she wanted the king to ameliorate. Though Poniatowski was willing to consider these grievances, his Czartoryski uncles refused for fear of undermining the chances of their reform program. Prince Repnin, the sole Russian envoy since Keyserling's death in September 1764, encouraged Poniatowski to disregard his uncles' advice. Caspar von Saldern, a veteran Holstein diplomat in Rus-sian service, was sent from Petersburg to assist Repnin in preparing the presentation of the dissidents' desires at the next Diet, whose favorable actions would be ensured by surrounding the assembly with Russian troops.[16]

Meanwhile antidissident and antimonarchical agitation revived like wild-fire, sparked by ardent Catholic spokesmen such as Bishop Soltyk. The Diet when it met refused to budge on rights for the dissidents, but it also scuttled the Czartoryskis' reform program. Furious at such intransigence, Catherine instructed Repnin to sponsor confederations that would force the convocation of an extraordinary diet, which would be forced to endorse rights for the dissidents and a treaty with Russia guaranteeing the Polish constitution minus the reforms of 1764. Soon after this extraordinary confederated diet started meeting in October 1767, with Warsaw surrounded by 10,000 Russian troops, Repnin arrested Bishop Soltyk and several other opponents of the Russian presence in Poland, exiling them to Russia. Thus cowed, the extraordinary diet grudgingly accepted the Russian conditions by late February 1768. Catherine then ordered her troops home in the belief that she had achieved all her purposes and broken all opposition.[17]

Before the Russian troops left, though, Polish patriotism burst into open rebellion in the southeastern town of Bar, close to the Turkish border, where several magnates declared a confederation in defense of Catholicism and Poland's liberty. Ill prepared and uncoordinated with other centers, the Confederation of Bar received no immediate help from abroad, and when Russian units finally marched southward they dispersed the confederates handily. Nevertheless, the movement encouraged other anti-Russian and anti-Poniatowski confederations elsewhere, forcing Catherine to send large forces back into Poland, which antagonized Ottoman and Austrian authorities alike. Egged on by lavish French bribes and calls to challenge Russian arrogance, the Ottoman Porte prepared for war with Russia after a marauding band of Ukrainian cossack freebooters sacked the town of Balta, a dependency of the Crimean Khanate. The Turks declared war on 25 September/6 October 1768 by locking the Russian envoy, Aleksei Obreskov, in the Castle of the Seven Towers when he refused an ultimatum to remove Russian troops from Poland. Catherine's policy in Poland thus led to a civil war there that provoked war with Ottoman Turkey. The peaceful policy of her early reign had ended in war, a war that Panin's "Northern System" had done nothing to prevent and which threatened to involve other powers. "Good God, what does one not have to endure to make a king of Poland," Frederick II groaned.[18]

Russo-Turkish Hostilities

Though Catherine protested her innocent surprise at the Turkish declaration of war, she eagerly embraced the opportunity for martial glory against a weak foe. Her derision of Polish political sagacity, military prowess, and religious fanaticism transferred blithely to the Turks. Well aware of Russia's military successes against the Turks and their Crimean Tatar vassals in the war of 1736–1739, she relished the chance to make good Peter the Great's humiliating defeat in the Pruth campaign of 1711. Russian operations in Poland could serve as a valuable training exercise for the new conflict. Indeed, the Empress and her advisers all waxed confident they could thrash the Turks in short order and make great gains in the bargain. Territorial acquisitions in the south, direct access to the Black Sea, and stabilization of borders with the Crimean Khanate, the Polish-Lithuanian Commonwealth, and the principalities of the Caucasus—all were traditional Russian aims pursued for almost two centuries. Catherine's abolition of the military colony of New Serbia and of the Ukrainian hetmanate was predicated on plans for colonization of the southern Ukraine, which would be transformed from a frontier desert into a fertile granary with thriving river towns and seaports. Peter the Great's campaigns in the 1690s and in 1711, surpassed by Field Marshal Münnich's triumphs in the 1730s, had blazed the way of empire to the Sea of Azov and the Black Sea, the Crimea and the Balkans.

Fulfillment of this Petrine legacy dazzled the Empress. Moreover, she was confident of success on two counts: the power of her newly reformed army and rebuilt fleet versus the obvious slippage of Ottoman military might, as reported by her consul in the Crimea, her governors in the Ukraine, and her envoy in Constantinople. Incited by French diplomatic intrigue, the Turks had awakened in Russia a slumbering cat that would massacre the mice. Frustration in Poland and with the Legislative Commission added another incentive beckoning Catherine in pursuit of glory against the Turks. "If we are successful in this war," she told Voltaire, "I shall have much to thank my enemies for: they will have brought me a glory to which I never aspired." Modest words! But Catherine aspired to glory throughout her life.[19]

Within days after word of the Turkish declaration the Empress convoked a council of nine top advisers at ten in the morning of 4 November 1768. Those in attendance were Kirill Razumovskii, the two princes Alexander Golitsyn (the general and the vice-chancellor), Nikita and Peter Panin, Zakhar Chernyshev, Mikhail Volkonskii, Grigorii Orlov, and Alexander Viazemskii. This council resembled Panin's project of 1762 and Elizabeth's conference during the Seven Years' War, but Catherine chaired its first sessions as an informal body. She kept its powers purely advisory even when its permanence was formalized two months later. Establishment of the council simply regularized the consultative style of administration the Empress had already become accustomed to.[20]

Catherine asked the councilors how to conduct the war, where to assemble the troops, what precautions to take on the other borders, and how to finance the conflict. From her councilors she sought broad concepts without details. All agreed the war should be waged offensively after the pattern of the 1736–1739 conflict, but Grigorii Orlov urged them to define their aims beforehand; otherwise, they should seek means to avoid bloodshed. Nikita Panin, obviously stung by the implication that his Polish policy had provoked the Turks, favored an immediate all-out attack; yet when Orlov rejected that as impossible, he argued for a war of attrition to force peace. Not to be outdone by Panin's aggressive stance, Orlov casually mentioned an enterprise of truly Petrine scope: a "cruise" by several ships into the Mediterranean to surprise the Turks from the rear. The venture would require British approval, he admitted, so it was shelved for the time being. Concerning finances, Viazemskii suggested raising the tax rate on all state peasants and making use of Polish funds seized in the confiscation of confederates' estates. His was the first hint of the appealing possibility of tapping Polish resources to prosecute the Turkish war. At the council's second session on 6 November they reviewed operational strategy in light of several different Turkish modes of attack and defined their initial war aims: free navigation on the Black Sea (previously a Turkish lake), possession of a port and fortress there, and stabilization of firm and defensible borders with Poland. When Orlov reintroduced the idea of a naval expedition, Catherine authorized him to begin plans for one. The session ended with her naming Alexander Golitsyn and Peter Rumiantsev in command of the two armies to operate in the south.[21]

At three-hour council sessions on 12 and 14 November the Empress and her advisers refined their strategy and planned their military mobilization, calculating supply requirements in light of the deficiencies encountered during the southern campaigns of the 1730s. Grigorii Orlov elaborated plans for the Mediterranean expedition, which obviously fired Catherine's imagination. The councilors resolved to follow Petrine precedent in appealing to the Orthodox subjects of the Ottoman Porte in Georgia, Greece, Dalmatia, and Montenegro, the latter to serve as a possible headquarters for the proposed expedition. Prince Volkonskii, nephew of the late Bestuzhev-Riumin and no friend of the Panin party, wondered what allies Russia could call on—none was the silent answer—and he complained about the complications stemming from the uproar in Poland. In support, Orlov inquired why Poland had revolted against Russia. Nikita Panin responded with a long explanation of the causes and complications, assuring the other councilors of the efforts underway to pacify Poland so as to avoid a two-front war. Accordingly, the Empress devised a tactful solution to her advisers' disagreement over Poland. From Warsaw she recalled Prince Repnin, the Panins' relative, to serve in the Turkish campaign and designated Volkonskii in his place.[22]

The Russo-Turkish War opened impressively for Catherine in the late winter and spring of 1769. Cold weather and Russian arms repulsed Tatar raids around Elizavetgrad; Russian troops occupied and fortified Azov and Taganrog, both landmarks of Petrine expansion. The Empress crowed to Voltaire of her army's eagerness for battle: "My soldiers are off to fight the Turks as if they were going to a wedding . . . wherever the Turks or the Tatars show themselves, we send them away with a sound thrashing, and the Polish rebels most of all." Lauding her achievements in the Petrine tradition, Voltaire lamented the war's cost, the drain on the Empress's time and energy, yet encouraged her "to review your troops on the road to Adrianople." Such praise inspired Catherine to scoff at the supposed burdens caused by the war (quoting Henry IV of France or paraphrasing Voltaire's *Henriade*): "Our taxes are so low there is not a peasant in Russia who does not eat chicken whenever he pleases; indeed, for some time now there are provinces where they prefer turkey to chicken. . . . We are at war, it is true; but Russia has long been used to that occupation, and emerges from each war in a more flourishing state than before." These last sentiments were to be a recurrent theme in Catherine's wartime correspondence abroad. Her public disdain for the costs of Russian aggression concealed a constant private concern about the necessary financial resources. Extraordinary taxes were instituted at the very start of the war, the banks for the nobility in both capitals began issuing paper money (*assignats*), and Russia negotiated its first foreign loans to finance the Mediterranean expedition—an extraordinarily expensive venture.[23]

Like Peter the Great at the start of his military career, Catherine displayed little patience in her avid pursuit of brilliant triumphs on the battlefield. Thus she had General Golitsyn's first victory over the Turks, in early July 1769, publicly celebrated in Petersburg on Sunday, 19 July. But when Golitsyn failed to follow this up with the capture of Khotin on the Dniester and even withdrew to block an invasion of Poland, the Empress angrily announced his recall to the council on 13 August, transferring his command to Rumiantsev, his brother-in-law, who was replaced by Peter Panin. Before these orders could reach the front, however, Golitsyn routed the Turks, seized Khotin, and invaded Moldavia. Catherine was embarrassed by her hasty action and tried to soothe Golitsyn's wounded pride by promoting him to field marshal, awarding him a sword encrusted with diamonds that was inscribed "For the clearing of Moldavia as far as Jassy itself," and appointing him governor-general of St. Petersburg. Torrential rains and an early winter foiled her hopes for the immediate capture of Bender lower down the Dniester, while Rumiantsev's forces occupied all of Moldavia and much of Wallachia up to the Danube. "The new Moldavian Princess bows to you," Catherine laughingly informed General Bibikov. The campaign had achieved a great deal without significant losses in combat; nevertheless, the Empress was eager for earthshaking victories. She was displeased at the slow outfitting and leisurely dispatch of the two squadrons of ships to the Mediterranean, and further perturbed by their losses from sickness and need for major repairs en route. Transmitting funds to the fleet perplexed the Empress, who griped to Nikita Panin: "You know that I am no merchant." Aleksei Orlov, who had suggested the Mediterranean expedition while convalescing at Livorno in southern Italy, anxiously awaited the fleet's arrival to launch operations in the spring of 1770.[24]

The war's second full year began inauspiciously with spring floods in southern Poland, and the outbreak of plague in Moldavia forced the Russian garrison out of Jassy and killed its commander. Nevertheless, as the plague meandered northward into Poland, General Rumiantsev brought his army across the Dniester and inflicted two devastating defeats on the Turks and Tatars at the battles of Larga and Kagul on 7 and 21 July 1770, respectively. News of these triumphs reached Petersburg before word of an even more amazing feat—total destruction of the Turkish fleet in the Aegean Sea at Chesme on 24–26 June 1770. Catherine joyously celebrated a *Te Deum* and a special memorial to the founder of the fleet, Peter the Great. On Aleksei Orlov she bestowed the title of Chesmenskii. Rumiantsev was promoted to field marshal and his victory at Kagul commemorated with an obelisk at Tsarskoe Selo. "If this war continues," Catherine joked with Voltaire, "my garden at Tsarskoe Selo will resemble a game of skittles: for after each of our noteworthy actions, I put up some new monument there." Yet when General Peter Panin captured Bender in September after a thunderous siege and bloody assault, he felt so affronted by the meager awards tendered him that he retired in a huff to his Moscow estate. The influence of the Panin party was waning rapidly.[25]

The Chesme victory, "Russia's first naval victory in nine hundred years," delighted the Empress, who described it lyrically to Voltaire: "They say that the earth and sea trembled with the huge number of exploding ships. The quakes were felt as far as Smyrna, twelve leagues away. . . . Count Orlov tells me that the day after the burning of the enemy fleet, he saw with horror that the water in the harbor of Chesme, which is not very large, was stained with blood, so many Turks had perished there." In commemoration of the triumph Catherine commissioned two sets of large paintings, by Jacob Hackaert and Richard Paton, to adorn one wall of the Great Hall at Peterhof and the adjacent Chesme Room. In 1780 she renamed the Kekerekinskii Palace, begun in 1773 between Petersburg and Tsarskoe Selo, the Chesme Palace. Voltaire, who despised Islam even more than Christianity, compared Catherine's victories to those of Hannibal and hailed her as "the avenger of Europe." She herself affected modesty: "The fact is that it is only since I have enjoyed good fortune that Europe finds me so clever. At forty, however, one scarcely improves in intelligence or looks, in the sight of the Lord."[26]

The Russo-Polish-Turkish imbroglio stimulated a bellicose superpatriotism in Catherine that brooked no criticism from Europe. Her militance in defense of Russian national honor found elaborate expression in an anonymously issued tract, published in two parts in French in 1770 without indication of place or publisher, entitled *The Antidote*. A detailed demolition of Chappe d'Auteroche's acclaimed travelogue of 1768, *The Antidote* righteously rebutted the French scholar's arrogant ignorance and malicious stupidity. Citing Catherine's *Great Instruction* several times, the anonymous author defended the Russian government and people against foreign charges of despotism and slavery, cruelty and lawlessness, ignorance and immorality. She also flayed the Frenchman's misogyny (yet twitted his weakness for girls) as well as his titillating treatment of Russian marriage customs and bathing manners. Refuting his claims of sexual promiscuity at the public baths, Catherine condemned the book's purveyance of Le Prince's salacious prints, especially the "most indecent" bath-house scene, which she deemed a fictitious "bacchanal." *The Antidote* apparently found few readers despite republication at Amsterdam in 1771–72 and translation into English in 1772 by one Maria Johnson, who dedicated her work to the Empress, "the first and greatest woman of the present age."[27] Though a failure as an exercise in publicity, the work revealed Catherine's mastery of polemical prose in an earnest affirmation of Russian history, Russian "manners," and her administration. Moreover, the hundreds of hours invested in *The Antidote* underscored Catherine's devotion to Russian interests, just as her tract offered a lode of ready-made counterattacks for zealous Russian apologists. Catherine had mounted the steed of Russian nationalism.

Russia's dazzling victories, she soon learned, excited more anxiety than admiration in the other European powers. The anarchy and the plague in Poland allowed Austria and Prussia to occupy frontier districts ostensibly as a protective measure, which Russia's commitment in the Danubian Principalities prevented her from vigorously opposing. Both the Germanic powers feared excessive Russian gains at Ottoman expense, Catherine's continuing domination of Poland, and the threat of a wider conflict. Prince Henry of

Prussia, Frederick II's brother, visited Petersburg and Moscow in the autumn and winter of 1770–71 with the object of promoting the partition of Poland. Catherine entertained him lavishly. "From October to February, there has been nothing but banquets, dances, and spectacles," she wrote Voltaire. "I do not know whether it is the effect on me of the last campaign, or whether joy is really universal in Russia." At a party on 28 December the Empress jokingly broached the possibility of Prussia taking Polish territory after the Austrian example. Zakhar Chernyshev, the proponent of annexation in 1763, seconded her sentiments. "It is necessary, after all, that everyone have something," Prince Henry quoted Cherynshev to his brother, the King. Although Nikita Panin continued to oppose the idea of partition, his ebbing influence could not counteract the determination of Catherine, urged on by Chernyshev (and possibly Grigorii Orlov as well). In May 1771 the council agreed that Russia might take Polish Livonia and compensate Poland with Moldavia and Wallachia. The idea of recouping the costs of the Turkish War in Poland moved a step closer to adoption.[28]

Events in 1771 hardly improved Russia's international position. General Vasilii Dolgorukii's quick conquest of the Crimea that summer, though it resulted in a new monument in the park at Tsarskoe Selo, failed to faze the Turks; whereas Austria massed troops on the Hungarian border and initiated secret negotiations for an alliance with the Ottoman Porte. King Frederick talked of seizing Danzig. A quick visit to Petersburg by Aleksei Orlov convinced Catherine not to seek an island stronghold in the Greek archipelago, but to blockade the Dardanelles and raid the coastal cities. By early August, she admitted to Voltaire that peace with the Turks was "still very far off." She harbored little hope for an early end to Poland's "insane quarrels." Even so, she exulted in Russia's military successes, past and future: "This war will win Russia a name for herself; people will see that this is a brave and indefatigable people, with men of eminent merit and all the qualities that make heroes; they will see that she lacks no resources, that those she has are by no means exhausted, and that she can defend herself and wage war with ease and vigour when she is unjustly attacked." The next two months severely tested Catherine's confidence as a massive epidemic of bubonic plague ravaged greater Moscow and triggered disorders in September 1771 that she sent Grigorii Orlov to master. By the end of 1771, the Empress decided to open peace talks with the Turks the next summer. The heroic Grigorii Orlov, just back from plague-stricken Moscow, was appointed plenipotentiary to the peace congress along with Aleksei Obreskov, released from Turkish confinement with Prussian and Austrian assistance.[29]

Early in 1772 Prussia and Russia renewed their alliance with a convention specifying their shares of Polish territory, an agreement Austria joined in March. The three partitioning powers then reached final agreement on their shares in August 1772, but they needed another year to force the rapacious arrangement on the Polish Diet, which abjectly ratified the loss of about thirty percent of the Commonwealth's territory and thirty-five percent of its population. Russia's share included the lands Cherynshev had advocated annexing a decade earlier. Indeed, Catherine named him governor-general of the two new guberniias carved out of the gains from Poland.[30]

The settlement in Poland relieved much of the pressure on Catherine to make concessions to the Turks. In fact, Prussian and Austrian representatives attended the Russo-Turkish peace talks at Focsani in Wallachia in August 1772, but they and Catherine were taken aback when Grigorii Orlov disrupted the negotiations by suddenly departing for Petersburg. Frustrated by Turkish intransigence on the Russian demand that the Crimea be declared independent, Orlov had also learned of his replacement in the Empress's favor.

Orlov's Removal and Paul's Marriage

On 2 September 1772 Catherine appointed Alexander Vasil'chikov, a twenty-eight-year-old lieutenant in the horse-guards, to the post of chamberlain. Installed in the palace, Vasil'chikov began dining almost daily with the Empress's inner circle and, everyone assumed, visiting her nightly. At the same time she promoted his brother, Vasilii, who was married to Kirill Razumovskii's daughter Anna, to the lesser court office of gentleman of the chamber. These abrupt changes signaled a species of political turnover: a sharp fall in the Orlovs' influence and a sudden resurgence by the Panin party. For Catherine's personal life the break amounted to a divorce.[31]

Exactly what caused her estrangement from Orlov remains obscure. Both showed signs of experiencing a mid-life crisis; Catherine was then forty-three, Orlov thirty-eight. Both sought younger partners. Their personal crisis probably began a year or two earlier, when the Empress sadly admitted to Voltaire: "At forty-two, I am hardly likely to improve in looks or intellect; in the nature of things I must and will remain as I am." Later she maintained (to Potemkin) that she had discovered Orlov's affair with a teenaged cousin on the very day of his departure for the peace congress. His betrayal "cruelly tormented me and forced me from desperation to make a choice at random."[32]

Orlov was not one to yield his position without a struggle, however, and when he stormed back to Petersburg in mid-September the Empress was so frightened she barred him from court. From his Gatchina estate he negotiated the terms of his retirement. On 14 September the Empress awarded him and his brother Aleksei 10,000 serfs in whatever region they chose. Three days later, citing Grigorii's "attacks of illness," she granted him a year's leave to recover his health at home or abroad.[33] He held out for more. Finally Catherine agreed to a full-scale settlement. She began by conferring on him the previously procured title of prince of the Holy Roman Empire and ended with a fourteen-point agreement designed to lead both of them "out of spiritual anguish and to return them to a tolerable state." All bitterness she consigned to oblivion; neither party offered any explanation of their actions. She assured him she did not hold him responsible for the collapse of the peace talks. He received an annual pension of 150,000 rubles, 100,000 rubles to set up a household, ownership of the Marble Palace then under construction across the square from the Winter Palace, two silver services, 10,000 serfs, paintings and other furnishings, and the use of all imperial palaces outside St. Petersburg until his should be completed.

Although he was to take leave for a year, Catherine reiterated her desire for him to resume state service thereafter. "From my side, indeed, I shall never forget how much I am obligated to all your clan and those qualities with which you are adorned and how much they can be useful to the fatherland, and I hope that this is not the last sign of that honesty which you also respect in me. I seek in this nothing else but mutual tranquility, which I intend to preserve completely." During these negotiations she directed the Petersburg postmaster to withhold from Prince Orlov any foreign gazettes that discussed his situation, perhaps to spare his nerves and keep him in the dark. Later she composed a sarcastically indignant letter to a German gazette protesting its allegations about Orlov's supposed disfavor.[34]

In fact, Orlov's leave did not last a year. He briefly reappeared at court before the end of 1772 and resumed all offices on 20 May 1773. Still he did not regain Catherine's love or her full respect. Neither could young Vasil'chikov fill the void. The Empress later told Potemkin of her boredom and tearful depression throughout Vasil'chikov's fifteen-month tenure. In May 1773 Frau Bielcke's congratulations on Catherine's forty-fourth birthday prompted a surprised confession: "My God! How long ago it has been and yet how recently it seems that I was an infant, and here I am old now; if the gazettes speak the truth, I am soon to become a grandmother."[35]

The breakdown of Russo-Turkish peace talks affected the Empress all the more deeply because it happened on the heels of a political revolution in Sweden on 8/19 August 1772. King Gustavus III's suspension of the Swedish constitution, to which Russia had been a guarantor, signified the restoration of absolutism with the financial backing of France. Many diplomats believed the headstrong young Swedish sovereign would seek glory in a war with Russia for the recovery of Baltic territories. Catherine could not countenance a third conflict on top of her Polish and Turkish involvements; so she made conciliatory advances to Sweden while reinforcing her garrisons in Finland and pressing for progress in negotiations with the Turks before the truce ran out in March 1773. Since the Turks refused any further concessions, warfare resumed that summer. Rumiantsev crossed the Danube briefly before he withdrew in disarray, complaining that his forces and supplies were unequal to the task. In the eastern Mediterranean, meanwhile, Orlov's naval forces occupied several Middle Eastern seaports and aided Arab rebels against the Sultan. Still the Porte refused to sue for peace.[36]

These events left Catherine nonplussed. Rumiantsev's strike across the Danube filled her with hope for an early end to the war and with pride in its historic rarity. His withdrawal a month later sobered the Empress, who dismissed its significance to Voltaire as "on the level of a spelling-mistake" (like Frederick the Great and the Peter the Great, she spelled poorly in all languages). There was bite, though, in her jocular explanation of Rumiantsev's retreat "because, he says, he found nothing to eat for dinner around Silistria, and the Vizier's cooking-pot was still at Shumla. This may be so, but at least he should have made sure of his dinner without counting on his host." Though disappointed with Rumiantsev's actions and explanations, she reassured him of her confidence, sent him some reinforcements (albeit far fewer than he had demanded), and urged new attacks to coerce the Turks into negotiations.[37]

In the fall of 1773, moreover, family and domestic strains added to the emergent crisis as Catherine faced complications over Paul's attainment of maturity and rumbles of revolt on the southeastern frontier. Explosions looked imminent. The Empire had been virtually at war with Poland for a decade, with Turkey for half a decade. Peace still seemed distant. Privately nervous and worried, Catherine publicly bluffed, brazened, and barged through the multifarious pitfalls of personal and political crisis.

At court, she recalled Grigorii Orlov to all offices, "except that of fucking," sneered King Frederick. "It is a terrible business when the prick and the cunt decide the interests of Europe."[38] With the support of Orlov and his allies, the Chernyshev brothers in particular, the Empress made arrangements for Paul's marriage, completed the long delayed exchange of Holstein to Denmark for the duchies of Oldenburg and Delmenhorst, which Paul then formally ceded to his great-uncle the coadjutor of Lübeck, and signed a new alliance with Denmark. The effect of all these moves was to remove Paul from the tutelage of Nikita Panin, to abolish his sole territorial claim to independent sovereignty, and to guard Russia against a Swedish attack.[39]

Selection of a bride for Paul posed other perils. From the very start of the process two years earlier, Catherine had decided against any Russian candidates. This decision sprang from her desire not to offend the various Russian aristocratic clans by selecting one of their number, her resolve to keep Paul out of Russian and European high politics, and her insistence on controlling the line of succession. Oddly enough, all these calculations resulted in a selection process remarkably similar to the one followed by Elizabeth in 1744. For Paul's bride Catherine wanted a healthy young German Protestant princess no older than he and who came from a minor house, uncommitted to Prussia or Austria. Catholic candidates were expressly rejected as unacceptable to Russian national sentiments. Several candidates were vetoed on grounds of age or because of bad reports about their character and intellect. Evidently the Empress really hoped to find a lovematch for her son; she rejected in principle marriages of convenience or cold financial calculation. Of course, she may have figured that a lovematch would divert Paul from political meddling and render him more tractable. To improve the chances of a successful match, she invited the Landgravin of Hesse-Darmstadt to visit Petersburg with her three daughters, ages eighteen, seventeen, and fifteen. Even before they embarked for Russia she secretly arranged for Holstein officials in Lübeck to check into the personal qualities of mother and daughters, such as "the goodness of their hearts, the liveliness of their manners, *the earnestness or joy of their atttiude, the fearfulness* or fearlessness in traveling and other important qualities of spirit" (Catherine's emphasis). Furthermore, she gently warned the mother against hearkening to advice from anyone in Russia besides herself, a warning probably based on memories of her own mother's inept conduct and one intended, besides, to forestall intrigues by the different court parties. She also drafted a series of maxims to guide the future grand duchess.[40]

This remarkable document testified to Catherine's deep concern that her new daughter-in-law behave so as to win the affection and respect of her spouse, her mother-in-law, and her adopted nation. It revealed, in addition, her effort both to profit from her own experiences as grand duchess and to forewarn her future daughter-in-law of potential dangers. Indeed, an outsider familiar with Catherine's earlier life could see in her maxims peculiar object lessons of the "do as I say, not as I did" variety. The new grand duchess was told, for example, that she must not only learn Russian at once (just as Catherine had done); she must live modestly, stay out of debt, and keep out of politics (none of which Catherine had managed). To help the grand duchess, the Empress allotted her an annual allowance of 50,000 rubles as compared to the paltry 30,000 she herself had overspent. Memories of Poniatowski and Hanbury-Williams may have animated Catherine's prescription that the grand duchess avoid compromising situations and, especially, the flattery of foreign ministers. Naturally, Paul's spouse was charged to love, respect, and support the grand duke—all things Catherine had not been able to achieve with her own hapless husband. On the issue that had preoccupied Empress Elizabeth, namely, the production of an heir, Catherine's maxims were mute. Not that she was indifferent to the question, for she endorsed Frau Bielcke's hope for "a little grand duke" within a year while noting that "a little grand duchess" would be welcome, too. Painfully aware of the loneliness and boredom at a strange court, the Empress advised her daughter-in-law to improve her mind with reading and conversations with enlightened persons, crafts and music. Fulfillment of Catherine's prescriptions would assure the grand duchess of "the most fortunate future."[41]

Paul immediately fell for the middle daughter, Princess Wilhelmina, who converted to Russian Orthodoxy on 15 August 1773 with the new name of Natalia Alekseevna. The couple were officially engaged the next day, and they were married in St. Petersburg on 29 September. The consorts received no separate court, inasmuch as Catherine recalled all too well the political potential of an independent "young court." At first Catherine seemed quite happy with Paul's bride, whom she described as a "golden woman" endowed with "the most solid qualities." Yet she also felt the usual motherly trepidation in wishing the couple a long life together, "for, as someone said, the life of a man is long." Prophetic words! She could hardly have guessed the marriage would end in less than three years with the death of Natalia Alekseevna in childbirth.[42]

With Paul declared of age, he had no further need of a governor, so Nikita Panin moved out of his rooms in the Winter Palace. To soothe the pain of Panin's parting with the Grand Duke (and perhaps the abrupt decline of his political influence in general), the Empress bedecked him with honors and awards including an estate with 9,000 serfs on the territory taken from Poland—an ironic touch in view of his opposition to the partition. At the same time, she promoted Zakhar Chernyshev to field marshal and president of the War Collegium, but she ordered Prince Mikhail Volkonskii, now governor-general of Moscow after a stormy stint in Warsaw, to maintain surveillance over the outspoken Peter Panin, who was reportedly castigating her policies from retirement on his estate near Moscow. Inside her council the Panin and Orlov-Chernyshev factions wrangled about peace terms and military strategy toward the Turks. Panin favored concessions to gain an early peace; Orlov held out for greater gains via one more campaign. Catherine wavered. Increasingly worried by the progress of the Pugachev revolt on the southeastern frontier, she pursued both policies at once, authorizing Rumiantsev to negotiate directly with the Turks while preparing another, more powerful strike across the Danube in the spring of 1774. The death of Sultan Mustafa III on 13/24 December 1773 gave her hopes of peaceful concessions from his elderly, inexperienced brother and successor, Abdul-Hamid I.[43]

As the Empress deftly made these political arrangements, emotional anguish buffeted her mental equilibrium. She could not bear to reconcile with Orlov, despite his gift of the "Nadir Shah," a fabulous 196-carat diamond from Persia that she eventually paid for and had set in the imperial scepter and renamed the "Orlov diamond." Yet she needed someone strong like him, someone trustworthy with whom she could share burdens and hopes and fears. On 16 December 1773 she wrote Lieutenant-General Grigorii Potemkin a polite note that he took for an invitation to return from the Danube front in quest of her favor. Within two months he became her adjutant-general (i.e., the official favorite) and the head of a new court faction. In him Catherine found the passionate lover, intellectual companion, devoted friend, and shrewd statesman that she needed at this critical juncture of her life and of the Empire's fortunes. From late February 1774 the two were inseparable. Multiple appointments confirmed his new political prominence as member of the council, vice-president of the War Collegium, commander of cavalry and irregular forces, honorary lieutenant-colonel of the Preobrazhenskii Guards, and governor-general of Novorossiia guberniia. Several relatives also received important offices.[44]

Potemkin's meteoric ascent to power resulted in the sudden dispersal of the Orlov-Chernyshev court party. After a stormy scene with the Empress in May, Grigorii Orlov retired temporarily to his estates and in 1775 left Russia for a two-year European tour. His brother Aleksei also left state service at the end of 1775. Zakhar Chernyshev strove to retain power by cultivating Nikita Panin, but he finally resigned from the War Collegium in August 1774 to take office as governor-general of Pskov and Mogilev guberniias. In retiring Vasil'chikov the Empress showed her customary liberality to former favorites. She granted him estates, a mansion in Petersburg, 50,000 rubles to establish a household, an annual pension of 5,000 rubles, china, table linen, and a silver dinner service for twenty-four. That "excellent, but very boring citizen" was replaced, Catherine privately explained, "by one of the biggest, most droll, and most amusing originals in this iron century."[45]

Catherine had known Potemkin since the day of her coup and had periodically patronized his budding political career. He shared many attributes with

Grigorii Orlov: youthful vigor, amusing manner, sexual appeal, love of luxury, impressive physique (slightly marred by the loss of an eye), relatively obscure noble origins, military background, and self-conscious Russian nationalism. Otherwise he conspicuously outshone Orlov in culture and intellect, ambition and ability, versatility and ingenuity. Exactly when and how he and Catherine became intimate is uncertain. His abrupt ascent in early 1774 may have simply crowned a gradually developing romantic relationship, which assumed extraordinary political significance amid the foreign and domestic crises of the moment. Potemkin certainly reinforced the resolve that carried Catherine to a brilliant and timely peace with the Turks. To her Prussian ally, however, the elevation of "Tapukin" confirmed a law of life: "that a woman is always a woman and that in a feminine government the cunt has more influence than a firm policy guided by straight reason."[46]

In June 1774 Field Marshal Rumiantsev's forces recrossed the Danube in strength. Led by generals Suvorov and Kamenskii, the Russian vanguard shattered the Turks' main force in the field, invested their principal fortresses, and repulsed their reinforcements, forcing the Grand Vizir to sue for peace. On 10 July 1774 Rumiantsev and the Turkish representatives agreed on terms at the obscure Bulgarian village of Kuchuk-Kainardji, which lent its name to the peace treaty. When Rumiantsev's son reached Petersburg on 23 July with news of the triumphant peace, Catherine rushed out of a chamber concert to offer prayers of thanksgiving. The treaty excited her all the more because it registered greater Russian gains than she had dared hope for, and because it ended the protracted external war just when the internal war led by Pugachev seemed to pose a threat to Moscow. Informing Prince Volkonskii in Moscow of the peace terms, the Empress frankly acknowledged her feelings of relief: "I consider this day one of the most fortunate in my life, when the Empire has obtained the peace it so badly needed."[47]

The peace delighted Catherine, most of all, by capping a clear-cut Russian military victory over the Turks, a victory achieved through persistent effort that opened the Black Sea to Russian commerce and naval might. Russia's gains were so substantial, moreover, as to tip the balance of power in the region in Catherine's favor for several decades—much as Peter the Great's victory in the Great Northern War had accomplished in the northwest. As an adopted citizen the Empress rejoiced in the fulfillment of long-held Russian aspirations; she loved to think of herself as following in the footsteps of giants.

Truly, the peace terms were something to celebrate: "independence" for the Crimean Khanate from the Sultan's political sovereignty and cession to the Tatars of all Turkish forts and lands in the region; transfer to Russia of Kerch and Enikale, fortress-ports at the entrance to the sea of Azov, and of Kinburn and its hinterland, which gave access to the Dnieper-Bug estuary and thence to the Black Sea; free Russian navigation on the Black Sea (and, tacitly, the right to operate a fleet there) and the right of merchant ships to pass the Turkish straits; and 4.5 million rubles indemnity—approximately the cost of the Mediterranean naval expedition. Russia restored to Turkish sovereignty the Danubian Principalities, several strongholds in the Caucasus, and all Greek islands seized during the war, but also won the right to establish consulates throughout the Ottoman Empire and make representations on behalf of a particular Orthodox church in Constantinople—a provision later twisted to imply a special role for Russia in protecting all the Orthodox peoples under Turkish rule. Not only did Russia obtain a firm foothold on the northern coast of the Black Sea; she gained strategic handholds on either side of the Crimea with which to pull the Khanate into the Russian orbit. In short, Catherine presided over Russia's emergence as a Pontic power with expanding interests in the Middle East, the Caucasus, and the eastern Mediterranean.[48]

The lavish peace celebrations which Catherine and Potemkin staged in Moscow on 10–23 July 1775 had been delayed eight days when the Empress fell ill with fever and diarrhea, from which she was relieved by copious blood-letting. All the festivities celebrated Russia's multiple triumphs on land and sea, underscoring the theme of southward expansion and culminated by a stupendous firework. A grandiose Roman-style triumphal arch greeted Field Marshal Rumiantsev outside Moscow. Yet, to the spectators' dismay, the imperious commander swept past it so swiftly the evening of 8 July that none could savor the sight. However miffed Catherine may have felt privately over this slight, she richly rewarded Rumiantsev with a laudatory charter that styled him Zadunaiskii ("Beyond the Danube"), a diamond-encrusted commander's baton and sword, a crown of laurel leaves and an olive branch, the cross and star of the Order of the Apostle St. Andrew, a special medal, 5,000 serfs in former Polish territory, 100,000 rubles for a house, a silver service for his table, and paintings for his house. Rumiantsev's village of Troitskoe was renamed Kanardzhi, and Catherine dined there on 28 October 1775. Commensurate honors were given the other main commanders—General Vasilii Dolgorukii (who was styled Krymskii for his conquest of the Crimea), General Aleksei Orlov, Field Marshal Alexander Golitsyn, and General Peter Panin—with lesser rewards to a host of others.[49]

Catherine described the gigantic celebration to Voltaire with pride and delight:

> To provide a treat for the people, a fairly large open space was chosen, which we called 'the Black Sea' and covered with ships. The approach was by two roads, one called the Tanais, or Don, the other—the Borysthenes, or Dnieper. Both these roads were adorned with various scenes—farms, villages, windmills, etc. . . . Following the map, on the little hills overlooking the plain, ballrooms were set up, which were called Kerch and Yenikale. The banqueting-hall was called Azov and Taganrog. A fair was organized. There was a huge theatre called Kinburn; there were fireworks on the other side of the Danube; feasts, fountains flowing with wine, rope-dancers, and other popular amusements were set up where the Nogai Tartars usually camp. The rest of the place was decorated with illuminations; and buildings, serving as kitchens and for other purposes, were put up so that between sixty and

one hundred thousand people could have all their wants supplied for
between ten to twelve hours. . . . I would love to have danced with
you there, Sir, and I am sure you would have honoured me with your
choice.[50]

Ratification and celebration of the Russo-Turkish peace formally ended the
first foreign policy crisis that Catherine confronted as empress. It had been
a very complex, protracted crisis that she surmounted with great effort and at
great cost. She blundered into the crisis through her highhanded treatment
of Poland, which increased her dependence on Prussia and provoked war
with Turkey. Victories against the Turks increased her appetite for military
glory and territorial gain, but the two tastes did not blend easily; the prolonged character of the war forced the Empress to make compromises with
Prussia and Austria at the expense of Poland. The entire experience left the
idea of a "Northern System" in shambles. Nevertheless, Catherine seemed to
have solved the Polish problem for the time being and to have made great
progress in solving the Turkish problem. She had shown great determination
in pursuing her foreign policy objectives, managing their pursuit shrewdly in
her new council. In domestic politics the Empress deftly arranged the transition from balancing between the Panin and the Orlov-Chernyshev parties,
both of which had lost her confidence, to a new constellation centered
around Potemkin. She had also weathered the crisis of Paul's majority without allowing his rights to the throne to become a public issue and getting rid
of the troublesome Holstein question. All the same, the cost of Catherine's
successes in war proved much higher than the direct losses of men and
equipment or the strains of extraordinary tax and recruit levies, budget
deficits and foreign debts. Indirect costs showed up in two other dimensions
of the general crisis of the war period: the plague epidemic of 1770–1772
and the Pugachev Revolt of 1773–1775.

6

Pox, Pestilence, and Crisis in Public Health

Possessed of a robust constitution, Catherine experienced most of the ordinary afflictions of the age without great difficulty. She was no stranger to illness or professional medical treatment in Russia. Indeed, as grand duchess and brood mare of the Romanov dynasty, her health had prompted constant solicitude from Elizabeth and other interested parties at court. Once she became empress, such matters acquired broader political significance for her own and the Empire's future, subject as she was to an array of psychological pressures and an immense, constantly accumulating weight of routine and extraordinary business. Despite formidable powers of self-discipline, regular work habits, and inborn cheerfulness, the Empress felt the burdens of absolute authority more and more. It was no accident that she created the council as a permanent advisory institution in the year of her fortieth birthday. After the first several sessions she attended irregularly, but monitored its discussions and presided whenever crucial decisions loomed imminent. Under the congeries of crises associated with the Turkish war, the Empress gradually acknowledged some of the limitations on her activities imposed by age and the crush of state duties. Perhaps her absorption in work lay at the root of her break with Grigorii Orlov. In these same years she often complained privately of sickness and physical ailments, some partly psychosomatic in character, such as headaches and backpains.

Since Catherine held a rather low opinion of professional medical practitioners in relation to her own health, she occasionally treated herself as when she confided to Nikita Panin sometime in 1768: "It has been all of four hours since the pain in my head has left me. Yesterday I ate nothing the whole day, and I think that will be much easier for me, so let the English envoy know that before the court-day at six o'clock I shall give him an audience. For me it will be much easier if I go out once in the evening, but in the morning stay in.''[1] Like her predecessors and contemporary sovereign peers, the Empress employed several court practitioners to attend her. From February 1769 the Scotsman Dr. John Rogerson became a fixture at court and butt of her jokes about modern medicine. Indeed, she preferred to rely on nature's recuperative powers (i.e., rest, relaxation, dietary moderation, fresh air, and mild exercise) with an occasional resort to home remedies and such standbys as laxatives and blood-letting. Her health had become more robust, she confided to Madame Geoffrin in 1766, because she ignored her physicians and strengthened her body by continual and successive exposure to cold and heat. Many years later she advised Emperor Joseph II of Austria against reading long reports by candlelight without spectacles, a practice that had caused her severe headaches in the early 1770s. Her skeptical attitude toward medicine reflected popular European literary humor of the time, some of which was expressed in the Russian satirical journals that she encouraged in the late 1760s and early 1770s. For example, an item in *Adskaia pochta* (Hell's Post) in 1769 derided the physician for obscurantist devotion to tradition: "he always swears by the science of ancient Medics and his own Rhubarb, that all innovations in Medicine are in fact extremely dangerous inventions." Such an ignorant practitioner was, therefore, "in a better position to kill forty persons in the old way than to cure one by the new."[2]

Still, when Catherine herself felt ill or worried about Paul's or somebody else's health, she sought and recommended professional care. Thus she described one illness to Nikita Panin in 1768:

> I am quite sick, my back hurts worse than I ever felt since birth; last night I had some fever from the pain, and I do not know what to attribute it to, I swallow and do everything that they wish; yesterday I took a powder, which was so small that, of course, in all its ingredients it did not amount to a grain; and therefore one could expect little effect from it, as proved to be the case in actual fact. They ascribed to this powder the power of causing perspiration, yet, to my extreme regret, although I even accepted the artfully composed dust, perspiration did not dutifully show itself.[3]

Paul's health worried Catherine as much as her own. She and Nikita Panin constantly fretted about the Grand Duke's being exposed to smallpox, one of the most prevalent and dangerous afflictions of that era. Indeed, the Empress was quite exceptional in having attained adulthood without contracting "the pocks," for which she preserved great apprehension. The memory of her fiancé's suffering and hideous disfigurement from smallpox excited mortal dread. Consequently she and Panin strove to isolate Paul from known carriers or large crowds, and in November 1765 the Petersburg police reaffirmed Elizabeth's prohibition from attendance at court or church by anyone with smallpox or other exanthemata at home.[4] Even so, Catherine conceded that Paul's future and her own were in doubt so long as neither had conquered the ogre of smallpox. As early as 1764 she considered inoculation for him, only to be dissuaded by the risk to his frail constitution.[5]

Naturally Paul, who had inherited his parents' "prodigious vivacity of thought with an astonishing facility and sharpness of expression," chaffed at the constraints placed on him on this account. Sir George Macartney recorded an instance of the twelve-year-old Grand Duke's "very strong turn for satire and ridicule" concerning the bugaboo of smallpox in 1767. Asked if he would attend a masquerade, Paul referred the query to Nikita Panin, remarking: "You know I am a child and cannot be supposed to be a judge whether I ought to go there or not, but I will lay a wager that I do not go; Mr. Panin will tell me there is a great monster called the small-pox, walking up and down the ball-room, and the deuce is in it, but that same monster has very good intelligence of my motions, for he is generally to be found precisely in those very places where I have the most inclination to go."[6]

Outside Russia the horrible experience of the Austrian Hapsburgs with smallpox in 1767 certainly gave Catherine cause for alarm about possible dynastic complications. Empress-Queen Maria Theresa herself and her daughter-in-law, Maria Josepha, both came down with the rash in May. Maria Josepha died five days later, whereas Maria Theresa recovered with some scarring. Her widowered son, Joseph II, refused to marry again and had no surviving children. Her own daughter Maria Josepha, engaged to the king of Naples, succumbed to smallpox the following October; two other daughters survived with terrible pockmarks. These horrific ravages spurred Maria Theresa to secure the services of a Dutch physician, Jan Ingenhouz, who successfully inoculated three of her younger children by 1 October 1768, only a month before Catherine's own inoculation.[7]

This menace assumed alarming dimensions in the spring of 1768 when Nikita Panin's own fiancée, Countess Anna Sheremeteva, described by a British diplomat as a "lady of almost unlimited ambition" and "of uncommon merit, beautiful, and immensely rich," contracted smallpox.[8] From Tsarskoe Selo the Empress watched the situation with mounting anguish. At first she hoped the affliction would not prove to be smallpox, but when she learned on 5 May that it was and that Panin had been quarantined for two weeks, she secretly ordered Paul brought to her. Although concerned about Panin and his fiancée, Catherine placed Paul's safety first; "for (God preserve us), if the Grand Duke will contract the smallpox in these minutes, then it will not be without reproaches from the public." She asked Elagin to explain her thinking and make the arrangements with Panin. "I am very upset," she confessed, "not being able to focus thought on anything better; for everything is awful in this critical situation." Panin's term of isolation seemed excessive to her, but she ruefully excused the doctors and herself for their trepidation. Paul joined his mother at Tsarskoe Selo the evening of 6 May and wrote Panin the next day a touching note in French to buck up his spirits.[9]

The Empress and the Grand Duke nervously waited for the threat to pass. When Catherine herself felt ill on 14 May, she hastened to inform Panin of her recovery overnight and relay the doctor's assurances that "these difficult days for your fiancée will pass propitiously." Two days later she was stunned by Sheremeteva's death. "I, having this hour learned of the demise of Countess Anna Petrovna, could not help letting you know my real sorrow about it," she wrote Panin on 17 May. 'I am so touched for you by this grievous misfortune, that I cannot sufficiently explain it. Please, watch your own health; I fear that you will fall ill." This news "infinitely touched" Paul, too, who regretted his governor's loss and absence. Catherine's anxiety persisted for weeks, as she informed Governor-General Saltykov at the end of May: "I am already living here at Tsarskoe Selo the seventh week with my son, while across the city there is such smallpox, and still the very worst kind, that I considered it best to live here." In fact, as a safety precaution she anxiously spent the entire summer with Paul moving from one suburban estate to another. As early as 8 June she remarked on the weird weather, warning Nikita Panin to have her son bring along his fur coat when they drove over to Peterhof for the St. Peter's day celebrations; "For en route you will find ten different weathers in one day."[10] Commonplace though it was to associate bad weather with disease, Catherine could scarcely foresee how menacing the association might become.

This fright also galvanized the Empress into investigating the controversial medical procedure of variolation: that is, inoculation with matter from the pustules of a convalescent from mild smallpox. An ancient folk technique practiced in many lands, variolation had been rediscovered by Greek physicians at Constantinople early in the eighteenth century and then popularized in Britain and her North American colonies. The technique was known in Russia by mid-century, but it remained suspect there (and in other Continental nations) from fears of harming those who gave or received the inoculant and of infecting non-immune segments of the population. Variolation was typically employed only amid actual epidemics, as happened in Russia in the late 1760s. Catherine sent for a British practitioner, Dr. Thomas Dimsdale, whose bestselling treatise of 1767 had won him the reputation of an expert in variolation. By adopting the new techniques of Robert Sutton and his sons— a superficial incision, minimal preparation and isolation, and "secret" medicine, all of which rendered variolation much easier, cheaper, and safer— Dimsdale claimed to have minimized all risks. He was hired by the Russian ambassador in London and departed with his son Nathaniel, a medical student at Edinburgh, for Russia at the end of July 1768.[11]

The Dimsdales reached St. Petersburg a month later, and Catherine privately received them on 28 August and dined with them that afternoon. Impressed by the Russian court, the fifty-six-year-old Quaker physician was charmed by the Empress and amazed at "her extreme penetration, and the propriety of the questions she asked, relative to the practice and success of inoculation." She smiled at his stumbling French and professed to understand some English. The next day she informed Dimsdale of her resolution to be inoculated as soon as possible. Moreover, when Dimsdale cautiously requested assistance from the court physicians, Catherine brushed aside his reservations, assured him of her confidence and previous good health, but asked him to keep the preparations secret. Thus the official court registers ignored Dimsdale's presence altogether, although the British ambassador reported on 29 August that the Empress's intention "is a secret which everybody knows, and which does not seem to occasion much speculation." The circumspect Dimsdale persuaded her, however, to wait a few weeks while he experimented on several local youngsters. For it was widely believed that diseases such as smallpox varied significantly from one region and climate to another. Although these experiments yielded mixed results that sapped Dimsdale's own confidence, Catherine never wavered in her resolve, certain of his competence and the benefit to herself, her son, and the Empire.[12]

On the evening of 12 October 1768 she quietly underwent inoculation at Dimsdale's hands. The inoculant was taken from a young boy named Alexander Markov, later ennobled with the honorary surname of Ospennyi—from *ospa,* Russian for smallpox. (Gossip proclaimed him Catherine's own offspring—by Orlov?—and she herself joked evasively about his parentage.) The next morning the Empress went to Tsarskoe Selo for a period of isolation in the country air. Following the "cool regimen" prescribed by Dimsdale, she went outdoors each day for two or three hours. She kept active, displayed only a few pustules that dried up within a week, and felt quite healthy "except for some slight uneasiness, indispensable in this sickness." Her return to Petersburg on 1 November occasioned a public celebration. Paul was inoculated the next day without difficulty. The dates of his and his mother's recovery were declared national holidays thenceforth.[13]

Catherine made the most of the occasion. Responding to the congratulations of the Senate and the Legislative Commission on 20 November, she reiterated her maternal concern for the entire Empire. "My objective was, through my example, to save from death the multitude of my subjects who, not knowing the value of this technique, frightened of it, were left in danger." Four years later the Senate thanked her anew in the name of the people and awarded her twelve gold medals engraved with her portrait on one side and on the other a temple of healing with a vanquished Hydra before it, the Empress leaving with the Grand Duke to meet the children of Russia. The inscription proclaimed: "She gave the example by herself—12 October 1768." Nationwide *Te Deums* and noble festivals, laudatory odes and an "allegorical pantomime ballet" at court entitled *Prejudice Defeated* all hailed the triumph of Minerva/Catherine, assisted by Ruthenia/Russia, the Genius of Science, and Alcind/Paul, in freeing the populace from Superstition and Ignorance. Grigorii Orlov, Kirill Razumovskii, an archbishop, and 140 aristocrats immediately imitated her example in seeking inoculation. Dimsdale and his son, richly rewarded and styled barons of the Russian Empire, were swamped with would-be patients in Petersburg and Moscow. Variolation clinics were established in both capitals, at Tsarskoe Selo, and in several provincial cities including distant Irkutsk in Siberia in 1772. A Russian translation of Dimsdale's treatise explaining his technique was published in St. Petersburg in 1768. Catherine named him her personal physician and took him shooting with her. Before leaving Russia in 1769 he treated the Empress for a "pleuritic fever" that kept her in bed "six long days," as she lamented to Frau Bielcke. Two years later he requested permission to dedicate an English translation to Catherine, who readily approved while lauding the rapid adoption of variolation in Russia since Dimsdale's visit. He returned in 1781 to inoculate her grandsons.[14]

Thanks to Voltaire's enthusiastic efforts, Catherine's bold adoption of inoculation won her much favorable publicity in western Europe. The great philosophe, who had long advocated variolation after the English example, cited her enlightened act to castigate "our ridiculous Sorbonne and . . . the argumentative charlatans in our medical schools!" With playful blasphemy he teased her: "You have been inoculated with less fuss than a nun taking an enema." The practical effects of variolation in Russia and on Catherine remain problematic. She and Paul both escaped smallpox, to be sure, and nearly 20,000 persons were supposed to have been inoculated in Russia by 1780 and some two million by 1800. Possibly variolation had greater impact on the foundling homes and in Siberia where 3,784 persons were inoculated at Irkutsk by 1776 with only 28 deaths. Catherine herself hired Dr. Charles de Mertens from Vienna to attend the Moscow Foundling Home, where he utilized the Sutton-Dimsdale method of variolation. Yet the overall effect was not dramatic, as mortality at such institutions regularly surpassed fifty percent in the next three decades. Nonetheless, Catherine's public endorsement of variolation advertised a practical application of her general effort to conserve population by lowering mortality, especially infant mortality. The same was true of her sponsorship of syphilitic "homes" or "secret" hospitals for victims of venereal disease, a subject addressed in her *Great Instruction* in 1767. Unlike Peter the Great, Catherine apparently did not suffer from venereal disease herself. Rather, her interest in the subject stemmed from a general concern for public health and from cameralist prescriptions.[15]

The Pestilential Distemper

In retrospect, it is a tragic irony that Catherine's vaunted triumph over smallpox occurred on the eve of her Empire's encounter with an even more fearsome and mysterious affliction—bubonic plague. Russia had not been visited by the "pestilential distemper," as plague was termed then, since 1740 although its southern frontiers were threatened almost annually through the 1760s. In any event, by 1770 few medical practitioners in Russia had ever seen the scourge, which was generally associated with southern locales and warm climates, filth and backwardness, such as prevailed in the Ottoman Empire and Persia. Nobody anywhere then understood the plague's link to fleas and rodents, house rats in particular, or its bacterial basis, which was only discovered in 1894. Indeed, most people thought that plague somehow originated from subterranean sources in the form of invisible vapors that spread in poisonous clouds (miasmata), through direct personal contact, or through contaminated articles (fomites) such as textiles, money, and paper. Another popular notion conceived of plague not as a specific affliction—the concept of separate diseases from separate germs was scarcely known—but as the apogee of a general infective process. Thus it was thought that less dangerous infections such as "putrid fever" (typhus) could, in certain circumstances, be transformed into "pestilential distemper." Everywhere the traditional defenses against plague relied on rigid isolation: quarantines for suspected carriers, pesthouses for those infected, and cordons of troops to seal off impested or suspect regions. Russia in fact already had a rudimentary network of quarantine stations along its western and southern borders, but these were too few to effect surveillance of the vast expanse (even had they known what to look for). Besides, the problems of border security worsened after 1768 with the population migration to the south and the military movements of the Russo-Turkish War.

If Catherine gave any thought to plague before 1770, she evidently shared the general notions outlined above. She was vaguely aware of the threat of epidemic disease in the south, and was concerned that the army and the fleet employ sufficient medical personnel to protect themselves. At Riga she authorized Governor-General George Brown to hire local surgeons and send to Königsberg for others. Furthermore, in 1769 she hired a Greek physician from Constantinople to supervise surveillance in greater Petersburg, apparently apprehensive that the prospect of disease might increase from troop and supply movements. Scattered reports of plague in the Danubian Principalities in late 1769 caused no commotion in Petersburg, where Catherine scoffed at the foreign gazettes for their attempts "to make our army die of plague." To Voltaire she sarcastically predicted: "In the spring, evidently, those who have died of the plague will rise to fight again. The truth is that none of our troops has had the plague." Voltaire seconded her scorn with blasphemous derision of the Turks and the Jews: "I hope your Majesty will soon be chasing the plague and the Turks out of Istambul."[16]

News of plague at Jassy in Moldavia in mid-March 1770 could not be confirmed for several weeks until General Rumiantsev sent Dr. Gustav Orraeus there early in May. Orraeus found pestilence ravaging Jassy and its Russian garrison, which was soon evacuated to the countryside where its commander, General Christopher von Stoffeln, perished suddenly on 30 May. Fearful of disrupting the spring campaign, Rumiantsev instituted a cordon along the Dniester and around Khotin, the assembly point for his offensive. The threat to the field army finally caught Catherine's attention.

On 28 May she dispatched posthaste to General Peter Panin's Second Army, en route to besiege the fortress of Bender, the Empire's foremost authority on pestilence—Dr. Johann Lerche. Former acting head of the Medical Chancery, a veteran of the plague of 1738–1740 during the earlier Turkish war, and currently St. Petersburg city-physician, Dr. Lerche enjoyed Catherine's full confidence. His departure for the south relieved whatever anxiety she had felt initially, whereas Rumiantsev's double defeat of the Turks in July gave the lie to fears of plague-related military complications. Although the two official Russian gazettes kept silent about any threat to the Empire while reporting the plague's ravages in Turkey and southern Poland, its steady progress northward reactivated Catherine's apprehensions. On 25 August she informed Nikita Panin of her hope that Aleksei Orlov had seized the Dardanelles, "but the condition of Moscow greatly disturbs me, for besides sickness and fires there is much stupidity there. All this recalls the beards of our ancestors." It is not known what sickness the Empress referred to, inasmuch as pestilence was not reported in Moscow for another four months, but her black view of the old capital had obviously been reaffirmed. Two days later she secretly ordered quarantine precautions taken quietly in Kiev, which overlooked the Polish border and served as a major supply depot for the Turkish campaign—it was the logical entry for pestilence from the south. Catherine's logic was good albeit tardy; the plague reached Kiev weeks before her orders did.[17]

As often happens with plague, however, its early manifestations went undetected. Governor-General Voeikov of Kiev only reported the outbreak on 9 September 1770. Meanwhile Petersburg denied the need for any further precautions on the Prussia-Kurland border. Ten days later the Empress finally ordered cordons established all around the Ukraine, and her council began coordinating the antiplague efforts. About Moscow she stayed acutely apprehensive, directing Governor-General Saltykov on 19 September to place a checkpoint at the river crossing in Serpukhov, a major junction of road and river traffic from the southwest. This flurry of precautions seemed effective at first. The Kiev authorities reported steady diminution of the local epidemic, and by 3 October they mentioned "fever with spots," commonly thought to be less dangerous than plague. At Riga, Governor-General Brown withheld proclamation of a quarantine so as to avoid disrupting commerce, a policy the Empress approved on 1 October by citing the prophylactic effect of "the present cold autumn season." (Conventional wisdom held that cold weather inhibited plague, although nobody knew why exactly.) In Kurland the Russian authorities called for the expulsion of Jewish merchants who were suspected of spreading pestilence through the rag trade. From Smolensk, Governor Tekut'ev reported all precautions in place and no outbreaks on Russian territory, despite the pestilence across the border in Poland.[18]

Yet Catherine's equanimity began to wear thin as the local weather cooled while the epidemic in the Ukraine still raged. She could not know that the Kiev authorities had systematically underestimated mortality in the city, but she smelled a rat (figuratively) when the disease persisted past mid-October, suspicious outbreaks erupted elsewhere, and Saltykov reported that refugees from Kiev were circumventing the cordon that guarded Moscow guberniia. On 1 November the Empress therefore detached a special emissary to oversee all antiplague precautions in the Ukraine. When Major of the Life Guards Mikhail Shipov, a protégé of Grigorii Orlov, arrived in the Ukraine, cooler weather had averted a near crisis in Kiev, where Dr. Lerche had arrived to supervise precautions on 10 October. But the Petersburg authorities were already more worried about Moscow. Reports of plague at Sevsk, only 330 kilometers south of Moscow, and hordes of refugees fleeing northward prompted Catherine to reinforce the cordon in those quarters in late November. She worried all the more about the situation in Moscow because Prince Henry of Prussia was scheduled to visit the old capital incognito in early winter. He did so in mid-December 1770, completely unaware of the epidemic then in progress. The Moscow authorities themselves only learned of the outbreak on 22 December, and Catherine got wind of it five days later.[19]

Though displeased, the Empress received the news calmly. The epidemic fortunately proved to be a small one limited to two wooden barracks at an annex of the Moscow General Infantry Hospital on the northeastern outskirts. Its nature baffled the local practitioners. Thus the hospital's chief doctor, Afanasii Shafonskii, asserted its pestilential properties and closed the premises to outsiders. But Dr. Andrei Rinder, the Moscow city-physician, denied that it was plague, noting that only twenty persons had died there in four weeks. The Moscow police and Governor-General Saltykov took the usual precautions: isolating the hospital and the annex, setting out fumigatory pyres to cleanse the tainted air, ordering all corpses examined before burial. All these measures received Catherine's approval after the fact. Hopeful the danger would soon pass, she charged Saltykov to encourage Muscovites with the promise of God's mercy. She was upset, though, by evidence that the epidemic had been hidden for more than a month. Furthermore, the Moscow outbreak persuaded the Empress and her council to end their public silence on the subject. On 3 January 1771 they published a proclamation summoning everyone to institute the precautions that had been covertly ordered four months earlier. This announcement did not explicitly admit the plague's arrival in Russia, but a week later the Senate publicly acknowledged the fact, reaffirmed the ban on textile imports from Poland, and later summoned all governors to enforce the antiplague precautions. Nothing was said about Moscow, evidently in the hope that the threat had already ended.[20]

The whole scare did seem over by mid-January 1771. Three months later than normal, frosts chilled the old capital at the end of 1770 and arrested the incipient epidemic, which killed only twenty-five persons at the hospital annex. Catherine and the Moscow authorities kept their precautions in force till early March 1771. In the meantime doctors Rinder and Shafonskii elaborated their debate over the disease's identity, with Saltykov forwarding their contradictory reports to Petersburg for consideration. Rinder denied it had been plague, whereas Shafonskii insisted that it was and warned of its possible revival with the return of warm spring weather.[21]

Before Petersburg considered this controversy, a second outbreak was suddenly discovered in Moscow at the start of March 1771, when the winter freeze broke into a brief thaw. On 9 March the police got word of unusual mortality in the heart of Moscow at a huge textile manufactory known as the Big Woolen Court. Investigation disclosed the death of 113 persons working or living there since 1 January; on the premises 16 others were found ill with alarming symptoms: dark spots and swollen glands. The police quietly isolated the manufactory that very night.[22]

This renewed threat to Moscow loomed much larger than the first because of the involvement of such a big, centrally situated, heavily populated enterprise (2,528 workers and dependents, 730 living at the mill) producing one of the most notorious "plague-goods"—cheap textiles made from imported raw materials. Moscow officials suspected the "pestilential distemper" had been brought to the city in raw wool transported by Greek merchants from the plague-ridden Ottoman Empire. As in the earlier outbreak, moreover, there was obvious evidence of negligence or willful concealment. Somehow the disease had gone unreported for ten weeks. Yet Dr. Rinder, who admitted having visited the mill on 30 January, could not be held accountable; he was then in bed with "a gangrenous ulcer on the leg" (from plague?) and died on 21 April. Other physicians checked the site again on 11 March, decided the disease closely resembled plague, and recommended immediate evacuation of the 640 persons left at the Big Woolen Court. On the night of 13–14 March the police stealthily convoyed the mill's residents to suburban quarantines and pesthouses.[23]

Catherine heard the awful news in Petersburg on 17 March. To Saltykov's report she replied icily, inquiring what precautions had been taken with the "soldier cloth" produced at the Big Woolen Court since the start of the sickness there. She also asked President Cherkassov of the Medical Collegium to convoke a meeting of all court practitioners and local physicians for the purpose of resolving the Rinder-Shafonskii dispute about the identity of the first outbreak. Unfortunately, the conclusions of this conclave have not been found. Probably their opinions were as diffuse and divided as the two reports they considered. In any event, Catherine's confidence in the various practitioners' expertise began to waver. When her councilors heard the first reports on 21 March, they saw in them a shocking indictment of Governor-General Saltykov's competence. Some wanted the seventy-two-year-old war hero replaced at once; others favored naming an assistant to take charge of the public health crisis. Catherine vacillated a few days. But when further reports depicted worsening confusion in Moscow—confirmed in person by Governor Yushkov of Moscow guberniia and by Dr. Orraeus, who had stopped there on the way back from Moldavia—she endorsed an emergency program of precautions on 28 March to save the old capital. To administer these precautions in Moscow she appointed Lieutenant-General and Senator Peter Eropkin, a respected official closely connected to the Panin party. Furthermore, to protect Petersburg's commerce from foreign embargo, the Empress placed Count Jakob Bruce, husband of her longtime confidante, in charge of quarantine measures in the new capital and its hinterland. On 3 April she also ordered a halt to foundation work on the new Kremlin palace for fear of releasing subterranean vapors.[24]

While Senator Eropkin took control of the antiplague campaign in Moscow, appointing officials in each of the city's fourteen police districts to cooperate with the police and the medical practitioners in removing the dead and evacuating the stricken and the suspect to pesthouses or quarantines, Catherine tensely awaited events. Eropkin hastened to locate personnel and dependents of the Big Woolen Court who lived outside the manufactory, and evacuate them to suburban quarantines. His efforts appeared to be effective, in conjunction with the return of freezing temperatures from mid-March onward, for the number of dead and newly sick abruptly declined by early April. Indeed, so suddenly did the mortality subside that Saltykov and Eropkin jointly decided against full implementation of Catherine's emergency program. Since Archbishop Amvrosii discerned no unusual mortality in the reports of the parish clergy, he also opposed extreme measures and even withheld special prayers sent by the Holy Synod to inspire the people.[25]

The epidemic's second abrupt abatement elicited dissension among the practitioners anew, further shaking public faith in them. It convinced Catherine and many others that the disease had not been plague after all. As she remarked to Nikita Panin in a postscript of 14 April: "In Moscow everything is correcting itself and there are no sick except in two monasteries, in the Greek one and the Simonov." Four days later she even poked fun at some of the precautions. "Evidently, with us they do not spare the vinegar," she commented about the widely prescribed disinfectant, "and not only do they strive to take the distemper out of letters, but already even wash out the ink, one can hardly read the letters." By mid-May she denied to Frau Bielcke that the disease had been plague, blaming the recent scare on scattered cases of "putrid fever and spotted fever." Neither the Empress nor anybody else divined any link to the strange weather, though she joked with Frau Bielcke on 31 March about the Russian climate following the fleet and causing the extraordinarily cold spring in Hamburg and Italy. Moreover, she informed Saltykov in surprise at the Petersburg frosts on 2 May 1771. Snow fell on Moscow at the same time. Indeed, the seasons in these years were almost reversed all over Europe, perhaps in consequence of dust veils from volcanic eruptions elsewhere.[26]

The waning of this second scare in Moscow gave Catherine an opportunity to look into various prophylactic and therapeutic measures. On 2 April, for example, she asked Saltykov to engage an enterprising surgeon for an experiment in plague therapy. The practitioner should isolate some hopelessly infected patients in cool, dry accommodations, give them cold water with vinegar to drink, and massage them with ice at least twice daily. The ice massages should be increased or decreased according to the patients' progress. Catherine wished the entire experiment kept secret and the results reported only to her. A month later she sent 500 rubles to surgeon Friedrich Margraf who, though he declined to appraise the treatment in general, had applied it to one patient, who survived anyway. The treatment, later grandiloquently termed *Remedium antipestilentiale Catherinae Secundae,* represented an application of the popular "cool regimen" to the worst fever known. It epitomized the Empress's amateurish, activist approach to epidemic disease and public health. On a different plane Catherine recommended a temporary ban on masquerades and theatrical performances, in order to discourage dangerous crowding indoors. To lift Muscovite spirits, however, she proposed outdoor amusements such as swings, seesaws, and the like. "Public promenades especially are very good and can be expected to be filled with people, if various diversions are set up there," she advised Saltykov on 12 April, authorizing the expenditure of state funds for such purposes. "One might still also make harmless bonfires that serve the spectators' satisfaction and cleanse the air . . . my main desire being to seek out modes for diminishing the action of the infection, and the means prescribed here have often produced good successes in such circumstances in other lands." These suggestions reveal Catherine's appreciation of Muscovite psychology and her endeavor to heed the cameralists' warning about the danger of provoking discontent by excessively stringent antiplague measures. On her forty-second birthday (21 April 1771) she began a new draft of memoirs, this one dedicated to Countess Bruce, "to whom I can speak freely without fear of consequences." Perhaps this tug of nostalgia foretold a mid-life crisis.[27]

Despite the onset of warm, rainy spring weather in mid-May, the Moscow epidemic showed few clear signs of reviving before the summer. The Empress and the Moscow authorities lifted the precautions slowly and cautiously. Chary of allowing the multitude of quarantined clothworkers to return to the confines of the Big Woolen Court, Senator Eropkin began investigating in late May the possibility of permanently relocating outside town the huge manufactory and others like it. This was an idea after Catherine's heart. She had long favored the proposal in principle, hoping to spread prosperity to the provinces while saving the capitals from all the social and environmental abuses spawned by huge manufactories that relied on bondaged labor. The senate departments in Moscow endorsed Eropkin's idea, and Catherine's council in Petersburg considered it independently at the same time in her absence, but neither body advocated immediate action, apparently anticipating resistance from the manufactory operators and thinking the issue was not yet urgent. But the plan was not forgotten.[28]

Just when Moscow's affairs seemed to be returning to normal, other concerns beset the Empress. On 23–24 May 1771 a series of conflagrations swept central Petersburg so severely that Catherine suspected arson and sent Grigorii Orlov to captain the fire-fighting efforts. And just as she undertook to seek a German bride for sixteen-year-old Paul, the Grand Duke and her assistant Grigorii Teplov both fell desperately ill. From Peterhof on 19 June the Empress shared her gloom with Nikita Panin: "My son is ill, we have lost Zhurzha [to the Turks], [Admiral] Seniavin has lost a bomb ketch, and furthermore in these weeks I have received six different denunciations about babblers, who really exhaust one's patience, and I ordered three lashed in the Semenovskii Regiment on parade." The next day she promised to come see Paul, whose gradual recovery cheered her, but on 25 June she still cautioned Panin against endangering her son's health with a visit to cold and damp Peterhof for his nameday. By the end of June she reported Paul on the mend and, a month later, merrily informed Frau Bielcke that some attributed the Grand Duke's five-week illness—a catarrhal fever—to the growth of his beard.[29]

The Plague Riot

At the end of June 1771 the Petersburg authorities reinstituted most anti-plague precautions in response to Eropkin's reports of resurgent disease in Moscow's suburbs (he did not term the infection plague). Catherine also ordered Dr. Lerche to leave Kiev for Moscow, where he arrived on 13 July. A week later, however, she approved the shipment of cloth produced at the Big Woolen Court, provided it had been aired for six weeks beforehand, and stipulated that the workers who washed and aired it should be quarantined for six weeks, too. Such encouraging developments left the Empress and her councilors quite unprepared for the shock of Eropkin's revelation, received in Petersburg at the start of August, that pestilence was ravaging

Moscow worse than ever. Even though Dr. Lerche confirmed the disease as definitely pestilential, and none of the other practitioners contested his verdict, both Eropkin and Catherine hesitated to believe the worst. Memories of the previous ambiguous alarms gave them hope.[30]

On 11 August the Empress and her councilors were dumbfounded by Eropkin's request for a month's leave to receive medical treatment and Saltykov's report of deaths among the soldiers under Eropkin's direct command and adjacent to his house. Catherine gently refused Eropkin's plea on grounds that his leadership could not be spared at that critical moment. Moreover, she promised him reward, assigned Senator Mikhail Sobakin to assist him, and sent twelve Guards officers to reinforce his command. Further alarming reports persuaded her on 20 August to order the immediate imposition of her emergency program of late March, which contemplated isolating the city by a series of cordons. Before the council six days later the Empress still expressed doubt that the disease was really plague, yet insisted they press all efforts against it.[31]

In these weeks of rapidly building tension and nerve-wracking uncertainty, Catherine suddenly recalled the issue of removing large manufactories from Moscow. She asked Viazemskii to look into the matter, in view of the cessation of all work at the manufactories since their closure on 20 August, thinking it might be an opportune moment to pursue the proposal. Viazemskii presented the plan to the Senate, which approved it in principle but took no immediate action. Soon senators and sovereign alike became absorbed in the disturbing reports from Moscow, each more explosive than the last.[32]

On 5 September 1771 the Empress chaired the council session that heard full confirmation of the impending disaster in Moscow: 300–400 persons dying daily, scores of abandoned corpses in the streets, collapse of the local network of quarantines and cordon checkpoints, worsening hunger in the impested metropolis, suspicious outbreaks in Pskov and Novgorod guberniias. They were further dismayed at the urgent request of Eropkin, Saltykov, and the senate departments in Moscow to abolish the practice of compulsory quarantine and to allow free movement in and out of the city. This request, which the Moscow authorities hoped would defuse an imminent upheaval, the Empress and her councilors flatly rejected in the belief that quarantines and cordons were essential to contain the pestilence. They doubted the severity of the hunger crisis, although they authorized the Moscow authorities to restrain victualers from leaving and to commandeer supplies from the hinterland. At the conclusion of this session Catherine announced her intention to send an exhortatory manifesto to calm Muscovite fears. The text was approved at the council session of 12 September, printed and dispatched the next day. It was too late.[33]

Sensing catastrophe, the Empress felt sick herself; "my whole left side aches from head to toe," she confided to Nikita Panin. Final warning of disaster arrived in Saltykov's desperate plea of 12 September to leave the impested metropolis temporarily, until winter set in. Two days later he left town as he deemed the situation out of human control with mortality exceeding 800 per day. Eropkin, left in charge, estimated the daily death toll at 600–900. Furious and frustrated, Catherine decided to send a "trusted personage" to save unruly Moscow from "utter ruin."[34]

Grigorii Orlov seized the opportunity. The Empress accepted his offer, "such a fine and zealous one on his part," she told Voltaire, "not without feelings of acute anxiety over the risks he would run." She knew his eagerness for action, his dissatisfaction at having been kept in Petersburg while his military peers won triumphs on land and sea. That very spring he had impressed her with his cool efficiency in battling the terrible fires in Petersburg. With Catherine's grant of full authority, Orlov and a considerable entourage, including military men, administrators, and doctors, galloped off toward Moscow on the evening of 21 September. The Empress sent with Orlov another manifesto for publication in Moscow that stated her desire to head the antiepidemic campaign in person, a desire that the burden of other business prevented her from fulfilling. Relieved by this resolution of the tremulous confusion, the Empress was thunderstruck two days later at word of rioting in Moscow that had resulted in the murder of Archbishop Amvrosii by a mob, the death of more than one hundred rioters, and the arrest of almost three hundred.[35]

These tragic events shocked, grieved, and outraged the Empress, who could scarcely imagine such bizarre happenings even in benighted Moscow. She saw in the catastrophe a direct effect of Saltykov's untimely desertion of his post, an unforgiveable abandonment of imperial sovereignty in the Empire's second capital. Amvrosii's violent death saddened her all the more because she had appointed him to his post, she admired his vigorous efforts to regulate the city's notoriously lax ecclesiastical establishment, and she applauded his prudent support of the antiplague campaign. To forestall panic from inflammatory rumors, such as live burials and robberies of plague corpses, Catherine authorized publication of an official account of the Moscow riots in the Petersburg gazette on 27 September 1771, an account that she personally edited and which foreign newspapers quickly circulated, just as she intended.[36] An English version recounted the tragedy in these terms:

> The malignant Distemper which has broke out at Moscow, has caused great Disturbance and Confusion among the common People, which is the particular Reason why the Remedies and Industry of the Physicians to stop its Progress have been ineffectual; and by the following Account received from thence, the 4th instant [23 September, old style], the Populace have carried their Excesses to the highest Pitch. Ambrosius, Archbishop of Moscow, perceiving that many Abuses had crept in among the common People, through the Artifice of some designing Persons among them, thought it his Duty to put a Stop to their Progress. These Impostors found Means to collect the major Part of the People to one of the City Gates, where there is an image of the Virgin Mary, and worked on their Credulity, by false Appearance of Religion, to gratify their own lucrative Intentions. The People, even many of the Sick, came in vast Crouds to this Place, and threw Money into a Chest put there for that Purpose, by which Means the Distemper was

spread surprisingly, and the Croud was so great, that many People were trod to Death. To put a Stop to such villainous and impious Practices, the Archbishop sent proper Officers to seal up the Chest; but the blinded Multitude, who looked upon this Action as a Disrespect to, and Disturbance of their Religion, immediately gathered themselves together, and plundered the Archbishop's house; but not finding him there, they went to the Convent, where this worthy Archbishop was killed by them in the most cruel and barbarous Manner. As soon as the Government of Moscow heard that the People were in an Uproar, they sent the Troops against them; by whose Hands many of these Wretches fell victims to their own Credulity, and blind Bigotry. A vast Number of them were taken Prisoners, who will be punished as the Law directs for so great a Trespass.[37]

Selectively accurate, this account reflected Catherine's own perspective on the events, which she later reiterated to Voltaire.[38] She relayed elements of the story with the express intention of minimizing the violence, explaining the plague's persistence by lack of public cooperation with the Moscow authorities, and blaming the riots on vaguely defined criminal instigators. Naturally there was no mention of any threat to Petersburg, nor any indication of the governmental collapse in Moscow or the disagreements between the two capitals on the question of quarantine policy and food supplies. In fact, Catherine herself may not have grasped the significance of these last two issues in provoking the riots; for the violence overshadowed the tense situation of the preceding weeks, and she remained several days behind the swiftly accelerating calamity.

Distraught over the riots, Catherine groped for a constructive outlet for her outrage. One phrase in Eropkin's first report of the riot caught her eye: "In this villainy there were found boyar people [house serfs], merchants, clerks, and factory workers, and especially schismatics."[39] Since his mention of factory workers called to mind the recently discussed proposal to remove large manufactories from Moscow, the very next day she scrawled the following note, designated "secret":

> To Our Senate we hereby give as a rule which it is never to lose sight of, that all big manufactories be taken out of the city of Moscow, and not a single one left except for handicrafts in homes, the methods to begin upon this we leave to the consideration and judgment of the Senate, but certainly one ought to begin upon it.[40]

This extraordinary proposal, though much discussed in governmental circles over the next two years, was scarcely implemented. The plague itself brutally resolved the problem by killing so many bondaged workers at Moscow's large manufactories that the enterprises shrank as a result, so only a few were relocated.[41]

The shock of the "plague riot" perturbed Catherine for several months afterward. At first she endeavored to suppress the news, ordering all letters from Moscow that called it a riot to be burned; but when word leaked out anyway and she was assured that no conspiracy had contrived the brief bout of violence, she attributed it all to Muscovite fanaticism. "The famous Eighteenth Century really has something to boast of here!" she exclaimed to Voltaire after recounting Amvrosii's death. "See how far we have progressed!" And to Alexander Bibikov she sadly confessed on 20 October 1771: "We have spent a month in circumstances like those that Peter the Great lived under for thirty years. He broke through all difficulties with glory; we hope to come out of them with honor." Catherine was learning the heartache of measuring up to the Petrine standard, despite Voltaire's stalwart encouragement.[42]

Confidence in Grigorii Orlov, together with hope for the timely onset of winter, sustained the Empress through these hectic weeks. Though the daily death toll in Moscow still hovered between 600 and 700 in October, Orlov took command of the city from Saltykov at the end of September and quickly revised the antiplague campaign. After arranging to investigate the captive rioters and bury the Archbishop, he cooperated with Dmitrii Volkov and Peter Eropkin to establish a special Commission for the Prevention and Treatment of the Pestilential Infectious Distemper that would coordinate the new policies. The commission represented a Russian adaptation of cameralist advice. Above all, it provided a vehicle for securing public support for reimposition of the policy of compulsory quarantine, the very policy that had sparked the riots. Chaired by Eropkin, the commission comprised medical practitioners, administrators, police officials, and two public representatives— one from the clergy, another from the merchantry. The new body superseded Eropkin's antiplague organization in exercising jurisdiction over all matters of public health. In effect, it temporarily administered Moscow under Orlov's general authority. Beginning on 12 October 1771, the commission met every day in the Kremlin for the next twelve months, presiding over the plague's end. Fortunately for everybody, freezing weather chilled Moscow by 19 October, which fact facilitated the epidemic's natural decline and ended the horror by early December. On 6 November the Empress dispatched Prince Mikhail Volkonskii to replace Saltykov as governor-general of Moscow and to recall Orlov, who oversaw the trial and punishment of the rioters before leaving for Petersburg on 22 November. In all, four persons were executed— two accused of murdering Archbishop Amvrosii, two chosen by lot for abetting the riot—62 others were knouted, their nostrils torn with tongs and then sent to hard labor, whereas 89 only received lashings and 142 were released without corporal punishment. Welcoming Orlov on 4 December, Catherine celebrated his heroism with a gold medal and marble medallion, and she commissioned a set of triumphal gates in his honor at Tsarskoe Selo, where they still stand.[43]

Perplexingly sporadic and relentlessly terrifying, the plague preoccupied Catherine for several months not only because of the devastation it caused in Moscow and the embarrassment it elicited in Petersburg; it also exhibited frightening powers of mobility. For several weeks the Empress and her advisers trembled in apprehension lest the pestilence move northwestward. Extraordinary precautions were therefore taken to protect Petersburg: another cordon of checkpoints on all roads; extra care in handling mail and tax monies; special commissars to inspect the hinterland; a police proclamation of detailed individual precautions; medical inspection of government offices, suspect groups, and occupations such as the personnel of the palace stables. At Tsarskoe Selo the Empress instituted extra security measures under a special officer that included locking the palace and its gardens and forbidding entry without documentation or after sundown. In greater Petersburg medical practitioners inspected all suspicious deaths. None caused serious consternation, however, and the plague scare subsided by the end of October 1771, when Catherine informed her council of the epidemic's rapid decline in Moscow and frosts blanketed Petersburg.[44]

If the Empress felt relief at the plague's apparent abatement, the confusing course of the epidemic left her fearful of its recrudescence in the springtime. By mid-January 1772 the Moscow authorities assured her that the horror had passed and proposed to reopen the government offices after offering public prayers. Just then several cases with ominous symptoms excited Catherine's dread anew, so she cautiously postponed any public celebration of the epidemic's end while maintaining most precautions until the onset of another winter. In August 1772 a brief scare seized Moscow when an old man came down with fever accompanied by dark spots; but Eropkin and the Plague Commission took instant precautions, thoroughly investigated the incident, and the victim recovered within two weeks without incident. While praising such speedy countermeasures, the Empress asked Governor-General Volkonskii to report "more often, so long as doubt remains," and she halted further excavation for the new Kremlin palace from fear that exhalations might "spoil the present autumn air." By mid-November 1772, winter having arrived without any other alarms, Catherine allowed public prayers of thanksgiving in Petersburg and Moscow, where all government offices finally reopened on 1 December 1772, more than fifteen months after the plague had closed them. Quarantine precautions persisted along the Empire's southern borders until most of the army returned from Turkish territory in August 1775, when the Plague Commission was abolished in Moscow and Major Shipov left the Ukraine.[45]

The plague of 1770–1772 proved to be one of the most puzzling crises that Catherine ever encountered, even in retrospect. To be sure, it baffled everyone at the time. Throughout the experience, the Empress felt exasperated at the contradictory, irresolute advice she received from practitioners and administrators alike. Even after the epidemic's apogee she still hesitated to pronounce the fatal word plague to Voltaire and his readers, terming it "an epidemic of various fevers, which are causing numerous fatalities." Voltaire applauded her restraint. "That word used to be the terror of the southern countries," he remarked in discounting the significance of the Archbishop's murder. "Everyone had his tale of woe. The printed lies which pour forth every day about your Empire show very clearly how history used to be written at one time. If the King of Egypt lost a dozen horses, it was said that the Angel of Death had come to slay all the quadrupeds in the land." The Empress was "born to instruct men as well as to govern them," Voltaire exulted, before the horrors of the Plague Riot made him conclude sadly: "The common people will be hard to instruct; but all those who have had

even a modicum of education will benefit more and more from the enlightenment which you spread." Although Catherine privately doubted the efficacy
of the various plague therapies—"all remedies have been found useless,
except those which induced perspiration," she told Voltaire—she vetoed proposals for antiplague inoculations. Still, she hoped to learn from the tragedy
by supporting the expansion of medical education, recruitment of more
foreign practitioners, a permanent network of border quarantines, and several scholarly treatises on the subject in Russian.[46]

Naturally, both the plague and the rioting darkened the Empress's already
somber view of Moscow, the epitome of Russia's traditional backwardness,
ignorance, and mindless violence. "Moscow is a world of its own, not just a
city," she told Voltaire in explanation of the Plague Riot. To guard against
future incitement to violence, Catherine decreed removal of the clapper from
the huge bell in the Kremlin's Alarm Tower. And she took literary revenge
in an anonymously issued satirical comedy, *O, Time!,* supposedly "written
in Yaroslavl during the plague of 1772," that lampooned Muscovite credulity
and rumor-mongering.[47]

The epidemic killed 100,000 persons in Moscow, she reported, probably
meaning the metropolis and its hinterland. A French report later inflated the
toll to 200,000 and blamed the plague on "pestiferous merchandize out of the
warehouses of the Jews." Actually the carnage resulted in several improvements in the old capital that Catherine had long favored: a curtailment of
overpopulation, shrinkage of the size and labor force of large manufactories
(mainly bondaged workers), elimination of thousands of small wooden
houses, removal of cemeteries and slaughterhouses outside the city limits. It
also gave impetus to completion of a new plan for the old capital in 1775,
loosely followed for the next several decades. Yet the plague dealt a blow to
her plans for a new Kremlin palace. The year-long disruption delayed site
preparation several years and, although the cornerstone was finally laid in
July 1773, the Empress suddenly countermanded further construction. Financial strigency certainly governed her decision against the costly project,
but fears of disturbing dormant pestilence in Moscow's subsoil also dissuaded
her. The project was never resumed.[48]

Catherine vividly remembered the plague for years afterward. With the
other alarms of the early 1770s it gave her more gray hair. Her forty-fifth
birthday in April 1774 elicited a pang of rage. "I hate this day like the
plague," she remarked, before joking wryly: "Tell the truth, would it not be
charming to have an Empress who remained fifteen years old all her life?"
And to Bielcke she confided that "it is a most disagreeable thing to grow
old." In 1775, while revisiting Moscow for the first time since 1768, the
Empress devoted considerable attention to matters of public health and epidemic disease in drafting the Guberniia Reform of 1775. In addition, she
endowed a new public hospital and poorhouse in the city in buildings formerly used as a quarantine and a manufactory.[49]

Pestilence did not remain merely a memory. It posed a perennial threat in
the south for the rest of Catherine's reign. It haunted her dreams and consistently complicated conflicts with the Turks. Even so, she chose not to

commemorate the epidemic itself in pictorial form, coldly receiving a proposal for a mural in 1782, although she apparently approved a dual portrait of Aleksei and Grigorii Orlov with an indistinct scene of persons collapsing on Red Square behind the latter. Otherwise she strove to forget the whole terrifying experience in hopes that time would expunge the dreadful blot from the glorious record of her enlightened reign.[50]

7

Plots, Pretenders, Pugachevshchina

From the moment Catherine seized power she periodically had to contend with various plots against her authority. These assumed two disparate guises: conspiracies among the elite (the Guards regiments in particular) that aimed at a new palace revolution, and stirrings among frontier communities in defense of local autonomy against the centralizing policies of the expansive, absolutist state. The worst political nightmare for the Empress, the most threatening prospect, would have fused the two different types of revolt into a regional or mass movement with elite leadership. Behind the gracious, confident façade that Catherine presented in public, she often worried about bizarre plots amid the societal strains generated by the prolonged Polish and Turkish conflicts, unforeseen calamities like the Moscow plague, and renewed speculation about Paul's political prerogatives. In such psychically tense circumstances the Empress suffered occasional bouts of paranoia. "It is not surprising that Russia had many tyrants among her sovereigns," she later philosophized. "The nation is naturally restless, ungrateful, and filled with informers and men who under the pretext of zeal try to turn everything in their path to their own profit."[1] Doubly disturbing was the fact that many incidents invoked the names of Peter III and Paul. Catherine therefore labored to exorcise a ghost and defend her sovereignty against her own son.

Conspiracies among the Guards regiments posed the most direct menace in view of their role in previous coups. Although only a few thousand men strong, the Guards wielded the requisite military muscle, inside political information, and social prestige for a serious bid for power; thus Catherine's persistent patronage of the Guardsmen and her efforts to control them through the Orlovs. Yet jealousy of the Orlovs in itself proffered a potent incentive for conspiracy. In 1769 four officers of the Preobrazhenskii Regiment fell afoul of the Secret Branch for criticizing state policies, alleging that the

Orlovs controlled Catherine, and advocating her overthrow in favor of Paul. The Empress reacted to such talk very seriously. A special court of Nikita Panin, Procurator-General Viazemskii, Policemaster-General Chicherin, and Ivan Elagin sentenced the four to death. But Catherine, as was her wont, altered the verdict: "As God himself delivered these traitors into my hands, it is not for me to judge them, but I leave them the rest of their life for repentance, and decree for them the following: Zhilin and Ozerov, after losing all ranks, noble status, and calling, are sent eternally to Nerchinsk to factory work, but do not keep them together; Stepanov and Panov, after losing ranks and noble status, are sent to live in Kamchatka, where they will be fed by their own labor."[2] These banishments inadvertently created a colony of enterprising anti-Catherine exiles in distant Kamchatka.

Later that year two other young Guardsmen, Il'ia Batiushkov and Ippolit Opochinin, were denounced to the Secret Branch for a similar plot. The Empress sent Senior Procurator Vsevolod Vsevolozhskii, a prominent participant in her coup, to investigate the incident in cooperation with Nikolai Arkharov, subsequently police chief of Moscow and governor of Moscow guberniia, and Senate secretary Ivan Zriakhov, an experienced operative of the Secret Branch. Interrogations and confrontations, threats and promises elicited a tangle of testimony to the effect that the suspects had aspired to install Paul on the throne after slaughtering the Orlovs and confining Catherine in a convent. Batiushkov, a retired cornet who had a history of "hypochondria," defended Peter III's regime and accused the Orlovs of masterminding the coup of 1762, which he had personally witnessed. God would punish the usurpers, he averred, and if the Empress married Grigorii Orlov, then "not only will the troops come out, but all the rabble as well." Vsevolozhskii blamed "the infection of this malice" on provincial idleness and drunkenness. Apparently the conspirators' grudge against the Orlovs, to whom they were remotely related, arose from their sister's dismissal from the court service and from their own lack of promotion. Catherine's mortification over this plot resulted in her singling out Batiushkov for exile in irons to hard labor in Siberia, but his place of exile was kept secret even from his relatives. Furthermore, when a younger sister petitioned Viazemskii for her brother's release in 1782, she got no response. Although Emperor Paul ordered the exile's ranks and freedom restored in December 1796, it is not certain whether Batiushkov was still alive by then.[3]

Also transferred to Kamchatka in 1769 was Ioasaf Baturin, the former officer who had languished in Schlüsselburg Fortress for sixteen years since his abortive plot in favor of Grand Duke Peter Fedorovich. Peter III had declined to release Baturin, but he vetoed a senate verdict consigning him to hard labor at Nerchinsk and granted him better subsistence. Baturin reciprocated by refusing to believe in his benefactor's death. Peter III was not dead, Baturin protested to his guards in 1768; scrutiny of the stars showed he was alive, wandering in other lands, and he would return to Russia soon. Baturin even wrote notes to Peter III and to Catherine, persuading several guards of the truth of his contentions. When the Empress heard about Baturin's ravings, she ordered "the agitator and instigator" exiled to Kamchatka.⁴ At Fort Bol'sheretsk he joined a tiny community of exiles who included Semen Gur'ev and Peter Khrushchev, the Guardsmen-conspirators banished in 1762, and one Turchaninov, a chamber lackey who had been exiled in 1742 for conspiring against Empress Elizabeth. In 1770 the exiles received a flamboyant leader in "Count" Mauritius Augustus de Beniowski.

A young Slovak nobleman from Hungary, Beniowski had embarked on a career of escapades after feuding with his brothers at home. He was one of several foreigners who joined the Polish Confederates in their guerrilla warfare against the Russian-backed King. Captured by the Russians in 1768, he was released on condition that he cease fighting, whereupon he promptly rejoined the fray and fell into Russian clutches again. This time he was interned in Kazan with a Swedish Confederate named Winblod. The two captives contrived to flee Kazan and were about to ship from Petersburg when they were recaptured in November 1769. Exiled to Kamchatka, they joined the other political prisoners at Bol'sheretsk in the summer of 1770.

Beniowski, resolute and resourceful (and increasingly fluent in Russian, almost an early Pan-Slav), quickly won a following among the other exiles right under the nose of the drunken local commandant, Captain Nilov. Among other ploys to win support, the loquacious newcomer alleged that he and Winblod had been banished for their fidelity to Grand Duke Paul, buttressing this claim with a green velvet envelope said to contain a letter from Paul to the Holy Roman Emperor seeking his daughter's hand. By the spring of 1771 the conspirators had concerted wide backing for a revolt against Captain Nilov and his garrison of seventy cossacks. They struck at night, killed Nilov, grabbed the local treasury as well as arms and ammunition, and forced the populace to swear allegiance to "Emperor Paul Petrovich." On 30 April the mutineers struck out for the harbor of Chekavinskoi, where they seized the galliot *St. Peter,* which they prepared for sea under the Emperor's flag. Constituting themselves "the Assembled Company for the name of His Imperial Majesty Paul Petrovich," the mutineers addressed a proclamation to the Senate protesting Paul's illegal deprivation of the throne and roundly denouncing all current government policies in the same spirit as the Guardsmen-conspirators of 1769 combined with the passion of the Polish Confederates.

Indeed, this proclamation rehearsed a whole catalogue of government abuses under Catherine. The destructive war in Poland was decried, for example, as being waged solely for Poniatowski's profit, and the salt and spirits monopolies were scorned as corrupt and burdensome. Ecclesiastical estates had been confiscated from the Church to support care of the illegitimate, it was alleged, whereas legitimate children suffered from callous neglect. Taxes and extraordinary impositions were levied on the infirm and minors; justice was for sale; gold and silver extraction was reserved for court favorites. Meanwhile the common folk wallowed in ignorance, and loyal service went unrewarded. Captain Nilov had provoked the revolt, the mutineers declared, blaming his death on paralysis from drunken terror.

The Empress only learned of these events many months later, by which time Beniowski and company were leaving a trail of international incidents along the Asiatic coast. Driven off the shores of Japan, the mutineers forced a landing on Formosa, losing Panov among others. By September 1771 they reached Macao in south China, where they sold their ship and fell to squabbling. Turchaninov and fourteen others died there from disease. Finally, Beniowski hired two French frigates to take the survivors to France, which they reached in the fall of 1772, with Baturin dying en route. Beniowski and some others entered French service, but several petitioned Catherine for pardon through her envoy in Paris and returned to live as free men in Siberian towns. After other adventures including two trips to revolutionary North America, Beniowski died in 1786 in battle on Madagascar, where he had been supervising French colonization efforts. His was one of the most romantically intrepid personalities of the eighteenth century.[5]

Such intrepidity dismayed Catherine, of course, when it advertised her officials' incompetence, and when it linked an inflammatory political program to analogous aspirations of the Polish Confederates and the explosive issue of Paul's sovereign rights. So suspicious was the Empress of outside incitement of unrest in Russia that in 1772 she had the Secret Branch investigate Maksim Vysotskii, an elder of the Zaporozhian cossacks, for clandestine contacts with Polish Confederates. He was stripped of his ranks and sent to Siberia. A year earlier the Empress read an anonymous letter addressed to "beloved fellow citizens" that excoriated all ten years of her rule as "an unbearable yoke." Blasting the burdens incurred from the "untimely war" and the plague, the anonymous author blamed everything on "the villainous Orlovs, traitors to the fatherland and murderers of the tsar [Peter III] and the prince [Ivan VI]." The Empress suspected that this letter was the work of a retired army colonel who had lodged several complaints against Governor Sievers of Novgorod guberniia, but nothing could be proved. Particularly worrisome was the author's call for a coup: "Already regiments of the Guards and other fighters are ready to save the innocent."[6]

Catherine's suspicions turned into near panic in the spring of 1772 when another plot in favor of Paul was discovered among youthful noncommissioned officers of the Preobrazhenskii Regiment. As before, the conspirators talked in loose and confused terms, but revelation of their plot was tied to her trip to Vyborg on 17–20 July 1772, fanning rumors that she had fled to Finland to save her crown. She was shocked to learn from the interrogations that the conspirators had contemplated incarcerating her in a monastery or, if Paul refused the throne, killing him and her before they announced the execution of the Empress for murdering the Grand Duke. Their other professed motives were equally abhorrent: allegations that Catherine intended to cashier the Guards, complaints about injustice and beatings without cause, vague sympathy for the common folk ("all the rabble are lost"), and fearful envy of Grigorii Orlov, whose departure for the peace negotiations with the Turks was taken as proof of his determination to become prince of Moldavia or even emperor.[7]

In pursuing the investigation Catherine tried to cloak the arrests, which foreign diplomats estimated at 30 to 100, with denials or countertales. She was astonished, most of all, that "such young kids have fallen into such lewd affairs"; one conspirator was twenty-two, two others eighteen and seventeen. Even so, she sanctioned severe punishments. One ringleader was knouted and sent to hard labor at Nerchinsk. Another was driven through the gauntlet twice and then assigned to the ranks in a remote Siberian garrison. Two minors were beaten with sticks in private and transferred to Siberian regiments; an unspecified number of others were lashed and exiled forever to Nerchinsk. As a result of this plot, the Empress considered purging the Guards as a whole, but she never dared challenge that Petrine institution head-on.[8]

At the same time the Empress surmounted the problems of Paul's achievement of political adulthood by arranging his marriage, which undercut the Panins' tutelage. From mid-1772 she devoted extra attention to her son, whom she proclaimed "a jolly lad" to Frau Bielcke, and in late August, barely two weeks after the young king of Sweden seized absolute power, she pointedly lauded Paul's filial devotion and the rarity of such complementary dispositions as his and hers. His eagerness to rule she met partway by allowing him to assist her twice a week as she reviewed reports. Inwardly, however, Catherine harbored constant suspicions about Paul's political pretensions. She deftly impeded his path to power by ceding Holstein to Denmark in the fall of 1773 and by refusing to establish a separate court for him and his bride. How she justified these arrangements to Paul remains little known. Possibly she hinted at a greater political role as he reached full maturity, confident that she could later put him off again. In fact, sometime in the first half of 1774 Paul asked to sit on the council. Catherine flatly refused on grounds that he lacked the maturity necessary to sort out the councilors' frequent disputes and that the council was merely a temporary body that would be abolished once the Turkish war ended. Actually the council lasted the rest of her reign, but Paul never entered it.[9]

Whatever her explanation, her fearful suspicions erupted anew after the fact when she belatedly learned, in late 1773 or early 1774, some particulars of another plot in Paul's favor, this time hatched by a prominent aristocrat and longtime adherent of the Panin party—the Holsteiner diplomat Caspar von Saldern. Although many details of Saldern's intrigues are still unclear, he apparently proposed to Paul and Panin that the Grand Duke assume an equal share in the government after the manner of Maria Theresa and her son Joseph II. The naive Paul supposedly agreed and even signed a paper pledging to heed Saldern's directions, but Panin repudiated the proposal and destroyed the paper to protect his ward, without informing Catherine of the scheme or publicly denouncing its author. The shrewd Panin evidently discerned in Saldern's plot an attempt at entrapment and self-aggrandizement. By compromising Paul and the Panin party, the arrogant Saldern might obtain leverage with the Orlov faction, then in disrepute because of Grigorii's "retirement" as favorite, and with the Empress in hopes of succeeding Panin in charge of foreign affairs. Whatever his motives, his intrigue inadvertently advanced Catherine's temporary rapprochement with the Orlovs and her "emancipation" of Paul from the Panins' tutelage by paralyzing them all with frightful guilt and mutual mistrust. Meanwhile, Saldern skipped the scene in

August 1773, dispatched to Holstein to complete its cession to Denmark. Several months later, when Catherine finally learned what Saldern had attempted, she angrily vowed to have "the wretch tied neck and heels and brought hither" for condemnation. The wily Holsteiner never set foot again in Russia, although someone later pursued posthumous, historical revenge on the Empress by publishing in his name a laudatory biography of Peter III. Yet the discovery of Saldern's pseudo-plot may also have demolished Catherine's brief renewal of confidence in the Orlov faction, clearing the scene for Potemkin's sudden emergence early in 1774.[10]

The various plots on Paul's behalf all involved members of the elite. By contrast, the parallel phenomenon of plots in favor of pretenders—persons who professed to be Peter III or Ivan VI—percolated down the social scale and outward into the borderlands, assuming in the process all the trappings of a myth. The myth took shape quickly. Within weeks of Peter III's death and burial, tales surfaced with claims that he was alive. In 1763, for instance, rumors spoke of Peter III's finding refuge with the Yaik cossacks on the southeastern frontier, and a priest sang prayers for him in the village of Chesnokovka near Ufa in the southern Urals. Actual impostors appeared the very next year. By the end of Catherine's reign, their numbers amounted to at least twenty-four. The Empress's first decade of rule alone witnessed ten instances of pretenders or their avowed agents. All levels of government regarded these incidents with the utmost gravity. Each impostor was quickly arrested, extensively interrogated, and severely punished—usually with the knout, sometimes with branding as well, always with exile.[11]

A profile of the typical pretender gradually emerged. They were invariably common, little people, outsiders: deserters from the army, peasants, petty freeholders, cossacks, or religious schismatics. Their appeals to followers were oral not written, since most were illiterate, and their promises were usually specific and localized. As proof of authenticity they sometimes displayed "tsar's marks," since stigmata were associated with saintly images of sovereignty. Often they sought recognition from local clergymen to legitimatize and publicize their appearances.

Since Peter III's name had become essentially taboo under Catherine's rule, she felt personally affronted by such impostors and sanctioned harsh punishments in most cases to discourage would-be imitators. This policy rested partly on her knowledge of Russian history, for most Russians remembered the disastrous Time of Troubles in which pretenders had figured so prominently in civil conflict. She was particularly wary that literate persons or foreign powers might undertake to sponsor such impostors. Indeed, one false Peter III popped up in faraway Montenegro in 1766 and actually ruled parts of that country for several years until he was assassinated by Turkish agents. Called Stepan Malyi, this man affected holy powers and attracted a large following, widely reported in the European press. He may have heard the legend of Peter III via travels to south Slav colonies in Russia. In the spring of 1768 Catherine alerted the governors along the western borders lest the impostor or his agents seek entry. The next year she dispatched General Yurii Dolgorukov to investigate. Several months of negotiations persuaded Dolgorukov that

Stepan Malyi did not himself claim to be Peter III and that he posed no threat to Russian interests.[12]

Just as Catherine evinced little appreciation of deep religious belief, so she underestimated the potent appeal of the various pretenders, the magic that so many projected on the imaginary virtues of her late husband. In some cases she must have divined actual lunacy, such as the ravings of an inmate of one Moscow monastery in 1766 that Peter III was not dead. With the British press the Empress publicly downplayed the significance of impostors: "This is not a suitable period of time for the revival of counterfeit Demetrius's; nor could they now set capital cities in flames, lay nations waste, and wade through torrents of blood as hertofore."[13] Little did she anticipate just such a revival.

Three instances will illustrate the impostor phenomenon and Catherine's reactions. In 1765 Gavrilo Kremnev, a fugitive soldier of petty freeholder origins, assembled a band of *odnodvortsy* in Voronezh guberniia with promises of freedom to distill spirits and of exemption from recruiting levies and taxes for twelve years. At first he called himself Captain Bogomolov—literally supplicant or pilgrim—but then took the name of Peter III, had his followers swear an oath of fidelity with the schismatics' two-fingered sign of the cross, and named two disciples "General Rumiantsev" and "General Pushkin." Several priests and deacons recognized him as tsar. Apparently the impostor and his band, which took in at least seventy persons, planned a visit to Voronezh from where they would send an announcement of his appearance to Moscow and Petersburg before going there themselves. An emissary sent to Voronezh to hire quarters, however, was arrested and troops captured the impostor. After investigation, the local authorities recommended cutting out his tongue, breaking him on the wheel, and then beheading. This sentence seemed excessive to the Empress, who detected no conspiracy involving significant figures and attributed the affair to drunken ignorance. She therefore altered Kremnev's punishment to knouting in each village he had visited, to branding the letters for "fugitive and impostor" on the forehead, and to dispatching him to perpetual hard labor at Nerchinsk. The clergy implicated in recognizing the impostor were all sentenced to one week in prison on bread and water.[14]

Concurrently another impostor with almost identical characteristics, Peter Chernyshev, was captured not far away in Slobodsko-Ukraina guberniia. Under torture, he and a priest denied any connection with Kremnev, although they had instituted the same rituals as he. They received the same punishments, too. Five years later, when the Nerchinsk authorities reported that Chernyshev and several followers still maintained that he was tsar and had made several attempts at escape, Catherine ordered him publicly lashed, branded, and exiled to the far north, where he died in 1771.[15]

The third incident fused features of the first two with appeals to another key social group—cossacks. A runaway serf and army deserter, Fedot Kazin alias Bogomolov—note the significance of his adopted surname, which Kremnev had also used—proclaimed himself Peter III in the spring of 1772 to a group of Don cossacks resettled at Dubovka on the lower Volga. Captured and imprisoned at Tsaritsyn (present-day Volgograd, formerly Stalingrad), Bogomolov persisted in his imposture even behind bars. "Tsar's marks" on the chest helped convince the guards, a priest, the local citizenry, and several cossacks of his authenticity. A mob sprang him from jail. Nevertheless, he was soon recaptured, other rescue attempts were repulsed, and agitation on his behalf among the Don cossacks was suppressed. On 31 December 1772 he suffered the knout, branding, and torn nostrils before being sent to Siberia. Death on the road did not prevent Bogomolov's story from sparking intense curiosity up and down the Volga. Some of his followers supported the impostor Riabov, a former brigand chief who had escaped from Nerchinsk before he was recaptured near Astrakhan. Others rallied to the most famous impostor of them all—the Don cossack Emel'ian Pugachev.[16]

"Amperator" Peter III

It is doubtful that Catherine had ever heard of Pugachev before the spring of 1773, when she confirmed his sentence to be knouted and exiled to Siberia for attempting to foment new unrest among the rebellious Yaik cossacks. Cossack revolts were more familiar to her from reading and recent events. Indeed, in the first six months of 1772 the Empress had approved the removal and exile of Stepan Efremov, ataman of the Don cossacks, for resisting government attempts to restrict cossack autonomy and levy recruits for the Turkish war. When the cossacks tried to free their ataman from confinement, they suffered severe repression from tsarist troops. Almost the same thing happened at the same time to the Yaik cossacks farther to the east in the steppes north of the Caspian Sea and south of the Ural mountains. Strife among the cossacks culminated in a mutiny in January 1772 that tsarist forces suppressed five months later with brutal reprisals. This was the tense situation that Pugachev, a Don cossack and deserter from the army, happened on late in 1772.

Like previous pretenders, Pugachev came from obscurely humble origins. Not even his date of birth is known. And, though illiterate, he proved to be a wily conspirator, a gifted tactical commander, and a charismatic demagogue. Posing as an itinerant schismatic merchant, Pugachev visited the cossack capital of Yaitsk in November 1772 and, probably inspired by Bogomolov's example, displayed his "tsar's marks" (actually scars from an illness) to several dissident cossacks and proposed to lead them as Peter III in reclaiming their recently lost autonomy. Eager for revenge on tsarist and cossack officials alike, the dissident cossacks concerted plans with the would-be impostor, but they had to postpone action when Pugachev was denounced, captured, and taken off to Kazan in irons. Within six months he contrived to escape and return to the Yaitsk region by August 1773. When the tsarist commander of Yaitsk learned of his whereabouts and moved to nip the plot in the bud, Pugachev and the cossack dissidents hastily proclaimed their revolt in mid-September.[17]

As "Amperator" Peter III, "the sweet-tongued and softhearted Russian tsar," the illiterate pretender started dictating appeals to the cossacks and nearby Kazakh nomads that promised "every freedom" from Catherine's repressive regime and all sorts of specific favors—lands, food, money, arms, freedom of religion, exemption from taxes and recruiting levies. Though the small band of rebels failed to capture Yaitsk, their ranks multiplied daily as they rode upriver taking several tiny outposts without much resistance. By early October 1773, they loosely invested the tsarist headquarters at Orenburg while their agitators carried the pretender's eloquent manifestos northward into the Urals. In less than a month the local cossack revolt escalated into a regional rebellion as the Turkic and Muslim Bashkirs joined the pretender in force, the rebels took over many metalworks in the southern Urals, and Kazakh nomads in the steppes along the Yaik threatened to join the fray.[18]

News of Pugachev's revolt reached Catherine by 14 October 1773, only a few weeks after she had married off Paul and ratified the partition of Poland. The new alarm caught her attention if for no other reason than because it involved a pretender in a recently rebellious, notoriously unstable region. Yet her initial response was simply to dispatch General Vasilii Kar from Petersburg to captain a small punitive expedition of the same sort that had suppressed the cossack mutiny one year earlier. She and her council, with which she discussed the matter on 15 October, considered the revolt a minor repetition of the previous year's troubles on the Yaik and the Don. To counter the impostor's appeals, moreover, the Empress had the council frame an "exhortative manifesto" for distribution only in the revolt-afflicted areas; otherwise the troubles were to be kept strictly secret. Her manifesto denounced Pugachev's imposture as "this madness" and "this godless turmoil among the people," calling for cooperation with General Kar to curb the revolt and to capture "that chief brigand, incendiary, and impostor." Additional precautions were ordered on the Don should the rebels head that way, and the Senate reissued a decree of 1762 warning against belief in any orders not printed by the government. Catherine obviously hoped the frontier ferment would soon dissipate, preoccupied as she then was with high politics at home and abroad.[19]

Imagine her agonized reaction, six weeks later, at the news that General Kar had not only failed to capture the "miscreant" (now reported to have seventy cannon) but had been routed and was fleeing back to Moscow! Even before the Empress met with her council to consider the worsening crisis, she decided to dispatch another punitive expedition under the trustworthy leadership of General Alexander Bibikov. This appointment revealed Catherine's political sagacity, for Bibikov had seen extensive military service in Prussia and Poland and possessed firsthand knowledge of the Urals frontier, where he had investigated industrial unrest in 1764. He enjoyed great public prestige as marshal of the Legislative Commission and associate of the Panin party. Catherine sensed the need for nonmilitary qualities of leadership, contemplating the appointment in a civilian capacity of Senator Dmitrii Volkov, the veteran administrator and former governor of Orenburg. Her councilors blocked Volkov's appointment, however, on grounds that the situation required military action first and unity of command second. They approved substantial forces under Bibikov's command, urging him to enlist the assistance of the provincial nobility against the rebels.[20]

Grigorii Orlov, with whom Catherine privately discussed the appointments of Bibikov and Volkov, speculated aloud in the council that the revolt might have begun in Kazan because rebel letters in Turkic had been captured there. Besides, he doubted that an impostor could appear by accident with so many followers. Similar suspicions inspired the Empress's order that Bibikov make Kazan his headquarters, from where he could investigate the revolt of "this motley crowd which is moved only by seething fanaticism or by political inspiration and darkness." Perhaps absolute rulers are especially prone to conceive of all opposition in terms of conspiracy or dumb credulity. Moreover, the Turkish war naturally incited apprehensions of outside meddling; so did the presence of large numbers of interned Polish Confederates in the guberniias of Kazan and Orenburg. To ferret out the causes of the astonishingly powerful revolt, Catherine empowered Bibikov to establish a temporary local department of the Secret Branch called the Kazan Secret Commission. Three Guards officers, assisted by an experienced secretary of the Secret Branch, were to interrogate captured rebels with "gentleness and moderation or real severity and intimidation" in order to ascertain whether there was "any outside promotion of the miscreant and through whom?"[21]

In connection with Bibikov's expedition Catherine composed a second manifesto against Pugachev. Like that sent with General Kar, her new proclamation was not an empire-wide announcement; it was secretly entrusted to Bibikov for use only in the rebellious region. Printed in the old-fashioned Church letters to lend it weight with the uneducated, Catherine's pronouncement compared Pugachev to the False Dmitrii of the previous century and recounted in lurid phrases the dire consequences of civil strife, pretenders, and foreign invasion. When the council discussed Catherine's text, however, Grigorii Orlov and Zakhar Chernyshev chided her for inflammatory hyperbole. She agreed to soften the language, but balked at a proposal to offer a reward for Pugachev dead or alive, authorizing Bibikov to reward only the pretender's capture alive. Within two more weeks, after further reports confirmed the revolt's explosive expansion, the Empress decided it could no longer be concealed from the public. On 9 December 1773 the council endorsed reintroduction of the local security precautions taken against the plague in 1771, limiting them to the provinces around Orenburg. At the same time, the councilors welcomed Nikita Panin's proposal for a public acknowledgment of the revolt.[22] Recalling the plague crisis, Catherine candidly explained this announcement to Governor Sievers of Novgorod guberniia:

> Two years ago I had a plague in the heart of the state, yet at the present moment on the borders of the kingdom of Kazan I have such a political plague, from which stem many cares. Your esteemed and worthy comrade Reinsdorp [governor of Orenburg] has already been besieged two full months by the crowd of a bandit, who is committing frightful cruelties and ravages. General Bibikov is departing thither with troops, who will pass through your guberniia, in order to curb this distemper

of the eighteenth century, which will bring neither glory nor profit to
Russia. I hope, however, that with God's aid we shall prevail, for this
riffraff has on its side neither order nor art: it is a rabble of miscreants
who have at their head a deceiver as brazen as he is ignorant. Probably
it will all end on the gallows; but what sort of expectation is that for
me, Mr. Governor, who has no love for the gallows? European opinion
will relegate us to the time of Tsar Ivan the Terrible! That is the honor
we must expect from this contemptible escapade. I have ordered that
no further secret be made of this occurrence, because it is beneficial
that substantial people should voice their opinions about it and speak
of it in the desired spirit.[23]

Panin's announcement, which was issued in Catherine's name on 24 December 1773 and proclaimed in Petersburg the next day, followed her usage
in alluding to the False Dmitrii and in deriding "the absurdity and madness
of such a deception, which cannot present the slightest credibility even to a
person who possesses only common human sense." To reassure the public,
the Empress admonished all to scorn the rebels, assured them the threat was
far away, and announced Bibikov's expedition. As compared to the plague
crisis, the government's news blackout about Pugachev lasted less than half
as long. Her quicker reaction sprang from Pugachev's clearer threat to the
social order, keener concern to mobilize armed aid from the provincial nobility, and greater anguish over the protracted Turkish war.

Compounding Catherine's worries in these very months was the visit to
St. Petersburg of Denis Diderot, the famous French philosophe whom she had
patronized from the start of her reign. The single philosophe ever to see the
Empress and her court at first hand, he arrived quite ill, "more dead than
alive," on 28 September 1773 and stayed for five months. On the one hand,
Catherine warmly welcomed the renowned editor of the *Encyclopedia;* he was
inducted into the Russian Academy of Sciences and received free access to
the Empress, who spent many hours in serious conversation with him on all
manner of subjects. The timing of his sojourn, on the other hand, could
hardly have been less propitious. Court politics were still unsettled in the wake
of Paul's marriage and the disintegration of the Panin and the Orlov parties.
The Turkish war refused to be resolved, and a bizarre pretender had just appeared at the head of a frontier revolt. Everything seemed to be conspiring to
tarnish the graven image of Catherine's competence.

If Diderot's brilliant mind lightened Catherine's boredom with the vacuous
Vasil'chikov, his probing queries may have discomforted her inwardly more
than the bruises his gesticulations supposedly inflicted on her knees. To be
sure, his intellect impressed her as "extraordinary." But he knew hardly anything about Russia and showed a disconcerting penchant to raise awkward issues such as the need for a better law of succession, for judicial reform, for
the creation of a third estate. To his query about the effect of servitude on
agriculture, for instance, she responded evasively: "I know of no country
where the worker loves his land and his home more than in Russia." Diderot
even had the temerity to intercede, however half-heartedly, on behalf of French
diplomatic intrigues aimed at mediating the Russo-Turkish war. That pro-

posal Catherine tossed into the fire. Using her womanly wiles and intellectual spirit, the Empress held her own with the garrulous, irrepressible philosophe, who told friends in admiration that she "is the soul of Caesar with all the seductions of Cleopatra" and "the soul of Brutus in the body of Cleopatra."

Whatever Catherine thought of Diderot's proposals at the time, she acted as if his visit were a great triumph. Many years later, with Diderot already in the grave, she grumpily branded his critical notes on her *Great Instruction* "a piece of genuine twaddle in which can be found neither knowledge of circumstances nor prudence nor perspicacity." Yet her more elaborate private repudiation of his ideas, in which she discerned impracticable theories, bespoke a sense of ideals abandoned, of purposes betrayed. She blamed their disagreements on the disparity between abstract theory and actual practice, the role of the thinker versus that of the ruler. At a deeper level it pained her to admit that the two roles—philosopher-sovereign and sovereign-administrator—could not always be successfully combined.[24]

Diderot's disconcerting visit may have been partially saved in Catherine's eyes by closer acquaintance with his companion, Frederick Melchior Grimm, minor philosophe and major literary operator. He and the Empress already knew each other by reputation. Six years older than Catherine, Grimm shared with her many qualities: German origins, French educations, high ambitions, cosmopolitan interests, love of literature, passion for witty conversation. She immediately invited him into her service. He refused, citing his age and his ignorance of Russian and of the Russian court. She protested without pressing further. They quickly discovered an extraordinary rapport that lasted and deepened over twenty years. For the Empress, Grimm functioned as a confidant and all-purpose sounding board in whom she preserved complete trust. While he was in Petersburg they conversed at length almost daily for some six months. When he left for Italy in April 1774 they commenced a correspondence that ended only with her death. He returned to Petersburg in September 1776 for almost a year, during which time the Empress asked him to head a new commission on public schools. Again he declined, although he later agreed to serve as her cultural and artistic agent in Paris for which she awarded him an annual pension of 2,000 rubles; the court at Vienna granted him the title of baron. Their friendship became one of the most important relationships in Catherine's life, particularly from an intellectual and psychological perspective. He was like a doting older brother.[25]

If Bibikov's departure against Pugachev restored some of Catherine's confidence, she watched his counterattack in early 1774 with nervous impatience. An anonymous letter found in the Winter Palace on New Year's Day scalded her already taut nerves. Signed "An Honest Man," this missive apparently condemned Procurator-General Viazemskii for injustice and inefficiency, accusing many other high officials, Grigorii Orlov in particular, of corruption and abuses of power. The Empress was furious. She ordered additional security at court and had the police announce that the "Honest Man" should substantiate his charges in person to Prince Golitsyn, marshal of the court. Nobody came forward, so the public executioner burned the letter in front of the Senate on 11 January 1774. That same day the Senate published a manifesto branding the anonymous denouncer a "real good-for-nothing filled with depraved insolence" and directing that such letters be publicly incinerated unopened.[26]

Concerning Catherine's suspicions of foreign or other highly placed conspirators behind the revolt, she received reassurance from Bibikov that "the suspicion of foreigners is completely unfounded." Even so, when Voltaire facetiously linked "Monsieur Pugachev" to "this farce . . . put on by the chevalier de Tott," a French soldier of fortune in Ottoman service, Catherine curtly denied the connection. Through Voltaire and other foreign correspondents the Empress strove to puncture inflated stories in the European press and advertise her confidence. To Voltaire she attributed "this freakish event" to backwoods superstition, ignorance, and idleness, insisting that the Orenburg region "is inhabited by all the good-for-nothings of whom Russia has thought fit to rid herself over the past forty years, rather in the same spirit in which the American colonies have been populated." Worried though she was by the revolt's expansive explosion, the Empress privately regretted the employment of torture in the investigation. "In twelve years under my eyes the Secret Branch has not scourged a single person during the interrogations," she informed Bibikov, "and yet every matter was sorted out entirely, and always more came out than we desired to know." So, when Catherine informed Frau Bielcke of Bibikov's victorious advance, she airily dismissed talk of his brutal treatment of captured rebels: "Since you like hangings so much, I can tell you that four or five unfortunates have already been hanged; such rare punishments produce a thousand times more effect on us here than on those where hangings happen every day." Russian diplomatic representatives abroad propagated similarly restrained or dismissive accounts.[27]

The Empress likewise allowed the two official gazettes, starting in late February 1774, to print accounts of Bibikov's triumphs over the rebels. She also commissioned an historical account of pretenders in Russia and elsewhere from the court historiographer, Prince Mikhail Shcherbatov. Although the aristocratic scholar found fewer foreign examples than Catherine might have wished, he executed her summons in six weeks in an anonymously published book of 200 pages. These efforts were the Empress's last public thrusts at Pugachev for several months, however, because she thought the revolt had been largely throttled by his defeats in March and early April 1774 which broke the siege of Orenburg and scattered the besiegers. For the next three months Catherine turned her gaze to Rumiantsev's offensive on the Danube. Bibikov's sudden death from fever on 9 April dismayed her, of course, but she assumed his commanders could easily complete the final mopping-up operations. Hourly expecting Pugachev's capture, she anticipated no further trouble.[28]

Investigation and Rebel Resurgence

With the revolt all but over, Catherine's interest sharpened in the investigation of its causes. To speed the processing of the thousands of rebels captured at Orenburg, she transferred several members of the Kazan Secret Commission to a new Orenburg Secret Commission, empowering the latter to look into all dimensions of the revolt—motives, plans, intentions, contacts, instigators—and to determine Pugachev's personal role. A rebel manifesto in German startled the Empress, hinting as it did at the involvement of educated persons, presumably noblemen or foreigners. She particularly feared upper-class incitement or leadership of mass discontent—what later generations would call "the Pugachevs from the universities"—and ordered the Kazan Secret Commission to find the author of the manifesto. The paper proved to be not an original product but merely a translation of another rebel manifesto done by Mikhail Shvanovich, a young grenadier officer captured by the rebels when they defeated General Kar.[29]

By 21 May 1774 the Orenburg Secret Commission compiled a report in answer to Catherine's queries which one member, Captain Savva Mavrin, supplemented with his own conclusions. Both reports played down the possibility of conspiracy or foreign meddling, although they admitted that the circumstances of Pugachev's escape from prison in Kazan were still unclarified and that the Bashkirs had always revolted when Russia was at war with the Turks. Both blamed the revolt on Pugachev's shrewd exploitation of the dissension among the Yaik cossacks, his appeals to other discontented groups such as the Bashkirs and the peasants assigned to the Urals metalworks, and his cunning capacity to capitalize on the local authorities' spineless inaction and vacillation. Pugachev's personal role received ambivalent assessment. The investigators depicted him as crude and uneducated, and thus by implication not a person who could have masterminded a massive revolt. Yet they also cautioned that all evidence showed him to be perceptive, crafty, resourceful, and persuasive—fully capable of tapping diverse discontents. Captain Mavrin in particular attributed greater initiative to Pugachev than to the rebellious Yaik cossacks, portraying the impostor as a dangerous man in search of circumstances to exploit. These reports comforted Catherine. Mavrin's reflections impressed her especially, and she began considering various reforms to ameliorate some of the problems dramatized by the revolt. Furthermore, to coordinate the work of the two secret commissions and to supervise reforms on the spot, she appointed Potemkin's cousin, Pavel Potemkin, in charge of both commissions on 11 June. He arrived in Kazan as Catherine's personal representative on 9 July 1774, three days before Pugachev stormed the city with a horde of 20,000.[30]

After sacking and burning most of Kazan, Pugachev's motley legions were defeated three times within four days before the pretender escaped with a handful of followers, forded the Volga, and headed southwestward, destination unknown. Pugachev's sudden resurgence and surprise swing to the northwest appalled Catherine when she heard the news in early July. She immediately discharged General Fedor Shcherbatov, who had succeeded Bibikov in general command of antirebel operations, in favor of General Peter Golitsyn, the vice-chancellor's younger brother. Through Potemkin she brusquely informed Count Chernyshev of her exasperation that "a crude brigand like Pugachev is still able to recoup his losses from our generals." She designated three regiments to reinforce Governor-General Volkonskii in Moscow and, to forestall panic, she instructed the Petersburg postmaster on 9 July to withhold all mail to the interior for three days. Still, at the council session of 14 July the Empress asserted her confidence in General Golitsyn and her conviction that Rumiantsev's victories on the Danube had brought Russia to the brink of peace.[31]

Amid such hopes and fears the news of the Kazan disaster packed a potent punch when it struck St. Petersburg by 21 July, two days before Rumiantsev's courier confirmed the peace with the Turks. Catherine convened her council at Peterhof that Monday morning, all the more stunned by Pugachev's triumphal revisit to Kazan inasmuch as she did not yet know of his multiple defeats there. The councilors recommended rushing four regiments with artillery to Moscow post-haste and recruiting cavalry squadrons from the Moscow nobility. They also agreed to send a "distinguished personage" to Kazan with the full powers that Bibikov had exercised. "Extremely shaken," Catherine broke into the deliberations by declaring her intention to leave immediately for Moscow in order to calm the situation by her presence. Her declaration shocked the councilors into silence. Some probably remembered the Empress's similar resolution amid the Moscow plague three years earlier.

Catherine then asked Nikita Panin, senior member of the council, for his opinion. Panin opposed her intention as unnecessarily provocative. But she insisted that it would have beneficial effects, with Potemkin endorsing her view. Grigorii Orlov begged off, lamenting that he had slept badly and had no ideas. Kirill Razumovskii and both Golitsyns sat silently. Zakhar Chernyshev, already feeling his lame-duck status in the War Collegium, muttered that the Empress's plan would be harmful and then enumerated which regiments were going to Moscow. Since nobody forced the issue, the councilors adjourned in the hope that Rumiantsev's courier would soon bring news of the expected peace. That same afternoon, however, Nikita Panin drew Potemkin aside and impressed him with the gravity of the crisis. He offered to lead the campaign against Pugachev or to answer for the dispatch of his brother the general, then in sullen retirement near Moscow. After Potemkin sounded Catherine of the subject, Nikita Panin discussed it with her at length and won her agreement to approach his brother.

The Empress knew Peter Panin's abilities perfectly well. Still, she was reluctant to seek his aid in the renewed crisis because of her doubts about his political reliability, notably his support for Paul's right to rule. Miffed at his abrupt retirement after the capture of Bender in 1770, Catherine resented his outspoken criticism of government policies and had authorized surveillance over "the insolent windbag" in the fall of 1773. Besides, appointing Peter Panin to such a sensitive post offended her pride, as she confessed to Potemkin: "before the whole world, frightened of Pugachev, I commend and elevate above all mortals in the Empire a prime big-mouth and my personal insulter." In this instance Catherine the practical politician won over Catherine the insulted sovereign.[32]

More flexible than ever in the face of adversity, and buoyed by her victory over the Turks, the Empress hedged Panin's appointment with political safe-guards. She confined his authority to the regions directly affected by the re-volt, directing him to cooperate with Governor-General Volkonskii in the defense of greater Moscow. Both secret commissions remained under her direct supervision. And as Panin's second in command she named General Suvorov, at Potemkin's suggestion, instead of the Panins' choice of their nephew General Repnin, whose pride was later mollified by his appointment to deliver the peace ratification to Constantinople in 1775–76. Thus Cath-erine rapidly recovered from her momentary panic, concerted new coun-termeasures under fresh operational leadership, and carefully followed her armies' pursuit of Pugachev southward throughout August 1774.

If her fears for Moscow subsided by mid-August, she remained so eager to shorten "this vile comedy" that when a mysterious rebel envoy, sup-posedly sent by dissident cossacks, approached Grigorii Orlov with a pro-posal to hand over Pugachev for 34,000 rubles, she assigned an officer to arrange the transaction. Whatever her misgivings about the impromptu in-termediary, she found "this sum a moderate one in order to buy peace among the people." (The emissary turned out to be an impostor in his own right who tried to abscond with the ransom, but he was eventually caught, knouted, and exiled to hard labor in irons.) At the same time word reached the Empress at Tsarskoe Selo about supposed rebel emissaries sent to mur-der her, Paul, and his bride. Even though she predicted to Potemkin that "the mountain will give birth to a mouse" (a favorite quotation), she or-dered a search for "these scape-graces" in the immediate vicinity. Nobody was found.[33]

Catherine spent most of August at Tsarskoe Selo fretfully following Puga-chev's destructive rampage—half flight, half invasion—through the Volga towns and villages before he suffered final defeat south of Tsaritsyn on 25 August 1774. After fleeing across the Volga into the steppe, the cossack remnant of his forces betrayed the impostor to save their own necks and handed him over to Captain Mavrin at Yaitsk on 15 September 1774, almost exactly a year since they had launched the revolt in the same place.

Either Voltaire was unaware of Catherine's absorption in "the Marquis de Pugachov," or he thought to lift her spirits by protesting the lapse in their correspondence, which he jokingly attributed to his own disgrace and her fickleness. Amused as well as irritated, the Empress denied any neglect of her venerable mentor, admitted that Pugachev had occupied her undivided attention for the past six weeks, and chided Voltaire for ignoring her "good peace with the Turks, your enemies and mine." By the end of August she was already expecting "something decisive" because she had not heard from General Panin for ten days, and since "bad news travels faster than good, I am hoping for something good, and best of all would be if they had tied up the enemy." Pugachev's capture became known to her by 26 September. "We are filled with joy that the miscreant has come to an end," Potemkin wrote General Panin. Catherine's joy was clouded, though, by her conviction that "this vile story" had set back Russia in European opinion by two or three hundred years. That was no laughing matter for the history-minded, glory-seeking Empress. In Pugachev she discerned an even darker blot than the Moscow plague on her record of enlightened rule.[34]

Whatever verdict posterity might pass on Pugachev, the Empress was determined to resolve her own doubts about the rebellion by a thorough investigation. If Voltaire playfully proposed to ask Pugachev—"Sir, are you master or servant? I do not ask who employs you, but simply whether you are employed"—Catherine wished to know all the facts of his employment and, above all, the identity of his employers. She still could not believe that a crude cossack had instigated the revolt alone. Thus she had the pretender and his closest cohorts brought to Moscow on 4 November 1774 for the final inquiry, which was conducted by Governor-General Volkonskii and General Pavel Potemkin in cooperation with the Secret Branch's notorious "knout-wielder"—Senate Secretary Stepan Sheshkovskii. These three interrogators grilled Pugachev nonstop for a month, confronted him with the contradictory testimony of his cohorts and other eyewitnesses, and checked out Catherine's many queries and other leads. From Petersburg the Empress carefully monitored the proceedings.[35]

With Pugachev in custody, Catherine eagerly anticipated full answers to her many questions about the pretender and the revolt. She was already planning a lengthy visit to Moscow for the peace celebrations and therefore wished the whole embarrassing business to be settled before her arrival. Pugachev's punishment must not upstage her own visit. The pretender's motives and character intrigued her, but she had no desire to see him in person alive or dead. Even before the final interrogations in Moscow the Empress concluded that "there was never a single foreign person close to Pugachev." To Voltaire (and for foreign consumption in general) she was still more positive: "So far there is no shred of evidence that he was the tool of any outside power or intelligence, or under anyone's influence. It is to be supposed that Monsieur Pugachev is the master-brigand, and not a servant." Nevertheless, certain odd details excited lingering trepidation. Thus Catherine directed the Moscow investigators to ask Pugachev about a Holstein banner captured from rebels near Tsaritsyn. She also inquired whether the pretender had coined money, who had painted his portrait, and what medals he had granted his followers.[36]

Pugachev's testimony settled all these queries to Catherine's satisfaction. The Holstein banner, he said, had been found in a trunk in the town of Dubovka. Although he did not know who had painted his likeness, appropriately executed over a portrait of the Empress seized from some government office, the artist proved to be an Old Believer icon-painter. Captured silversmiths had made about twenty medals for him, but he denied minting any coins and could not remember who had fashioned a silver seal for him. The investigators pursued several leads linking Pugachev to religious schismatics, but they could never establish any firm ties, and the pretender himself denied ever embracing the Old Belief. Pressed by the Empress to complete the inquiry, Governor-General Volkonskii and General Potemkin compiled their final report on 5 December 1774. Their report condemned Pugachev

Princess Sophia of Anhalt-Zerbst in 1740, as depicted by Rosina Lischevska. This early portrait suggests a precocious Catherine, who is being prepared for an advantageous marriage.

Grand Duchess Catherine about 1760 in a painting by Rotari. In comparison with the portrait of 1740, Catherine has certainly matured in face and figure and determination.

ELISABETA PRIMA,
Imperatrix et Autocratrix
Omnium Russiarum.

Elizabeth I, Empress and Autocratrix of All the Russias, in an etching by E. Chemesov, presumably from early in her reign, 1741 to 1761. Though Catherine privately criticized Elizabeth's erratic rulership and capriciousness, she owed her a great deal and learned much about Russian court politics and customs from her.

Emperor Peter III in 1762 by A. Antropov. This portrait shows Catherine's husband at the peak of his career, which lasted barely six months before he was overthrown by her partisans and soon murdered.

Empress Catherine II astride Brilliant on 29 June 1762, the day of her triumph over Peter III at Peterhof, by Vigilius Ericksen, 1765. A huge copy of this picture, seven feet square, still decorates the east wall of the Great Hall at Peterhof.

Catherine II at the time of her coronation in September 1762, by Torelli. Her face seems to show the pressures already starting to weigh on the new sovereign.

Ivan Antonovich (Ivan VI) in 1741, by I. Leopold. A great grandson of Peter the Great's half-brother Ivan, this boy reigned briefly under his mother's regency in 1740–41 until he was overthrown and imprisoned by Elizabeth. He grew up in captivity, solitary most of the time, and was killed by his guards at Schlüsselburg Fortress in July 1764 after Vasilii Mirovich attempted to free him while Catherine was on her trip to Estland and Livland. His strange death was added to the accusations that portrayed Catherine as a murderous usurper.

Jean-Baptiste Le Prince, *The Public Bath,* 1764. This titillating drawing, in combination with Abbé Jean Chappe d'Auteroche's critical remarks about Russian popular mores, provoked Catherine into publishing *The Antidote* anonymously in 1770 with this comment: "And here, good reader, you will find a most indecent print which the *Abbé* intends should be supposed to describe a Russian *bania,* but which in reality far more resembles a bacchanal."

Coat of arms of Alexander Markov, renamed Ospennyi and ennobled in 1769 for donating the inoculant for Catherine's inoculation against smallpox.

Medal commemorating Catherine's inoculation for smallpox in 1768. One side reads: "By the Grace of God, Catherine II, Empress and Autocratrix of All the Russias"; the other depicts Hygeia, the Greek goddess of health, sheltering three girls and four boys, under the heading "For the Inoculation of Smallpox."

Medal commemorating Grigorii Orlov's heroism against the Moscow plague. On one side, his bust is surrounded by the inscription: "Count Grigorii Grigor'evich Orlov, Prince of the Roman Empire." The obverse side shows him mounted on horseback, galloping into the abyss like the Roman hero Curtius. The upper legend proclaims: "Russia Has Such Sons Within Herself"; the lower explains: "For the Saving of Moscow from the Distemper in the Year 1771."

The Moscow mob assaulting Archbishop Amvrosii on 16 September 1771, in a print of unknown origin. The violent death of Amvrosii, whom Catherine had appointed Archbishop of Moscow in 1768 and greatly admired, stunned and outraged the Empress, compounding her animus against the old capital.

The Orlov or Gatchina Gates at Tsarskoe Selo, built by Antonio Rinaldi between 1777 and 1782 to celebrate Grigorii Orlov's bravery in conquering the Moscow plague of 1771. (Photograph by the author in 1971.)

Portrait of Aleksei and Grigorii Orlov by Jean Louis de Veilly, about 1775, showing two stalwarts of Catherine's reign with scenes of the Battle of Chesme in the left background and the Moscow plague in the right.

Portrait of Pugachev at the start of his revolt in 1773, as portrayed by an Old Believer icon painter who used a portrait of Catherine II as his canvas. This picture excited her curiosity and apprehension because it suggested a broader conspiracy than the violent revolt seemed to convey at the time. The original now hangs in the State Historical Museum in Moscow.

"Princess Tarakanova" in her death throes in a flooded casemate of the Peter and Paul Fortress in St. Petersburg. Painting of an imaginary scene by K. D. Flavitskii around 1864. The true identity of this impostor has yet to be established.

Elizabeth Chudleigh, Duchess of Kingston, as Iphigenia at the Venetian ambassador's masquerade in London in 1749.

The Duchess of Kingston in the dress in which she was presented to Catherine at Tsarskoe Selo in September 1777. Her flamboyant personality may have been confused with the legend of "Princess Tarakanova."

Prince Grigorii Potemkin (1739–1791), Catherine's longtime favorite and probably her secret spouse, by Lampi the Elder.

Count Peter Zavadov-skii (c. 1739–1812), shortime favorite and longtime high official, in a painting by F. G. Slezentsov, c. 1797.

Statue of Catherine by an unknown sculptor at Lialichi, formerly Ekaterinindar, Zavadovskii's opulent estate near Chernigov in the Ukraine.

Prince Platon Zubov (1767–1822), Catherine's final favorite, in a print of unknown origin. Gossip derided him as her "Platonic" lover.

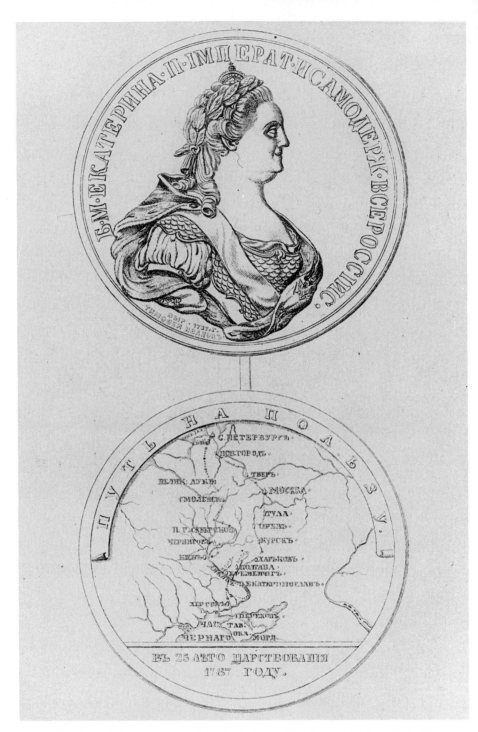

The official medal commemorating Catherine's Tauride Tour in 1787. Her bust portrait is encircled by her monogram. The map of the route is bordered by the legend, "The Way to Benefit," and below it, "In the 25th Year of the Reign, the Year 1787."

Your Sublime Highness, is to blame I Fear,
Thus forcibly to Enter My Fron....tier,
In Rearing Rampant, on each Slight pretence,
You Risk the Blush, which Shame Gives Impotence;
My Shield is tested, and Approved as Staunch.

THE CHRISTIAN AMAZON, with her INVINCIBLE TARGET,
Alias, the Focus of, Genial Rays, or
Dian of the Rushes, to much for 300,000, Infidels.
Published as the Act directs Oct.' 24.'' 1787, by J. Langford N.° 7 Middle Row Holborn.

By Every Artist famous in the ....Rennoch,
Should then each Member in your Salique Land,
Rise up Against My Power, and make ....a Stand.
They Shall yield Victory, to this potent Hand.
Creek

"The Christian Amazon, with Her Invincible Target," 24 October 1787, anonymous satirical engraving. Such attacks heralded the more scurrilous satirical prints released at the time of the Ochakov Crisis in 1791. (See discussion on pp. 265–266.)

"Amsterdam in a Dam'd Predicament—or—The Last Scene of the Republican Pantomime," by James Gillray, 1 November 1787. This satirical drawing focused on the political upheaval in the Netherlands, where the pro-French Patriots revolted against the Stadholder, who was supported by his brother-in-law, King Frederick William II of Prussia, with British backing. Catherine is shown in the upper left box shaking her fist at the Sultan, while her ally Joseph II of Austria fondles her breast. (See discussion on p. 266.)

"An Imperial Stride!" by Thomas Rowlandson, the English caricaturist, published on 12 April 1791. (See discussion on p. 289.)

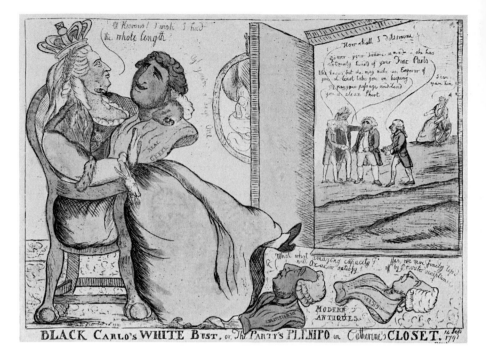

"Black Carlo's White Bust, or The Party's Plenipo in Catherine's Closet," by Joseph Dent, 14 September 1791. A satire on Pitt's anti-Russian foreign policy and Catherine's cultivation of opposition leader Charles James Fox, whose bust she placed in her sculpture gallery. On the wall is a peculiar oval portrait hanging upside down, possibly an image of her murdered husband. (See discussion on p. 289.)

"The Balance of Power—or—'The Posterity of the Immortal Chatham, Turn'd Posture Master'," by James Gillray, 21 April 1791. This engraving satirizes Pitt's foreign policy with snide remarks on Catherine's lascivious reputation. The phrase "posture master" came from Sheridan's speech in Parliament on 15 April 1791 attacking the Anglo-Prussian ultimatum to Russia. (See discussion on p. 289.)

Jeanne Moreau as Catherine in *Great Catherine* (1967), a film adaptation and elaboration of Shaw's playlet of 1913.

Marlene Dietrich as Grand Duchess Catherine in *The Scarlet Empress* (1934), Josef von Sternberg's film.

Mae West in *Catherine Was Great* (1944), a Mike Todd production that ran for six months on Broadway before a brief road tour.

Jayne Meadows Allen as Catherine the Great in a segment of the television series "Meeting of Minds" (1980). Depicted here is Catherine's flamboyant entrance preceded by two guardsmen.

Jayne Meadows Allen and Steve Allen with guests Oliver Cromwell and Daniel O'Connell. (See discussion on pp. 339–340.)

as unrepentant and deserving of the cruelest punishment, but they traced the revolt less to any individual than to the rebellious Yaik cossacks as a whole, with the evident implication that the cossack community must be radically transformed.[37]

Concerned to dissociate herself publicly from the grim details of Pugachev's trial and execution, the Empress empowered the Senate to pronounce the sentence, as announced in her manifesto of 20 December 1774. Privately, however, she sent Procurator-General Viazemskii to Moscow with secret instructions to end the affair as quickly and cleanly as possible. She specifically vetoed any torture at the executions, which she thought should include no more than three or four of the worst offenders. "Please help to inspire everyone with moderation both in the number and in the punishment of the criminals," she wrote Volkonskii. "The opposite will be regrettable to my love for humanity. We do not have to be clever to deal with barbarians."[38]

In Moscow for Pugachev's trial and punishment, Viazemskii faced a double challenge in fulfilling Catherine's orders. First, he hastened to get through the trial as quickly as possible, fearful that the hapless pretender might die before he could be sentenced. Second, he strove to limit the number and severity of death sentences in the heatedly vengeful local atmosphere. To avoid public pressure and unseemly outcries, Viazemskii conducted the trial secretly in the Kremlin on 30–31 December. Pugachev, who had become very weak from confinement and constant questioning, was brought before the court on the second day. On entering the trial chamber, the pretender fell to his knees, acknowledged all his crimes, and proclaimed his repentance. He was then led out, and the judges considered the sentences. At first they agreed he should be quartered and then beheaded. But when they passed the same sentence on one of his cohorts, several judges suddenly protested the first sentence as too lenient. "So therefore they wanted to break Pugachev on the wheel," Viazemskii wrote Catherine, "in order thereby to distinguish him from the rest." In response the Procurator-General persuaded the court to leave Pugachev's punishment as it stood. But he conceded that the pretender's severed head and limbs would be placed on public display in the four corners of Moscow before they were burned. After passing four more death sentences, the judges reluctantly agreed to commute still others to severe corporal punishments. Even so, Viazemskii knew the Empress would not countenance the public spectacle of a man being quartered alive. He therefore arranged, in consultation with the Moscow police, to have the executioner "accidentally" alter the sentence by beheading Pugachev first and later cutting off his hands and feet.[39]

Catherine accepted the necessity of this arrangement in the circumstances. Though saddened at the prospect, her outlook betrayed no sympathy for Pugachev, who, she uncharitably informed Voltaire, "lived a villain and will die a coward. He showed himself so timorous in prison that he had to be carefully prepared for sentencing, lest he die of fright on the spot." To her satisfaction, the executions proceeded without incident on 10 January 1775 before a huge throng on Bolotnaia Square near the center of Moscow. Two months later the Empress privately apprised Frau Bielcke of her part in the arrangements. In Russia, by contrast, she never publicly admitted the act, preferring to forget the entire episode.[40]

A few days after Catherine received confirmation of Pugachev's demise she set out for Moscow. There she initiated additional steps designed to obliterate all traces of the late rebellion. The Yaik cossacks, for example, were renamed the Ural cossacks, and their capital and the river were renamed Ural'sk and the Ural, respectively—names they preserve to this day. On the Don she decreed that Pugachev's home village be razed, relocated across the river, and renamed Potemkinskaia; she also stipulated that the pretender's brother, Dementii, who had not been involved in the revolt, cease using his family name. Furthermore, in a decree of 17 March 1775 the Empress issued a general pardon for all who had participated "in the internal mutiny, uprising, unrest and disarray of the years 1773 and 1774," consigning "all that has passed to eternal oblivion and profound silence." Among the people at large, memories of Pugachev lived on to inspire other pretenders—more than a dozen in the next twenty years. And a new term entered the Russian vocabulary (but not Catherine's): *Pugachevshchina*— the dark deeds of Pugachev, a synonym for mindless anarchy and bloody violence.[41]

"A Notorious Woman" and Other Scares

In the same weeks that Catherine began to relax after Pugachev's final defeat and capture, she got word of a new kind of pretender: a woman who claimed the throne as Elizabeth's daughter and who, in the company of prominent Polish rebels and French diplomatic agents, was said to be in touch with Pugachev and the Turks as she travelled through southern Europe. Aleksei Orlov, in Livorno with the Russian fleet, heard about her escapades in several Italian cities. Perturbed and perplexed by the pretender's claims, the wily Orlov sent an officer to interview her and obtained a copy of a letter she had written to British envoy Hamilton, which he forwarded to Catherine with the suggestion that he entice the "madwoman" on board a Russian ship for dispatch to Petersburg. The Empress approved Orlov's plan, noting that Nikita Panin had received a similar letter from the pretender. Moreover, since she knew the woman had visited Ragusa (present-day Dubrovnik) in July 1774 with Prince Radziwill, a leading emigré Polish Confederate, she ordered Orlov to send a ship for her. If the Ragusans did not heed his threats to surrender the pretender, "one can toss a few bombs into the town," although she preferred a quieter solution.[42]

Orlov humored the pretender, lent her money, professed love for her, invited her to review his fleet, and then arrested her when she ventured aboard. Admiral Greig delivered her and her entourage—two Polish aides and six Italian servants—to Petersburg in May 1775 while Catherine was away at Moscow. As in the case of Pugachev, so with this pretender, too, the Empress supervised the interrogation from a distance. She delegated Prince Alexander Golitsyn, the governor-general of Petersburg, to interview the pretender in isolated quarters in the Peter and Paul Fortress, whither she was clandestinely delivered at two o'clock in the morning of 26 May. Prince Golitsyn began politely interrogating her later that day in French, for she spoke no Russian. She impressed him as sensitive and temperamental, knowledgeable and perceptive, widely travelled and gifted in languages, slender and stately with dark hair, gray eyes, and a long, Italianate nose. Her romantic appearance was enhanced by a consumptive cough that occasionally brought up blood. Cross-examination of her entourage convinced Golitsyn that they all believed she was a princess of some sort. Although she denied ever calling herself Elizabeth's daughter, she recounted a convoluted tale of mysterious travels, strange acquaintances, and constant concern about money from Holstein through Russia to Persia and back to Prussia, England, France, and Italy. "The story of her life is filled with fantastic affairs and rather resembles fairy tales," Golitsyn concluded in perplexity. A month later Golitsyn allowed her to write the Empress, in hopes that she might reveal something new.[43] But her plea for a personal interview enraged Catherine, who angrily instructed Golitsyn:

> Send someone to tell the notorious woman that if she wishes to lighten her petty fate, then she should cease playing the comedy which she has continued even in her last letters, and even extended her insolence to the point of signing herself as Elizabeth; order her informed in addition that nobody entertains the least doubt that she is an adventuress, and that you therefore advise her that she should moderate her tone and wholeheartedly confess who forced her to play this role, and where she was born, and were these tricks invented long ago. Meet with her and tell her quite seriously that she should come to her senses. Here is a rank scoundrel! The insolence of her letter to me exceeds all expectations, it seems, and I begin to think she is not fully sane.[44]

At the same time Procurator-General Viazemskii sent word that the Empress had just learned from the British envoy that the pretender was the daughter of a Polish tavernkeeper. Despite Golitsyn's exhortations, threats of eternal imprisonment, physical and psychological pressures on the prisoner, who was kept in isolation and given less food and creature comforts, she steadfastly refused to repent. "The different fairy tales repeated by her show clearly," Golitsyn informed Catherine, "that she is a person perfidious, lying, shameless, evil and without conscience." By late October her health was failing fast. Citing medical testimony that her condition was incurable and that she could not live long, Golitsyn denied any mistreatment and forewarned Catherine of the prisoner's natural death, which followed on 4 December 1775 "from the indicated illness by God's will." Her body was hastily buried on the grounds and the guards sworn to perpetual secrecy about the entire affair.[45]

Nobody has yet determined who the "notorious woman" was. Her obscurity and notoriety were subsequently overshadowed by a romantic legend of martyrdom, expressed most poignantly in K. D. Flavitskii's famous painting of 1864 depicting "Princess Tarakanova" in her death throes in a flooded rat-infested casemate. Other tales insisted that she had given birth to a son before her own death, which had allegedly stunned a conscience-stricken Aleksei Orlov. Numerous novels were written about her exotic career. Posterity compounded the mystery by awarding the impostor the strange name of Tarakanova, literally "of the cockroaches," evidently a corruption of Daraganova (Sof'ia Daraganova had served as a maid of honor at court in 1763 before her marriage to Colonel Prince Khavanskii, but she had no known connection to any impostor).[46]

The romantic legend arose, we may speculate, from a peculiar conflation of dramatic events and personalities. The catastrophic Petersburg flood of 10 September 1777—fourteen feet above the Neva's normal level—appalled the Empress by its destructive fury and chastened her enthusiasm for the Petrine capital's location and topography. Barely a week earlier at Tsarskoe Selo she had received the flamboyant Elizabeth Chudleigh, Duchess of Kingston (1720–1788), an aging glamor girl renowned for irregular marriages, reckless expenditures, wide travels, and daring dress. Intrigued by her reputation, Catherine paid for the repair of her flood-damaged yacht, but soon tired of the visitor, who had bought an estate in Livonia and became enmeshed in various scandals during four visits to Russia. Though Kingston's empty life could be seen as a parody of Catherine's in most respects, her appearance unleashed a flood of gossip that may have sprouted into the "Princess Tarakanova" legend.[47]

Several lesser scares punctuated Catherine's year-long sojourn in Moscow in 1775. A letter composed by one Ivan Smirnov, a crazy clergyman, exhorted people not to believe in Pugachev's death. Another anonymous missive, addressed to Governor-General Volkonskii, warned of a conspiracy of 320 armed nobles to redress grievances against the Senate, implicating the Guards regiments and five dignitaries. These accusations seemed "mystification" to the Empress, whose investigators could find nothing. Some kind of letter was sent to Potemkin, but its contents remain unknown although, strangely, Governor-General Volkonskii and Procurator-General Viazemskii declined to have it publicly burned for fear of stirring up "empty rumors and conversations."[48]

More worrisome was the case of Grigorii Rogov, a former voevoda who was arrested for composing "insane manifestos" in Moscow taverns. Interrogated by the formidable Sheshkovskii, Rogov gave no reason for his actions. But the Empress felt very suspicious since his manifesto was written in Paul's name, the Grand Duke having supposedly succeeded his deceased mother, and it asked him to return the Church's confiscated lands, reduce taxes, and lower the price of state-sold spirits. Catherine questioned Rogov's testimony and urged the interrogators to discover, using threats if necessary, "whether he himself or someone else is the instigator." Since they found nothing, Rogov was sentenced to incarceration in Schlüsselburg, and his wife and two daughters were sent to settle in Siberia—probably more as a charitable measure than a punishment, since Rogov seemed incapable of supporting them. Finally, just after the Empress left Moscow for Petersburg in December 1775, still another anonymous letter appeared with charges of a conspiracy among bondaged servants in Moscow and other towns to renounce their allegiance to their masters on 1 January 1776. Nothing significant happened on that date, however, and nothing further is known about the letter or its author. Indeed, this kind of "underground" political literature diminished abruptly in volume and frequency after 1775, as the tensions of war and rebellion eased for almost a dozen years.[49]

By the end of 1775, Catherine had weathered the worst phase of the prolonged, complex, and multiple crises of the past eight years. In the Legislative Commission she had initiated a fundamental review of the Empire's government and policies, a review that provoked widespread tensions and fears within and between the major social estates. In the partition of Poland and the Turkish war of 1768–1774 the Empress had achieved great victories abroad at the cost of great domestic burdens. Both the plague and the *Pugachevshchina* were widely seen as products of the extraordinary economic and social strains of the prolonged war. Even Grand Duke Paul viewed them in this light, advocating in private that the Empire must have a long period of peace to regain stability and security.[50] In the matter of Paul's own right to rule, Catherine had diverted him temporarily by removing him from the direct control of the Panin party, arranging his marriage to a German princess, and disposing of his Holstein patrimony. Yet the many plots against Catherine in Paul's name pointed to her persisting problem of legitimacy, an issue that Pugachev's imposture and revolt dramatized for all to see. If the Empress could feel some satisfaction in her triumphs over foreign and domestic foes, she shuddered at how close she had come to worse disasters, how dangerous such strange phenomena as pretenders could become in times of tension (what if a pretender had visited plague-stricken Moscow?), and how deficient many parts of her administration had proved to be under stress. All these lessons dictated an early revision of basic policies and institutions, a task Catherine felt better prepared to undertake in partnership with the remarkable Potemkin.

8

"Legislomania": Reactions to Crisis

Catherine spent most of 1775 in Moscow, where she arrived two weeks after Pugachev's demise and which she left in the third week of December. This was her longest sojourn as empress in the old capital. She lingered there because of insistent political imperatives. Indeed, to Frau Bielcke she boasted of covering the distance between the two capitals in only fifty-six hours, aside from short stops in Novgorod and Tver, and praised the progress and prosperity in evidence all along the way. Despite an elaborate official entry with Paul and his consort on Sunday afternoon, 25 January, the Empress felt no more at home in the Golovin and Kolomenskoe palaces than she had eight years earlier. That spring she bought Prince Kantemir's picturesque estate south of the city. Changing the name from Chernaia Griaz' (Black Muck) to Tsaritsyno, she commissioned a new palace for summer visits and stayed at her new estate most of August. By early March she was already bemoaning the persistent rigors of the Moscow winter, in pointed contrast to Petersburg's constantly variable climate. Winter resurged in late May with intense cold and heavy snowfall, bitter winds and hail. "Putrid fever" in April caused consternation in pestilence-shy Moscow, whereas "fever and ague" afflicted thousands in September. Catherine herself suffered periodic illness from April onward, one "indisposition" making her miss the celebrations of Paul's birthday and her coronation on 20 and 22 September, respectively. Fever, sore throat, and other alarming symptoms confined the Empress to her rooms the first week of December.[1]

Just as tranquility returned inside Russia, rebellion seemed rife abroad: peasant disorders in Bohemia and Moravia that supposedly involved a "Russian prince," the "flour war" bread riots in Paris, and armed conflict around Boston that induced the British government on 1 September 1775 urgently to request 20,000 Russian infantry for service in America—an invitation

184

Catherine graciously declined. To Frau Bielcke on 30 June 1775 the Empress predicted the independence of America from Europe in her lifetime.[2]

Her Moscow visit encompassed much more work than pleasure. Even before she left St. Petersburg she warned Melchior Grimm that "a new sickness called legislomania" had struck her again: "the first time it concerned principles only; this time it is all earnest work."[3] First on the Empress's political agenda was a fundamental reorganization of local and regional administration, as prescribed in the Guberniia Reform issued on 7 November 1775. This reform consolidated many previous piecemeal changes, and represented the most ambitious and comprehensive institutional innovation till that point of Catherine's reign. It was largely the direct product of her pen. Five months of singlehanded labor, she crowed to Voltaire immodestly, had resulted in a work of 215 pages in quarto that "yielded in nothing as compared to the *Instruction* for the law code." Indeed, she told Grimm her earlier work now seemed "mere verbiage" in comparison. Half a year later, however, she apologized for having failed to send the Sage of Ferney a French translation of the new ordinance (it appeared in 1778); "but I warn you beforehand that this work is very dry and tedious, and if one searches in it for anything other than order and common sense, one will be mistaken. In all this farrago, assuredly, there is neither genius nor wit, but still much utility." She was especially proud of the preface to the statute, which she depicted as only one part of the "legislative edifice" that her *Great Instruction* of 1767 had foreseen. Regulations for finances, commerce, police, and other spheres were to follow, "after which even the law code will be a quick and easy work." On the last point, the Empress proved to be overly sanguine; she never completed the codification of the Empire's laws.[4]

Catherine could draft the Guberniia Reform in barely nine months (not five) because she considered it so urgently needed. Both the plague and the *Pugachevshchina* had dramatized the many defects of local government, notably, weakness and inefficiency. Moreover, the general principles behind the reform had already been assembled—some on paper, others in practice— and she hastened to use the respite from foreign pressures. Encouraged by her multiple triumphs over internal and external foes, the Empress sought to consolidate the Empire's gains and revitalize its governmental institutions. Potemkin's personal support and political assistance boosted Catherine's resolute re-entry into the intricacies of law making. If thirteen years on the Russian throne had made her a more confident ruler, her impatience for rapid results had grown apace. She could no longer abide the dawdling disputations of a reconvened Legislative Commission. It was time for bold action.[5]

Catherine brought abundant preparatory materials to Moscow, where she plunged into the process of drafting even as she solicited additional guidance. Procurator-General Viazemskii provided constant counsel, of course, and she obtained much practical advice from Governor Jakob Sievers of Novgorod guberniia, Governor George Brown of Livland, Governor Nikolai Engel'gardt of Finland, Governor-General Mikhail Volkonskii of Moscow, and Gustav Reinhold von Ulrich, an official from Livland. It was significant that officials from the Empire's western marches were called on so extensively; for Catherine meant to adopt a modified form of the local government of the Baltic Provinces, "which, having possessed it four hundred years, consider themselves extremely fortunate."[6]

This last remark was made in response to Volkonskii's reform project of 9 February 1775, many provisions of which the Empress found close to her own, swiftly crystallizing draft. Her other comments to Volkonskii show that, at this early stage, she already contemplated closing many of the central collegia, transferring their functions and personnel to the reformed guberniias, and absorbing remnants of the Legislative Commission into a reorganized Senate. The guberniias as reformed would be smaller in size and run by administrations divided functionally into four departments. Governors-general or vicegerents (*namestniki*) would oversee groupings of two or three guberniias, whereas officials elected from the nobility would assist at the district and intermediate (province) levels. Division of duties (especially the separation of judicial organs from local administration), delimitation of jurisdictions, decentralization of nonmilitary functions, all under the supervision of the Empress's personal appointees as governors-general—these concepts became hallmarks of the reform. Catherine needed several more months to work out the details, but these basic features remained intact.[7]

The whole statute went through at least six distinct drafts, with some sections revised as many as eleven times. Of the 1,200 pages preserved from the process, some 800 belong directly to Catherine, 600 in her own hand. She took great pains with her work, particularly with its explanatory preface, the duties of local officials, the functions of the new bureaus of public welfare, and the reorganization of the judicial system. When first printed, the law comprised 28 chapters with 412 articles in part I. Chapter 29, though written in 1775, only appeared in print in 1780 along with two more chapters that together constituted part II (19 articles in all). Catherine presented the new institutions to her council, joined for the occasion by Field Marshal Rumiantsev, for review on 2 and 4 November 1775. The councilors acclaimed her work for its "wise foresight, maternal concern for subjects, love for mankind and mercy of Her Imperial Majesty," urging its speedy implementation. After reviewing the reform three days later, the Senate also called for its immediate introduction first in Tver and Smolensk guberniias, and only then in the rest of the empire. These reactions delighted the Empress. "The gratitude of all the Empire and the Senate cannot be unpleasant to ME," she informed Prince Viazemskii. "I do not doubt, indeed I expect and desire, that your implementation completely accord with My zealous intention in the publication of my new institutions for the benefit of the Empire."[8]

Like Peter the Great, Catherine explained her purposes and justified the need for the new institutions in a florid preface. Here she repeatedly contrasted the Empire's current brilliant status with the decadence and disorders that had allegedly deformed the post-Petrine decades. The general need for administrative changes was linked to territorial gains, population growth, economic expansion, and "enlightenment." Her own earlier efforts, culminating in the Legislative Commission, were proudly recited, their non-completion blamed on the six-year struggle in defense of faith and fatherland. The primary failings of the old institutions—confusion, inefficiency, injustice—were indicted for undermining "good order, general tranquility, and security." The Empress pledged to restore these virtues by strengthening local and regional institutions through greater numbers of trained personnel, clarification of functions, specification of duties, and simplification of procedures—all of which would, she vowed, "hasten the best and most exact execution of the most useful legislation issued in the future." In other words, the Guberniia Reform was only the start of comprehensive institutional change. In closing she called on "every right-thinking person and every zealous son of the Fatherland" to heed the new laws and appealed for divine assistance in the fulfillment of duties in the fight against luxury, laziness, negligence, and carelessness in matters of administration.[9]

According to the final draft of the Guberniia Reform, its major provisions were to increase the number of guberniias and standardize their numbers of population while decreasing each guberniia's size and eliminating the intermediary unit of the province (additional subdivisions remained an option, though). Notions of order, regularity, and rationality permeated the statute, whose main intent stemmed from the cameralist concept of bringing the government closer to the population. This was also Catherine's way of answering the criticism expressed in the *nakazy* to the Legislative Commission about bureaucratic rigidity, red tape, and lawlessness. Hence the Empress sought to strengthen local government and buttress security by assigning more functions to localities and eliciting service by election from local noblemen. In rural areas the land-captain (*zemskii ispravnik*), a sort of sheriff elected by the district nobility, was to oversee local security. In towns the same functions devolved on the commandant or police chief (*gorodnichii*). Both these offices had evolved out of proposals made at the Legislative Commission and from local experiments. One of the commandant's duties (article 262) registered Catherine's indignant reaction to the weakness shown by local authorities during the Moscow plague and the *Pugachevshchina*: "The *gorodnichii* may not forsake the town in any dangerous situation at the risk of forfeiting his office and honor."[10]

Welfare concerns went hand in hand with security considerations in the thinking of those cameralist theorists, such as Bielfeld, Justi, and Sonnenfels, on whom Catherine drew so liberally. Thus she projected bureaus of public welfare in each guberniia to coordinate welfare policies and institutions, supervising schools, hospitals, poorhouses, work houses, and insane asylums. In delineating the requirements for urban hospitals, the Empress lifted provisions from the charter for Paul's Hospital in Moscow, which she then supplemented in practice by founding a new public institution in a former pesthouse, later known as Catherine's Hospital. An invalid home and poorhouse were founded there at the same time. By such practical steps the Empress advertised her own concern for public welfare. In the 1780s she undertook the establishment of a public hospital in St. Petersburg, a separate lazaret for venereal patients (whose names and afflictions were to be kept strictly secret), and an empire-wide network of free public schools.[11]

Reorganization of the courts received great attention from Catherine, who had been impressed by the volume of criticism on that score at the Legislative Commission. The thrust of her effort was to simplify procedures and curtail the stages of possible appeal. To handle cases involving minors, lunatics, sorcery or other extenuating circumstances and to discourage lengthy litigation, she provided for "conscience courts" in each guberniia comprised of an appointed judge and two assessors elected from the nobility, the townspeople, and the state peasantry. But to reiterate the central government's commitment to the maintenance of legality both in state administration and in public life, she expanded the numbers of procurators at all levels, from 50–60 in the 1760s to 650–750 by the 1790s. Judicial reform preoccupied Catherine for several more years. On 4 January 1780 she published three more chapters of the Guberniia Reform that prescribed the establishment in the imperial capitals of special upper and lower courts, evidently needed because of the rapidly expanding urban population and the crush of litigation in both cities.[12]

One curious feature of the Guberniia Reform was Catherine's occasional use of archaic Russian terminology. The new bureau of public welfare, for example, was called *prikaz obshchestvennogo prizreniia,* even though the word *prikaz* recalled Muscovite times and had rarely been used since the Petrine reforms, which themselves introduced hundreds of foreign administrative terms. Perhaps in deference to Muscovite mores she also introduced in 1775 the Stone Bureau (*kamennyi prikaz*), a seventeenth-century name for her new administration to supervise the planned reconstruction of the old capital. Other old-fashioned sounding terms were *gorodnichii, zemskii ispravnik, striapchii,* and *namestnik.* Possibly the Empress used such archaic language in an effort to russify the new institutions, hoping they would prove better adapted to Russian conditions than some of the foreign-inspired Petrine institutions had been. Then too her reform expunged from Russia's official administrative idiom one venerable office synonymous with corrupt ineptitude—the voevoda.

Catherine's interest in judicial reform exploited another famous foreign source: the recently released French translation (Brussels, 1774–1776) of Blackstone's *Commentaries on the Laws of England.* "Sir Blackstone, who did not send me his commentaries, alone enjoys the honor of being read by Her Majesty for two years," the Empress informed Grimm in August 1776; "oh, his commentaries and me, we are inseparable; he is an unstinting supplier of facts and ideas; I have not made any of that which is in his book, but it is my thread, which I unwind in my own manner." She was not simply jesting. Diligently plowing through the six volumes, pen in hand, she accumulated 386 folio pages of notes, remarks, queries, and proposals over a period of some eight years (1774–1782).[13]

Reading Blackstone prompted Catherine to reconsider notions of more ambitious political reforms. For several years she mulled over the possibility of creating a Chief Executive Chamber, to consist of three or four departments staffed by appointed officials, a small number of councilors, and— most remarkable—a number of assessors elected every three years from each guberniia. This body would exercise supervisory, judicial, consultative, and legislative functions under the authority of the Senate and the sovereign. Apparently she saw the chamber as a russified version of the French parlements with a few attributes of the British parliament. It also resembled the Austrian Imperial Council and recalled something of Nikita Panin's council proposal of 1762–63. Whatever its origins, the institution did not materialize under Catherine. But its consideration testifies to her persistent search for useful political-administrative reforms, and her recognition of the need for intermediary bodies to bridle bureaucratic arbitrariness and foster wider political participation.[14]

Having drafted the Guberniia Reform in haste, the Empress favored its gradual implementation, but the Senate urged her to give it a brief trial in Tver and Smolensk before extending the new institutions to the entire Empire. She therefore authorized Governor-General Sievers to oversee the foundation of Tver guberniia in January 1776. The ceremonies and nobility elections that Sievers instituted in Tver, a new guberniia capital, became standard for the "opening" of Russia's other new guberniias, fifty in number by the end of Catherine's reign. Lavish official hospitality aimed at attracting maximum turnout by the provincial nobility and active participation in the new elective institutions. The statute itself was read aloud, and then the Empress usually sent a personal message to the newly elected marshal of the guberniia nobility. Typically, the nobility reciprocated by sending a delegation to thank Catherine in person and to ask permission to build a statue to her. She graciously declined the honor in proposing that they donate their funds to the new bureau of public welfare. Delighted with the results at Tver, Catherine pushed for the reform's general introduction in the next few years.[15]

Beyond the pomp and rhetoric of the new institutions, their most immediate practical effects were to pump new money and new officials into the Russian provinces. (The Guberniia Reform was introduced into the non-Russian borderlands somewhat later, in the mid-1780s.) Within two decades the number of officials more than doubled. Well aware of the shortage of qualified personnel, the Empress had recommended that Viazemskii find positions for former voevodas and their assistants: "for it is impossible that they have not acquired some knowledge." Dozens of new towns were founded in bringing the reform to life. Led by the noble assemblies, civilized social life in the European style penetrated more widely and rapidly into the Russian countryside. The Empress decided to see for herself in 1780.[16]

Departing from Tsarskoe Selo with a substantial suite on 9 May 1780, Catherine undertook a month-long inspection tour of the newly reformed western guberniias and vicegerencies. This journey took her as far west as Mogilev, where she received Emperor Joseph II disguised as "Count Falkenstein." Her inspections were carefully planned beforehand. At each town she visited she delegated four veteran officials—senators Jakob Bruce and Alexander Stroganov, brigadier Alexander Bezborodko and colonel Peter Turchaninov—to collect detailed information about the workings of the new institutions.[17]

The imperial itinerary took her to Narva, Pskov, Polotsk, Mogilev, Smolensk, Novgorod, with briefer stops in smaller towns in between. In the course of this inspection tour she visited guberniias administered by eminent officials who were also close friends. To establish the new institutions on a sound basis she selected men of experience and stature, men in whom she had the utmost confidence based on their record of distinguished state service and personal loyalty. Naturally they exerted themselves in welcoming the Empress with grandeur and in showing off her new institutions and subjects in the most positive light. Music, processions, parades, balls, dinners, outings, church ceremonies, and other diverse entertainments enlivened Catherine's triumphal progress.[18]

Local officialdom unanimously lauded the new administrative arrangements. Almost everywhere the new institutions were found in place and working efficiently, with few tax arrears, few unresolved cases, and even fewer prisoners in jail or inmates in poorhouses. Schools, hospitals, and poorhouses were being organized in many localities. The conscience courts won general approbation. Towns seemed to be growing, trade flourishing. Only a few petty complaints were heard. Were others suppressed? Perhaps so, for the burgomeister of Narva was advised to deliver his speech of welcome in writing to avoid "alarm." To the scattered criticism concerning urban deficiencies the Empress held out the ideal answer: any problems would be treated in future general legislation about towns and their trades and enterprises. Besides, she conducted herself as a most gracious guest, bestowing grants and gifts far and wide, on high and low alike. She greeted hundreds of people in the crowds that accompanied her over hundreds of kilometers.[19]

On the way back Catherine became annoyed at word that the nobility of St. Petersburg guberniia, led by their marshal Prince Alexander Kurakin, were planning a massive turnout in support of a renewed attempt to confer on her the titles of "The Great, Most Wise Mother of the Fatherland." Denouncing these plans as "superfluous and improper," the Empress pointedly instructed Governor-General Alexander Golitsyn to countermand any assembly and hand over any donations to the bureau of public welfare. "This is absolutely My will," she enjoined Golitsyn. No formal welcome occurred. But Catherine had not heard the last of this notion, and several speeches reported in the Russian press used the phrase.[20]

Not that she was averse to private summations of her achievements, for she complained to Grimm in June 1779 that Bezborodko's preliminary list of notable decrees, victories, etc., had omitted far too much. Two years later his expanded summary won her approval:

During the last 19 years

Guberniias organized according to the new form	29
Towns organized and built	144
Conventions and treaties concluded	30
Victories recorded	78
Memorable edicts prescribing laws or institutions	88
Edicts for the amelioration of the people	123
total	492

These included only matters of state, not private affairs, she joked to Grimm: "Well, Sir, are you satisfied with us? Have we not been lazy?"[21]

Police, Nobles, and Towns

The Guberniia Reform, concentrating as it did on issues of local administration, largely overlooked urban affairs and issues concerning the status, social role, and internal organization of the various estates. Yet Catherine's vision of a reformed Empire required more towns—richer, tidier, better administered urban centers. If St. Petersburg exemplified her Europeanized ideal and Moscow its "Asiatic" antithesis, she hoped to pursue the transformation of the latter, to see flourishing provincial towns replace the charred wooden ruins of Kazan and Saratov left after the *Pugachevshchina,* and to plant new towns along the recently expanded southern frontier. Even as she drafted the Guberniia Reform the Empress began preparing other institutional innovations that culminated in the Police Code of 1782 and the twin charters to the nobility and to the towns of 1785. All three statutes shared Catherine's authorship. All three shared with the Guberniia Reform her extensive use of materials and proposals generated by the Legislative Commission and its subcommittees. All displayed different dimensions of her general reaction to the crises of 1767–1775.

Catherine's concern to found "all sorts of estates" in Russia and, in particular, to stimulate the formation of a "third estate," a "middling sort of people" midway in status between the nobility and the peasantry, had sparked much discussion at the Legislative Commission. Indeed, one subcommittee had drafted a "charter of rights of the middling sort of state inhabitants" that the Empress pronounced "the best one which has yet been done" and from which she borrowed extensively in subsequent urban legislation. She started the process by issuing an omnibus decree of 17 March 1775 that celebrated ratification of the peace with the Turks by awarding forty-seven "favors" to the various estates. This decree launched a lengthy, sporadic process of urban reform by abolishing thirty-two separate taxes and imposts. More important, it redefined the urban estate and the basis of its tax obligations.[22]

Intent on introducing order and hierarchy into Russia's traditionally amorphous urban communes, Catherine divided the registered urban population into a merchant elite (*kupechestvo*) no longer subject to the socially demeaning head-tax, and a mass of burghers (*meshchanstvo*). By a stroke of her pen the Empress abolished the long tradition of joint tax responsibility for the registered urban population. The merchants were subdivided into three "guilds" on the basis of their declared capital, on which they paid a tax of one percent annually. In effect, the Empress singled out some ten percent of the urban population for privileged treatment, lessening their proportional tax burden and elevating their social status and corporate autonomy by a measure of imperial confidence. Nevertheless, the same decree restated her rejection of exclusive economic privileges by declaring that thenceforth any free person might establish a trade or manufactory without special authorization—that is, the central government would no longer restrict entry into nonagricultural pursuits. Furthermore, it was stipulated that all freed serfs might enter the merchantry or the burghers. These last two stipulations amounted to a rebuff of merchant pretensions to a monopoly of urban trade and manufacturing, a reaffirmation of the value of free enterprise as practiced by an open, numerically growing "middle" estate.[23]

That Catherine adopted the characteristic Russian (and cameralist) priority of politics over economics may be deduced from her issuing the Police Code three years before the Charter to the Towns. Although the precise process of drafting the Police Code remains obscure, she obviously used much foreign and domestic legislation and treatises. Cameralist writings bulked large among the latter. The Empress knew well the multivolume works of Bielfeld and Justi, for she had sponsored their translation into Russian in the 1760s and 1770s. Probably she was also acquainted with the ideas of Sonnenfels, whose work only appeared in Russian translation in 1787. Evidently she consulted the classic formulations of Nicholas de la Mare (Paris, 1713), and she sampled such russified cameralist works as the lengthy police nakaz of 1767.[24]

Enacted on 8 April 1782, the Police Code's 174 articles applied minute bureaucratic regulation and pious moral suasion to the administration of the urban population. The very title of the ordinance, literally "Code of Good Order" (*Ustav blagochiniia*), resounded with regulatory and moralistic imperatives. It followed the Guberniia Reform in dividing urban space, as measured by population, into conveniently manageable units—districts (200–500 households) and quarters (50–100 households) under a police board (*uprava blagochiniia*) comprising the *gorodnichii,* two provosts for criminal and civil affairs, and two councilmen. Each district was assigned a provost, each quarter a supervisor. The provost commanded the police corps in each district (34 men per district in the capitals). Both capitals received in addition an *oberpolitseimeister* and a *politseimeister,* appointed by the Senate with high ranks and substantial salaries, but the central office of policemaster-general was abolished. An uncharacteristically short preface explained the code's issuance in terms of supplementing earlier reforms to promote "good order," better execution of the laws, and more efficient governance. "These considerations induced Us, having completed the first part of the aforementioned Code, to issue it for the necessary implementation, in anticipation of the time when, with God's aid, we shall succeed in completing the ones that follow after it." Thus were additional reforms promised, but part two of the Police Code never appeared.[25]

According to the code, the police board was charged to function as "the mirror of justice in regard to the mutual obligations of citizens among themselves." After outlining the board's structure and functions, Catherine inserted a peculiar list of moral injunctions, largely borrowed from de la Mare, to guide its actions. This "mirror of justice" had first been conceived as a general introduction to the code, but the Empress later narrowed its application; it specified rules of morality, social duties, personal qualities, and official duties of police personnel. The police were to exercise common sense, good-will, humanity, loyalty to the imperial service, zeal for the common good, concern for duty, honesty and incorruptibility. These injunctions ended with an exhortation against accepting bribes; "for they blind the eyes, pervert the mind and heart, and bridle the tongue."[26]

Such idealism quickly faded before a panoply of duties and procedures, prohibitions and punishments, the latter mostly left to determination by the courts. Besides upholding public order and morality, protecting against fire and health hazards, overseeing trade, and regulating domestic servants, the police were to enforce sumptuary legislation against luxury. Political or social dissidence in the form of unauthorized organizations or "suspicious" meetings was strictly prohibited, of course; such disobedience was to be punished by the courts. Public gambling and drunkenness were condemned along with sorcery. Prohibitions on spreading infection and selling spoiled foodstuffs concluded the Police Code, which Catherine began to institute in St. Petersburg within a month of its publication. On 19 May 1782 she sent a copy of the code to Potemkin with model ranks and budgets, calling for its immediate introduction in provincial towns.[27]

The Police Code displayed Catherine's ambitious attempt at codification of civil and criminal law for the urban population with a renewed accent on bureaucratic hierarchy and paternalistic control. Issued three years before the charters to the nobility and to the towns, the new police institutions underscored her government's basic priorities—firm control and "enlightened" moral leadership of a slowly evolving, loosely structured society.

The twin charters to the nobility and to the towns, both published on 21 April 1785, signified the end of Catherine's second attack of "legislomania." The first codified the privileges of the Empire's primary estate; the second redefined the structure of urban society and reorganized its governance. Both were designed by the Empress to promote social consensus and political stability, economic advance and cultural enlightenment. Both drew on, and selectively reworked, the plethora of precedent—foreign and domestic—accumulated over the previous quarter century. Both underwent perfunctory review before they received warm acclamation from Catherine's council on 31 March and 3 April 1785.[28]

The Russian nobility—how it should be defined, what status it should have in society, what political role it should play—these questions had puzzled Catherine from the start of her reign. Acutely aware of the political risks entailed in reforming the Empire's principal political estate, the Empress had postponed such issues until she felt more securely in power; yet the Legislative Commission had witnessed acrimonious discussions of noble privileges that showed few grounds for achieving consensus. Evidently this experience convinced Catherine that further public airing of such issues would only delay or even block their resolution. Besides, she needed time to digest the multitude of noble opinions expressed in the hundreds of *nakazy,* in the few debates at plenary sessions, and in the work of the subcommittee that drafted a project for rights of the well-born.

With the role of the nobility in local government redefined by means of the Guberniia Reform, Catherine next initiated a wider inquiry into noble services and status in the past, preparatory to new legislation. "Is there not in the Appointments Archive any legislation concerning the nobility?" she asked Procurator-General Viazemskii on 25 February 1776. "Secondly, which have been noble services, which are they now, and can one extract from the Appointments Archive proof of nobility?" She had Viazemskii consult the Moscow archivist-historians Gerhard Müller and A. T. Kniazev. Within a few months these men gave the Empress extensive materials elucidating the history of noble ranks and services. Müller and Kniazev both underlined the vagueness and ambiguity of the terms noble and nobility (*dvorianin/dvorianstvo*). Indeed, when Kniazev told Catherine that many nobles had no genealogies at all, she had him start compiling a genealogical register that resulted in a large compendium of historical information about the Russian nobility. Kniazev and his assistants also drafted a "plan for the compilation of extracts from laws concerning the nobility," a document Catherine carefully utilized in writing the charter.[29]

The Empress used all this historical information to fashion a charter clarifying the basis of noble status and privileges, and reiterating her special solicitude and gratitude for the nobility's zealous leadership and loyal service in war and peace. Apparently she worked on the charter fitfully for several years, and then chose the occasion of her fifty-sixth birthday in the notably tranquil year of 1785 to proclaim her confidence in the Russian nobility as the pillars of the Empire and her throne. This proclamation marked quite a contrast to the nervous anxieties of her first decade of rule. As she privately remarked to one secretary in 1786 as her toenails were being clipped: the "boyars" of Elizabeth's time had been tamed; "the points of all daggers have been blunted and they cannot stab."[30]

It is clear from the charter itself, and from Catherine's responses to some changes suggested by an unidentified senior official, that she deliberately anchored the new law in Russian precedent. In fact, the charter granted no new privileges to the nobility. It simply defined the estate more precisely, confirmed the privileges it already enjoyed, guaranteed them "for eternal times and steadfastly," and specified its corporate functions. On the delicate question of different types of nobility, for example, particularly the distinction between hereditary and service nobles, the Empress cited Russian precedent in recognizing six categories: actual nobility as attested by grants from the sovereign, military nobility as indicated by the rank of commissioned officer, nobility by civil service as shown by the achievement of one of the top eight ranks in the Table of Ranks, nobility from foreign sources, titled Russian nobility, and old noble families that lacked documentary proof of their status. Thus she acknowledged different kinds of nobility; but she accorded no practical significance to such distinctions and made it clear that she would countenance no purge of lesser nobles in the process of compiling the official genealogical registers, which were to be supervised by the elected district marshals of the nobility and a copy submitted to the guberniia marshal. Her criteria for determining noble status were both broad and loose. Furthermore, nothing was said about one category taking precedence over another.[31]

The charter explicitly and eternally confirmed the hereditary nobility's "freedom and liberty": its right to continue or retire from state service according to the established rules, enter the service of friendly powers, and travel abroad. The ancient tradition of noble service to the state was not forgotten, however, as article 20 stipulated:

> But as the name and dignity of well-born nobility are acquired by service and labors useful to the Empire and to the throne in the past, the present, and in the future, and as the actual station of the Russian nobility is dependent upon the security of the fatherland and the throne; so therefore at any such time as needed by the Russian autocracy, when the service of the nobility is needed and necessary for the common good, then every well-born nobleman is obliged, at the first summons from the sovereign authority, not to spare either labor or life itself for the state service.[32]

That state service was regarded as normal and expected for noblemen, moreover, was reiterated by provisions barring those who had never served from voting at the district and guberniia noble assemblies held every three years or from standing for elective service. At such assemblies they were also to be seated separately from former servitors.

The question of noble economic privileges, which had triggered fierce controversy at the Legislative Commission, received another kind of compromise solution in the charter. Laconically confirmed was their right to buy villages (that is, to own serfs), but nothing further was mentioned about their authority as masters. Indeed, their judicial authority was explicitly circumscribed by injunctions that the nobility was protected by, as well as subject to, the jurisdiction of the established courts; "for it would be unjust and not in accord with the general order, if each in his own case thought to make himself the judge." Their property rights were reaffirmed, including their right to forests and minerals on their lands, as were their rights to operate enterprises on their estates, to hold fairs, and to build or own handicraft shops in towns. But to enjoy urban rights they must obey urban laws.[33]

The charter therefore reasserted Catherine's conviction that the nobility should devote itself primarily to agricultural pursuits and state service, military or bureaucratic, national or local. With Montesquieu, she believed that the involvement of noblemen in urban retail trade and industry would undermine their traditional estate functions, causing harm to the state service, social chaos, and injury to other estates. If formation of the new middle estate were to signify economic progress and bolster social stability, it must not dignify such derogation of status and functions on the part of a few noblemen. Catherine assumed few noblemen would wish to enter urban pursuits. But when ten enrolled in urban guilds on the basis of article 92 of the Charter to the Towns, she forbade such participation, even for recently ennobled persons. Moreover, she solicited a wider ruling from the Moscow guberniia authorities and the Senate that found commerce incompatible with noble education, honor, and duties. The news that several aristocrats had leased spirits concessions in 1789 annoyed Catherine, who maliciously remarked that Prince Alexander Kurakin, a close friend of Grand Duke Paul, could not even manage his own household. In slightly expanding the concept of service by the nobility, the Empress stopped well short of endorsing the emergence of a "trading nobility" as advocated by some European pamphleteers and a few capitalistically oriented aristocrats in the capitals. Her ideal of societal organization and evolution, although not altogether static, accented balance and order, agriculture before industry, gradual change in preference to stagnation or (God forbid!) disruption.[34]

Just as Catherine in her preface to the Charter to the Nobility lauded their martial and administrative achievements in governing, expanding, and defending the Empire, so she introduced the Charter to the Towns by citing the appearance of 216 new towns during her twenty-three-year reign; this was proof positive of her resolve to multiply and enrich the urban citizenry through patronage of crafts and trades, industry and commerce. Townbuilding benefited urban and rural populations alike, she declaimed grandiloquently. "Beginning with antiquity shrouded in darkness, we meet everywhere the memory of townbuilders exalted on par with the memory of legislators, and we see that heroes, glorified for their victories, endeavored to give their names immortality through townbuilding." Obviously she dreamed of ensuring her own immortality by similar means. Following the usage adopted in the Charter to the Nobility, she bestowed the new privileges and institutions on the towns, their societies, and their citizens "for centuries steadfastly." Intimations of mortality enlivened the Empress's greater concern for posterity.[35]

The Charter to the Towns drew on a plethora of Russian and foreign materials to redefine urban society and reform its governance, applying in the process some of the principles adumbrated in the Guberniia Reform, the Police Code, and the Charter to the Nobility. Indeed, great significance inhered in the simple fact that the charter focused exclusively on the urban estate—for the first time in Russian history. The townspeople were the only social category besides the nobility to receive such formal, legal recognition, which in itself certified a substantial elevation in social prestige. Even the timing of the charter's publication implied a certain parity in the sovereign's solicitude for the needs of townsmen and nobility. Other parallels between the two charters and the two social groups included a sixfold division of town inhabitants into real citizens who possessed property in the town, guild merchants, artisans, foreigners and other outsiders engaged in urban pursuits, honorary citizens (a new category), and traditional members of the urban commune, the so-called *posad* people. Like the noble assemblies, these six urban categories were authorized to meet together every three years to consider common needs and elect officials to posts in the town administration. This general gathering also held custody of the town seal and archive.[36]

If the general gathering reflected Catherine's attempt to enlarge the definition of urban inhabitants and lend them some corporate identity, she knew full well that smaller, less inclusive bodies were required for everyday urban administration. These functions she conferred on the common council (*obshchaia duma*), a curiously archaic Russian term. Comprised of varying numbers of representatives of the six categories of urban inhabitants, the common council assembled only once every three years. It was essentially an electoral body that chose a six-man council (*shestiglasnaia duma*), whose daily meetings served as the actual executive arm of urban self-government. In her eagerness to create the new urban institutions Catherine left open the issue of their interrelationships, perhaps because she recognized the considerable overlap and duplication between them, the police, and the traditional municipal administrations (the *magistraty*).[37]

The charter further specified privileges for particular segments of the urban estate. The three merchant "guilds," for instance, were made more exclusive by raising the capital qualifications for entry. They also gained honorary distinctions—the right to use equipages of specified sizes—and, more important, exemption from recruiting levies in return for a money payment. All these gains set the merchantry farther apart from the burghers. The honorary distinctions all represented imperial responses to requests and complaints expressed in the town *nakazy* to the Legislative Commission.[38]

In granting the charter, Catherine had no thought to weaken central control over the towns or to concede any national political role to the urban estate. Like the nobility, the townspeople were authorized to petition the governor about their common needs and interests. But, unlike the nobility, they were not accorded the right to choose deputies to carry such petitions to the Senate or the sovereign. Thus, the Empress took pains to delineate a basic legal equality between the nobility and the townspeople, while maintaining some distinctions between the two, functionally and historically different, estates. Like Peter the Great before her, Catherine took umbrage at the customarily obsequious language of petitions. Her decree of 19 February 1786 called for replacement of the term slave/servant (*rab*) by loyal subject (*vernyi poddannyi*).[39]

Catherine's second bout of "legislomania" did not forget the Empire's most numerous estate—the peasantry. Although she avoided the inflammatory issue of regulating relationships of masters and serfs, she applied the principles of the twin charters of 1785 to one for the state peasantry. It provided corporate rights to state peasant "societies," even the right to make collective petitions. It also divided the state peasantry into the prescribed six categories of registered village dwellers, the wealthiest group of which would enjoy freedom from corporal punishment—a privilege shared with the nobility and the merchantry. Yet this charter was never promulgated. Perhaps the crises of the late 1780s and early 1790s soured Catherine's hope for further social and institutional reforms.[40] A note to herself in the fall of 1787 hinted at a deepening pessimism about the effects of her reform efforts:

> Use the winter of 1787 and the beginning of 1788 to compose the chapters on the Senate and the Senate's procedures and instruction, do this with application and honest industry, if however the information [received] and criticism reveal barriers and tedious or wily difficulties,

then put the whole work into a deep drawer, for we do not see for whose sake I labor and will not my labors, care, and warm concern for the good of the Empire be in vain, for I do see that I cannot make my frame of mind hereditary.[41]

Here Catherine candidly acknowledged her cautious approach to institutional change: her worry lest it provoke unforeseen or intractable problems, her apprehension that Paul might revoke her laws. If she publicly reveled in the bombast of her reform decrees and the ceremonies that celebrated their introduction, she harbored secret doubts about their longevity and ultimate utility. The exhilarating effects of "legislomania" subsided fairly soon. In her own estimation it began "to limp along" in growing confusion by August 1777. "I do not know whether it is the material or the head," she confided to Grimm at the end of 1777, "but great strides are becoming rare; it is a slow fever without spirit." The following May she complained anew of feeling exhausted and ill from the recent attacks of "that devil of a disease: dear legislomania."[42] She already felt restless for other kinds of glory.

III

An Aging Empress

9

Nymphomania? Favorites and Favoritism

It is an oddity of Catherine's career that her second attack of "legislomania" coincided with the onset of another kind of mania: a parade of male favorites whose youth and social inexperience contradicted the dignified demeanor of their rapidly aging imperial patroness. The contrast in age and station bemused and befuddled contemporaries, unleashing a flood of gossip and speculation that has alternately titillated and scandalized posterity. Thus Samuel Schmucker apprised his American readers in 1855 of the instruction to be derived from the life of Catherine, "a woman of extraordinary genius; an historic meteor, the splendour of whose glittering transit across the political heavens struck every beholder with awe and wonder." Yet he discerned equally great dangers in "such a living embodiment of passion" and "one of the most corrupt, sensual, and licentious of women," warning: "There was no depth or excess of impurity which she had not fathomed and exhausted."[1] For his readers' safety, therefore, Schmucker discreetly suppressed the ostensibly indelicate details—a time-honored come-on.

In truth, there is precious little hard fact to cite.[2] If the progression of favorites is clear enough, its meaning for Catherine's emotional life, not to speak of her statecraft, rests in obscurity. It seems highly probable that her passages from one favorite to another entailed intense psychic crises. Only in a few instances, most notably the obviously exceptional case of Potemkin, do we enjoy access to sizable swatches of their intimate correspondence. Yet even here the chronology of their relationship remains uncertain, and several salient questions vainly beg for elucidation. How, for example, did their romance begin? Were they ever formally married? And what caused their passionate affair to cool? Although our twentieth-century curiosity may hanker after the physical facts of Catherine's romantic involvements, her own love notes offer scant hints about sexual preferences and practices. Rarely

201

can we peep past the bedroom door. In this situation, scandalous speculation may run amuck.

Predictably, male contemporaries displayed intense interest in Catherine's sexual foibles, tended to dwell on such matters and attach great significance to them. Foreign ministers at the Russian court followed the Empress's amorous affairs with particular attention, searching for political meaning in each change of favorites. Russians had to be more careful about recording their firsthand reactions. In a posthumously published tract written in 1786–87, for instance, the aristocratic curmudgeon Prince Mikhail Shcherbatov primly passed over any particulars in condemning the Empress for licentiousness, ostentation, and selfish absorption in personal glory, all of which had accelerated "the corruption of manners in Russia."[3] "To add to the corruption of women's manners and of all decency," Shcherbatov averred, "she has set other women the example of the possession of a long and frequent succession of lovers, each equally honored and enriched, thus advertising the cause of their ascendancy. Seeing a shrine erected to this vice in the heart of the Empress, women scarcely think it a vice in themselves to copy her; rather, I suppose, each thinks it a virtue in herself that she has not yet had so many lovers!" A British visitor to St. Petersburg in 1792 sanctimoniously proclaimed "in low life the women are all whores, i.e., the married women," and he echoed Shcherbatov's adage: "When any woman of rank or indeed any woman in low life is reproached with her gallantries, her answer is that our mother does the same."[4]

These comments from males may misrepresent actual female opinion, about which we know little. The prissy Princess Dashkova, for one, piously denied any contact with the various favorites and, in her memoirs written after Catherine's death, expressed outrage at Grigorii Orlov's sly suggestion that she groom her spoiled son for the imperial bed. In 1785–86, when Potemkin's nephew mentioned that his uncle wished to see Colonel Dashkov early in the afternoon, the "lovers' hour," the Princess declined the proposal, noting that if her son ever became the favorite she would go abroad for several years.[5]

Some of the ups and downs of Catherine's love life may be linked to her entry into middle age. At some point in the late 1770s she must have undergone menopause with its attendant gyrations of mood—intimations of mortality compounded by fears of faltering femininity. "She has lately missed a court or two in the morning," commented Sir James Harris, the newly arrived British special emissary, in January 1778, "from a slight indisposition, often dangerous at her time of life, but which is not attended with the least alarming symptom." Perhaps that fact explains the turbulence of her romance with Potemkin and some of the instability of her subsequent relationships. Certainly her appetite for passion grew with the eating. As she ruefully confessed to Potemkin in denying that fifteen others had preceded him in her affection (she admitted only five), "the trouble is that my heart would not willingly remain one hour without love."[6] Besides, the atmosphere at court spawned constant temptations.

In reflecting on her early years at the Russian court under the flirtatious Empress Elizabeth, Catherine offered a candid assessment of her own contribution to the atmosphere of temptation and romantic intrigue:

> I have just said that I was pleasing, consequently half the road of temptation was already traversed, and it is the very essence of human nature that, in such cases, the other half should not remain untracked. For to tempt, and to be tempted, are things very nearly allied, and, in spite of the finest maxims of morality impressed upon the mind, whenever feeling has anything to do in the matter, no sooner is it excited than we have already gone vastly farther than we are aware of, and I have yet to learn how it is possible to prevent its being excited. Flight alone is, perhaps, the only remedy; but there are cases and circumstances in which flight becomes impossible, for how is it possible to fly, shun, or turn one's back in the midst of a court? The very attempt would give rise to remarks. Now, if you do not fly, there is nothing, it seems to me, so difficult as to escape from that which is essentially agreeable. All that can be said in opposition to it will appear but a prudery quite out of harmony with the natural instincts of the human heart; besides, no one holds his heart in his hand, tightening or relaxing his grasp of it at pleasure.[7]

For intimacy, companionship, and moral support in the loneliness of her dedication to sovereign duty—duty that could be crushingly tedious and nerve-wracking—Catherine became more than ever vulnerable to physical temptation. At the same time she had less need to worry about an inconvenient pregnancy and more leisure to indulge her fancies. Even so, she felt haunted by the specter of a lover who might exploit her vulnerability to attain political domination. Hence the constant endeavor to compartmentalize her life, to separate passion from statecraft, to keep everything (but not everybody) in its place. This effort gave rise to the paradox of institutionalized favoritism: regulated passion that seems in retrospect to have been long in outward show and short in psychic satisfaction. Indeed, its very predictability and regularity may have reflected Catherine's inability to maintain a relationship of intimate equality. Her urge to dominate, coupled with her fear of domination by another, made for unstable romantic affairs. Yet the persistence of her search for love attested to a deep unfulfilled need, a need that intensified as the years flew by.

Potemkin

The sudden rise to prominence of Grigorii Potemkin was connected, on the one hand, with insistent political imperatives: Catherine's need for fresh advice and support to resolve the extended crisis of 1767–1775. On the other hand, it also functioned in an intimate sense as a means of transition from her emotional dependence on Grigorii Orlov to greater autonomy and, perhaps, higher self-esteem. The Empress could thrill to Potemkin's passion and delight in his wit. In the physical sense their affair lasted barely two years, 1774–75, although when it started is uncertain. In other respects it lasted until his death in 1791.

Catherine and Potemkin may well have been secretly married. In several affectionate letters she calls him "my dear husband," "dear spouse," "my darling husband," and "my master." Another speaks of their attachment "through sacred bonds"; "I love you and I am attached to you by all possible bonds."[8] Whether they were formally united or not, theirs evidently became an "open" union after the first two years. They no longer lived together and they spent long periods apart. Nevertheless, they constantly corresponded and obviously treasured their political and personal ties. In case of need each could always call on the other. Both pursued other partners quite openly (Potemkin's affections extending even to his nieces, the three Engel'gardt sisters), yet they mostly avoided public displays of jealousy. They found much satisfaction in their joint pursuit of glory and power for the Russian Empire.

The first year or so of their intimacy had witnessed a torrid romance, which must have given Catherine great comfort and renewed confidence after her breakup with Orlov and boredom with Vasil'chikov. Indeed, she could readily see that Potemkin outshone Orlov in intellect and political insight; he was just the sort of capable helpmate she longed for. Her joy in discovering his zealous devotion radiates throughout their correspondence, many specimens of which abound with affectionate or playfully derisive expressions: my dear soul, my beautiful Golden Pheasant, ghiaour, Muscovite, cossack, my sweet friend, my little Grisha, Grichifichetchka, my pigeon, my heart, my beauty, my jewel, my little father, Papa, imbecile, Tartar, Pugachev, golden cock, peacock, cat, golden tiger, lion in the jungle, doggie.[9] Her penchant for animal names may imply vigorous loveplay. Apparently they both enjoyed extended trysts in the steambath. Both were also subject to bouts of hypochondria. Reinforcing the defense of Russian bathing customs voiced in *The Antidote* of 1770, Catherine reiterated in the Police Code of 1782 her predecessors' prohibition of mixed bathing in public. She stipulated that the sexes must be separated above age seven, that male and female sections must be clearly designated, and that offenders should be sent to a work house for half a day.[10]

In their first years together, Potemkin's jealousy upset Catherine, who constantly assured him of her undying love. In fact, he may have been the first to tire of their rapture, and to neglect the constant reassurances that she so eagerly sought. In several notes she upbraided him for coldness, negligence, and—above all—moodiness. In theory, she desired a warm and constant relationship. In actuality, her own moodiness and her absorption with state duties made it almost impossible for a man like Potemkin, who valued his own autonomy, to dance attendance in the fashion desired. He could not match her devotion to work, subject as he was to fits of lassitude and periods of depression or religious contemplation. Acutely conscious of the distance between them in social standing, Potemkin must have felt terribly insecure much of the time. His overwhelming dependence on Catherine for his political preeminence could only have exacerbated minor quarrels and disagreements. For her part, the Empress had trouble understanding his constant need for reassurance and independence. Her prodigal gifts of money, palaces, titles, honors, and offices ought to have satisfied any man, in her view. Her loving notes and gestures begged for constant reciprocation. Apparently her eagerness outlasted his, perhaps partly in consequence of the ten-year difference in age. She pined for constant displays of affection; he became bored after a while. They began to quarrel more frequently.

A revealing dialogue records one stage of their relationship and the end of one of their quarrels:

Potemkin	Catherine
Allow me, Dear, to say the last,	I allow you.
which, I think, will end our dispute.	The sooner the better.
Do not be amazed that I am uneasy in	Be calm.
the matter of our love. Beyond your innumerable	One hand washes the other.
benefactions to me, you have placed	Firmly and solidly
me in your heart. *I wish to be*	You are and will be.
there alone above all predecessors,	I see and believe it
because not one has loved you so well;	I rejoice in my soul.
whereas I am the work of your hands, so I desire	My first satisfaction
that my peace be built on you,	It will come by itself.
that you enjoy doing me good;	Rest easy in your
that you devise everything for my comfort	thoughts, so that
and therein find rest for yourself in	the feelings can act
your difficult labors, whereby you are	freely; they are
occupied according to your high station.	tender, they will
Amen	themselves seek out the
	best way.
	End of quarrel.
	Amen[11]

Of course, theirs was much more than a love match. She initiated him into virtually the whole spectrum of statecraft—and found a willing pupil, industrious viceroy, and a fellow dreamer of glorious dreams. The Empress valued Potemkin's political abilities so highly, and trusted him so thoroughly, that she allowed him greater freedom of action and wider access to resources than anybody else in the Empire. Recognizing his restless ambition and gradually tiring of his temperamental outbursts and bilious sulks, Catherine may have endeavored to avoid a repetition of her relationship with Orlov by gently encouraging Potemkin's involvement in myriad projects that took him away from St. Petersburg for long periods. Their romance could continue by courier, to some degree. As she remarked in the middle of one businesslike note: "Although I do not like it when you are not by my side, my dear Lord, I must confess that your four-week sojourn in Kherson has ultimately included significant utility in itself, as you yourself mention."[12]

It is not certain what caused the crisis or crises that resulted in the lovers' loosening their bond. Perhaps the intensity of their passion simply wore them out. According to Catherine, however, "the essence of our disagreement is

always the question of power and never that of love."[13] Power in what sense
and how manifested? Did Catherine apprehend that Potemkin was trying to
manipulate her with his moodiness? Did she think he was trying to dictate
policy like a Turkish pasha to her, a cultured German princess become the
all-powerful Russian empress? Or did she suspect that he was in love with
her power above herself? So long as Paul lived she could not make her ties
with Potemkin any more official than they already were. She could not make
Potemkin co-sovereign in any event; for the essence of absolute sovereignty
was rule by a single person, and the most serious threats to the principle of
absolutism in eighteenth-century Russia had come during periods of female
rule. To be sure, she could (and did) share some of the burdens of absolute
rule with favorites and subordinates. But she could not share any of the final
responsibility. If the burdens of awesome power made her need constant love
and attention more than ever, then her failure to find these in sufficient
measure in Potemkin led to a wider, more insistent search. Power she had.
Love she powerfully desired. The dilemma was to find a man who could love
her without cramping her power.

"Petrushinka" Zavadovskii

The second day of 1776 Catherine discreetly, albeit ambiguously, switched
favorites. Many observers avidly awaited Potemkin's "dismission." Nevertheless, he kept his offices and, with Catherine's permission, even received
several foreign decorations including the illustrious title of Prince of the Holy
Roman Empire. He was given a Petersburg palace and funds to furnish it
sumptuously, but meanwhile maintained his quarters in the Winter Palace.
Some wondered whether he had not yielded his place in Catherine's bed in
favor of supervising his successors. To confuse matters further, Grigorii
Orlov unexpectedly returned from abroad in mid-January 1776. The warm
welcome he received at court excited rampant speculation. Indeed, gossip
blamed his "Stroke of Palsy" on poison from Potemkin, whose ambition was
said to covet the Duchy of Kurland. Orlov himself, though visibly declining,
showed amorous aspirations in activating anew the courtship of his teenaged
first cousin Ekaterina Zinov'eva, whom the Empress had appointed a maid
of honor in 1775. Despite strenuous and prolonged criticism from family and
clergy because of the close degree of consanguinity—criticism that Orlov
allegedly sought to deflect by procuring testimony that his cousin was a
changeling—their marriage was celebrated in a meadow outside Petersburg
on 5 June 1777, with the stout Orlov dancing for joy. Blessing the nuptials,
the Empress immediately promoted the new Princess Orlova to lady in
waiting and dined with the couple at their Gatchina estate. In September
1777, during the celebration of the fifteenth anniversary of Catherine's
coronation, she awarded Orlova the Order of St. Catherine. Thus did she
assist a former favorite even as she promoted a new one. This unusual union
produced no live children, for the consumptive Orlova rapidly wasted away

before her death at Lausanne in June 1781, a loss that hastened her husband's slide into insanity.[14]

Catherine's new protégé was Colonel Peter Zavadovskii, a thirty-seven-year-old Ukrainian generally considered to be a client of Field Marshal Rumiantsev and Kirill Razumovskii. Potemkin also knew him well and as early as November 1774 recommended him to Catherine, who had appointed him to her personal cabinet on 10 July 1775 and granted him an estate, Lialichi, with several hundred serfs adjoining the family home in the Starodub district of Chernigov guberniia. A handsome officer with an excellent classical education and much governmental experience under Rumiantsev in the Ukraine and in battle against the Turks, Zavadovskii assisted the Empress in her final work on the Guberniia Reform (for which she awarded him the cross of St. George, fourth class, on 26 November 1775) and evidently impressed her with his efficiency, elegant Russian prose, and willingness to work long hours. Exactly how and when they became more than co-workers remains obscure. He was manifestly a man on the make, as it were, but we do not know whether he or she (or Potemkin) took the initiative in their amorous alliance.

A peculiar kind of *ménage à trois* became evident by the start of 1776. On 2 January "heaven chose" the new favorite as "general's-adjutant," a title rarely used in public. Catherine, Potemkin, and Zavadovskii had worked closely together for several months, and they often dined together alone or in small parties. If only we could retrieve what they said on such occasions and how they said it. ("Body language" can be so instructive.) Zavadovskii must have struggled to compete with two such accomplished conversationalists as Catherine and Potemkin.[15]

Though Zavadovskii later professed not to be in awe of Potemkin (whom he knew all too well), Catherine's charisma clearly captivated the socially inexperienced and sexually innocent Ukrainian. Did the Empress encourage their amicable rivalry for her affections? The same age, both men shared several other attributes: modest provincial noble origins, excellent higher educations, varied civil and military service, love of luxury, good looks, and high ambitions. In personality the two were quite different: Potemkin excessive and expressive in everything, Zavadovskii modest and reserved, almost shy. Perhaps these last qualities attracted Catherine initially by the sharp contrast to Potemkin's ebullience. The new French *chargé d'affaires*, the canny Chevalier de Corberon, forecast after one month of observation that Zavadovskii was "probably no more than an amusement," while Potemkin accepted his own diminished role at court.[16] The Empress's newly expanded favor only emerged in full public view by the summer of 1776. On 28 June, the fourteenth anniversary of Catherine's coup, Zavadovskii was promoted to major general with a grant of 20,000 rubles and 1,000 serfs. This appointment was only announced in the capital gazettes a month later, with the cryptic comment that Zavadovskii would continue in his previous (unspecified) position. "It was expected by many that he would likewise be made chamberlain," reported the British envoy, "but as this has not taken place, I am still of opinion that it is not meant to bring him much forwarder on the scene, and though he has hitherto no declared rival, I cannot think him likely to preserve his present favour for any length of time, or to make any other use of it, than to secure his own fortune, which, indeed, he has already done to a more than competent degree."[17] These predictions proved quite accurate. Zavadovskii's emergence never eclipsed Potemkin's eminence, whereas his period of full favor lasted barely a year.

However the new affair began, Catherine's love notes to Zavadovskii show that it was a passionate interlude on her part. These little known notes, translated in full in the Appendix, are mostly undated and the sequence of their composition is thus uncertain; yet they deserve careful study for the psychological illumination they cast on the Empress's post-Potemkin emotional state. Unfortunately, they are less numerous and just as one-sided as her better known correspondence with Potemkin. Only some stray letters to friends (none to Catherine) offer an inkling of Zavadovskii's view of their romance.

Catherine's notes gush with affectionate effusions and endearments. "Thank you, Dearest; 150 kisses shall I joyfully give you each hour," she assures him. "Petrusa, you laugh at me, yet I am out of my mind over you. I love your smile immemorably."[18] Flaunting her mastery of Russian, she plays affectionate variations on his name—Petrinka, Petrukha, Petrusha, Petrusinka, Petrushinka—and occasionally refers to herself as Katia and Katiusha.[19] Her epithets for him are less flamboyant than those she bestowed on Potemkin. Indeed, "dear lordling" (*Sudarushichka*) and "Dear Little Angel" (*Angeliushichka*) might be taken for silly condescension were they not part of her passionate reply to his "most kind and most affectionate little letter": "I kiss you a hundredfold and press you to me." His tender attention excites her. "You feed my passion heart and soul," she confesses; "your tenderness and sensitivity cannot be compared to anything. Dear Little Angel, my friend, Petrusa, I love you like my soul, my beauty, and shall love you for a century; only do not change yourself, darling."[20]

She frequently reassures him of her love, just as she had done for Potemkin: "Petrusa, dear, all will pass, except my passion for you." Or again: "It is resolved that, I love you and shall love you, and remain firmly committed therein, yet you grieve over a trifle. At present I do not demand an answer, for I am going to get dressed, but after dinner I beg you to send word or bring it yourself. Priceless darling, Petrusa, do not grieve."[21] Sometimes she complains of neglect, as she plaintively pleads in one note: "Petrusa, you leave me all alone just when one wishes to see him [a grammatical slip or a reference to some part of his person?]. Petrusa, Petrusa, come to me! My heart calls you. Petrusa, where are you? Where have you gone? The priceless hours pass without you. My darling, Petrusa, come soon! I wish to embrace you."[22] Not even his temperamental outbursts deterred her. To one she replied with mock outrage, remarking that "You are Vesuvius itself: when you least expect it, an eruption appears; but no, never mind, I shall extinguish them with caresses. Petrusha dear!"[23]

Some of her notes allude to the physical manifestations of her passion, as in the following enigmatic mention of "little pillows"—evidently a euphemism for breasts:

> Petrushinka, I rejoice that you have been healed by my little pillows, and if my caress facilitates your health, then you will never be sick. Darling, you have no fault before me; stretch out your arms, I shall embrace you. Being kind, as you are, you have no cause to change yourself, I am extraordinarily contented with you and hour by hour adore you on par with the love that will be with you irrevocably. Dearest, dear darling, you are born for me, and our feelings, for the most part, and particularly in endearment, are essentially the same; your soul when it flies toward me, then it is met midway en route from my [side].[24]

In many notes Catherine reiterates her love and devotion, and refutes his charges of indifference and neglect. "I am healthy and the upset has passed," she informs him calmly and then exhorts him: "Petrusa, love me, and I will not only respond to you, but even anticipate. Dearest, My Dear!"[25] His protest that she persecutes those who speak frankly to him, however, triggers an explosion of rage. "Such a hellish invention, not conformable with my kind heart, does not dwell in me; these Machiavellian rules do not dwell in me." But then she concludes philosophically: "When fools blather, however, Katiusha ought not pay with her own tranquility. Please, be indulgent toward her, and do not act, and do not judge her so harshly. Really, she is all alone and nobody till now has busied himself with her justification, and yet it is tedious for her, loving justice and truth, always to be engaged in the refutation of false notions."[26]

Catherine did not entrust Zavadovskii with significant, independent political responsibilities, as she had done with both Orlov and Potemkin. Why not? Perhaps she wished to spare him the burden, thinking (after Potemkin) that love and duty could not mix. Perhaps she did not think him ready for such a role, or perhaps she did not fully trust him. In any event, her need for such assistance had lessened with the emergence of Potemkin, whom she may have feared to antagonize by an overly rapid advancement of his successor. It seems strange, too, that the Empress conferred only one decoration—the Polish Order of the White Eagle—on her Ukrainian lover, and that she awarded him no court rank. It may be significant that he was the single one of her native-born favorites who had not served in the Guards, nor did she bring any of his relatives into court service—a common practice with other favorites.

Zavadovskii apparently continued his cabinet duties as before, spending most of each weekday in close contact with his mistress/employer preparing reports, composing decrees, overseeing orders, and so on. It was work he was accustomed to, but at a level and in a setting that were new and strange. He began to feel the perils of proximity to great power: constant concern about his standing with the Empress vis-à-vis other courtiers (and former favorites), frequent requests from others to intervene on their behalf with Catherine, private life under the close scrutiny of others, as if "under a microscope," Zavadovskii wistfully confided to a friend.[27] To the same correspondent he hastened to contradict rumors of the sybaritic existence that he supposedly enjoyed at court. His workday began at nine in the morning (he explained) and lasted till dinner in the early afternoon, when he dined with the Empress and a few courtiers. Then they resumed work till evening, when he hardly had time for three rubbers of whist (not sixteen, as his detractors asserted) before retiring for the night at ten.[28] A discreet lover, he made no mention of hours for lovemaking, but there could not have been much time free for him or Catherine—"those dear hours that I spend with you," she called them.[29] It had to be a wearisome regimen for sovereign and favorite alike, more than enough to deflate the most robust passion.

Equally demanding as administrator and as mistress, Catherine found it difficult to grasp the psychic pressures that Zavadovskii labored under—the threat he espied in experienced courtiers such as Orlov, Potemkin, and Rumiantsev; his omnipresent insecurity in view of the Empress's changing moods, his sense of awkwardness in hardly speaking French at the cosmopolitan Russian court, his boredom with court routine. (Catherine may have helped him overcome his deficiency in French by regularly dining with him in the select company of Baron Grimm—who spoke no Russian—and a few other intimates; Zavadovskii was included at least thirty-five times between October 1776 and June 1777.)[30] For her part, Catherine worried when Zavadovskii became ill, yet she declined to visit until he recovered, and she even suggested on one occasion that he was feigning sickness to avoid her. Twice she complained of headache and pain in the legs, the latter perhaps an early indication of an ailment that dogged her last decades as she steadily put on weight. His professed passion pleased her, she acknowledged, but then she reprimanded him for failure to understand her situation and for foolish jealousy. "Had you thought as much about despotism as I have, you would not mention it much," she instructed him. "Secrets, I repeat, I do not keep from you. The suspicion about Popov [Potemkin's factotum], I confess that I laughed, for your sensitivity in this instance is really delirium itself. Believe, Petrusha, that I love you fervently, and in nowise and nothing do I deceive you."[31] His tears and sulks saddened her. On one occasion, seeking to relieve his sorrow, she even suggested he unburden himself to a friend, on condition that they both act "discreetly" and that he not show her letters to anyone. "I love you, love to be with you," she reassured him. "As often as possible, I am only with you, but Majesty, I confess, interferes a lot."[32]

In truth, the sovereign's role as Catherine conceived it often "interfered" with her desire for intimacy. Thus she tactfully explained her workaholic ways and needs to Zavadovskii in the following remarkable letter:

> Petrusa, in your ears a cry of falsehood has taken root, for you do not enter into my station at all. I have set myself the rule to be assiduous to state affairs, to lose the least time possible, but whereas a time for relaxation is absolutely necessary for life and health, so these hours are dedicated to you, and the time remaining belongs not to me, but to the Empire, and if I do not use this time as I ought to, then in me will take root against myself and others my own indignation, dissatisfaction,

and *mauvaise humeur* from the feeling that I am spending time in idleness and not as I ought to. Ask Pr[ince] Or[lov] whether I have not been this way long since. Yet you immediately cry out and blame it on lack of affection. It is not from that, but from an orderly division of time between state affairs and you. See for yourself, what other diversion do I have except strolling. This I must do for health.[33]

Beyond her needling reference to Orlov, it should be noted that "strolling" in this context might also mean "going out" for amorous purposes. Whether Catherine was a devotee of recreational romance or simply a believer in the benefits of regular exercise, she clearly enunciated her priorities here—duty before diversion.

To be sure, in the reversal of traditional sex roles that favoritism under Catherine entailed, it was only natural that her lover should resent her absorption in work and jealously complain of being ignored, neglected, humiliated. His only defenses were such typically "feminine" artifices as tears, recriminations, deprivation of attention, and (if all else failed) threats of abandonment. This last apparently worked at first. Catherine certainly reacted strongly, as the following note discloses:

> Petrusa, you have gone out of your mind! What nonsense! Where will you go? I feel nothing except affection; I show you nothing except some affection; and yet here are your conclusions! How well you use logic! Petrusa, you are unjust in regard to me; I do not seek causes to become angry, and indeed I am not angry by nature, even the little irascibility in me changes with one glance from you. Little Darling, truly, you jest. What do you lock yourself in your room for? Truly, hypochondria is good for nothing. Give me back my dear Petrusa, do not lock him away: me loves the darkhaired man; but leave the wrathful master home. Darling, if you do not wish to be deemed mean, then come with a caress.[34]

After a time their emotional upsets cooled her ardor. A "wrathful master" was not what she needed. Since most of her love notes cannot be precisely dated, it is well nigh impossible to chart exactly the decline of her passion or deduce all the reasons for the lovers' estrangement. Probably it all occurred gradually over several months and culminated in his near mental and physical collapse. For a while she laughed off his complaints as so much childish pouting and vain pride. She made repeated attempts to cheer him up. Finally his gloom caused her to fear for his sanity and to protect her own peace of mind. Apparently she even had Orlov and Potemkin intercede on her behalf, yet cautioned Zavadovskii against assuming that she had resumed intimacy with either.[35] "Never ascribe to me the qualities of base and weak souls," she warned him before explaining her coolness in pointedly masculine political terms: "the tsar knows how to reign, but when he has nothing but tedium the whole day, then he is tedious; he is all the more tedious when a dear visage looks on stupidly and the tsar, instead of merriment, gets from it a supplement of tedium and vexation. All this is past and forgotten."[36]

Their strained relationship could not be concealed for long. By early May 1777 outside observers confidently predicted Potemkin's "Reestablishment" and Zavadovskii's "approaching Retreat." Through Ivan Elagin, Catherine's longtime intermediary in affairs of the heart, she arranged a settlement of sorts: Zavadovskii to cool off at his Ukrainian estate for two months, his sabbatical sweetened by grants of 4,000 serfs in Belorussia, 50,000 rubles for the rest of that year and 30,000 for the next, a silver dinner service for sixteen. Advising him to rest and relax in the country, she held out hope for their future: "Your return depends on you every hour and be assured that my friendship will remain with you and yours inalienably for centuries." Ever the maternal adviser/confidante/teacher, she counseled him to translate Tacitus or read Russian history, and she sent him the ring she had promised. They dined together for the last time on 2 June. "Every meeting is painful," the lovelorn Zavadovskii confessed to Semen Vorontsov, an aristocratic army buddy. The breakdown of their romance caught him by surprise, he sorrowfully admitted on 8 June: "Amid hope, amid passion full of feelings, my fortunate lot has been broken, like the wind, like a dream which one cannot halt: [her] love for me has vanished." He left town that same day, already officially replaced by Potemkin's supposed new nominee—major of the hussars Semen Zorich, a fiery Serb who was quickly named a chamberlain and aide-de-camp and heaped with gifts and decorations. (Zavadovskii knew Zorich slightly, the two having sat next to each other at a banquet six months before.) As the British envoy saw it, these changes signified that "Prince Potemkin is now again at the highest Pitch."[37]

Barely six weeks later Zavadovskii dashed back to Petersburg in answer to Catherine's summons. (His passion for her—"like a stricken stag"—had not waned at all, just as he had predicted on leaving.) Warmly greeted, he soon detected a new coldness in his imperial mistress, who (he was informed by intermediaries) "respected" him wholeheartedly but restrained her exterior manifestations "in order to extinguish the alarm." Whose alarm? Her own or Potemkin's? Patronized by "all the boyars, big in rank but not in soul," Zavadovskii found himself scorned as soon as they concluded that he would not be reinstated. He stayed by turns at the Vorontsovs' house in Petersburg or their nearby dacha, and the Orlovs often consoled him at Gatchina. By contrast, the official court registers ignored his presence altogether, as if he had become an eighteenth-century "unperson." Soon he left again for the Ukraine, convinced that he lacked the qualities of a courtier. Yet life in the provinces palled within months. "From S. [the sovereign Mistress] herself I have twofold permission to return," he wrote Peter Bakunin, a friend in the Collegium of Foreign Affairs, on 25 February 1778, "nonetheless I still cannot put myself in that situation with equanimity; I foresee that there I will be rubbing salt in my wound, for which rationality is still not a powerful plaster." On 6 June he dined again at court and did so three more times by the end of the month. He resumed his administrative duties with the cabinet and added new ones with the Senate at the same time, but only occasionally attended court functions thereafter. His return to service may have been eased by the retirement in May 1778 of his successor Zorich after a stormy falling out with Potemkin. Some predicted his reinstatement as favorite, a move that Potemkin was said to have blocked, and it was rumored that he had been promised a seat on the Senate.[38]

Indeed, Zavadovskii had to recognize, however reluctantly, Potemkin's ascendancy in Catherine's councils. "Prince G. P. has no balance against him," he confided to Rumiantsev. "In actions I do not discern the previous rules, the previous opinions." Like many other court observers, Zavadovskii nursed ambivalent sentiments about the hegemony that Potemkin exercised. As he informed Rumiantsev with sarcastic admiration: "In all the centuries rarely has God produced a person so universal as that which is Prince P.: he is everywhere and everything." For several years after their breakup Zavadovskii pined for Catherine, "a fierce and unfortunate passion" that left no room in his heart for another. His infatuation only began to ebb in 1780 when she publicly snubbed him at her meeting with Joseph II in Mogilev. That summer he began to talk of taking a bride.[39]

Although Catherine quickly found a series of successors to Zavadovskii, she respected his administrative skills and loyalty sufficiently to promote him to privy counselor and appoint him to the Senate in 1780, to send him on inspection tours in 1780–81, and to put him in charge of the St. Petersburg bank for the nobility. Likewise she acceded to his request in 1781 to name his favorite estate Ekaterinindar (Catherine's Gift). With her financial assistance and architectural advice through Quarenghi, one of her favorite builders, Zavadovskii constructed a splendid palace at Ekaterinindar with 250 rooms, mosaic parquet floors, porcelain stoves, malachite fireplaces, a huge park, a library of 3,750 volumes, a bronze statue of Rumiantsev, and a full-length marble statue and full-length portrait of Catherine. The Empress never visited this million-ruble monument to her favor. The palace still stood in 1910. In 1786 Zavadovskii also bought the Panins' Petersburg palace, which he sumptuously refurnished at a cost of some 125,000 rubles. Catherine's confidence in his enlightened outlook and bureaucratic skills was further reflected in his appointment to head the new commission on public schools in 1782. In 1784 he was appointed to reform the Imperial Corps of Pages and to reorganize medical-surgical instruction in St. Petersburg. She also asked him in 1787–88 to assume the guardianship of Count Bobrinskoi, her son by Orlov, who had accumulated huge debts while abroad.

Zavadovskii preserved tender feelings for Catherine many years later. Before he finally married seventeen-year-old Countess Vera Apraksina on 30 April 1787 he solicited (and received) Catherine's "maternal" advice, encouragement, permission, and blessing for which he fulsomely thanked her: "From you I have all the goods of life. You are my protection and hope." At the start of the second Turkish war in 1787 she placed him in her council, the only favorite besides Orlov and Potemkin to enjoy that honor. In 1794 she obtained for him and his two brothers the title of count of the Holy Roman Empire.[40] He survived Emperor Paul's short reign and under Alexander I became Russia's first minister of public education.

Catherine's affair with Zavadovskii may disclose certain parallels and tangents in comparison to her association with Potemkin. First, it was obviously passionate and stormy, just as her first years with Potemkin had been. (Years later, gossip accused Potemkin of engineering Zavadovskii's removal amid tumultuous scenes of physical passion and near assault on sovereign and favorite alike; he supposedly hurled a candlestick at her.)[41] Second, it ended strangely and indefinitely, similar to her break with Potemkin. Perhaps Catherine really hoped they might be reconciled after some time away from one another. Indeed, the rather modest awards she conferred on Zavadovskii— modest only in comparison to the largesse heaped on Orlov and Potemkin over a longer period—may have implied that his eclipse was only temporary; but then again he may have seen them as a deliberately insulting measure of his past services. Third, Zavadovskii was the only favorite besides Potemkin to retain public prominence after his period of favor. The Empress certainly made less of Zavadovskii in public than she had for Potemkin. In this sense she may have considered him a transitional figure, someone with whom she could find the intimacy she had lost with Potemkin but not someone she wished to advertise to the greater world. Perhaps with Zavadovskii she really was seeking to defend their intimacy against the prying public. How fortunate for her that Russia lacked gossip columnists, scandal sheets, investigative journalists, and paparazzi! (Diplomats and courtiers filled the void, to some extent.) Even so, she must have felt deeply disappointed at her latest failure to secure the longer term intimacy that would help her bear the burdens of great power as she entered the new uncertainties of middle age.

Youth on Parade

Zavadovskii's "retirement" after some eighteen months of favor was followed by similarly short preferments of Semen Zorich in 1777–78 and Ivan Rimskii-Korsakov in 1778–79. Several other figures also sparked speculation for even shorter periods: Stakhiev and Strakhov in 1778, Levashev and Rontsov in 1779, Vysotskii and Mordvinov in 1780–81. (Rontsov was the bastard son of Count Roman Vorontsov and the half-brother of Princess Dashkova; he incurred Catherine's wrath and temporary disgrace for involvement in the Gordon Riots in London in 1780.) Probably these latter incidents were mere speculation, but gossip cited them as the eighteenth-century equivalent of one-night stands. The parade slowed slightly in 1779 with the installation of Alexander Lanskoi, who held center stage until his sudden death in June 1784. Then the steady succession resumed with Alexander Ermolov in 1785– 86, Alexander Dmitriev-Mamonov in 1786–1789, and, finally, Platon Zubov in 1789–1796, with briefer, shadowy appearances by several nonentities: Stoianov, Miloradovich, and Miklashevskii.[42] Since none of these confirmed and unconfirmed favorites left inside accounts of their experiences, and because only a bit of Catherine's correspondence with them has been found (presumably more once existed, judging from her previous romantic graphomania), little definite can be surmised about their significance.

James Harris, disappointed in his efforts to gain a Russian alliance, indicted the machinations of court factions in grooming the various studs for Catherine's delectation. Yet by August 1778 he predicted Korsakov's imminent dismissal, the Empress allegedly preferring multiple lovers, "as the Gratification of this disgraceful Passion is now become a Distemper rooted in the Blood." These serial dissipations, Harris foretold, would soon ruin her health and shorten her reign. Did Catherine delight in the conspicuous competition for her favor? Surely it afforded her some psychic as well as physical satisfaction. Baroness Dimsdale, who met her at Tsarskoe Selo in 1781, recorded this portrait: "Fine looking woman, not tall, fine expression, blue eyes and a sweet sensible look, a handsome person in her fifty-fourth year." And she long outlived Harris's pessimistic prediction. The coupling of her sexuality with themes of excess and death, however, long outlived her, taking on a sensuous life of its own.[43]

The aging Catherine lavished great wealth and attention on these favorites, evidently in something of a *quid pro quo* spirit. Several of them disappointed her and hastened their own dismissal: Zorich for his gambling and breaking with Potemkin, Rimskii-Korsakov for being caught in an assignation with Countess Bruce (who supposedly served as Catherine's "éprouveuse" or tester of male capacity, competing with Potemkin to control the succession of favorites), Dmitriev-Mamonov for falling in love with maid of honor Princess Shcherbatova. Countess Bruce's "betrayal" must have hurt her longtime friend deeply, the more so as she went off with Korsakov to despised Moscow.[44] All except Zubov followed Zavadovskii's example in that Catherine gave them no public political responsibilities. Like Zavadovskii, his successors received lessons in culture from the Empress, who treated them with a mixture of motherly affection and girlish admiration. The growing discrepancy in their ages and hers exercised the imaginations of court gossips ever more copiously.

Notions of Catherine's sexual insatiability assumed virtually mythic proportions in Russia and abroad. John Parkinson, an Oxford don who visited St. Petersburg in 1792–1794, heard an anecdote that linked the Empress's "building-mania" (*bâtissomanie*) in the decoration of St. Petersburg with her sexual promiscuity: "A party was considering which of the Canals had cost the most money; when one of them archly observed there was not a doubt about the matter; Catherine's Canal (this is the name of one of them) had unquestionably been the most expensive."[45] This particular tale may well have reflected a specifically English fascination with sensuality; for the same observer recounted how he and his noble pupil had made the obligatory visit to view the women's bath-house and had come away unimpressed: "Nothing could be more disgusting than most of the figures, their breasts hanging down in a most hideous manner."[46] Back home in England the former envoy extraordinary to Catherine's court, Sir George Macartney, recalled his Petersburg sojourn twenty years earlier with a mixture of cultural condescension and sensual satisfaction (he had been recalled for sexual indiscretion, having sired a daughter with Anna Khitrovo, a maid of honor who had been banished from court as a result).[47] When Macartney heard about the parade of Catherine's favorites, he deduced from it a policy and a preference:

It is evident from the lists given of the Empresses [sic] Favourites that she has always of late preferred a Russian to one of any other Nation. This may be partly owing to a fear of exciting any jealousy in the Nation, but by some is attributed to an idea that the Russians excell even the Irish in a certain *Manly* accomplishment, or rather feature of their Persons. The Russian Nurses it is said make a constant practice of pulling it, when the child is young, which has a great effect of lengthening the *virile instrument*. It is very certain that pulling and stroking the nose lengthens and raises it much and a similar plan may have some effect on other parts of the body.[48]

Catherine's patronage of Alexander Lanskoi, a twenty-three-year-old officer of the horse-guards, revealed her strongly pedagogical streak in seeking to cultivate promising young noblemen of mediocre background. She deluged "Sashin'ka" with presents to the tune of several million rubles, or so gossip proclaimed, and encouraged him to correspond in French with Baron Grimm. In fact, when Lanskoi's younger brother Yakov tried to elope with a foreign mistress from Dresden to Paris, Catherine prevailed on Grimm to arrange the young man's return. Promoted to chamberlain and General, Lanskoi received petitions and also accompanied the Empress on her inspection tour of the newly reformed western guberniias in 1780. With Potemkin's approval (and ignoring seniority) she promoted his cousins Stepan and Paul to ensign rank in the Preobrazhenskii Guards. His sisters Elizaveta, Avdot'ia, and Varvara she appointed maids of honor and awarded Elizaveta a house in St. Petersburg; all married aristocrats in ceremonies at court. Like his predecessors, Lanskoi was constantly rumored to be on the verge of dismissal, ostensibly because of differences with Potemkin.[49] In August 1783 his fall from a horse alarmed her greatly, as did his ensuing illness of six weeks.[50] "He was a very strong man, though ill made below," reported one foreign visitor ambiguously, "and without the appearance of being a muscular man."[51] Lanskoi's sudden death on 25 June 1784 after a short bout of "a malignant fever accompanied by quinsy" (i.e., inflammation of the throat, possibly from diphtheria) threw Catherine into a deep, prolonged depression—one of the most severe psychic crises of her life. "I have been plunged into the most acute sorrow and my happiness is no more," she confided to Grimm; "I thought that I myself would die from the irreparable loss of my best friend, a loss I experienced a week ago." His youth and her plans for their future redoubled her sense of loss. "I had hoped that he would become the support of my old age: He applied himself, he profited, he had adopted my tastes, this was a young man that I was educating, one who was grateful, gentle and honest, who shared my pains when I had any and who rejoiced in my joys."[52]

She personally wrote his mother the day after his death, and although he left his fortune to his imperial mistress, she divided it equally between his mother, brother, and five sisters.[53] Crazed by grief, Catherine took to her bed and, in her own words, "hovered for two weeks between life and death."[54] For more than three weeks she kept to her rooms. A bleeding on 27 July seemed to relieve her grief temporarily, for Dr. Rogerson assured her the first two cups of blood had been "extraordinarily inflamed." Still, she was tormented by a sore throat, flatulence, and chestpains, all of which may have been exacerbated by Rogerson's pills and purges. She kept asking about Lanskoi's body, which was buried at nearby Sofiia on 27 July in her absence. Her secretary Bezborodko summoned Potemkin from the Crimea and Fedor Orlov from Moscow to comfort her.[55] "They helped, but I could not endure the help," she told Grimm a year later. "No one was able to speak, to think in accord with my feelings. . . . One step at a time had to be taken, and with each step a battle had to be endured: one to be fought, one to be won, one to be lost." Gradually Potemkin succeeded in diverting the Empress, "and thus he awakened us from the sleep of the dead."[56] By early September 1784 she had recovered sufficiently to assure Grimm that, even at the height of her ordeal, she had not shirked her duties. "During the most frightful moments I was asked for orders for everything, and I gave them well, with order and intelligence." Her own devotion to duty and Potemkin's skillful intervention pulled her through this psychic crisis, a loss she sadly remembered years later.[57]

Another who helped her was Dr. Johann Zimmermann, court physician at Hannover. His widely translated and often reissued disquisition, *Solitude considered with Respect to Its Influence upon the Mind and the Heart,* received Catherine's thankful public endorsement "for the excellent precepts he has given to mankind," sentiments that she accompanied with gifts: a ring "enriched with diamonds of an extraordinary size and lustre," and a gold medal with her portrait. She also added him to her roster of valued foreign correspondents and, though he declined to visit Russia, he assisted in the recruitment of physicians and surgeons for Catherine's service. His tract on solitude appeared in Russian translation (St. Petersburg, 1791).[58]

Curiously, Lanskoi's death became the object of several scurrilous indictments of Catherine and her court. He was said to have expired "in place," some hinting that he had been worn out by the use of aphrodisiacs. "He had obtained such an influence over the Empress that it was thought he would have ruined Potemkin," averred a tale circulating in Petersburg in the early 1790s. "It is certain that after his death his legs dropped off. The Stench was also insufferable. The boy who gave him his coffee disappeared or died . . . the day after. All these circumstances lead [one] to suppose that he was poisoned." The prim Princess Dashkova, who had quarrelled with Lanskoi over a bust of the Empress, maliciously remarked upon his death: "he quite literally burst—his belly burst."[59] Naturally such stories also accused Potemkin, whose power and influence with the Empress made him the target of much jealous hatred.

Catherine's liaison with Dmitriev-Mamonov in 1786–1789 resembled that with Lanskoi, except that it ended not with her lover's death but with his surprise marriage at court. The same age as Lanskoi, Dmitriev-Mamonov was a Guards officer and an aide-de-camp to Potemkin, who may have recommended him to Catherine as a replacement for the ungrateful Ermolov.[60] The Empress called him "the redcoat," perhaps in reference to a portrait, and to Grimm she praised his command of French.[61] His installation, tenure, and retirement were all chronicled closeup by his friend Alexander Khrapovitskii, secretary and literary assistant to the Empress from 1782 to 1793, who kept a clandestine diary of court life with many jottings of Catherine's private comments and remarks on her moods. Indeed, she may have retired Khrapovitskii "upstairs" to the Senate after learning of the existence of his secret chronicle. Other details about Catherine's new affair were collected by Potemkin's Petersburg administrator, Mikhail Garnovskii, who drew on a variety of sources including Mamonov himself.[62]

Ermolov had been suddenly dismissed on 15 June 1786. After an "explanation" with Zavadovskii, who with Bezborodko had predicted Ermolov's retirement a year before because he was too timid for court politics, he was awarded the Polish Order of the White Eagle, 4,300 serfs in Belorussia, 130,000 rubles in cash, a silver dinner service, and leave to live abroad for five years. (In fact, he visited London in 1787, causing some embarrassment by his insistence on meeting George III). That very evening Mamonov was brought in to meet the Empress, who wrote him a letter the next day, presumably confirming the arrangement.[63] Apparently this change of partners was orchestrated by Potemkin, who is supposed to have denounced his former protégé Ermolov as "this young monkey, this white nigger." (All-knowing gossip blamed the break on his "incapacity.")[64] Ermolov left town the next day and Mamonov reappeared in the evening, to be ushered into Catherine's boudoir. "They s[lep]t until 9 o'clock," Khrapovitskii cryptically commented. The same thing occurred the next evening. "They closed the door. M-v was there after dinner and according to custom—[she was] powdered." Perhaps this last phrase hinted at exuberant loveplay.

On 19 June 1786 the new favorite was proclaimed aide-de-camp to the Empress. When Potemkin returned to court the next day Mamonov gave him a gold teapot with the inscription: *plus unis par le coeur que par le sang* (more united by the heart than by the blood; perhaps they were distantly related).[65] Two months later Catherine promoted Mamonov's father to the Senate and sent his mother a jeweled snuffbox.[66] She then distinguished the younger Mamonov with promotions, titles, gifts, and miscellaneous duties. In June 1787, for example, he was promoted to premier major in the Preobrazhenskii Guards, in May 1788 he rose to adjutant-general with the rank of lieutenant-general ("since he conducts himself like an angel"), and later that same month he received the title of count of the Holy Roman Empire.[67] She presented him with a silver dinner service purchased from Fitzherbert, the British ambassador; a team of English horses bought from Procurator-General Viazemskii for 2,000 rubles; and a jeweled walking stick for which she paid 3,700 rubles. Mamonov was unhappy with the last gift, however, feigning illness to avoid his mistress, but he confidentially informed a friend that he coveted the Order of St. Alexander Nevskii. The Empress gave it to him ten days later.[68] Eager to surprise her favorite, she arranged for an English theatrical troupe to stage a performance in his apartments, paying the seven players 200 rubles apiece. He hosted at home a production of one of Catherine's own plays in French. The Empress showed Mamonov various state papers and asked his advice about certain decrees and other matters. Nevertheless, she did not appoint him to her council (although she considered doing so) and confined most of his advice to literary activities.[69]

Like Catherine's previous liaisons, her relationship with Dmitriev-Mamonov started to cool after about two years, or so she later learned. In fact, rumors of his dismissal or voluntary departure had circulated for years. He came under attack from several directions. He was not on speaking terms with Bezborodko, Catherine's chief minister. He seemed neurotically attached to François de Ribaupierre, a courtier and soldier of Swiss extraction; his relationship with "Ivan Stepanovich" was stronger than "lover toward mistress," Garnovskii opined. To counteract Mamonov's support for the absent Potemkin, Zavadovskii and his confidant Alexander Vorontsov sought to wine and dine the young man, Garnovskii reported in alarm, while frightening him with a rival. Worst yet, as early as the spring of 1788 Mamonov was known to be involved with Shcherbatova, openly "beckoning" to her that summer. By contrast, he was on terrible terms with Anna Protasova, Catherine's confidante and chief "hen" at court. His hypochondria, physical revulsion, and growing coldness toward the anxious Empress boded ill for them both. Why were so many of her lovers sick so frequently? Or did they just pretend to be, to manipulate their mistress? After dinner on 11 February 1789 they quarreled. "Tears," recorded Khrapovitskii. "They spent the evening in bed . . . . He has asked to resign."[70] She wept the whole next day and declined to see anybody except Bezborodko. But Potemkin made peace between them after dinner. Four days later Khrapovitskii's friend the chamberlain Zakhar Zotov confided that "the laddie considers his life a prison, is very bored, and supposedly after every public gathering where ladies are present, she attaches herself to him and is jealous."[71]

On 21 February 1789 it was "tears" and isolation again, but the Empress reappeared at court the next day although Khrapovitskii tersely remarked that "the confusion continues." When word was received of the death of Dmitriev-Mamonov's sister, Catherine spent the evening publicly with her favorite; the next day she had Khrapovitskii correct the spelling of a letter of condolence to Dmitriev-Mamonov's father. At the same time she openly complained to Zotov about the favorite's "coldness and preoccupation" for nearly four months—"that is," Khrapovitskii calculated, "since the time that his absences began."[72] During the next few months the Empress showed no clear signs of emotional anguish, but she spent little or no time with her favorite, rarely dined with him, and seemed increasingly preoccupied with the tense international situation. On 8 March "she lay on a skiff, feeling a pain in the waist," and on 1 April she missed church because of a stiff neck.

Nobody at court could figure out what was going on, as Khrapovitskii anxiously noted on 29 March: "Not a word to me from anybody." That Catherine was in low spirits, however, may be deduced from her strong reaction to news of Emperor Joseph II's mortal illness; "since yesterday evening she has been weeping and spent all day in bed," Khrapovitskii recorded on 21 April 1789, Catherine's sixtieth birthday, which she passed in seclusion. The next day he still noticed a "remnant of illness and anxiety." The death on 24 April of Count Andrei Shuvalov further depressed the Empress, who sent to inquire about the circumstances. "What a melancholy time!" Khrapovitskii quoted Catherine as saying on 5 May. "Three persons slashed themselves. This is from the weekly governor's report, and was said in relation to her own anxiety."[73]

Some courtiers either saw what was happening before the Empress did, or they were misled by her composed countenance amid the flurry of intrigues. Zubov first appeared officially at court at Tsarskoe Selo on 29 April; he was supposedly sponsored by General Nikolai Saltykov, governor of the grand dukes, whose tour of court duty beginning on 20 May might have assisted his protégé. Whatever the case, her former favorite Zavadovskii knew by 1 June that Mamonov was going to marry Princess Shcherbatova, "a girl most ordinary,.not possessing either looks or other gifts." The whole affair had been "a secret only for one woman," the same observer commented maliciously before unleashing a bitter tirade on court morals and a denunciation of Dmitriev-Mamonov:

> Intrigue and cuckoldry are committed at court most casually. Treachery is no less rewarded than even heartfelt devotion. The same crimes at a different time have not the same revenge. Imagine this one and the example of Korsak and Briuussha! [i.e., Korsakov and Countess Bruce] Be that as it may, but all are glad that this man has ceased to be the favorite. An arrogant and haughty animal, he was filled with malice and cunning. In the face he resembled a Kalmyk or Bashkir, only the eyes are bulging and larger than usual in that breed. Being taken from the officers, he attained such power that all affairs, which he could not even comprehend, passed through his hands. The face of a haughty and arrogant person he did not drop for a minute. He spoke French, busied himself with the theater, and from these signs they attributed to him both good breeding and a universal mind. The least ray of sense in the favorite seems a blazing sun. Not being in a position to proceed along the course of the prince [Potemkin], he only imitated his laziness and deviousness. Our common friend, Ct. Al. Andreevich [Bezborodko], he has discredited forever; it was easy for him to succeed in that, for society and his life have supplied modes most abundantly thereto. In the broader sphere he is the same as he was at Jassy [with Rumiantsev in 1774–75]. I know not what will be further; but usually, once one is dislocated at court, then no bonesetter can help. A holy place does not remain empty. A new favorite is rising—an officer of the horse-guards, a twenty-year-old boy, whose outward appearance and innards do not promise longevity.[74]

To be sure, Zavadovskii had many reasons to denigrate the falling favorite and disdain the presumed successor. Probably he exaggerated Dmitriev-Mamonov's political influence in general, perhaps from envy and malice. But he may have been right in predicting the imminent decline of Potemkin and Bezborodko in high policymaking. At any rate, it is curious that he (and Garnovskii) knew so much several weeks before the public denouement, and that they both believed Catherine to be blind to her favorite's romantic involvement. Presumably he knew her psyche and political practices from his own stint as favorite a decade before and from his subsequent state service in the capital. In that regard, the virtual paranoia associated with court politics shines forth in his injunction to his correspondent, Count Semen Vorontsov, to burn his letters at once.

Zavadovskii's description of the transition from Dmitriev-Mamonov to Zubov suggests a couple of different explanations: first, that the matter may have been arranged without Catherine's knowledge or, second, that she may have arranged it herself, yet carefully concealed the fact. Why would she do the latter? Simply to preserve the social fiction of male initiative and female passivity? That might have been partly the case, but she may also have been so absorbed in state affairs (and too proud to face an imminent loss) that she could not see an obvious escape from her own emotional turmoil. One can only speculate about her thoughts at the time, or deduce them from her subsequent explanations/justifications—a notoriously perilous procedure.

Against this confused, somber psychological backdrop Khrapovitskii and the other courtiers witnessed in mid-June 1789 "a Russian *cosa rara;* they have quit." Tears all day on 18 June preceded the revelation that the Empress was releasing her "laddie" to marry Princess Shcherbatova, age twenty-seven. Catherine spent the next two days closeted with her confidante, Anna Naryshkina, whom Zotov suspected of arranging Zubov's succession.[75]

Dmitriev-Mamonov's "duplicity" was for the Empress a surprise that was no surprise; yet she was much affected all the same. As she recounted the events to Khrapovitskii a few days afterwards, when the favorite had appeared on Monday, 18 June, he complained at first of her coldness and then began to berate her. She had coolly reminded him of how she had been and how much she had suffered since the previous September—evidently allusions to earlier disputes. Later he had asked her advice on what to do. Ever the generous friend, Catherine had suggested that he marry Count Bruce's nubile, already mature thirteen-year-old daughter, one of the richest heiresses in Russia. "Suddenly he answers with trembling hands that for a year he has been in love with Shcherbatova and six months ago gave his word to marry her."[76] Whatever the degree of Catherine's surprise at this disclosure—she fainted, she confessed to Potemkin, and when Mamonov asked her to call in Naryshkina, the latter "abused him so much that I have never in my life heard anybody so scolded"—the Empress quickly "pardoned" the young lovers, granted them permission to marry, even insisted that the ceremony be performed at court. "God be with them!" she exclaimed to Khrapovitskii. "Let them be happy." To prove her goodwill she awarded the couple estates with 2,250 souls and 100,000 rubles in cash.[77] She had not been surprised, she assured Khrapovitskii, who believed her, knowing that Zubov was already waiting upstairs in her bedroom and that he stayed till eleven o'clock in the evening of 21 June. Thereafter the new favorite began dining with the Empress and her close circle and visiting her upstairs in the evenings.[78]

Catherine's abrupt promotion of Zubov served in some measure to camouflage her pain at parting with Dmitriev-Mamonov. Her mood oscillated wildly. On 29 June she boasted to Potemkin of how much better her health was as compared to the previous year; but twelve days later she admitted having just recovered from a powerful chill that resulted in three days of fever, sore throat, and delirium. In letters to Potemkin, who later cursed Mamonov for prematurely deserting his sinecure "in a stupid manner," the Empress bewailed her former favorite's strange conduct—why had he not told her sooner? "Can you imagine," she informed Potemkin a few days after the wedding had taken place at court (in her conspicuous absence) on 1 July 1789, "there are signs that he had a desire to stay with his wife at court as before, finally a thousand contradictions and contradictory ideas and irrational behavior, such that his closest friends do not justify him."[79]

Two weeks later she still ruminated over the causes of the breakup. Potemkin had tried to tell her that winter and spring, she admitted, but she had not believed him and had defended the youth. Why had Potemkin not been more insistent, she inquired sorrowfully, and thereby saved them all from "much superfluous grief?" Dmitriev-Mamonov's intimate friend, Ribaupierre, had known all about the affair, she concluded; for when summoned he had turned "white as a sheet," but she had declined Potemkin's prompting to question him further.[80] She took umbrage at the suggestion that she had kept her lover against his will. Thus she castigated Potemkin: "I have never been anybody's tyrant and hate constraint, is it possible that you have misunderstood me on this point! and that the generosity of my character has vanished from your head and you consider me a vile egoist, you would cure me in a minute by telling me the truth." After this emotional explosion she reiterated her confidence and favor in Potemkin, scorned his unnamed critics, and advised him to ignore petty vexations. "Comfort me, treat us kindly," she begged for herself and Zubov: "NB, we have a kind heart and a manner most pleasant, without malice and cunning and a very determined desire to do good; four rules we possess that there will be an endeavor to preserve, namely, be *loyal, modest, devoted,* and *grateful to an extreme.*"[81]

As with previous favorites, so with Dmitriev-Mamonov the Empress parted on officially cordial terms, and she later praised his mind and courage, and boosted his military career. For his part, he wrote her occasionally from Moscow and even lamented his youthful "folly" in precipitating the unfortunate loss of her favor, a memory that "constantly tortures my soul," as he informed her in 1792. Gossip about this switch of favorites gave rise to the story (almost certainly false) that Catherine revenged herself on the loose-tongued Shcherbatova by secretly sending policemen disguised as women to whip her in her husband's presence.[82] Yet Catherine did take a kind of revenge in releasing maid of honor Maria Shkurina from court service in the fall of 1789 to join the Mamonovs in Moscow, granting her 12,000 rubles as a "dowry" (?!) and commenting acidly: "this one will bring the disorder to its height." (She suspected Shkurina of facilitating the intrigue and had learned that Mamonov had quarrelled with his father and was living apart; rumor had it that he had gone mad, but the Empress denied this to Potemkin.) About this *ménage à trois* Catherine chortled: "these two busybodies will kill him." A year later, however, she coldly noted Shkurina's return to court. Excluded from court service, Shkurina later retired to a convent. "He cannot be happy," Catherine summed up Mamonov as lover and prospective spouse; "there is a difference in strolling with somebody in the garden and seeing her for a quarter of an hour, or to live together."[83]

Rid of one lover, the Empress eagerly embraced his replacement. On 3 July 1789 she promoted Platon Zubov to colonel in the horse-guards and adjutant. She showered cash on him; he in turn made cash gifts to Zotov and Naryshkina, presumably for their assistance in his ascent. Eager to educate her new young lover, she had Khrapovitskii order a parcel of French books for him from a catalogue and laughed merrily when she noticed one title: "Lucine without intercourse—a letter in which it is demonstrated that a woman can give birth without commerce with a man." "That's a sunbeam," she hooted, repeating a favorite gibe, "and in ancient times Mars, Jupiter, and other gods served as an excuse." In elevating Zubov the Empress followed her customary practice and promoted his father and three brothers.[84] She strove to ingratiate them with Potemkin, but their greatest influence emerged only after the latter's death in October 1791.

From a psychological perspective, Zubov's installation gave Catherine a definite lift: "I am healthy and merry and have come alive like a fly," she crowed to Potemkin on 5 August 1789. Her high spirits did not last long, however, for on the evening of 17 August she fell ill. "There were powerful spasms," Khrapovitskii reported. "She agonized [all] night." She felt better the next day, but then suffered a relapse that kept her in bed several days. When she got up on 25 August she complained of noise in her ears—perhaps evidence of a circulatory ailment. Illness afflicted her again in mid-September. The anniversary of her coronation a week later brought her only momentary pleasure. Told that she would reign another sixty years, she replied: "No, I will be without mind and memory, I shall live another 20 years, the past year has been difficult, in the present one the only vexation is Pushkin's inaction" (against the Swedish army in Finland).[85] Catherine's feelings of being old and overburdened could no longer be lightened by a new favorite's ministrations.

System and Significance

What can be concluded about Catherine's "system" of favorites from Potemkin onward? For one, she did formulate a sort of system in this regard, a regular pattern of behavior on her part. For another, she sought to preserve appearances to some extent; she neither flaunted nor concealed her attachments. As concerns the attributes of her system, one should reiterate its political foundations. Except for Zavadovskii, all her main choices singled out Guards officers, a blatant example of her assiduous attention to them as a mainstay of her rule. From a practical angle, moreover, Guardsmen were especially likely to catch her attention in view of their youth, robust physiques, their ubiquity at court, and their employment in all manner of governmental duties. Since all her favorites came from fairly obscure noble families, their rise thus reminded the nobility of the rewards that state service (servicing the autocratrix in this instance) could gain for an individual and his relatives. In one sense Catherine used her selection of favorites to restock the elite, promoting newcomers and rescuing old families fallen from eminence in recent decades. Never did she choose a favorite from an already prominent noble clan. To have done so would have risked inciting the jealous ire of other established families. In another sense her system of patronizing favorites and their relatives offered a substitute for the wider family that she had missed earlier in life.

Foreigners were impressed by her liberality toward former favorites and her astuteness in arranging alternative employment for them. As *The Daily Universal Register* (soon to become *The Times* of London) commented in July 1787:

> Nothing can more clearly prove the strength of mind which the Imperial Catherine possesses, than her conduct toward her favourites, *quand cela ne plait plus.* —In lieu of suffering them to intermeddle in politics (too often the case among favourites here of both sexes in an inferior station) she wisely dismisses them with a handsome allowance, to travel into foreign countries.[86]

In economic terms the institution of favoritism exemplified Catherine's policy of prodigal expenditures in pursuit of glory, fame, and prestige. It is estimated that the court's share of state expenditures rose only slightly in the period 1767–1781, from 10.9 percent to 11.4 percent—probably a negligible increase in real terms. But from 1781 to 1795 the share increased substantially both in proportional and absolute terms: from 11.4 to 13.5 percent, and from 4.6 million rubles per year to 10.6 million.[87] Contemporaries believed the favorites reaped colossal sums from their imperial mistress. This was partly true, yet it cannot be precisely determined in many instances and, besides, the practice cannot be completely divorced from Catherine's general patronage of the nobility and from her expenditures on such policies as colonization and town-building in the newly acquired southern territories. Apparently Catherine did not lavish pensions on her favorites or, if she did, she kept the accounts separate from the other funds disbursed by her personal cabinet.[88]

With the exception of Potemkin, it seems Catherine did not permit her favorites to play much of an independent role in politics. But one cannot be entirely certain on this score, for some of them may have exerted a subtle or indirect influence that escapes detection. If the Empress's treatment of Zavadovskii was typical, however, her conception of absolute sovereignty did not permit her to cede any permanent authority to anyone else. And she appears to have exerted herself to keep her statecraft separate from her love life. No doubt she sometimes fuzzed the line in certain situations, but she certainly postulated a distinct separation. Indeed, her crushingly conscientious concept of duty made romance a physical and psychological necessity in a purely recreational sense.

The progressively younger ages of Catherine's favorites, a quality all the more striking as she herself assumed the shape and status of a grandmother, shocked contemporaries and posterity alike. Then as now many observers reacted to the idea of intimacy between the aging Empress and her youthful favorites with disgust, incredulity, or disdainful mirth. Perhaps in the present-day sexually emancipated world with its much longer lived population, such evidence of "senior sex" looks less startling than in Catherine's time. But then the notion of a dominating, voracious, insatiable, promiscuous, castrating female has threatened male psyches from time immemorial.

The youthfulness of Catherine's favorites also focused attention on another aspect of her system: its pedagogical and cultural function. In cultivating a succession of bright young men, the Empress gave an unusual exhibition of her broad effort to enlighten Russian society and enrich its elite with the refinements of European culture. Her favorites were supposed to ornament her sophisticated, cosmopolitan court; they were to be ambitious, attractive, accomplished young men worthy of emulation. Furthermore, several possessed some literary talent, Zavadovskii, Lanskoi, and Dmitriev-Mamonov in particular. They helped her in her Russian literary pursuits even as she initiated them into European culture, encouraging them by her own example to broaden their cultural and intellectual horizons.

Paradoxical features of favoritism under Catherine were the brevity of her lovers' tenure and their steady succession. Is it too simple to explain this pattern by nymphomania—a gargantuan appetite for sex and variety in sexual partners? Because it is so difficult to penetrate past the bedroom door and, moreover, to determine the specific causes for Catherine's several changes of favorites, one cannot be certain what the typical pattern of her relationships actually was, or what it meant for her psyche. Surely an element of chance shaped the apparent pattern. Lanskoi's death, for example, ended one of the longer terms of the Empress's favor. In more cases than not, it seems, Catherine clung to the relationship longer than her lover did. Potemkin, Korsakov, and Dmitriev-Mamonov all apparently took the initiative in ending or loosening their ties with the Empress. Yet she appears to have made the decision to terminate in the case of Zavadovskii, who may have alienated her by his jealousy of his predecessors. Did Catherine feel inadequate in her inability to "hold" one man, or did she think it natural to be involved with many over the course of the years? Was her power as much of an aphrodisiac for her as it was for her favorites? Was she really searching compulsively for the ideal bedmate, or did she rationalize the matter to herself and blame the instability of her relationships on bad luck or her partner's defects? Was the passion she manifested in writing to Potemkin, Korsakov, and Zavadovskii only a paper sentiment? Whatever it was, she certainly excited passion in many of her lovers. Passion, whether paper or palpable, permeated an important part of her psyche, but one can only guess how large (and how controlled) that part was of her personality.

All told, the number of her documented lovers did not exceed twelve, and that over a period of forty-four years. With five—Poniatowsky, Orlov, Potemkin, Lanskoi, and Zubov—she maintained multiyear romantic relationships that amounted to serial monogamy. Of those favorites who enjoyed shorter terms—Saltykov, Vasil'chikov, Zavadovskii, Zorich, Rimskii-Korsakov, Yermolov, and Dmitriev-Mamonov—at least two (Zavadovskii and Dmitriev-Mamonov) retained strong feelings for her years after. All her lovers received bounteous gifts and perquisites. None experienced any evident vindictiveness from Catherine, who certainly had cause for such in the case of Rimskii-Korsakov and Dmitriev-Mamonov. Notwithstanding all the gossip and insinuations about many other lovers (their ranks exhibited a mythic propensity to endless expansion, especially after her death, in a female version of "George Washington slept here"), Catherine strove to conduct her court with great decorum. As the overburdened ruler of an "immense and turbulent Empire" first and a proud, passionate woman second, she had neither the time nor the inclination to dabble in ostentatious dissipation.[89] Amid the welter of state duties and court routine she sometimes felt achingly lonesome. A nymphomaniac she was not, but a normal person in an abnormal position.

10

Succession Concerns
and Southern Vistas

The question of the succession to the Russian throne bedeviled Catherine's entire adult life. In one form or another it complicated and confused much of her statecraft. It would not go away. It would not be solved. Moreover, it was a peculiar kind of issue for which political theorists offered no guidance. By arranging Paul's marriage in September 1773, Catherine had hoped to make a start on resolving this most delicate dilemma. A healthy male heir was the primary object of this union. Indeed, so concerned was the Empress about the provision of an heir that she considered delaying her visit to Moscow in 1775 to allow Grand Duchess Natalia's recovery from a brief illness. The young woman's health "is becoming steadily worse," Catherine complained to Grimm from Moscow in February 1775, "and we are dying of fear that she not become consumptive: she has all of the symptoms." No dynastic help could be expected from Catherine's teenaged son by Orlov. Recently returned to Petersburg from years abroad, he was finally given the surname of Bobrinskoi (after an estate the Empress had purchased for him) and enrolled in the Noble Cadet Corps under the watchful eye of Ivan Betskoi.[1]

The frailty of Paul's wife only compounded Catherine's dissatisfaction with her daughter-in-law. "Everything is excessive in this woman's household," she declared to Grimm before unleashing a veritable tirade on the Grand Duchess's defects of character:

> If one goes for a walk, it's twenty versts; if one dances, it's twenty quadrilles, as many minuets, not counting the allemandes; to avoid heat in one's rooms, they are not heated at all; if somebody rubs their face with ice, then the whole body becomes the face: in short, moderation in everything is very far from our household. Apprehending evildoers, we do not trust the whole world and listen to neither good nor bad advice; in a word, up till now there has been neither consideration,

nor prudence, nor shrewdness in anything, and God knows what will come of it, since one listens to nobody and wants to do everything in one's own way. Just imagine, after more than a year and a half one still speaks not a word of the language; we wish for someone to teach us, but we do not give an hour a day to it; everything is trifles; we cannot bear the one nor the other; we are in debt for twice what we have, and yet we have as much as anyone in Europe.[2]

By mid-summer 1775 the Grand Duchess was thought to be with child. "Her friends are, with Reason, very anxious that She should prove so," the British ambassador reported on 27 July. "Pretty plain Hints have been already dropt of the Necessity of a Divorce should She not soon become pregnant." A month later, however, such concerns yielded to anxious anticipation at news that the Grand Duchess was pregnant. Her pregnancy proceeded so smoothly that the Empress even ordered a search for wet-nurses for the new baby, superstitiously stipulating that no redheads be selected. Catherine's old friend and admirer, Prince Henry of Prussia, arrived on 2 April 1776 to witness the happy event.[3]

After three o'clock in the morning of Sunday, 10 April 1776, Paul awakened his mother with word that the Grand Duchess had been in torment since midnight. Catherine arose at once and, finding that true birthpains had yet to begin, stayed with the expectant couple until ten in the morning, when she left to dress for the day. Back with the grand ducal pair by noon, the Empress and Countess Rumiantseva, an experienced midwife, winced while the contractions became so powerful that parturition looked imminent. A doctor and surgeon waited outside in the anteroom. The night passed without result, though, the pains alternating with periods of restless sleep. The next day witnessed more of the same; so doctors Kruse and Tode were summoned to advise Countess Rumiantseva, "but our best hopes remained without success," Catherine later lamented. On Tuesday the physicians called in doctors Rogerson and Lindemann, the senior specialists in St. Petersburg, "for the midwife rejected the possibility" of saving mother or child. Dr. Tode was admitted on Wednesday, but he could do nothing. All agreed that the child, too large to enter the birth canal, was already dead. The Grand Duchess was given the last rites on Thursday and died on Friday, 15 April 1776, about five P.M.[4]

Catherine and Paul had kept a constant vigil for five days in a row. "Never in my life have I found myself in a more difficult, more hideous, more painful position," the Empress confided to Grimm on 17 April: "I forgot to drink, to eat, and to sleep, and my strength sustained me I know not how. I begin to believe that if this misadventure did not derange my nervous system, it is underangeable." Yet only one day later she admitted that "on Friday, after the fatal end, I turned to stone and at this moment [Monday] I am still numb." She began to worry about Paul's own health and future even more. He did not attend the burial on 26 April at Petersburg's St. Alexander Nevskii Monastery, where his mother, accompanied by Potemkin and Grigorii Orlov, "shed many tears and appeared deeply affected at this melancholy Ceremony." Her sorrow was redoubled by knowledge that her dead grandchild had proved to be a "perfectly formed" boy.[5]

Exhausted as well as mortified by the tragedy, Catherine immediately accompanied Paul and Prince Henry to Tsarskoe Selo for several weeks, obviously in hopes that the change of scenery would lighten their grief. A postmortem persuaded her that a deformity of the spine had dictated both deaths. The Grand Duchess's birth canal had measured only four fingers wide, whereas the baby's shoulders had been eight or nine fingers across. Feelings of guilt and recrimination wracked the Empress for weeks afterwards. She and Baron Asseburg, who had helped her select Paul's spouse, were both shocked by German press reports that the late Grand Duchess had been injured in childhood, with her capacity to bear children ruined by a quack's ineptitude. Stung by such charges, Asseburg denied any knowledge of the defect and protested to the Empress that Natalia's late mother had repeatedly ("a thousand times") assured him of her daughter's healthy "constitution." All of which led Catherine to conclude privately: "I am very persuaded of the innocence of Mr. d'Assebourg, but it is no less true that fourteen physicians, surgeons and the midwife have been convinced by opening the body that he was misled and that the gazette article is true."[6] To Grimm and other correspondents the Empress reiterated her stoic conviction that the tragedy had been the product of unforeseeable circumstances— *"Sic transit gloria mundi"*; "Man proposes and God disposes." "My grief has been great," she confessed to Prince Volkonskii on 1 May, "but, trusting in God's will, one must think about recouping the loss." Catherine's grief was cut short not only by political considerations. Within days of Natalia's demise evidence came to light of her "disposition to gallantry and intrigue" with young Count Andrei Razumovskii, the Grand Duke's favorite chamberlain, who was banished from court forthwith. Years later gossip proclaimed that he had infected her with venereal disease, which she communicated to Paul.[7] Both assertions appear doubtful.

Actually, Catherine had begun arranging for a replacement the very day of Natalia's death—clear testimony to the urgency she felt in the matter. She resolved to have Prince Henry immediately sound out his niece about the availability of her eldest daughter, Princess Sophia Dorothea of Würtemberg. Born in Catherine's hometown of Stettin, the now sixteen-year-old princess, one of three daughters and eight sons, had been considered too young for Paul three years before. The Empress wished the mother to bring her daughters to Berlin at once with a promise of recompense for the journey (40,000 rubles). While the preliminary negotiations with her parents were being settled, Paul and Prince Henry would journey to Riga, from where they could quickly visit Berlin if a match looked promising. Paul must approve the choice and then write for his mother's blessing, which she empowered Prince Henry to give the parents on the spot. The Grand Duke would then return to await his bride-to-be, who should travel with her mother and sister to Memel, where they would be met by Countess Rumiantseva and her suite. (Presumably Rumiantseva's knowledge of midwifery would allow her to

ascertain the princess's childbearing capabilities; there must be no more surprises in this particular dynastic department.) After bidding farewell to her
mother and sister—did Catherine not wish them to witness the wedding because she recalled the problems with her own mother thirty years before, or
did she nurse a grudge against the late Natalia's mother for misrepresenting
her daughter's qualities?—the bride-to-be should come to Petersburg to embrace Orthodoxy and be officially betrothed and married. Complete official
silence was to shroud these arrangements until the matter was well under
way. Such was Catherine's bold, urgent initiative.[8]

Alert to the political (and financial) potential in the proposed match,
Prince Henry and his brothers, King Frederick and Prince Ferdinand, exerted themselves to make it all happen as Catherine desired. They urged
their niece to accept the marriage as a unique opportunity for family prestige, political service to Prussia, and the financial salvation and future
security of the house of Würtemberg, conveying Catherine's pledge of dower-
ies for all three daughters (hence the parents might pocket the dowry provided by the duchy!), 60,000 rubles for the journey to Memel, and pensions
for them all. Furthermore, they pointed out that Paul's favor would open
career prospects—ranks, offices, and titles—for the family's two eldest sons
that they could hardly aspire to in Prussian service. That the prospective
bride was already engaged to Prince Louis of Hesse Darmstadt, Paul's
brother-in-law through the late Grand Duchess, proved no obstacle at all.
He was persuaded to withdraw from the betrothal and promised the hand of
a younger daughter, with the threat of Prussian and Russian disfavor if he
stood in the way. The parsimonious Frederick even provided 10,000 thalers
for the bride's wardrobe. He also briefed her beforehand about the Russian
court, just as he had done for Catherine thirty-two years before. Naturally
Paul's Prussian partisans extolled the Grand Duke's merits to the bride and
her parents, dismissing the necessity of her conversion to Orthodoxy as a
matter of slight significance. Indeed, Prince Henry sent ahead the form of
abjuration used by the late Grand Duchess so that Paul's intended could
begin memorizing it.[9]

In making these arrangements Catherine sought to please Paul. Mother
and son became closer than ever for a time. When he drove over to Peterhof
with Prince Henry at the end of May 1776, for example, she lauded his
affectionate note of greeting and regretted their temporary separation: "Really,
the house is empty without you, and no less do I await the minute in which
I may embrace you." Since Paul had inherited his father's and the Panins'
Prussophile proclivities, the prospect of a trip to Frederick the Great's Berlin
appeared certain to delight the young widower, who had never ventured
abroad. Even so, the Empress kept the arrangements secret from Nikita
Panin, who was ill in Petersburg with "a violent Attack of Piles in the Blad-
der" while Paul recovered from a fever at Tsarskoe Selo. She made certain
the Grand Duke would travel in comfort and splendor with a large suite
headed by General Nikolai Saltykov, governor of the grand ducal household,
and ornamented by the great war hero Field Marshal Rumiantsev-Zadunaiskii. All these preparations thrilled Paul, as Catherine confided his sentiments

to her lover Zavadovskii (who had privately begged the prickly Rumiantsev to honor Catherine's invitation) "that everything is being prepared so well and so swiftly to his satisfaction that he considers it all a special good fortune." And when word arrived of the parents' permission for Sophia Dorothea to wed, the Empress wrote her prospective daughter-in-law a tactful note in French placing Paul's happiness in her hands and promising an affectionate welcome in Russia. As signs of *"l'amour et de la patrie,"* moreover, she sent with her son the Order and ribbon of St. Catherine with the further assurance that Russia spoke through her with open arms.[10]

Paul departed for Riga the evening of 13 June 1776. As usual, Catherine worried about his health, wrote him frequently (Potemkin corrected her Russian in several instances), and praised his letters and his rapid progress. She constantly reassured him about her own good health. The memory of Natalia's death still haunted the Empress, who ruminated to Voltaire about the strange succession of "sad spectacles" and "fortunate events" before reiterating the tragic inevitability of the loss of her daughter-in-law and unborn grandson: "No human aid could ever have foreseen, prevented, or saved both or at least one of the two. . . . We are presently preoccupied with repairing our losses."[11]

With Catherine's evident encouragement, Paul acted like a ruler by inspecting the local government, garrisons, and economic conditions along the way to Prussia. Did he hope his insights would eventually convince her to share power with him, as Maria Theresa had done with Joseph II? When, for instance, Paul complained from Riga on 20 June about the shabby uniforms and footwear of the local garrison, blaming the situation on dissension between General Elmpt and Governor-General Brown, Catherine vowed to look into the matter although she partly explained it as a clash of personalities and jurisdictions. She responded more enthusiastically to Paul's praise of the orderliness and manners of Livland, remarking: "I hope that in time the main part of Russia will not yield to this guberniia in anything, neither in order nor in the correction of manners, and that your lifetime will be sufficient to see such a change."[12]

Here Catherine restated her conviction that Russia must follow the pattern of the more Europeanized western portions of the realm. Perhaps there was also a hint that the end of her reign and Paul's succession might come sooner than either of them could foresee. In reply to Paul's admiration for Riga's flourishing commerce and his criticism of its decrepit citadel and miserable garrison, she took credit for the first, agreed with him about the second— "God forbid that one should see the need for reinforcement of its garrison"— and blamed the third on blind imitation of Prussian military methods. This last dig may have been intended to caution Paul against the dangers of indiscriminate admiration for all things Prussian. For if the Russian military leadership had erred in this instance, "then this failure proves, as do so many others as well, that in borrowing from others we do not always act in conformity with our own benefit." What did she think about Paul's later laudatory description of Prussian prosperity, especially his conclusion that Prussian society surpassed Russian in all respects by two centuries? In private

Catherine shared these sentiments, for she pronounced Paul's observations "well founded." In public she could never admit such notions.[13]

Accompanied from Memel onward by Prussian representatives, Paul reached Berlin on 10/21 July 1776. Frederick the Great exerted himself in honoring his Russian allies. Paul rode with Prince Henry into Berlin through triumphal arches, amid music and cannon salutes, in a chariot sheathed in silver and drawn by eight beautiful horses. A medal was struck to commemorate the occasion, and a special pamphlet published in German. Sir James Harris, soon to be transferred to Petersburg, recorded a quip to the effect that a zealous Pomeranian mayor had ordered the welcoming banners to read "Paul *Von* Petrowitz"! To Catherine's letter delivered by Paul, the King responded warmly, reaffirming his devotion and gratitude, and showering the Grand Duke with attention at supper that evening and throughout his visit. All this Prussian hospitality pleased the Empress greatly. She was even happier about Paul's enthusiastic endorsement of his prospective bride's good looks and good sense, her determination to fulfill her marital duties, her intellectual interests (even geometry!), and her resolve to learn Russian, "knowing how necessary this is and remembering the example of her predecessor." The Empress eagerly sent her blessing on 22 July. But she insisted that the bride come to Russia without any relatives, only one maid for the first three months (a concession requested by Paul). To Sophia Dorothea she wrote three days later, praising her willingness to follow the King's and her parents' advice to make herself "my daughter." "Be assured in advance that I shall neglect not a single occasion where I may prove to Your Highness the sentiments of a tender mother." To assist her rapid progress in Russian (Paul reported that she already knew the Cyrillic alphabet by heart), Catherine sent a cabinet secretary, Peter Pastukhov, to meet her in Memel and begin language lessons on the way to St. Petersburg.[14]

Paul left Berlin a few days before his bride-to-be and arrived in Memel with a Prussian convoy by early August. A Russian escort met him in Kurland, where he passed Countess Rumiantseva with her huge suite on 8 August. To Sophia the Empress sent with Rumiantseva a diamond necklace and earrings, and to her parents a jewel-encrusted snuffbox and saber. She gave Paul a choice of three gifts for his mother-in-law. News of the convoys that King Frederick had insisted on providing, a precaution in response to an anonymous letter delivered to Paul in Berlin, caused Catherine some momentary anxiety; she wrote her son at Riga on 5 August to question the need for extraordinary security and to regret the rumors it might evoke. His calm explanation of the alarm allayed her fears so completely that she blamed it all on her eagerness to see him after such a long separation. Escorted by Countess Rumiantseva, Princess Sophia crossed the Russian border at Riga on 24 August and joined Paul at Yamburg on 30 August. The next evening they were received at Tsarskoe Selo by Catherine and her court.[15]

The Empress had made extraordinary preparations to welcome the couple, supervising the splendid decoration of their rooms and providing new bedclothes and linen. Sophia Dorothea she greeted warmly. Within days Catherine sent Frau Bielcke a delighted evaluation of "this charming princess":

She is precisely that which is desired: shapely as a nymph, with a face the color of the lily and the rose, the most beautiful skin in the world, tall and proportionate in carriage, she is still light; modesty, goodness of heart, candor are expressed in her physiognomy; the whole world is enchanted with her, and whoever does not love her is unjust, for she has been born and does everything to please. . . . In a word, my princess is everything that I desired, so there, I am content. I had wished to have her for a long time; it has been ten years that I have had my eye on her; yet when it was necessary, three years ago, that the Grand Duke marry, my princess was only thirteen. During the last three years I therefore lost sight of her. But as soon as the position became vacant, I asked about my princess; three days later I received word that she was engaged and to whom? During those three years five matches with her had been broken by singular hazards, and thus everything conjoined to give her to me.[16]

On Tuesday afternoon, 6 September, Catherine and the grand ducal pair left Tsarskoe Selo in a magnificent parade coach to enter St. Petersburg and the Winter Palace, where a rocket signalled a 101-gun salute in welcome and the imperial party attended a Russian comedy in the court opera house before dinner. A round of court festivities preceded Sophia Dorothea's official conversion on 14 September, when she accepted the new name of Maria Fedorovna. Her official betrothal followed the next day. The wedding took place at court on 26 September 1776. Modelled after the celebrations of Paul's first marriage, the ceremony was witnessed by the entire court and the foreign ministers. In the procession to the court chapel Potemkin preceded the Empress, in full regalia, and Grigorii Orlov held the wedding crown over Paul during the ceremony. Conspicuously absent was Nikita Panin, former mentor to the Grand Duke. He was either ill or still sulking about his exclusion from the marriage arrangements. Twenty days of festivities ensued including a public feast on the square before the Winter Palace, with roast oxen and fountains of wine, all of which culminated on 15 October with a magnificent firework.[17]

Catherine left Petersburg by sleigh for Tsarskoe Selo on 16 November, leaving behind Paul and his suddenly sick spouse. As always, she kept in daily communication with her son and sympathized with his wife's feverish condition. "I imagine that this has happened, from the transpiration, which usually happens after a paroxysm, no matter how it might have been broken, and therefore it is desirable that she keep warm," she advised him on 17 November. The next day she was relieved to learn of Maria Fedorovna's recovery, rejoiced that they would soon rejoin her, and remitted two grouse she had shot that morning. Paul and his wife reappeared at Tsarskoe Selo on 19 November. All spent the next days in various games and outings, celebrations and entertainments, before returning to St. Petersburg by carriage on 25 November. The next day Catherine, dressed in a long army coat and decoration, hosted at court a banquet and ball for the military order of St. George, the martyr and conquerer, with fifty-seven cavaliers of the four grades in attendance.[18]

The new Grand Duchess repaid her mother-in-law for all this attention in the best way possible: Grand Duke Alexander Pavlovich, Catherine's first grandchild, was born on 12 December 1777. King Frederick was honored to be named godfather. The Empress immediately took charge of her grandson, whom she named after Alexander Nevskii, the famous Russian princely warrior. From birth "Monsieur Alexandre" was the apple of her eye. Yet her appropriation of the new tsarevich, the urgently desired heir, added new strain to her ambivalent relationship with Paul and his wife. It reminded them of their subordinate position at court. And it showed a lack of trust and confidence in their competence as adults and parents.[19]

Only weeks after the wedding the Empress even developed some doubts about Paul's marital fidelity. She suspected a liaison with Ekaterina Nelidova, a recent young graduate of the Smol'nii Institute whom she appointed maid of honor to the Grand Duchess in June 1777. That same year Catherine built summer cottages for the consorts not far from Tsarskoe Selo naming them Paulust and Marienthal. These eventually evolved into the elaborate estate of Pavlovsk, presided over by Maria Fedorovna although largely financed by the Empress. Catherine's joy in the role of grandmother rose even higher with the birth of a second grandson on 27 April 1779. By giving him the Greek name of Constantine (Konstantin in Russian) and a Greek nurse, possibly at Potemkin's behest, she underscored the new prince's political mission and historical value. Both grandsons were guarantees of Russian greatness. Konstantin's godfather ought to be "my dearest friend Sultan Abdul Hamid," the Empress hooted to Grimm.[20]

The Empress devoted great care to the upbringing and education of her grandsons. They were trained to be Russian rulers in the European context. The five granddaughters who were born after Alexander and Konstantin interested her less, since their chances of ruling were slight. "The girls will all make very unfortunate matrons," she quipped to Grimm in 1778 before any had appeared, "for nothing will be more disagreeable and more insufferable than a Russian princess. They will not know how to accommodate themselves to anything; everything will appear parsimonious to them; they will be ill-natured, shrewish, faultfinding, beautiful, inconsistent. . . . The worst one of them will be Mademoiselle Catherine. The name she bears will cause her to have more wrong with her than her sisters." In time, however, the Empress manifested greater appreciation for her granddaughters and even sought to console Maria Fedorovna, disappointed at the birth of a fourth daughter on 10 April 1788, by naming the child Catherine.[21]

The birth of Catherine's grandsons promised great political benefits. Above all, it began to settle the succession issue. Unlike their father, both boys proved to be healthy (although Catherine worried about Konstantin for his first few years), and both got along beautifully with their doting grandmother. If their arrival aggravated tensions between Catherine and Paul, it reinforced the ruling family's future. The Empress could forget about the possible need to legitimize her bastard son Bobrinskoi. When he graduated from the Noble Cadet Corps in the spring of 1782, she sent him on a tour of Russia that took him to Moscow, Kazan, Astrakhan, Kherson, and Kiev before he visited

Poland and Italy and settled in Paris for several years. Moreover, she could dispose of another political skeleton in the shape of the Brunswick family, the two brothers and two sisters of the late Ivan VI. With the next generation of her own family assured, Catherine could have no conceivable need for any Brunswick heir, nor anything to fear from their dispatch abroad. Their father, Anton Ulrich, had died in 1774 in remote Kholmogory, where he was buried without ceremony or marker. In the spring of 1780 the Empress therefore arranged their passage to Denmark to be placed under the supervision of their aunt, Queen Juliane Marie, who reigned as regent. To establish them at a makeshift court in the small town of Horsens, Catherine provided 200,000 rubles in gold and an annual pension of 32,000 rubles to the Queen. Under heavy security and utmost secrecy they embarked from Arkhangel'sk on 30 June 1780 and reached Horsens by October. Supported by the Danish and the Russian courts, the Brunswick heirs survived under virtual house-arrest until 1806. They considered Catherine a great benefactress—as well they should have, for she spent more than a million rubles on their upkeep. At Tsarskoe Selo on 29 July 1780 Catherine directed Elagin to seal all pertinent documents for safekeeping in the vaults of the Secret Branch. One more political rival was gone forever.[22]

New Allies and New Territories

While Catherine worked at resolving the succession issue, she and Potemkin pursued territorial gain and imperial consolidation in the south. They had scant choice in the matter, for the Russo-Turkish war of 1768–1774 had left many issues open between the two empires. Demarcation of boundaries, spheres of influence, navigation rights, and the balance of forces were all disputed. Nobody imagined that the Crimean Khanate, an Ottoman vassal for three cenuries, could preserve its newly proclaimed independence between such imperial giants.

Proud though the Empress was of her recent triumph over the Turks, she carefully considered its costs, the animosity Russia's gains had excited in other powers (especially Austria and Prussia), and the necessity of fortifying her empire's new southern outposts. In the short run, she wished to avoid any more large-scale conflicts. With Potemkin supervising Russian policy in the south, therefore, Catherine followed a cautious course in relations with the Crimea and the Ottoman Empire. From Austrian policy during the recent conflict she drew a crucial conclusion: Vienna would not tolerate any further Russian unilateral aggrandizement at Ottoman expense, particularly in the Balkans. Indeed, Austrian animus over such gains had been dramatized in the spring of 1774 when they seized the Bukovina region on the withdrawal of the Russian occupation forces. This easy acquisition seemed certain to whet Emperor Joseph II's appetite for more Turkish territory, portions of which he had personally inspected in 1773; so Catherine wrote him in May 1774 protesting Austria's enlargement of its share of Poland. In January 1775 she apprehended an attempt against Kamenets-Podol'skii and Khotin.

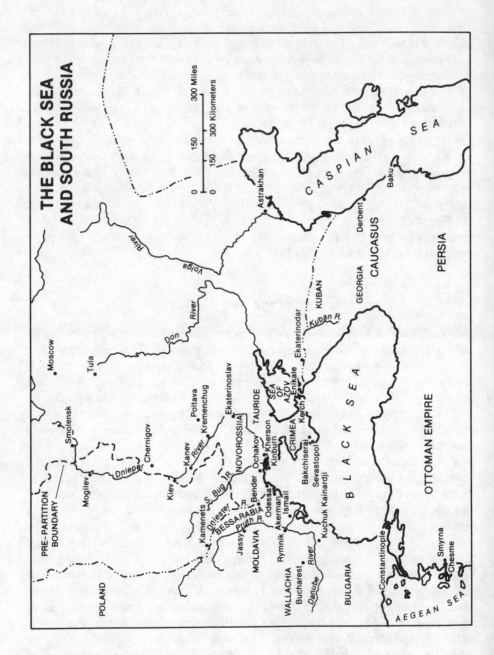

THE BLACK SEA
AND SOUTH RUSSIA

300 Miles
300 Kilometers

POLAND

PRE-PARTITION
BOUNDARY

Mogilev
Smolensk
Moscow

Tula

Chernigov

Kiev
Kanev
Poltava
Kremenchug
Ekaterinoslav

Kamenets
S. Bug R.
Dniester R.
Pruth R.
NOVOROSSIIA
Ochakov
Kinburn
Kherson
TAURIDE
SEA
OF
AZOV
Enikale
Kerch
CRIMEA
Bakchiserai
Sevastopol

Bender
Odessa
BESSARABIA
Akerman
Ismail

Jassy
MOLDAVIA
Rymnik
WALLACHIA
Bucharest
Danube River
BULGARIA
Kuchuk Kainardji

Constantinople

Smyrna
Chesme

AEGEAN SEA

OTTOMAN EMPIRE

BLACK SEA

Dnieper River

Don River

Volga River

Astrakhan

CASPIAN SEA

Baku
Derbent

GEORGIA
CAUCASUS
KUBAN
Kuban R.
Ekaterinodar

PERSIA

236

"The impudence of the Austrians is great," she informed Field Marshal Rumiantsev in forewarning him to scotch any sudden move. "Kamenets is no more than two hundred and fifty versts from our border, and I do not desire to have the imperials as neighbors."[23]

Whatever Catherine's misgivings about Austrian policy in the Balkans, in December 1774 she rejoiced to Voltaire over the spectacle of four Russian frigates sailing from the Greek archipelago into the Black Sea past the harem of "my brother and friend Sultan Abdul-Hamet." Russia was about to become a new naval power on the Black Sea, a fact vigorously publicized by completion of the Chesme column at Tsarskoe Selo in the spring of 1775 and by the exuberant celebrations in June and July 1776 of the sixth anniversary of the Chesme victory and the Baltic fleet's triumphant return from the Mediterranean. On land Catherine's visions of southern glory emerged even earlier and developed faster. On 6 September 1775 she authorized Potemkin to name two new southern fortresses Kherson and Slavensk. The name Kherson conjured up memories of the ancient Greek colonies in the Crimea (the Greek *chersonesos* means "peninsula"), whereas Slavensk hinted ambiguously at Slavic glory (*slava*) in southern climes. Catherine and Potemkin were already considering Russia as the patron of a revived Greek Empire that could supplant the Ottoman and Tatar presence around the Black sea. Indeed, on 9 September 1775 the Empress appointed Eugenios Voulgaris, a cosmopolitan Greek monk who had translated her *Great Instruction* into modern Greek, to be archbishop of the new diocese of Slavensk and Kherson, the boundaries of which were as yet undetermined. This appointment also showed the trend of Catherine's thinking about southern expansion, for Voulgaris was a militant, outspoken foe of Turkish tyranny over Greek Orthodoxy. At the same time several thousand Greek and "Albanian" veterans of the Orlov naval expedition were resettled in the Russian-held sectors of the Crimea around the forts of Kinburn, Kerch, and Enikale—a potential Trojan horse under Russian command.[24]

Some of Catherine's new advisers, notably Potemkin and Bezborodko, advocated more aggressive policies toward the Crimean Tatars. In 1776 Bezborodko, a Ukrainian client of both Potemkin and Rumiantsev whom the Empress had promoted to state secretary in December 1775, drafted a historical survey of Russo-Tatar wars from the mid-tenth century that stridently recounted the continual ravages and costly treacheries suffered at Turko-Tatar hands. Probably the Empress and Potemkin commissioned this work as a "feasibility study." In any event, Bezborodko's historical analysis and political conclusions advocated aggressive action. Thus he underlined the utility of historical knowledge in present-day politics, remarking that "King Janus" was depicted with two faces so as to view simultaneously the past and the future. Moreover, his elaborate survey of Turko-Tatar (and Mongol) raids concluded on a militant offensive/defensive note: "From this it is abundantly clear, how necessary it is to adopt the right measures against these our eternal enemies, so as to lead ourself into security from them once and for all, and thereby to obtain for our fatherland a reliable peace forever." Pointing to Ivan the Terrible's glorious conquests of Kazan and Astrakhan

in the 1550s, Bezborodko played on Catherine's penchant for historical precedent at the same time that he proclaimed the golden opportunity Russia now
enjoyed versus the minimal risks posed by the Tatars' manifest weakness.
Ideas such as these evidently crossed the Empress's desk, whereas Bezborodko's rapid rise in government stature afforded him ample opportunity to
champion his hard line against Tatars and Turks alike. With the death of
Grigorii Teplov in 1779 Bezborodko gained greater weight among Catherine's
close advisers.[25]

The uncertain situation in the Crimea, when considered together with the
Khanate's centuries-long hostility toward Russia, impelled Catherine and
Potemkin to capitalize on the Tatars' disarray by rapidly asserting Russian
control over the southern steppelands—Novorossiia. Suppression of the
Zaporozhian cossacks in June 1775 opened the way for colonization of the
region. Since military calculations held top priority, many of the new settlements were fortresses that commanded the strategic rivers. The southernmost
strongpoint was Kherson. Founded by Potemkin in 1778 on the lower
Dnieper, only a few kilometers upstream from the shallow Bug-Dnieper
delta (liman), Kherson was intended to be a multipurpose military base:
sentinel, fortress, dockyard, and naval station. The name Slavensk was applied in 1784 to the small settlement of Tor, which, however, failed to
develop into a commercial center. In 1778 Potemkin also awarded the
grandiose title of Ekaterinoslav—"Catherine's Glory"—to a new town on
the Kilchen' River, but the site proved to be so unhealthy that the community was moved ten kilometers to the Dnieper in 1784 (Paul I vindictively
renamed it Novorossiisk in 1797). In the northern Caucasus, the easternmost
end of Potemkin's viceroyalty, another town was named Ekaterinodar
("Catherine's Gift") in 1794, renamed Krasnodar in 1920. Catherine's son
and first two grandsons were likewise memorialized by Pavlograd and Pavlovsk, Aleksandriia, Aleksopol', and Aleksandrovsk, Konstantinopol', Kon-
stantinograd, and Konstantinogorsk.[26]

Besides strategic colonization, Catherine utilized political, diplomatic, and
military maneuvers in her effort to stabilize Russia's new southern frontier.
Just as she had worked through Poniatowski and noble confederations to
control Polish politics, so she found convenient tools in the various Tatar
hordes and the person of Shagin-Girei, younger brother of the first "independent" khan, Shahib-Girei. She had first met the young Tatar in St. Petersburg in 1771 while negotiating the Treaty of Karasu Bazaar, signed on 1 November 1772, which made the Crimea independent of the Ottoman Empire,
established an alliance with Russia, and proclaimed the Khan to be freely
elected and to wield all administrative authority. European in outlook and
habits, "the dauphin of the Crimea" charmed the Empress. "The young
Tatar prince has a gentle character," she told Voltaire; "he has spirit, he
makes Arabic verses; he never misses a play; the theater pleases him."[27]

To be sure, his political potential attracted Catherine most of all. He was
ambitious and anti-Ottoman, and as a member of the ruling Girei clan he
enjoyed excellent prospects to become the kind of friendly, pro-Russian khan
who could sustain Tatar independence vis-à-vis the Porte. Worried about the

machinations of Devlet-Girei, a pro-Ottoman former khan whom the Porte had sent to the Kuban in 1773 to rally dissident elements against the Russian-sponsored independence, Catherine and her councilors secretly allocated Shagin-Girei 150,000 rubles in 1774–75 to get himself "elected" khan by the Nogai hordes of the Kuban. Meanwhile, the Russian representatives in Constantinople spent substantial sums on the Sultan's favorites in hopes of winning Turkish ratification of the Treaty of Kuchuk-Kainardji and acceptance of Crimean independence.[28]

Early in 1776 the Empress secretly arranged with Potemkin and Rumiantsev for reinforcement of the land and naval forces in and around the Crimea. By late fall everything had been prepared for the ouster of Devlet-Girei, who had been invested as khan that spring. To forestall an Ottoman invasion in support of an alleged conspiracy by Devlet-Girei to renounce independence, General Prozorovskii seized Perekop, gateway to the peninsula, on 21 November without resistance. Shagin-Girei, though elected khan by the Nogais, mismanaged an attack on the Ottoman garrison at Taman in January 1777, but he soon arrived in Enikale under Russian protection. Since Devlet-Girei received neither Ottoman nor Crimean support, he decamped for Constantinople in March 1777 and Shagin-Girei was installed as khan a month later. The Russians recognized that this easy triumph could not last without Ottoman and Crimean acquiescence. So, in administering the new oath of loyalty to Shagin-Girei and dispatching deputies to the Porte to obtain the Sultan's religious investiture of the new khan, General Prozorovskii concealed a bold political innovation: the khan's authority was thenceforward to be absolute and hereditary. Both qualities were sharp deviations from Tatar tradition and provocative parallels with Russian practice.[29]

Entertaining "Brother Gu"

Though preoccupied with southern vistas, Catherine kept her eyes open to developments in European politics that might affect Russian interests. Ever since the Swedish revolution of 1772 she had heard contradictory reports about her first cousin, King Gustavus III. Some said he wished to visit her. Others warned of his quixotic desire for revenge for Russian meddling in Swedish internal politics and of his plans to wrest Norway away from Denmark, Russia's longtime ally. Sixteen years younger than Catherine, Gustavus was the son of her uncle Adolf Frederick and Louisa Ulrika, sister of Frederick the Great of Prussia. The cousins shared many qualities and experiences: high ambitions and overbearing mothers, wide reading and unhappy marriages, admiration for French culture and yearning for nationalistic glory. Their close family ties only abetted the traditional rivalry of their adopted homelands. As early as January 1774 Catherine insisted to Frau Bielcke that she and her Swedish cousin were born opposites: he was a blind imitator of all things French, whereas she was an English "original" who chose her own way. If Gustavus ever did visit her, she concluded, he would be bored to tears.

So it was with a mixture of pride and foreboding that the Empress received the King incognito in the summer of 1777. The "count of Gotland" arrived by sea in St. Petersburg on 5 June. Catherine met him at Tsarskoe Selo that afternoon. They dined together the same evening and met several more times during his month-long sojourn. The Empress arranged to show "brother Gu" (her sarcastic name for him to Grimm) all the local sights and the intellectual attractions of St. Petersburg—the Academy of Sciences, the Smol'nii Institute, the Mining Institute, and numerous theatrical performances. Wearing the Swedish Order of St. Seraphim, Catherine proudly treated her royal guest to a display of Russian naval might that only incited him to build up the Swedish fleet, which Potemkin derided as "so rotten a royal salute would shake it to pieces." Rich gifts were exchanged. He gave her a huge ruby; she reciprocated with a pelisse of black foxtails said to be worth 30,000 rubles. Still, Catherine felt relieved when her guest departed on 5 July, though she began a friendly correspondence with Gustavus III from then on. She had succeeded in impressing the King. He did not impress her at all. Even so, his widely reported visit enhanced Russia's international prestige, for Gustavus was the first European monarch to meet the Empress in person, hat in hand. She could therefore concentrate even more single-mindedly on southern glory.[30]

Catherine's latest success in the Crimea seemed so easy and virtually cost-free that she awarded Potemkin 150,000 rubles on 30 September 1777 for his birthday and saint's day. Nevertheless, both the Empress and her viceroy anticipated war with the Ottomans and renewed unrest in the Crimea. When full-scale revolt erupted against the inept Shagin-Girei in late 1777, Russian forces were ready. Whereas the Khan fled for his life while the rebels pillaged his palace and an "Albanian" detachment sacked the Tatar town of Kaffa, Catherine calmly watched to see whether the Turks would intervene (she assumed their clandestine involvement). "In case of war there is nothing else to do," she advised Potemkin in November, "than to strike the Turks defensively in the Crimea, or wherever they show themselves; if it extends to another campaign, then I expect action already ought to be prepared against Ochakov; it would be good to seize Bendery, too, but Ochakov on the river is more needed." Her idea was to wage an aggressive defense. Potemkin championed the same concept in person before the council on 6 November, urging massive preparations for war while pursuing a negotiated settlement. The councilors authorized Rumiantsev to recommend conciliatory policies to Shagin-Girei and, if war broke out anyway, to evacuate him to the Kuban and to ravage the Crimea itself. Russian patience was draining away.[31]

How drained soon became apparent. Shagin-Girei was brought back to his palace in Bakchiserai in February 1778, and an Ottoman squadron was repulsed from the harbor of Akhtiar by Russian shore batteries on 11 March. Yet Catherine's confidence in her puppet khan gradually seeped away. Fearful of further bloodshed, she invoked a variant of her council's evacuation scheme. An enforced exodus of the Christian population, Shagin-Girei's last source of local support, began that very spring. By mid-September 1778 some 31,000 civilians had left. The hapless Khan abdicated temporarily, but he was talked into another attempt at ruling. Another Ottoman fleet was driven away from Akhtiar on 12 August without a landing. This was the last, futile Otto-man protest against the Russian military occupation.[32]

Stymied at every turn, the Porte grudgingly agreed to a new settlement. The Convention of Aynali Kavak, mediated by France and signed at Con-stantinople in January 1779, pledged the Ottoman Empire to recognize Shagin-Girei as the lawful khan of the Crimea for life. The khanate was declared to be independent in all matters except religion, wherein it recog-nized the Sultan as caliph. Russia, for its part, promised to remove all its forces—except the garrisons at Kinburn, Enikale, and Kerch—from the Crimea and the Kuban within ninety days, and to cede to the Tatars the territory between the Bug and the Dniester taken in 1774. The Turks pro-posed that neither empire have permanent representatives at Bakchiserai, but Catherine rejected that proposal. Her independent and absolute puppet could not be allowed to forget who pulled his strings.[33]

The Emperor-King with Two Faces

If by 1779 the Empress could feel confident in her stronger grip on the Crimea, she still had to wonder how long the Sultan would countenance Russia's growing might, and how her gains could win European recognition. Despite occasional bluster, Catherine was eager to avoid conflict—hence her renewed support for the battered Shagin-Girei. As she jokingly summarized her attitude to Frau Bielcke in April 1778: "For the Turks and me, I will tell you that it's been so long that we have been frowning at one another that I believe nobody minds it anymore; let them do as they please; I sing them the song from a comic opera: I am good, I am modest, but I kept ahold of my peace."[34] Pertinacity became her watchword.

The Turkish and Polish crises of past years had revealed afresh the limits of Catherine's alliance with Prussia. Frederick II would not help her against the Turks. He and Maria Theresa of Austria—"Saint Teresa" in the Em-press's cynical estimation—had crudely taken advantage of Russia's difficul-ties in the past conflicts with the Polish Commonwealth and the Ottoman Empire. Some of Catherine's resentment toward Frederick II ("Herod" she privately dubbed him to Grimm, presumably because of his attempts to "slaughter innocents" such as herself) peeked out of her wry comment in March 1778 about a Dutch medal depicting the Empress of Russia and the Empress-Queen of Austria in a coach driven by the King of Prussia; asked where they wish to go, the passengers reply, wherever it pleases the coach-man to take us. "I found this very droll," Catherine confided to Grimm; "it lacks only the truth or the music of a French comic opera: the first in order to make it piquant, or the second in order to make it a complete platitude."[35] She would not be driven by anyone.

What could be more welcome in this diplomatic stalemate than a feeler from Joseph II, "the man with two physiognomies," as Catherine sarcasti-cally termed him to Grimm. In the spring of 1779 the Austrian Emperor-King took the initiative in communicating his desire to meet incognito during her already announced tour of the western provinces. To Grimm the Empress scoffed at Joseph's silly incognito, recalled in mock horror her anxiety at meeting Gustavus III two years earlier, and affected to be frightened by the prospect; but she quickly assented anyway. Joseph's proposal held out intriguing possibilities. At the very least his visit would burnish Russia's soaring international prestige through recognition by the Holy Roman Emperor. It would also tweak Maria Theresa's sanctimonious nose, for Catherine would cultivate the son despite his aging mother's admonitions about the immoral-amoral "princesse de Zerbst."[36]

Besides, what did Joseph want? From earlier Austrian approaches Catherine could guess that the Emperor-King and his wily chancellor, Prince Kaunitz, hoped to pry Russia away from her Prussian alliance. Indeed, Joseph privately avowed "to stimulate the bile of the dear Frederick so that he dies of it." Catherine, too, had already cooled to the Prussian alliance, a coolness that turned icy from Frederick's recent foolhardy proposal of a Russo-Prusso-Turkish alliance. From St. Petersburg on 2 April 1780 the Austrian envoy passed on Potemkin's account of Catherine's frigid reaction: "The King of Prussia may ask what he will, but the Empress will do only what is in her interests, and in particular she will never enter into an alliance with the Turks. She will join an alliance with anyone in order to drive the Turks out of Europe." Before leaving for Mogilev she had Bezborodko draft a plan for Russo-Austrian cooperation in the dismemberment of the Ottoman Empire. This formed the crux of her famous-notorious "Greek Project."[37]

Because Catherine and Joseph II both wanted something from the other, and because both had a shrewd idea of what the other coveted, their summit meeting at Mogilev in May 1780 proved a great success. In fact, the Empress took pains to conciliate her guest by ordering Governor-General Zakhar Chernyshev not to allow any public references to the Peace of Teschen of 1779, a diplomatic defeat for Austria against Prussia in the War of the Bavarian Succession that had been terminated by Russo-French mediation. Nervous and sweaty from the warm spring weather and pestered by clouds of mosquitoes, Catherine met "Count Falkenstein" at Mogilev after morning mass on 24 May 1780. Joseph's compliments and cultivated conversation quickly won her approbation. "He loves to talk, he is knowledgeable, he wishes to make everybody everywhere very much at ease," she wrote Paul and his wife in hopes of weaning them from their Prussian proclivities. She and Joseph found they shared a deep interest in educational policy for multinational empires; both admired Voltaire and the Jesuits' role in education.

In the sphere of foreign policy they gingerly fished for common prey. Catherine showed off portraits of her grandsons, with Konstantin in Greek surroundings. She teased her guest about making Rome the capital of his empire, while he touted Constantinople as the natural capital of the Orthodox world. "Her project of establishing an empire in the East rolls around in her head and broods in her soul," Joseph told his mother afterwards. Knowing the Prussian persuasion of Count Panin, who was conspicuously absent from the trip and the meetings, the Emperor-King quietly quizzed Bezborodko about the Empress's practices in formulating foreign policy—he was told that she saw every dispatch in full—and about the other officials under Panin, Peter Bakunin in particular. He also praised Grand Duke Paul and declared his eagerness to meet him.[38]

Their witty and wide-ranging conversations delighted Catherine. After laying the foundation for a new church dedicated to St. Joseph, the Empress and the Emperor-King left Mogilev in the same carriage on 30 May 1780 for a brief sojourn at Zorich's estate in Shklov on their way to Smolensk, where they met a gigantic reception from the local nobility. Catherine then returned to St. Petersburg while "Count Falkenstein" went on to Moscow with Potemkin. On 12 June he rejoined her for three weeks in St. Petersburg, where he attempted to win over Paul by ridiculing his mother's "Greek Project." Paul was neither amused nor impressed. Maria Fedorovna, however, was captivated by the visitor, who told his mother he would have married her himself, had they met ten years before. Instead he wooed her with the prospect of marrying her youngest sister to his nephew Franz, heir to the Austrian throne. When Joseph got back to Vienna he praised Catherine to the skies. "Her spirit, the elevation of her soul, her courage, and with that the pleasantness of her conversation must be known and experienced for one to be able to appreciate their extent." The Empress pleased the Austrians even more by her warm reception on 2 August of the Prince de Ligne, an Austrian military agent and witty courtier, and her cold reception of the September visit of Frederick the Great's nephew and heir, Frederick William. An alliance was only a few steps away.[39]

Beginning a regular correspondence in the fall of 1780, the new imperial friends avidly stroked each other's ego. Catherine lauded Joseph's "natural eloquence and the charm of his conversation," applauded the naval assistance received in the Mediterranean from his brother, Grand Duke Leopold of Tuscany, and seductively suggested the virtues of bold, risk-flaunting action spurred by courage and inspiration as opposed to cold calculation and passive prudence.[40] Praising Catherine's insightful analysis of the indecisive military activities surrounding the revolutionary war in North America, the Emperor-King contrasted such incompetence and ineptitude with her finesse and resolution:

> You knew how to use all circumstances in order to elevate the glory of
> your nation, to conquer your foes, and to compel other nations to seek
> your friendship and to value it more than any other European nation
> has ever succeeded in doing. If all of that fell to your ministers to con-
> ceive and to arrange, while you only followed their suggestions: you,
> Madame, would be, of course, far from that degree of glory and that
> right to self-satisfaction which you have accumulated. To your energy,
> your bravery, your constancy, and to that which you knew how to
> make others obey you, to these qualities, for which the Russian Empire
> will eternally bless your reign, to them and them alone is this Empire
> obliged for the rapid and, I daresay, almost incredible successes which
> during seventeen years of your rule she has succeeded in attaining,
> both in the opinion and esteem of foreigners, and in the power, wealth,
> and enlightenment within the state.[41]

Their mutual admiration surged beyond the realm of rhetoric as soon as the last obstacle to rapprochement vanished with the death of Maria Theresa on 18/29 November 1780. Catherine sent three letters of condolence with a special envoy. Urging the newly elevated Emperor to rule his twenty million subjects wisely and energetically, she retrieved the idea of a mutual guarantee of the two empires' possessions. Joseph assented at once. Though privately lamenting Catherine's female vanity and egocentricity, the Emperor resolved "to howl with the wolves" and proposed a full-scale defensive alliance. She wanted more: a clear promise of assistance against the Turks, whose repeated violations of the Treaty of Kuchuk-Kainardji she indignantly recounted. Joseph agreed only to give diplomatic aid, noting politely that Russia needed no military help against the Turks, and he restated his common interest with Russia in keeping Poland confused and weak, while warning Catherine of Frederick's machinations there.

In St. Petersburg the Austrian ambassador accepted Russia's conditions in principle, but then undercut the entire venture by questioning its form. Would the Empress be content to sign second on both copies of the treaty, as Hapsburg custom ordained? She would not. Was this female vanity, Joseph wondered, or a clever trick by Frederick II and Nikita Panin to foil the alliance? Nevertheless, he would not budge, either.[42]

Catherine thereupon flashed her ingenuity in arranging with Kaunitz for an artful compromise to confound all their enemies. There would be no treaty in the usual sense. Catherine and Joseph would merely exchange private letters detailing their obligations, letters that they both would keep strictly secret, under lock and key in their own cabinets. Consequently, neither sovereign need admit the existence of any treaty. Both would officially acknowledge the failure of the negotiations over questions of protocol. It was a brilliant scheme that worked like magic.[43]

Catherine signed the copy of her letter to Joseph II at Tsarskoe Selo on 24 May 1781, a year to the day since they first met: "the anniversary of the best and most memorable day of my life," she enthusiastically informed her new ally and closed her letter by recalling his promise to revisit her in Kherson. Despite her complaints about rheumatism in the left hand, the Empress had every reason to rejoice in the alliance. Their agreement pledged a mutual defensive guarantee of Russia's current European possessions for eight years, promising armed assistance (10,000 infantry and 2,000 cavalry) in case of attack, with these forces to be replaced by an annual subsidy of 400,000 rubles if the hostilities should pit Sweden against Russia. But the alliance's main value for Catherine concerned the Ottoman Empire, where special stipulations committed Austria in support of all Russia's treaty relations with the Porte. If diplomacy failed to resolve Ottoman nonfulfillment or open violations of the Treaty of Kuchuk-Kainardji and its supplements, or if the Porte declared war, then Austria was obligated to enter the conflict with forces equal to her ally's and within three months of Russian notification. Should Russian naval operations be contemplated on the Sea of Azov or the Black Sea, the sovereigns agreed to consult about coordinating their forces. They pledged to share equally all gains from any Russo-Ottoman hostilities, to coordinate strategy and military operations, and to make no separate peace or truce without consultation. In case of an attack by a third party during any Russo-Turkish war, both allies promised to consider it cause for invoking the alliance and vowed full, active support. Although the new alliance said nothing about the "Greek Project" or any other specific territorial gains, it underlined the commonality of Russian and Austrian interests in the fate of the Ottoman Empire. It represented a large insurance policy for Catherine in dealing with the troublesome Crimea.[44]

The secret Austrian alliance altered Russian domestic politics almost immediately. Above all, it signified the end of the Panin party's influence and the dispersal of the pro-Prussian, pro-Paul court faction. Humiliated at being bypassed in the negotiations, Nikita Panin sought to delay any agreement and, having failed in that, left St. Petersburg in despair in April 1781 for his estate in Smolensk guberniia. Catherine was unperturbed. Panin's departure gave her full latitude to reorganize the Collegium of Foreign Affairs under the direction of her pupil Bezborodko, with the help of such former Panin clients as Peter Bakunin and Arkadii Markov. She did not disgrace Panin publicly; he kept his official positions, but he received no specific duties or significant papers. Vice-Chancellor Ivan Osterman assumed everyday direction of official foreign affairs. Other, less adaptable Panin appointees were removed. In particular, the Russian minister at the Porte, Alexander Stakhiev, was replaced by Yakov Bulgakov in May 1781. In a parallel move Governor-General Sievers resigned on 20 May his vicegerency of Novgorod and Tver guberniias.[45]

The existence of the secret new alliance was known for certain to only five of Catherine's advisers: Potemkin, Bezborodko, Osterman, Bakunin, and Markov. (Sir James Harris learned of it only one month later.) Somehow Grand Duke Paul had to be told. In view of his Prussophilia, the Empress could foresee his probable reaction to such an underhanded cancellation of Russo-Prussian ties. She accordingly arranged for him to learn the secret from Emperor Joseph II himself in Vienna the following November. Paul's own desire to visit Italy and his wife's Würtemberg relatives facilitated his departure from Tsarskoe Selo in mid-September 1781, by which time his sons were both recovering from their inoculation against smallpox. To the consternation of Paul and Maria Fedorovna, who travelled under the pseudonyms "Count and Countess of the North," Catherine flatly vetoed any visit to Berlin. She handpicked their entourage and closely monitored their correspondence. Potemkin (with the Empress's knowledge?) went so far as to persuade the Austrian ambassador to cooperate in intercepting the suspected correspondence between Paul, the Panin faction, and the Prussian court, but Joseph II virtuously refused this ploy. When the Emperor informed the Grand Duke of the new alliance, Paul professed to be delighted at Catherine's confidence in sharing the secret. Six months later in Florence, however, he raged against the pro-Austrian faction in St. Petersburg.[46]

Catherine's suspicions of antigovernment machinations among Paul's entourage burst into frightened fury in the spring of 1782. Her outrage was triggered by interception of an apparently seditious letter from Pavel Bibikov, son of the late general, to Prince Alexander Kurakin, a nephew of the Panins who was accompanying the Grand Duke abroad. In lamenting the sad situation at court and in the empire at large, Bibikov alluded to other clandestine correspondents and lambasted the nefarious influence of Potemkin, "the Cyclops par excellence." Russia's salvation could only come from the Grand Duke, Bibikov asserted, and he asked Kurakin "to offer my allegiance to Their Imperial Majesties and assure them that I would be the happiest man on earth if I had the opportunity to prove my attachment and devotion to them not only in words but in deeds."[47]

Angry as well as apprehensive, Catherine ordered Bibikov arrested and interrogated by the Secret Branch. To Paul in northern Italy she wrote on 25 April 1782 of Bibikov's "impudent acts" and sent along a copy of the offending missive, "filled with such dark utterances." The Empress herself framed forty-seven questions for the interrogators, Procurator-General Viazemskii and the baleful Sheshkovskii. Question number thirty-seven instructed them to exhort the accused, with a promise of mercy, to disclose what "deeds" had been contemplated and with whose assistance. The ogre of conspiracy still gnawed at Catherine. But Bibikov steadfastly declined to implicate anybody else. Despite his criticism Potemkin repudiated revenge and advised mercy; so Catherine refused Bibikov's plea for death if anything seditious were found, and the Secret Branch condemned him on 28 April to lifelong banishment. By June 1782, with the offender exiled to Astrakhan where he died two years later without direct heirs, Catherine blamed the entire incident on ingratitude and slanderous lies. "My principles pulled this young man by the hair back from the abyss into which he had been about to plunge, because my manner is less tragic than that of my predecessors," the Empress pointedly lectured her son and his spouse. "I tell you this, my dear children, because my tenderness for you wishes that you make use of this for the present time and that to come." It was a blunt warning. Only in December 1782 did Paul return to St. Petersburg, where he found the Panin party completely scattered and silenced. He was by then so alarmed about his own future that for one month he did not even dare visit the dying Nikita Panin. The frightened Empress had frightened her son even more than herself. Rumors arose just then of her alleged intention to remove Paul from the line of succession.[48]

Conquest of the Crimea

The risk of war with the Turks over the Crimea lay at the basis of Catherine's secret alliance with Austria. With that weapon in reserve she and Potemkin undertook stricter measures to secure their position in the Crimea. The Empress kept hoping that Shagin-Girei, her puppet khan, could somehow stabilize his sprawling, splintered state. Although the Khan was completely dependent on Russian financial largess—some 150,000 rubles in 1778–1780, that is, far too little to manage a modern state—he ignored Russian advice, acted like a pocket despot, and moved to expand his borders, all without any local means of support. Renewed revolt resulted. The Nogais never accepted his authority, and others followed their lead in 1780–81. Deposed again by rebels in the Kuban and the Crimea proper, Shagin-Girei fled to Kaffa in May 1782 and then to Russian protection at Kerch. On 3 August the Empress ordered Potemkin, who had returned to St. Petersburg for the unveiling of the new statue of Peter the Great, to invade the Crimea once more. Tatar resistance evaporated in the face of Russian arms, with Shagin-Girei returning to his palace by early October, less secure than ever. His brutal repression of the rebels alienated Catherine still further. Emboldened by reports from Constantinople that the Turks feared war and were incapable of rapid deployment, the Empress proposed to Joseph II on 10 September 1782 that they frame a plan of action in case war resulted from the Turks' rejecting her recent ultimatum, which called for freedom of navigation through the straits, settlement of the revolt in the Crimea that had allegedly been provoked and supported by the Porte, and resolution of conflicts over Moldavia and Wallachia.[49]

At this juncture Catherine retrieved her "Greek Project," as drafted by Bezborodko more than two years earlier. But now she presented it as a practical possibility. To counter Joseph's skepticism, she prefaced the plan with an elaborate survey of the current European political scene, from which she concluded that circumstances were uniquely propitious for Russo-Austrian success against the steadily declining Porte. In her view the allies' principal aim should be to drive the Turks back into Asia. The Ottoman Empire's European provinces could then be reorganized into two Christian buffer states between Austria and Russia: a reconstituted "Dacia" encompassing the Danubian Principalities and Bessarabia, and a restored Greek Empire under the suzerainty of her grandson Konstantin. Dacia would be ruled by an Orthodox sovereign acceptable to the allies; apparently Catherine had Potemkin in mind for the post. Austria's direct share of Turkish territory would comprise the western Balkans. Russia would expand her borders to the Black Sea—a step that implied annexation of the Crimea—and westward to the Dniester River, thereby incorporating Ochakov and its hinterland. Catherine also wanted one or two islands in the Greek archipelago for commercial purposes. "No matter how remote and grandiose these views may appear," the Empress exhorted her ally, "I think that little exists that is impossible for the might of our two states, in the close unity between them."[50]

Within weeks, on 22 September 1782—the twentieth anniversary of her coronation—Catherine gave further evidence of her romantic political aspirations by founding the new Order of St. Vladimir, named for the grand prince of Kiev whose conversion to Christianity in 988 had been confirmed in ancient Kherson. She was already contemplating a triumphant visit there herself as early as the summer of 1783. The first recipients of the new decoration comprised the leading commanders and statesmen.[51]

Joseph II's cool response to the "Greek Project" and his concern about "leaks" from their confidential correspondence made little difference to Catherine's immediate plans for the Crimea. Her stiffening resolve was revealed in a private remark of 28 November 1782: "About the Tatars a notion was given by Shagin-Girei; he said that one need not tickle a Tatar." Besides, her "Greek Project" did not have to be accomplished all at once; it offered both maximum and minimum objectives. In the last three months of 1782 annexation of the Crimea gradually became her immediate, minimum objective.[52]

In answer to Potemkin's worried request of mid-September, she promised additional shipwrights for "the young Colossus of Kherson!" and approved his reinforcement of Kinburn to overawe the Turks at nearby Ochakov, comparing both these enterprises to Peter the Great's Baltic conquests. (Petrine precedents were on her mind more than ever, since the unveiling on 7 August 1782—the centennial of Peter's enthronement—of Falconet's magnificent equestrian statue on Petersburg's Petrovian Square. The blunt inscription on the boulder-base, "To Peter the First—Catherine the Second," boldly proclaimed the historical significance of her reign as the rightful successor to the creator of modern Russia.) By early October she praised Potemkin's preparations of troops and provisions for another campaign in the Crimea including seizure of the strategic port of Akhtiar. Catherine also had her eye on the Caucasus as a possible springboard for a diversionary action against the Turks. On 25 April 1782 she had privately mentioned the opening of a new road to Georgia that bypassed the mountains, commenting: "through that all of Turkey has become open."[53]

Potemkin returned to St. Petersburg in late 1782 for final consultations about the Crimean campaign. "His eye they consider the eye omniscient," Zavadovskii grumbled to Rumiantsev. On 14 December he received Catherine's "most secret" instructions authorizing seizure of the peninsula in the event that the Porte refused her latest joint ultimatum with Joseph II in support of the three conditions previously stipulated, or in case of a half-dozen other contingencies. Russia would never enjoy peace with the Ottoman Empire, the Empress explained to her viceroy, so long as the Crimea remained "a nest of brigands and insurgents" whose continual unrest and alarms had strained Russian vigilance and arms, costing 7.5 million rubles in extraordinary expenses over the past nine years alone. Potemkin was to fasten on any of the following contingencies to accomplish the annexation: the death or kidnapping or overthrow of the Khan; betrayal by the Khan or his refusal to yield Akhtiar; refusal by the Porte to accept the three conditions; Ottoman attacks on the Crimea or the Kuban, naval action on the Black Sea or attempts to incite Tatar revolt; Ottoman action against Russia elsewhere—open, concealed, or through third parties; and if Austria should advance its frontier cordon into Moldavia or Wallachia, Russia must seek recompense in the Crimea. Even if the Porte conceded her three conditions, Catherine insisted that Russia must at least acquire Akhtiar, but she left Potemkin free to execute the plan as local circumstances required. By way of preparing a surprise diversion against the Turks should war ensue, the Empress empowered Potemkin to follow Petrine precedent in occupying the Persian provinces along the west coast of the Caspian Sea. She was certain "the moment is very favorable in order to acquire a lot," beginning with the occupation of Akhtiar.[54]

If, by mid-January 1783, the Empress could congratulate Potemkin on his success in reinstating Shagin-Girei, a scant three weeks later she urged her viceroy to make the Khan cease repressions against the former rebels and surrender his brothers and nephew as hostages and as security for his own good conduct. Should Shagin-Girei refuse compliance, Potemkin might arrest him and proceed to annexation forthwith. Catherine's hardening resolve to act boldly and decisively was abetted by Joseph II's bland assurances that the Turks seemed inclined to compromise without armed conflict. The Empress thought otherwise, or at least she subsequently professed to have less regard than her secret ally for Ottoman assurances and more confidence in the force of Russian arms. About Joseph's vacillation she wrote Potemkin on 14 April 1783: "I am not making any reflection about all this because I am firmly resolved not to count on anybody but ourselves. When the cake will be baked, each will have an appetite. As I rely little on an ally, so do I little apprehend and respect the French thunder or, better to say, heat lightning." This last phrase referred to Joseph's concern about French support for the Turks. In fact, the day before she issued definitive orders to Potemkin about annexation she wrote Joseph explaining her dissatisfaction with the Ottoman response, accusing the Porte of new provocations in the Crimea, and declaring her readiness for war if the Turks did not yield. Conquest of the Crimea, Catherine informed the Emperor, represented a scaled-down version of their previous "grand designs." Moreover, it was more practical in current circumstances and less likely to provoke hostile reactions in Europe. Convinced that Prussia and France would stay out of any Russo-Ottoman confrontation, and anxious to capitalize on the preoccupation of the other European powers with the American war of independence, the Empress declared her forces sufficient alone to obtain from the Porte "a peace that is secure, advantageous, and glorious," delicately reminding Joseph II of her desire that he "unsheath the sword, so as to confer on his own prosperous reign the glory of ringing victories and useful conquests." In short, she would take the first step herself.[55]

Just what Catherine had in mind she explained in detail to Potemkin in her orders of 8 April 1783, with which she enclosed undated copies of her manifesto proclaiming the annexation, his announcement to the Crimean populace, and a duplicate of her instructions to Bulgakov in Constantinople. (Copies were sent to Joseph II within a few weeks.) The Russian annexation was justified on political and economic grounds: namely, since the Tatars had shown themselves unfit for freedom and independence because of their "ignorance and savagery," the Empress felt compelled to restore order, forestall further Ottoman intervention, and recoup the "many millions" already spent on Crimean affairs. She was hopeful that Russia's obvious preparedness for war would cow the Porte. In pursuit of a peaceful settlement she allocated Bulgakov 100,000 rubles in hush-money for the Sultan's notoriously craven ministers. Even so, she sketched a contingency plan of land and sea operations that, following occupation of the Crimea, the Taman peninsula, and the

Kuban, envisaged an attack on Ochakov in the autumn. Potemkin's announcement of the annexation would give the Tatars thirty days to take the oath of loyalty to the Empress or decamp peacefully.[56]

Of course, annexation meant the end of Shagin-Girei's rule in the Crimea. Yet Catherine did not wish to abandon her puppet altogether. She charitably designated 200,000 rubles annually in support of a plan to install him as the Shah of Persia! This was to be only one of several Russian moves in the Caucasus aimed at diverting Ottoman forces and, through alliances with the local Georgian and Armenian sovereigns, erecting firm barriers against Turkish and Persian power. Shagin-Girei must be sent off to Persia, the Empress stipulated, not as a deposed exile, "but with an army and with the splendor that befits Asiatics." Here was a romantic design that held the additional attractions of providing an honorable retirement of her loyal puppet and of provoking further Ottoman-Persian enmity.[57]

After approving all these arrangements Catherine waited impatiently at Tsarskoe Selo for Potemkin to make his way leisurely back to the south to implement their glorious designs. On 4 May 1783 she wrote him of her recent recovery from a severe siege of fever and pain in the cheek that had been "transformed into a colic" (stomach pains) after three days, thanks to a blood-letting and without drugs. Joseph II's recent letters reaffirmed her determination to act alone, but she considered that "war is inevitable." The warm season encouraged her to think it would help Potemkin provision his troops. The very next day Catherine calmly accepted the news of Shagin-Girei's renunciation of authority, reminding her viceroy to treat the ex-Khan kindly and respectfully. She approved at the same time a proposal by General Pavel Potemkin to take under Russian protection Khan Ibrahim of Susha, an ally of Tsar Irakli of Georgia. By late May the Empress received word of Potemkin's arrival at Kherson, although she complained of the long lapse in their correspondence. She had just awarded the cross of the Order of St. Vladimir, first class, to General Ivan Gannibal, supervisor of the construction of Kherson. "I don't doubt," she assured Potemkin, "that in your hands and with your solicitude everything will proceed as it should." Four days later she reassured him of her return to health and lauded the realization of his prophecy that Joseph II would welcome the annexation, inasmuch as "their appetite grows with the eating." Her spirits remained high, inflated by the beautiful spring weather, and she even looked forward to meeting Gustavus III on the Finnish border in June.[58]

By 5 June 1783 the Empress began relaxing somewhat since her meeting with Gustavus III had been postponed because of a fractured arm he suffered in a fall from a horse. At Potemkin's request she ordered a special award for Shagin-Girei: the blue ribbon of the Order of St. Andrew with an oval medallion framed in diamonds and inscribed with the word "Fidelity," a jewelled star of the same order but without the usual cross (since the former Khan was not a Christian), and the rank of lieutenant-general. These decorations were dispatched to Potemkin by the end of the month. "I impatiently await from you news about completion of the Crimean affair," she informed her viceroy; "please take it before the Turks succeed in twisting [the Tatars] into resistance to you." Sending howitzers for the defense of Akhtiar, she informed Potemkin of Field Marshal Rumiantsev's apprehensions of Ottoman attacks. "As war has not been declared, so it seems that everything may still be hastened in time," the Empress calmly concluded. Meanwhile Joseph II played his part in the drama by informing the French government (Queen Marie Antoinette was his sister) of the Austrian alliance with Russia, a diplomatic bombshell that stunned the French and infuriated the Prussians.[59]

Within days old and new worries gripped Catherine, who lamented Potemkin's absence, the lack of news from the Crimea, and rumors of pestilence in the south. Russo-Ottoman hostilities always seemed to incite plague. Still, Ottoman proposals for a trade treaty piqued her interest, but she rebuffed the notion of an offensive and defensive alliance; "it's a French ploy against Konstantin II." On 12 June she forwarded 100,000 rubles to Potemkin for the naval fortifications at Kherson. The very next day she urged him again to make haste with the annexation, which was already being talked about in Constantinople. On the eve of her departure to meet Gustavus III, she wondered wryly how he would be: "Alexander of Macedon did not fall from his horse in front of his army from his own negligence." Her meeting with the King of Sweden took place at Fredericksham on 18–21 June 1783. Catherine and her small entourage left Tsarskoe Selo on Thursday, 15 June, and returned by Saturday afternoon, 24 June. A total of 51 carriages with 296 horses conveyed the court. Nothing of political weight was discussed, although the Empress informed Gustavus III of her imminent conquest of the Crimea and the likelihood of war with the Turks. To Potemkin she scoffed afterwards at the King's vanity and eccentricity, just as she disdained the Finnish countryside: "Good God! What a country! How is it possible that one wished to sacrifice human blood in order to possess a desert that even marsh fowl do not choose to inhabit!"[60]

Omitting the customary visit to Peterhof for the late June holidays, Catherine returned directly to Tsarskoe Selo, where she became increasingly concerned over Potemkin's uncertain health and, most of all, his apparent laggardness in occupying the Crimea. Still, she strove to support his spirits. "That you have knocked yourself out of strength, about that I am most sorry," she wrote on 29 June; "you know that you are for me very, very necessary; thus I beg you in all ways to preserve your health." And she hoped that "by now the fate of the Crimea has been decided, for you write that you are driving there." By mid-July the Empress had become almost desperate, tormented by apprehensions, fears, and doubts. "It's very long since, my sincere friend, that I have had no letters from you," she plaintively pleaded on 10 July; "I think that you have left for the Crimea; I apprehend that the illnesses there somehow not extend, God preserve, to you. From Tsargrad I received the trade treaty completely signed, and Bulgakov says that they know about the occupation of the Crimea, only nobody will crow about it, and they themselves seek to extinguish the rumors. An amazing affair!" Potemkin, for his part, informed Field Marshal Rumiantsev on 12 July that all had proceeded calmly "except that the plague is generally in all the Crimea, excluding Kozlov district."[61]

On 15 July she wrote Potemkin again, protesting that she had gone without word from him for five weeks. "I had expected the occupation of the Crimea at the latest by the middle of May, and yet now it is the middle of July, yet I know no more about it than the Pope of Rome." Imploring Potemkin to report more frequently, she confessed to being tortured by "a thousand ideas." "Hither arrive all sorts of tales about the distemper; by frequent notification you will calm my spirit." And she glumly inquired "when is it that your story of the Crimea will finally be terminated?"[62]

Only on 19 July 1783 could Catherine rejoice at last over the oath of submission by the Crimea and two Nogai hordes that Potemkin had administered on 10 July at Karasu Bazaar. Even so, her joy and sense of relief were restrained by fears for Potemkin's health and the threat of pestilence. "The plague frightens me," she wrote him on 20 July; "God grant that you succeed in preserving your troops from it and to end its sojourn in the Crimea." At the same time the Empress worried about the arrival of a new grandchild (Grand Duchess Alexandra Pavlovna finally appeared on 29 July) while suffering a scare from the injuries her favorite Lanskoi had sustained in a fall from a horse. To Potemkin she sent an official acknowledgment of his achievement on 28 July, granting the Order of St. Vladimir, first class, to Generals Suvorov and Pavel Potemkin, and the Order of St. Alexander Nevskii to General de Bal'men. Her initially cool recognition of Potemkin's success reflected the long months of anxious anticipation and the frustration at being kept in the dark during a critical situation. Within a few more weeks, however, Catherine and Potemkin settled their latest snit. She accepted his explanation of the delays and difficulties involved in the takeover, vowed not to mention their misunderstanding again, and chuckled over his witty dismissal of the inflated tales of plague that were bandied about by "those who gather at Spa and Paris."[63] More important, she fervently reaffirmed her appreciation and regard in support of their political partnership:

> For all the labors exerted by you and the boundless cares for my affairs I cannot sufficiently expound my recognition to you; you yourself know how sensitive I am to merits, and yours are outstanding, just as my friendship and love for you are; God grant you health and an extension of bodily and spiritual forces; I know that you will not stick your face in the mud; be assured that I shall not subordinate you to anyone, except myself.[64]

Catherine's spirits were boosted even higher by her hope that the Turks might not opt for war after all, a decision that she expected to be made after the Muslim feast of bairam (30 August 1783). Furthermore, on 18 August she thanked Potemkin effusively anew, this time for arranging Tsar Irakli's recognition of Russian authority and protection. "Plainly you are my sincere friend," she exulted. "Upon the envy of Europe I look quite calmly, let them jest, yet we do our business." And she ended with her usual good wishes for his health and another avowal: "As concerns me, know that I am committed to you for a century." From her cabinet the Empress gratefully allotted 100,-000 rubles to speed the construction of Potemkin's new Tauride Palace in

St. Petersburg. Yet by the end of August she became distraught once more over Potemkin's report of plague at Kremenchug and of his own fever there. As September flew by, the Empress grew more confident that unless the Porte declared war before October, winter would postpone any hostilities. Nevertheless, Potemkin's persistent illness perturbed her powerfully in conjunction with the reports of plague at Kremenchug and "infectious diseases" at Kherson. Indeed, the Kherson epidemics convinced the Empress that her plan to visit the south could not be accomplished the next spring.[65]

Toward the end of September all the old worries resurged to shake Catherine's confidence. Rumors of pestilential ravages in the Crimea and Kherson kept filtering in. Despite Austrian pressure on France, the Empress still scented war, as she warned Potemkin: "I now expect at any moment a declaration of war from the intrigues of the French and the Prussians." Potemkin's letters of late September from Nezhin evoked in the Empress "mortal fears" at the thought of his galloping through the steppes while dangerously ill. In motherly/wifely tones she urged him not to neglect his health. Yet while counseling peaceful rest the Empress herself kept suggesting various political stratagems to her viceroy. "It has occurred to me," she wrote him on 3 October 1783, "that if Shagin-Girei will still play pranks, then he should be reminded that Khans replaced by the Porte have never received two hundred thousand in pension." That same day Catherine informed Potemkin of her hope that Franco-Prussian machinations in support of the Porte would come to nothing. All the same, she authorized him a day later to reinforce Russian diplomacy by keeping Russian land forces on the ready in winter quarters, and to speed the construction of twelve fifty-gun frigates for service on the Black Sea. She also exempted the guberniias under Potemkin from the newly proclaimed levy of two recruits from every 500 peasant "souls." About war and peace Catherine took no chances.[66]

In mid-October 1783 the Empress ordered Shagin-Girei's removal to Voronezh. This move was intended to pacify the Crimea and prepare the ex-Khan for his new career in Persia. He would not budge for several months, however, and further strained Catherine's patience by refusing his Russian decorations. Still apprehensive of war with the Turks, she temporized until early 1784, by which time her envoy in Constantinople had signed a new convention of Aynali Kavak on 28 December. This Russo-Ottoman agreement reconfirmed the Treaty of Kuchuk-Kainardji while dropping all references to Crimean independence. The deed was finally done. Catherine personally approved the medal struck to celebrate the occasion. One side laconically proclaimed "the results of peace"; the other, depicting a map of the Crimea, the Taman peninsula, and the Kuban, declared them "acquired without bloodshed on April 9, 1783." To this the Empress added an inscription: "profit, honor, and glory." Catherine was well satisfied. A year later she confided to Khrapovitskii that all politics is based on three words: "circumstance, conjecture, and conjuncture." All three figured in the conquest of the Crimea.[67]

By way of crowning her latest conquest, the Empress on 26 February 1784 ordered Shagin-Girei transferred to Russian territory, forcibly if necessary. He was brought to Voronezh under heavy guard on 20 July 1784. Subsisting on a paltry stipend of 20,000 rubles per year, the former Khan lived in Russia under virtual house arrest until early 1787, when he was allowed to leave for Ottoman territory. At first the Sultan treated him generously. But with the Ottoman declaration of war on Russia in August 1787, Shagin-Girei was denounced as a godless renegade from Islam and a Russian spy. He was beheaded on the island of Rhodes that same month. Catherine's Crimean puppet never had a chance at the Shah's throne in Persia.[68]

Incorporation of the Crimea was formally signified on 2 February 1784 when the former khanate was renamed the Tauride Region, a subdivision of the newly "opened" Ekaterinoslav vicegerency under Potemkin's overall authority as governor-general. The harbor of Akhtiar was renamed Sevastopol. In the meantime the danger of war with the Turks waned so rapidly that Catherine authorized withdrawal of most Russian troops from Poland by the end of March. Still, the pestilential perils of the south made her vacillate over plans to inspect her new acquisitions. As she dolefully inquired of Potemkin on 15 April: "Tell me, my friend, frankly, if you think that due to the distemper or other obstacles it will not succeed for me to visit Kherson next year, I could then go to Kiev." Two days later she left for Tsarskoe Selo for five months, a sojourn that fanned rumors of ill health and depression. It was the second year in a row she missed the June holidays at Peterhof.[69]

From the ominously late spring of 1784 well into the fall Catherine nervously followed reports of scattered outbreaks of plague. As usual, she angrily admonished Potemkin against putting himself in danger, advised him to oversee all antiplague precautions and to soak his swollen legs in water, and argued for his early return "a bit merrily." Their mutual dreams of southern glory continued to blossom as she authorized on 4 September 1784 the foundation of a university in Ekaterinoslav. A month later she procured for Bezborodko, a principal architect of the conquest, the title of count of the Holy Roman Empire. On 3 October she sent Potemkin the schedule of her proposed southern tour, publicly announced on 26 September 1784 for the next spring. Seven weeks later she postponed it until January 1786 because of the plague. Only in the spring of 1785 did the threat of pestilence diminish sufficiently for the Empress to approve the removal of quarantines from the Smolensk region and Belorussia. In May 1786 she also endorsed a new quarantine statute. By then she had finally set her southern tour for early 1787. In compensation for the postponement of the Tauride tour, Catherine's friends raised her spirits by a quick trip in May and June 1785 to inspect the new canal works at Vyshnii Volochek, from where she visited Moscow for three days before returning to Petersburg by water—a journey of 1,800 kilometers all told. The new palace at Tsaritsyno dismayed her by its resemblance to a coffin.[70]

Conquest of the Crimea afforded Catherine and Potemkin enormous satisfaction. Despite formidable obstacles and the omnipresent prospect of full-scale war, they had contrived to accomplish the annexation without significant bloodshed. Furthermore, they succeeded with minimal aid from their Austrian ally. Joseph II magnanimously claimed no equivalent in Turkish territory; he was content with only commercial concessions. If the "Greek

Project" had been achieved only in part, its possibilities had been demonstrated in the potent Russo-Austrian alliance. Certainly the Turks had been intimidated. The future of Ottoman possessions in Europe was in more serious doubt than ever. The Russian bear and the Austrian eagle were both poised on the borders of "the sick man of Europe," only a few days' dash or sail from his vulnerable heartland. Incorporation of the Crimea and Russia's new protectorate in Georgia lengthened the southern frontier appreciably, of course, complicating its defense. On 14 January 1785 Catherine therefore authorized the army to increase its infantry strength by 40,000 men.[71]

If 1783 denoted a year of political triumph for Catherine, her joy was beclouded by constant worries and a series of sobering deaths among her lieutenants and friends. When General Bauer died on 11 February, she wept for days and cursed the entire medical profession. The demise of Nikita Panin on 31 March and Grigorii Orlov on 12 April, although both had been anticipated, depressed her all the same. The deaths of statesmen who had served the Empress three decades or more left her wondering who would be next and when her turn would come. Commiserating with Potemkin over his illness in October 1783, Catherine sadly commented: "for me it's a black year; this week died fm. pr. Alex. Mikh. Golitsyn, and it seems to me that whoever falls into Rogerson's hands is already a dead man." The next few years brought more grief. She was distraught over the death of Grimm's longtime mistress, Louise d'Épinay, in early 1784. Besides, the sudden death of "Sashin'ka" Lanskoi on 25 June 1784, followed two days later by the demise of senator and state secretary Adam Olsuf'ev, brought the Empress herself close to despair for almost a year. Indeed, by late 1783 European newspapers circulated reports of her declining health or imminent death, stories that she blamed on "Herod" in Potsdam. At Milan in November 1784 her son Bobrinskoi heard rumors that Catherine was dangerously ill with breast cancer, without hope of recovery. Such false rumors would not cease. Another longtime admirer and supporter, Count Zakhar Chernyshev, expired unexpectedly on 31 August 1784. Her former confidante Countess Bruce, born the same year as she, died in Moscow on 7 April 1786. Finally, King Frederick II's death on 17 August 1786 removed a sometime benefactor and lifelong role-model. All these losses fortified her doubts about modern medicine and her faith in home remedies such as "Bestucheff Drops," an iron "nerve tonic" named for the late Bestuzhev-Riumin whose secret recipe she purchased in 1780 and published in the Russian press. In 1786 she quipped that she would take eighty drops at age eighty. Nature seemed in sorrow too. Drought that summer in central and southern Russia resulted in poor grain harvests, rising prices, and hunger among peasants and livestock. And Catherine's oft-postponed trip to the south, when completed in 1787, provoked a new siege of crises.[72]

11

Wars, War Scares, and European Revolution

Catherine's long delayed Tauride tour in 1787, the grandest spectacle of her reign, celebrated her quarter of a century on the Russian throne. More than six months of travel by land and water over 6,000 kilometers amounted to the longest journey of her life, a political progress surpassed in length and ambition only by Peter the Great's Persian campaign of 1722–23. It involved much more than a pleasure tour. Organized by Potemkin, Bezborodko, Rumiantsev, and a host of others, Catherine's splendid journey set the seal of sovereignty on Russia's latest southern conquests even as it heralded additional ambitions and fanned speculation in the European press. Almost a year in advance anonymous accounts from Petersburg alleged an intention to be crowned "sovereign of her new possessions" in brilliant ceremonies that would cost seven million rubles. Meeting Joseph II at Kherson and touring the Tauride with him advertised the past and future benefits of the Russo-Austrian alliance. All along the way the Empress ostentatiously reviewed her army regiments and naval squadrons. She and Potemkin were determined to show that Russian military power in the south was no mirage.[1]

At the end of May 1786, seven months before her departure, the Empress privately remarked on the 15 million rubles set aside "in case of war." "The future is very beautiful," she concluded. A month later she let her expansive dreams float freely: "The border is not finished. Time is demanded for the execution of a great enterprise. The border will be the Black Sea and the subjugation of the Persian rulers, equalizing them with the Duchy of Kurland, will facilitate that." The "Greek Project" still held sway over Catherine's imagination, and it showed signs of spinning off a "Persian Project." Indeed, in August 1786 she ordered Potemkin to cultivate the various sovereigns of the Caucasus, using for the purpose 60,000 rubles of Shagin-Girei's annual pension.[2]

Planning for the Crimean tour had begun years ahead. Until the very last moment Catherine intended to take both grandsons with her, despite their parents' protests. Only when both suddenly became ill shortly before their scheduled departure did she finally relent and leave them behind. Her tight schedule allowed no delay. Her spirits were exceptionally high. After a brief illness in September she felt better than she had in years.[3]

Before Catherine could leave St. Petersburg she was unexpectedly confronted by one other, quite messy family problem. The long brewing marital disputes of Grand Duchess Maria Fedorovna's brother Prince Frederick and his wife, Princess Augusta of Brunswick—better known as Zelmira—landed literally in her lap the evening of 17 December 1786. The distraught princess begged the Empress on her knees for refuge from her husband's abuse. Catherine granted her temporary asylum in the Winter Palace, assured the young mother of three that she would not be abandoned, and advised "Don Feroce" to take leave abroad. He left town before the end of the month. His adjutant, Major Baron von Hersdorf, was imprisoned at Schlüsselburg for eight months on suspicion of treasonous contacts with Sweden and of baneful influence on Grand Duke Paul. Unwilling to keep Zelmira in St. Petersburg near Paul and Maria Fedorovna, who were both unsympathetic to her plight, the Empress arranged asylum at the castle of Lode, an imperial estate west of Reval. While on her Tauride tour Catherine kept tabs on Zelmira and corresponded with her father, whom she found unsupportive of his daughter's wish for a divorce. The Empress insisted that Zelmira not be compelled either to reconcile with her brute of a husband, whom she discharged from Russian service, or to return to her parents.

This embarrassing stalemate persisted some twenty months until abruptly terminated by Zelmira's sudden death from an unspecified illness on 16 September 1788. No public announcement of the event was made, nor were the parents of the deceased informed for some weeks. Try as Catherine might to hush up the whole affair, scandalous tales circulated for decades afterwards. It was alleged that Zelmira had died in childbirth, or that she had been buried alive with her newborn child, or that she had been poisoned by Catherine or Potemkin to keep her quiet. These allegations were absorbed into the same accusatory tradition that blamed Catherine for the demise of "Princess Tarakanova" and Grand Duchess Natalia Alekseevna.[4]

Catherine's huge entourage left Tsarskoe Selo the morning of 7 January 1787. Traveling over the snow swiftly and smoothly in two hundred gilded coaches mounted on runners, the imperial suite included three foreign ministers: Count Louis Cobenzl of Austria, Count Louis-Philippe de Ségur of France, and Alleyne Fitzherbert of Britain—"my pocket ministers," Catherine called them. The Empress herself rode in a six-place conveyance with her favorite Dmitriev-Mamonov and maid of honor Anna Protasova; the other three seats were rotated daily among the invited guests. As usual, Catherine worked as she was whisked along, keeping in close communication with Paul and her officials. From Porkhov on 9 January she dispatched a journal of the tour to governor-generals Bruce and Eropkin in St. Petersburg and Moscow "for the deflection in the capitals of empty utterances." Public relations occupied the Empress constantly, on several levels. In the towns that her cavalcade passed through she received local notables and dispensed a shower of presents and awards. At Smolensk in mid-January she stayed four days longer than planned because of her favorite's illness (a high fever and sore throat that Dr. Rogerson treated with James's powders and Spanish fly), which allowed her to attend a "gigantic" ball on 17 January. Concerning her grandsons she sent a stream of advice and instructions. She wrote Paul that Konstantin's rash sounded like scrofula. The inoculation for smallpox of two granddaughters also worried the Empress, who had Paul's letters to Count Ivan Chernyshev secretly opened. On 24 January the imperial party stopped for dinner at Field Marshal Rumiantsev's Vyshenki estate. He accompanied them the rest of the way to Kiev, where they arrived on 29 January 1787 shivering in twenty degrees of frost.[5]

Catherine's second visit to Kiev contrasted sharply to her first view of the "Mother of Russian towns" in 1744. Festivities and decorations greeted her everywhere for the next ten weeks as she thoroughly explored Kiev and its environs. The old town's shabby condition combined with the slush of winter and the mud of spring to dampen her spirits. Potemkin kept his distance, morosely residing at the venerable Monastery of the Caves. By contrast, scores of foreign dignitaries flocked to see the Empress. Among them were two dashing soldiers of fortune, the German-French Prince Charles de Nassau-Siegen, who became a great favorite of Potemkin, and the Spaniard Francisco de Miranda, who dazzled the Empress herself. Although Catherine declined to invest 20,000 rubles in Miranda's schemes to liberate South America from Spanish oppression, she invited him to join her service and, despite his refusal, she granted him 1,000 rubles on departure in August 1787 and ordered Russian embassies in Europe to assist his travels and protect him from Spanish plots. Her patronage of the handsome young Spaniard set tongues awagging. As Stephen Sayre, a boastful American who had worked in St. Petersburg in 1780–81, slyly reported Miranda's purported conquest: "nothing has escaped his penetration—not even the Empress of all the Russias, as I believe—a mortifying declaration for me to make, who was 21 months in her capital without ever making my self acquainted with the internal parts of *her extensive & well known dominions*." Another young American, the Virginian Lewis Littlepage, a secretary to King Stanislas Poniatowski, was presented to Catherine at Kiev; but he made no claim of intimacy.[6]

From Kiev on 15 March Catherine ordered the Petersburg mint to strike a special medal commemorating the Tauride tour and the twenty-fifth anniversary of her reign. This medal depicted her portrait on one side and her itinerary on the other, encircled by the motto "The Way to Benefit." One hundred gold and five hundred silver medals were cast from 36 pounds of gold and 128 pounds of silver at a cost of 13,361 rubles.[7]

By early April, the Dnieper having opened on 27 March, Catherine impatiently declared herself ready to proceed, despite Potemkin's unfinished preparations and rumors that she would go no further. Indeed, she may have wished an earlier departure to ascertain whether her viceroy planned to hoodwink her with phony evidence of progress and prosperity, the "Potemkin villages" that his Russian and foreign detractors were already disparaging. Hostilities with the Turks did not worry her. To Khrapovitskii she confidently confided that "we can start it ourselves," pointing to Ottoman inroads in the Caucasus and their deposition of the pro-Russian hospodar of Moldavia, who had taken refuge in Russia. She scoffed at newspaper speculation about her supposed plan to be crowned "Queen of Taurida," a transparent ploy designed to incite Ottoman ire. On 22 April 1787 the imperial party boarded a flotilla of eleven specially constructed (and armed) galleys, with an escort of barks and lesser vessels, to visit Novorossiia and the Tauride. Catherine rode in a galley named *Dnieper;* Potemkin followed on *Bug* with his nieces.[8]

At Kanev on the Dnieper south of Kiev the Empress greeted her old friend Stanislas Poniatowski, whom she had not seen for thirty years, on 25 April. The King staged a magnificent reception replete with grandiose fireworks— an imitation of Mt. Vesuvius erupting—and asked her to stay several days. But Catherine politely refused, having privately resolved months before that their reunion should not exceed one day. King Stanislas was told that, for the Empress to meet Joseph II on time, her schedule could not be changed. "Furthermore, every change of intention, you yourself know," she assured Potemkin, "is unpleasant for me." The next day Catherine relaxed, glad to be rid of her royal visitor. "Pr. P. said not a word," she groaned to Khrapovitskii; "I was compelled to talk endlessly; my tongue dried up; they almost became angry, begging us to stay. The King bartered for 3, then 2 days, or at least for dinner the next day." As the Prince de Ligne mordantly summarized Poniatowski's fiasco: three months and three millions expended for three hours of empty conversation with the Empress. She never saw Poniatowski again. His offer to ally with Russia against the Turks was brusquely declined as inopportune.[9]

Soon the voyage became tedious, the winds contrary and sultry. The galleys had to be steered close to the riverbank because of shoals, but these unforeseen obstacles were stricken from the official journal to stifle speculation and rumors. Catherine lauded the economic and military benefits Russia would reap from the new territories and lamented that Petersburg had not been located amid the fertile region and mild climate. To flaunt her good spirits before the widowered Governor-General Bruce of St. Petersburg, the Empress appended to her regular report five catty queries devised in concert with Lev Naryshkin and Anna Protasova "on the galley *Dnieper* 4 May 1787 under a soft breeze, from boredom:"

1. Has Zavodovskoi married and is the rumor about his marriage not false?
2. Are maid of honor Passek and chamber-gentleman Shkurin alive?
3. Have you not had a gain or loss of people?
4. Who are you in love with right now and is she biting?
5. Are your old amourettes healthy? and are they not angry with you?[10]

Alerted that "the eminent traveler Count Falkenstein" had reached the vicinity, Catherine hastily disembarked and hurried by coach to meet her ally near Kaidak on 7 May. That evening Potemkin presented a prodigious girandole, a radiating and revolving firework that encircled Catherine's monogram with a bouquet of 4,000 rockets and a flaming hill with lava. The Empress knew Joseph II had come reluctantly, fearful of his health. His presence was essential to her, however, to amplify the tour's political purposes. They entered Kherson on 12 May where they met Yakov Bulgakov, Russian minister at Constantinople, and three days later all witnessed the launching of two ships of the line, *Vladimir* and the 80-gun *Joseph II*. Catherine professed herself delighted with Kherson, writing her grandsons on 13 May in praise of its fortifications, wharves, and fleet. "I am healthy," she remarked, "we have fresh breezes and it is not at all hot." By contrast, Joseph II privately scoffed at Kherson; he arose early each morning and was ready to tour by six A.M. The Empress in turn quietly chided his frenetic pace. "Everything do I see and hear, although I do not run, like the Emperor." His conversation and veiled criticism irritated her so much that she privately predicted his eventual undoing; "he does not know the Russian proverb: to confuse business with idleness; the man was himself the cause of two riots." Although Catherine did not explain these allusions, her prediction proved uncannily accurate. Joseph's short reign ended in disaster.[11]

Intent on impressing her imperial ally, the Empress took him on a whirlwind tour of the Crimea from 21 May to 1 June. At Inkerman on 22 May they reviewed the new Russian Black Sea fleet, fifteen ships of the line and frigates, and Catherine demonstratively drank the health of her best friend, the Emperor-King, whom she thanked for his aid in conquering the Crimea. One of the Russian ships, *Slava Ekateriny* (Catherine's Glory), raised the Emperor's flag, to a fifteen-gun salute. Joseph was dazzled, unaware that her toast would be expunged from the official journal the next day. Even so, he noticed that the cutter on which she inspected the fleet was an exact replica of the Sultan's. And he was even more enthralled by the monster firework at Sevastopol that involved 20,000 rockets, a spectacular exhibition that terrified the Tatar spectators.

Potemkin spared no effort or expense in showcasing Russia's power and resources. He even surprised the Empress with a battalion of "Amazons"— 100 Greek women dressed in crimson skirts and gold-trimmed jackets (spencers) topped by gold-spangled turbans with ostrich feathers. Joseph II disconcerted the commander of these musket-bearing Amazons by greeting her with a kiss. Gratified by this strange spectacle, Catherine embraced the commander, offered her hand to the "troops," and awarded their commander a jeweled brooch and 100 rubles each to the rank and file.[12]

All these sights enraptured the Empress. To her grandsons, then en route to Moscow to meet her for the June celebrations, she wrote on 28 May praising the Black Sea fleet—1,500 kilometers from St. Petersburg, but only forty-eight hours from Constantinople—the amenities of Sevastopol's harbor, the beauty and abundance of the Crimea's scenery and soil. Yet, after returning to Kremenchug on 4 June, her mood darkened for several days, possibly from a combination of fatigue, bad news about Turkish intentions, and foreboding about the Moscow celebrations. At Poltava on 8 June, the Empress awarded Potemkin the title of "Tavricheskii" (Tauride) and 100,000 rubles. Travel northward by coach was slower and less comfortable than by sledge or galley, of course, and when Catherine reached Tula on 20–21 June she was too tired to appear at a ball. Moscow greeted her on 27 June.[13]

The Empress spent scarcely a week in Moscow—her last sojourn in the unloved old capital—before returning to Tsarskoe Selo on 11 July 1787, utterly exhausted. She had vetoed any large welcome. Delighted with her Tauride tour although concerned about reports of crop failures, Catherine lauded Potemkin and his works extravagantly, but she was already worried that revolts in Flanders and Brabant might prevent Joseph II from assisting her against any Ottoman attack. Nevertheless, the prospect of hostilities with the Porte did not faze her, when Bezborodko mentioned the likelihood on 5 August in St. Petersburg, where she had arrived after a quick visit to her new palace at Pella to escape the northern summer's rains and mists. Apparently she asked Khrapovitskii on 17 August to hunt up Potemkin's secret project to create an "Albanian" realm for Konstantin from Persian territory by occupying Derbent and Baku and uniting them with Gilian.[14]

After celebrating the holiday of the Preobrazhenskii Guards on 6 August, the Empress was disconcerted the very next day by a new kind of crisis: labor unrest in Petersburg. A delegation of 400 peasant-workers assembled that morning on the square before the Winter Palace in hopes of delivering their petition of grievances into Catherine's own hands. Their complaints alleged abusive, barbaric treatment by the merchant-contractor Dolgov, who had hired 4,000 laborers to work on the granite embankments along the Fontanka River and the Catherine Canal—one of Catherine's favorite embellishments of the new capital. The dispute had simmered for several weeks, notwithstanding efforts by Governor-General Bruce and Senior Policemaster Ryleev to pacify the "muzhiks." The workers became more militant when two delegates sent to state their case at Tsarskoe Selo had been arrested. Moreover, they had refused to discuss their complaints with adjutant-general Count Anhalt, scorning him as a foreigner. The crowd of petitioners was quietly insistent. Every time they caught sight of a woman through the windows of the imperial apartments, they bowed low and waved their petition. Throughout the morning they defiantly ignored exhortations to disperse. Catherine did not show herself, directing arrangements from inside the palace. Early in the afternoon the palace guards suddenly seized seventeen petitioners, who were hustled off to face criminal charges of illegal assembly and conspiracy. The rest of the crowd decamped immediately. Horse-guards and Don cossacks patrolled the palace precincts that evening and night to prevent any new assemblages. Catherine's dinner was delayed until three P.M. The affair occupied her the next day, too, as she angrily dictated orders to Governor Konovnitsyn to prevent such illegal gatherings; but the tension quickly eased after the prompt release of those arrested and the start of an official inquiry. Evidently Dolgov had to raise his payscale and improve working conditions. This was the only labor disturbance the Empress ever witnessed. It did not impress her, but she may have worried about a recurrence.[15]

At the same time the issue of the succession perturbed Catherine anew.

On 19 August she read the preface to Peter the Great's Naval Code, in which the question of divided inheritance was condemned. The next day she had Khrapovitskii read sections of *The Justice of the Monarch's Will,* the Petrine political tract that justified substitution of the sovereign's wish for the practice of succession by seniority. Five days later she requested all edicts dealing with the succession since the time of Catherine I. What Catherine did with all these materials we do not know. Perhaps she contemplated a new succession law that would exclude Paul.[16]

The Christian Amazon in Action

By mid-August 1787 a rumor on the streets of Petersburg sensed war with the Turks. At the end of August word arrived of the Ottoman arrest of the Russian minister in Constantinople, Yakov Bulgakov, for refusing a Turkish ultimatum. It meant war. Though not unexpected, the Ottoman action still incensed Catherine, who reportedly wept before convening her council on 31 August. The membership of the council, which had not met all year, reflected the confused composition of Catherine's government. Vice-chancellor Count Ivan Osterman and Count Alexander Bezborodko, jointly in charge of foreign affairs, were the only regular members present. Joining the council for the occasion were Governor-General Jakob Bruce; General Count Valentin Musin-Pushkin, vice-president of the War Collegium; General Nikolai Saltykov, tutor to the grand dukes; Count Andrei Shuvalov, chief director of state banks; Count Alexander Vorontsov, president of the Commerce Collegium; Stepan Strekalov and Peter Zavadovskii, both cabinet secretaries.[17] In the council room of the Winter Palace the Empress opened the session after eleven o'clock in the morning with a short speech:

> I suppose you know that the Turks have violated the peace with our empire and have even dared to incarcerate in the Castle of the Seven Towers a minister of MINE. You yourselves are to consider which measures ought to be taken from My side in such circumstances. For an explication of all the wily and treacherous conduct of the Porte since the conclusion of the peace at Kainardji until the present time you will be supplied with a note from the Department of Foreign Affairs which I urgently ordered to be compiled.[18]

Then Catherine presided while Bezborodko detailed Russian grievances against the Porte. All the councilors agreed to wage the war defensively at first. They welcomed Austrian assurances of armed support. The councilors and the Empress both thought of the new war in terms of the old; its cost concerned them. They also apprehended domestic disorders, especially among the Muslim nomads of the southeast. Nobody mentioned Pugachev, but his specter could hardly be forgotten. To avoid cannibalizing the garrison forces and thereby inviting internal disturbances, Catherine's initial proposal for a levy of two recruits per 500 census "souls" was increased to one recruit per 100 souls. "We scared the Turks, they prepared themselves—and declared war on us unexpectedly," Zavadovskii complained to Field Marshal Rumiant-sev on 6 September. "Every war is unpredictable, but to defend ourselves is a necessity, while this one has happened in a hungry year." Flour prices were rising, Catherine admitted to Grimm, but she denied any shortages of bread or brandy.[19]

The threat of pestilence was not forgotten either. Catherine inquired about the number of sick in Potemkin's army, particularly at Kherson. On 9 September the council recommended that precautions be adopted in the border guberniias as well as those adjacent. Rumors of plague at Ochakov prompted the council to endorse internal precautions on 14 October. Four days later the councilors likewise approved Governor-General Eropkin's proposal, based on his bitter experience of the plague in 1770–71, to institute a sanitary cordon along the southern edge of Moscow guberniia.[20]

While the councilors worked on a counterdeclaration to be issued on 7 September, the Empress privately declared her confidence in Russian readiness: "Now we are more ready than at the start of the last war; in two weeks all troops can be in place." A day later she reiterated her conviction that the people, grown confident through the twenty-five years of her beneficent reign, would support the new war with enthusiasm. Bezborodko assured her that Russian forces in the south were fully prepared, the Black Sea fleet in particular. On 14 September the Petersburg press printed a detailed account of the naval action off Ochakov on 21 August whereby two Russian vessels bravely repulsed the Ottoman fleet, an action that Catherine later lauded to Grimm. Equally sanguine, Catherine asked her council to fit out a new naval expedition from the Baltic to the Mediterranean, possibly under the leadership of Aleksei Orlov-Chesmenskii himself. Command of the armies in the south was split between Potemkin and Rumiantsev, to their mutual consternation.[21]

All this confidence was quickly undercut by events in the south. A storm scattered the Sevastopol fleet before it could engage the Turks, who attacked Kinburn by land and sea. One Russian ship was blown into the Constantinople canal, so Catherine jokingly recommended to Potemkin better timing for such visits. Her namesake, *Slava Ekateriny*, lost all three masts, yet managed to escape Ottoman clutches, to the Empress's grateful relief. She advised renaming the ship to avoid future complications. The captured Russian ship, she pointedly informed Grimm, was the *Maria Magdalina* (Mary Magdalene) whose commander was not a Russian but a British officer. The vaunted Black Sea fleet seemed to be turning into a "Potemkin village." Potemkin himself panicked. Complaining of illness, he dolefully reported these disasters only in late September. He begged to be relieved of his command and to come to Petersburg, even advised evacuating his own Tauride realm.[22]

Catherine kept calm. She alternately cajoled and coaxed her mercurial viceroy, hopeful his hypochondria would lift. His "spasms" she blamed on gas pains. "I know how tormenting they are, most especially to sensitive and impatient people, like we and you." Naturally she dissuaded Potemkin from abandoning the Crimea and promised to build new ships on the Don as reinforcements for the Black Sea fleet. Kinburn she urged him to defend, Ochakov she urged him to attack. "I do not demand the impossible," she insisted, "but only write what I think." In mid-October the Empress rejoiced at word of General Suvorov's gallant, bloody repulse of an Ottoman amphibious attack on Kinburn. Public prayers in St. Petersburg celebrated this first victory on 17 October 1787. The Empress implored Potemkin to take the offensive, cheering him on with the possibility that the Ochakov garrison might turn tail like their compatriots at Khotin in 1769. To follow military movements in the Kuban and beyond, she dug up a map which, on study, convinced her that these operations in the Caucasus were essential for the security of the entire Tauride region. On 21 October she invited Aleksei and Fedor Orlov in Moscow to take command of the naval expedition to the Mediterranean in the spring; "for their name alone will add weight to the measure of naval armament," she assured Khrapovitskii. They declined the invitation. Aleksei Orlov was said to covet field marshal rank so as to be senior to Potemkin. On the way to the theater that evening Catherine fell down. Perhaps she felt the political world slipping beneath her. A dispatch from Paris the next day describing the rapprochement of England and Prussia, France and Russia, and Swedish designs on Denmark persuaded her that Europe was headed toward a general war.[23]

With Potemkin preoccupied in the south, Catherine felt increasingly isolated, overburdened, and out of control in the winter of 1787–88. Accidents alarmed her, as in mid-February when a torch fell off the wall of the Winter Palace just after she passed. Her health failed frequently, too. On 30 November 1787 she kept to her rooms and refused to eat. "Since the 12th I have not been very healthy, a cold fever," she lamented to Potemkin on 16 December; "today is the first day I am on my feet, but my head is weak and I cannot write." To Khrapovitskii she complained of sleeplessness on 3 January 1788, headache on 17 March, illness on 20 and 21 March, "unbearable colic" on 22 and 25 April. The variable Petersburg winter depressed her as usual. One-third of the capital seemed sick with colds, coughs, and fevers in late January; influenza was reported to be rife in Poland, and despite rumors of plague in Wallachia, the Empress pined for the warm climes of Ekaterinoslav. On 11 April 1788 *The Times* breathlessly announced: "The news of the day is, that the *Empress of Russia is suddenly dead!*" Death had in fact been on Catherine's mind in the early months of 1788, when she privately surveyed her life in a brief epitaph. By the end of April she was already worried her Austrian allies might rout the Turks in Moldavia and reveal Potemkin's laggardness. "God grant good weather there, so that there not be sicknesses and so that the Prince soon take Ochakov." In actuality, epidemic disease and Ottoman counterattacks slowed the Austrian advance as well.[24]

Potemkin's hotheadedness reminded Catherine of the dead Grigorii Orlov and Zakhar Chernyshev and the retired Peter Panin. Orlov had always said Potemkin was smart as the devil, and she trusted her viceroy completely: "he knows no other sovereign; out of a sergeant I made him into a field marshal." Yet his practice of reporting only once a month provoked Catherine's constant consternation. "It makes me die a thousand deaths, not just one," she exclaimed at the end of 1787. "You could in no wise show devotion and gratitude more vividly, than to write me more often, but to write from month to month, as now, this is the harshest deed, from which I suffer every hour and which can have the most evil and unexpected and undesirable consequences from you." What did these last hints signify? That she might hearken to his many critics, such as Aleksei Orlov, who had supposedly denounced Potemkin to her at the end of 1787? Or was she simply pleading for some psychic support herself? His reports, however tardy, invariably evoked her empathy and eloquent encouragement. As always, she sympathized with his illnesses, no matter how trivial (such as hangnails), and confided her own fears and concerns: "Sick persons and sicknesses scare me." Paul's announced intention to join the field army alarmed her, too, but she hoped his wife's pregnancy would stop him. To inspire Potemkin she sent him several of her own fur coats and two Chinese dressing gowns.[25]

About the upcoming war Catherine showed mixed feelings. Her initial confidence in a quick and easy victory soon gave way to doubts and distractions. In mock horror she begged Grimm in February 1788 not to follow the Prince de Ligne in calling her Catherine the Great "because, first, I do not like any sobriquet, second, my name is Catherine II, and third, I do not wish that anybody say about me, as they did about Louis XV, that he is badly named; fourth, I am neither large nor small in size: tell those to whom it pertains that I yield all sobriquets to those who deserve them, like Gegu and company" (i.e., George III and Gustavus III). Her troubles with the latter two sovereigns had just begun.[26]

Mobilization exacerbated stresses in an already taut economy, fueling inflation and the hoarding of foodstuffs and currency, even copper coins, all of which complicated the provisioning of the enlarged army. Reluctant to impose new taxes, the Empress borrowed 9 million Dutch gulden and 1.2 million Genoese piasters abroad in 1788, and sought to cut domestic expenditures by partially postponing administrative reforms such as implementation of the Charter to the Towns and reorganization of the financial administration, road repairs, and so on. To Dr. Zimmermann in Hannover she denied rumors in Europe that Russia aimed to overthrow the "immense," heavily populated Ottoman Empire. "Do you believe the thing is possible?" she asked rhetorically. Nevertheless, she hoped to teach the Turks and their European sympathizers a lesson of respect for Russia's newly consolidated power. With new victories she and Potemkin would show the world that Russia's armed might was no "Potemkin village."[27]

European opinion also expressed mixed sentiments about Russia's latest military venture. Fastening on Potemkin's "Amazon battalion," a British satirist in October 1787 coupled Catherine's foreign policy with her checkered personal reputation in a pictorial assault on "The Christian Amazon, with Her Invincible Target, Alias the focus of Genial Rays, or Dian of the Rushes, too Much for 300,000 Infidels." The Amazon Empress leans back to strike the Sultan with her saber, revealing breeches and jackboots under her petticoats. Louis XVI of France, a small crowned ape, appeals to the Sultan for moderation while Joseph II hides behind his Amazon ally, whose shield wards off the Turkish cannonballs and grenades. The Empress and the Sultan bandy ribald rhymes, Catherine charging:

> Your Sublime Highness, is to blame I Fear,
> Thus forcibly to Enter my Fron . . . tier
> In Rearing Rampart, on each Slight pretence,
> You Risk the Blush, which Shame gives Impotence;
> My Shield is tested, and Approved as Staunch.

To which Abdul Hamid retorts:

> By Every Artist, famous in this . . . Branch,
> Should then each Member, in your Salique Land,
> Rise up against My Tower, and make . . . a Stand,
> They Shall yield Victory, to this potent Hand.

Another print of the same time, "Amsterdam in a *Dam'd* Predicament,—or— The Last Scene of the Republican Pantomime," depicted an audience of European sovereigns in a fantastic theater witnessing the turmoil of Dutch politics. From an upper box Catherine leans out to brandish her fist at the Sultan below, exclaiming: "Blast you, you old Goat! to keep so many Women shut up in your Seraglio. I'll turn over a new Leaf & allow every Woman 20,000 Men." The Sultan stands to draw his sword, swearing "By our holy Prophet & sacred Mecca, I'll curb that wanton Spirit."[28] Because Catherine carefully read the British press she probably knew about such scurrilous prints.

Since the new Russo-Turkish war would obviously involve large naval as well as land forces, Catherine strove to bolster Russian naval power by recruiting experienced foreign commanders. The naval fiasco of the first few weeks made her painfully aware of Russian ineptitude at sea. The most celebrated foreign naval commander she recruited was none other than the Scottish-American corsair, John Paul Jones. "Pavel Dzhones" (or Paul'zhons), as the Russians called him, was recommended to the Empress by Thomas Jefferson, among others. He was promptly hired. Taken by his reputation for defeating the British navy with tiny forces, Catherine thought to use his name as well as his skills. "This man is extremely capable of multiplying fear and trembling in the foe," she informed Potemkin in sending him "one more bulldog for the Black Sea." Appointed captain of the fleet with the rank of major-general, Jones was elevated to "Rear Admiral" even before he arrived in St. Petersburg on 23 April 1788. "Paul Jones has arrived; I saw him today," Catherine notified Grimm on 24 April. "I believe he will make a miracle here." She graciously accepted his gift of the new American federal constitution and dined with him the day after. He was invited to dinner with the court at Tsarskoe Selo on 30 April and again on 6 and 7 May, when he left for the south. Jones made a good impression on the Empress, who tactfully undertook to win him Potemkin's favor. "He burns with desire for our service," she wrote Potemkin on 1 May, and she sent with Jones a personal note to Potemkin reiterating her regard: "I love you greatly, my friend, without ceremony."

Potemkin's affable reception of Jones at Ekaterinoslav on 19 May delighted Catherine, who may have sensed the likelihood of conflict between two headstrong individuals. Jones' enthusiasm and anti-British reputation appealed to her all the more because of her deepening suspicions of British complicity in the Ottoman declaration of war and incitement of Sweden to threaten Russia with an arms buildup. "England is hindering us everywhere," she complained to Khrapovitskii on 19 May.[29]

Even as Catherine urged Potemkin to open the spring campaign early, so as to force peace on the Porte by the next fall "and so that you might return here and I not be without hands as now," she bemoaned the disarray among her councilors. The emergent "triumvirate" of Bezborodko, Vorontsov, and Zavadovskii was explicitly warned against any anti-Potemkin machinations. No doubt the Empress also heard about Osterman's attack on Bezborodko for neglecting his duties to dally with "girls," an accusation that almost led to blows before Zavadovskii reconciled the rivals. Court gossip referred to the lascivious Bezborodko as "the Reis Effendi" with his own "Seraglio," which included one Grekova, a sister-in-law of the governor of Saratov, two Italian girls, and the actress/singer Sandunova. "In the council they stop everything," the Empress growled to Khrapovitskii; "they were about to confound Paul Jones, but I finally set things right." Equally worrisome were the persistent reports of Sweden's war preparations on land and sea. In mid-May the arrival of a shipment of gunpowder sparked rumors of a Turco-Swedish plot to blow up Kronstadt. Catherine suspected the erratic Gustavus III was simply posturing, but the threat of a wider war had to be heeded. The border fortresses were hastily repaired and reinforced, and naval forces were mobilized.[30]

Amid these alarms another appeared with the birth of a new granddaughter, Ekaterina Pavlovna, on 11 May at 3:40 P.M. Joy, relief, and consternation all washed over Catherine, who observed the difficult birth of her namesake and took credit for saving her daughter-in-law's life after two and a half hours of anxious attendance. An immediate consequence of this birth was to free Grand Duke Paul to join Potemkin's army, a prospect that both mother and viceroy dreaded. In fact, the idea chilled Catherine as much as the erratic weather. "It is so cold with us," she informed Potemkin on 11 May 1788, "that in writing I almost froze."[31]

Two weeks later Catherine wrote Potemkin that "Swedish affairs are now in the same crisis." She was still unsure what Gustavus III intended, but she was certain the Turks or other powers were financing his armaments. A report from Hamburg maintained that 700,000 gulden or "no less than ten tons of silver specie" had been transmitted to Sweden from Turkey (these funds never arrived). That very day the Empress ordered three light vessels to check Swedish naval preparations. A report on 2 June (which later proved false) that the Swedish fleet had appeared off Reval resulted in orders for Admiral Chichagov to put to sea at once. Her councilors also offered conflicting advice. Vice-chancellor Osterman advocated a preventive strike at the Swedish fleet; others thought the Swedes would attack only after the Russian fleet left for the Mediterranean in mid-June, an expedition that Catherine was reluctant to countermand. "Perceptible is uneasiness, or more, vexation,"

Khrapovitskii noted. Maps and atlases were brought to permit the Empress to visualize the Russo-Swedish border in Finland. Catherine still hoped the Swedes were just bluffing, but she wondered how to call their bluff. Potemkin's sagacity was sorely missed. "If you were here, I would have decided in five minutes what to do, talking it over with you," she wrote him on 4 June. A two-front war might entail unforeseen consequences, she ruminated in requesting Potemkin's counsel. Ambivalent feelings agitated the Empress. On the one hand, she was tempted to kill two birds with one shot by teaching the Turks a lesson through the quick destruction of Swedish naval power. She saw the political benefits, on the other hand, of allowing Gustavus III to cast himself in the role of the aggressor and violator of his own constitution of 1772, a role his constitution-minded subjects might refuse to finance; "and so I propose to give him time to play the fool, to spend his money, and to consume his bread."[32]

Catherine found her psychological turmoil reflected in the weather. Five days of tree-breaking storms and "most abominably cold weather" at the end of May gave way to "most powerful heat" and rains in mid-June. Noticing how profusely the corpulent Khrapovitskii perspired as he lumbered to discharge his secretarial duties, Catherine mischievously advised him to take cold baths, "but with the years it will pass," she advised philosophically: "I myself perspired a lot at first."[33]

By mid-June 1788 the Empress concluded that Gustavus III was bent on war. Would he desist, she wondered, if she recognized his authority as sovereign? That she would not do. Admiral Samuel Greig's squadron, designated for the Mediterranean, was therefore diverted to cruise off Reval until Swedish intentions could be clarified. Catherine's concern became all the more intense inasmuch as she believed she was confronting an unpredictable madman who might decide to assault Kronstadt and Petersburg first. That possibility kept her awake all night on 17/18 June, when she ordered Kronstadt on full alert and its defenses reinforced.[34]

The Russo-Swedish war began not with a bang, as Catherine anticipated, but with a series of military-diplomatic feints. On the morning of 20 June the Empress received a courier from Count Andrei Razumovskii, her ambassador in Stockholm, with reports of the King's demand for Razumovskii's expulsion within eight days for his intrigues and insults to sovereign and nation alike. It was pure pretense, Catherine concluded, but she had her council convene at six o'clock that evening to consider defense measures. The Russian government reacted precipitously. The Swedish ambassador was told to leave immediately. "We shall not begin hostilities," the Empress declared vehemently. "It is necessary to be a Fabius [i.e., to adopt delaying tactics], yet one's hands itch to thrash the Swede." Swedish troops bombarded the border fortress of Nyslott on 22 June, supposedly in retaliation for an incursion by "cossacks," whom Catherine believed to have been Swedish soldiers in disguise.[35]

Outrage animated the Empress. Though anxious to avoid bloodshed, she would not consider terms humiliating to Russia, such as the acceptance of Gustavus III's absolute authority, Swedish interference in the disposition of Paul's portion of Holstein, or Swedish pretensions to Kurland. After returning "with perceptible uneasiness" from a short walk on 23 June, Catherine ranted to Khrapovitskii over her councilors' lack of resolve. She was used to managing great affairs and knew how to fortify herself, she declared, "but it is impossible to be calm until September" (i.e., the end of the campaign season). "From love for the fatherland and from natural sensibility, it is impossible not to feel uneasy now." Russia must use her naval superiority to defeat the Swedish fleet and then attack Stockholm. Chastened, Khrapovitskii underlined his sovereign's swings of mood: "From cares there are alterations, and then she naturally weakens."[36]

In these same critical days Catherine rejoiced at news of Russian naval victories over the Turks in the Bug-Dnieper estuary on 6 and 7 June 1788. Dressed in a long naval uniform, the Empress celebrated these triumphs on Sunday morning, 25 June, at the Catherine Palace in Tsarskoe Selo. Later that day when Grand Duke Paul paraded his Life Cuirassiers regiment past the palace on their way to the Finnish border, his wife broke into tears while the Empress displayed "perceptible confusion." To Potemkin she frankly admitted feeling overwhelmed: "not one minute empty or without cares do I have now, yet I am healthy"; nevertheless, she deplored his report of the sailors' animosity toward John Paul Jones. "God grant that they stop being angry, we need him."[37] (This was the first sign of Potemkin's disapprobation of the imperious Jones, who participated in another Russian victory on the same site on 17 June for which he received the cross of St. Anna. This modest award offended him, and his relationship with the all-powerful Potemkin rapidly deteriorated. They disagreed over basic strategy in the siege of Ochakov and, in October, Potemkin requested that Catherine recall Jones, whom he accused of being "sleepy" and insubordinate. The Empress promised to find him a command against the Swedes. Ill with pneumonia, Jones recuperated at Kherson before returning to St. Petersburg, where he was well received at court on 6 December. But he was not invited to dinner and his presence was ignored in the official court journal until New Year's Day, 1789, when he dined at court for the last time. The next spring, moreover, Jones got into trouble with the law. He was accused of raping a young girl. Though the middle-aged bachelor denied the charge and the case never came to trial—his friends believed he had been framed, possibly by British intrigues—his reputation was ruined with the Empress, who coolly granted him two years' leave on 26 June 1789. She ordered his journal of his Russian campaigns sealed so as to stifle complaints from rival commanders. He never saw Russia again, dying in revolutionary Paris three years later. His death caused Catherine scant remorse. "This Paul Jones was a wrongheaded fellow," she wrote Grimm in 1792; "very worthy to be celebrated by a rabble of detestable creatures."[38])

By 26 June the Empress decided that, despite the hot weather, the Swedish threat required her presence in St. Petersburg. There she hoped to inspire the populace and, if necessary, accompany the Guards regiments to their camp in the suburbs. Why had Peter the Great built his new capital so close to Finland? She answered her own question with stout resolve: because he relied on himself. The next day, while signing orders for Russian and Danish naval raids on the Swedish coast, she chuckled at Khrapovitskii's jest that on the holiday of the Russian victory at Poltava she should issue orders against the Swedes. Even so, she was incredulous at intercepted dispatches that depicted Gustavus III's war aims as conquest of Finland and the Baltic Provinces by direct attack on Petersburg, or failing that, he would renounce the throne, convert to Catholicism, and move to Rome. The holidays of Catherine's accession and Paul's nameday (28–29 June) were accordingly celebrated at Tsarskoe Selo without the usual crowds and fanfare. On Friday morning, 30 June, Catherine signed her declaration of war against the Swedes and then accompanied Paul and her court into St. Petersburg, where she crossed the Neva on her sloop to celebrate a *Te Deum* in the Peter and Paul Cathedral for the naval victory of 7 June. After dinner at the Winter Palace she tearfully bade goodbye to the Grand Duke, who left that afternoon for the Finnish front.[39]

Catherine's declaration of war was proclaimed by Bezborodko on Sunday, 2 July, after the morning service at the chapel of the Summer Palace. Only a day before the Empress had received an official ultimatum signed by Gustavus III. "This insane note," as Catherine termed it, threatened war unless Russia punished ambassador Razumovskii for his intrigues, returned all Swedish territory in Finland and Karelia ceded by the treaties of 1721 and 1743, accepted Swedish "mediation" of the Russo-Turkish war, and restored the Crimea and all Ottoman territory seized since 1768. To sharpen the insult the King referred condescendingly to his "aid" in not attacking the Empress when she had been menaced by Pugachev. Furthermore, on leaving Stockholm for the army, Gustavus III boasted to the ladies that they would breakfast at Peterhof. He would go straight to Petersburg, overturn the statue of Peter the Great, and substitute one of himself! All this confirmed Catherine's conviction that she was confronting "Sir John Falstaff." To Potemkin she derided the King's martial mania in donning "breastplate, thigh-pieces, armlets, and a helmet with an enormous number of plumes." To Joseph II she compared Gustavus III to Don Quixote, "the vagabond knight," a quip that one courtier russified into the King's *"donkishotsvo."*[40]

Joke as she might, Catherine arose the next morning at five o'clock grumbling that Bezborodko should still be lounging at his dacha (with his mistresses?) when she needed him every hour. At eleven she visited briefly with Grand Duchess Maria Fedorovna before joining her council until one P.M. Not since the outbreak of the Turkish war had the Empress personally presided over her council, which she questioned about the sufficiency of Russian defenses. The councilors reassured her that the border commanders would block all invasion routes so as to win time for the Russian forces to assemble. Together with the Empress they inspected a map of Finland to ascertain likely avenues of Swedish advance. Foreseeing supply difficulties in barren Finland, Catherine ordered an inventory of provisioning needs so that she might coordinate deliveries of beef and mutton. She directed Count Chernyshev to expedite the dispatch of more ships to Admiral Greig for an attack on the Swedish fleet or the interdiction of Swedish troop landings. So wary was Catherine of an assault on Petersburg that she pardoned 153 Russian sailors under court-martial to bolster the defense forces at Kronstadt. She likewise approved seizure of Swedish trading vessels, requisition of horses from the peasants of Petersburg and Novgorod guberniias to haul military provisions, and provision of horses from the palace stables to transport twenty cannon for a newly created reserve corps. In addition, she endorsed a proposal to recruit two artillery battalions from free estate groups such as merchants, burghers, state peasants, churchmen, and lamplighters. Satisfied with all these countermeasures, the Empress left for dinner after informing the councilors of Paul's arrival at Vyborg and of the provocative Swedish ultimatum, which the council recommended sending to all Russian ministers abroad for use as proof of Gustavus III's aggressive intransigence. "In Her Majesty the spirit of bravery is always present," councilor Zavadovskii remarked after this session. "By invoking 'God is with us' she inspires everyone."[41]

That Catherine remained seriously perturbed about Swedish designs was underscored three days later by her second appearance before her council in the Winter Palace. On this occasion, however, she stayed only half an hour to hear Count Chernyshev's report about naval defenses, approving reinforcements for the Kronstadt garrison and floating barriers to augment its seawalls. "This time is difficult for me, it is true," she confided to Potemkin; "but what can one do? I hope in a short time to receive great reinforcement, inasmuch as men and munitions are being brought from everywhere." The "awful, suffocating heat" added to her discomfort, which included pressure on the chest beginning on 6 July. (By 17 July the heat wave had peaked at a temperature of 39.5°C [103°F] in the sun.) Against this extraordinary heat she sought refreshment in a carriage ride after nine o'clock in the white night of 7 July. Dr. Rogerson mixed a "weakening" powder in her drink before bed on 10 July, but it gave her no rest; she awoke at five A.M. Skipping the council session later that morning, Catherine did not feel well enough to dine with the court.[42]

The tension began to relax somewhat by nine o'clock in the evening of 9 July, when word was received of Admiral Greig's success against the Swedish fleet three days before off the island of Hogland. To Potemkin the Empress exulted on 17 July over this victory and the delivery of his battle trophies, the captured Turkish flags and banners that were ceremoniously marched around the Winter Palace and past the Admiralty and the statue of Peter the Great on the way to the Peter and Paul Fortress the next day, where they were draped over Peter the Great's magnificent tomb. "Petersburg has at this moment the look of an armed camp, and I myself am like the quartermaster-general; the day of the naval battle of 6 July the smell of gunpowder was scented in town; and so, my friend, I too have smelled gunpowder." Her martial spirit in full bloom, Catherine assured Potemkin of her calmer spirits since his successes against the Turks, and urged him to take Ochakov with as few losses as possible. For his naval triumphs she ordered a magnificent gold plate with an inscription to the commander-in-chief of the Ekaterinoslav land and sea forces. At the same time she expressed annoyance over the abrupt, imperious arrival from Moscow of Aleksei Orlov, "like snow dumped on one's head." His appearance seemed to show Muscovite overreaction to the crisis as well as a lack of confidence in her leadership. Although Orlov stayed in

Petersburg from 17 July to 10 August, the Empress caustically denied to Potemkin any morale boost from the presence at court of the old warhorse: "he's like a nanny goat's horns."[43]

Even the weather turned cooler with a breeze from the north, and the Empress found some diversion in a surprise visit on the evening of 16 July to the suburban dacha of Alexander Naryshkin and his wife, who entertained her entourage with fresh fruit from the garden and a parting cannon salute. Still, on 20 July when Krapovitskii affirmed that his perspiration had ceased the past three days, the Empress admitted feeling weak for the thirteenth day in a row. She neither attended the council that day nor dined with her court.[44]

At the end of July the Empress could finally relax further in the knowledge that Russian prospects in the Swedish war looked more favorable with the King's failure to capture any borderposts, his sudden retreat because of short supplies, and, most of all, a Russian-abetted mutiny among his Finnish forces (the Anjala Confederation). She merrily noted the contrast between the situation on 1 August and the panic of 1 July when the Swedish ultimatum had been delivered. With the Swedish fleet now bottled up in Sveaborg by Admiral Greig and with reports of Denmark's imminent entry into the war on the Russian side, Catherine looked forward to clipping "the wings of the vagabond knight, so that he will fly lower in the future." On 2 August she took great pleasure in launching two new 100-gun ships, named *Konstantin* and *Alexander,* from the Admiralty yards in central Petersburg. All the same, her successes in the north made her worry afresh about Potemkin's dilatory advance in the south. His own plea for more frequent reports irked her, since by 31 July she had had no word from him for three weeks. As she complained to Khrapovitskii on 14 August: "here the war is under one's nose, but there I know not what they do." Yet when Potemkin whined about hangnails, she suspected him of covering up more serious wounds and, visualizing his difficulties at the siege of Ochakov, she disdained the "foolish Swedish war" in hopes that the peace negotiations might still allow dispatch of the fleet to the Mediterranean in the fall.[45]

Catherine's health problems flared up again on 7 August when she felt feverish. Five days later she fell ill with a "bilious colic" that Dr. Rogerson treated with some kind of drops. She felt weak and dizzy; "my head is not my own," she told Khrapovitskii. But after a difficult night and two days in bed she felt better by mid-August, despite backpains. A month later she confessed retrospectively to Potemkin that "my cares are presently almost beyond my strength, the more so as the month of July was such that I thought I would fall ill, now it is a little better." Paul's return to Petersburg on 18 September may have eased one such concern, along with a truce on the Finnish front.[46] Nevertheless, Catherine's concerns continued into the fall when she was stunned by Admiral Greig's sudden death from fever at Reval on 15 October. Dr. Rogerson had not been able to save his fellow countryman. According to Khrapovitskii, the Empress exhibited "acute sorrow and tears" in declaring: "This is a great loss, this is a loss to the state."[47]

As winter came, she became more impatient than ever for Potemkin to capture Ochakov, a feat she felt certain would expedite peace in the south as well as the north. "Nothing in the world do I desire so much as that you could, upon taking Ochakov and upon completing winter arrangements in the course of the winter, come here for an hour in order that, first, I might have the satisfaction of seeing you after such a long separation and, secondly, that I might talk over many things with you in person." On 26 October she attributed the pain in her waist to a presentiment of Ochakov's capture. The news of Potemkin's conquest of Ochakov reached Catherine the evening of 14 December 1788, by which time she had become despondent from a week-long attack of colic. Her hopefulness started to return on 17 December, Khrapovitskii observed, but the very next day he dolefully recorded the night's torments: "unbearable pain inside, in the back and left side, compelled her more than a hundred times to change position on the bed, so that until the fourth hour after midnight she did not find a [comfortable] place. By leaving under the head one pillow and lying flat on the back, she finally calmed down." Later in the day she decided she must have caught cold during the *Te Deum* honoring the fall of Ochakov (frosts of 25° to 28° paralyzed Petersburg just then). On leaving her bed on 20 December, the Empress felt so weak and chilled that she rested on a sofa the next two days before suffering a relapse that confined her to bed for three more days. After consulting Dr. Rogerson, she postponed a blood-letting. The last day of 1788 Catherine celebrated the full reports of Ochakov's bloody capture, noting that Potemkin had ordered the Turkish corpses thrown into the sea to float back to Ottoman shores. Despite Russian victories, the year had severely strained Catherine's nerves. She felt terribly alone. The new year promised more of the same.[48]

Catherine's low spirits at the start of 1789 were strained in different directions as the new year unfolded. In January she took fright at Mamonov's two-week bout with what appears to have been "strep throat." Perhaps his ailment reminded her of Lanskoi's death. Possibly she thought he might have contracted it from her. Certainly she was already aware of their deteriorating relationship. Even more unsettling was the prospect of Potemkin's long-anticipated arrival. She never knew what he might think or say or do. According to his Petersburg agent and administrator, Mikhail Garnovskii, court sentiments were polarized like those forecast for the Second Coming: some trembled, others rejoiced. "The Prince has not yet arrived," Peter Zavadovskii grumpily wrote Field Marshal Rumiantsev on 20 January 1789: "without him— nothing."[49]

Catherine herself reportedly confided to Zakhar Zotov: "My God, how I need the prince now." When she inquired whether Potemkin was loved in the capital, however, Zotov's reply—"only by God alone, and by you"—left her pensive. The Empress's obviously declining health was said to have made her resolve never again to allow her viceroy to leave her side. Yet while she desired his support for her current policies, she felt uncertain about both them and him. For instance, she wanted to recall Rumiantsev and entrust Potemkin with the command of both armies in the south, but she worried about the political repercussions of such a step and whether the double burden might be too much for one man. About the Swedish threat to Petersburg she still felt nervous. In similar circumstances, she ruefully confessed to Khrapovitskii,

Peter the Great had banged his forehead against a wall. More than once she had already considered dividing the capital into defensive quarters, to be manned by armed townsmen. But when Khrapovitskii protested her plan as a foolhardy product of panic, she calmed down and agreed with him that Petersburg was no fortress and the Russian fleet offered its best defense. European affairs looked no brighter, with Frederick William II of Prussia, "the stupid successor" to Frederick the Great, intriguing in Sweden, Poland, and the Ottoman Empire against the Russo-Austrian alliance.[50]

Preparations for Potemkin's reception in Petersburg and the celebration of his conquest of Ochakov also agitated the Empress. On 26 January 1789 she suddenly remembered the triumphal gates erected in honor of Grigorii Orlov's heroism during the Moscow plague and Rumiantsev's triumphs in the first Turkish war, upbraiding herself for overlooking Potemkin's comparable exploits. Khrapovitskii assured her that they knew each other so well no such accounts need be kept, but she insisted awards would be expected. Orders were issued to illuminate the marble gates at Tsarskoe Selo and to decorate them with land and naval armaments, the whole to be capped with a crown of laurels and a line from Vasilii Petrov's ode on the capture of Ochakov: "You will in splashes enter the temple of Sophia." This ambiguous political proclamation delighted the Empress, for she could silence the critics of Russian expansionism by placidly pointing to the cathedral in the new town of Sofiia near Tsarskoe Selo. But Potemkin "will be in Tsargrad this year," she ambivalently exclaimed to Khrapovitskii, "only don't you tell me about it all of a sudden." The same synthetic optimism colored her avowal to Ivan Shuvalov on 27 January that in her sixtieth year she would live twenty more and then some. At the same time Catherine and Khrapovitskii rushed the final preparations of their comic opera, *The Errant Knight* (Gorebogatyr'), a rollicking burlesque of Gustavus III that was first staged at the Hermitage Theater on 29 January, with the Austrian and French ambassadors conspicuously present.[51]

Two days before Potemkin's appearance Catherine admonished him in writing for neglecting his health in his mad dash northward, jokingly threatening to pull his ears: "that's the greeting we have prepared for the victor!" On Sunday evening, 4 February 1789, Potemkin finally arrived in town amid the festivities of Grand Duchess Maria Pavlovna's birthday. Only a week later was he officially received at court while 200 Turkish banners from Ochakov were ceremoniously trooped and trumpeted past the Winter Palace to the Peter and Paul Fortress. "The Prince we see is extremely affable and most gracious to everyone," his old rival Zavadovskii notified Rumiantsev on 26 March; "his arrival we celebrate every day." Warning the field marshal that his failure to return to Petersburg had undermined his credit with the Empress, Zavadovskii reminded his old patron of the current facts of political life: "All faith is in *one person*."[52]

Eager to please Potemkin, Catherine complained to her secretary on 18 March at their failure to make awards for the capture of Ochakov. The awards received her signature on 14 April and were presented the next day with the usual pomp. Potemkin received a magnificent mace decorated with diamonds and other precious stones, a gold medal with a charter commemorating the victory, and 100,000 rubles (actually a loan) to finish the Tauride Palace. General Suvorov was awarded a sprig of diamonds for his hat, whereas three other generals were given jeweled or gilded swords. Many officers were granted the Order of St. Vladimir, others were given gold medals, and the rank and file were all awarded silver medals. Potemkin disbursed another 3,000 gold rubles to those courtiers who built a model of Ochakov, who played Turkish music, and who danced at the ceremonies. Asked about the effect of these awards, Khrapovitskii assured the Empress the next day that the Guards regiments had been inspired. Besides, surveillance of the local foreign ministers' dispatches revealed, to Catherine's delight, their envy of her liberality.[53]

Potemkin's three-month sojourn in Petersburg did not resolve Catherine's multiple equivocations. In particular, he could not reconcile her with Mamonov. Potemkin had already left town when the final blowup transpired in mid-June, and he had no say in Catherine's rapid promotion of Platon Zubov, his father, and his three brothers. Neither could Potemkin resolve Russia's foreign policy dilemma. Indeed, he and the Empress and the council all continued to dispute the policy alternatives. Toward Sweden the Empress favored a defensive policy on land until command of the sea could be achieved, at which point she would seize the offensive: "This will produce a revolution," she assured Khrapovitskii. At the end of March she issued instructions to Admiral Chichagov to attack the Swedish fleet. Crossing herself as she signed these orders, Catherine sent him an icon of St. Nicholas the Wonderworker, "Our Neptune." This time she expected a decisive victory.[54]

Gustavus III's antics caused constant apprehensions, such as a scare in early March over the discovery of a plot to set fire to the Russian squadron wintering in Denmark. Another "churlish" plot was rumored to be aimed against Catherine herself. Her own suspicions were reinforced by Potemkin's. When he relayed a letter from the imprisoned ambassador Bulgakov that had been sent via the French envoy in Constantinople, he denounced the French for their longtime patronage of the Turks: "they have been our enemies and forever will be." Consigning the British and the Prussians to the same hostile camp, the Empress paranoically prophesied Berlin's willingness to undertake her assassination.[55]

With Ochakov in Russian hands, both Catherine and Potemkin were eager for peace with the Porte. Indeed, the Empress in early 1789 announced her desire for a general peace, her only stipulation being that negotiations not begin until Bulgakov had been freed. She even agreed that her Austrian ally might make his own separate peace, counting on Joseph II subsequently to neutralize Prussian pressure in Poland, Sweden, and the Baltic. Though distrustful of French motives, she welcomed their attempts to mediate a peace settlement with the Turks and flirted with the prospect of an alliance with France as well as Spain, by way of offsetting British hostility on the seas. Sultan Abdul Hamid's death on 28 March/7 April 1789 boosted hopes, temporarily, for an early peace with the Turks. But Selim III, the new sultan, resumed hostilities with renewed intensity.

By the second week of April the Empress felt stricken by cabin fever.

Deploring the muddy roads, she playfully inquired of Khrapovitskii whether the King of Prussia had reached Riga yet—a sardonic riposte to rumors of Prussian military preparations at Königsberg. "It smells of Tsarskoe Selo," she sighed on 11 April. Before she left town at the end of the month, however, she had to endure the painful passage of her sixtieth birthday. Her annual depression was darkened further by the news of Joseph II's mortal illness and concerns about his successor. Death and decay seemed to surround her. Within twenty-four hours arrived news of the death of Peter Panin, whose passing left her outwardly unmoved, and of Andrei Shuvalov, whose demise mortified her. Several other ministers and commanders were manifestly failing. Physically and mentally wasted by a stroke, Prince Viazemskii had lost his grip on internal affairs, the aged Ivan Betskoi had begun to revert to childhood, Field Marshal Rumiantsev had asked for leave to take the waters (but then, unable to sit on a horse, he had sat stolidly in Moldavia for two years), and Count Ivan Chernyshev gave off such a sickening stench that when he left the Empress's rooms the floors had to be swabbed with lavender water.[56]

After Potemkin departed for the south on 6 May the Empress worried anew about his health and that of his troops. Just before his departure she warned him again about the danger of plague being brought into the Black Sea by French merchantmen. In the next weeks she was heartened, however, by Potemkin's comparatively frequent reports and by the splendid spring weather. These felicitous circumstances helped Catherine surmount in short order the crisis of Mamonov's dismissal. In fact, she displayed new confidence and independence in rapidly arranging the installation of young Zubov, the first favorite in more than a decade to receive her patronage without Potemkin's endorsement.[57]

Political Distemper in Paris

While the Empress rearranged her love life at Tsarskoe Selo in the summer of 1789 and waited anxiously for diplomatic and military successes in the north and the south, a new kind of crisis gradually preempted her attention. Revolution seized France. It puzzled and perplexed everyone. To be sure, Catherine had long harbored ambivalent sentiments toward France and the French. She admired French culture past and present; and her affection for the Count de Ségur, together with her hopes for French aid in reaching a settlement with the Turks and for an alliance that might counterbalance the new Anglo-Dutch-Prussian combination, made her respectful of France's international political potential. In historical perspective, the France of Henry IV and Louis XIV represented Catherine's ideal of prudently progressive monarchy. She kept hoping that Louis XVI would live up to his illustrious forebears. Accepting Montesquieu's axiom—"no nobility, no monarch"—Catherine thought the King should rally the nobility behind him in seeking solutions to France's financial and foreign difficulties. All the same, these pro-French sentiments floated uneasily on the surface of deep doubts about French motives and modes of political action. Decades of French machinations in Russian domestic politics, coupled with recent and past attempts to thwart Russian aims in Sweden, Poland, and Turkey, left the Empress decidedly distrustful of French foreign policy. For instance, when one Count Roger Damas, a French gentleman adventurer who had earned colonel's rank at the storm of Ochakov, petitioned through envoy Ségur for appointment to the Guards and as adjutant to the Empress, she vetoed the proposal on 15 April with a stern comment: "I did not wish to have in my interior rooms a French spy."[58]

A month later similar suspicions prompted the rejection of Ségur's proposal to speed peace negotiations at Constantinople by permitting French merchant ships into the Black Sea, where they could deliver diplomatic dispatches under the cover of purchasing grain. In repudiating this transparent ploy, Catherine's council cited the triple danger of greater pressure on the armed forces' food supplies, untimely relief of Constantinople's reportedly deficient provisions, and the compromise of military security along the Black Sea. Hence the proposal was politely declined on the pretext of the ubiquitous pestilential perils attached to grain shipments from the Ottoman capital. Ségur's response, that the Russian action violated the trade treaty of 1787 with France, was also rejected. These discussions repeated the criticisms of French policy toward the Turks that Potemkin had pressed on "Ségur-Effendi" several years before. In defending the Ottomans, "an empire in agony," the French covered themselves with shame as "protectors of barbarism and of the pestilence."[59]

Although Catherine and her councilors closely followed the accelerating turmoil of French politics in the spring of 1789, they were as surprised as everybody else when the doubled Third Estate "willfully" proclaimed itself the National Assembly. At the end of July the Empress was shaken at the violent seizure of the Bastille, blaming it on the King's drunken ineptitude. No wonder all the eminent and the princes of the blood were fleeing to Flanders. She was equally baffled by Ségur's enthusiastic support of his cousin Lafayette and the "fortunate revolution."[60]

Catherine reacted to the news from France all the more vehemently because of her mounting frustration over the two wars that she could not seem to end by arms or diplomacy. She started to suspect that her orders were not being carried out. So, when word was received on 6 August that Admiral Chichagov's squadron had been attacked by the Swedish fleet off Karlskrona in mid-July, the Empress exploded. In her eyes Chichagov had violated her precise orders to seek out and attack the foe. After the action, moreover, he had withdrawn to Russian waters with the loss of one captain, several hundred men, and two ships disabled by the explosion of their Petrine vintage cannon. "I believe that all the world is in accord with the King of Sweden," she raged to Khrapovitskii, condemning her commanders' inaction. Later that day she sent Bezborodko to the council session with orders to consider Chichagov's actions in the light of her signed instructions. The council was to submit a signed report explaining whether or not her instructions had been executed. The results of this inquiry would guide future policy-making, the Empress thundered:

for it is becoming notable in the Swedish war, as if inaction had become the subject of all commanders just when lively and united action everywhere could have given superiority over the foe, and obtained for the Empire the peace desired by everyone; yet from all this has now arisen a triple threat to the Empire: first, disobedience in the nonfulfillment of prescribed instructions, through which France is presently going to ruin; second, great expenditures vainly employed and augmented by delay; third, vain losses of people and time.[61]

Chastened by this imperial broadside, the councilors nervously recorded their inability to solve the issue that day at Tsarskoe Selo in the absence of the relevant documentation. They resolved to reconvene the next morning in town. Meanwhile, they bent all efforts at coordinating the conquest of Swedish Finland.

Actually, Catherine's tantrum started to subside the very next day when she learned of the Russo-Austrian victory over the Turks at Focsani. "This will shut the mouth of those who have been bruiting it about that we are not in accord with them," she crowed to Khrapovitskii. On 9 August she returned to St. Petersburg for a *Te Deum* at the Kazan Cathedral. In the meantime the council assured her that Admiral Chichagov had made all appropriate efforts against the Swedish fleet. Blaming the wind for Chichagov's failure, the councilors reminded the Empress that "fighting at sea does not always depend on the wish on one side." As to Catherine's other charges against the commanders fighting the Swedes, her councilors coolly requested specific orders for each. Prince Nassau-Siegen's victory over the Swedish galley fleet on 13 August heartened the Empress, who celebrated it at the court chapel three days later.[62]

Still, Catherine's animus did not disappear entirely. The events in France and their spread to Brabant upset her. She was particularly perturbed by ruminations about Russia's own revolutionary potential, frankly confessing her fears to Khrapovitskii on 10 August:

> From my accession to the throne I always thought that there must be fermentation there; now they have failed to make use of the disposition of minds: Lafayette, as one of the ambitious, I would have taken into my councils and made him my defender! Do you see what I have done here since my accession? With us a ferment among the rabble can be produced not by a recruiting levy of one per 500 souls, but of five per 500, and now we must proceed to that.[63]

An official account of the Paris revolution appeared in the St. Petersburg press on 17 August with editorial additions that showed the Russian government's disapprobation. Catherine only ordered the new levy of recruits on 27 August, having just left her bed after a ten-day bout of "bilious colic." It was the third year in a row for such a heavy recruitment.

To Potemkin she announced on 6 September her complete recovery, which she attributed largely to pillows soaked in chamomile, as recommended by the Metropolitan of St. Petersburg. *The Times* in mid-October pronounced her health "rapidly on the decline," a result of exhaustion caused by "disappointment and misfortune." "The too frequent use of the bottle and glass has been resorted to as a means to drown reflexion, which has brought on a nervous fever, from which her *Imperial Majesty* will scarce ever recover." Nevertheless, within two weeks the same newspaper found her "perfectly recovered" and in mid-December denied another gazette's report of her death. Yet she also apprehended transmission of "the French disorders" to Brabant and Holland; "you will hear soon that they will crop up in the [nearby] Prussian regions as well, for the people are naked and the troops are foreigners." By early December she was convinced "this infection" was spreading into the German lands.[64]

Further reports from France fired Catherine's indignation. When Khrapovitskii branded the constraints on the royal authority "a veritable anarchy," she emphatically agreed: "Yes, they are capable of hanging their King from a lamp-post, it's frightful!" Louis XVI should flee Versailles for Metz, where the nobility would flock to his defense. Still, when Ségur sighed over this strategy for monarchical salvation, Catherine acidly retorted: "And how is it possible for cobblers to govern?" Her gloom over the disorders thickened at the abrupt appearance in France of books on the private life of Queen Marie Antoinette and a history of the Bastille. The riot that forced the royal family in early October to move from Versailles to the Tuileries Palace in Paris convinced the Empress that Louis XVI could not survive the revolution.[65]

Despite Catherine's alarms over revolutionary France, she took heart in the fall of 1789 from Potemkin's "multitude of victories" over the Turks. Suvorov's brilliant triumph at the Rymnik River on 11 September was rewarded with a jeweled sword and the title of Count Suvorov-Rymnikskii, the military Order of St. George first class, and the diamond cross, star, and epaulettes of the Order of the Apostle Andrew—"an entire cart of diamonds," Catherine blithely informed Potemkin. To the latter she prepared to send a golden crown of laurels said to have cost 200,000 rubles. The allies made rapid gains on both sides of the Balkans. Belgrade surrendered to the Austrians on 27 September. Three days later the Russians captured another Belgrade (Akerman) on the Dniester, and on 4 November the fortress of Bender capitulated without a fight while the Austrians occupied Bucharest. The Empress kept hoping that these victories would force the Ottomans to sue for peace. But with the campaigning season over for the winter, she concluded on Christmas Eve, 1789, "now we are in a crisis: either peace, or threeway war, i.e., with Prussia." A week later she repeated her fears: "Now is a crisis. . . . The Prussians have gone mad, they hinder peace and are ready to begin a war with us and with the Emperor; all the Powers are in ferment, only Spain is calm. . . . Now everything depends on the Prince [Potemkin], if he will make peace."[66]

The new year, 1790, opened anxiously for Catherine. Disenchanted with Musin-Pushkin's ineffectual leadership of the Russian troops in Finland, she received him icily on 5 January, censured his ignorance of the epidemics among the Swedish forces that were reportedly killing 100 men per day, and replaced him with General Count Ivan Saltykov. Sickness seemed to reign everywhere, from the army hospitals, where 2,000 men had supposedly died, to the court itself. Platon Zubov, whose slim physique betrayed a tendency toward consumptiveness, scared his imperial mistress by spending a week in bed with fever and swollen glands behind the ears. Reports of Potemkin's ill health constantly perturbed her, too. Along with a sable hat and coat of fox furs, she sent him a special chest of medicines for external use only, inasmuch as she herself had long ago given up internal drugs. For his rheumatism she prescribed camphor salve or spirits of soap, but only under a field surgeon's supervision. When he complained of a cold and cough, she regretted the "frozen ink" he had to write with, and urged him to use the little flask and goblet she sent with a courier. His headaches she blamed on congestion, advising him to warm his forehead. The closer the opening of the spring campaign approached, the more she worried about his condition. "I am upset most of all by your illness," she wrote on 19 April 1790; "take care of yourself for God's sake, you may not be one of the weak, but with the years certain precautions become necessary that preserve health more than in one's first youth. God grant that you are soon recovered completely."[67]

Emperor Joseph II's death on 9/20 February 1790 further confused the tense international situation. The long expected sad news reached Catherine five days later. Although she mourned the deceased as a sincere friend and steadfast ally, she blamed Austria's troubles in Brabant and Hungary on his political ineptitude and loquacity; and while assuring his successor, Leopold II, of Russia's support she foresaw no alteration in Prussia's devious policy. Indeed, reports of Prussian (and Polish) preparations for an attack on Russia in the spring prompted Catherine and Potemkin to organize an observation corps at Riga. Hopes for an early peace with the Turks also plummeted at word of Prussia's secret alliance (31 January 1790) with the Ottoman Empire, an arrangement known in Petersburg by mid-March. The Empress first reacted by suggesting that Potemkin bribe persons at the Porte to gain peace, but his dispatches quickly quashed her hopes.[68]

Eager as usual for spring, Catherine bemoaned to Potemkin in mid-March the persistent grip of winter: "Here it is cold now and we still sit in ice up to the ears." Even so, she erupted in fury on 9/10 March over a Swedish raid on Baltiiskii Port west of Reval. A landing force of only forty men forced the local commandant's capitulation and then burned the munitions, spiked the cannon, and extorted an indemnity of 4,000 rubles. "A Russian would not have done that," the Empress erupted to Khrapovitskii in condemnation of Colonel de Roberti, contrasting his cowardly conduct to Major Kuzmin's gallant defense of Nyslott in 1788. Her council, equally displeased, recommended investigating the incident while troops and ships were rushed to reinforce the coast of Estland.[69]

When the Russian land offensive against the Swedes commenced on 18 April 1790, Catherine crossed herself. Her apprehensions swiftly proved justified as one Russian column was repulsed with heavy losses including its foreign commander, the dashing young Prince Victor Amadeus of Anhalt-Bernburg-Shaumburg. The Empress had thought to appoint him successor to Musin-Pushkin, but evidently Potemkin vetoed the nomination. His death made her weep at Tsarskoe Selo, where the court took up residence on 28 April. She wrote his wife and mother to offer assistance, and she later commissioned a mausoleum in his honor. Her grief and discontent became all the greater a few days later on reading fuller reports of the action. The Swedes had been alerted beforehand to Anhalt's advance, she concluded bitterly, as the loss of 503 killed and wounded also indicated. Reading a translation of Plutarch with Platon Zubov gave her some consolation. "It fortifies my soul," she told Khrapovitskii.[70]

Delayed by ice till late April 1790, the opening of naval operations in the Gulf of Finland made Catherine even more nervous. Reports of an attack on Chichagov's Reval squadron by twenty-six Swedish sail kept the Empress awake all night on 3/4 May while Bezborodko blubbered. Fortunately, this clash resulted in a small Russian victory. Outfitting was rushed on Admiral Alexander Cruse's battle fleet and Nassau-Siegen's galley fleet at Kronstadt. Catherine's excitement showed on her face: "From the alteration has remained a red spot on the cheek," Khrapovitskii observed on 5 May. A week later the Empress predicted full-scale naval combat, but contrary winds postponed Cruse's departure till 20 May. She also approved the formation of a police battalion in St. Petersburg. "The King of Sweden is being marked everywhere, like a mad cat, and of course he is expending all his possibilities on the present season," Catherine notified Potemkin on 13 May; "whether this will be for long, I know not; I know only that God's wisdom alone and His omnipotent miracles can create a good end to all this."[71]

On 23 May the Empress at Tsarskoe Selo and her ministers in Petersburg listened from daybreak till dusk to a "terrific cannonade." Their anxiety rose and fell through two more days of firing, which slowly receded as confused reports trickled in. Amid the action Catherine got word of a weird inquiry from the eccentric Gustavus III: were his gift chalices of 1777 still intact, and could she hear his cannon in Tsarskoe Selo? "Does he really think that I take chalices out of churches?" she quipped, before adding acidly: "I have listened to empty cannons more than 25 years." Informed that Chichagov's Reval squadron had joined Cruse's Kronstadt fleet, backed by Nassau-Siegen's galleys and bomb vessels from Fredericksham, the Empress drove over to Peterhof on 28 May and spent the next day at Kronstadt watching the action through a telescope. That same day she gratefully accepted an offer by the Petersburg city duma to underwrite a 200-man auxiliary corps till the war was over. An accidental explosion of 500 bombs in the artillery laboratory on the Vyborg side of Petersburg startled the townsfolk, who thought it signaled a Swedish assault. Two hundred windowpanes were shattered in the Tauride Palace. To calm the populace, a prohibition was issued against the firing of cannon, rockets, and fireworks at dachas. With the Swedish naval forces trapped in the skerries off the Gulf of Vyborg, a decisive battle appeared in the offing if the winds held steady from the south.[72]

The first three weeks of June 1790 the Empress impatiently watched the weather: cold and rainy with west winds from the sea as in the autumn, these conditions lasted throughout the summer. Rumors of unrest in Sweden also quickened hopes for an early peace. Finally the winds shifted, so that Nassau-

Siegen attacked Gustavus III's battle and galley fleets on 22 June in a five-hour engagement. The next morning, with the wind having veered around to the north, the Swedes concerted a breakout spearheaded by three fireships. These drifting destroyers drove into entanglements with two other Swedish ships, however, demolishing all five; the Russians captured seven ships of the line. Somehow the King slipped through by skipping from one vessel to another as he fled, leaving his breakfast still warm in one instance. A relieved Catherine celebrated this victory at Tsarskoe Selo on 27 June, the day of Peter's Poltava triumph, and three days later in St. Petersburg, the day she had signed her declaration of war two years before.[73]

Hardly had she savored her latest triumph than it was soured by a surprise defeat. On 28 June, the holiday of Catherine's coup, Nassau-Siegen's galley fleet was routed at Rochensalm with a loss of gun-prams, four galleys, four frigates, and (Khrapovitskii remarked) "his own head." Russian losses in killed and captured totaled almost 6,000 men. This setback hit the Empress harder than any since the losses of the Black Sea squadron to the storm at the start of the Turkish war. Nevertheless, as confused reports of the debacle filtered in, she recommended to Bezborodko and the other councilors that they follow the heroic example of Frederick the Great in his comebacks from near disaster. She herself sought to calm the incipient panic in Petersburg by visiting the capital on 6 July to launch a new 100-gun ship, which she christened *St. Evsevii* in honor of the victory of 22 June. Nassau-Siegen's sorrowful request for a court-martial was magnanimously rejected, his defeat blamed on the fickle fortunes of war.[74]

All the Empress's anguish over Swedish affairs suddenly dissipated with the peace agreement signed at Verela on 3 August 1790. This peace, as sudden as the rupture that opened the war, left the Russo-Swedish border unchanged. Catherine felt immense relief over the war's timely end. "God ordained to free one paw from a tight place," she exulted to Potemkin on 5 August. The peace, together with the celebration on 3 August of yet another naval victory on the Black Sea, boosted Catherine's spirits with renewed hope for peace with the Turks. "One paw we have pulled out of the mud," she reminded Potemkin, "as soon as you pull out the other, we'll sing alleluia." For all its surprises, the Swedish war ended in reaffirming Catherine's confidence. Khrapovitskii heard her boast: "I managed everything like a commanding general, and there were many cares." She smiled ironically at his reminder of her readiness to lead the Guards in defense of Petersburg. "Yes, if need had required it, then I would have put my head in the last battalion-square." Barely a year later, on 19 October 1791, she agreed to an alliance with "cousin Gu" aimed against France, whose emigré princes she subsidized with 500,000 rubles.[75]

An Anonymous Journey

As if Catherine were not sufficiently preoccupied with multiple military-diplomatic dilemmas in the stormy summer of 1790, a new kind of political problem arose abruptly in June with the appearance of an anonymously issued book innocently entitled *A Journey from St. Petersburg to Moscow*. Its contents and the circumstances of its publication struck Catherine as anything but innocent. After reading thirty pages she detected "the sowing of the French infection: an aversion toward authority; the author is a Martinist" (that is, a follower of Saint-Martin, a mystical freemason). The same day she ordered a police investigation that immediately cast suspicion on a certain Radishchev. The bookseller offering the volume was arrested at once and interrogated. Released on 29 June, he was exhorted to keep the matter secret, but he told the author, who was arrested the following day. Radishchev was incarcerated in the Peter and Paul Fortress for interrogation by Stepan Sheshkovskii, venerable operative of the Secret Branch.[76]

The Empress vaguely knew who Alexander Radishchev was. As a well-to-do nobleman educated at the Imperial Corps of Pages who had also attended the University of Leipzig at government expense, Radishchev exemplified the kind of enlightened officials Catherine had been striving for decades to multiply. Her Montesquieuian-cameralist concepts of government required such new men. So it was doubly unsettling to discover that such an educated person not only entertained radical ideas, but that in privately publishing his anonymous work he had taken advantage of Catherine's own efforts to foster book publication by the legalization of individual ownership of presses. Furthermore, the censor's stamp of approval on the book enraged the Empress as much as its incendiary message. How could any of her officials have endorsed such a tract?

Catherine prided herself on her wide reading, for bibliomania had been one of her earliest, most durable passions. As a lifelong devotee of the European enlightenment she took ideas very seriously. Yet the French Revolution had shown her how dangerously double-edged some political and social ideas could be. Her careful reading of Radishchev's tract convinced her that he was "a rabblerouser, worse than Pugachev"—an indictment that she proclaimed to Khrapovitskii on 7 July "with ardor and feeling." Sheshkovskii's interrogation of Radishchev she directed from a distance; her extensive comments on the book told him what to look into.[77]

Everything about the book galled the Empress. A strange Old Testament passage concerning defecation "is so indecent it cannot even be mentioned," she fumed. Above all, it pained her inwardly to see ideals she had formerly held (and still held privately in some cases) perverted in the service of attacks on time-honored institutions: absolutism and bureaucracy, nobility and serfdom, war in pursuit of national defense. "The purpose of this book is clear on every page," she quickly discerned: "its author, infected and full of the French madness, is trying in every possible way to break down respect for authority and the authorities, to stir up in the people indignation against their superiors and against the government." His discussion of the rights of man incensed her: "The questions brought up here are the ones over which France is now being ruined." Radishchev's advocacy of equal rights among estate groups was derided as "the present French system," whereas his criticism of injustice was branded "the French venom." Praise for the regicide Cromwell alarmed the Empress by the author's ostensible "criminal intent, completely revolutionary," and she disdained his praise of the French moderate Mirabeau, "who deserved not once but many times over to be hanged." Catherine ended her commentary by urging Sheshkovskii to determine whether Radishchev had accomplices, how many copies of the tract had been printed, and where they were. For "it seems probable that he has appointed himself the leader, whether by this book or by other means, in snatching the scepters from the hands of monarchs." Catherine's wrath peaked on 13 July in her order transmitting the case to the St. Petersburg Criminal Court: Radishchev's book, she concluded, was permeated with "the most harmful philosophizing, destroying the social peace, disparaging the respect due to authorities, seeking to arouse in the people disgust against their superiors, and finally it is filled with insulting and rabid utterances against the dignity of sovereign authority."[78]

Taken aback by the authorities' vehement reaction, Radishchev endeavored to lighten his fate by blaming the book on his vanity and begging for Catherine's forgiveness. Meanwhile, the St. Petersburg Criminal Court issued its verdict on 26 July 1790: death. It was the first death sentence imposed on a nobleman since the issuance of the Charter to the Nobility. Confirmed by the Senate on 8 August with the specification that Radishchev, now bereft of noble status, be beheaded in faraway Nerchinsk, this sentence was immediately commuted (in honor of the peace with Sweden) to ten years' exile at hard labor. This amended sentence the Empress then referred to her council for review—a most unusual step, since the council was not a judicial body. In transmitting the Senate's report to the council on 11 August, the day Swedish ratification of the peace was brought to Tsarskoe Selo, Catherine directed "with perceptible feeling" that her councilors consider the case impartially; they were not to be swayed by the insult to her person, which she despised. On 19 August the councilors dutifully reviewed Radishchev's offenses in the light of his civic duty as manifested in his oath of fidelity and the laws against conspiracy and designs against the sovereign. These were the same laws that had been cited against Pugachev fifteen years before. The council concurred with the amended verdict without further recommendation. Stripped of noble status, all ranks and decorations, Radishchev was dispatched in chains to Siberia on 8 September 1790, the same day that Catherine sumptuously celebrated the peace with Sweden.[79]

Exhausted, the Empress spent the entire next day resting on a couch, barely able to move. Her head spun. She had no energy. Probably she felt pangs of conscience about the Radishchev case. If general fears of the French infection caused her on 26 August to order the return forthwith of all Russians in Paris, including young Count Stroganov and his tutor who had attended the Jacobin Club, she detected no more specific cases in Petersburg. No accomplices of Radishchev could be found. Only some thirty copies of his tract had been sold. He had destroyed the other 600 copies himself. And as he had told Sheshkovskii, his book had not been addressed to the common people, who in any case did not read books like his. To a Catherine rapidly recovering her composure, Radishchev looked less and less like a "Pugachev from the university." His chains had been removed the day after he left Petersburg.[80]

The Ochakov Crisis and Potemkin's Demise

In any event, the Empress felt increasingly eager to end the Turkish war, now entering its fourth year. The surprisingly sudden, highly satisfactory conclusion of the Swedish war made her more sanguine than ever that a policy of firmness, of maintaining military pressure while displaying readiness to negotiate, would terminate the costly conflict. On 18 September 1790 she ordered a new levy of four recruits per 500 census souls. Besides, the Austro-Prussian Convention of Reichenbach (June 1790), whereby Leopold II ignominiously accepted Anglo-Prussian mediation of peace with the Turks on the basis of no territorial gain, offered Catherine an object lesson in what to avoid. Repudiating the Reichenbach negotiations, she complained to Potemkin of Prussian arrogance and avarice, duplicity and deceit. A bizarre accident fanned hopes that Prussian haughtiness would not go unavenged. At the peace celebrations in Petersburg the Prussian *chargé d'affaires* fainted, collapsing so heavily that he bloodied his nose and forehead. The crowd took it as an omen: The Prussian had broken his nose on the steps of the Russian throne.[81]

With the campaign season almost over, Catherine worried anew about Potemkin and the Turkish front. At the end of August his visit to the Black Sea fleet, together with storms in Petersburg, reminded her so forcibly of the maritime perils of autumn that she advised him to keep all ships in port. Even so, she rejoiced in mid-September at Admiral Ushakov's victory over the Turks off Gadzhibei (the future site of Odessa), a triumph she celebrated at a splendid banquet for the four Guards regiments on 15 September. Naval victories gave her special pleasure because of their novelty, and because Russia had long been deficient at sea. With Potemkin she gloried in their joint achievement; "the Black Sea fleet is our creation, consequently it's close to the heart." Along with gifts for the commanders she sent Potemkin a gold coffee service for the Turkish pashas with whom he would negotiate for peace.[82]

Yet all her old physical ailments recurred in late September 1790: congestion in the chest, cough, backpains, gas and hemorrhoidal colics, fever, diarrhea, and weakness. Steambaths afforded scant relief. Nevertheless, she took no medicine, only walks and carriage rides when the pain permitted. By late December she decided her affliction was gout that had passed into the stomach and intestines. Her remedy was to drive it out with pepper and a daily glass of Malaga wine. "It is much better for me," she wrote Potemkin on 8 October, "but I had been very sick and now I'm still rather weak." Only Zubov's attentions, which she lauded to Potemkin in sending him a jeweled ring on his nameday, lifted her spirits. Like a true Russian, the Empress perked up at winter's onset by 1 November 1790, finally ending a whole year of unbroken rains. The week before she even danced a polka and launched secret plans for a grand transvestite ball and supper in the Hermitage on 10 November. "Everybody was very merry," Khrapovitskii reported. Delighted with the results, the Empress praised the French actors and actresses who manned the booths selling costumes on credit for the masquerade—Persian veils for the men, Turkish turbans for the women. Catherine strove to recapture the joys of her early years in Russia, and perhaps also to show Potemkin that she could mount a spectacle without him. The year ended on a gleeful note when young Valerian Zubov arrived with the news of Suvorov's bloody storm of the Turkish fortress of Ismail on 11 December 1790. Surely the Sultan must now sue for peace.[83]

Feeling better as the new year opened, Catherine eagerly awaited Potemkin's full account of his Ismail triumph and encouraged him to visit Petersburg before the spring. Within weeks after his arrival on 28 February 1791, however, the Empress succumbed to a new onslaught of depression, weeping in indignation at the threat of war with Prussia abetted by Britain and Poland. She rejected Potemkin's advice to write King Frederick William II directly. She refused to consult a doctor, sticking to her reliance on nature. Her spells of weakness made her neglect state affairs. "If you wish to roll the stone from my heart, if you wish to stop the spasms," she despondently implored Potemkin in March 1791, "dispatch a courier at once to the army and let the land and sea forces commence action as soon as possible, or else you will drag out the war still longer, which of course neither you nor I desire."[84]

All Catherine's apprehensions of a new conflict crystallized into specific threats in the first weeks of April. Rumors of British intentions to send naval squadrons into the Baltic and the Black seas, together with reports of great troop movements in Prussia and suspicions of Swedish intentions, prompted "various racing around" on 7/8 April. "Vexation," Khrapovitskii tersely remarked. "Stubbornness is leading to a new war." The Empress became almost apoplectic over an Anglo-Prussian ultimatum opposing any further territorial gain by Russia from the Ottoman Empire and summoning her to clarify, within ten days, her readiness for peace on reasonable terms. In Catherine's view her peace terms had been reasonable all along. Besides, the ultimatum was all the more outrageous for being proffered on the tip of a sword. From London, ambassador Semen Vorontsov urgently reported that Parliament had approved George III's request for additional funds for the fleet's "Russian armament." Although Potemkin sought to calm the agitated Empress, his well-known Anglophilia depreciated his advice, as did his wry remarks on the folly of fighting the English with raw recruits and his bitter sarcasm about Catherine's impetuosity: "Wasn't the Swedish cannonade here tiresome?" He felt his own position slipping beneath Zubov's rapid rise in favor, and had returned to Petersburg intent on removing this latest "toothache" (a play on names and words: *zub* means tooth in Russian). Some thought he had gone mad, others that his madness was limited to the pursuit of young women. He told the Swedish envoy he could still manage Catherine the woman.[85]

In no mood for jocularity, the Empress asked her council on 10 April 1791 whether the Reval squadron should be brought back to reinforce the main

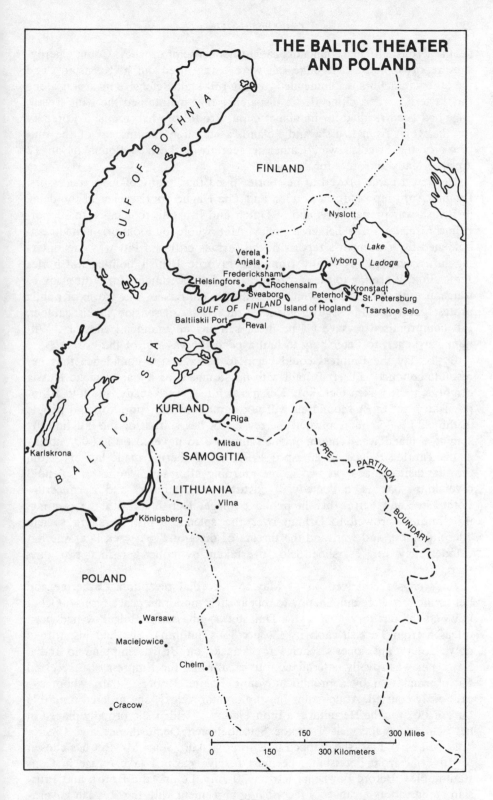

THE BALTIC THEATER
AND POLAND

GULF OF BOTHNIA

FINLAND

Nyslott

Lake Ladoga

Verela
Anjala
Fredericksham
Helsingfors   Rochensalm   Vyborg
Sveaborg   Kronstadt
GULF OF FINLAND   Peterhof   St. Petersburg
Baltiiskii Port   Island of Hogland   Tsarskoe Selo
Reval

BALTIC SEA

KURLAND   Riga

Mitau

Karlskrona   SAMOGITIA

LITHUANIA   Vilna

Königsberg

PRE-PARTITION BOUNDARY

POLAND

Warsaw
Maciejowice
Chelm

Cracow

| 0 | 150 | 300 Miles |
| 0 | 150 | 300 Kilometers |

fleet at Kronstadt. The councilors caught her sense of urgency. Count Cherny-shev reported that twenty-nine sail were being fitted out at Kronstadt, and the other councilors recommended rushing full-scale defensive measures along the western border, citing Berlin dispatches that maintained the King's equipage had been readied for imminent departure to join his troops. To prepare for the worst from Prussia and Poland, a situation reminiscent of the outbreak of the Swedish war, Catherine secretly authorized Potemkin on 12 April to ready all forces for action.[86]

Her latest panic proved to be shorter-lived than many of its predecessors. By mid-April reports from London and The Hague apprised her of the delay in British war preparations and of Dutch and Prussian reluctance to support Prime Minister Pitt's bellicose policy. Her whole outlook brightened, emboldened by Vorontsov's reports of the furious criticism Pitt was encountering in Parliament, especially from her favorite British politician, Charles James Fox. Warming to the task, she dispatched documents for Vorontsov to transmit to the opposition, which he skillfully cultivated. The storm of public protest paralyzed Pitt's government. Wracked by dissension in his cabinet, Pitt compromised to save his position, sending an unofficial emissary, William Fawkener, to Petersburg to find a peaceful way out of the crisis.[87]

By 1 May the Empress could begin to relax in the confidence that her resolute conduct had left Britain with no stomach for a war to make Russia disgorge godforsaken Ochakov. Her naval forces were ready, she told Khra-povitskii, "yet those scoundrels will not come, but they only torment people in the cold." Potemkin assisted the revival of her spirits for the last time by staging a magnificent entertainment (rumored to have cost 150,000 rubles) at his Tauride Palace on 23 April 1791. As Catherine made her exit from the "fantastic palace" at two in the morning after seven hours of splendid diversions—dances, a comedy, a costume ball, supper, and a concert—Potemkin knelt before her in public homage. Delighted with the evening, the Empress crowed to Grimm over the splendors of Petersburg society "despite noise, and war, and the threats of dictators!" A week later she left clandestinely for Tsarskoe Selo, overtaken by colic her first two days there.[88]

Pitt's emissary arrived on 14 May to a cordial reception. Catherine and her councilors were quite happy to repeat their moderate peace terms—Ochakov and the territory west to the Dniester (ambassador Bulgakov had been released from Turkish captivity the previous autumn). She had just turned down John Paul Jones's scheme for attacks on British shipping to India. Fawkener was royally entertained, but meanwhile the Empress also received an informal visit by a prominent young Foxite, Robert Adair, whom she cautiously courted. Anticipating her diplomatic victory, she ordered a marble bust of Fox for the Hermitage, a bronze copy of which she proudly placed in her sculpture gallery at Tsarskoe Selo between Demosthenes and Cicero. "Pitt will envy this," she quipped to Khrapovitskii. "Since Mr. Pitt has chosen to drive me from Petersburg, he must forgive me if I take refuge in Constantinople." Before Fawkener left on 20 July, he and the British and Prussian ambassadors arranged a face-saving agreement with the Russian government, which pledged free navigation on the Dniester if peace terms with the stipulated territorial gains were reached within four months; otherwise, if the Turks refused this deal, Russia could seek different terms alone. At Fawkener's farewell reception Catherine presented him with a jeweled snuffbox worth 6,500 rubles. His rival, Robert Adair, she favored with an elegant brooch with her portrait.[89]

The "Ochakov crisis," as it became known in British politics, resulted in a stunningly easy victory for Catherine over Pitt's inept plan. Among its byproducts was a plethora of critical editorials and satirical prints lampooning the Prime Minister, his rivals, and the Empress alike. In "The Fate of Despotism, A Vision," one anonymous critic blamed the carnage of the Russo-Turkish war on "the whim of a weak vindictive woman," remarking: "Hundreds of thousands has her despotism consigned to the other world, hundreds of thousands has she sent prematurely to the grave." An elegant engraving showed the Empress put to sleep so as to prevent "other enormities"—an indictment that recalled Radishchev's the year before.[90]

"An Imperial Stride!" satirized the grandeur of Catherine's political aims in the "Greek Project" by reference to her supposedly gargantuan sexual appetite. Her colossal figure is depicted stepping from Petersburg to Constantinople before an appreciative chorus of the European powers, who make ribald comments in gazing under her petticoats. Says the Doge of Venice: "To what a length Power may be carried," while the Pope remarks, "I shall never forget it." "By Saint Jago, I'll strip her of her Fur!" blusters the King of Spain, as Louis XVI of France thoughtfully observes, "Never saw anything like it." Britain's stuttering George III declaims "What! What! What! What a prodigious expansion!" To which Leopold II of Austria adds: "Wonderful elevation." And the Sultan of Turkey concludes in amazement: "The whole Turkish Army wouldn't satisfy her." In elaborating the same themes a French copy, "The Imperial Embrace," portrayed the Empress barebreasted with disheveled hair.[91]

Catherine's well-publicized patronage of Fox also came in for its share of sexual-satirical assault in "Black Carlo's White Bust, or the Party's Plenipo in Catherine's Closet." Gazing amorously at a bust of Fox in her lap, the Empress wistfully remarks, "O Heavens! I wish I had the whole length." Leeringly, the bust, inscribed "Real Greek," replies: "Ay! You're a deep One." The busts of Demosthenes and Cicero, which the Empress has kicked over, are labelled George III and Pitt. "What what amazing capacity will Oxacow satisfy?" inquires the King. To which Pitt smugly retorts: "Yes, we are finely toss'd off by Private acceptance"—an acid commentary on the Fawkener mission and Adair's intrigues. Another satirical blast at Pitt and his policy, by James Gillray, showed the Prime Minister on a high wire struggling to balance the Sultan and the Empress at the opposite ends of a pole. Catherine defiantly derides Pitt's attempt and his Prussian ally: "Both Billy the Flat, and yourself may do your worst, you circumcised dog! Get me down if you can! I'll match you all, and swallow Thousands More." Did such satires attract Catherine's attention? Almost certainly she knew about them, and they must have chilled her already detumescent opinion of the

British government. Apropos of British maneuvers at foreign courts she commented to Khrapovitskii on 6 June: "We never start wars, but we know how to defend ourselves."[92]

The opening of the campaign season made her more eager for decisive results. New victories, she hoped, would wring peace out of the Turks before their negotiations with the Austrians at Sistova could sunder the Russo-Austrian alliance with a separate peace. At Peterhof for the June holidays her spirits were tugged in divergent directions by momentary joy at the news—contradicted later in the day—of Louis XVI's escape from Paris with noble and foreign assistance (the abortive "flight to Varennes" in which Catherine may have had a clandestine hand), and by Potemkin's notification on 2 July of the seizure of Anapa ten days before. In celebration of the latter she supped with Potemkin that evening at the horse-guards barracks before returning to Tsarskoe Selo. On 11 July she rejoiced further at Prince Repnin's defeat of the Grand Vizir at Machin. Congratulating Potemkin on these victories, which were celebrated at the Kazan Cathedral two days later, she prayed that peace would soon follow. At the same time she became upset over Grand Duke Paul's surprise visit to the Kronstadt fleet amid stormy weather. Potemkin himself finally left Tsarskoe Selo for the southern front at five o'clock in the morning of 24 July. The Empress and her viceroy sensed that they would never see each other again.[93]

As before, she worried as much about Potemkin when he was out of sight as when he was in town. On 3 August 1791 she thanked him for his letters from Mogilev. "I confess that there is nothing in the world I wish so much as peace." Though concerned that withdrawal of the Turkish fleet from the Black Sea would foil Russian attacks, she praised Potemkin for keeping her informed and assigned General Kamenskii to assist him. By 9 August she looked forward frantically for signs of peace, fearful that the Turks' naval retreat would prevent further combat in anticipation of the autumn storms, the alarming memory of which still haunted her. Another old apprehension agitated her anew. The plague, reported at Cairo in July, had supposedly reached Constantinople. "For God's sake, take all possible precautions in order that it not be drawn into you, and from you inside Russia." This threat increased her concern for his own health. "That you have been tormented and are sick, about that I regret with all my heart; may God help you. Farewell, amiable friend." Time was running out for them both.[94]

The very next evening Potemkin's courier brought word of a preliminary peace with the Turks. From caution, much concerned about "leaks," Catherine withheld public word of the peace until her council reviewed the proposed terms on 11 August. As soon as Bezborodko reported the council's endorsement, except for the articles calling for an eight-month truce before the final treaty and prohibiting new fortifications on the territory ceded to Russia, the Empress set the public announcement and celebrations in Tsarskoe Selo and Petersburg for 15 August, the anniversary of the peace with Sweden. Urging Potemkin on 12 August to complete the peace treaty as soon as possible, she regretted the great heat and bad roads that had undercut his health at such a critical moment, "'when each minute demands new labor." The peace had caught her by surprise, she told Potemkin. "With us here everybody is terribly glad." It had come none too soon; news of the Peace of Sistova between Austria and Turkey, signed on 24 July/4 August 1791, had reached the Empress only three days after Potemkin's courier. In stark contrast to Catherine's gains, Leopold II had obtained nothing except (in a separate convention) the town of Orsova and a minor rectification of the border between Wallachia and Serbia. The "Greek Project" had petered out.[95]

Happy as Catherine was with the preliminary peace and with Admiral Ushakov's defeat of the Ottoman fleet on 29 July only sixty versts from Constantinople, her joy turned to sorrow on 24 August at word of the death of Grand Duchess Maria Fedorovna's brother, Prince Karl Alexander of Würtemberg-Stuttgart. Two days later she drove over to Pavlovsk to comfort her daughter-in-law. Within another forty-eight hours she burst into tears on learning of Potemkin's worsening illness. His warning that he felt too weak to surmount his fever panicked the Empress, who begged him to spare her from "such a blow, about which I cannot even think without extreme grief." After a week, however, she relaxed somewhat at word of his recovery. She routinely sent Zubov's greetings and reassured Potemkin of her own good health amid the current "warm and beautiful days." By mid-September all her fears resurged over Potemkin's four-day fever with headache. Her own health had improved in the interim. At the end of September panic arose afresh. "My sincere friend, Prince Grigorii Aleksandrovich," she wrote Potemkin on 30 September. "Your sickness upsets me utterly; for the love of Christ, if needed take that which, in the doctors' estimation, will afford you relief; and having taken it, I beg you also to save yourself from food and drink that oppose the medicine. I beg God that He will soon return to you strength and health. Farewell, my friend. Platon Aleksandrovich [Zubov] thanks you for the greeting and greatly regrets your condition. Upon your nameday I congratulate you and send a little fur coat."[96]

On 3 October 1791 two couriers delivered reports of Potemkin's dangerous decline amid persistent fever; he had been given the last rites. Catherine wept despite the doctors' hopes that the patient was improving. The next morning Dr. Rogerson told her that Sutherland, the court banker, would not survive another twenty-four hours; he died after midnight. A week later another courier reported that Potemkin had suffered a relapse on 1 October. The next afternoon toward five o'clock a courier brought the final news: Potemkin had expired in the steppe outside Jassy on 5 October 1791 before noon. His last note, dictated the day before, implored:

[In Popov's hand]

Little Mother all-merciful Mistress,

There is no more strength to bear my torment; salvation alone remains—to leave this town and I have ordered myself taken to Nikolaev. I know not what will be with me. Most loyal and most grateful subject. [In Potemkin's scrawl]: salvation alone—to drive away.[97]

Catherine collapsed. "Tears and desperation," recorded Khrapovitskii on 12 October. "At 8 o'clock they let blood, at 10 o'clock she went to bed." At two A.M. she poured out her grief in a letter to Grimm. Awakening in tears the next morning, the Empress bemoaned her failure to train men to replace Potemkin. Now she had nobody she could depend on.[98]

Catherine contradicted herself. While she was being bled the night before, the council had met at her behest to consider who should succeed Potemkin in command of the army and the peace negotiations. She had already accepted, and the councilors immediately endorsed, Bezborodko's offer to conduct the peace congress at Jassy; they urged him to leave at once. The council likewise approved General Kakhovskii as the temporary new commander-in-chief and advised General Gudovich to follow any orders Potemkin had left concerning the Caucasus and the Kuban. The councilors were greatly concerned to hurry the peace negotiations to a beneficial conclusion, so they advised the Empress as a precaution to appoint a new chief commander and, if he were not in the capital, to recall him immediately for consultations about the next campaign. Catherine acted on all these recommendations the next day. Bezborodko departed on 16 October thinking, Khrapovitskii maliciously noted, that he would manage everything, whereas that "little fool Zubov" had already won Catherine's confidence.[99]

Throughout these hasty improvisations the Empress continued to weep and lament. How could she replace the irreplaceable Potemkin? Who would ever have dreamed that sick old men like Alexander Viazemskii and Ivan Chernyshev would outlive him? "Yes, and everybody now, like snails, will start to stick their heads out," she moaned to Khrapovitskii, whose protest that such matters were beneath her only prompted a sad retort: "So I, too, am old." Sobbing afflicted her off and on the rest of the year. Her grief redoubled on 29/30 November with the deaths of Ivan Orlov and Jakob Bruce, and on 22 December at word of the "strange death" of Mikhail Potemkin, sent south to wind up his late cousin's tangled financial affairs. After Christmas she stayed in her rooms three days in a row, laid low by a cold and a feeling of weakness. Even the peace treaty with the Turks brought only tears when delivered on 6 January 1792. Prayers were offered in the palace and 101 cannon roared a salute. But banquet invitations and toasts at the supper table were sternly vetoed. When Potemkin's confidant Vasia Popov delivered the Prince's papers to Catherine on 12 January, they both wept amid much frenzied activity. Potemkin's papers were locked in a special cabinet and the key hidden. When General Samoilov arrived on 30 January with the Turkish ratification of the peace, the Empress dismissed her company and wept with Samoilov. The next day she rewarded Bezborodko and Samoilov with the Order of St. Andrew and 50,000 and 30,000 rubles, respectively.[100]

Catherine could take scant pride in her latest triumphant treaty with the Turks. She was too aware of the costs involved, too tormented by grief that its chief architect and builder had left her alone against the terrors of old age amid a new era of revolutionary turmoil across Europe.

12

Spring Surprises,
Autumn Anxieties

The spring of 1792 confronted Catherine with another complex of crises new and old, predictable and unforeseen, political and personal, physical and psychological. These spanned the gamut of anxieties from international war to domestic subversion, from the sudden demise of fellow sovereigns and relatives to concerns for her own health. All the while she felt more alone than ever. Her longevity threatened to turn into a liability. Yet she could not bear the thought that she might outlive her glory. She felt old. She looked old albeit well preserved. She thought old, so to speak, afflicted as she was with nostalgia for earlier times, with her place in history. She intensified her preoccupation with Russian history and renewed her efforts at autobiography.[1]

Both her advancing age and her declining health stirred sporadic feelings of being overwhelmed by work, of losing her grip on political affairs. On 12 February she hired two more court physicians, doctors Freygang and Timan, for Grand Duke Paul and for herself. On 7 March she complained to Khrapovitskii of fatigue amid the welter of affairs that demanded her attention, particularly the preparations for intervention in Poland. Can a sovereign rule Russia, she wondered aloud, and not be assiduous and active? Khrapovitskii sympathetically remarked on the diverse involvements necessitated by the Empire's size, its multiple political ties abroad, and the current chaos in Europe, all of which magnified the burdens of the center (i.e., Catherine) that impelled movement and direction to the whole. "Yes," she replied with a wave of a hand, "only my movement gives the direction where it ought to go."[2]

Three days earlier she had proclaimed six weeks' mourning for her ally Emperor Leopold II, whose sudden death on 19 February/1 March 1792 forcibly reminded her of unpleasant possibilities. In mid-March another stroke

293

of anxiety hit with the news that her relative and ally, King Gustavus III of Sweden, had been wounded—shot in the back by an aristocratic assassin at a masked ball on 5 March. A courier from Count Stackelberg, Russian minister in Stockholm, delivered the shocking story directly to Platon Zubov on Saturday evening, 13 March. Reassured on 26 March that the king was out of danger, Catherine complained of pain in the waist and spent the morning in bed. Gustavus, who had always feared the month of March, was dead by the end of it (29 March/9 April). Catherine's courtiers donned their mourning attire anew on 12 April for six weeks: black ribbons on the women, black stockings on the men. A British visitor to the Russian court in 1792–1794 recorded an observation of the Prussian envoy: "N.B. The Empress does not like the black colour. She does not like either to be left alone. She must always have some living creature with her; at least a dog or something of that kind."[3]

Catherine found her administration in greater disarray than ever, from the sudden demise of the supposedly omnicompetent Potemkin and the palpable decline of the formerly omnipresent Viazemskii. No individual could replace either of these trusted wheelhorses of her regime. If she had been shocked by Potemkin's death in the far south, Viazemskii's daily decline before her eyes excited a different order of dread. Gossip might proclaim the ailing procurator-general to be "never a day without a girl," but the Empress had to think how to ease him out of his multiple offices and redistribute his duties to others.[4] Not surprisingly, she procrastinated, confiding her horror at Viazemskii's pitiable condition to Platon Zubov, the young favorite whose meteoric rise in government status created as many problems as it solved.

> The person that you made inquiries about yesterday by my orders, has been to see me today; he is in a state that one cannot imagine; he does not eat or sleep, as he says himself, his heart races continually, his head is so feeble that when he sits it falls on his shoulder; from weakness, sitting on a chair, he rocks to and fro; he says that every movement is unbearable, that the air takes his breath away; in a word, it is not certain what will come of this; he told me that he looks on his condition with a philosophical eye; only it is evident that he suffers terribly.[5]

Catherine knew what the outcome must be. But neither she nor Viazemskii could face the problem squarely before the summer. He no longer attended court. When he declined to sign any papers for two weeks, the Empress lamented to Zubov the "extreme anarchy" that would result from further delay. Officially retired on 17 September 1792 with full salary, Viazemskii died less than four months later on 8 January 1793, having lived sixty-five years, five months, and five days—a calculation that could not have cheered Catherine, then in her sixty-fourth year. Alexander Samoilov, a nephew of Potemkin, replaced Viazemskii as procurator-general and in charge of the Secret Branch.[6]

Amid this governmental drift and indecision, the Empress steadily entrusted Platon Zubov with new duties and new honors. In January 1792 she quietly provided Zubov with his own chancery headed by Adrian Gribov-skii, a former Potemkin aide. With his father, three brothers, one sister, and one sister-in-law at court, the twenty-four-year-old Guardsman looked like the kingpin of a new "party" under the Empress's wing. His rapid emergence into the political limelight naturally upset the established court factions—above all, the Vorontsov "party" led by three senior council members: Alexander Vorontsov, Alexander Bezborodko, and Peter Zavadovskii. Such long-time critics of Potemkin-style politics could only disdain a young parvenu like Zubov, who seemed about to replace Potemkin in Catherine's confidence and in her newly narrowed process of decision making, for she did not deign to put him on the council. All the rancorous feelings of rivalry toward Potemkin were accordingly projected on Zubov. His hold over Catherine, it was alleged, must be sexual. "The War with Poland is entered into at the instigation of the present favourite of the Russian Empress," it was whispered in Sweden in mid-summer 1792. "She sleeps with him in a bed separated by a partition, which whenever she chuses, is removed by means of a spring and serves as a signal to her lover." Later court gossip maintained that Catherine, "as she is now old," tailored her schedule to Zubov's, reserving time for him each afternoon: "From two to four is the Time of Mystery." It may well have been her naptime.[7]

Zavadovskii, himself a former favorite, saw the situation in a more sober light. The change in personalities in power reflected the Empress's own decline. "But the chief thing is, the sun is setting: it does not possess that light which acts in the east and at mid-day." With Bezborodko away for the peace negotiations at Jassy, Zubov had seized control of foreign and domestic policy. Bezborodko's relative eclipse was registered two days after his triumphant return to Petersburg on 10 March 1792 when Zubov was promoted to lieutenant-general and adjutant-general. "Not one of the previous favorites, not even the all-powerful Prince Potemkin himself, possessed such a broad sphere," observed Zavadovskii; "for his hegemony pertained to only one department, but to the present one all are drawn close." Zubov he credited with a good soul and mind, but he faulted his lack of experience and consistency, persistence and balance. With Markov's assistance in foreign affairs, Zubov was accused of secretly drafting the plan for intervention in Poland, which Zavadovskii vainly opposed. The problem was not that Zubov controlled the Empress, but that though sensible and assiduous in executing her wishes, he was too young and too new to thwart her folly. So appalled at the changes in personnel and politics was Zavadovskii that he vowed to follow Alexander Vorontsov into retirement as soon as possible, meanwhile scorning his friend Bezborodko's craven opportunism in bowing to the new order at court. But since Zavadovskii did not retire, he too adapted to Zubov's dominance. Within a few months he joined the chorus of court "outsiders" who ridiculed Zubov's "manners as uncommonly haughty."[8] For her part, Catherine probably remembered the constant criticism of Potemkin by nameless rivals. "This g-1 Zoubof is hardworking, trustworthy, possessed of good will and of a most excellent frame of mind; this is a man about whom people will soon be talking," she informed Grimm on 9 May, just as Russian troops crossed the Polish border: "it depends upon me again, to make of him a factotum."[9]

Aggravating these anxieties at the same time were apprehensions about French (or French-inspired) machinations in Poland and even in Russia itself. Just as the Empress coordinated armed intervention in Poland in consultation with Polish republican confederates, to overthrow the "Jacobin" constitution of 3 May 1791, she was distressed by disputes among her top advisers, several of whom feared that war with Prussia, Poland's ally, would result from an ill-disguised invasion. For several days after the council session of 29 March the Empress fumed, censuring Bezborodko for the councilors' irresolution. With Platon Zubov and Arkadii Markov the Empress worked out the plan for intervention in Poland without consulting the council, which insisted that Prussia and Austria must be forewarned of Russian intentions. At first Catherine spurned this implicit reminder of the difficulties spawned by the partition twenty years before, but after a few days she reluctantly agreed. On 10 April both Berlin and Vienna were sent notification of the imminent invasion.[10]

Russia's relations with revolutionary France rapidly deteriorated in the first months of 1792. War looked close. After clandestine conversations with Louis XVI and Marie Antoinette, Ivan Simolin, the Russian ambassador, left Paris at the start of February and visited Vienna on his way back to St. Petersburg. Baron Grimm departed at the same time. On 14 February the Empress ordered special surveillance over all Frenchmen in Moscow, particularly newcomers of uncertain standing. Any found guilty of suspicious or reprehensible acts were to be expelled at once and reported to the Empress. In Petersburg the French embassy had been under virtual house arrest since 30 August 1791, when *chargé d'affaires* Edmond Genet (subsequently notorious in the United States as "Citizen Genet") had been forbidden to appear at court. Treated as a complete pariah, the volatile Genet found his correspondence purloined (the Russians had a key to his cypher) and his house "surrounded" in an atmosphere of "daggers, pistolets, and poisons." He repaid his persecutors with inflammatory dispatches, copies of which came into Catherine's hands, dilating on the supposedly rampant revolutionary ferment about to engulf every level of Russian society, from the enserfed peasantry to the national minorities, from the grand dukes to the Guards regiments.[11]

Apprised at the end of February that Princess Varvara Shakhovskaia in Paris had married her daughter to a French aristocrat, Prince Arenberg, and that the newlyweds might return to Russia, Catherine publicly barred the Frenchman from Russia for his part in "two riots," in France and Brabant. The princess might enter Russia, the Empress stipulated, but her property must be secured against Arenberg's rascality. Accordingly, she directed the governor-general of Moscow to find out whether her father knew and approved of his daughter's marriage. Her decree warned that such marriages of aristocratic Russian heiresses with foreigners had been increasing and must be regulated by legislation so as to preserve future tranquility in the

Empire's "womb." It is symptomatic of Catherine's worries that this incident elicited so stern a reaction. (Princess Shakhovskaia later returned with her daughter to Russia, where the Holy Synod annulled the latter's marriage to Arenberg.)[12]

Catherine's anxieties peaked in the first week of April. On Easter Sunday, 4 April 1792, the Empress abruptly announced the cancellation of a ball scheduled two days later, and she forbade toasts or salutes at dinner that day and the next. These prohibitions may have been motivated by an attack of nerves over "all the horrors" reported abroad, and exacerbated by "excessive fatigue" from four straight days of church-going. The very next day Catherine authorized the governor-general of Moscow to secretly investigate a "pasquinade" mailed from there against Synod and Senate officials. Confirmation of Gustavus III's death reached Petersburg on 7 April. The Russians were shocked to learn that the fatal shot had included spikes and pellets as well as a square bullet.[13]

The very next day a report arrived about a Frenchman, a certain Baseville, supposedly sent via Königsberg on 22 March to murder the Empress. Security precautions were instituted at once along the western border and in the capital; all visitors to Tsarskoe Selo and Sofiia—foreigners especially— were to be strictly watched. Rumors of poison pointedly dismayed Catherine. "If you find that man, about whom I have just instructed you," she directed Senior Policemaster Ryleev, "then, if phials or powders are discovered on him, then proceed more cautiously with them, preserve them and try not to break or scatter them accidentally, and most of all, nobody should open them, for it could be dangerous." By mid-April these apprehensions subsided sufficiently for her to jest with Grimm about the boastful predictions voiced in Paris and Warsaw concerning her imminent demise. "As soon as I can, I shall deliver some blows of the stick to these rogues, so as to teach them how to speak." She was doubly distressed by the news from France— outraged at attempts to justify assassination by appeals to Voltaire's authority, and affronted by the willingness of the European courts to condone the vacillations of Louis XVI and Marie Antoinette.[14]

Catherine's concern about France sharpened after more than an hour's conversation with Simolin on 17 April. A week later, pointing to her troops through the window, she punned: "they have no patriotic piques." To which Khrapovitskii muttered: "nor red hats." On 28 April the Empress rejoiced at news that France had declared war on Austria. The day before, several Polish republican magnates had signed the Confederation of Targowica, as drafted by Catherine's subordinates. Dated "May 14, Targowica" so as to foster the fiction that it had been written by patriotic Poles on Polish territory, the pact assailed "the usurpers" in Warsaw for "the contagion of democratic ideas" after the fatal French example that had destroyed the Republic in favor of "despotism." The benevolent, invited Russian invasion was set for 10 May.[15]

After dinner on 28 April 1792 the Empress left Petersburg for Tsarskoe Selo. In gathering up her papers for the change of residence, Khrapovitskii scanned an undated testament in Catherine's hand. This document divulged the depth of her mental turmoil in past months and her despair about the future.

> If I die in Tsarskoe Selo, then lay me in the Sofiia town cemetery.
>
> If—in the city of Saint Peter—in the Nevskii Monastery in the cathedral or burial church.
>
> If—in Pella, then transport me by water to the Nevskii Monastery.
>
> If—in Moscow—in the Donskoi Monastery or at a nearby city cemetery.
>
> If—in Peterhof—in the Trinity-Sergiev hermitage.
>
> If—in some other place—in a nearby cemetery. The coffin is to be carried by horse-guards, and by nobody else.
>
> My body is to be laid out in a white dress, with a golden crown on the head, on which my forename will be inscribed. Mourning clothes shall be worn half the year, and no longer, the less the better.
>
> After the first six weeks all the popular amusements should be reopened.
>
> After the burial, marriages should be permitted—weddings and music.
>
> My library with all manuscripts and everything found in my papers written in my hand, I bequeath to my beloved grandson Alexander Pavlovich, also my cut gems, and I bless him with mind and heart. For the purpose of a better fulfillment, a copy of them will be deposited and has been deposited in such a safe place, so that sooner or later shame and disgrace shall overtake those who do not fulfill my will. My intention is to place Konstantin on the throne of the Greek Empire.
>
> For the good of the Russian Empire and the Greek I advise that the Princes of Würtemberg be removed from the affairs and concerns of these Empires and made known as little as possible, likewise remove the half-Germans from the concerns of both empires.[16]

The omissions in this testament speak as eloquently as its stipulations. Why did she not wish to be interred with Peter the Great and his successors in the Cathedral of Peter and Paul in the heart of her beloved St. Petersburg? Indeed, the Nevskii Monastery was where her unlamented husband had been buried. Perhaps her wish in this regard was another expression of prideful modesty, to distinguish herself from the imperious Petrine legacy and reassert her innocence in Peter III's death.

Paul is not mentioned directly. At the very least she did not wish to contemplate his enthronement. Her dismissal of the Princes of Würtemberg, Maria Fedorovna's eight brothers, likewise looks to have been directed at Paul. The hope and trust she vested in Alexander were inversely proportional to her expectations of Paul. Had she already drafted a document proclaiming her eldest grandson and excluding her son from the succession? None has ever been found. But many believed then and later that she had penned such instructions. Her dreams for Konstantin had not evaporated, either. Perhaps Potemkin's recent death had reinforced her resolve to realize the "Greek Project." As for her own fate, the multiple places mentioned in the will may show that she sensed her death in the near future. Either she still worried about bullets or poison, or she simply prudently provided for various eventualities. Considering her animus against Moscow and her aversion to travel in recent years, it seems odd that she envisioned the possibility of dying there. Perhaps this notion sprang from half-hidden hopes for another triumphal tour before her days had ended. Less than two years later she would assure Grimm that if she travelled before departing this world, her aim would be to breathe the restorative airs of Novorossiia that Potemkin had vainly sought in his death throes. It could hardly have comforted Catherine to think that none of her testament's provisions would be implemented, even if "shame and disgrace" did overtake her successors.[17]

The strained relations between Catherine and Paul became manifest by this time. Even foreign visitors noticed in the Grand Duke's "very vulgar, insignificant, disagreeable countenance," blatant testimony of disregard: "a very melancholy air, an air of chagrin and discontent." Privately, several Russians predicted that he would never gain the throne. "The Grand Duke has no friend because he cannot be trusted." If he did succeed Catherine somehow, it was foretold that his reign would be tyrannical and short. His mother evidently thought the same.[18]

"Martinists" in Moscow

In mid-April 1792, just when the Empress was assailed by threats of assassination from abroad, she initiated an inquiry into suspicious circumstances in Moscow that divulged more than she could have foreseen. This evolved into the infamous case of Nikolai Novikov and his fellow freemasons.

Novikov had been known to Catherine since the late 1760s when she patronized several of his journalistic and editorial ventures. Her favorable attitude toward him had hardened, however, after his move to Moscow in 1779 and his involvement with freemasonry. To the Empress, freemasonry, which she tended to lump together with the European Illuminati and Martinists, represented "one of the greatest aberrations to which the human race had succumbed," a strange fad among males only that she scorned as "a mixture of religious ritual and childish games." Indeed, in 1785–86 she publicly ridiculed its practices and practitioners in three crudely satirical comedies: *The Deceiver, The Deluded,* and *The Siberian Shaman,* translated titles that exemplified her mocking attitude. She could not understand why Novikov, a prosperous nobleman who had retired from state service to become the Empire's preeminent private publisher, subscribed to such a bizarre doctrine. Furthermore, she was suspicious of freemasonry for its secretive organization, its contacts with foreign courts (especially Prussia), its apparent ability to mobilize substantial funds, and its powers of proselytism among the "do-nothing" Moscow nobility. Indeed, Novikov had come into conflict with state publishing regulations in 1788 for printing religious books without the permission of the Church authorities. As early as February 1790, when she appointed Prince Alexander Prozorovskii to be governor-general of Moscow, she charged him to look into rumors that "a certain gang of persons harmful to society under the name of Martinists" had been multiplying there and had even enticed into their ranks Governor Lopukhin. Two months later she reiterated her resolve that the Moscow police not tolerate any covert meetings, a prohibition that applied especially to "Masonic lodges and other similar secret and absurd gatherings." Prozorovskii was to determine quietly whether masonic membership was increasing or decreasing.[19]

A report of an unauthorized book treating religious matters from the perspective of the schismatic Old Believers prompted Catherine's order of 13 April 1792 to search Novikov's Moscow residence and his provincial estate for the book, others like it, or the old-fashioned church letters in which it had been printed. In confiscating these articles, moreover, she directed Prince Prozorovskii, a former general notorious for his blunderbuss approach to civil affairs, to investigate the sources of Novikov's suspiciously substantial wealth.[20]

Moscow had long perturbed the Empress with its reputation for gullibility and chicanery, volubility and prodigality—all vices that some deluded Martinists might exploit for their own purposes. Catherine's suspicions of Novikov were also fed by the zealous efforts of Prince Prozorovskii, whose idea of a "comprehensive and immediate" investigation was to wait until the Empress's sixty-third birthday on 21 April 1792 before sending three officials to search Novikov's estate and bring him to Moscow for interrogation. Although this search party found neither the specific book nor type fonts in question, they discovered other prohibited books and several clandestinely printed masonic works. Besides, their surprise visit unhinged the ailing, recently widowered Novikov, who almost fainted "from extraordinary spasms" while they collected piles of masonic books and personal papers. In Moscow some twenty banned titles were turned up, so fifteen booksellers were arrested and their shops sealed. Rummaging through all these materials on 23–24 April, Prozorovskii wrote Catherine immediately, imploring the assistance of Stepan Sheshkovskii, the ancient senior operative of the Secret Branch, and urgently sent a company of hussars to convey Novikov to his Moscow residence, which stood conveniently close to the local premises of the Secret Branch. Almost overnight the search for an illegal book escalated into a political witchhunt.[21]

Indeed, when Prozorovskii interrogated Novikov for three hours on his arrival on 25 April and again the next day, he deduced that the suspect was dissembling in a crafty ruse to conceal his crimes behind a cloud of rhetoric. Novikov's verbal agility and the sheer volume of his papers made Prozorovskii importune Catherine anew for Sheshkovskii's special skills.[22]

These inflammatory reports reached Catherine on Wednesday morning, 28 April, whereupon she consulted Sheshkovskii about the questions to put to the suspect. Sheshkovskii was summoned to dinner three days later, by which time the Empress had directed Prozorovskii to pursue the investigation and prepare for a trial. The very next day, 2 May, when another report arrived from Prozorovskii she ordered it shown to Zubov before it went to Sheshkovskii. Maybe this was the testimony that Catherine told Zubov was devoid of political significance but which revealed Novikov to be "a very great rogue." In any event, the import of all this evidence persuaded Catherine that Prozorovskii was quite right in refusing Novikov a public trial, which was bound to be complicated, perhaps inconclusive, and provocative in political terms. "I applaud the conduct of Prince Prozorovskii, that he halted my order about judging Novikov," she noted on 9 May after dining again with Sheshkovskii, "and it is necessary to write, as I have already ordered this morning, to bring this rogue to Schlüsselburg."[23]

The following day her order went out to Prozorovskii to dispatch the suspect clandestinely, under heavy guard and by roundabout roads, to Schlüsselburg Fortress for interrogation by Sheshkovskii. Such extraordinary security attested to Catherine's stomach-churning apprehensions over the ramifications of the Novikov affair. Suspecting a conspiracy of fanatical "Martinists," well-financed and well-connected noblemen with ready access to the newly expanded media of public expression, the Empress sought to forestall Novikov's martyrdom (suicidal or otherwise: under interrogation one of his typesetters had tried to slit his own throat) and to squelch negative publicity by keeping his associates in the dark and silencing any imitators. Delivered to Schlüsselburg by the end of May, Novikov was treated as a nameless state criminal (though accompanied by his doctor and a manservant). He was incarcerated in the same casemate in which Ivan VI had perished almost twenty-eight years before.[24]

By the time Sheshkovskii confronted the hapless Novikov, he and Catherine had expanded her initial list of twelve questions to a grand total of fifty-seven. Her first concerns on reading Novikov's interrogation transcripts from Moscow had been to discern his motives in founding the "new sect or schism," and to pinpoint its participants, their disciples, and their contacts with foreign and Russian dignitaries. Their correspondence with the Prussian minister Wöllner piqued Catherine's curiosity, as did his interest in "G.D." (Grand Duke Paul). Linking Paul to the Prussian royal court redoubled the Empress's recent animosity toward Potsdam. Moreover, she was startled to learn that Paul still corresponded with Prince Alexander Kurakin, the Prussophile confidant she had banished to the provinces in 1782. On 26 May another secret packet of "Martinist papers" arrived from Prozorovskii among which was discovered the political explosive that blasted any possibility of mercy for Novikov.[25]

This was a note written by the architect and Moscow freemason Vasilii Bazhenov mentioning visits and gifts of masonic books to Paul, most recently in the winter of 1791–92. Paul, when shown this note by his mother, categorically denied any involvement with freemasonry, and Catherine acted as if she believed him. But she and Sheshkovskii fastened on the incident as evidence of the freemasons' wily endeavor to "entice" the Grand Duke into their nets. Twice Novikov was asked about Bazhenov's note, which he was shown. Nowhere in the proceedings was Paul named. Novikov's terrified remarks were coldly recorded in reference only to "a certain personage." Sensing the inquiry's import, the prisoner begged for mercy even before he answered. "Here, not saying anything more, as a perfect criminal in my true and heartfelt repentance and contrition, I prostrate myself at the feet of Her Imperial Majesty, as one who does not deserve any mercy or pardon, but who is guilty of any sort of punishment that the will of Her Imperial Majesty shall ordain for me." To Novikov's rambling response, which Sheshkovskii kept separate from the rest of his replies, the "inquisitor-general" cryptically retorted: "in this point he himself acknowledges himself to be a criminal."[26]

The interrogations were over by the last weeks of June, but then Catherine dawdled strangely before sealing the case. Her spirits were depressed, she told Count Esterhazy, envoy from the emigré French princes, by the rainy weather that prevented her daily walks and confined her to a chaise longue to ease the pain of a swollen calf. Fatigue and fever troubled her till the end of July. The decree sentencing Novikov to fifteen years in Schlüsselburg was ready for her signature by 14 July, yet only signed on 1 August. Such delay betokened doubts as well as conflicts in Catherine's mind. She could not overlook the absence of direct evidence to confirm her suspicions; her decree admitted as much. Perhaps she also suspected that Prozorovskii and Shesh-kovskii had "cooked" the testimony to prove "the harmful designs of this criminal and his associates," in the words of her decree, "infected with a spirit of insubordination and cupidity." Still she might wonder whether all the roots of the plot had been scotched. Certainly it was no matter for public discussion, so her decree sentencing Novikov was not published, as Radi-shchev's condemnation had been. It was quietly sent to Prozorovskii in Mos-cow, who was to call in Novikov's three main colleagues—the noblemen Prince Nikolai Trubetskoi, retired brigadier Ivan Lopukhin, and brigadier Ivan Tur-genev—for further questioning, notably on the point of Paul's alleged entice-ment. Even so, without waiting for their testimony the Empress prescribed banishment to the provinces, a sentence that was commuted for Lopukhin because of his aged father. Strangest of all, Bazhenov, author of the crucial note, was not even interviewed, possibly in deference to Paul. Catherine did not soon reward any of her subordinates in the case. Indeed, when Prozorov-skii visited court five months later the Empress sarcastically remarked on his expectation of reward, whereas Sheshkovskii's rumored elevation to the Sen-ate did not occur. On 20 May 1793, however, she quietly awarded Shesh-kovskii 10,000 rubles and 1,000 for his chancery. These gifts may not have been related to any particular case. In fact, the money may have been Sheshkovskii's retirement award, for he died almost exactly one year after-ward at age seventy-four. A month later his wife was granted 5,000 rubles for her late husband's service, a sum supplemented by 10,000 rubles at the end of August 1794.[27]

The secrecy surrounding the Novikov affair, together with its ambiguous disposition, left the public in some confusion. Nikolai Bantysh-Kamenskii, a well-connected noble official in the Moscow archives of the Collegium of Foreign Affairs, wrote in perplexity on 25 August 1792 to Prince Alexander

Kurakin, long-time friend of Paul and former associate of Novikov then living in exile on his Saratov estate:

> The case of Novikov is resolved; but a contradiction has come out: some say it is ordered for him to sit in a guarded place forever, others say for 15 years. His partners Ivan Volod. Lopukhin, Pr. Nikolai Trubetskoi, and Turgenev are exiled from the capital; but yesterday the first, for his elderly father, was granted a pardon; perhaps those others will not be punished for long, either. And will the maternal heart bear it! All that is ascribed to them in guilt, according to rumor, is correspondence with the Jacobins. If so, tell me now in good conscience, aren't these people blackhearted? We see what these Jacobins are doing in Paris. What good can one expect from acquaintance with them?[28]

These last sentiments would have won Catherine's assent. For when word of a new revolt in Paris on 30 July/10 August—a mob invaded the Tuileries, imprisoned the royal family, and abolished the monarchy—reached Tsarskoe Selo three weeks later, she declared hotly: "this is horrible!" Her outrage burned even hotter at the news that Paris mobs had overturned and destroyed statues of her two favorite French kings, Louis XIV and Henry IV.[29]

From this tension-filled and illness-ridden summer break Catherine returned to Petersburg later than usual on Wednesday afternoon, 1 September 1792. Within days she was startled by an inundation of the Neva six feet above normal, which fortunately subsided so swiftly that the streets were not submerged. Her mood swings mirrored the waters. On 9 September she ratified the treaty with Prussia and accompanied the foreign ministers to a French comedy that evening at the Hermitage Theater. Still she was angry all day and wept unaccountably after returning from the theater. Probably she was thinking of Potemkin, for she visited his horse-guards' palace the next day with her grandsons, Platon Zubov, Count Esterhazy, and Anna Protasova. The adults strolled in the gardens and inspected several rooms while the boys played with boats on the pond. The palace, which Catherine had taken over after Potemkin's death, she now officially renamed the Tauride Palace, a name retained ever since. Saddened by its deteriorating condition, the common fate of many buildings in damp and overcast Petersburg, she asked for estimates of the cost of renovation. "Everything there used to be charming," she murmured to Khrapovitskii, "but now everything is not right." With the entire court she returned to spend five days and nights there, 14–18 September. At the end of the month, on Potemkin's nameday, Catherine wept again in private before greeting her court clear-eyed. The first anniversary of his death, on 5 October 1792, she stayed quietly alone, apparently calm, in her rooms all day. Nobody could replace Potemkin in her eyes.[30]

Revolutionary Fears and Celebrations of Peace

In fact, the progress of the French Revolution had preoccupied the Empress at the same time that the Novikov affair vied for her attention. The day after her troops invaded Poland she assured Grimm of her resolve to let the French emigrés and the allied powers, Austria and Prussia, assault the Jacobins of Paris while she would "beat and defeat" those of Warsaw. The Russian invasion proceeded so smoothly, and King Stanislas's will to resist proved so ineffectual, that Russian ambassador Bulgakov stayed safely in Warsaw throughout the nine weeks of hostilities. In desperation, the king begged Catherine for a truce and for her grandson Konstantin to be named heir to the Polish crown. The Empress referred the matter to her council on 21 June, where it was rejected as a juvenile ploy to gain time. Besides, she had in mind for Konstantin a bigger and better throne, in Constantinople. Stanislas she told to cease fighting and accede to the Confederation of Targowica, which he finally did on 13 July. Overt resistance promptly ended. Meanwhile, the Empress solidified her international position by separate treaties with Austria (3/14 July) and Prussia (27 July/7 August), pacts ensuring that neither Berlin nor Vienna would aid the rebellious Poles. With her generous financial support King Frederick William II and Emperor Francis II would lead the "promenade to Paris." Informed that the Russian *chargé d'affaires* in Paris had arrived in The Hague on 5 June, Catherine and her council began preparing in late June for the expulsion of the despised Genet. On 19 July he was given eight days to leave, "with his head sunk in a hat of red wool," as she jibed to Grimm.[31]

Amid these preparations for war the Empress received a new granddaughter, Ol'ga Pavlovna, on 11 July. The baby did not delight her grandmother, fatigued and upset by two sleepless nights of waiting for another grand duchess. When cannon salutes signaled the birth, Catherine muttered to Khrapovitskii about all the noise for "a mere girl." When he congratulated her again the next morning she still regretted the surplus of grand duchesses: "too many maidens, all of them will not be married off, they will grow old as maidens." To Khrapovitskii's suggestion that she emulate Maria Theresa in using the marriages of daughters to secure alliances, she objected: "I do not make alliances that way." Her disapprobation was displayed anew a week later at the baby's baptism, when none of the customary promotions were made.[32]

Less than a month later, by contrast, Catherine confided to Grimm her high hopes for her eldest grandson: "My Alexander will be married, and in time crowned with all the ceremonies, all the solemnities and all possible public festivities." Her search for a suitable bride was already well advanced. The princesses of Baden Durlach, Louisa Augusta and Fredericka Dorothea, ages thirteen and eleven, were welcomed by Catherine on Sunday evening, 31 October 1792. Both were awarded the Order of St. Catherine the next day. They met Grand Duke Paul and his wife and sons a day later in Catherine's presence. On 3 November a splendid court reception greeted the deputies of the Polish Confederates with speeches, a state dinner, and in the evening a French comedy at the Hermitage Theater.[33] On this occasion John Parkinson, an Oxford don recently arrived in St. Petersburg with his aristocratic pupil, Edward Wilbraham-Bootle, observed Catherine closely:

Her Majesty sat with a very dignified and imperious air; supporting her right hand with her fan. She wore a star and I think a red rib-band. . . . Her manner was much more majestic than it was on Monday. On Sunday she appeared very gracious and condescending. . . . Count Osterman not venturing to depend on his memory held a copy of his oration in his hat, to which he was continually turning his eyes like the Dean of a College presenting a young man to his degree for the first time. Bootle says that while he was speaking the Empress smiled at her Minister's embarrassment and spoke to some person behind her.[34]

After following the allies' invasion of France closely in August and September 1792, the Empress had been taken aback by the French triumph at Valmy on 20 September and the allies' abject retreat. Of the 42,000 Prussian troops that invaded France, less than half returned, most of them sick. All her anxieties of the previous spring resurged. Miliotty, an Italian artist at court, was suspected of organizing a Jacobin Club and placed under surveillance. At the end of October, when some Petersburg ladies appeared at the English Club wearing "red Jacobin hats," all the clothing merchants of the capital were strictly forbidden, in Catherine's name, to sell such wares. At a court reception on 26 November celebrating the military order of St. George, the Empress was seen "to be agitated in a very unusual manner," an occurrence that rumor blamed on her fear of assassination. Toward the end of the year she felt ill and stayed in her rooms three days in a row. Still weak on 29 December, she exploded the next morning at Zubov's report on the Guards regiments. As usual, her ire did not last long. On 28 January 1793 she quietly conferred on Zubov, his father, and brothers the title of count of the Holy Roman Empire, procured from the Austrian ally that she adroitly kept out of the new partition of Poland. The Zubovs' place in the Russian aristocracy was thereby assured.[35]

The very next day Catherine's trepidation over the critical situation in France froze into mortification at news of Louis XVI's execution. The date of the deed—10/21 January 1793—plucked a fateful chord in her memory: Pugachev had been beheaded in Moscow the same day in 1775. Sick and sorrowful, the Empress took to her bed. On 1 February, the first day she had appeared in public for a week, official mourning was proclaimed for six weeks. She had already asked her council how to respond to the outrage. The councilors shared her "extreme horror and mortification" in advocating the policies adopted by Tsar Aleksei on the occasion of the execution of King Charles I of England: a total break in relations until the French monarchy was restored. The trade treaty of 1787 was suspended; no French vessels would be allowed in Russian waters, nor Russian vessels in French-controlled ports; all French nationals in Russia were given three weeks to leave, except for those who publicly took a prescribed oath forswearing the revolution; all Russians in France or French-controlled territories were to depart immediately, and no Russians would be authorized to visit France or maintain any contact with French citizens at home or abroad; the importation of French publications was banned; no French citizens might enter Russia for service or business unless they were attested by Russian consular representatives and swore the prescribed oath.

After unanimously endorsing this package of countermeasures, the councilors reiterated their alarm by spelling out the urgent need for immediate, diligent implementation of these prescriptions by the police, so as to assure strict surveillance of all French nationals in Russia, especially in both capitals, and to avoid any sizable assemblages of them anywhere. Furthermore, in the course of the discussion another ominous fact was raised: namely, "that almost all the Russian and noble youth is educated by the French, for the greater part of this nation are actually schoolmasters and schoolmistresses, who are found both in public schools and in private houses." And, one might have added, such teachers even instructed the Empress's grandchildren. Catherine's decree announcing the break with France was published on 8 February 1793, supplemented nine days later by her instructions to Bezborodko and Samoilov that banned the importation of French wares. Of some 1,500 French citizens in Russia, only 43 refused the new loyalty oath. In effect, Russia was already at war with revolutionary France. To Khrapovitskii the Empress excoriated the barbarities in Paris: "Equality is a monster, it wishes to be king."[36]

These anxieties assumed greater immediacy toward the end of February with appeals from Polish Confederates questioning her approval of any new partition. "I thought to enter Poland to a prepared confederation," she told Khrapovitskii with a bitter laugh before ordering Zubov to prepare an answer; "but instead of that my troops went to Warsaw and the confederation was opened in back of the army. They themselves did not keep their word, and now I am taking the Ukraine in recompense for my expenses and loss of people." Russia's annexation of Polish territory was proclaimed on 27 March 1793. Meanwhile, she worried about the arrival of the Count of Artois, brother of Louis XVI, fearful he might raise pretensions to Poland.[37]

On Tuesday, 8 March, the first day of Lent and Bezborodko's birthday, Catherine fell on her way to the bath and slid down fifteen steps. Chamberlain Zotov heard the noise and could hardly lift the fat and frightened Empress, who was bled as a precaution. Though she felt better the next day, rheumatism in her bruised knee tormented her ever after, whenever the weather changed. This new evidence of old age could hardly have cheered her on the eve of meeting the Count of Artois, the most resolute leader of the French emigré aristocracy and a potential successor to the monarchy that she hoped to reinstitute by international action. Neither he nor his hostess could have guessed that he would become Charles X thirty years later, or that he would be overthrown by another revolution in 1830 led by Lafayette.[38]

In Petersburg from 12 March to 15 April 1793, Artois and his companions were courted and coddled. Catherine greeted him at a magnificent reception arranged by Zubov on 13 March. The Russian court continued to wear mourning attire in memory of Louis XVI until 15 March, whereupon a new period of four weeks' mourning was initiated to commemorate the death of

Catherine's sole surviving brother, Prince Frederick August of Anhalt-Zerbst, her junior by five years. Artois's prospects suddenly looked more promising when word arrived of the signing in London on 14/25 March of Anglo-Russian commercial and political conventions aimed against France, which had declared war on Britain on 1/12 February. Lord Grenville, the British secretary of foreign affairs, was awarded a diamond solitaire worth 25,000 rubles and a snuffbox with Catherine's portrait. On 11 April the Empress prepared for Artois's departure by granting him a gold sword with a diamond solitaire and the inscription "With God for the King." Consecrated by the Metropolitan of Petersburg at the tomb of St. Alexander Nevskii and sprinkled with holy water, the gold sword symbolized Catherine's aspirations for his success. "M. d'Artois loves me like his mother," she trilled to Grimm after the count's departure for Reval to take ship for England; "the whole world is very satisfied with him; he is a prince who has an excellent heart, a very quick understanding, good sense; he willingly listens to good advice, and he will follow it, I am sure." Although she lamented the lack of a good general in Artois's entourage, she foresaw a fortunate future. "Misfortune is a great teacher, and, in truth, I think that Henry IV did not know any more than he does. Great affairs are achieved through four or five axioms: if he maintains these, he will achieve them." Just then a Russian squadron under Admiral Chichagov was fitting out to police the Baltic for French ships and French contraband, and to pressure Sweden and Denmark into joining the maritime blockade and economic embargo against France.[39]

Amid these festivities and preparations, however, Catherine's conscience was gnawed by private concerns about excessive expenditures—"from this very thing France has been ruined," she moaned to Khrapovitskii—and suspicions about Zubov's recent "promenades." The evening of 14 April she had Zotov watch where Zubov went after the farewell supper for Artois. Her chamberlain reported that the favorite had driven straight home. A restless loneliness seized the Empress as her sixty-fourth birthday approached. On 17 April she secretly arranged with Khrapovitskii to leave the Winter Palace after dinner for the Tauride Palace, whither she went after four P.M. Four days later, on Holy Thursday, her birthday was quietly celebrated. Back in the Winter Palace on 23 April, the day before Easter, she revisited the Tauride Palace on the 28th. Probably she was thinking of Potemkin as she made these moves.[40]

Certainly she was thinking of the succession. On 15 April, Khrapovitskii noted it was the day of Grand Duchess Natalia's death. He did not mention her unborn son, but the Empress could not have forgotten him, not with her fifteen-year-old grandson's anxiously anticipated bethrothal in prospect. His bride, Princess Louisa Augusta of Baden Durlach, recently turned fourteen, converted to Russian Orthodoxy on 9 May with the new name of Elizaveta Alekseevna. The couple were officially betrothed the next day. The Empress left town for Tsarskoe Selo on 12 May. Two months later she lauded Alexander's physical and moral education. "If he has a son, and he will likewise be educated for seven years by the same Englishwoman, then the legacy of the Russian throne is guaranteed for 100 years," she exulted to Khrapovitskii. "What a difference between his education and his father's." Alexander would soon be ready to rule (she secretly hoped).[41]

Usually this springtime change of residences hiked Catherine's spirits. Gloom greeted her instead: the deaths of General Mikhailo Krechetnikov in Poland on 10 May, four days after his elevation to count, and of Maria Naryshkina, an intimate friend since Catherine's early years in Russia and a year younger than she, on 28 May. Was the latter's older sister, Princess Natalia Shcherbatova, still alive? the Empress dolefully inquired. Dead more than a year was Khrapovitskii's whispered reply. At the end of May it was reported that the British had refused to let the Count of Artois land at Hull, citing legal threats from creditors. Catherine raged at what she regarded as a chicken-hearted excuse to mollify Prime Minister Pitt's domestic critics. The crusade against France showed signs of stumbling.[42]

No significant awards were made at the late June holidays, and on 1 July the Empress received another jolt: Count Bezborodko's resignation. He grumbled at being bypassed and demeaned in the conduct of Polish affairs. His main gripe was with Zubov, whom he did not name. But she knew. She talked Bezborodko out of resigning, sympathized with his faltering health—wounds on the legs, probably phlebitis—and granted four weeks' leave to visit his palace under construction in Moscow. Ill on 5 July, Catherine sorely missed Bezborodko the following weeks when she suddenly realized all the arrangements that must be made in his absence for the long postponed celebration of the Treaty of Jassy with the Turks.[43]

Platon Zubov stepped forth to assist her, using Bezborodko's draft of the manifesto that was issued on 12 July announcing the celebrations, now specified to include the newly annexed lands from Poland, to commence in both capitals on 2 September. He was handsomely rewarded before dinner on 23 July with a portrait of the Empress in diamonds (a gift only Orlov and Potemkin had enjoyed) and the Order of St. Andrew, while Arkadii Markov received the Order of St. Alexander Nevskii and Jakob Sievers, her ambassador in Poland, the Order of the Apostle Andrew. Two days later she signed decrees appointing Zubov to Potemkin's old post, governor-general of Ekaterinoslav guberniia and the Tauride. The young favorite "is flying high, despite his years and that not everything will be placed on one person," Zavadovskii remarked bitterly; "he is minister of all parts of the administration." Bezborodko returned on 4 August, still seething with resentment toward Zubov and Markov.[44]

Catherine brought her court back to the Tauride Palace in Petersburg on 16 August and, a week later, publicly reconfirmed the peace festivities for 2–15 September. The council approved her proposed "favors" on 25 August. It was the first great public spectacle staged without Potemkin's guidance. His successors—Zubov, Markov, and Samoilov—may have planned to dazzle the Empress with a spectacular affirmation of public acclaim. Or did she herself orchestrate it all behind the scenes?[45]

The festivities began early Friday morning, 2 September 1793, when 12,029 Guardsmen and other troops thronged around the Winter Palace. At ten o'clock the courtiers gathered, the gentlemen in dress uniforms, the ladies in Russian dresses. With trumpets and kettledrums two heralds then led a procession of court officials that preceded the Empress, who wore a small crown and the imperial mantle, with six chamberlains carrying her train, to the palace chapel for a service, blessing, and the singing of "We praise Thee God," accompanied by cannon salutes from the Admiralty and Peter and Paul fortresses and a thrice-repeated "running" fire from the troops. Church-bells clanged throughout the day. After a brief recessional the Empress reappeared in the gallery and seated herself on the throne, flanked by two tables covered with red velvet and golden gossamer on which were displayed the imperial regalia and the various awards to be presented. From an adjoining room the members of the Senate marched in, by pairs in order of seniority, and bowed three times before the Empress.[46] Procurator-General Alexander Samoilov then greeted her with a speech from the Senate "in the name of all the loyal-subject people":

MOST GRACIOUS MISTRESS!

More than thirty years have Russians [Rossy] been blessed through THEE; but today the triumphant Victrix will hear three times the voice of the Senate, the exclamations of the zealous people exalted through THEE. We loudly inquire of the universe: WHO is the Tsar as great as our Tsarina and Mother? And we do not hear of anyone even similar to THEE. More than all THOU alone hast gained the crown of unsullied glory, being meek, most merciful and beneficent to your own subjects, terrible only to foes, when to correct the laws of peace they compelled THEE to unsheath the sharp sword in defense of the fatherland and be punished for their deeds. Three wars from the countries of the South and the North have envy and malice directed at us, tormented by the felicity which has been created in THY days. Not depleted was THY valor fighting in many years: from THY spirit the leader took wisdom, the warrior fortitude: THOU guidest their hand, may they exalt THY name, may they glorify armed Russia with renowned victories on the seas and dry land; THY People knew neither wounds nor burdens therefrom, warring to be amazed at the peace. Sons of the Fatherland dance for joy! The foes are thrown down and will not arise; Our Mistress in recompense for labors has brilliantly triumphed! Arise PETER the First and be amazed at the second transformation of Russia! Behold the regiments that in new order and in a multitude CATHERINE II, ever victorious, leads out in Europe and Asia! behold the Baltic Fleet left by THEE in infancy, how by HER care it has grown up and filled out, destroys in near and far seas the water forces of our adversaries. Three parts of the world that for many centuries have been terrified by Turkey, broken by THINE own intense exploit, look with what wounds it has twice fallen under the arms of the valiant CATHERINE. THOU left defeated Azov, the Meotic and Euxine waters closed to Russia; the powerful hand of CATHERINE restored this city and many anew, tore off disgraceful reins, conquered the realm of Tauride, the ancient country of Tmutorakan, where a branch of the Russian Princes had reigned, drove from the face of the earth the rapacious clans of Tatars, eternally in enmity to our Fatherland: created a new fleet on the Black Sea, which in its birth is already a victor; and through it extended the limits of Russia into all ends of those waters; for on them HER creation rules. For the Persians, for the Greeks and for the Romans themselves, omnipotent in their time, the impenetrable Caucasus is opened for entry by the arms of Catherine and the power of Russia flows into it. . . .

THOU didst travel to foreign countries to acquire knowledge, deficient in the fatherland, our eyes see the tsars who come to CATHERINE the Second to contemplate HER deeds and to learn how to rule. The posterity of Greece, which has poured out its wisdom to all peoples, drinks now at the source of sciences in our fatherland.

Having delighted in the joy from these successes, honor the immortal soul overshadowed by so much glory of CATHERINE: for not one of the successors of THY throne has esteemed Thy memory so worthily as She.

AND THOU MOST AUGUST MONARCH, grant us your will, that on this triumphal day may triumph the perfect gratitude of THY people before THEE. THOU hast cherished it as the offspring of THY benefactions, which will not fit into a brief speech that fulfills all circumstances. Not one out of the subjects has shed drops of tears for something lost, whereas they poured out streams of them from joy, when THOU hast rewarded the merits of each, when both favors and pardons flowed by the millions. For this virtue of THY most merciful heart, for the indefatigable concerns for the common weal, we sought to proclaim THEE MOTHER of the Fatherland; according to the majesty of THY spirit, that THOU hast vanquished foes by arms, and through THINE OWN wisdom. returned the inheritance of Russia lost for centuries, glorified and increased the power of the fatherland, expanded the boundaries of it by the acquisition of extensive countries, settled by millions of people: to dedicate to THY forename the sobriquet GREAT.[47]

What was Catherine thinking during this flowery oration, the general tenor of which she must have known beforehand? Indeed, its recitation of the accomplishments of her reign repeated that published the same day in announcing twenty-one specific favors to the military and the populace at large. Russia's gains from Turkey and Poland were lauded, especially the powerful fortress of Kamenets-Podol'skii and 20,000 Polish troops transferred without a shot. In proclaiming public prayers for these successes, Catherine's manifesto exhorted pastors and teachers to spread true concepts of Orthodoxy and piety in opposition to superstition and errors that provoke "idleness and false reasoning under the name of false societies, that like actual schisms lead weak persons often into becoming the victim of self-interest, diverting them from service and other useful pursuits." Presumably these criticisms were aimed at the French Revolution and freemasonry. Before enumerating her favors, the Empress summoned all officials and estates to fulfill their duties.[48]

The proposal that Catherine assume the titles of Mother of the Fatherland and the Great put her in a quandary. She had already refused such honors several times. Did she blush at their reiteration now, or did she secretly relish the gesture in hopes of solidifying her claim to immortality, whatever the number of her remaining years? Her response, apparently prepared in advance, was announced by Vice-Chancellor Osterman. She thanked her subjects for their zeal, yet graciously avoided direct denial of their request.[49] Although she did not accept the proffered titles, observers on the spot could be forgiven for thinking she had done so. In any event, she proceeded to confer a plethora of awards. Estates with some 110,000 male serfs (or 11 million rubles in capital, Bezborodko estimated), on lands annexed mostly from Poland, were lavishly distributed to such worthies as Bezborodko (7,000 souls, producing an income of 40,000 rubles annually), whose pride was also rejuvenated with a jeweled olive branch for his hat valued at 25,000 rubles. No less than 111 crosses of St. Vladimir were handed out. All the troops were awarded medals and coinlike counters were tossed to the crowds in five squares around Petersburg. The festivities, which included a ball on 5 September for Grand Duchess Elizaveta's nameday, climaxed the evening of 15 September with a magnificent firework on Tsaritsyn Meadow.[50]

Barely two weeks later another, shorter and quieter, ceremony solemnized the marriage of Grand Duke Alexander and Grand Duchess Elizaveta. After the wedding festivities and dinner the Empress escorted her new granddaughter-in-law to her grandson's apartments. She certainly hoped that their first night alone together would not repeat her own, forty-eight years in the past. Paul almost did not attend the ceremony, alienated as he had become from mother, wife, and son alike; but his wife and lady-friend Nelidova talked him out of creating a public scandal. Soon thereafter Catherine called in La Harpe, Alexander's Swiss tutor, apparently in an attempt to enlist his assistance in persuading her grandson to endorse the exclusion of Paul from the succession. La Harpe refused.[51]

In the meantime the changing of the guard in Catherine's government continued. Khrapovitskii, her longtime assistant, was appointed to the Senate—and thenceforth ceased his close chronicle of Catherine's moods and conversations. The death on 22 September of Senior Courtmaster Ivan Elagin, another longtime intimate, cleared the way for the appointment a few weeks later of Bezborodko to that ceremonial post. At the Empress's urging he also made peace with Platon Zubov. She regretted Elagin's failure to finish his history of Russia, which she had patronized, whereas the writings about freemasonry that he left behind she branded "a farrago of nonsense, which proves that he had lost his mind."[52]

Sensational events in France perturbed the Russian court on 27 October with the proclamation of six weeks' mourning for Queen Marie Antoinette, guillotined three weeks before (5/16 October 1793). Catherine's ire sputtered for words strong enough to denounce the gang of "prosecutors, lawyers, and other scoundrels" who had perverted the teachings of the philosophes to rouse the rabble of Paris to "the most atrocious crimes," crimes they dared to call liberty instead of "a tyranny as cruel as it is absurd." Her last hope was that hunger and pestilence would sober the deranged multitude, and when the murderers of the king and queen had killed each other off, then one might hope for a change for the better.[53]

Contributing to Catherine's indisposition in late 1793 was a surprise wrangle with Princess Dashkova, president of the Imperial Academy of Sciences, over Yakov Kniazhnin's posthumously published play, *Vadim Novgorodskii*. Released by the Academy earlier that year, the play with its republican sentiments suddenly came to the Empress's attention just when she learned of Marie Antoinette's disgraceful demise. Catherine's ancient suspicions of Dashkova, her Vorontsov brothers, and their clients abruptly revived. Their patronage of the exiled Radishchev was recalled in the tongue-lashing that Catherine privately administered to Dashkova. The haughty princess, although she denied all knowledge of Kniazhnin's ideas, resented the allegations and suspected Zubov was behind the imperial ire. Following her brother Alexander's example, she requested and received two years' leave from state service and moved to Moscow the next spring. Such retirements of sulky aristocrats to benighted Moscow only inflamed Catherine's animus against the old capital and its indolent elite. The Senate ordered Kniazhnin's play destroyed for its "insolent and damaging utterances against the lawful sovereign power." On 11 November 1793 Governor-General Prozorovskii was directed to quietly trace and impound the 400 copies taken by merchant Ivan Glazunov for sale in Moscow. Only 160 copies could be found.[54]

Russian precautions against the French infection intensified in 1794. In March the sale of French calendars, which adopted the new revolutionary neoclassical chronology, was expressly prohibited in Moscow; in July three barrels of confiscated French vodka were turned into "punch" in Petersburg (i.e., dumped into the Neva) while other French wares were publicly burned. That same summer a French emigrant, one Montague, who had served in the Russian Black Sea fleet, was arrested as a French agent. Interrogated in Petersburg, he was accused of plotting to blow up the entire Black Sea squadron with secret chemical substances. He was condemned to be keel-hauled, but Catherine commuted this sentence to public defamation in Petersburg on 19 November 1794. Taken to the gallows, he lost his military rank and noble status. His sword was broken over his head before he was banished to convict labor in Siberia forever.[55]

Catherine's own outlook had darkened at the start of 1794. Russia's strait-ened finances prompted her order to Grimm not to buy any more European art; "I wish to pay my debts and to amass some money." An anonymous proposal that she send troops to the Rhine against the French invasion stirred an incredulous response: how could she spare troops so far away when the Turks, egged on by the British and the French, threatened to renew hostili-ties on her southwestern border? Yet Fedor Rostopchin, a new courtier who aspired to replace Khrapovitskii as a source of court gossip, believed the Empress herself avidly desired another war with the Turks, to complete the unconsummated "Greek Project." On 13 March she granted an official in the Collegium of Foreign Affairs 500 rubles for his historical account of diplomatic relations with the Crimea. Both Platon Zubov and Arkadii Markov were expected momentarily to be awarded the titles of prince and count of the Holy Roman Empire, which ambassador Cobenzl had delivered on 23 March, for their services in the recent peace. But in fact this did not happen for two years. Even so, Zubov in March moved into Potemkin's rooms in the Winter Palace; he was also accused of coveting the rank of field marshal and thirsting for the military glory that Potemkin had attained. Rostopchin reported fears for the security of the Russian share of Poland, which had become a haven for brigands and where the Russian troops were restive from going without pay for eight months. Catherine herself he thought "bored" with French affairs.[56]

Three gala court weddings at once with 165 guests on Thursday, 10 February 1794, reminded Catherine vividly of her advanced age. She found no joy the day before in celebrating the fiftieth anniversary of her arrival in Russia. Indeed, looking around she was shocked to count barely ten persons in Petersburg who could have witnessed her arrival. Only relics like the blind, decrepit Ivan Betskoi, who kept asking youngsters whether they had known Peter the Great; or the seventy-eight-year-old (actually seventy-four) Countess Anna Matiushkina, who danced at the weddings that day; the Naryshkins, or Ivan Shuvalov, who was too frail to leave his house, or her ancient chambermaid, who had forgotten everything: "Such in short are my contemporaries," she sighed to Grimm before switching briefly to German; "that is very strange: all the rest could be my children or children's children. That's how aged I am. There are families in which I know the fifth or sixth generation." All the same, she marvelled at the merriment she felt making faces like a five year old and playing silly games with her grandchildren.[57]

Other observers commented on the Empress's age and the likelihood that she could not last much longer. Before John Parkinson left Petersburg in March 1794 he collected some medical testimony about Catherine's condition, supposedly supplied by one of her court physicians:

> . . . the Empress was subject whenever she caught any little cold to certain obstructions from which the vigour of her constitution had hitherto been able to relieve her by means of a looseness. This lasted two days or thereabouts; she took nothing for it, but when it began to abate, made use of her diet I think of rice and milk. His opinion was that whenever Nature should at last prove too weak to make these efforts an Apoplexy or a dropsy capable of carrying her off in three days would be most probably the consequence. So that her death bids fair to be sudden.[58]

This prediction proved to be remarkably accurate. In March 1794, however, Catherine was reported to be planning to delay her annual migration to Tsarskoe Selo until June, so delighted was she with her walks in the gardens of the refurbished Tauride Palace.[59]

The Hydra of Jacobins in Warsaw

The spring of 1794 began with a new upheaval in Poland, a radical national rebellion that Tadeusz Kosciuszko, the patriotic military leader who had served in the American Revolution, launched in Cracow on 13/24 March. It spread to Warsaw on 6/17 April, Easter Thursday, when the rebels surprised the Russian garrison and seized the city in a bloody massacre. General Baron Igelstrom, the Russian plenipotentiary, barely managed to fight his way out of the city to the Prussian camp. He was recalled in disgrace. Fired by revolutionary rhetoric, the rebellious Poles "spoke with the highest contumely of the Empress and the King of Prussia, in the true Jacobin style calling the former Catherine Tyranne and the latter Guillaume Traitre." The Empress's portrait was pillaged from her Warsaw embassy by a mob, which "insulted it, stamped upon it, treated it with every indignity and tore it to pieces." More than 3,000 Russians were killed or captured, many of their corpses stripped. Disorders also erupted at Vilna in Lithuania and in neighboring Kurland. Postal service between Russia and Poland was temporarily cut.[60]

If Catherine scorned the initial actions as Jacobin posturing, she was already upset when the news arrived because of a surprise inundation of the Neva seven feet above normal that briefly engulfed Petersburg on the eve of her sixty-fifth birthday. General Count Nikolai Zubov and the Prince of Nassau-Siegen both galloped in from Poland to confirm the gravity of the situation there. She had Platon Zubov present the first reports of the "treacherous and perfidious" conspiracy to the council meeting at the Tauride Palace on Thursday morning, 20 April 1794, his sole appearance before that body. In Catherine's name he demanded their advice. His new role before the council reaffirmed his primacy among Catherine's top advisers, even as it thrust him into the maelstrom of crisis management. Was she completely confident the young man could hold his own with her aging councilors, or did she secretly worry that he might embarrass her or himself? Why did she no longer attend the council in person?[61]

It was obvious to all that things had gone badly awry. Both Bezborodko and Zavadovskii must have gloated inwardly over the arrogance and ineptitude of Zubov and Markov in thinking they could manage Poland and Prussia all by themselves. Still, the councilors all advocated an immediate military riposte against this "Hydra of Jacobins" on their doorstep. Russian troops in and around Poland should assemble in battle formation at once to support each other, guard against other surprises, and protect Russian borders. Since all assumed King Stanislas Poniatowski and other magnates were in league with the rebels, their estates in the newly ceded territories were sequestered, and the counterattacking Russian forces were to confiscate food and fodder on the way. Doubtful of the loyalty of the Polish units taken into Russian service after the second partition, the councilors urged that they be withdrawn to Russian territory, dispersed, and disarmed. The Poles would be shown no mercy. A bloodbath was in prospect. Soon there was talk of another, final partition that would expunge Poland from the map of Europe. To captain the campaign Catherine accepted Bezborodko's advice and prevailed on the venerable Field Marshal Count Rumiantsev-Zadunaiskii, who had been in ill favor and ill health since the Russo-Turkish war. She hoped his name alone would frighten the faint-hearted. Nevertheless, she cautiously limited his authority to the armies under Generals Saltykov and Suvorov.[62]

Russians were appalled at the public executions the rebels visited on prominent Russophile Poles. They were frightened, too, by the revolutionary government that proclaimed nationwide rebellion and called for emancipation and mobilization of the enserfed peasantry. Suspecting French machinations behind the Polish rebellion, the Empress on 26 April 1794 ordered Governor-General Passek in Belorussia to refuse entry to four Frenchmen who had reportedly crossed the Prussian border into Poland. Kosciuszko was alleged to have dispatched emissaries to Paris (or to have received French funds) and to be counting on revolts in Sweden, Denmark, Prussia, Austria, Hungary, and perhaps aid from Turkey as well. Reports of an abortive Jacobin coup in Naples and rumors of another in Genoa also reached Petersburg at this tense time, fanning the fears of widespread revolution.[63]

Such extreme fears started to fade within a month, however, when Russian forces trounced the ill-armed Polish rebels at Chelm on 29 May and recaptured Cracow by 4 June. Meanwhile, Frederick William II personally assumed command of the Prussian counterattack in concert with the Russian effort.[64]

Driving out to Tsarskoe Selo with Platon Zubov and other courtiers on Friday afternoon, 12 May, Catherine anticipated warmer weather as well as some relaxation from the Petersburg bustle. Neither awaited her. The summer of 1794 turned out to be "a frightful season," continually cold and rainy. Her old bones ached worse than ever. She returned to the Tauride Palace in Petersburg unusually early, on 11 August. But its dampness combined with a late summer chill to drive her back to the Winter Palace by the end of the month. Although an Indian summer set in after 8 September, it hardly helped her health or spirits. To Grimm she complained of a stiff neck on 4 September, an affliction that prevented turning her head to the left and which she blamed on her indignation against "the dumb Devil" Prussians for lifting their siege of Warsaw. The burdens of being Empress oppressed her more than ever, she groaned to Grimm: "In my position you have to read when you wish to write and to talk when you would like to read; you have to laugh when you feel like crying; twenty times interfere with twenty others; you have not time for a moment's thought, and nevertheless you have to be constantly ready to act without allowing yourself to feel lassitude, either of body or spirit; ill or well, it makes no difference, everything at once demands that you should attend to it on the spot."[65]

The news from France, coupled with the leisurely pace of Russo-Prussian operations against the Polish rebels, had kept the Empress preoccupied with politics throughout the summer. In revolutionary Paris the guillotines only slowed their bloody work after the downfall and execution of Robespierre on 25 July 1794 (10 Thermidor by the revolutionary calendar), but the allies lost ground in Flanders and Brabant. The allied maritime blockade produced little effect, even though Catherine reaffirmed on 14 June her ban on French goods. The Russian state financial deficit had ballooned to such dimensions that after six weeks' discussion in her council the Empress on 23 June 1794 announced the first hike in the head-tax since its imposition by Peter the Great seventy years before, a thirty percent increase that was publicly justified on grounds of recent inflation, greater circulation of money, and dictates of imperial defense. This was only one of several new or increased taxes that were projected to produce 12 million rubles of new revenue which, along with 20 million in new paper currency, would, it was hoped, cover the soaring internal and external debt. Cognizant of the dangers of tax increases in times of tension, Zavadovskii privately prayed they would be the last in his lifetime. They were not. To cushion the impact of the new levies, Catherine directed the Senate to arrange their collection partly in grain; but this had to be abandoned by early September because harvest failures in several guberniias delayed deliveries, so the amounts due were converted to a money-tax (something Zavadovskii had favored all along). In fact, the new levies, the spirits monopoly above all, did produce new revenue: nearly twenty percent more in 1795. The annual deficit was cut in half. In July the Empress also authorized the establishment of grain magazines in the Tauride region, in response to Governor-General Platon Zubov's report of shortages the previous year and remembering those of 1789.[66]

The same day that Catherine converted the tax in kind to a money-tax she announced several measures to strengthen the army and the fleet. Foremost was a new levy of five recruits per 500 census souls, the very level that the Empress herself had privately cited five years before as politically provocative. She now felt pressured to adopt the higher level in connection with the imminent occupation of more Polish territory and the international complications that were certain to follow. At the end of September she approved, too, another expensive military undertaking proposed by Platon Zubov in his role of General of Ordnance: the formation of five horse artillery companies with seventy cannon for an initial investment of 234,954 rubles and an annual upkeep of 115,552 rubles. This venture would expand eventually to twenty companies with 280 cannon. Platon Zubov was now presumed to command military expertise as well as political clout.[67]

By comparison, eight weeks earlier Catherine had given evidence of her devotion to Zubov in a distinctly minor matter. On 3 August an artillery sergeant-orderly sent by Zubov to Bezborodko with a packet of state papers had been stopped by a Petersburg police officer, beaten with a riding crop and fists, then dragged to the police station where he had been beaten again before being thrown into the street. This innocuous incident incited fury in the Empress, who on 10 August condemned the act as "particularly outrageous and insolent" for offending military honor and regulations, and for insulting both dignitaries the orderly had been serving. After the guilty party confessed in the presence of the Senior Policemaster, Catherine ordered Governor Ryleev to fire the offender, replace him, and send him to Procurator-General Samoilov for further (unspecified) orders. Though insignificant in itself, this altercation divulged Catherine's stressful state of mind in the summer of 1794 and her hypersensitivity to affairs involving Zubov's personal dignity. It may likewise hint at her awareness of the critical rumors about her favorite circulating in Petersburg, rumors that she could not allow to sap military morale in wartime.[68]

Field Marshal Rumiantsev's preparations to invade Poland, once his forces had cleared Lithuania and secured the Ukraine, compelled Catherine to consider the fate of the rump republic. A new partition was an obvious solution.

Moreover, it was urged by Bezborodko and Zavadovskii, and by Zubov too, whom the two veteran statesmen derisively labelled "the oracle" and "the universal minister" because of his overweening influence. Bezborodko grudgingly acknowledged Zubov's firmness in pushing for a military showdown; his younger brother Valerian had left court in mid-May to command a detachment in Poland. By mid-July the Empress agreed to sound Berlin on the prospect of partition, confident from leaks of secret Prussian correspondence that Frederick William II would settle for equal shares with Austria. It looked as if the headstrong king and his Prussians, stung by their defeat against France, would gain the honor of strangling the Warsaw Hydra. Indeed, the Prussian siege began by late July. Catherine and company were less than delighted with the prospect of Prussia winning Warsaw, whose imminent fall was reported by the ubiquitous Nassau-Siegen at the end of August. Hence the Empress's professed disappointment at the sudden lifting of the Prussian siege in early September rang hollow. She regretted that the Polish rebellion had not been quashed at the start, an omission blamed on the Prussians who, she complained to Grimm, had also ignored her predictions four years before of Louis XVI's fate. By October she knew that General Suvorov, a veritable whirlwind, had defeated a Polish contingent on the eastern border and was racing toward Warsaw. On 28 September/9 October another Russian force under General Ivan Fersen crumpled Kosciuszko's main army at Maciejowice, sixty kilometers southeast of Warsaw. Kosciuszko, the Polish "godlet" in some Russian eyes, was unhorsed, wounded in several places, captured, and dispatched to Petersburg where he arrived on 14 November 1794.[69]

Suvorov's "flying" corps reached Praga, the fortified suburb across the Vistula from Warsaw, on 18 October. His artfully prepared, devastatingly executed assault resulted in the infamous "massacre of Praga" on 24 October/ 4 November. This thunderous victory marked a vengeful end to the rebellion that in Russian eyes had begun with the massacre of 6/7 April—the "Warsaw Sicilian Vespers" according to Bezborodko. This time the rebellious capital surrendered unconditionally on 29 October/9 November 1794. Catherine, who received the news on 19 November, sent Suvorov a field marshal's baton. He arrested the revolutionary leaders including the king, disarmed their forces, and confiscated the royal regalia, archives, and library.[70]

Catherine's joy at this triumphant conclusion to the Polish revolt was tarnished, however, by grievous news: the gallant Valerian Zubov lost a leg to a Polish cannonball. The Empress was saddened by the misfortune of her favorite's young brother, whose bravery and resilience in undergoing amputation on the battlefield she trumpeted to Grimm. Furthermore, she awarded the wounded Zubov the Order of St. Andrew, a sable coat, and an annual pension of 12,000 rubles starting on 15 October. Fitted with a wooden leg, he reappeared at court on 8 February 1795. Soon he was appointed to head another Potemkin-style imperial enterprise: a Persian campaign.[71]

The victory in Poland was also undercut in Catherine's appreciation by a bout of illness, "a species of erysipelas in the head," she reported to Grimm, in late November and early December that kept her in bed or inactive, with little sleep and scant appetite, for almost two weeks. Finally she submitted to a blood-letting on 6 December for which Dr. Rogerson and two surgeon-assistants were granted rewards of 5,000 rubles. On 15 December she still complained of an earache, but looked forward to the evening's chamber concert. Perhaps the news from Poland helped her recovery. The full official account of Warsaw's surrender was delivered on 11 December by General Pavel Potemkin, who was promoted to general-in-chief at once. He died only months later.[72]

The new year opened with joy and sorrow in bewildering succession. On 1 January 1795 Catherine directed the Senate to provide Field Marshal Rumiantsev with a laudatory charter for suppressing the Polish rebellion and authorized a memorial monument on his estate or in the capital, whichever he chose. It was built in St. Petersburg. His officers were all awarded gold medals, the troops silver medals with the inscription "For toils and courage." Bezborodko was conciliated at the same time with a grant of 50,000 rubles and an annual pension for life of 10,000. A week later St. Petersburg celebrated the birth of Catherine's sixth granddaughter, Anna Pavlovna. The official announcement and christening on 14 January were followed two days later by another proclaiming the death of two-year-old Ol'ga Pavlovna the evening before, from a condition that had caused the infant to eat ravenously for many weeks. Terrible torments preceded the toddler's death. It was the first child Paul and Maria Fedorovna had lost, the first granddaughter Catherine had lost. The young grand duchess was buried at the Alexander Nevskii Monastery on 20 January 1795.[73]

The ban on importing French goods, especially wines, was loudly reaffirmed by the Empress on 3 February, four days before she signed a treaty of alliance and defense with Britain promising 10,000 infantry and 2,000 cavalry (or a subsidy of 500,000 rubles per year) if Britain were attacked, 12 ships with 708 cannon and 4,560 men if Russia were the victim. Ratified by St. Petersburg on 28 April, this pact represented an insurance policy in the event that Prussia objected to the settlement in Poland. Meanwhile, Russia consolidated its own position by annexing Kurland and Semigalia on 15 April and administering oaths of loyalty to the population of the newly established Minsk, Iziaslav, and Bratslav guberniias on 16 May. Voznesenskoe vicegerency and Podol' and Volyn guberniias were established on 13 June and 5 July, respectively. These territorial gains from the second and third partitions, which gave Russia a common border with Austria and Prussia, amounted to 376,200 square kilometers with a polyglot population of some six million. On 20 June, moreover, the Empress endorsed the sentences for the captive Polish rebel leaders recommended by the investigatory commission in Smolensk, sentences that resulted in exile for ten different groups. Kosciuszko, "my poor creature," Catherine chortled to Grimm, remained under house arrest in Petersburg, "quiet as a lamb." It was long rumored that King Stanislas Poniatowski would also be brought to the Russian capital, but he arrived only after abdicating at Grodno on 25 November 1795 (and died in Petersburg in 1798).[74]

In 1795 Catherine's annual sojourn at Tsarskoe Selo, from 17 May till 9 August, looked comfortably relaxed in contrast to the previous year's tribulations. Both her health and the weather improved. About the former she harbored some doubts, though, because on 17 July she hired an additional court physician, Professor Dr. Johann Christian Weltzien. With Zubov, other courtiers, and her grandchildren she took frequent strolls through the newly expanded palace buildings and gardens, and carriage rides through the park. As had become her habit in recent years, she did not go to Peterhof for the late June holidays. Nor did she make any promotions or awards on that occasion. Yet she sanctioned one odd innovation: a requiem on 26 June, eve of the Poltava celebration, in honor of Peter the Great and (wonder of wonders) of Peter Fedorovich, her husband and predecessor. That the latter was not designated Peter III suggested her ambivalent attitude. All the same, this was the first public reference to him in decades—and it was repeated the same day of the next year. It hinted that Catherine felt some guilty nostalgia toward her long-dead spouse and cousin, perhaps from the memories mobilized in the latest draft of her memoirs. Perhaps the memorial service was also intended to mollify Paul, for whose second son, Konstantin, she was just then completing the selection of a bride.[75]

On the international scene, moreover, affairs appeared to be tending toward peace and a return to stability. Her government's springtime apprehensions over Prussia's role in the Polish partition, now that Berlin had left the anti-French coalition by the Treaty of Basel of 4 April 1795, dissipated promptly as it became clear that Frederick William II would accept a three-way division of the rump including Austria. Although Catherine regretted the collapse of the coalition against France, she welcomed an interval of peace to clarify the settlement in Poland, where the king's abdication would set the stage for his country's extinction.[76]

In preparation for the final partition the Empress made amends on 19 August 1795 for her failure to make awards at the June holidays. From the lands in Poland she made colossal grants. First on the list was Platon Zubov with 13,199 souls. His grant overshadowed those to Rumiantsev (7,100 souls), Suvorov (6,900), and Bezborodko (4,981). Valerian Zubov received the castle of Ruhenthal in Kurland, estimated to produce an annual income of 18,000 thalers. Two other Zubov clients, Colonel Adrian Gribovskii, whom the Empress had just hired as a state secretary, and the Greek Altesti, were granted 653 and 535 souls, respectively. Dr. Rogerson was awarded 1,586 souls on choice properties in Minsk guberniia that were reckoned to yield more than 6,000 rubles a year. Count Esterhazy was also honored with 966 souls. Besides these prominent recipients, dozens of officers and their heirs were given a few hundred souls each in recompense for their own or their dead relatives' service against the Polish rebels. All told, lands with a total of more than 107,000 souls were distributed on this occasion.[77]

About Poland's fate Catherine admitted no remorse. Indeed, to Grimm on 16 September she boasted, like an early Pan-Slav ideologue, of not having taken "an inch" of ethnically Polish territory as distinct from the ancient Russian and Lithuanian lands that she felt justified in reuniting to the Great Russian core. The Poles merited no mercy, she declared: "venal, corrupt, liars, braggarts, oppressors, dreamers, they lease their own estates to be run by Jews, who suck blood from their subjects and give the lords very little: here in a word is the Poles' spitting image." Just then she felt relieved, too, by the return of Russian ships from the North Sea to the Baltic and with the launching on 11 September of a new ship of the line, the 74-gun *Elizaveta,* named for Grand Duke Alexander's wife. The military situation looked so benign that the new recruiting levy proclaimed on 8 October 1795 called for only one recruit per 500 souls, to begin on 1 November for completion by 15 January 1796.[78]

Within Russia neither "Jacobins" nor "Martinists" could be detected. When Count Aleksei Orlov-Chesmenskii forwarded from Moscow on 12 July 1795 an anonymous foreign letter that he implored Catherine not to unseal with her own hands—"for evil persons there are no limits"—she could have laughed at his concern. It proved to be merely a petition from a foreign merchant, she informed Orlov, whom she sent a snuffbox, remarking: "I would have sprinkled in the snuffbox tobacco that grows in my garden, some other of which I am not sniffing now, but I apprehend that it would dry out en route." His counteroffer of gift horses for her grandsons from his renowned stud farm brought a gracious acceptance with the proviso that he not provide any "head-breakers," and this time she sent him some tobacco. On 31 August, back in Petersburg, she calmly accepted the long anticipated news of Ivan Betskoi's death at age ninety-three. He had been one of her first acquaintances in Russia. Two days later she dispatched Count Golovkin to meet Princess Augusta Karolina of Sachsen-Saalfeld-Koburg with her three daughters, candidates for Konstantin's choice of a bride. They arrived safely in Petersburg on Saturday evening, 6 October 1795. Watching the three young princesses dismount from the carriage, the Empress is supposed to have singled out the youngest, Juliana Henrietta, who had just turned fourteen.[79]

Catherine loved matchmaking. It reminded her of her mother and her youth, but now she herself could call the tune. Besides, it was exhilarating to see how eager foreign houses were for a Russian connection, and to bemuse foreign visitors with the opulence of St. Petersburg, its glum grandeur made more majestic by her gift of granite embankments. On Sunday, 7 October, the Empress staged a splendid reception at the Winter Palace for Count Giulio de Litta, minister plenipotentiary from the Grandmaster of the Knights of Malta, before she awarded the three Koburg princesses decorations of the Order of St. Catherine. Bezborodko, the bachelor rake who considered himself an expert judge of feminine pulchritude, appraised all three as "very tolerable," but found fault with the faces of the older two while lauding the beauty of the youngest, who, however, he feared would soon grow fat. The Empress left the choice to Konstantin, who promptly endorsed her favorite. The decision had been made by 14 October, for the two sat together at dinner that day, and with Alexander and his wife they led the Polish minuet that opened the evening's ball. His formal proposal was made and accepted on 25 October; the festivities climaxed that same evening with a huge public promenade at the Winter Palace to which 5,655 persons were invited. The other Koburg princesses left Petersburg two days later for a night at Tsarskoe Selo and a visit to Gatchina before they headed homeward. They were showered with diamonds, and Catherine sent ahead a draft to pay the mother 60,000 rubles and her two other daughters 50,000 each on their return to Leipzig.[80]

After three months' language study and religious preparation, Princess Juliana converted to Orthodoxy on 2 February 1796 with the new name of Anna Fedorovna. She was also awarded a diamond solitaire ring for 20,000 rubles, six spicated diamonds for 11,000, and a diamond band for 15,000. Officially betrothed the next day, she and Konstantin were married on 15 February, two days later than planned because of her bout with fever and toothache. They moved into the Marble Palace, which the ghost of Grigorii Orlov was reputed to haunt, the same night. Despite all the splendor, the marriage proved miserable for both consorts.[81]

The Last Year

These expensive court entertainments came at an awkward time for Catherine in view of Russia's dangerously deteriorating finances. She privately acknowledged the excessive spending in an order of 22 December 1795 to the court office that demanded an explanation of its two million ruble debt since 1789 on an annual budget of three million. Six months earlier Bezborodko had privately complained that with revenues of 60 million rubles Russia was "incomparably poorer" than in 1784 with only 40 million. On the international scene both recent explosions—the French Revolution and the chaos in Poland—and the current financial and harvest crises in Britain, France, and Holland all underscored the political hazards of unchecked spending, profligate borrowing, and excessive emission of paper currency. Nonetheless, the Empress could not resist further rewards to her favorite Platon Zubov. He was finally awarded on 25 March 1796, the holiday of the Annunciation of the Virgin, the dignity of prince of the Holy Roman Empire—the same title bestowed on Potemkin. (Apparently Arkadii Markov was given his equally long awaited count's title a few weeks after Zubov.) How had she explained her three-year delay in conferring the title? Presumably she told Zubov she had been waiting for settlement of the Polish problem and for a propitious moment. Whatever her explanation, the day before her sixty-seventh birthday, 20 April 1796, she granted Zubov 100,000 rubles "in appreciation of his distinguished labors on behalf of the state service." His political potency appeared to rise even higher with the announcement in March of his brother Valerian's invasion of Persian territory along the Caspian, the opening wedge of a new "Oriental Project." When, moreover, Valerian Zubov swiftly seized Derbent in April and Baku by July, Catherine waxed jubilant at his rapid progress, which in two months had exceeded the gains of Peter the Great's costly Persian campaign in two years.[82]

The Zubovs' ascendancy displayed another dimension later that spring with Platon's appointment on 8 May to the new Committee to Extinguish State Debts and to Reaffirm State Credit, a small top-level body that seemed about to eclipse the State Council's jurisdiction over financial affairs. As if Zubov needed any more influence, on 19 July the Empress enlarged his role in military policy-making by entrusting to his care the Black Sea fleet and Admiralty with the right to make promotions up to the rank of lieutenant-captain. All these moves dramatized Zubov's extraordinary concentration of massive patronage and authority in the style of Potemkin. Solicitous of her favorite's favorable repute, Catherine crowed to Grimm on 11 May over the recall of Saxon diplomat Helbig, whose public criticism of the Russian court had long annoyed her. She would not have appreciated his subsequent book on Russian favorites, hers especially.[83]

Catherine had left Petersburg for Tsarskoe Selo on 16 May 1796, thereby missing by ten days a conflagration at the Galley Wharf and a terrible thunderstorm whose lightning bolts damaged the Winter Palace and the Hermitage. Privately she still criticized Peter the Great's choice of location for his new capital. While in the country she celebrated the birth of her third grandson, Nikolai Pavlovich (the future Nicholas I), on 25 June, delighting in his "giant" size, robust appetite, and rapid growth. He was christened on 6 July in a splendid ceremony. About this time Catherine allegedly sought Maria Fedorovna's signature on a document barring Paul from the throne. Incensed by her daughter-in-law's refusal, she later obtained, supposedly, Alexander's feigned agreement.[84]

Catherine's swollen, bleeding legs bothered her so much that she tried the remedy recommended by Colonel Lambro-Kachoni, a Greek client of Zubov's, to soak daily in seawater brought from near the island of Hogland. Dr. Rogerson's opposition to this unconventional treatment merely made her more certain of its "marvelous" effects. Her sight had also weakened such that she sometimes used a magnifying glass to read. Back in Petersburg by mid-August, the Empress welcomed a huge Swedish delegation (140 persons) headed by "Count Vasa," the regent Duke of Sudermania and brother of the late Gustavus III, and the uncrowned Gustavus Adolphus travelling as "Count Haga" (the name of his country estate). The Swedes were seeking the hand of Catherine's eldest granddaughter, Grand Duchess Alexandra Pavlovna.[85]

This match had been under discussion, fitfully, for more than a year. It had rattled around in Catherine's mind even longer, for she recalled Gustavus III's wish that his son (proclaimed illegitimate by Gustavus's own crazy mother) marry into the Russian imperial family. Hence the Empress had become furious when the regent arranged the young king's engagement to Princess Louisa Charlotta of Mecklenberg-Schwerin on 1/11 November 1795, the king's seventeenth birthday. Through blandishments, veiled threats, and multiple intrigues Catherine managed to dissolve the Mecklenberg match and coax both king and regent to Petersburg for the final arrangements. To ensure propriety of dress at court during the visit (Catherine jealously guarded the reputation of her court), she prohibited all ladies from wearing chemises or other *deshabille* except Grecian gowns. She received the Swedish delegation at the Hermitage on the evening of 15 August 1796. So excited and breathless was the Empress in meeting her young royal cousin, she botched the introductions of her own entourage, as she afterwards merrily admitted to Swedish ambassador Count Stedingk. "Count Haga" was introduced to Alexandra Pavlovna at once, the two leading the minuet that opened the evening's fancy dress ball. Contrary to her custom, Catherine stayed through the late night supper till midnight conversing gaily with each of her guests. Over the next three weeks daily entertainments and sightseeing visits regaled the Swedes. Senior Court-master Count Bezborodko hosted a magnificent dinner and ball on 28 August said to have cost him 40,000 rubles. Since he shared with the Empress obe-sity and phlebitis, he had a special ramp constructed to ease her entry into his Petersburg palace. Fatigued by the festivities, Catherine left after seven in the evening. Her granddaughter, though only thirteen, seemed charmed by her intended. The youngsters were given plenty of time and privacy to become acquainted. When Gustavus Adolphus made his formal proposal, the Empress sent a courier to Gatchina to inform the parents. Meanwhile, the alliance that the marriage would seal was busily negotiated with Osterman, Zubov, Bez-borodko, and Markov. Russia promised an annual subsidy of 300,000 rubles and back payments of 1,050,000 withheld since 1793.[86]

Catherine anxiously urged forward the marriage arrangements in hopes it could be consummated before winter. The formal betrothal she set for Thurs-day evening, 11 September 1796, at the Winter Palace. The single lingering point of dispute concerned the Empress's insistence on Swedish guarantees of her granddaughter's freedom to practice Russian Orthodoxy in Lutheran Swe-den, an issue the uncrowned king had posed on arrival. Devoted to his king-dom's established religion, Gustavus Adolphus contended that his queen should share his faith and scorned the "errors" of Orthodoxy, yet he orally as-sured the private practice of her own faith. To Catherine's protest that his ministers had already pledged the guarantees desired, the youthful monarch repudiated any such agreement, charging that the Empress had been misled by her own ministers. Suspicious, Catherine demanded the king make his pledge in writing. Gustavus Adolphus vacillated. To provide for a postpone-ment, the Empress obtained a ruling from the Holy Synod on 9 September that sanctioned a betrothal *in absentia* for a member of the imperial family.[87]

All these tensions came to a head the evening set for the formal betrothal. At the last moment the young king declined to appear, leaving the Empress and her court to wait vainly for several hours while Markov and Zubov rushed about in pursuit of a face-saving solution. According to Rostopchin, Cather-ine's public humiliation dealt her a mild stroke. This seems doubtful. Cer-tainly she was terribly shaken. Gossip maintained that rage goaded her into twice striking Markov with her scepter. That evening and night seemed far longer, she acknowledged ruefully, than the night before her seizure of power. By contrast, the official court register recorded no details of the scene, blankly noting that the crowd of courtiers assembled at six o'clock till past nine when they were sent home. Even though the Swedish delegation tarried in Peters-burg until noon on 20 September, agreement still evaded the negotiators. But the Empress did not yet concede failure. A shipload of gifts worth 141,785 ru-bles was dispatched with the Swedes, whose dire need for cash had usually made them compliant. In mid-October, Zavadovskii still forecast imminent agreement. It was not to be. Gustavus Adolphus, enthroned as Gustavus IV on 1/12 November 1796, wound up marrying Princess Fredericka Dorothea of Baden, younger sister of Grand Duchess Elizaveta Alekseevna who had supposedly shown him her portrait, on 31 October 1797. Grand Duchess Alexandra Pavlovna, the forgotten victim of the fiasco, was wed a year later to Joseph, Archduke Palatine of Hungary. Catherine knew neither of these outcomes.[88]

She survived the Swedes' departure by only six weeks. Besides the Swedish marriage fiasco, her last weeks of ruling witnessed other tensions. The upcoming campaign against the French invasion of northern Italy required a new, augmented recruiting levy of five recruits per 500 souls on 13 September to replace the 60,000 troops to be sent westward with Suvorov. Such a heavy levy foretold grumbling from lords and peasants alike. Three days later Catherine instructed the Senate to implement restrictions on the freedom of book publishing and the importation of foreign books, restrictions that gave birth to Russia's first comprehensive system of censorship. Three-man boards of censors were established at Petersburg, Moscow, Riga, Odessa, and on the Polish border. Only government presses or those expressly authorized by the Empress were allowed to remain in business; all others were prohibited. However reluctantly, Catherine opted for strict control of the newly expanded media of public expression that she had done so much to encourage. Busy with preparations for a new campaign against France, she was irked at the emigrés for having spent 8 million rubles in vain. To her old friend Grimm, driven back to Germany by the French Revolution, she sent 20,000 rubles for his losses and travel expenses to take on his new post of Russian consul at Hamburg. On 24 October four weeks' mourning was declared in commemoration of the death of the Dowager-Queen Juliane Marie of Denmark. A week later at a ball given by Grand Duke Alexander despite a new period of mourning for the deceased Queen of Portugal, the Empress commented sadly that the festivities were more like a German funeral than a ball with black spots and white gloves.[89]

On Wednesday morning, 5 November 1796, Catherine arose as usual at six o'clock, drank some black coffee, and sat down to write, which she did until nine. Sometime after nine chamberlain Zakhar Zotov, not having been summoned as anticipated, peeked in her bedroom and found nobody. In a closet adjacent he discovered the Empress on the floor. With two comrades Zotov tried to help her up, but she barely opened her eyes once before emitting a faint groan as she exhaled and lapsed into unconsciousness from which she never recovered. The strength of six men was required to drag her bulk into the bedroom, where she lay on the floor with eyes closed, snorting for breath, her belly writhing. Dr. Rogerson and other medical men were summoned to revive the Empress. Though they opened a vein in her arm, the blood barely seeped out, dark and thick. When neither emetics nor other powders, neither Spanish fly nor several clysters brought her around, chaplain Savva Isaevich was called. Fluid flowing from the mouth prevented her accepting Holy Communion, so around noon it was decided to administer the last rites with the arrival of Metropolitan Gavriil. This was done about three o'clock in the afternoon when, after the flow of blood slackened for a moment, Catherine was given communion and anointed with holy oil.[90]

Meanwhile, an officer and then Count Nikolai Zubov had been dispatched to Gatchina to apprise Paul of his mother's distress. Receiving the news at 3:45 P.M., Paul and Maria Fedorovna immediately drove to Petersburg, arriving at the Winter Palace at 8:25 in the evening. Falling to their knees at this "most shocking sight," the consorts kissed her hands in an effort to revive the prostrate Empress, with whom they stayed throughout the night. Joined by Alexander and Konstantin the next morning, Paul and his wife and the courtiers sadly witnessed further sufferings that left no hope for recovery. Around noon, therefore, Paul ordered Bezborodko and Samoilov to collect and seal the papers in the Empress's study, under the supervision of her grandsons, and to lock her study, delivering the key to him. If they found any testament, it was presumably destroyed at this moment. By five in the afternoon, with death imminent, the Empress was given the last rites. Her agony lasted almost to the end, according to the official account, her breathing obstructed by the flow of putrid dark fluid from the throat. She died at 9:45 P.M., having lived sixty-seven years, six months, and fifteen days. Sobbing, weeping, and wailing accompanied her last moments. Paul, Maria Fedorovna, and their children discharged their last duty by kissing the corpse.[91]

Paul immediately withdrew to an adjoining room to receive congratulations on his accession. His wife took charge of the arrangements for the body to be raised from the floor and placed on a table for the washing required by Orthodox custom. Dressed in suitable clothes, the corpse was placed on a bed used by the Empress and draped with a coverlet of gold silk brocade and gold gossamer. Paul then went to the court chapel, where Metropolitan Gavriil blessed him with the cross and sprinkled him with holy water. Procurator-General Samoilov thereupon read the manifesto proclaiming Catherine's death and Paul's accession. Maria Fedorovna was the first to take the oath of allegiance, embracing and kissing her spouse thrice on the lips and eyes. His sons, their wives, and his daughters followed suit. These ceremonies were completed by one A.M. Catherine's body was guarded by fourteen courtiers while clergy read the gospels in shifts.[92]

On Friday, 7 November 1796, the new Emperor celebrated his accession by granting awards: ranks, decorations, and money. An autopsy was conducted on the Empress's body the next day from eight in the morning till past one in the afternoon. The cause of death was determined to have been a cerebral stroke, with hemorrhages in two places from burst blood vessels, and two stones were found in the bile that had infiltrated the heart. At a church service on Sunday, 9 November, Paul promoted deacon Peter Pomorotsev to protodeacon for having first pronounced the imperial title, an act for which he was also awarded 1,000 rubles. The Emperor then accepted congratulations from all the foreign envoys and from a spokesman of the Petersburg merchantry. Numerous other awards were announced that day: Prince Nikolai Repnin and Count Nikolai Saltykov to field marshal, Vice-Chancellor Osterman to Reichs-Chancellor (a new designation reflecting Paul's Prussophile proclivities), and Senior Courtmaster Bezborodko to the first class, equivalent to field marshal. Metropolitan Gavriil was granted the Order of St. Andrew to wear on the neck, whereas Count Nikolai Zubov and General Nikolai Arkharov were both given Orders of St. Andrew.[93]

The first indication that Paul intended to redress old wrongs appeared the evening of 10 November when, after prayers at Catherine's corpse, he led the entire imperial family to the Great Chapel for a requiem in memory of his father, Peter III. On 15 November the Empress's body, now dressed in silver silk brocade with the imperial purple mantle under the legs, a fur-lined train twenty-two feet long, and all her decorations in place, was transferred to a splendid parade bed in the throne room for public display. Five days later a cortege of forty-two carriages conveyed Paul and his family, with a convoy of life hussars and horse-guards, to the Nevskii Monastery for a requiem over his father's newly unearthed casket. He is supposed to have insisted that everybody kiss his father's bones, an act the official description understandably omitted. Paul returned on the 25th to place a crown on the casket, the same day that Catherine's body was transferred to a casket in the Great Gallery that rested on an elevated structure surmounted by a circular tent of black velvet with silver fringe. On 2 December the Empress's casket was joined by that of her spouse. Paul led a solemn procession in subzero temperatures to the Nevskii Monastery, where his father's casket was loaded on a wheeled platform pulled by eight horses. Two and a half hours were required for this cortege, led by clergy and followed by the Emperor and courtiers (Aleksei Orlov among them), to make its way back across the city to the Winter Palace— "a procession the most grand, awful, and solemn, that could possibly be witnessed." Both caskets were interred on 5 December at the Peter and Paul Cathedral, side by side on a splendid catafalque, as cannon salutes reverberated in the frigid air.[94]

By the time Paul buried his mother and reburied his father he had already taken many measures to undo despised features of her thirty-four year reign. The recruiting levy of 13 September was countermanded on 10 November. Valerian Zubov was recalled from Persia and hostilities there suspended. Imprisoned Polish rebels including Kosciuszko, who was given 60,000 rubles, were released, as were the Russian noblemen dissidents Radishchev and Novikov. The roster of guberniias was pared down, Ekaterinoslav and the Tauride being prominent among those abolished. Several towns that marked Catherinean triumphs were renamed. The Zubovs were excluded from high office, but Paul reportedly offered Platon a glass of water when the latter fainted at his mistress's deathbed and, since he could no longer live in the palace, gave him a Petersburg house for 100,000 rubles. Within days of the succession Zubov's Greek minion Andrei Altesti was exiled to Kiev, where he was imprisoned for the duration of the reign. The Emperor brought his exiled friend Prince Alexander Kurakin back to court by 14 November, appointed him Vice-Chancellor, paid his debts of 150,000 rubles, and installed his younger brother, Aleksei, as procurator-general in place of Samoilov. Paul's own banished half-brother, Aleksei Bobrinskoi, was recalled from Reval and well received at court on 21 November when he was awarded the title of count. On only one point did the new Emperor endorse his predecessor's policies:

French-style clothing was publicly banned in both capitals and, a year later, he specifically prohibited ladies from appearing at court in the latest French coiffure, "à la guillotine"![95]

Catherine's death stunned other stalwarts of her regime. Bezborodko, who observed her final hours, and Zavadovskii, who did not, both mourned their benefactress long and deeply. Her demise scarcely left Field Marshal Rumiantsev time to lament, for he followed her to the grave on 8 December 1796. Foreigners commented copiously on her death, which had so often been falsely reported abroad in past years. For that very reason Sir James Harris, former ambassador to Petersburg, disbelieved the first press reports, only accepting when the fact was asserted "from so many quarters." His knowledge reflected the official court account: "The Empress was supposed to be writing; she remained so much longer than she usually did, shut up in her closet, that at last the door was opened. She was found nearly expiring of an apoplexy, her face upwards, and her legs close to the door, which, it was supposed she had attempted to open. Her Majesty continued to breathe for several hours, but no possibility of recovery existed from the beginning." An anonymous writer in Dodsley's *Annual Register* praised Catherine as "the most illustrious sovereign, after the exit of Frederick the Great, king of Prussia, on the theatre of Europe, for comprehension of mind, lofty ambition, courage, and perseverance in her designs, and the general influence of her policy and arms in the affairs of Europe." Comparing her favorably to Peter the Great, the same writer regretted "the love of glory that was her predominant passion; and the humane will regret that she pursued this through seas of blood: so that she will take her station in the temple of fame, among the great, not the good princes; and, in this speculative age, add to the odium of absolute monarchy, by displaying the miseries that flow from unbounded power, united with unbounded ambition."[96]

As regards popular reactions in Russia outside the imperial court and government circles, the diary of Ivan Tolchenov, a merchant from Dmitrov who was born in 1754 and lived till 1812 or later, recorded these impressions under "other memorable happenings" in 1796:

> November 6th happened the very most memorable day in the whole Russian Empire with the unexpected end of its possessor Catherine the Great, which followed from paralysis and the accession to the throne of Paul I. Soon thereafter not just daily, but one can say even hourly, there followed changes by the will of the new monarch both in the army as well as in the civil administration. And soon indeed we perceived the intemperate inconsistent character of the sovereign who had entered into the government, for he poured out both favors and punishments with excessive liberality, such that they followed without lawful rules and even through the uncustomary course of justice.
>
> Between the most august deceased mother and the enthroned son there had already long been estrangement and even hatred. And the late Catherine had had the intention upon her own death to give up the crown to her favorite grandson Alexander, for in her son she did not find the abilities to administer so extensive an empire, enlarged by her.

And this intention of hers she divulged to favored and trusted personages, but to fulfill it in fact she had postponed from time to time,
whereas swift and unexpected death left this plan without action and
fulfillment. For this and other reasons, the Paul I who appeared on the
throne rendered little duty of gratitude to the authoress of his days and
even openly showed his estrangement to her ashes and changed in haste
all her arrangements and plans and even the great among women and
the benefactress of millions was deprived of the customary gratitude
that is rendered to the simple, but to great mortals at death by laudatory speeches or odes or something else, for all the Russian poets did
not dare to issue anything to the public, knowing the ingratitude about
this of the stern monarch. On the contrary, Paul I rendered all the filial
ardor due his mother to his father Peter III and his rotted body, which
had been buried in 1762 in the Nevskii Monastery in the Annunciation
Church, he ordered taken out of the earth with the rotted casket and,
arranging a splendid catafalque with all imperial honors and attendants, to place in that church for a time, laying on the casket the crown
which Peter III, when alive, had not wished to bestow upon his own
head, this the zealous son bestowed for him on the casket against his
will. And even to such a laughable honor he extended his authority,
that whoever of the people happened to be in the Nevskii, each was
compelled to ascend into the church and to fall down unwillingly
before the putrescent finger of the former emperor.[97]

Particularly notable in Tolchenov's account is his calling her Catherine
the Great as a matter of course. Notwithstanding her efforts to postpone that
designation during her lifetime, it had become widely used informally among
the populace at large and also abroad. On her death it quickly assumed even
wider acceptance, perhaps partly in silent protest of Paul's ill-considered efforts to demean his mother. Within Russia only in the Soviet era after 1917
did this appellation incur official disdain and censorship. But among ordinary
Soviet citizens today she is still commonly called Catherine the Great, even
though they may be hard put to account for her greatness.

EPILOGUE

The Legend of Catherine the Great

Catherine was indeed a legend in her own time. Her markedly dualistic reputation—images of splendor contending with the specter of scandal—took shape even before she mounted the Russian throne. Her fame and notoriety grew throughout her long reign and, unleashed by her death, developed in divergent directions over different times and territories, cultures, and media of expression. Soon the legend assumed mythic proportions. Her checkered repute has proved long lasting, far reaching, and dynamically changeable. Like all authentic legends, Catherine has encompassed fact and fantasy, tradition and invention. The very tension among rival sets of images energized her enduring historical identity, an identity equally charged with power politics and sexual ones. Catherine's presumed hunger for power, fame, and love or sex—attributes more commonly applied to men in the late eighteenth century—set her apart from most past female sovereigns in Russia and Europe.[1] Her indelible identification with the expansive Russian Empire in an era of political consolidation amid revolutionary challenges brought in its train glorious affirmation and calumnious denial of her life and ideas and deeds. From the grave, her lifelong concern for her place in history cannot dodge constant questions, charges, and countercharges from individuals and groups.

The two sides of her renown may blend bewilderingly in unexpected places. Thus, some descendants of the Volga German immigrants who carried her name to remote middle America by founding the village of Catherine near Hays, Kansas, in 1876, still complain about the broken promises that lured their forebears to Catherinian Russia. The township of Catherine still survives, centered on the limestone St. Catherine's Catholic Church dedicated in 1893.[2] What would their compatriots who stayed behind in Katharinenstadt, later Baronsk then Marxstadt and now Marx, say about the Empress who in-

vited them to Russia? In the USSR she is presently ignored as an archaic embarrassment or attacked as a despotic foreign adventuress who mouthed enlightened phrases so as to mask tyrannous practices—"a Tartuffe [hypocrite]
in skirts," in Alexander Pushkin's withering phrase. Elsewhere her reputation
is associated less with politics and ideology, more with scandalous sexuality.
Just pronouncing her name may elicit leers or jeers.

Images of splendor, progress, and power—all carefully cultivated throughout Catherine's reign—assumed constancy and currency with her death. In
her native Germany laudatory accounts of her life immediately appeared, accounts that echoed the official propaganda of her reign. An anonymous German tract of 1796, translated into Russian and published in Moscow in 1801
(after Paul's downfall made it safe to mention his mother's name again), saw
in her passing "an event which in all Europe, in all known parts of the world,
will produce a more or less powerful feeling; in proportion to the relations
and actions of Her government upon the states of the whole world, in proportion to the recognition of the political greatness of Russia, and of Her com-
mandrix till now; *She who made one third of the eighteenth century her own
epoch.*" This was mere prelude to more vociferous praise in world-historical
terms:

> CATHERINE, from the thousand millions of people that inhabit the
> known earth, had more than a quarter part as her foes or friends. She
> possessed an expanse of earth twice as large as the whole of Europe,
> and half as large as the whole of Asia, a seventh part of the firm land
> of all the globe. Never did any state in the world, neither the Roman
> in the time of its greatest extension, nor the so called conquest of the
> world by Alexander, nor the Chinese Empire, never was any realm in
> universal history so colossal as that which submitted to the scepter of
> CATHERINE. Thus in tsarish majesty and might was she the first subject
> in the species of humanity. Irrefutable truth demands from the impar-
> tial Historian the attestation, that the force of Her Spirit in a life full
> of achievements was equal to the Greatness of Her dignity.[3]

Naturally, the contrast between Catherine's lengthy, successful reign and
the short, sorry tenures of Peter III and Paul I cemented her posthumous
claim to greatness. Princess Dashkova, her friend and sometime rival who
suffered persecution under Paul, lauded the Empress as greater than Peter
the Great, in whom she discerned a coarse, brutal tyrant absurdly overpraised
by those ignorant of Russian history and culture.[4]

Even critics conceded Catherine's greatness. "Whatever difference of opinion may be entertained with regard to the public and private character of the
late Empress of Russia," proclaimed an anonymous memorialist in Edinburgh in February 1797, "we conceive that there will be a general concur-
rence in this, that she was a most extraordinary woman." In rhetoric that
would sound familiar to American critics of Russia two centuries later, the
same author debunked Catherine's military conquests as bloodstained oppression that resulted in agricultural neglect, "and her dominions were only

manured with the blood of her subjects." Nevertheless, she was praised for
her self-control—"a perfect mistress of all her passions, even love itself"—
and lauded for her looks and good taste, her discrimination and intelligence:
"in short, such were the extraordinary talents of this woman, that her death
has suspended the plans of all the cabinets of Europe, and on a serious review of her character, we may exclaim with Doctor Johnson,

> She left a name at which the world grew pale,
> To paint a Moral, or adorn a Tale."[5]

As if in defense against an onslaught of sensationalist writings expected to
be unleashed by Catherine's death, another anonymous English obituary
plaintively predicted: "It is an invidious thing to pry, with too much curiosity, into the frailties of such a character. The severest critic has not been
able to charge her with anything unnatural, or, in her predicament, and situation, not easily forgiven." This fond hope was rudely punctured even before
it was printed. Within months of Catherine's burial, signed and unsigned
accounts circulated abroad charging her with many "unnatural" transgres-
sions. "No more MURDER'S lurid face / Th' insatiate Hag shall gloat with
drunken eye!" proclaimed Coleridge's "Ode to the departing year" at the end
of 1796. Euphemism and insinuation became favorite tools in the hands of
a coterie of critics who trampled Catherine's repute.[6]

Radical politics inspired some of the early attacks on Catherine's posthumous reputation and Russia's enlarged role in Europe. In France in 1802
there appeared, anonymously, the first printed rendition of Catherine's "Testament," a document whose existence and contents had been debated inside
Russia since the last years of her reign. Indeed, the Zubov brothers had artfully exploited their presumed knowledge of this document to rally aristocratic support for Paul's overthrow. Never published in Russia in full, this
forgery was the work of the radical writer and poet Pierre Sylvain Maréchal
(1750–1803), a member of the utopian communist "Conspiracy of Equals."
The "Testament" itself offers quite a positive picture of the Empress, who is
represented as imparting tender advice to her son (in ironic contrast to their
actual tension-laden relationship shortly before her death). Besides, by comparison with the "Testament of Peter the Great," a much more notorious
forgery that circulated widely in France at the turn of the eighteenth and
nineteenth centuries (and elsewhere to the mid-twentieth century), Catherine's "Testament" uttered no imperialistic threats to European freedom. The
benign thrust of the document conceals an ironic contrast with the Empress's
glorified triumphs in wars with Poland and Sweden, Turkey and Persia.
Nevertheless, the author's radical politics were revealed in sallies against
Napoleon and scorn for Voltaire's defense of absolutism. "The supposed
philosophes became worshippers of the good deeds of a woman who, perhaps,
was the most daring of all those who ever carried a crown." Predictably,
Catherine's reign was denounced as bloody and tyrannical. Although at least
three manuscript versions circulated in Russia, the tsarist censors prevented

its publication. In fact, the tsarist censorship steadfastly protected Catherine's positive image against radical and foreign attacks.[7] The official stance of the Soviet regime has been strikingly similar, albeit for quite different reasons.

Bestiality and Death

Scandalous stories had circulated underground in Russia during Catherine's lifetime, as evidenced by the pornographic poetry attributed to Ivan Barkov, the gossip collected by foreign diplomats and travelers, and the indictments of noble critics as diverse in their politics as Prince Mikhail Shcherbatov and Alexander Radishchev. Russian ribald "barracks" satire added coarser elements to the salacious underground stew by linking the Tauride Tour to Catherine's excessive appetite for sex:

> And, having taken his . . . into his hands
> He asked, having saluted:
> How many . . . a day
> Do you desire a supply report about?
>
> C. said:
> It is Lent, so it is a sin;
> I am tired from the road,
> Three will be sufficient![8]

Outside Russia lewd images of Catherine enjoyed easier access to public expression, notably in the British and French satirical prints that bespangled the "Ochakov Crisis" of 1791. These prints, it will be remembered, explicitly assaulted Catherine in crudely sexual terms, expatiating on her supposedly insatiable appetite for barnyard sex. Possibly these prints were the proximate seedbed for the most outrageous tale about her sexuality: the horse story.

For decades, perhaps centuries, this titillating tale was rarely written down, probably because it was considered too crude and offensive. Only in our cultured, enlightened, sexually "liberated" century has it received typographical fixation, as it were, and something like acceptance in polite discourse. Before discussing its evolution and meaning, here (for the innocent) is a recent, nonpornographic version:

> Catherine the Great of Russia had an immense sexual appetite which led to her death when a horse was lowered on her too suddenly.
>
> NOT TRUE.   The Empress suffered an attack of apoplexy at the age of sixty-seven, while sitting on her commode, and died in her bed two days later.
>
> Catherine reached the throne in 1762 by overthrowing her husband, Peter III, who died in prison not long after. With no husband to restrain her, the Empress amused herself with a steady stream of lovers during her thirty-four year reign, mostly handsome young army officers. French historians, writing with a clear anti-Russian bias, later

built these affairs into a legend of debauchery that has attached itself firmly to Catherine's memory. From the French writers came the story that her lovers were all examined by a palace doctor before being admitted to her bed, so great was her fear of venereal disease. Also French, and unconfirmed by any firsthand Russian sources, is the myth that the Empress employed a trusted aide to test and approve her choices. Two women of Catherine's court, Countess Bruce and Madame Protasova, have been unfairly labeled *les eprouveuses*—the testers.

While Catherine's sexual appetite was admittedly large, it did not require staff assistance, and it did *not* run to horses. An item of rumor lore often told to back up the legend of her death is equally false: that in the depths of the Kremlin Armory in Moscow sit the horseshoes worn by Catherine's favorite steed. According to the tale, they are made of pure silver, forged in the shape of hearts.[9]

For sober historians, the significance of this silly story resides less in its ridiculous particulars than in the time and manner of its appearance, its political-biographical-psychological slant, and its fascination for mass audiences of later generations. The precise moment of its appearance remains uncertain. It may well have circulated orally for a long time, swelling in the telling, before some intrepid soul committed it to paper. Possibly it arose outside Russia, although it might just as easily have sprung from Russian court gossip.

An intriguing possibility is a strange phrase in Gribovskii's memoirs. He refers to the imprisonment of one Passek in 1795 or 1796 with what might be a paraphrase of Catherine's words: "That the young people have used scholarship for evil purposes. A pasquinade found with him against her person and a steed. . . ." The association of prison with pornography recalls the case of John Cleland, who while in jail for debt wrote *Fanny Hill,* a work probably known in late eighteenth century Russia.[10]

Another apparent reference is contained in the most notorious Russian pornographic poem or song, *Luka Mudishchev* (Luka the Hose), often albeit mistakenly attributed to Ivan Barkov. Some versions contain a vague allusion to *Matiushka* Catherine in whose times Lev Mudishchev was promoted, thanks to his huge "machine." Even though the body of this poem, generally considered a product of the nineteenth century, does not refer further to Catherine, its stress on the fatal consequences of inordinate female sexual demands echoes, in psychological terms, the horse story. That is, *Luka* may be interpreted as an archetypical story of male/female sexual rivalry that could easily be transformed into the horse story simply by substituting a stallion for the gigantic genitalia of the legendary Luka. In any event, the denouement of most versions of the horse story is the same as that in *Luka:* death by penile impalement, the ultimate punishment for "unnatural" female sexual voracity.[11]

The biographical-psychological implications of the horse story appear aimed at undercutting Catherine's claims to greatness, by aggressively asserting that her primary motivation was unbridled sex, the excesses of which resulted in monstrous death. The symbolism of the horse may entail multiple meanings. By inversion, so to speak, the horse story debunks Catherine's well-attested equestrian skill as well as her political adroitness. We should remember how politically potent and popular with Catherine personally was Ericksen's 1765 portrait of the Empress atop Brilliant on the day of Peter III's surrender at Peterhof. The horse story depicts her in the reverse posture, with manifest intent to degrade. By the same token, the tale belongs to a tradition of male sexual fantasies, powerful yet ambivalent. According to testimony gathered by amateur sexologist Nancy Friday, these male fantasies focus on the apogee of a presumed female eagerness for vivid sex, with images of "women in heat, women hungry for sex, the woman out of control, who masturbates, takes another woman to bed, or even seduces the male—all these notions about the wantonness of women find ultimate expression if she will turn to a dog or a horse for sex. . . . Women like Catherine are Queens of Fantasy." Though Catherine has rarely been accused of dalliance with other women or dogs, the horse story has, to male minds, insistently underscored her sexual excess.[12]

For women, the story seems to hold a somewhat different fascination. If my own limited experience is any guide—twenty-two years of instructing male and female students, mostly undergraduates, at the University of Kansas over three decades of "sexual revolution," 1966–1988, and giving talks on Catherine at various institutions at home and abroad—females evince a franker appreciation of the tale than males. In bygone days it was only an occasional, invariably embarrassed male student that diffidently asked about the horse story. In recent years, however, female students are as likely to pose the question, often amid a mixed crowd of classmates. Ordinarily they do not seem shocked by the notion, as do most males. Even in the officially straitlaced Soviet society some women show the same interest, at least in private conversation. Indeed, the first female ever to mention it to me was a middle-aged matron I had just met casually, through a scuffle of our respective small children, in a Moscow park in 1971. Her inquiry made me blush, not her. She thought the matter both serious and amusing. Furthermore, according to another survey by Nancy Friday of female sexual fantasies, the horse story belongs to a broader category involving animals:

> With barnyard studs, imagined or not, it's all about the visible turn-on of the prick, the incredible size of it more than anything. Imagine something *that* big—which you reacted to with such fascination, at least the first time you saw it, even if you almost immediately glanced away with embarrassment—imagine that penetrating you! How can a woman look at a prick that big and not imagine it going into her?[13]

The frequent association of the horse story with Catherine's death also accents its undercut to her historical reputation. Because horses often symbolize power and mastery, depicting a horse as the agent of her demise dramatically denotes her loss of primacy as well as life. Male horses, whether stallions or geldings, may connote control vis-à-vis the common concept of the female as wilder and closer to nature. The common role of horses in funerals may suggest, too, the widely held conviction that Catherine's personality was essentially masculine: Catherine Le Grand as she was jokingly called at times. This judgment may apply to other female sovereigns: "The women who have accomplished works comparable to those of men are those exalted by the power of social institutions above all sexual differentiation," affirms Simone de Beauvoir. "Queen Isabella, Queen Elizabeth, Catherine the Great were neither male nor female—they were sovereigns. It is remarkable that their femininity, when socially abolished, should have no longer meant inferiority: the proportion of queens who had great reigns is infinitely above that of great kings." Besides, the mythical function of horses in conveying the dead to the "other world" is slyly perverted in the case of Catherine's monstrous death. There can be no doubt which world she will be consigned to.[14]

To conclude our discussion of this most scandalous story about Catherine, two very recent fictional accounts may be analyzed to portray the decline of restraint in treating the topic and its purported grip on the popular imagination. The pornographic romance of one Hillary Auteur (a pseudonym?), *The Courtesans: The Carnal Confessions of Catherine the Great* (1984), may represent a culmination of the sleazy stories about her. It recites the standard repertoire of pornographic fantasies, popularized by works such as *Fanny Hill,* loosely projected on Catherine's life as gleaned from her memoirs. Most of all, it is utterly obsessed with the horse story from first page to last, where a truly gross denouement is described. In between, Catherine's sexual awakening is tortuously traced.[15]

On a slightly more elevated plane, the neo-Freudian concept of polymorphous perversity takes on literary clothing in the fantastic fiction of Sasha Sokolov, *Palisandriia* (1985), where the hero imagines himself reincarnated in the form of the stallion that serviced Catherine in a *ménage à trois* with Potemkin. Accused of causing her death, the steed is sent to the glue factory, his hide turned into a pair of boots, his skeleton consigned to the St. Petersburg cattle grave as "Literary Footbridges," his skull buried in a field, his flesh ground into sausage. So ends the dreary epic of Catherine and the horse, rightly relegated to the sphere of literature of the absurd.[16]

The horse story epitomized only one variety of the scandal that dogged Catherine's posthumous repute. Russian revolutionary radicals joined with foreign critics of Russia to repeat the litany of charges against Catherine in campaigns to discredit the Romanov dynasty and Russian political prominence in Europe and Asia.[17] In camouflaged form, this critical tradition carried over into the Soviet period, accounting for the peculiar official neglect of Catherine that only recently shows signs of waning, especially in historical fiction.

Images on Stage and Screen, in Sculpture and Painting

If the historical treatments have oscillated between panegyrical and pornographic poles, fictional and artistic works attempted to bridge the polarity in dramatizing Catherine's personality and life for broader audiences. For example, a more complex portrayal found expression in *Catharina the Second,* a now forgotten work by a once popular nineteenth-century German play-

wright, Albert Lindner. This Shakespearean style tragedy in verse was brought
to New York City in October 1868 by Fanny Janauschek and "Her Company
of German Artists." Billed as "the eminent German tragedienne," the tem-
pestuous Czech actress (1830–1904) could not carry the play beyond three
performances in German, whereas the English translation remained scarcely
known.[18]

In relation to historical images of Catherine, Lindner's tragedy offers a
sympathetic view of her final days. The play's plot may be summarized as
follows. While arranging her granddaughter's betrothal to the future king of
Sweden, Catherine confronts a multilayered conspiracy by the regent of Sweden in cahoots with Princess Dashkova to inveigle Dmitri Yurieff, her long-
lost son by Potemkin, into assassinating the Empress in defense of Swedish
and European freedom against Russian imperialism. Yurieff, stamped at
birth with Peter III's physiognomy, grew up in France and is brought back
from revolutionary Paris disguised as a monk to become court chaplain at
Peterhof. Averse to violence, he vows to save Russia by wringing freedom
from Catherine through the power of faith alone. Placards appear proclaiming that Peter III is alive, so Catherine, who does not know Yurieff's true
identity, agrees to a midnight meeting at Schlüsselburg—supposedly to deliver
her testament, actually to flush out the conspirators. As the clock tolls midnight, Yurieff (knife in hand) denounces her reign in a twelve-point indictment including "Lust! Lust! The devil only knows / A name for it." He ends
this catalogue by evoking the spirit of her murdered husband as he tears off
his disguise. Catherine feigns bewilderment in an effort to clarify his identity,
then has her grenadiers shoot the impostor. In the last act Catherine learns
the details of the plot and Yurieff's identity. Thunderstruck by this revelation
and by the news of Bonaparte's defeat of her European allies, she proclaims Paul's accession, lies down beside Yurieff's coffin, and, donning a veil,
avows: "One more is added to my victories!" Throughout the drama Catherine is shown to be intelligent, shrewd, courageous, and far-sighted (although haunted by Peter III's memory).[19]

By contrast, George Bernard Shaw's *Great Catherine: A Thumbnail Sketch
of Russian Court Life in the XVIII Century (whom Glory still adores),* written and first performed in London in 1913, presented the Empress as a
witty woman of the world, determined to flout tiresome convention and find
gaiety amid court routine. In the playlet's second scene Catherine, bored with
the ceremony attendant on arising in the morning, complains comically to
Naryshkin about the scant rewards of her office:

> No: what maddens me about all this ceremony is that I am the only
> person in Russia who gets no fun out of my being Empress. You all
> glory in me: you bask in my smiles: you get titles and honors and
> favors from me: you are dazzled by my crown and my robes: you feel
> splendid when you have been admitted to my presence; and when I say
> a gracious word to you, you talk about it to everyone you meet for a
> week afterwards. But what do *I* get out of it? Nothing. [She throws
> herself into the chair. Naryshkin deprecates with a gesture; she hurls
> an emphatic repetition at him] Nothing!! I wear a crown until my neck

aches: I stand looking majestic until I am ready to drop: I have to smile at ugly old ambassadors and turn my back on young and handsome ones. Nobody gives me anything. When I was only an archduchess, the English ambassador used to give me money whenever I wanted it—or rather whenever he wanted to get anything out of my sacred predecessor Elizabeth [The Court bows to the ground]; but now that I am Empress he never gives me a kopek. When I have headaches and colics I envy the scullerymaids. And you are not a bit grateful to me for all my care of you, my work, my thought, my fatigue, my sufferings.[20]

Shaw's comic Catherine proved exceptionally attractive, inspiring several imitations in the new medium of films. Several early European film stars portrayed Catherine: Polish-born Pola Negri in Ernst Lubitsch's *Forbidden Paradise* (1924), Louise Dresser with Rudolph Valentino in Clarence Brown's *The Eagle* (1925), Paule Andral in Raymond Bernard's *Tarakanova* (1928), Elisabeth Bergner in Paul Czinner's *Catherine the Great* (1934), Marlene Dietrich in Josef von Sternberg's *The Scarlet Empress* (1934), and Suzy Prim in Fedor Ozep's *Tarakanova/Betrayal* (1938). After World War II American, British, and German films revived the theme with Tallulah Bankhead in *A Royal Scandal/Czarina* (1946), Hildegard Neff in the German language *Catherine of Russia* (1962), and most recently the film version of Shaw's play (1967) with Jeanne Moreau as Catherine, Peter O'Toole as the British officer, and Zero Mostel as Potemkin. Cameo roles as the Empress were played by Viveca Lindfors in *The Tempest* (1958) and by Bette Davis in *John Paul Jones* (1959). In a brief instructional film, *Catherine the Great: A Profile in Power* (1974), Zoe Caldwell portrays the Empress in an interview wherein her feminine wiles and genius for public relations seduce her interlocutor away from awkward subjects.[21]

Except for the "adipose epic" of *John Paul Jones,* where Bette Davis resented the director's insistence on "voracious sexual intensity," most of these films elaborated Shaw's comedic treatment, which reached its zenith on the American stage in Mae West's *Catherine Was Great.* Indeed, the superstar sex siren felt captivated by Catherine's persona. The novelty of the theme intrigued Mae West, dissatisfied as she was with the portrayals by Bergner and Dietrich in the 1934 films, both of which concentrated on Catherine's career before she seized the throne. Aware that the Dietrich film had been "an arty disaster" at the box-office, the American actress pursued another interpretation altogether. "Not the hollow-cheeked doll portrayed in the Von Sternberg film. I saw the Empress as a warm, gay, very sensual woman, and yet a monarch who was a skillful politician and master statesman." In four months, by September 1938, Mae West compiled a screenplay about Catherine's life as empress. She quickly filled in the historical background. "History, I found out, is almost anything that can happen—and most of our great heroes created more than they could use." Catherine herself was frankly characterized as "a *pre-incarnation* of myself: A Slavic-Germanic Diamond Lil [one of her most successful stage roles in 1928–29 and later], just as low in vivid sexuality, but on a higher plane of authority." Despite her manager's enthusiasm for the project, the Hollywood studios reacted frigidly. Mae West resolved to have it produced independently, but this proved impossible too. She therefore converted the material into a stage revue, whereas Lubitsch in 1946 produced a remake of his silent comic hit *Forbidden Paradise* starring Tallulah Bankhead at the huge salary of $125,000. "Although Miss Bankhead gave a good performance, as she always does," commented Mae West cattily, "still the picture didn't do well. It played the smaller drive-ins."[22]

By comparison, Mae West's reworked screenplay scored a surprising success. *Catherine Was Great,* "A Comedy in a Prologue and Three Acts by Mae West," opened in Philadelphia in July 1944 for three weeks before a financially lucrative Broadway run: 191 performances from 2 August 1944 through 13 January 1945. The opulently costumed, costly ($150,000) production by Mike Todd was, predictably, panned by the critics. "Mae West slips on the steppes . . . the siren of sex lies half-slain by her pen," groused one. "I'm afraid *Catherine Was Great* will be a bust," predicted another, "which will give Miss West one more than she needs." Producer Todd reportedly argued with the star to play the revue less seriously, but she was so wrapped up in the role that she declined his suggestions with an imperious "The Empress would never do that." Still, she did regret limiting herself to a single song, "Strong, Solid, and Sensational." The elaborate, heavily brocaded costumes tested her endurance; her seventy-pound train in the final scene required four men to lift gracefully.[23] All the same, she savored the triumph for herself and for her great forerunner:

> I was the Empress of all the Russias at last in a court of violence, seduction, intrigue and comedy—choosing my lovers not only for personal pleasure but also for the good of Russia. At the final curtain, the ovations I received from that jam-packed audience would have warmed the heart of Catherine II herself if she were looking down, or *up,* at the proceedings. When I was finally permitted to leave the stage after my curtain speech, I discovered unaccustomed tears in my eyes.

That curtain speech, incidentally, reiterated her snappy treatment of the subject: "Catherine was a great empress. She also had three hundred lovers. I did the best I could in a couple of hours" (confining herself to only fourteen, mostly muscular young Guardsmen). After her box-office triumph on Broadway "the Queen of Sex" took the show on tour to Baltimore, Washington, Boston, Chicago, St. Louis, Kansas City, and Columbus, Ohio.[24] Certainly her portrayal impressed more deeply than ever in the popular psyche Catherine's association with extravagant, theatrical sexuality.[25]

The several films about Catherine's life, however widely seen, achieved scant critical acclaim. Yet Josef von Sternberg's *The Scarlet Empress* did win some notoriety. Featuring Marlene Dietrich in an oddly asexual, wooden performance against a weirdly expressionist background, "a gorgeously mad tapestry of Catherine's Russia," the film had to be retitled because of the prior release of *Catherine the Great* with Elisabeth Bergner and dissatisfaction with a second title, *Her Regiment of Lovers.* Jinxed from the start, it was withheld eight months in hopes of a more propitious moment of release, but still flopped, compromising the director's reputation. Certainly the film ranks as one of the strangest ever made. Intended primarily as a comedy, the picture is memorable mostly for its bizarre sets and the eerie performance of Sam Jaffe as Grand Duke Peter, "a spidering white-haired idiot, prematurely senile yet trapped in the sexual obsessions of childhood." Denigrated though it was at the time, *The Scarlet Empress* later gained a following as a kind of cult classic.[26]

By comparison to the rather staid, censorship-wary films of the 1930s through 1960s, the two-part television presentation by Steve Allen and Jayne Meadows Allen in 1980 harked back to Mae West's unzipped interpretation, but in a new talk-show format. These two segments of the Allens' biographical-historical series, "Meeting of Minds," placed Catherine, drolly played by Mrs. Allen, in the distinguished company of Oliver Cromwell, the seventeenth-century English Puritan leader, and Daniel O'Connell, the nineteenth-century Irish liberator. The Empress was introduced grandly in words and gestures: "one of the most powerful women of European history," and "perhaps the most gossiped-about woman in history." Catherine enters the room third through doors flung open by two strapping young Guardsmen just after the moderator, Mr. Allen, has mentioned the "popular legends" about her love life in which she is "likened to the most lascivious, depraved women of ancient history." A wolf whistle accompanies her entry, which she accentuates by patting one Guardsman on the cheek, the other on the backside with her fan. After some banter about her lovers and her gifts to them the moderator abruptly, almost sheepishly, inquires "about the matter of bestiality—the—er—animal? Your death—"[27]

Catherine, whose role was largely researched by Mrs. Allen, scotches this salacious sally: "Death? I do not know what you mean. I was alone in my apartment—I was exhausted. I had had an exceptionally thrilling night in the arms of my young lover, and—went to sleep." To O'Connell's interjection that she is said to have perished with a smile on her face, Catherine giggles: "Wouldn't you?" This lively introduction soon turns into a conversation about Catherine's arrival in Russia and her "disastrous" marriage, with satirical asides about arranged marriages, political marriages, and contemporary nonmarriages. Soon the Empress declares that "the only *lasting* love I ever knew—my passion for *Russia* penetrated to the very marrow of my bones." Despite the poverty and squalor, the barbarism and ignorance, "and yet the sheer beauty—the *masculinity* of this untamed giant, Russia, kindled in me a love beyond any I would ever know. You gentlemen certainly understand what I mean." Later, in discussing the "unconsummated marriage that was pure hell," Catherine becomes almost tearful, explains her search for solace in books, and acidly excuses Paul's birth as done to order: "The prize bitch had done her duty and whelped a living son!" To Cromwell's bluff challenge that she murdered her husband, she heatedly retorts: "Sir, you presume. My huband was murdered in Ropsha. I was, at the time, in St. Petersburg." O'Connell's remark that the Orlovs assassinated Peter for her elicits a proud rejoinder: "it was for *Russia*." This segment of the show concludes, as it began, on a jocular note with the moderator's wish to hear more about "your great love affairs with Potemkin and—what were their names: Zaed . . . Zada . . . (Can't pronounce it)." In the best Mae Westian style Catherine cunningly comments: "Oh yes, Zavadovskii. Wonderful legs . . . and Lanskoi, and one who got away, what was his name?—oh, yes, Ermolov, and Zorich and Mamonov, who died so young, Rimskii and my darling Zubov—dear Zubey—"[28]

Part two of this segment of "Meeting of Minds" begins less boisterously with sober discussions of religion in politics, the place of established churches in society, and the issue of national expansion or imperialism versus nationalist self-determination or liberation. The question of revolution is also debated, with Catherine scorning the French monarchs for their ineptitude and defending the necessity of suppressing Pugachev. The sexual theme arises again later in the show with Catherine's candid confession that she was attracted by her lovers' physical charms. Cromwell and she then enter into a brief fiery fray over sex roles and public propriety. Asked how she could degrade herself by having Potemkin play the pimp, the Empress acerbically answers: "I had been degraded by men all my life. Now it was I who chose the time and the place." Cromwell rages that she surpasses "even the whore of *Babylon*." Undaunted, she coolly counterattacks in defense of female equality: "What *is* it that outrages you so, Cromwell? My sexual activity or my gender? An older *man* who shows favor to a young *woman* is treated as some paragon of *virility*. It's the image of an older *woman* in bed with a muscular young *man* that repulses you, is it not?"[29]

Toward the end of the episode the Empress is asked why she became known as "the Great" in contrast to other famous female sovereigns. She sidesteps the inquiry at first, then later points to territorial expansion as a standard of achievement and mentions the long hours she dedicated to the good of the realm. Finally, she contends in exasperation: "I wanted to be greater than any man." The moderator endorses this resolution, remarking: "You performed a man's job—and succeeded." Her riposte is immediate: "No. I performed a job and succeeded." At the close of the program she expresses surprise at the moderator's explanation of "Potemkin villages," a bit of ignorance quite out of character with her image of omniscient competence. And after his account of her "bizarre" funeral she calmly inquires, "Does the world remember my husband or am I still called 'Catherine the Great'?" So ends this modern television reinterpretation of Catherine, a revisionist view that considered critical issues raised by historians with current debates over sex roles and attitudes, all in the unstuffy aura of after-dinner repartee. A similarly positive portrayal was offered quite recently in Peter Ustinov's television series, wherein he interviews the Empress, imperiously and coquettishly played by Soviet actress Valentina Azovskaya. Probably as many persons watched these presentations as ever saw any of the plays or films about Catherine.[30] But then the video cassette and cable television booms of recent years have retrieved some of these films from obscurity for new generations of viewers.

In terms of graphic images, Catherine had consistently vetoed statues in her lifetime, just as she had refused the title of the Great. Potemkin placed a smallish statue of her by Fedot Shubin in the Tauride Palace, but Paul banished it on his accession. Another that Potemkin ordered cast in Berlin in the 1780s for Catherine's Tauride Tour had only arrived after her death and was erected in Ekaterinoslav in the nineteenth century. Paul's animus prolonged her own veto on statuary into the nineteenth century. At long last, on 24 November 1873, a splendid statue of her and her collaborators was unveiled in central St. Petersburg on the square between the Alexandrinskii Theater and the Public Library. Designed by M. O. Mikeshin and sculpted by M. A. Chizov and A. M. Opekushin, this complex still towers majestically over the noble square. Catherine stands in ceremonial robes, scepter in hand, on a rostral column around which stand and sit eight prominent personages representing different dimensions of her reign: field marshals Potemkin, Rumiantsev, and Suvorov; chancellor Bezborodko, Admiral Chichagov, philanthropist Betskoi, poet and official Derzhavin, and president of the Imperial Academy of Sciences Princess Dashkova. In bronze it is certainly the grandest depiction of the Empress and her regime, the more impressive for its location amid huge neoclassical buildings and abundant greenery. Catherine would have appreciated such a tasteful, yet grandiose, complex of statuary with her in the center.[31]

As concerned painted portraits, to be sure, the Empress had never stinted throughout her reign. She was undoubtedly the most frequently painted Russian sovereign till that time. Some 171 engraved frontal portraits were catalogued by 1887. Counting profiles and group pictures, prints and busts, medals and caricatures, the total at that time was 526, a figure that did not include those not engraved or all foreign-held representations. Toward the end of her life she sat for several portraits. Lampi and Borovikovskii both painted her in 1796; their compositions reflected a simpler vision in comparison to Levitskii's opulent rendition of Catherine as legislatrix in the early 1780s.[32]

In the pictorial realm it was only to be expected that photography would discover pornographic analogues to the horse story. A batch of photographs purportedly obtained from the Gatchina Palace reproduces frescoes or tapestries that show frisky satyrs copulating athletically with lush nymphs, and carved furniture portraying various sexual acts and organs. Catherine's connection with these artifacts is vigorously asserted, of course, with one amateur historian blithely maintaining that she may have posed as a model for the sexual activities depicted. Although two contradictory claims are advanced as to the provenance of these photographs, no shred of proof is offered for their authenticity. They might have been snapped in anybody's attic or clipped from some porno pulp.[33] If there is any historical value in such pornographic potboilers, it stems from their testimony to the extraordinarily durable potency of the two centuries' old lubricious images of Great Catherine, the Scarlet Empress. Would she have appreciated the publicity, however misguided, or scorned posterity's prurience? Perhaps both. Her legend lives on.

APPENDIX

Catherine's Love Notes
to Peter Zavadovskii, 1776-77*

1
Thank you, dearest; 150 kisses shall I joyfully give you each hour.

2
Petrusa, you laugh at me, yet I am out of my mind over you. I love your smile immemorably.

3
Petrusa dear, all will pass, except my passion for you.

4
It is resolved that, I do love and will love you, and am committed therein, yet you grieve over a trifle. At present I do not demand an answer, for I am going to get dressed, but after dinner I beg you to send word or bring it yourself. Priceless darling, Petrusa, do not grieve.

5
Petrusa, you leave me all alone just when one wishes to see him. Petrusa, Petrusa, come to me! My heart calls you. Petrusa, where are you? Where have you gone? The priceless hours pass without you. My darling, Petrusa, come soon! I wish to embrace you.

6
You, dearest, recollected what I begged you a hundred times to order your brother to come, and so now there is nothing for me to ask, for I long ago said I would be glad for his arrival.

Goodbye, friend of the heart, take a stroll for your health.

* Source: Russkii istoricheskii zhurnal, bk. 5 (1918), 244–57.

7

You are Vesuvius itself: when you least expect it an eruption appears; but no, never mind, I shall extinguish them with caresses. Petrusa dear!

8

Because of the great frost today I cannot be at the monastery for the examination; will you not consult with I[van] I[vanovich] [Betskoi] to postpone it till another day?

9

If I set out to do a commentary on your letter, then I would be late to the monastery for Mass. If you mourn, then know that I desire nothing in the world so much as to see you merry and content. Sweetheart, Petrusa!

10

Dearest, my legs are better; about the rest we shall talk it over, but I shall not give you cause to complain, for everything is as it has been.

11

My dear sir, it is unforgiveable that you permit your reason such considerations that embitter the soul; believe me for your own tranquility: truly, I do not deceive you, I love you with all my soul. Go out, be healthy and merry, live; you have no cause to sadden yourself and, please, do not write nonsense; for your honor I throw your letter into the fire.

12

I congratulate you, dearest, with the ribbon and return to you Stakelberg's letter; about the rest we beg you not to bother.

13

Go ahead, dear friend, and, talking about the matter, remember also that I too do not utter empty words when I swear to you that I love you more than all.

14

With extreme feeling I accept your affection! for myself I love you like a soul.

15

Petrusa, today's smart one, thank you for your note, and entering yesterday into your station I knew that it will pass, to mention the unpleasant I will not, only believe that not a single minute was I angry and that I love you like a soul.

16

Friend of the heart, in all ways I beg of you to calm your spirit; it is necessary and needful in order that in both of us thoughts be settled; I am very sorry that you are ailing.

17

Petrushinka, I am yearning; those dear hours have come which I spend with you; will you be coming to me, or are you not able; my darling, let me know. There is a big dinner at Ct. Ostermann's. I love you and shall not cease loving. Write at least how you are.

18

Dearest, my dear friend, our love is equal; I promise you willingly, while I am alive, not to part with you, for this desire also is properly mine. I am healthy, sweetheart Petrusinka.

19

My darling, my affection is always the same; I love you like a soul; I slept overly much and from that my head aches; the leg, it seems, is far better than yesterday. Goodbye, dear little darling.

20

Dearest, aside from affection alone, in answer to your letter I have nothing to declare to you; I see that I am loved by you, and I beg you to believe that I also love you.

21

You end the postscript thus: love aggrieved; but, my darling, love by means of me I do not consider aggrieved, for I am not guilty before you in thoughts, but I love you fervently heart and soul.

22

Dearest, thank you for the most affectionate little letter; I am better; I love you mutually in soul.

23

My advice is—stay with me; 2) believe it when I say something; 3) do not quarrel hourly about trifles; 4) reject hypochondriac thoughts and replace them with amusing ones; 5) Conclusion: all this feeds love, which without amusement is dead, like faith without kind deeds.

There's your answer.

24

Petrusa, you have gone out of your mind! What nonsense! Where will you go? I feel nothing except affection; I show you nothing except some affection; and yet here are your conclusions! How well you use logic! Petrusa, you are unjust in regard to me; I do not seek causes to become angry, and indeed I am not angry by nature, even the little irascibility in me changes with one glance from you. Dear little darling, truly you jest. What do you lock yourself in the room for? Truly hypochondria is good for nothing. Give me back my dear Petrusa, do not lock him away: me loves the dark-haired man; but leave the wrathful master home. Darling, if you do not wish to be deemed mean, then come with a caress.

25

Petrusa, dear, I coughed less tonight than in the last ones, now occasionally after a strong sweat. Darling, keep healthy and love us at least a little, if a lot is not possible. However, it is your choice, but I love you as strongly as today's wind was rich in snow.

26

You are capricious, Petrinka, I beg you to remember the point from which we set out, the time when we came back from Moscow, and compare it with the present and then judge about the future, also remember the related circumstances too and from that draw the conclusion that my aspirations are essentially in yours and my favor. Divert me with both a merry and an affectionate face, which will encouragize me to guide everything to the desired position. The letters I shall read, and then I shall say how it will be. You jest, Petrinka: you remember only the bad alone, but the good you do not mention so easily.

27

Peter Vasil'evich, from three or four thousand souls of your choice in Belorussia and in the Ukraine, plus fifty thousand rubles in the present year and thirty thousand rubles in the future year with a silver service for 16 persons, I hope this will repair the station of your house. Incidentally, as pertains to living in the district, you know that I advised this to you more for promenades and dissipation than from any other view. Your return depends on you every hour and rest assured that my friendship will remain with you and yours irrevocably for centuries.

28

Petrusha, I do not betray, rest assured and I beg you, do me the kindness, believe that I do not lie when I say that I love you. Think to yourself: do I possess the selfishness to assure you about that which I do not feel? I confess, it is miserable to bear reproach and distrustfulness, for neither the one nor the other is just, and oppresses passion, robbing it of freedom and turning even its display into sham pretense. Think to yourself: just what is my position. For God's sake, lead us both out of such painful circumstances, turn your distrustfulness into belief and calm your spirit. You yourself will see that I love you, and love ardently. The less doubt you show me, you yourself recall, then the more content you will be with me and my love.

29

The passion which all your letter shows cannot be other than pleasant to me. Had you thought as much about despotism as I have, you would not mention it much. Secrets, I repeat, I do not keep from you. The suspicion about Popov, I confess that I laughed, for your sensitivity in this instance is really delirium itself. Believe, Petrusha, that I love you fervently, and in nowise and nothing do I deceive you. Calm your spirit. You are precious to me.

30

Be kind, darling, how have I offended you such that you wept all night? It seems that yesterday we did not part at all sadly. Dear friend, of course there is some kind of misunderstanding. If it is that Betskoi summoned you to sit on the Council, well you will stay with me besides. My dear sir, for God's sake do not weep! I do not understand why you cannot look at me without tears. Would I desire to see you in sorrow. If not for the damn painter, then I would have learned in the morning that you did not go out, and would have hastened to find out your sadness; but he kept me from nine till two o'clock. Petrusha, my darling, with impatience I shall await the evening, in order to see you, alas, catching sight of my caress, you will see how precious you are to me. Sweetheart, I do not know, really, what to do to give you comfort.

31

My dear sir, sweetheart, for God's sake I beg you not to grieve. I certainly do not have the slightest vexation about you; I love you as a soul, and I am not inclined to part with you at all; do not ever go out of my room without reconciling with me and without a caress; that saddens me and you too; and thus is my anguish increased.

32

Petrusa, your tears are incomprehensible to me. If you feel the need for it or if it will be a relief for you to unburden yourself to someone, then unburden yourself to your friend, perhaps he will bring relief to your station, but only such that he, the same as you, proceed discreetly. My letters I beg you not to show. I love you, love to be with you. As often as possible I am only with you, but Majesty, I confess, interferes a lot. Dear little darling, calm yourself! I desire to cause you satisfaction, not tears.

33

Petrusa, in your ears a cry of falsehood has taken root, for you do not enter into my station at all. I have set myself the rule to be assiduous to state affairs, to lose the least time possible, but whereas a time of relaxation is absolutely necessary for life and health, so these hours are dedicated to you, and the time remaining belongs not to me, but to the Empire, and if I do not use this time as I ought to, then in me will take root against myself and others my own indignation, dissatisfaction, and *mauvaise humeur* from the feeling that I am spending time in idleness and not as I ought to. Ask Pr[ince] Or[lov] whether I have not been this way long since. Yet you immediately cry out and blame it on lack of affection. It is not from that, but from an orderly division of time between state affairs and you. See for yourself, what other diversion do I have except strolling. This I must do for health.

34

Dearest darling, Petrusa, your ravings I received and see and feel with what love they are written; I love you fervently, all else will follow from this. I am extremely content with your heart and soul; would I really be unjust? At the first occasion I shall pay you with love; the rest will not depart and will not pass you by, but forced marches are not apt now, for without need they exhaust more than the good they bring. Favorite little lord, to the rest I do not answer, for we are fasting and matins have begun. I see what your dream was, and am sorry about it, but what for I shall say. Goodbye, Petrusa darling.

35

Petrushinka, I rejoice that you have been healed by my little pillows, and if my caress facilitates your health, then you will never be sick. Dear little darling, you have no fault before me; stretch out your arms, I shall embrace you. Being dear, as you are, you have no cause to change yourself. I am extraordinarily contented with you and hour by hour honor you on par with the love that will be with you irrevocably. Dearest, dear darling, you are born for me, and our feelings for the most part, and especially in endearment are essentially the same; your soul when it flies toward me, then it is met midway enroute from my [side].

36

My dear sir-darling, I arose later than usual and, being exercised by you in spirit and not thinking at all that you were upset, I did not come to you, but calmly sat down to write. For God's own sake, I beg you, do not set out with a lively imagination into fanciful tsardoms; it is not I who has hardened, not I who is hardening, I love and respect you on the same level as before, and my upset yesterday stemmed from nothing else but that, it seemed to me, you had changed your manner of treating me and you sit in deep silence with me for hours, which your pleasant discourses had decorated before this. Amiable Petrusa, I embrace you a hundredfold; if you love me, you will not start grieving.

37

Petrusinka darling, with this I send you the field marshal's letter. The Grand Duke was so glad that he will come that he told me that everything is being prepared so well and so swiftly to his satisfaction that he considers it all a special good fortune. Petrusa, as if it is easy that I have not seen you for three days. I wander about your little windows, on the off chance you will glance out, and God knows how many times a day I go past. Let me have Petrusa! Where is he, the darling? Will your ailment be long, but the doctor says there is no fever.

38

Little sweetheart, for the most kind and most affectionate little letter I kiss you a hundredfold and press you to me. I arose with a headache and because of the bad weather I set out to walk about the hall during the watering, when I unexpectedly found Levshina, Alimova and both nightengales Barshchev and Nelidov, and a little later, when the rain passed, we set out along the boards of the sledding hills and returned home. My darling, I completely reciprocate your amiable madness, myself I love you immemorably. And how could it not be so? You feed my passion heart and soul; your tenderness and sensitivity are utterly incomparable. Dear little angel, my friend, Petrusa, I love you as a soul, my beauty, and shall love you a century; only do not change yourself, dearest.

39

In vain do you weep, in vain is repentance too. You did not grieve me, I forgot it all long ago and do not reproach; but for us both is needed a restoration of spiritual peace! I have been suffering on par with you for three months, torturing myself and expecting relief from reason, but not having found it I am handing it over to time. I will talk to Prince Gr[igorii] A[leksandrovich] [Potemkin]. About your honesty I do not doubt; you know the inclination of my soul as well. Time alone can do what is not in your and my power. I beg you, calm yourself in spirit and body; I want the same for myself as well.

40

I thank you, dearest, for the affectionate letter. Your feelings, really, correspond to mine; I do not love anyone on par with you; your love is a comfort to my soul; I love you and shall love you eternally and have just as much friendship for you and I see how much you are also fervently attached to me, from all your actions. I shall come to you after dinner, but Prince Or[lov] is not here. I have sent to ask about him. My little darling, God sees that I pay you with fervent and impassioned feeling; goodbye, I embrace you, I am going to get dressed.

41

I could have written a whole dissertation on the legislative postscript received by me; from it I see unsoftening casuistic pride; you have been weeping about trifles, yet nobody seeks offense anywhere with a torch in hand. A prophecy will disappear by itself when it is founded not on far-sighted healthy consideration, but on impassioned empty-thinking imagination alone. Since you extend your hand and heart, so I pardon you your childish weaknesses and set your repentance and interpret it in favor of love. You tried yesterday, but I knew beforehand that you could not be without me. The Lord does not judge anyone, for neither I nor anyone else, I expect, is guilty before you; you impose God's judgment on me, yet I say: God be with you; you yourself know not what you do.

42

Neither old nor new nor any crimes against you, dearest, do I know, and you are in all ways worthy to be loved; you ought not have regret about any matter in the world. Before you I have no guilt in actual fact up to this time. Comforting you, I followed my own inclination, which endured much distrust; to pretend to be affectionate does nothing for me—affection was inborn in me. For both of us it is most fitting of all for mutual agreement to avoid every kind of disputes, quarrels, and irrelevant alarms that harm health, lead the mind out of its natural and proper position. I am ending from an apprehension that this not be taken for irrelevant moralizing.

43

Petrusa, for God's own sake I beg you, do not take every trifle to heart; yourself and me will sit down, dearest, and your grief will go away. Do not respond, dear darling, to this letter, so as not to increase mutual sensitivity, and rest assured that I love you fervently.

44

Petrusa, they tell me that you are ill, but it seems to me that you are enraged with me or I have offended you with my considerations; but be that as it may, I love you and desire greatly to see you healthy, merry, and healthy. Petrusa darling, away with sadness, rage, and ailment; dearest Petrusa, I beg you, dear friend.

45

Petrusha, the world is this way: one is lauded for that which another is cursed for. This depends solely on what is convenient or proper. That there is nobody similar to you, in much about that I agree, but it is in no way agreed that one is to consider you in a sorry position, and I hope that there will never be an occasion to have pity upon you. It has been ordered to find a gift for Rebinder. I am sending the signed decree about the Ap[raksin] affair. Goodbye, most amiable Petrukha.

46

I am healthy and the upset has passed. Petrusa, love me and I will not only respond to you, but even anticipate. Dearest, little father!

47

I do not know for what cause you seize upon to quarrel; the snuffbox you removed from my room; I request you to send it back for me, for I do not like compulsion in any thing and I shall not bear it at all. Besides, I am not guilty of anything before you, and your snuffbox I am returning to you at your demand for I do not attach significance to trifles.

48

Dearest little soul, stop grieving, I love you as a soul, and I desire your contemplation; do not lock yourself at home; I swear to God, you will be more content with me hour by hour; little lord, do not respect that which is not worthy of respect; my heart is completely occupied with you.

49

I would have come to you willingly, but nothing will come from that except mutual tears; so I beg you in all ways that you should accept food according to the prescription of [court-surgeon] Kel'khen; and when you accept it and become stronger and perceive that my visitation will bring you relief, then rest assured that I shall come. Prince Orlov will be here today, if he has not already arrived. I am going to get dressed for dinner.

50

I ask your healthy reason, is it possible to consider as banishment that which necessity forces one to do? Is it possible to consider as oppression that which heretofore according to circumstances was still not opportune? And ought one not consider as melancholy visions and intolerance, not peculiar to you, all the contrary constructions about that? That you love, I believe, and by the same token I pay you. Just calm your spirit and mine by your peace.

51

Twice I sent after Petrusa, twice Petrusa was not found home; where is my Petrusa? I am going to sleep, not having seen Petrusa the whole day. I cry out, he does not come; my God, how tedious! I sustained a powerful siege and Prince Orlov is chosen as a mediator. The affair proceeds decisively, however much he prevaricates and, really, there was little merriment and none of my joy, from which the impossible is made possible and for which any kind of yoke seems lighter. I took paper to scribble; I scribbled. Here you are, read the scribbling; how does it seem to you? Do not become enraged, share my tedium, read, then go to sleep, and tomorrow come a bit earlier.

52

Not without reason was I both bored and sad all day. Petrushinka, you really are ailing, as I glimpsed from your letter, now received, just when I wanted to send after you, thinking to have comfort in my own melancholy. My darling, you order me to justify myself. About the elephant and about dinner I learned no earlier than twelve o'clock, and wanted to tell you about it at the meeting with you, but this I leave, in order to express to you my feeling. My darling, amidst your sickness and sorrow I see your love for me; believe, that this alone constitutes my satisfaction. I love you and, loving you, of course, I surmount and do not cease to surmount and shall in the future all obstacles; but still some time is necessary, and all will come by itself. I am extremely thankful to you that you justly look into my feelings. Without you I am so melancholy that tears are all in my eyes. Priceless and dear friend, I implore God that you be given relief.

53

Is it really impossible that, having consideration for everyone, both to me and mine people cannot have an ardent, but willing manner to show at least half as much as I show them? Yesterday I explained myself to the prince [Orlov] and it appeared that we parted the very best and most sincere friends, as we have always been and shall be eternally, at least from my side. I beg you for God's sake to extinguish from your thoughts the mean, insulting, and utterly untrue accusation that I supposedly persecute and am hateful toward all those who are sincere with you. Such a hellish invention, not conformable with my kind heart, does not dwell in me; these Machiavellian rules do not dwell in me. With this I append the signed decree about prince Golitsyn. It is a pity that affairs which I ought to do, sending them packing, when they are halted even a little then you ascribe it to other than the actual causes. When fools blather, however, Katiusha ought not pay with her own tranquility. Please, be more indulgent toward her, and do not act, and do not judge her so harshly. Really, she is all alone and nobody till now has busied himself with her justification, yet it is tedious for her, loving justice and truth, always to be engaged in the refutation of false notions.

54

My darling, the destruction of ambition I have never demanded from you, I regret that I give cause for the mobilization of forbearance; that you scorn scornful vexations, this is laudable. Temper the desire for benevolence with justice and with the necessary cautions, in order not to encourage the vice of human caprices. It is impossible to give Katiusha to you, for she is always with you and is yours, you please her more than all and according to her heart, which also makes merry with you. I embrace you mentally and desire to be with you. My love is fervent. Dear and priceless friend, whom I respect as much as I love. I see and feel how much you also love. Goodbye, dearest.

55

I embrace you a hundredfold for the affection described in your letter. My heart is filled with feelings, love and trustfulness for you. The field [marshal] [Rumiantsev] this minute departed from me, it seems, fairly merry; he asked when he is to go; I said that the place of his sojourn depends on him.

56

Your affection and love are really my sole comfort. It seems to me I am the same to you in all the 24 hours that constitute a day, but the difference is this, that the signs are not always on the outside, but the heart is the same one. You chose an unpleasant time for a walk, and that you are not tired, I am amazed, why is that, dearest. Petrusha, I love you as a soul, and shall not cease loving.

57

Petrushenka-darling, I share with you the torture you have endured, and I desire that you be eternally healthy, merry and content, but however you will be, my passion for you will not be broken. My little darling, be calm. The Gr[and] D[uke] has come. Goodbye.

58

Petrusa, really, you will not regret being patient. Spit on niggardly souls. They are worthy of scorn. I shall stamp my foot, they will shake, and you know Katia is yours. Pras[kov'ia] A[leksandrovna] [Bruce] is driving into town, and she is taking her niece too. Dear darling, I love you as a soul.

59

Little father, what is this sadness for? Be kind! you see this sadness, permit me to say, is really weakness and faint-heartedness. Say it yourself: well, how can you not go out of my room when propriety demands it? You see, all your grief is about that. You see, with friends too, when you know that it is proper to leave a friend alone or because of decorum, then you will go away from him without heart or sadness. Really, darling, you behave like a child. I thought to spend the evenings with you in complete contentment, but on the contrary you exercise yourself with empty melancholy and, God sees, and in your letter the cause of your great grief is not described at all. I search for it, but I know not from what. I shall complain to Pr[ince] Or[lov] about you: let him judge us, and the other went off to Lev Narishkin. Dear darling, dearest, let go of irrelevant sadness, otherwise I shall think you are losing your mind.

60

To a person most valuable and dear, who however is extremely, extremely mistaken, when he attributes the commotion of thought to boredom, I beg you that you not be mistaken in me, never ascribe to me the qualities of base and weak souls; the tsar knows how to reign, but when he has nothing but tedium the whole day, then he is tedious; he is all the more tedious when a dear visage looks on stupidly and the tsar, instead of merriment, gets from it a supplement of tedium and vexation. All this is past and forgotten [*crossed out:* but if you will be].

61

When you pull any thing whatever from both ends, then the thing usually breaks at both ends. But when three grab hold and each pulls it toward himself, then does the thing come out whole or the three ends, I ask you. I have a wish to see quiet, peace, harmony; I have my wish, you have another, that one has a third; is it impossible for people to agree to live peacefully and serenely? If you went to congratulate the new Highness, the Highness will receive you affectionately. If you locked yourself up, neither I nor anybody will be accustomed to see you. Patience is lacking in you. Bearing so much, the term of this position is already brief. You scribbled off the sheet in a dream. Dreams—are nonsense. That you are ill, I regret, that you are loving and raving, this happens with everyone. I love you, that is the truth, here's your answer; yet if I answer your letter properly, then the answer will be longer than the Charter of the treasury department, which I am drafting. I am affectionate, and not angry, Petrusa.

62

I shall see you the hour your present weakness permits it and therefore I send Kel'khen to you. Prince Or[lov] told me that you desire to go, and to that I agree. I did not answer at a time when you did not accept any reasons and I feared that you were falling ill, and I confess that this was vexing to me. After dinner, if you will be eating, I can meet with you. Besides, rest assured that I do not withdraw from you either friendship, nor trust, nor benevolence.

63

Your letter with the appendices I received on Friday. For the assurance of fidelity and attachment I thank you, not doubting about that at all. Rest assured that I shall be excellently disposed to you forever. About your arrival I leave it to your will. Most of all, calm your spirit and be healthy and merry, and I advise you to follow the advice of S[emen] R[omanovich] V[orontsov] to translate Tacitus or to practice Russian history. His letters to you I am returning: they are written with excellent spirit and style. In order that pr. Gr[igorii] A[leksandrovich] [Potemkin] be friendly with you as before about this, it is not difficult to make the effort; but facilitate it yourself; there will not be ambiguity in that; on the contrary—your minds will approach the same notion about me and thereby become closer to one another than they themselves understand. Envy and slander, just the same as persecutions, I am accustomed to keep in fetters; and so, be calm. I shall send the promised ring; I[van] I[vanovich] B[etskoi] has already been ordered about it. Besides, your house together with you remain and will remain in my memory and protection.

Abbreviations

AGS	*Arkhiv gosudarstvennogo soveta*
AHR	*American Historical Review*
AKV	*Arkhiv kniazia Vorontsova*
AR	*Annual Register* (London)
CASS/CSS	*Canadian-American Slavic Studies/Canadian Slavic Studies*
ChIOIDR	*Chteniia v imperatorskom obshchestve istorii i drevnostei rossiiskikh pri Moskovskom universitete*
CMRS	*Cahiers du monde russe et sovietique*
DA	*Daily Advertiser* (London)
DCB	*Despatches and Correspondence Buckinghamshire*
DKH	*Dnevnik Khrapovitskogo*
IV	*Istoricheskii vestnik*
JGO	*Jahrbücher für Geschichte Osteuropas*
Kfzh	*Kamer-fur'erskii zhurnal*
MERSH	*Modern Encyclopedia of Russian and Soviet History*
MV	*Moskovskie vedomosti*
OSP	*Oxford Slavonic Papers*
OV	*Osmnadtsatyi vek*
PROSP	Public Record Office, State Papers (London)
PSZ	*Polnoe sobranie zakonov*
RA	*Russkii arkhiv*
RS	*Russkaia starina*
SA	*Senatskii arkhiv*
SEER	*Slavonic and East European Review*

SG	*Starye gody*
SGECRN	*Study Group on Eighteenth Century Russia Newsletter*
SIRIO	*Sbornik imperatorskogo russkogo istoricheskogo obshchestva*
SJC	*St. James Chronicle* (London)
SPV	*Sanktpeterburgskie vedomosti*
TCM	*Town and Country Magazine* (London)
TsGIA-SSSR	Tsentral'nyi gosudarstvennyi istoricheskii arkhiv USSR
ZG	*Zapiski Garnovskogo*

Notes

Chapter 1

1. V. A. Bil'basov, *Istoriia Ekateriny Vtoroi*, 2 vols. (Berlin, 1900), 2:22–23.
2. Bil'basov, 1:467–468; Katherine Anthony, ed., *Memoirs of Catherine the Great* (N.Y. and London, 1927), 265, 267.
3. R. Nisbet Bain, *Peter III, Emperor of Russia* (Westminster, 1902; reprinted New York, 1971), 110–111.
4. Ibid., 45, 93–94, 106–107.
5. Marc Raeff, "The Domestic Policies of Peter III and His Overthrow," *AHR*, 75 (1970):1289–1310.
6. Ibid., 1308–1310; Bain, *Peter III*, 45, 47.
7. D. A. Korsakov, "Nekotorye iz storonnikov votsareniia Imperatritsy Ekateriny II," *Iz zhizni russkikh deiatelei XVIII veka* (Kazan, 1891), 369–416; Kyril Fitzlyon, ed., *The Memoirs of Princess Dashkov* (London, 1958), 39–41.
8. Carol Scott Leonard, "A Study of the Reign of Peter III of Russia," unpub. diss. (Indiana University, 1976), 254, 280.
9. Claude C. de Rulhière, *A History or Anecdotes of the Revolution in Russia, in the Year 1762* (London, 1797; reprinted N.Y., 1970), 4–6; *Memoirs*, 276.
10. Bil'basov, 2:24–25.
11. Ibid., 25–27.
12. Ibid., 27–29.
13. Ibid., 29–30; Ruhlière, 102.
14. Ruhlière, 113–114.
15. Bil'basov, 2:97–99.
16. Ibid., 32–34.
17. Ibid., 35–38.
18. Ibid., 40–41.
19. Ibid., 42.
20. Ibid., 68–69; Ruhlière, 118–119.
21. Ruhlière, 128.

22. Bil'basov, 2:43–46.
23. Ibid., 47–48.
24. Ibid., 49–56.
25. Ibid., 56–58.
26. Bain, *Peter* III, 160; quoted by Bil'basov, 2:137.
27. Bil'basov, 2:69–74.
28. Ibid., 74.
29. Ibid., 77.
30. Ibid., 78–79.
31. Quoted by Bil'basov, 2:81, 565.
32. Ibid., 83–84.
33. Ibid., 88.
34. Ibid., 88, 91.
35. *DA,* 26 Aug. 1762; *AR* (1762), 20.
36. Bil'basov, 2:84, 92.
37. N. K. Shil'der, *Imperator Pavel Pervyi* (Spb., 1901), 37; Arthur M. Wilson, *Diderot* (N.Y., 1972), 443.
38. Bil'basov, 2:120–124.
39. Ibid., 128; Bain, *Peter III,* 171.
40. John Parkinson, *A Tour of Russia, Siberia and the Crimea, 1792–1794,* ed. William Collier (London, 1971), 85.
41. Bil'basov, 2:129–136.
42. V. Nashkerov, "Gosudarevo slovo i delo," *RA,* bk. 1 (1912), 326–331.

Chapter 2

1. *PSZ,* 7:no. 5,007 (7 May 1727).
2. Brenda Meehan-Waters, *Autocracy and Aristocracy* (New Brunswick, 1982), ch. 6.
3. Bil'basov, 1:27–29.
4. Ibid., 30–31.
5. Ibid, 1–5.
6. *OV,* 1:4.
7. O. E. Kornilovich, "Zapiski Imperatritsy Ekateriny II," *Zhurnal Ministerstva narodnogo prosveshcheniia,* n.s., 37 (January 1912), 37–74.
8. *Memoirs,* 73.
9. Ibid., 7–8.
10. *Zapiski Imperatritsy Ekateriny Vtoroi* (Spb., 1907), 15.
11. Ibid., 8–11.
12. Ibid., 17.
13. *Memoirs,* 18, 76, 223; *Zapiski,* 204–209.
14. *Zapiski,* 23–24.
15. Peter Petschauer, "The Education and Development of an Enlightened Absolutist: The Youth of Catherine the Great," unpub. diss. (New York University, 1969), 191–194.
16. *Zapiski,* 26-28, 30, 76.
17. Bil'basov, 1:30–34.
18. Ibid., 37–52; *Zapiski,* 32–34.
19. Bil'basov, 1:52–57.
20. *Pridvornye zhurnaly 1743–1748 gg.* (Spb., 1913), 35–36; Bil'basov, 1:57–65.

21. Bil'basov, 1:65–68.
22. *Memoirs*, 39–41.
23. Bil'basov, 1:70, 85.
24. *Memoirs*, 44–45, 229–230; *Zapiski*, 209–210.
25. Bil'basov, 1:82, 149–154, 182–183; *Memoirs*, 62, 236–237.
26. Bil'basov, 1:98.
27. Ibid., 97; *Memoirs*, 42–43, 231–232; *Zapiski*, 211–212.
28. Bil'basov, 1:105; *Zapiski*, 212–213.
29. Bil'basov, 1:106, 119–120.
30. Ibid., 117–120.
31. Ibid., 121–131.
32. Ibid., 132–134; *Memoirs*, 50, 234.
33. Bil'basov, 1:137.
34. N. O. Mikhnevich, "Grafinia M.A. Rumiantseva," *Istoricheskie ocherki i razskazy* (Spb., 1900), 2:296–339; *Memoirs*, 57.
35. *Memoirs*, 51–55, 57, 235.
36. Bil'basov, 1:140–148.
37. *Memoirs*, 55–58.
38. Ibid., 66.
39. Bil'basov, 1:149–150.
40. Ibid., 150–154; *Memoirs*, 236.
41. Bil'basov, 1:154–159; *SIRIO*, 42:465–466; *Memoirs*, 60, 62–63.
42. Bil'basov, 1:178–183.
43. *Zapiski*, 59, 124, 233, 236; *Memoirs*, 124.
44. *Memoirs*, 66–68; Bil'basov, 1:184.
45. Bil'basov, 1:185–186; A. A. Goncharova, *State Armoury in the Moscow Kremlin*, tr. Alexandra Ilf and Natasha Johnstone (M., 1969), no. 169.
46. *SIRIO*, 7:50; *Memoirs*, 69–70, 92–93.
47. Bil'basov, 1:191–192, 245–247.
48. *Memoirs*, 63, 94–96, 99, 237–238.
49. *Memoirs*, 97–98; *Zapiski*, 239–240.
50. Bil'basov, 1:210–212; *Memoirs*, 100.
51. *Memoirs*, 101; *Zapiski*, 241–245.
52. Bil'basov, 1:219–228.
53. Ibid., 286; *Memoirs*, 100–104, 240–243.
54. Bil'basov, 1:242–243; *Memoirs*, 107–108, 188.
55. *Memoirs*, 120.
56. *Memoirs*, 29–30, 60–62; Petschauer, "Education and Development," 196–200, 202, 511–514.
57. *Memoirs*, 93, 124, 168, 184, 209, 244; Joanot Martorell and Marti Joan de Galba, *Tirant Lo Blanc*, tr. David H. Rosenthal (N.Y., 1984), 40.
58. Ibid., 108, 120; Bil'basov, 1:280–283.
59. *Memoirs*, 103, 110, 112, 117, 131–136, 147, 175, 178, 185, 190, 194–195, 198–200, 209, 212, 242.
60. *Memoirs*, 106–110, 138–143, 244–245.
61. Ibid., 110, 125, 138, 147, 178–180; 212; *Zapiski*, 304–307.
62. *Memoirs*, 125, 168, 178–180, 187, 197–198, 213.
63. *Memoirs*, 205–206; *Zapiski*, 297.
64. *Memoirs*, 169–170.
65. Ibid., 181, 192–194.
66. Ibid., 194.

67. *Zapiski,* 295–297; *Memoirs,* 199–205.

68. *Memoirs,* 200, 247–248; Bil'basov, 1:533–544.

69. *Memoirs,* 102, 105, 117–118, 131–132, 156–167, 174, 180, 211.

70. Ibid., 97, 217, 235; *Zapiski,* 315, 323–325; "Liubovnye zapisochki vysokoi osoby XVIII veka," *RA,* bk. 1 (1881), 390–401.

71. *Memoirs,* 151, 248–249; *Zapiski,* 307–308, 319–320, 327–336, 342–348, 352.

72. *Zapiski,* 353, 356.

73. *Ibid.,* 356–364; E. N. Shchepkin, *Russko-avstriiskii soiuz vo vremia semiletnei voiny 1746–1758 gg.* (Spb., 1902), 464–465.

74. Quoted by Herbert H. Kaplan, *Russia and the Outbreak of the Seven Years' War* (Berkeley and Los Angeles, 1968), 109

75. *Zapiski,* 366; Bil'basov, 1:319–326.

76. *Zapiski,* 301–303, 317–318; Kaplan, *Russia and the Outbreak,* 103.

77. *Zapiski,* 372–373, 392–97, 399, 406–407; Bil'basov, 1:316–317; *SIRIO,* 7: 92–97.

78. *Memoires du roi Stanislas-Auguste Poniatowski,* ed. A. S. Lappo-Danilevskii and S. M. Goriainov (Spb., 1914), 1:156–157.

79. *Zapiski,* 376, 379–381, 386–388.

80. *Correspondence of Catherine the Great When Grand-Duchess, with Sir Charles Hanbury-Williams and Letters from Count Poniatowski,* ed. and trans., The Earl of Ilchester and Mrs. Langford-Brooke (London, 1928), 183.

81. Ibid., 59–60, 101, 128, 191, 216, 235, 238–239, 243.

82. Ibid., 90–92, 183, 275, 282.

83. *Zapiski,* 382, 406, 410, 433–434; *Memoirs,* 258; Korsakov, "Nekotorye," 400–401.

84. N. D. Chechulin, "Chetyre goda zhizni Ekateriny II, 1755–1758: Ekaterina i Poniatovskii." *Russkii istoricheskii zhurnal* (Petrograd, 1922), bk. 8: 165–169; *Zapiski,* 408, 415–418, 465–466.

85. *Zapiski,* 408–411, 421–422; Bil'basov, 1:518–534.

86. M. de Swart to Holderness, 16 October 1757, *ChIOIDR* (1870), bk. 3: 11–15.

87. *Zapiski,* 410–412; Bil'basov, 1:368, 372.

88. *Zapiski,* 422–423, 425–426.

89. Ibid., 430–438.

90. Bil'basov, 1:375; *SIRIO,* 7:77; *Memoirs,* 259–260.

91. *Zapiski,* 441–456.

92. Ibid., 443, 456–461; Chechulin, "Chetyre goda," 165; Shchepkin, *Russko-avstriiskii soiuz,* 672.

93. *PSZ,* 15: no. 10,930 (9 March 1759); *MV,* 20 April 1759.

94. *Zapiski,* 456; *MV,* 20 April 1759; Bil'basov, 1:411–418.

95. Bil'basov, 1:423–424, 427, 445–446; *MV,* 20 April 1759.

96. *Zapiski,* 419; Bil'basov, 1:426–428.

97. I. S. Barkov, *Utekhi Imperatritsy* ("Rassvet": Tel Aviv, n.d.); Bil'basov, 1:452, 454.

98. *Correspondence with Hanbury-Williams,* 181; David Ransel, *The Politics of Catherinian Russia: The Panin Party* (New Haven and London, 1975), 10–11, 23–24, 33–37, 44–54.

99. *Memoirs of Dashkov,* 28, 39–41.

100. *Memoirs,* 94, 283–287; Bil'basov, 1:464–465.

101. "Zapiski Fav'e," *IV,* 29 (1887), 387–388.

Chapter 3

1. V. Z. Dzhincharadze, "Iz istorii tainoi ekspeditsii pri Senate (1762–1801)," *Uchenye zapiski Novgorodskii gos. ped. inst.*, 2, fasc. 2 (1957), 100.

2. *Memoirs*, 299–302.

3. Bil'basov, 2:104–108.

4. *SIRIO*, 1:216; vol. 7:126–128, 131, 135–143, 155, 169, 197; vol. 42: 470–471.

5. *SIRIO*, 7:120; vol. 42:475, 480; Bil'basov, 2:507, 510.

6. *Pis'ma i zapiski Imperatritsy Ekateriny Vtoroi k grafu Nikite Ivanovichu Paninu* (M., 1863), 4–5, 129; *SIRIO*, 7:149–150; vol. 42:476; P. V. Dolgorukov, *Rossiiskaia rodoslovnaia kniga*, 3 vols. (Spb., 1854–1856), 2:74.

7. *SIRIO*, 7:121; vol. 42:471; Bil'basov, 2:160–162.

8. Raeff, "Domestic Policies of Peter III," 1302.

9. Bil'basov, 2:163–165.

10. Ibid., 168.

11. Ibid., 170; E. V. Anisimov, *Rossiia v seredine XVIII veka* (M., 1986), 152.

12. Bil'basov, 2:179–182; *SA*, 12:265.

13. *SIRIO*, 12:78; *Zapiski*, 589–590; *DCB*, 1:100.

14. S. A. Poroshin, *Zapiski* (Spb., 1844), 12; *SIRIO*, 12:44.

15. *DCB*, 2:56; Bil'basov, 2:172; Shil'der, *Pavel Pervyi*, 37.

16. *DA*, 20 Dec. 1762; Bil'basov, 2:188–198; *SIRIO*, 7:170–172.

17. *Memoirs*, 280; Bil'basov, 2:203; Dzhincharadze, "Iz istorii," 96.

18. *SIRIO*, 7:162; Bil'basov, 2:198, 213–214; Dzhincharadze, "Iz istorii," 112; *MV*, no. 10, 2 February 1767.

19. *SIRIO*, 12:46.

20. *PSZ*, 16:no. 11,665 (16 September 1762); *SA*, 14:200.

21. *SIRIO*, 7:319; Iu. V. Got'e, "Proizkhozhdenie sobstvennoi e.i.v. kantseliarii," *Sbornik statei po russkoi istorii, posviashchennykh S. F. Platonovu* (Petersburg, 1922), 346–355.

22. *SIRIO*, 7:324, 351; vol. 42:312.

23. *PSZ*, 16:no. 11,912 (4 September 1763); *SIRIO*, 7:157–158; S. M. Troitskii, *Rossiia v XVIII veke* (M., 1982), 168.

24. Troitskii, *Rossiia*, 187–192.

25. Ransel, *Politics*, 153–170.

26. *SIRIO*, 7:346.

27. Ibid., 345–348.

28. D. V. Tsvetaev, ed., "Sobstvennoruchnye ukazy i pis'ma Imperatritsy Ekateriny Velikoi," *Zhurnal Ministerstva iustitsii*, no. 10 (December 1915), 196–197.

29. Ibid., 188, 191, 193, 195.

30. *Memoirs of Dashkov*, 78–79; *DCB*, 1:67, 101.

31. *Memoirs*, 311–312, 317, 319; *Correspondence with Hanbury-Williams*, 239; Bil'basov, 2:281.

32. Ransel, *Politics*, 125.

33. *Memoirs*, 318; *SIRIO*, 7:290–291; vol. 12:106.

34. Bil'basov, 2:289; *SIRIO*, 7:290.

35. Bil'basov, 2:294–296; *SIRIO*, 7:298.

36. Ransel, *Politics*, 126; *SIRIO*, 7:321–322.

37. Bil'basov, 2:265.

38. Isabel de Madariaga, *Russia in the Age of Catherine the Great* (New Haven and London, 1981), 116–117.

39. *DCB*, 2:58.

40. *DCB*, 1:102.

41. Bil'basov, 2:209–213.

42. *Memoirs*, 301; *PSZ*, 16:no. 11,606 (12 July 1762).

43. Bil'basov, 2:207, 559, 574; J. T. Alexander, "Petersburg and Moscow in Early Urban Policy," *Journal of Urban History*, 8 (1982), 149, 151–152, 157–158.

44. Bil'basov, 2:583; *SIRIO*, 7:285.

45. J. T. Alexander, "Catherine the Great and Public Health," *Journal of the History of Medicine*, 36 (1981), 189–190; N. A. Zhivopistsev, *Bol'nitsa Imperatora Pavla I-go v Moskve* (M., 1914), 3–8.

46. Bil'basov, 2:214–218, 572; *SIRIO*, 7:187, 323.

47. Bil'basov, 2:575; Roger P. Bartlett, *Human Capital: The Settlement of Foreigners in Russia, 1762–1804* (Cambridge, 1979), 65–66, 108.

48. *SIRIO*, 7:116, 119, 126–127, 175–176; vol. 42:475–476; *PSZ*, 16:no. 11,728 (19 December 1762).

49. Alexander, "Catherine and Public Health," 191–195; *PSZ*, 16:no. 11,965 (12 November 1763).

50. *SIRIO*, 7:137; *Pis'ma Ekateriny II k Adamu Vasil'evichu Olsuf'evu, 1762–1783* (M., 1863), 85.

51. Bil'basov, 2:572–574; *SIRIO*, 7:230; S. M. Troitskii, *Finansovaia politika russkogo absoliutizma v XVIII veke* (M., 1966), 210–211.

52. *SIRIO*, 12:188, 200–201.

53. *Memoirs*, 299, 304; S. M. Troitskii, "Finansovaia politika russkogo absoliutizma vo vtoroi polovine XVII i XVIII vv., *Absoliutizm v Rossii* (M., 1964), 313; Arcadius Kahan, *The Plow, The Hammer, and the Knout: An Economic History of Eighteenth-Century Russia* (Chicago, 1985), 346.

54. *PSZ*, 16:no. 11,648 (20 August 1762).

55. Bil'basov, 2:576–577; *SIRIO*, 7:322, 327.

56. *SIRIO*, 7:327–328, 350–351; Wallace Daniel, "The Merchantry and the Problem of Social Order in the Russian State: Catherine II's Commission on Commerce," *SEER*, 5 (1977), 185–203; idem, "Grigorii Teplov and the Conception of Order: The Commission on Commerce and the Role of the Merchants in Russia," *CASS*, 16 (1982), 410–431.

57. *Memoirs*, 299, 04–305; *PSZ*, 16:no. 11,593 (3 July 1762).

58. *SIRIO*, 7:182.

59. Ibid., 196, 278–279, 324–326, 329–330; vol. 42:303; *Pis'ma Olsuf'evu*, 422–423; A. S. Orlov, *Volneniia na Urale v seredine XVIII veka* (M., 1979), 84–85.

60. *SIRIO*, 10:32–33; M. N. Martynov, *Gornozavodskoi Ural nakanune velikoi krest'ianskoi voiny 1773–1775 gg.*, diss. summary (L., 1967), 9–10; Orlov, *Volneniia*, 169–182.

61. *PSZ*, 16:no. 11,594 (3 July 1762); no. 11,595 (5 July 1762); no. 11,650 (12 July 1762); no. 11,707 (11 November 1762); Shil'der, *Pavel Pervyi*, 36–38; L. G. Beskrovnyi, *Russkaia armiia i flot v XVIII veke* (M., 1958), 304–305.

62. Beskrovnyi, *Russkaia armiia*, 306–308, 317–318, 326–327; *SIRIO*, 7: 274–275, 331–333, 336; vol. 12:169–170.

63. *DCB*, 2:128, 136, 154, 160; *Kfzh* (1763), 142–148, 153–162; (1764),

272–293; (1765), 98–118, 263–318; *SIRIO*, 7:336–338; vol. 12:297–300; vol. 42:310.

64. Bartlett, *Human Capital*, 19, 109, 111; *SIRIO*, 7:291–292; *SA*, 13:12–13.

65. *Zapiski*, 711; *SIRIO*, 7:187, 348, 359–360, 375; vol. 12:160, *Pis'ma Olsuf'evu*, 427–429; Bil'basov, 2:449–456.

66. *SIRIO*, 7:375–391.

67. Bil'basov, 2:585; *DCB*, 2:159, 177, 179, 182, 191–198.

68. Bil'basov, 2:347; *SIRIO*, 7:365.

69. Bil'basov, 2:353.

70. Ibid., 344, 347; *SIRIO*, 12:173.

71. Bil'basov, 2:360–361, 590.

72. Ibid., 373; *SIRIO*, 7:171.

73. *SIRIO*, 7:365–367; vol. 12:172.

74. *SIRIO*, 7:370, 372; *Kfzh* (1764), 120–121, 323–329; *DCB*, 2:213.

75. Bil'basov, 2:386–389; *DA*, 3 Sept. 1764; *Kfzh* (1764), 139.

76. Bil'basov, 2:389–394.

77. *SIRIO*, 7:374; *Kfzh* (1764), 150, 157.

78. Bil'basov, 2:536.

79. *SIRIO*, 12:174.

80. *AR* (1764), 15; *Monthly Review* (London), 31 (1764), 316.

81. *SIRIO*, 57:237; *DCB*, 2:215, 217, 236.

82. Bil'basov, 2:404; *SIRIO*, 12:188; Anon., *Authentic Memoirs of the Life and Reign of Catherine II, Empress of All the Russias*, 2nd ed. (London, 1797), 40–41; *DCB*, 2:248.

Chapter 4

1. *SIRIO*, 1:274; *DCB*, 1:101.

2. *SIRIO*, 1:272–273; vol. 10:1, 5–6, 27, 36–37, 42, 250, 280–281; vol. 42: 353; Poroshin, *Zapiski*, 541–542.

3. *Zapiski*, 711–712; George Macartney, "The Court of Russia, 1767," Macartney papers, Osborne Collection, Yale University, 16.

4. *SIRIO*, 10:45–46; *Memoirs*, 324; Parkinson, *Tour*, 211.

5. *DCB*, 1:205, vol. 2:232.

6. *Pis'ma Olsuf'evu*, 435–436; *SIRIO*, 12:202–203; Bil'basov, 2:519–521.

7. Macartney to Lady Holland, February 1766, British Museum Add. Ms. 15,875.

8. Paul Dukes, *Catherine the Great and the Russian Nobility* (Cambridge, 1967), 86, 92–93, 95, 99; Roger Bartlett, "I.E. and the Free Economic Society's Essay Competition," *SGECRN*, 8 (1980), 58–67; V. S. Lekhnovich, "K istorii kul'tury kartofelia v Rossii," *Materialy po istorii zemlevladeniia* SSR, vol. 2 (M. and L., 1956), 259–325; *MV*, no. 8, 26 January 1767; supplement to no. 73, 11 September 1767.

9. *SIRIO*, 1:268; vol. 10:75–87; *Memoirs*, 306–307; Ransel, *Politics*, 182–183; A. Lentin, ed., *Voltaire and Catherine the Great: Selected Correspondence* (Cambridge, 1974), 49.

10. J. T. Alexander, "Nakaz of Empress Catherine II," *MERSH*, 24:45–49; A. Florovskii, "Shvedskii perevod 'Nakaza' Ekateriny II," *Zapiski russkogo istoricheskogo obshchestva v Prage*, 1927, bk. 1:149–152; Isabel de Madariaga, "Au-

tocracy and Sovereignty," *CASS*, 16 (1982), 381–382; Karen Rasmussen, "Catherine II and Peter I: The Idea of a Just Monarch (The Evolution of an Attitude in Catherinian Russia," unpub. diss. (Berkeley, 1973), 112–171; *Voltaire and Catherine*, 56, 69, 106, 111; Gary Marker, *Publishing, Printing, and the Origins of Intellectual Life in Russia, 1700–1800* (Princeton, 1985), 166–167; *SJC*, 29–31 March 1768.

11. W. F. Reddaway, ed., *Documents of Catherine the Great: The Correspondence with Voltaire and the Instruction of 1767 in the English Text of 1768* (Cambridge, 1931; reprinted N.Y., 1971), 215–217, 219, 243–245, 249–250, 256–257, 264, 303–304.

12. Robert V. Allen, "The Great Legislative Commission of Catherine II," unpub. diss. (Yale, 1950), 47–49; *SIRIO*, 13:6.

13. *Voltaire and Catherine*, 47.

14. *SIRIO*, 10:170–171; "Pis'ma Imperatritsy Ekateriny Velikoi k fel'dmarshalu grafu Petru Semenovichu Saltykovu, 1762–1771," *RA*, bk. 3 (1886), 51–52, 55, 60–61.

15. *SIRIO*, 10:180, 277; "Pis'ma Saltykovu," 56.

16. "Pis'ma Saltykovu," 42–45, 51.

17. *Nastavleniia politicheskiia Barona Bil'fel'da*, trans. F. Shakhovskoi, 2 vols. (Moscow, 1768–1775); *SIRIO*, 13:3–4.

18. Jacob Friedrich Bielfeld, *Institutions politiques*, 2 vols. (La Haye, 1760), 1:259; *SIRIO*, 10:186.

19. *PSZ*, 18:no. 12,872 (17 April 1767); Victor Kamendrowsky, "State and Economy in Catherinian Russia: The Dismantling of the Mercantile System of Peter the Great," unpub. diss. (North Carolina, 1982), 199–214; "Dmitrii Vasil'evich Volkov: Materialy k ego biografii," *RA*, 18 (1874), 496.

20. A. V. Florovskii, "K istorii ekonomicheskikh idei v Rossii v XVIII veke," *Nauchnye trudy risskogo narodnogo universiteta v Prage*, 1928, no. 1:81–93.

21. "Pis'ma Saltykovu," 55–58.

22. *SIRIO*, 10:185–186, 270; vol. 12:302, 338–339; *Pis'ma Olsuf'evu*, 448–449.

23. *SIRIO*, 10:179, 187–189.

24. *SIRIO*, 10:190, 219–220; Tsvetaev, ed., "Sobstvennoruchnye ukazy," 198.

25. *SIRIO*, 10:191; vol. 42:354.

26. *SIRIO*, 10:193–199, 201.

27. Ibid., 199–200.

28. Ibid., 201–202.

29. Ibid., 203; *Pis'ma Olsuf'evu*, 446–447.

30. *SIRIO*, 42:354; *Kfzh* (1767), 193.

31. *SIRIO*, 10:204, 206.

32. Tsvetaev, ed., "Sobstvennoruchnye ukazy," 197.

33. *SIRIO*, 10:205–207, 210, 464.

34. Ibid., 207.

35. Ibid., 210.

36. Ibid., 211–212.

37. Ibid., 212–218.

38. Ibid., 216–218; Kahan, *Plough, Hammer, and Knout*, 13, 59, 168–172.

39. *Kfzh* (1767), 273–276.

40. *SIRIO*, 10:235.

41. *PSZ*, 18:no. 12,978 (27 September 1767); *SIRIO*, 10:237; vol. 12:309; *MV*, supplement to no. 91, 13 November 1767.

42. *SIRIO*, 12:291, 307, 316.
43. Allen, "Great Legislative Commission," 67–72.
44. Ibid., 73–75.
45. *SIRIO*, 10:238–239.
46. Ibid., 240, 242, 253, 271, 279; vol. 27:15.
47. Tsvetaev, ed., "Sobstvennoruchnye ukazy," 201.
48. Ibid., 201; *SIRIO*, 12:359–360; vol. 42:297.
49. *OV*, 3:390–391; V. I. Semevskii, *Krest'iane v tsarstvovanie Imperatritsy Ekateriny II*, 2nd ed. rev. (Spb., 1903), 1:417–418.
50. "Pis'ma Saltykovu," 62; *SIRIO*, 10:276–279.
51. "Pis'ma Saltykovu," 63–68.
52. *SIRIO*, 42:297; Parkinson, *Tour*, 124, 258; Anon., "Brat'ia Choglokovy," *Pamiatniki novoi russkoi istorii* (Spb., 1873), 3:323–333.
53. *Zapiski*, 174–175.
54. *Memoirs*, 307.

Chapter 5

1. Bil'basov, 2:114.
2. Ibid., 113–115, 305–318, 559–560; *SIRIO*, 48:13, 32.
3. *SIRIO*, 7:92.
4. Herbert H. Kaplan, *The First Partition of Poland* (N.Y., 1962), 7–12.
5. Bil'basov, 2:422–423; *SIRIO*, 48:150.
6. Walter Leitsch, "Russo-Polish Confrontation," in Taras Hunczak, ed., *Russian Imperialism from Ivan the Great to the Revolution* (New Brunswick, N.J., 1974), 156–158.
7. Kaplan, 13, 22–24; Bil'basov, 2:428–429.
8. *SIRIO*, 7:321.
9. Kaplan, 28–29, 32; Bil'basov, 2:430; *SIRIO*, 51:5–8, 9–11, 136, 283.
10. Kaplan, 29; Bil'basov, 2:435, 438.
11. Kaplan, 32–41.
12. Kaplan, 41; Bil'basov, 2:446; *OV*, 1:56.
13. Bil'basov, 2:441–446; Kaplan, 43.
14. Kaplan, 43; *OV*, 1:56–57; *SIRIO*, 7:373–374.
15. P. H. Clendenning, "The Background and Negotiations for the Anglo-Russian Commercial Treaty of 1766," in A. G. Cross, ed., *Great Britain and Russia in the Eighteenth Century* (Newtonville, Mass., 1979), 145–163.
16. Poroshin, *Zapiski*, 35–36; *SIRIO*, 7:367; Kaplan, 50–51.
17. Kaplan, 81–90.
18. Kaplan, 95–105; Madariaga, *Russia in the Age of Catherine*, 204.
19. Solov'ev, *Istoriia*, 14:280; *Voltaire and Catherine*, 54; *SIRIO*, 2:275–283.
20. *AGS*, 1, pt. 1:i–xv; *SIRIO*, 10:303–305.
21. *AGS*, 1, pt. 1:2–8.
22. Ibid., 9–11; Kaplan, 116.
23. *Voltaire and Catherine*, 57–58, 61–62; Roger P. Bartlett, "Catherine II, Voltaire and Henry IV of France," *SGECRN*, 9 (1981), 41–50.
24. *AGS*, 1, pt. 1:29, 31; *SIRIO*, 10:389, 413; V. P. Nikiforov and A. V. Pomarnatskii, *A. V. Suvorov i ego sovremenniki* (L., 1964), 25.
25. *Voltaire and Catherine*, 108, 117; Ransel, *Politics*, 197–199.
26. *Voltaire and Catherine*, 86, 91; Abram Raskin, *Petrodvorets (Peterhof)*,

2nd ed. (L., 1978), 124–134; A. G. Cross, "Richard Paton and the Battle of Chesme," *SGECRN,* 14 (1986), 31–37.

27. *Sochineniia imperatritsy Ekateriny* II, ed. A. N. Pypin (Spb., 1901), 7: i–lvi, 311–312.

28. *Voltaire and Catherine,* 99–100; Kaplan, 138, 146.

29. *Voltaire and Catherine,* 115; Kaplan, 149–150.

30. Kaplan, 173–181, 188–189.

31. *Kfzh* (1772), 378–381; *SIRIO,* 13:360, 397.

32. *Memoirs,* 324; *Voltaire and Catherine,* 115.

33. C. to Senate, 14 and 17 September 1772, TsGIA-SSSR, f. 1329, op. 1, d. 133:99–100.

34. *SIRIO,* 13:271–276.

35. *Memoirs,* 324; *SIRIO,* 13:326.

36. Madariaga, *Russia in the Age of Catherine,* 215–218, 227–229; J. T. Alexander, *Autocratic Politics in a National Crisis* (Bloomington, 1969), 11–14.

37. *Voltaire and Catherine,* 151, 154.

38. Robert B. Asprey, *Frederick the Great* (N.Y., 1986), 600.

39. Madariaga, *Russia in the Age of Catherine,* 260–261.

40. *SIRIO,* 13:287, 310, 321, 323.

41. Ibid., 335–336, 353, 361, 400.

42. Ibid., 347, 353, 361, 388; vol. 27:79.

43. Alexander, *Autocratic Politics,* 5, 20–22, 79–83, 166–167; *SIRIO,* 13:392.

44. Alexander, *Autocratic Politics,* 84–85, 131–134; A. A. Golombievskii, *Biografiia kniazia G. G. Orlova* (M., 1904), 43; M. I. Pyliaev, *Zabytoe proshloe okrestnostei Peterburga* (Spb., 1889), 154.

45. Alexander, *Autocratic Politics,* 133–134; *SIRIO,* 13:397–398, 416; vol. 27:52.

46. Asprey, *Frederick,* 601–602.

47. Alexander, *Autocratic Politics,* 165.

48. Ibid., 162; E. V. Tarle, *Sochineniia* (M., 1959), 10:89.

49. *SIRIO,* 27:42–44, 48; A. T. Bolotov, *Zhizn' i prikliucheniia* (M. and L., 1931), 3:207–210; *Kfzh* (1775), 432, 702.

50. *Voltaire and Catherine,* 168.

Chapter 6

1. *SIRIO,* 10:247.

2. *SIRIO,* 1:289; Alfred Ritter von Arneth, ed., *Joseph II und Katharina von Russland* (Vienna, 1869), 137–138; V. I. Pokrovskii, "Smertodavy v satiricheskoi literature XVIII v.," *ChIOIDR,* 222, bk. 3 (1907), sect. II:9,11.

3. *SIRIO,* 10:249.

4. *PSZ,* 17:no. 12,505 (8 November 1765).

5. *DCB,* 2:177, 230.

6. Macartney, "Court of Russia, 1767," 8–9.

7. *SIRIO,* 12:328, 331.

8. Donald R. Hopkins, *Princes and Peasants: Smallpox in History* (Chicago, 1983), 63–65.

9. *SIRIO,* 10:290–291; *Pis'ma Paninu,* 160.

10. *SIRIO,* 10:294–295; *Pis'ma Paninu,* 160; "Pis'ma Saltykovu," 69.

11. W. J. Bishop, "Thomas Dimsdale, M.D., F.R.S. (1712–1800) and the Inoculation of Catherine the Great of Russia," *Annals of Medical History,* 4 (1932),

321–338; Peter Razzell, *The Conquest of Smallpox* (The Dock, Firle, Sussex, 1977).

12. *Kfzh* (1768), 167–168; *SIRIO*, 2:304; vol. 12:362–363; PROSP 91/79: 204; Thomas Dimsdale, *Tracts on Inoculation, Written and Published at St. Petersburg in the Year 1768* (London, 1781), 15–19, 24–26.

13. Dimsdale, *Tracts*, 71–91; Solov'ev, *Istoriia*, 14:613; "Pis'ma Saltykovu," 93.

14. *PSZ*, 19:no. 13, 801 (14 May 1772); no. 13,755 (1 February 1772); Dimsdale, *Tracts*, 58–69, 99–112; *SIRIO*, 10:332; vol. 13:127; Roger P. Bartlett, "Russia in the Eighteenth-Century European Adoption of Inoculation for Smallpox" (forthcoming).

15. *Voltaire and Catherine*, 53, 56; Alexander, "Catherine and Public Health," 197–201; Roderick E. McGrew with the collaboration of Margaret P. McGrew, *Encyclopedia of Medical History* (N.Y., 1985), 155.

16. *OV*, 3:241–242; J. T. Alexander, *Bubonic Plague in Early Modern Russia* (Baltimore and London, 1980), 54; *Voltaire and Catherine*, 78, 91.

17. Alexander, *Bubonic Plague*, 101–110; *SIRIO*, 10:436; *OV*, 3:249–250.

18. *AGS*, 1, pt. 1:391; *OV*, 1:249–250; vol. 3:246–247, 250; "Pis'ma Saltykovu," 84; *SIRIO*, 1:393.

19. *SIRIO*, 1:392; "Pis'ma Saltykovu," 88–91.

20. Alexander, *Bubonic Plague*, 116–121, 125–126; "Pis'ma Saltykovu," 92.

21. Alexander, *Bubonic Plague*, 121–124, 127–128.

22. Ibid., 129–130.

23. Ibid., 130–135.

24. Ibid., 145–148.

25. Ibid., 148–151; William Richardson, *Anecdotes of the Russian Empire* (London, 1784), 153.

26. *Pis'ma Paninu*, 47; *SIRIO*, 13:18–19; "Pis'ma Saltykovu," 101.

27. "Pis'ma Saltykovu," 100–101; *Memoirs*, 1.

28. Alexander, *Bubonic Plague*, 154–155.

29. *SIRIO*, 13:99–100, 114, 116–118, 138, 142.

30. "Pis'ma Saltykovu," 102; Alexander, *Bubonic Plague*, 153, 166.

31. Alexander, *Bubonic Plague*, 166, 173–174.

32. Ibid., 174.

33. Ibid., 175–176.

34. Ibid., 202.

35. Ibid., 203–204; *Voltaire and Catherine*, 121; *SIRIO*, 13:99–100.

36. Alexander, *Bubonic Plague*, 205.

37. *DA*, November 5, 1771.

38. *Voltaire and Catherine*, 121–122.

39. Ia. Rost, ed., *Vysochaishiia sobstvennoruchnyia pis'ma i poveleniia . . . Ekateriny Velikiia, k . . . Erapkinu . . .* M., 1808), 85.

40. TsGIA-SSSR, f. 1329, op. 2, d. 112:114.

41. Alexander, *Bubonic Plague*, 265–270.

42. *Voltaire and Catherine*, 122; *SIRIO*, 13:179–180.

43. Alexander, *Bubonic Plague*, 208–228.

44. Ibid., 245–250.

45. Ibid., 251–254.

46. *Voltaire and Catherine*, 121, 124–125.

47. Ibid., 122; Edward V. Williams, *The Bells of Russia* (Princeton, 1985), 158–60; I. K. Kondrat'ev, *Sedaia starina Moskvy* (M., 1893), 159–160; *Sochineniia Imperatritsy Ekateriny II* (Spb., 1901), vol. 1.

48. "On the plague in Turkey and Egypt," *Scots Magazine,* 49 (Feb. 1787), 58–60; Alexander, *Bubonic Plague,* 257, 264, 275.

49. Ibid., 277–278; *SIRIO,* 13:401, 406.

50. Alexander, *Bubonic Plague,* 300–301.

Chapter 7

1. *Zapiski,* 658.

2. Solov'ev, *Istoriia,* 15:154.

3. A. Barsukov, *Razskazy iz russkoi istorii XVIII veka* (Spb., 1885), 195–242.

4. Solov'ev, *Istoriia,* 14:132–133.

5. Ibid., 15:154–156; A. G. Brikner, *Istoriia Ekateriny Vtoroi* (Spb., 1885), 196–198; Nikolai N. Bolkhovitinov, *The Beginnings of Russian-American Relations, 1775–1815,* tr. Elena Levin (Cambridge, Mass., 1975), 149–152.

6. Dzhincharadze, "Iz istorii," 103–104; Alexander, *Autocratic Politics,* 29–30.

7. Ransel, *Politics,* 232; Solov'ev, *Istoriia,* 15:156–158; *Kfzh* (1772), 271–281.

8. Ransel, 232–233; Solov'ev, 15:159; Dzhincharadze, "Iz istorii," 98–99.

9. *SIRIO,* 13:260, 266; vol. 42:356.

10. Ransel, *Politics,* 241–249; *SIRIO,* 19:399–400.

11. K. V. Sivkov, "Samozvanchestvo v Rossii v poslednei treti XVIII v.," *Istoricheskie zapiski* (1950), 31:96–102; S. M. Troitskii, "Samozvantsy v Rossii XVII–XVIII vekov," *Voprosy istorii,* 1969, no. 3:142.

12. A. S. Myl'nikov, *Legenda o russkom printse* (L., 1987), 34–59, 145.

13. Michael B. Petrovich, "Catherine II and a False Peter III in Montenegro," *American Slavic and East European Review,* 14 (1955), 169–194; *Sbornik starinnykh bumag, khraniashchikhsia v Muzee P. I. Shchukina* (M., 1901), 8:387; *AR,* 1767, 11–12; *SJC,* 19–22 Dec. 1767.

14. Sivkov, "Samozvanchestvo," 103–108.

15. Ibid., 108–112.

16. Ibid., 113–117.

17. J. T. Alexander, *Emperor of the Cossacks* (Lawrence, Ks., 1973), 43–56.

18. Ibid., 56–76.

19. Alexander, *Autocratic Politics,* 1–10.

20. Ibid., 68–72.

21. Ibid., 71–72, 75.

22. Ibid., 72–74, 77–79.

23. A. A. Bibikov, *Zapiski o zhizni i sluzhbe Aleksandra Il'icha Bibikova,* 2nd ed. (M., 1865), 115–116.

24. Wilson, *Diderot,* 639–640, 647, 651, 657; Isabel de Madariaga, "Catherine and the *Philosophes,*" in A. G. Cross, ed., *Russia and the West in the Eighteenth Century* (Newtonville, Mass., 1983), 38–47.

25. *SIRIO,* 2:324–335.

26. Alexander, *Autocratic Politics,* 112–113.

27. Ibid., 106–107; *Voltaire and Catherine,* 158–161; *SIRIO,* 13:396.

28. Alexander, *Autocratic Politics,* 105, 119–122, 135.

29. Ibid., 139–141; R. V. Ovchinnikov, *Manifesty i ukazy E. I. Pugacheva* (M., 1980), 89–91.

30. Alexander, *Autocratic Politics,* 142–150.

31. Ibid., 162–163.

32. Ibid., 163–169.

33. Alexander, *Emperor*, 162–163; *SIRIO*, 13:407.

34. *Voltaire and Catherine*, 161–162; Alexander, *Autocratic Politics*, 184.

35. *Voltaire and Catherine*, 163; Alexander, *Autocratic Politics*, 195–196.

36. *OV*, 3:232; *Voltaire and Catherine*, 164.

37. Alexander, *Autocratic Politics*, 197–203.

38. Ibid., 203–205.

39. Ibid., 205–208.

40. *Voltaire and Catherine*, 167; *SIRIO*, 27:320.

41. Alexander, *Emperor*, 195–204.

42. *SIRIO*, 1:105.

43. Ibid., 170–181.

44. Ibid., 184–185.

45. Ibid., 188, 193; J. T. Alexander, "Tarakanova, Princess," *MERSH*, 38:173–177.

46. *Kfzh* (1763), 137.

47. *Kfzh* (1777), 737–738; A. G. Cross, "The Duchess of Kingston in Russia," *History Today*, 27 (1977), 390–395; A. Fel'kerzam, "Gertsoginia Kingston i ee prebyvanie v Rossii," *SG* (June 1913), 2–35.

48. K. V. Sivkov, "Podpol'naia politicheskaia literatura v Rossii v poslednei treti XVIII veka," *Istoricheskie zapiski* (1946), 19:71–73.

49. Ibid., 74–78.

50. Ia. Barskov, "Proekty voennykh reform tsesarevicha Pavla," *Russkii istoricheskii zhurnal*, 1917, bk. 3–4:104–145.

Chapter 8

1. *SIRIO*, 27:26–27, 30–32; Tsvetaev, ed., "Sobstvennoruchnye ukazy," 216–218; PROSP 91/99:107v.–108; *Kfzh* (1775), 314–315, 604–613, 772–778.

2. Myl'nikov, *Legenda*, 146–147; *SIRIO*, 19:477–505; vol. 27:44.

3. *SIRIO*, 23:13.

4. *SIRIO*, 27:39, 57, 86, 135–136; *Réglèments de Sa Majesté Imperiale Catherine II, imperatrice et autocratrice de toutes les Russies*, etc., *pour l'Administration des Gouvernements de L'Empire de Russie*, tr. from the original Russian (Spb., 1778).

5. Robert E. Jones, *Provincial Development in Russia: Catherine II and Jakob Sievers* (New Brunswick, 1984), 83–87.

6. *OV*, 1:160–161.

7. N. P. Pavlova-Sil'vanskaia, " 'Uchrezhdenie o guberniiakh' 1775 goda i ego klassovaia sushchnost'," kand. diss. (Moscow, 1964), 113; *OV*, 1:160–161; *SIRIO*, 13:355–356.

8. Pavlova-Sil'vanskaia, "Uchrezhdenie," 125–127, 186; *AGS*, 1, pt. 2:208–209; Tsvetaev, ed., "Sobstvennoruchnye ukazy," 218.

9. *Uchrezhdeniia dlia upravleniia gubernii vserossiiskiia imperii, v koikh stolitsy* (Spb., 1780), 1-3v.

10. Ibid., ch. 1, 18–19.

11. Ibid., ch. 25; Pavlova-Sil'vanskaia, "Uchrezhdenie," 276; *PSZ*, 21:no. 15,399 (18 May 1782); Henry Storch, *The Picture of Petersburg* (London, 1801), 201–204; Max J. Okenfuss, "Education and Empire: School Reform in Enlightened Russia," *JGO*, 27 (1979), 41–68.

12. Ibid., chs. 26–27; Pavlova-Sil'vanskaia, "Uchrezhdenie," 424; J. P. Le Donne,

"The Judicial Reform of 1775 in Central Russia," *JGO*, 21 (1973), 31–35; Janet M. Hartley, "Catherine's Conscience Court—An English Equity Court?" in Cross, ed., *Russia and the West in the Eighteenth Century*, 306–318.

13. *SIRIO*, 23:52; Marc Raeff, "The Empress and the Vinerian Professor: Catherine II's Projects of Government Reforms and Blackstone's *Commentaries*," *OSP*, n.s. 7 (1974), 18, 40.

14. Raeff, "The Empress and the Vinerian Professor," 28–36.

15. Robert E. Jones, *The Emancipation of the Russian Nobility, 1762–1785* (Princeton, 1973), 244–252.

16. Ibid., 227; Tsvetaev, ed., "Sobstvennoruchnye ukazy," 198; J. P. Le Donne, "Catherine's Governors and Governors-General, 1763–1796," *CMRS*, 22 (1979), 15–42; idem., "The Territorial Reform of the Russian Empire, 1775–1796," *CMRS*, 23 (1982), 147–185.

17. *SIRIO*, 1:385–386.

18. Ibid., 384–420.

19. Ibid., 388, 390, 409.

20. A. F. Bychkov, ed., "Pis'ma imperatritsy Ekateriny II-oi k raznym gosudarstrennym Sanovnikam," *ChIOIDR*, bk. 3 (1863), otd. V, 161–162; *MV*, 29 July, 5 Sept., 26 Sept. 1780.

21. *SIRIO*, 23:148, 216.

22. *SIRIO*, 1:276, 284–286; Tsvetaev, ed., "Sobstvennoruchnye ukazy," 201; *PSZ*, 20:no. 14,275 (17 March 1775).

23. J. Michael Hittle, *The Service City: State and Townsmen in Russia, 1600–1800* (Cambridge, Mass., 1979), 198–202.

24. *Iosifa Zonnenfelsa nachalnyia osnovaniia politsii ili blagochiniia*, trans. Matvei Gavrilov (M., 1787); V. Grigor'ev, "Zertsalo upravy blagochiniia," *Russkii istoricheskii zhurnal*, 1917, bk. 3–4:73–103; Marc Raeff, *The Well-Ordered Police State: Social and Institutional Change in the Germanies and Russia, 1600–1800* (New Haven, 1983), 222–230.

25. *PSZ*, 21:no. 15,379 (8 April 1782); *SIRIO*, 27:200–205.

26. *PSZ*, 21:no. 15,379, p. 465; Grigor'ev, "Zertsalo," 95.

27. Ibid., arts. 250, 256–257, 266, 272, 274; no. 15,390 (6 May 1782); no. 15,397 (18 May 1782); *SIRIO*, 27:200–206.

28. *AGS*, 1, pt. 2:351, 359.

29. Tsvetaev, ed., "Sobstvennoruchnye ukazy," 214; A. N. Filippov, "K voprosu o pervoistochnikakh zhalovannoi gramoty dvorianstvu 21 aprelia 1785 g.," *Izvestiia Akademii nauk SSSR*, no. 5–6, 7–8 (1926), 423–443, 479–498.

30. *DKH*, 13.

31. *PSZ*, 22:no. 16, 187 (21 April 1785), arts. 76–82; *SIRIO*, 42:435–436.

32. Ibid., art. 20.

33. Ibid., arts. 25–34

34. Victor Kamendrowsky and David M. Griffiths, "The Fate of the Trading Nobility Controversy in Russia: A Chapter in the Relationship between Catherine II and the Russian Nobility," *JGO*, 26 (1978), 198–221; *AGS*, 1, pt. 2:358; *DKH*, 274; A. V. Florovskii, "K istorii teksta zhalovannoi gramoty dvorianstvu 1785 goda," *Russkii istoricheskii zhurnal*, 1917, bk. 3–4:186–194.

35. *PSZ*, 22:no. 16,188 (21 April 1785).

36. Ibid., arts. 28–29, 36, 78, 80–81, 156–158, 171; Hittle, *Service City*, 221.

37. Janet Hartley, "The Implementation of the Laws relating to Local Administration, 1775–1796, with Special Reference to the Guberniya of Saint Petersburg," Ph.D. diss (University of London, 1980), ch. 4.

38. *PSZ*, 22:no. 16,188, arts, 92, 99, 106.

39. Ibid., arts, 5, 30; no. 16,329 (19 February 1786).

40. *SIRIO*, 20:447; Madariaga, *Russia in the Age of Catherine*, 299.

41. Quoted by Raeff, "The Empress and the Vinerian Professor," 38.

42. *SIRIO*, 23:61, 73, 87.

Chapter 9

1. Samuel M. Schmucker, *Memoirs of the Court and Reign of Catherine the Second, Empress of Russia* (Philadelphia, 1855), vii.

2. Irving Wallace, Amy Wallace, David Wallechinsky, and Sylvia Wallace, *The Intimate Sex Lives of Famous People* (N.Y., 1981), 366–369.

3. M. M. Shcherbatov, *On the Corruption of Morals in Russia,* ed. and trans., A. Lentin (Cambridge, 1969), 79, 235, 241–245.

4. *Ibid.*, 245; Parkinson, *Tour*, 22, 86.

5. *Memoirs of Dashkov*, 154–156, 161, 225–226.

6. Harris, *Diaries and Correspondence,* 1:162; *Memoirs*, 324.

7. *Memoirs of the Empress Catherine II* written by herself with a preface by A. Herzen (New York, 1859), 280. This passage was excised in the Academy edition of Catherine's writings: *Sochineniia Imperatritsy Ekateriny II* (Spb., 1907), 12:419.

8. Georges Oudard, ed., *Lettres d'amour de Catherine II à Potemkine* (Paris, 1934), 153–156, 160–162, 165, 169, 172, 177.

9. *Ibid.*, 37, 40, 42–43, 60–61, 163; *SIRIO*, 42:400.

10. George Soloveytchik, *Potemkin: Soldier, Statesman, Lover and Consort of Catherine of Russia* (N.Y., 1947), 93–94; *PSZ*, 11:no. 8,842 (21 December 1743); vol. 15: no. 11,094 (31 August 1760); vol. 21: no. 15,379 (8 April 1782), arts. 71, 220, 262.

11. *SIRIO*, 42:411.

12. *Ibid.*, 404.

13. Quoted by Soloveytchik, 154.

14. *SIRIO*, 19:511–515, 521–522; PROSP, 91/101:23v.; *Kfzh* (1777), 790; L. H. Labande, ed., *Un diplomat Français à la cour de Catherine II, 1775–1780* (Paris, 1904), 2:157; Alexander Polovtsoff, *The Favourites of Catherine the Great* (London, 1947), 83–84.

15. *Kfzh* (1776), 22–23, 25, 31, 43–44; *AKV*, 12:11; vol. 24:150.

16. Labande, ed., *Un diplomat Français,* 1:164, 190.

17. *MV*, 16 August 1776; *SIRIO*, 19:520.

18. Ia. L. Barskov, "Pis'ma imp. Ekateriny II k gr. P. V. Zavadovskomu (1775–1777)," *Russkii istoricheskii zhurnal*, 1918, bk. 5:244.

19. *Ibid.*, 246–247, 250, 254–255.

20. *Ibid.*, 250.

21. *Ibid.*, 244.

22. *Ibid.*, 244.

23. *Ibid.*, 244.

24. *Ibid.*, 249–250.

25. *Ibid.*, 252.

26. *Ibid.*, 254.

27. *AKV*, 12:10; see also *AKV*, 26:7–30.

28. *AKV*, 12:9–10.

29. Barskov, 246.

30. *AKV,* 12:12–13; Barskov, 239.

31. Barskov, 252–255, 257.

32. *Ibid.,* 249.

33. *Ibid.,* 249.

34. *Ibid.,* 246–247.

35. *Ibid.,* 251, 256–257.

36. *Ibid.,* 256.

37. *Ibid.,* 247, 257; PROSP, 91/101:86, 89, 108; *AKV,* 12:15–16; vol. 24:156; *Kfzh* (1776), 710; (1777), 356, 404.

38. *AKV,* 12:16–19, 316–317; vol. 24:158, 161; *Kfzh* (1778), 276, 327, 340, 358, 381, 809; Harris, *Diaries,* 1:199–202.

39. "Pis'ma grafa P. V. Zavadovskago k fel'dmarshalu grafu P. A. Rumiantsovu," *Starina i novizna,* bk. 4 (1901), 245–246; "Dnevnik grafa Bobrinskago vedennyi v kadetskom korpuse i vo vremia puteshestviia po Rossii i za granitseiu," *RA,* 10 (1887), 118.

40. N. E. Makarenko, "Lialichi," *SG* (July–Sept. 1910), 131–151; *AKV,* 12: 42–44, 52–58, 97; *SIRIO,* 27:404–405; "Pis'ma Zavadovskago Rumiantsovu," 227–231, 263; La Comtesse Brevern de la Gardie, ed., *Un Ambassadeur de Suède à la Court de Catherine II* (Stockholm, 1919), 1:48, 101.

41. Parkinson, *Tour,* 76.

42. Barskov, 227; *Kfzh* (1778), 23, 25; A. G. Cross, *"By the Banks of the Thames": Russians in Eighteenth Century Britain* (Newtonville, Mass., 1980), 239–240.

43. PROSP, 91/102:311–312; Elizabeth Dimsdale's unpublished diary, excerpt in Anthony Cross, ed., *Russia under Western Eyes, 1517–1825* (London, 1971), 220.

44. Shcherbatov, 257, 288–289, 293; Harris, *Diaries and Correspondence,* 1:227.

45. *SIRIO,* 23:250; Parkinson, *Tour,* 49.

46. *Ibid.,* 88.

47. P. F. Karabanov, "Stats-damy i freiliny russkago dvora v XVIII stoletii," *RS,* 4 (1871), 64–65.

48. George Macartney, "Macartney's Commentary on Russia in 1786," Macartney papers, Osborne Collection, Beinecke Library, Yale University—my thanks to Norman Saul for the loan of this material.

49. Shcherbatov, 289; *SIRIO,* 1:384; vol. 23; 195, 218–219, 230–232, 314–316; vol. 42:418; Polovtsoff, *The Favourites,* 192–197; Isabel de Madariaga, *Britain, Russia, and the Armed Neutrality of 1780* (New Haven, 1962), 129, 232, 242, 359.

50. *SIRIO,* 23:282–283.

51. Parkinson, 50.

52. *SIRIO,* 23:316–317.

53. *Ibid.,* 317; "Posle konchiny A. D. Lanskago," *RA,* 1880, bk. 2:151–152.

54. *SIRIO,* 23:344; *DKH,* 10.

55. *Kfzh* (1784), app., 31–32; *DKH,* 525; *SIRIO,* 26:280–281.

56. *SIRIO,* 23:344.

57. *Ibid.,* 317; *DKH,* 10.

58. *Solitude Considered with Respect to Its Effect upon the Mind and the Heart,* tr. J. B. Mercier, 2nd ed. (London, 1792), ix; *O uedinenii, sochinenie Io. Georg Tsimmermanna . . .* (Spb. 1791); A. G. Brikner, "Ekaterina II v perepiske s doktorom Tsimmermannom 1784–1791," *RS,* 54 (1887), 271–294, 591–612.

59. Parkinson, 45, 49; "Iz zapisok doktora Veikarta," *RA*, 1886, no. 3:244–245; *Memoirs of Dashkov*, 215, 229–230.

60. Soloveytchik, 261–263.

61. *SIRIO*, 23:381, 383.

62. *DKH*, xiii–xiv.

63. *SIRIO*, 27:372; *DKH*, 12–13; Ia. K. Grot, ed., *Sochineniia Derzhavina*, 5:520; A. G. Cross, *"By the Banks of the Thames,"* 243.

64. "Pis'ma Zavadovskago k Rumiantsovu," 291; *SIRIO*, 27:372–373; vol. 26: 378; Soloveytchik, 262; Parkinson, *Tour*, 84.

65. *DKH*, 13.

66. *DKH*, 15.

67. *DKH*, 39, 79, 85; *SIRIO*, 27:494.

68. *DKH*, 65, 139–141, 150, 276.

69. *DKH*, 77, 93, 139, 156, 165.

70. *ZG*, 15:15, 242, 244–245, 250, 252, 255, 690–691, 713–714; vol. 16:8, 26–27, 30, 211, 215–219, 225, 235; *DKH*, 252.

71. *DKH*, 254.

72. *DKH*, 255–256.

73. *DKH*, 260–261, 270, 277–278; *Kfzh* (1789), 169.

74. *AKV*, 12:63; *Kfzh* (1789), 180, 183–184, 217.

75. *DKH*, 290–291.

76. *DKH*, 293.

77. *DKH*, 291–292; *Kfzh* (1789), 273–274, 283, 290, 292.

78. *DKH*, 292; *Kfzh* (1789), 273–274, 283, 285, 292.

79. *DKH*, 308, 359; *SIRIO*, 42:15, 17, 21; *Zapiski*, 717.

80. *DKH*, 291, 297.

81. *SIRIO*, 42:22.

82. *SIRIO*, 42:254; "Pis'ma grafa A. M. Dmitrieva-Mamonova k Ekaterine II, 1790–1795," *RA*, 1865:852–860; [J. H. Castéra], *History of Catherine II, Empress of Russia*, tr. Henry Hunter (London, 1800), 532–533.

83. *DKH*, 306, 308, 337; Karabanov, "Stats-damy," 386–387.

84. *DKH*, 294–295, 297, 502–503.

85. *SIRIO*, 42:24; *DKH*, 304–305, 308–309.

86. *Daily Universal Register* (London), 18 July 1787.

87. S. M. Troitskii, "Finansovaia politika russkogo absoliutizma," 311, 316.

88. *200-letie Kabineta Ego Imperatorskago Velichestva, 1704–1904: istoriche-skoe izsledovanie* (Spb., 1911), 376–378.

89. PROSP, 91/103: 164v.

Chapter 10

1. *SIRIO*, 23:16; vol. 42:385; "Pis'ma I. I. Betskago k imperatritse Ekaterine Vtoroi," *RS*, 88 (1896), 393–420.

2. *SIRIO*, 23:12.

3. PROSP, 91/99:41; *SIRIO*, 23:33; vol. 27:66.

4. *OV*, 1:141.

5. *SIRIO*, 23:45–46; PROSP, 91/100:87v., 93; *Kfzh* (1776), 212–213.

6. *SIRIO*, 27:79–80, 95–97.

7. *SIRIO*, 23:45–46; *OV*, 1:142; PROSP, 91/100:90–90v., 93v.–94; Parkinson, *Tour*, 32, 125.

8. *SIRIO*, 27:78–79, 106, n.1.

9. *SIRIO*, 9:7, 13, 18–20, 32; E. S. Shumigorskii, *Imperatritsa Mariia Feodorovna* (*1759–1828*) (Spb., 1892), 67–82.

10. *SIRIO*, 20:411; vol. 27:83–84; PROSP, 91/100:88v.; Barskov, "Pis'ma Zavadovskomu," 250; "Pis'ma Zavadovskago k Rumiantsovu," 242–243.

11. *SIRIO*, 27:85–87, 89, 95, 107.

12. Ibid., 88.

13. Ibid., 91–92, 99.

14. Ibid., 85, 97–98, 100–101, 106, 109; Harris, *Diaries*, 1:147–154; "Tseremoniia i vstrechi vel. kniazia Pavla Petrovicha po pribytii ego v Prussiiu, 1776 goda," *Shchukinskii sbornik* (M., 1910), 10:473–475.

15. *SIRIO*, 9:1–8, 110–111, 114–115.

16. *SIRIO*, 27:117–118.

17. *Kfzh* (1776), 545–549; app., 23–31.

18. Ibid., 674–675, 680–710; *SIRIO*, 27:116–117.

19. *SIRIO*, 20:370; vol. 23:72–73; vol. 27:148–150.

20. *SIRIO*, 27:117, 577; *Kfzh* (1776), index, 18; A. M. Kuchumov and M. A. Velichko, *Pavlovsk: dvorets i park* (L., 1976), 10; Shumigorskii, *Imperatritsa Mariia*, 123, 149–151.

21. *SIRIO*, 23:92, 449.

22. "Dnevnik Bobrinskago," 135–165; I. Ia. Shchelkunov, *Pis'ma Imperatritsy Ekateriny II k datskoi koroleve Iuliane Marii* (Copenhagen, 1914), 5–9; *SIRIO*, 27:184–185; P. Ganzen, "Russkii kniazheskii dvor v gorode Gorsense, 1780–1807 g.," *Vestnik Evropy*, 211 (1901), no. 9, 5–37; no. 10, 625–655.

23. Karl A. Roider, Jr., *Austria's Eastern Question 1700–1790* (Princeton, 1982), 140–147; Arneth, *Joseph II und Katharina*, 1–4; *SIRIO*, 27:29.

24. *SIRIO*, 27:15, 51, 60–62, 91–94; Stephen K. Batalden, *Catherine II's Greek Prelate: Eugenios Voulgaris in Russia 1771–1806* (N.Y., 1982), 29, 43.

25. *SIRIO*, 26:93, 399, 369–370.

26. E. I. Druzhinina, *Severnoe prichernomor'e v 1775–1800 gg.* (M., 1959), 53, 80–81, 149, 176; V. I. Timofeenko, *Goroda severnogo Prichernomor'ia vo vtoroi polovine XVIII veka* (Kiev, 1984), 80–84, 88–91, 148–150.

27. *SIRIO*, 13:190, 201, 227.

28. Alan W. Fisher, *The Russian Annexation of the Crimea 1772–1783* (Cambridge, 1970), 66–67.

29. Ibid., 73–76, 82–83, 120, 124; *SIRIO*, 27:133–134.

30. *SIRIO*, 13:379; Ia. K. Grot, "Ekaterina II i Gustav III," *Sbornik Otdeleniia russkago iazyka i slovestnosti Imperatorskoi Akademii nauk* (Spb., 1878; reprinted Nedeln, 1966), 18:21–29; PROSP, 91/101:139; Romuald J. Misunias, "Russia and Sweden, 1772–1778," unpub. diss. (Yale, 1972), ch. 6; R. Nisbet Bain, *Gustavus III and His Contemporaries* (London, 1894); 1:195–207; Harris, *Diaries*, 1:327; *Kfzh* (1777), 488, 541.

31. *SIRIO*, 27:137–138, 140; *AGS*, 1, pt. 1:331–332.

32. Fisher, *Russian Annexation*, 107–108.

33. Ibid., 108–111.

34. *SIRIO*, 27:147.

35. *SIRIO*, 23:84.

36. Ibid., 75, 87, 128.

37. Roider, *Austria's Eastern Question*, 158–159; David M. Griffiths, "Russian Court Politics and the Question of an Expansionist Foreign Policy under Catherine II, 1762–1783," unpub. diss. (Cornell, 1967), 164–165; *SIRIO*, 26:385.

38. *SIRIO*, 9:52–53, 55, 57; vol. 23:183; vol. 26:65, 372–373; vol. 42:277;

A. G. Brikner, "Puteshestvie imperatritsy Ekateriny II v Mogilev v 1780 godu," *Russkii vestnik,* 155 (1881), no. 8:495; Isabel de Madariaga, "The Secret Austro-Russian Treaty of 1781," *SEER,* 90 (1959), 115–116.

39. *SIRIO,* 9:58–60; *Kfzh* (1780), 241–246; Griffiths, "Russian Court Politics," 181–184; *Kfzh* (1780), 578; Shumigorskii, *Imperatritsa Mariia,* 159–161.

40. Arneth, *Joseph II und Katharina,* 11, 13, 22.

41. Ibid., 16–17.

42. Harris, *Diaries,* 1:432; "Perepiska Ekateriny Velikoi s Germanskim imperatorom Iosifom II-m," *RA,* bk. 1 (1880), 222–223, 225, 227–228, 233, 236–237, 239.

43. Ibid., 248.

44. Ibid., 240–241, 254–257.

45. Ransel, *Politics,* 254–255; *SIRIO,* 27:190–191; Jones, *Provincial Development,* 157–158.

46. Harris, *Diaries,* 1:432; "Perepiska Ekateriny s Iosifom," 264, 266–268; *SIRIO,* 9:64, 66; Madariaga, "Secret Treaty," 129–131; Griffiths, "Russian Court Politics," 211.

47. Griffiths, "Russian Court Politics," 326–327.

48. Ibid., 216–227; idem, "The Rise and Fall of the Northern System: Court Politics and Foreign Policy in the First Half of Catherine II's Reign," *CSS,* 4 (1970), 566; *SIRIO,* 9:145, 158–159; Shumigorskii, *Imperatritsa Mariia,* 237–246; Harris, *Diaries,* 2:18–19.

49. "Perepiska Ekateriny s Iosifom," 277; *SIRIO,* 27:206–207, 210–213, 216–218, 281.

50. "Perepiska Ekateriny s Iosifom," 281–291.

51. P. M. Maikov, ed., "Pis'ma A. A. Bezborodka k grafu P. A. Rumiantsovu, 1777–1793," *Starina i novizna,* bk. 3 (1900), 260, 276; *SIRIO,* 27:215–216.

52. "Perepiska Ekateriny s Iosifom," 291–300; *DKH,* 3; Griffiths, "Russian Court Politics," 161–163.

53. *SIRIO,* 27:217–219; A. L. Kaganovich, *"Mednyi vsadnik": Istoriia sozdaniia monumenta* (L., 1975), 159–164; *DKH,* 1.

54. "Pis'ma Zavadovskago k Rumiantsovu," 275; *SIRIO,* 27:221–228.

55. *SIRIO,* 27:230–233, 251–253; "Perepiska Ekateriny s Iosifom," 306–311; Arneth, *Joseph II und Katharina,* 197–198.

56. "Perepiska Ekateriny s Iosifom," 313; *SIRIO,* 27:240–250.

57. *SIRIO,* 27:244.

58. Ibid., 255–256, 259–261.

59. Ibid., 262, 266–267; Madariaga, "Secret Treaty," 138–140.

60. *SIRIO,* 27:263–264, 266; *Kfzh* (1783), 263–297; suppl., 63–65; Grot, "Ekaterina II i Gustav III," 46, 48.

61. *SIRIO,* 27:266–268; "Sem' sobstvennoruchnykh pisem i zapisok kniazia G. A. Potemkina-Tavricheskago k grafu P. A. Rumiantsovu-Zadunaiskomu (1769–1788)." *Starina i novizna,* bk. 5 (1902), 69.

62. *SIRIO,* 27:269.

63. Ibid., 270–272, 274.

64. Ibid., 274.

65. Ibid., 276–280.

66. Ibid., 280–285.

67. Ibid., 283, 286–287, 290–291, 294; Fisher, *Russian Annexation,* 138; *DKH,* 4.

68. *SIRIO,* 27:293–295; Fisher, 151.

69. Fisher, 142; *PSZ*, 22:no. 15,920 (2 Feb. 1784); *SIRIO*, 27:296–300, 332; *Kfzh* (1784), 226, 380–384, 452.

70. *SIRIO*, 27:334, 336–342, 344, 351, 365; "Pis'ma Bezborodka k Rumiantsovu," 274, 279; *PSZ*, 22:16,057 (4 Sept. 1784); *DKH*, 4; A. G. Brikner, "Puteshestvie Imperatritsy Ekateriny II v Vyshnii Volochek i Moskvu v 1785," *IV*, 6 (1881), 681–702; *Kfzh* (1784), app., 71.

71. *PSZ*, 22: no. 16,128 (14 Jan. 1785).

72. *SIRIO*, 23:268, 284, 293, 303–304, 326, 330, 338, 361; vol. 26:455; vol. 27:287; "Pis'ma Zavadovskago k Rumiantsovu," 279–281, 285; "Dnevnik Bobrinskago," 160; *DKH*, 8; *MV*, 6 June 1780; I. Bondarenko, "Podmoskovnye dvortsy XVIII veka," *SG* (March, 1911), 23–30; Kahan, *Plough, Hammer, and Knout*, 13; [I. A. Tolchenov], *Zhurnal ili zapiska zhizni i prikliucheniia Ivana Alekseevicha Tolchenova*, ed. N. I. Pavlenko (M., 1974), 211–212.

Chapter 11

1. *SIRIO*, 27:381–387, 416; *TCM*, 18 (March 1786), 161–162.

2. Ibid., 376; *DKH*, 10, 12.

3. *Kfzh* (1787), app. 39–44; Shumigorskii, *Imperatritsa Mariia*, 286–293; *SIRIO*, 23:385; vol. 27:388, 472.

4. A. G. Brikner, " 'Zel'mira': Epizod iz istorii tsarstvovaniia imperatritsy Ekateriny II," *IV*, 41 (1890):277–303, 551–572; D. F. Kobeko, "Imperatritsa Ekaterina Alekseevna, pis'ma eia k komandantu Tsigleru (1786–1787 gg.)," *RS*, 73 (1892), 267–270; V. A. Bil'basov, "Vysylka iz Rossii printsa Viurtembergskago Fridrikha," *RS*, 73 (1892), 459–468.

5. *SIRIO*, 23:391, 393–394; vol. 27:403; *DKH*, 22–23, 26–29.

6. A. G. Brikner, "Puteshestvie Ekateriny II v Krym," *IV*, 21 (1885), 452–456; Joseph O. Baylen and Dorothy Woodward, "Francisco de Miranda and Russian Diplomacy, 1787–88," *The Historian*, 13 (1950), 52–68; John R. Alden, *Stephen Sayre: American Revolutionary Adventurer* (Baton Rouge, 1983), 130; Curtis Carroll Davis, *The King's Chevalier: A Biography of Lewis Littlepage* (Indianapolis, 1961), 147–152.

7. *Kfzh* (1787), app. 51, 91.

8. *SIRIO*, 27:417–418; *DKH*, 30; *ZG*, 15:20; *Kfzh* (1787), 309; A. M. Panchenko, " 'Potemkinskie derevni' kak kul'turnyi mif," *XVIII vek*, 14 (L., 1983), 93–104; *DA*, 24 March, 28 March, 9 April, 17 April, 12 May, 3 July, 13 July 1787; "Imperatritsa Ekaterina II v eia neizdannykh ili izdannykh ne vpolne pis'makh k I. G. Tsimmermannu," *RS*, 55 (1887), 247, 286.

9. *SIRIO*, 26:284; vol. 27:407–408; *DKH*, 33; "Perepiska Ekateriny II s kn. Potemkinym," *RS*, 16 (1876), 58, 239; Brikner, "Puteshestvie v Krym," 465; *Lettres du Prince de Ligne à la Marquise de Coigny pendant l'année 1787*, ed. M. de Lescure (Paris, 1886), 13.

10. *Kfzh* (1787), 344–345, 380–382, 384–387; app., "Pis'ma Imperatritsy Ekateriny II k Iakovu Aleksandrovichu Briusu, 1787 goda" (Spb., 1889), 23; *DKH*, 33–34, 36.

11. *SPV*, 28 May 1787; *SIRIO*, 27:408–409; *DKH*, 35–36; *Kfzh* (1787), 417; Roider, *Austria's Eastern Question*, 172.

12. *Kfzh* (1787), 473, 489–490; *DKH*, 36–37; G. Esipov, "Amazonskaia rota pri Ekaterine II," *IV*, 23 (1886), 71–75; Arneth, ed., *Joseph II und Katharina*, 363–372.

13. *SIRIO*, 27:410–411, 413, 447; *DKH*, 38–40.

14. *SIRIO*, 27:417, "Pis'ma Briusu," 33; *Kfzh* (1787), 748–752; app., 31–33; *ZG*, 15:237; *DKH*, 44, 46; *Memoirs and Recollections of Count Segur* (London, 1825–1827), 3:190–193.

15. *Kfzh* (1787), 752–760; *ZG*, 15:33–34, 237–239; *DKH*, 44–45; *PSZ*, 22: no. 16, 561 (8 Aug. 1787).

16. *DKH*, 46–47.

17. *ZG*, 15:243, 247; *SIRIO*, 27:421–422; *DKH*, 47; *AGS*, 1, pt. 1:x.

18. *Kfzh* (1787), 799–800; *AGS*, 1, pt. 1:459.

19. *AGS*, 1, pt. 2:25–28, 44, 416; "Pis'ma Zavadovskago Rumiantsovu," 297; *SIRIO*, 23:421.

20. *AGS*, 1, pt. 1:467, 484.

21. *DKH*, 47–48; *SIRIO*, 23:419; vol. 26:397–399; *SPV*, 14 Sept. 1787; *AGS*, 1, pt. 1:471–474.

22. *SIRIO*, 23:421; vol. 27:442, 455.

23. *SIRIO*, 27:424, 434, 436–439, 442–443; *DKH*, 53, 55; *ZG*, 15:494–495, 498.

24. *ZG*, 15:701; *DKH*, 57, 60, 65, 69–73, 76–78; *SIRIO*, 23:440; vol. 27:457, 469; *The Times* (London), 15 March, 11 and 18 April, 21 June 1788; *AGS*, 1, pt. 2:725–726; *Memoirs*, 326; Roider, *Austria's Eastern Question*, 181.

25. *DKH*, 72–73, 82; *SIRIO*, 27:454, 459–460, 465–466, 469, 477.

26. *SIRIO*, 23:438.

27. *SIRIO*, 27:472, 480; *DKH*, 71; *ZG*, 15:476; N. P. Pavlova-Sil'vanskaia, "K voprosu o vneshnikh dolgakh Rossii vo vtoroi polovine XVIII v.," *Problemy genezisa kapitalizma* (M., 1970), 308, 310; *AGS*, 1, pt. 2:416–455.

28. *Catalogue of Political and Personal Satires Preserved in the Department of Prints and Drawings in the British Museum*, ed. Mary Dorothy George (London, 1938), 6:424–426.

29. *SIRIO*, 23:446; vol. 26:289; vol. 27:474–475, 484–485, 487–488, 491; *Kfzh* (1788), 227–228, 238, 257, 261; *DKH*, 83.

30. *SIRIO*, 27:486; *DKH*, 80–81, 151, 345–346, 572; *ZG*, 15:26–27, 246, 488, 704; vol. 16:9, 19.

31. *DKH*, 81; *SIRIO*, 27:488–489, 492.

32. *TCM*, 20 (July 1788), 336; H. Arnold Barton, *Scandinavia in the Revolutionary Era, 1760–1815* (Minneapolis, 1986), 155–156; *SIRIO*, 26:292; vol. 27:492–493, 496–497; *DKH*, 86–87; *ZG*, 16:12, 15, 25.

33. *SIRIO*, 27:497, 501; *DKH*, 88, 91.

34. *DKH*, 92–93; *AGS*, 1, pt. 1:570.

35. *AGS*, 1, pt. 1:569–571; *DKH*, 93; *SIRIO*, 23:452.

36. *SIRIO*, 26:294; *DKH*, 95.

37. *DKH*, 96; *Kfzh* (1788), 385–390; *SIRIO*, 27:501–502.

38. *SIRIO*, 23:575; vol. 27:529; *Kfzh* (1788), 735–736; (1789), 23, 273; *DKH*, 313.

39. *DKH*, 97, 99; *Kfzh* (1788), 390–414.

40. *Kfzh* (1788), 416–422; *DKH*, 100–101; *SIRIO*, 23:454–455; Arneth, ed., *Joseph II und Katharina*, 315–316; *ZG*, 16:27.

41. *DKH*, 101–102; *Kfzh* (1788), 412; *AGS*, 1, pt. 2:47–48; "Pis'ma Zavadovskago Rumiantsovu," 311.

42. *DKH*, 104–105; *SIRIO*, 27:505, 512; *Kfzh* (1788), 430, 434–435.

43. *SIRIO*, 27:512–513; *Kfzh* (1788), 454–460.

44. *DKH*, 113; *Kfzh* (1788), 452–453, 464.

45. *SIRIO*, 27:514, 516–518; *DKH*, 121–123, 130; *Kfzh* (1788), 498–499; Barton, *Scandinavia*, 158–160.

46. *DKH*, 125, 128–129; *SIRIO*, 27:522; Barton, *Scandinavia*, 164.

47. *SIRIO*, 27:526; *DKH*, 169, 174–175.

48. *SIRIO*, 27:531–532; *DKH*, 179, 211–219, 224; "Imperatritsa Ekaterina II v pis'makh k Tsimmermannu," 300.

49. *ZG*, 16:235; "Pis'ma Zavadovskago Rumiantsovu," 320.

50. *ZG*, 16:226, 234; *SIRIO*, 42:2; *DKH*, 229, 238.

51. *DKH*, 245–247.

52. *SIRIO*, 42:6; *Kfzh* (1789), 65–70, 75–77; "Pis'ma Zavadovskago Rumiantsovu," 321.

53. *Kfzh* (1789), 354–357; app., 35–36; *DKH*, 265, 275–276.

54. *DKH*, 267, 269–271.

55. *AGS*, 1, pt. 1:677, 683, 686; *DKH*, 260; *SIRIO*, 42:8.

56. *DKH*, 269–273, 277–278, 310, 325; *SIRIO*, 23:475; "Pis'ma Zavadovskago Rumiantsovu," 326, 328.

57. *DKH*, 288; *SIRIO*, 42:9, 11–13, 15.

58. *DKH*, 275.

59. *AGS*, 1, pt. 1:693–694, 697–698; Frank Fox, "Negotiating with the Russians: Ambassador Segur's Mission to Saint-Petersburg, 1784–1789," *French Historical Studies*, 7 (1971), 53; *Memoirs and Recollections of Count Segur*, 2:274, 296; vol. 3:80, 87.

60. *DKH*, 296, 299, 301; *AGS*, 1, pt. 1:666–667, 668, 690–691, 696, 718, 720, 722.

61. *DKH*, 302, *AGS*, 1, pt. 1:724–726.

62. *SIRIO*, 42:25; *AGS*, 1, pt. 1:727, 729.

63. *DKH*, 303; *AGS*, 1, pt. 1:731.

64. *ZG*, 16:413–414; *DKH*, 304–305; *SIRIO*, 42:32–33, 52; *The Times*, 14 Oct. 1789; *AGS*, 1, pt. 1:738, 740.

65. *DKH*, 308–311, 314.

66. *SIRIO*, 42:37, 43; *DKH*, 312, 320–321.

67. *DKH*, 322, 324; *ZG*, 16:406, 410, 423; *SIRIO*, 42:51, 57–58, 62, 65, 75; Barton, *Scandinavia*, 190.

68. *DKH*, 328–330; *SIRIO*, 42:59, 61, 62, 65–67, 75, 78–79; *AGS*, 1, pt. 1:769.

69. *SIRIO*, 42:63; *DKH*, 327–328; *AGS*, 1, pt. 1:766–767, 770.

70. *DKH*, 313, 330–331, 388; *SIRIO*, 42:45, 86.

71. *SIRIO*, 26:423; vol. 42:73; *DKH*, 332–333; *PSZ*, 23:no. 16,863 (10 May 1790).

72. *DKH*, 335–336; *SIRIO*, 42:25; *ZG*, 16:430–433; *PSZ*, 23:no. 16,869 (28 May 1790).

73. *DKH*, 337–338; *SIRIO*, 42:87–88, 91–92, 103.

74. *DKH*, 339–340; *SIRIO*, 42:91, 103.

75. *SIRIO*, 42:99, 101; *DKH*, 345, 380, 382–383; Barton, *Scandinavia*, 194.

76. *DKH*, 338–339.

77. *DKH*, 340.

78. A. N. Radishchev, *A Journey from St. Petersburg to Moscow*, tr. Leo Wiener, ed. Roderick P. Thaler (Cambridge, Mass., 1958), 82, 239, 241–242, 248–249; Allen McConnell, *A Russian Philosophe: Alexander Radischev 1749–1802* (The Hague, 1964), 118.

79. McConnell, 119, 121; *DKH*, 334, 347; *AGS*, 1, pt. 2:737; *PSZ*, 23:no. 16,901 (4 Sept. 1790).

80. *SIRIO*, 42:106–107; *DKH*, 345; McConnell, 107–108, 115.

81. *SIRIO*, 42:100–101, 107–108.

82. Ibid., 107, 109.

83. Ibid., 110, 119–120, 122, 125, 132, 134–135; *DKH*, 350–353.

84. *SIRIO*, 42:137, 148; *DKH*, 359.

85. *DKH*, 361; *SIRIO*, 26:424; M. S. Anderson, *Britain's Discovery of Russia, 1553–1815* (London, 1958), 156–157; Jerzy Lojek, "Catherine's Armed Intervention in Poland: Origins of the Political Decisions at the Russian Court in 1791 and 1792," *CSS*, 4 (1970), 576, 581–582; *AKV*, 12:68; *Un ambassadeur de Suede*, 1: 112–113.

86. *AGS*, 1, pt. 1:841–844; *SIRIO*, 42:150–151.

87. *AGS*, 1, pt. 1:844–845; *DKH*, 361.

88. *DKH*, 362; Parkinson, *Tour*, 30; *SIRIO*, 23:517–520.

89. *SIRIO*, 23:541–542, 554; *AGS*, 1, pt. 1:851–875; *DKH*, 363–367, 373–374, 398; Allen Cunningham, "Robert Adair's 1791 Mission to St. Petersburg," *Bulletin of the Institute of Historical Research* 105, no. 132 (1982), 154–165; idem, "The Oczakow Debate," *Middle Eastern Studies*, 1 (1965), 235, n. 17.

90. *TCM*, 23 (March 1791), 104.

91. *Catalogue of Political and Personal Satires*, 6:777–778.

92. Ibid., 816–817; *DKH*, 364; *The Satirical Etchings of James Gillray*, ed. Draper Hill (N.Y., 1976), no. 19.

93. *SIRIO*, 42:189, 191, 193; "Baronessa Korf i eia sodeistvie pobegu Liudovika XVI iz Parizha v 1791," *RA*, 4 (1866), 800–816; K. E. Dzhedzhula, *Rossiia i Velikaia frantsuzskaia burzhuaznaia revoliutsiia kontsa XVIII veka* (Kiev, 1972), 318–320; H. Arnold Barton, *Count Hans Axel von Fersen: Aristocrat in an Age of Revolution* (Boston, 1975), 73–74, 107–108, 111, 142.

94. *SIRIO*, 42:192–193; *AGS*, 1, pt. 1:875.

95. *AGS*, 1, pt. 1:879–880; *DKH*, 371; *SIRIO*, 42:194; Roider, *Austria's Eastern Question*, 189–190.

96. *DKH*, 372–373; *SIRIO*, 42:196, 198–199, 202–203.

97. *DKH*, 376; *SIRIO*, 42:203; "Imperatritsa Ekaterina II i kn. Potemkin," *RS*, 17 (1876), 652.

98. *DKH*, 377; *SIRIO*, 23:561.

99. *AGS*, 1, pt. 1:893–895; *DKH*, 378.

100. *DKH*, 377–378, 383–385, 387.

Chapter 12

1. Kornilovich, "Zapiski Ekateriny," 47–48.

2. *Kfzh* (1792), app., 65–66; *DKH*, 392–393.

3. *Kfzh* (1792), 101, 144, 165; *DKH*, 393; Parkinson, *Tour*, 224.

4. Parkinson, *Tour*, 73; *DKH*, 396, 404–405.

5. *SIRIO*, 42:320–321.

6. *DKH*, 410, 418–419.

7. "Vospominaniia i dnevniki Adriana Moiseevicha Gribovskago," *RA*, bk. 1 (1899), 50; Parkinson, *Tour*, 14, 46, 48.

8. *DKH*, 383; *AKV*, 12:75–80.

9. Parkinson, *Tour*, 46; *SIRIO*, 23:566.

10. *DKH*, 394; *SIRIO*, 42:224; *AGS*, 1, pt. 1:906–912.

11. Dzhedzhula, *Rossiia i frantsuzskaia revoliutsiia,* 323–325; M. M. Shtrange, *Russkoe obshchestvo i frantsuzskaia revoliutsiia 1789–1794 gg.* (M., 1956), 118; *SIRIO,* 2:345; "Pis'ma Ekateriny k Moskovskim glavnokomanduiushchim," 564; William L. Blackwell, "Citizen Genet and the Revolution in Russia," *French Historical Studies,* 3 (1963), 87.

12. *DKH,* 391; *SIRIO,* 42:220–221; "Pis'ma Ekateriny k Moskovskim glavnokomanduiushchim," 565–566; "Moskovskiia pis'ma Bantysh-Kamenskago," 403.

13. *Kfzh* (1792), 151, 159; *SIRIO,* 23:564; vol. 42:221–223; "Pis'ma Ekateriny k Moskovskim glavnokomanduiushchim," 566–567; *DKH,* 394–395; *TCM,* 24 (May 1792), 217–220, 236.

14. Shtrange, *Russkoe obshchestvo,* 110; *SIRIO,* 23:565.

15. *DKH,* 395; Robert H. Lord, *The Second Partition of Poland* (Cambridge and London, 1915), 275.

16. *Zapiski,* 719–720; *Memoirs,* 327–328.

17. N. Ia. Eidel'man, *Gran' vekov* (M., 1982), 50–52; *SIRIO,* 23:597.

18. Parkinson, *Tour,* 22–23, 54, 62, 72, 85, 125.

19. Gilbert H. McArthur, "Catherine II and the Masonic Circle of N. I. Novikov," *CSS,* 4 (1970), 531–532; "Pis'ma Ekateriny k Moskovskim glavnokomanduiushchim," 533–534, 538–539; V. Bogoliubov, *N. I. Novikov i ego vremia* (M., 1916), 404; Marker, *Publishing,* 219–225.

20. G. P. Makogoneko, ed., *N. I. Novikov: Izbrannye sochineniia* (M. and L., 1954), 590–591.

21. Ibid., 591–593; Bogoliubov, *Novikov,* 409–410; *Kfzh* (1792), 212, 232.

22. Makogonenko, ed., *Novikov,* 600.

23. Ibid., 600–601; *DKH,* 397; *Kfzh* (1792), 232; *SIRIO,* 42:227.

24. Bogoliubov, *Novikov,* 412, 419–420; *DKH,* 398–399; *SIRIO,* 42:314–315; Marker, *Publishing,* 226–228.

25. *SIRIO,* 42:226; *DKH,* 400.

26. McArthur, "Catherine II and Novikov," 541, 544; Bogoliubov, *Novikov,* 433; Makogonenko, ed., *Novikov,* 638.

27. *Nouvelles lettres du Cte Valentin Ladislas Esterhazy à sa femme 1792–1795,* ed. Ernest Daudet (Paris, 1909), 62, 69, 79, 90, 106; *DKH,* 404, 406–407, 409, 419–420; McArthur, "Catherine and Novikov," 544; *Kfzh* (1793), app., 29; (1794), app., 88; "O S. I. Sheshovskim," *RA,* bk. 4 (1866), 263–264.

28. "Moskovskiia pis'ma Bantysh-Kamenskago," 273.

29. *DKH,* 407–408.

30. *Nouvelles lettres du Esterhazy,* 119, 130; *DKH,* 408–412; *Kfzh* (1792), 502–512.

31. *SIRIO,* 23:567; Lord, *Second Partition,* 292–297; *AGS,* 1, pt. 1:922–927; Blackwell, "Citizen Genet," 79, 90.

32. *DKH,* 404.

33. *SIRIO,* 23:574; *Kfzh* (1792), 592–625.

34. Parkinson, *Tour,* 34.

35. *SIRIO,* 23:577–578; Lord, *Second Partition,* 349; *DKH,* 413, 415, 417; "Moskovskiia pis'ma Bantysh-Kamenskago," 278; Parkinson, *Tour,* 58; *Kfzh* (1792), 668–673; (1793), 84; *Karlik favorita,* 199, n81.

36. *DKH,* 417, 420–421; *Kfzh* (1793), 72–74; *AGS,* 1, pt. 1:951–954; *PSZ,* 23:no. 17,101 (8 Feb. 1793); no. 17,103 (17 Feb. 1793); Charles de Larivière, *Catherine II et la Revolution Française* (Paris, 1895), 137.

37. *DKH,* 422–423; *PSZ,* 23:no. 17,108 (27 March 1793); *Kfzh* (1793), app., 6.

38. *SIRIO,* 23:667; *DKH,* 423.

39. *Kfzh* (1793), 163–166; app., 7–9; *SIRIO,* 23:583; vol. 42:240; Dzhedzhula, *Rossiia i frantsuzskaia revoliutsiia,* 359–364.

40. *DKH,* 424–425.

41. *DKH,* 434–435; *Kfzh* (1793), 334–358, 363–364.

42. *DKH,* 428–429.

43. *DKH,* 431–433; *SIRIO,* 29:231, 236–241.

44. *DKH,* 433–435; "Rostopchinskiia pis'ma," *RA,* bk. 2 (1887), 149; *PSZ,* 23:no. 17,143 (12 July 1793); *AKV,* 12:91.

45. *DKH,* 437; *AGS,* 1, pt. 2:762.

46. *Kfzh* (1793), 702–709.

47. *Kfzh* (1793), app., 98–102.

48. *PSZ,* 23:no. 17,149 (2 Sept. 1793).

49. *Kfzh* (1793), app., 102–103.

50. *AKV,* 13:276; *SIRIO,* 29:244, 248; "Rostopchinskiia pis'ma," 152; *Kfzh* (1793), 721–757.

51. *Kfzh* (1793), app.: *Zhurnal prebyvaniia v S.Peterburge ikh svelostei Printsess Badenskikh v 1793 godu* (Spb., 1892), 582–584; *PSZ,* 23:no. 17,156 (29 Sept. 1793); Shumigorskii, *Imperatritsa Mariia,* 394–395, 399–400.

52. *DKH,* 438; *SIRIO,* 23:589; vol. 29:250–251.

53. *SIRIO,* 23:587; vol. 42:243–244; *Kfzh* (1793), 831; *AKV,* 12:93.

54. *AKV,* 12:96; *Memoirs of Dashkov,* 242–244; K. A. Papmehl, *Freedom of Expression in Eighteenth Century Russia* (The Hague, 1971), 119–120; "Iz rozysknago dela o tragedii Kniazhnina Vadim," *RA,* bk. 1 (1863), 605–610.

55. "Pis'ma Ekateriny k Moskovskim glavnokomanduiushchim," 574; "Moskovskiia pis'ma Bantysh-Kamenskago," 392, 396, 401; *PSZ,* 23:no. 17,284 (18 Dec. 1794); Dzhedzhula, *Rossiia i frantsuzskaia revoliutsiia,* 380.

56. *SIRIO,* 23:590–591; "Rostopchinskiia pis'ma," 152–155; "Moskovskiia pis'ma Bantysh-Kamenskago," 385–386; *Kfzh* (1794), app., 72–73; *AKV,* 12: 95, 100.

57. *SIRIO,* 23:591–592; *Kfzh* (1794), 114–137; app., 69.

58. Parkinson, *Tour,* 227–228.

59. "Rostopchinskiia pis'ma," 156.

60. Norman Davies, *God's Playground: A History of Poland* (N.Y., 1982), 1: 538–540; Parkinson, *Tour,* 230–232.

61. *SIRIO,* 23:603; *AGS,* 1, pt. 1:978; *Kfzh* (1794), 296–300, 314.

62. *AKV,* 12:109–114; vol. 13:284–293; *AGS,* 1, pt. 1:978–981.

63. *PSZ,* 23:no. 17,201 (26 April 1794); *AKV,* 12:110–113; vol. 13:293; *AGS,* 1, pt. 1:980–981; "Moskovskiia pis'ma Bantysh-Kamenskago," 387–391.

64. "Moskovskiia pis'ma Bantysh-Kamenskago," 390–391.

65. *SIRIO,* 23:605–606, 608, 611, 613; *Kfzh* (1794), 358, 594.

66. *AKV,* 12:114–115, 125, 130; vol. 13:308–309, 331; *PSZ,* 23:no. 17,215 (14 June 1794); no. 17,217 (21 July 1794); no. 17,222 (23 June 1794); no. 17,248 (7 Sept. 1794); *AGS,* 1, pt. 2:505–512; Kahan, *Plough, Hammer, and Knout,* 341–342, 346.

67. *PSZ,* 23:no. 17,247; no. 17, 249; no. 17,250 (all 7 Sept. 1794); no. 17,258 (29 Sept. 1794).

68. *PSZ,* 23:no. 17,240 (10 Aug. 1794).

69. *AKV,* 12:118, 127, 134; vol. 13:314; *SIRIO,* 23:610–611; "Pis'ma Zavadovskago k Rumiantsovu," 336; "Moskovskiia pis'ma Bantysh-Kamenskago," 400; *AGS,* 1, pt. 1:990–991.

70. *AKV*, 13:465; *Kfzh* (1794), 796–797; Longworth, *Art of Victory*, 199–207.

71. *SIRIO*, 23:616–617; *Kfzh* (1795), 157; app., 117; "Moskovskiia pis'ma Bantysh-Kamenskago," 398.

72. *SIRIO*, 23:615, 617, 631; *Kfzh* (1794), 843–859; app., 107.

73. *PSZ*, 23:no. 17,286; no. 17,287 (both 1 Jan. 1795); no. 17,294 (14 Jan. 1795); no. 17,295 (16 Jan. 1795); *SIRIO*, 23:617–618; *Kfzh* (1795), 35–92; app., 99.

74. *PSZ*, 23:no. 17,303 (3 Feb. 1795); no. 17,305 (7/18 Feb. 1795); no. 17,319 (15 April 1795); no. 13, 343 (13 June 1795); no. 17,345 (20 June 1795); no. 17,352 (5 July 1795); Edward C. Thaden, *Russia's Western Borderlands, 1710–1870* (Princeton, 1984), 51; *SIRIO*, 23:650; "Moskovskiia pis'ma Bantysh-Kamenskago," 402–412.

75. *Kfzh* (1795), 420, 509, 627; app., 192–193; (1796), 536; *AKV*, 13:346.

76. *AKV*, 12:153, 158–159.

77. *AKV*, 13:351–356.

78. *SIRIO*, 23:645, 647; *PSZ*, 23:no. 17,394 (8 Oct 1795).

79. *Kfzh* (1795), app., 189–190, 193–194, 204; *SIRIO*, 23:644–645; E. P. Karnovich, *Tsesarevich Konstantin Pavlovich* (Spb., 1899), 42–44.

80. *AKV*, 13:361; Parkinson, *Tour*, 41, 67, 76; *Kfzh* (1795), 821–826, 845; app., 236.

81. *Kfzh* (1796), 69–81, 110–115; app., 11–12; *PSZ*, 23:no. 17,436 (3 Feb. 1796); Parkinson, *Tour*, 77; *SIRIO*, 23:668–669.

82. *Kfzh* (1795), app., 258–261; (1796), 233–235, 293; app., 34; *AKV*, 13: 331, 347; Georges Lefebvre, *The French Revolution from 1793 to 1799*, tr. John Hall Stewart and James Friguglietti (London and N.Y., 1964), 169, 174–175, 188; *SIRIO*, 23:671, 685–688; *PSZ*, 23:no. 17,451 (March 1796); "Vospominaniia Gribovskago," 54.

83. *PSZ*, 23:no. 17,455 (8 May 1796); no. 17,457 (11 May 1796); no. 17,490 (19 July 1796); *SIRIO*, 23:651, 674; vol. 29:317–320; *AKV*, 12:117, 165–166.

84. Tolchenov, *Zhurnal*, 314; *SIRIO*, 23:681, 690; *Kfzh* (1796), 396, 528–534, 575–587; *PSZ*, 23:no. 17,479 (6 July 1796); E. S. Shumigorskii, *Ekaterina Ivanovna Nelidova, 1758–1839* (Spb., 1898), 59–60; "Vospominaniia Gribovskago," 58.

85. *SIRIO*, 23:685; vol. 29:348; vol. 42:266; "Vospominaniia Gribovskago," 16, 59.

86. A. Chumikov, "Gustav IV-i i velikaia kniazhna Aleksandra Pavlovna," *RA*, bk. 1 (1887):59–79; *SIRIO*, 23:691–694; vol. 29:321, 491; vol. 42:266.

87. Chumikov, "Gustav IV," 79–83; *PSZ*, 23:no. 17,505 (9 Sept. 1796).

88. *Kfzh* (1796), 642, 665; app., 99–101; Chumikov, "Gustav IV," 84–98; *AKV*, 12:175; *SIRIO*, 29:322; N. V. Drizen, "Gustav IV i Velikaia kniazhna Aleksandra Pavlovna, 1794–1796 gg.," *RS*, 88 (1896), 193–207.

89. *PSZ*, 23:no. 17,508 (16 Sept. 1796); no. 17,523 (22 Oct. 1796); no. 17,538 (10 Nov. 1796); Kahan, *Plough, Hammer, and Knout*, 348; *SIRIO*, 2:383, 388–392; vol. 23:693–694; James W. Marcum, "Catherine II and the French Revolution," *Canadian Slavonic Papers*, 16 (1974), 199; Dzhedzhula, *Rossiia i frantsuzskaia revoliutsiia*, 415–418; *Kfzh* (1796), app., 109; Marker, *Publishing*, 228–232; "Ekaterina Velikaia v poslednie dni svoi," *RA*, bk. 1 (1898), 477.

90. *Kfzh* (1796), app.: *Opisanie konchiny Ekateriny Alekseevny Vtoryia 1796 g.* (Spb., 1895), 3–4.

91. *Kfzh* (1796), 737–742; app., 5–8; *SIRIO*, 29:348–354.

92. *Kfzh* (1796), 743–748; app., 8–12; *PSZ*, 23:no. 17,530 (6 Nov. 1796).

93. *Kfzh* (1796), app., 12–15.

94. *Kfzh* (1796), app., 15–42; N. Shil'der, "Konchina Ekateriny II i votsarenie Pavla I," *RS*, 88 (1896), 476; "Vospominaniia Fedora Petrovicha Lubianovskago," *RA*, 10 (1872), 147–148; Anon., *Authentic Memoirs*, 287.

95. *PSZ*, 23:no. 17,538 (10 Nov. 1796); no. 17,585 (29 Nov. 1796); no. 17,634 (12 Dec. 1796); *Kfzh* (1796), 782, 795; app., 116, 120, 127; (1797), app., 111; Muriel Atkin, *Russia and Iran, 1780–1828* (Minneapolis, 1980), 47; "Vospominaniia Gribovskago," 10–11, 54, 57; Tolchenov, *Zhurnal*, 36.

96. *AKV*, 12:179; vol. 13:365–366; Harris, *Diaries*, 3:348; *AR* (1796), 201–202.

97. Tolchenov, *Zhurnal*, 314–316.

Epilogue

1. Leo Braudy, *The Frenzy of Renown* (N.Y., 1986), 384–387.

2. Norbert R. Dreiling, *Official Centennial History of the Volga-German Settlements in Ellis and Rush Counties in Kansas, 1876–1976* (Hays, Kansas, 1976), 35–39, 54–58; Matthew Pekari, *History of St. Catherine's Parish, 1876–1942* (Catherine, 1942; reprinted 1976).

3. Anon., *Konchina imperatritsy Ekateriny Vtoryia: Istoricheskoe i statisticheskoe kratkoe nachertanie o nei, i o Rossii v Eia tsarstvovanie*, tr. from German (M., 1801), 4–5, 14, 21–22, 29; Michael Hadley, "The Sublime Housewife: An 18th-Century German View of Catherine the Great," *Germano-Slavica*, 2 (1977), 181–188.

4. *Memoirs of Dashkov*, 249, 286–288.

5. Anon., "Sketch of the Life of the Late Empress of Russia," *Edinburgh Magazine*, 9 (Feb., 1797), 126–130; Anon., *Authentic Memoirs of the Life and Reign of Catherine II*, 284.

6. *AR* (1796), 201–202, A. G. Cross, "O thou, great monarch of a powr'ful reign!': English Bards and Russian Tsars," *OSP*, 15 (1982), 86; David M. Griffiths, "Castéra-Tooke: The First Western Biographer(s) of Catherine II," *SGECRN*, 10 (1982), 50–61.

7. G. A. Likhotkin, *Sil'ven Mareshal i "Zaveshchanie Ekateriny II"* (L., 1974), 5, 15–16, 44–45; Hugh Ragsdale, *Détente in the Napoleonic Era: Bonaparte and the Russians* (Lawrence, 1980), 20–23, 109–110, 138–141; N. Ia. Eidel'man, *Gran' vekov* (M., 1982), 53, 298; Marianna Tax Choldin, *A Fence around the Empire: Russian Censorship of Western Ideas under the Tsars* (Durham, 1985), 152–156.

8. Shcherbatov, *On the Corruption of Morals in Russia*, 106–107; William H. Hopkins, "The Development of 'Pornographic' Literature in Eighteenth- and Early Nineteenth-Century Russia," Ph.D. diss. (Indiana, 1977), 188, 245–246.

9. Hal Morgan and Kerry Tucker, *Rumor* (Harmondsworth, England, and N.Y., 1984), 81–82.

10. "Vospominaniia Gribovskago," 61; Hopkins, "Development of 'Pornographic' Literature," 240–241.

11. Hopkins, "Development of 'Pornographic' Literature," 371–372, 377, 424; an appendix reprints the whole poem in Russian and English. See also Ivan Barkov, *Luka Mudishchev: A Poem in Four Parts*, tr. Ann Peet and Sharon Miller, illustrated by Alex Gamburg, published and edited by P. Agron (Manuscript Publishing House, Co.: N.Y., 1982).

384   *Notes*

12. Nancy Friday, *Men in Love* (N.Y., 1980), 274.

13. Nancy Friday, *My Secret Garden: Women's Sexual Fantasies* (N.Y., 1973), 166.

14. Simone de Beauvoir, *The Second Sex,* tr. H. M. Parshley (N.Y., 1953), 130; Elizabeth Atwood Lawrence, *Hoofbeats and Society: Studies of Human-Horse Interactions* (Bloomington, 1985), 139, 182–183.

15. Hillary Auteur, *The Courtesans: The Carnal Confessions of Catherine the Great* (N.Y., 1984).

16. Sasha Sokolov, *Palisandriia* (Ann Arbor: Ardis, 1985), 180–181.

17. *Catharine II, Memoirs of the Empress, written by herself with a preface by A. Herzen,* 12–14; N. Ia. Eidel'man, *Gertsen protiv samoderzhaviia: Sekretnaia politicheskaia istoriia Rossii XVIII–XIX vekov i Vol'naia pechat,* 2nd ed. (M., 1984), 87–88, 115–116, 141–142, 166, 256; A. V. Stepanov, *Ekaterina II: eia proiskhozhdenie, intimnaia zhizn' i politika* (Berlin: Heinrich Caspari, n.d.; reprinted Israel, c. 1981); Bernhard Stern, *Die Romanows: Intime Episoden aus ihrem Familien– und Hofleben* (Berlin, 1906), 209–281; idem, *Geschichte der öffentlichen Sittlichkeit in Russland* (Berlin, 1907–1908), 2:522–588; Edgar Saltus, *The Imperial Orgy* (N.Y., 1920); Betty Millan, *Monstrous Regiment: Women Rulers in Men's Worlds* (Shooters Lodge, 1982).

18. N. Dashkevich, *Literaturnyia izobrazheniia imperatritsy Ekateriny II-i i eia tsarstvovaniia* (Kiev, 1898); George C. D. Odell, *Annals of the New York Stage,* (N.Y., 1936), 8:66, 471, 529.

19. Albert Lindner, *Catharina the Second* (N.Y., 1868).

20. Bernard Shaw, *Complete Plays with Prefaces* (N.Y., 1962), 4:561–562, 583.

21. Leslie Halliwell, *The Filmgoer's Companion,* rev. ed. (N.Y., 1967), 139; John Baxter, *The Cinema of Josef von Sternberg* (N.Y., 1971), 113; Pola Negri, *Memoirs of a Star* (Garden City, N.Y., 1970), 15, 243–245, 248; Charles Higham, *Bette: The Life of Bette Davis* (N.Y., 1981), 249–250; Kaye Sullivan, *Films For, By and About Women* (Metuchen, N.J., 1980–1985), 1:49–50; 2:74; *Halliwell's Film Guide,* 5th ed. (London, 1986), 170, 517, 852, 958.

22. Mae West, *Goodness Had Nothing to Do With It* (N.Y., 1981; first published in 1959), 191, 196–198; Lee Israel, *Miss Tallulah Bankhead* (N.Y., 1972), 239–242.

23. West, *Goodness,* 221–223; Michael Todd, Jr., and Susan McCarthy Todd, *A Valuable Property: The Life of Michael Todd* (N.Y., 1983), 119–121.

24. West, *Goodness,* 197, 223–227.

25. Ibid., 223; Jon Tuska, *The Films of Mae West* (Secaucus, N.J., 1973), 169; Todd and Todd, *Valuable Property,* 121–122.

26. Baxter, *Cinema of von Sternberg,* 112–121; Homer Dickens, *The Films of Marlene Dietrich* (N.Y., 1968), 112–115.

27. [Steven Allen and Jayne Meadows Allen], "Meeting of Minds," shows no. 405 and no. 406, 5th draft typescript (Van Nuys, California, 1980), no. 405:1–2, 40–45.

28. Ibid., 45–59, 76–91.

29. Show no. 406:4, 6, 9–23, 36, 42–43, 49, 61, 73–81.

30. Ibid., 69–73, 77–78, 82–84; Marjorie P. K. Weiser and Jean S. Arbeiter, *Womanlist* (N.Y., 1981), 38; Peter Ustinov, *Ustinov in Russia* (N.Y., 1987), 40–45.

31. Audrey Kennett and Victor Kennett, *The Palaces of Leningrad* (London,

1973), 80; "Pamiatnik Ekaterine II, 24 noiabria 1873 g.," *RS*, 2 (1873), 633–648; V. Schwarz, *Leningrad: Art and Architecture,* tr. Olga Shartse (M., 1972), 208.

32. D. A. Rovinskii, *Podrobnyi slovar' russkikh gravirovannykh portretov,* 4 vols. (Spb., 1886–1889), 2:763–903.

33. Bernard Gip, *The Passions and Lechery of Catherine the Great* (London, Edinburgh, and Oslo, 1971); Herbert T. Altenhoff, *Catherine the Great: Art, Sex, Politics* (N.Y., 1975).

Selected Bibliography

I. Writings of Catherine II

"Bumagi Ekateriny II (1744–1796)," *SIRIO*, vols. 7, 10, 13, 27, 42.

Correspondence of Catherine the Great when Grand-Duchess, with Sir Charles Hanbury-Williams and Letters from Count Poniatowski, ed. and tr. the Earl of Ilchester and Mrs. Langford-Brooke. London, 1928.

"Imperatritsa Ekaterina II i kniaz' Potemkin-Tavricheskii, podlinnaia ikh perepiska," *RS*, 1876, vol. 16:33–58, 239–262, 441–478, 571–590.

"Imperatritsa Ekaterina II v eia neizdannykh ili izdannykh ne vpolne pis'makh k I. G. Tsimmermannu," *RS*, 1887, vol. 55:239–320.

Joseph II und Katharina von Russland: Ihr Briefwechsel, ed. Alfred Ritter von Arneth. Vienna, 1869.

Lettres d'amour de Catherine II à Potemkine: correspondance inedite, ed. Georges Oudard. Paris, 1934.

"Liubovnye zapisochki vysokoi osoby XVIII veka," *RA*, 1881, bk. 1:390–403.

Memoirs of Catherine the Great, tr. Katharine Anthony. N.Y., 1927.

Memoirs of the Empress Catherine II, Written by Herself with a Preface by Alexander Herzen. N.Y., 1859.

Nakaz, dannyi Komissii o sochinenii proekta Novogo ulozheniia, ed. N. D. Chechulin. Spb., 1907.

"Perepiska Ekateriny Velikoi s Germanskim imperatorom Iosifom II-m, 1774–1790," *RA*, 1880, bk. 1:210–372.

Pis'ma Ekateriny II k Adamu Vasili'evichu Olsuf'evu, 1762–1783. M., 1863.

Pis'ma i bumagi imperatritsy Ekateriny II khraniashchiiasia v Imperatorskoi publichnoi bilioteke, ed. A. F. Bychkov. Spb., 1873.

"Pis'ma Ekateriny Vtoroi k baronu Grimmu," *RA*, 1878, bk. 3:5–240.

"Pis'ma gosudaryni imperatritsy Ekateriny II-i k kniaziu Mikhailu Nikitichu Volkonskomu," *OV*, 1868, vol. 1:52–162.

Pis'ma imperatritsy Ekateriny II k Datskoi koroleve Iuliane Marii, ed. I. Ia. Shchelkunov. Copenhagen, 1914.

"Pis'ma imperatritsy Ekateriny II k Grimmu (1774–1796)," *SIRIO*, vol. 23. Spb., 1878.

"Pis'ma imperatritsy Ekateriny II k Iakovu Aleksandrovichu Briusu, 1787," *Prilozhenie k Kamer-fur'erskomu zhurnalu 1787 goda*. Spb., 1889.

"Pis'ma imperatritsy Ekateriny Velikoi k fel'dmarshalu grafu Petru Semenovichu Saltykovu, 1762–1771," *RA*, 1886, bk. 3:5–105.

"Pis'ma imp. Ekateriny II k gr. P. V. Zavadovskomu (1775–1777)," ed. Ia. Barskov, *Russkii istoricheskii zhurnal*, 1918, bk. 5:223–257.

"Pis'ma imperatritsy Ekateriny II-ii k raznym gosudarstvennym sanovnikam," *ChIOIDR*, 1863, bk. 3, otd. V:158–184.

"Pis'ma i reskripty Ekateriny II k Moskovskim glavnokomanduiushchim," *RA*, 1872, bk. 2:225–336; bk. 3–4:533–580.

Pis'ma i zapiski imperatritsy Ekateriny Vtoroi k grafu Nikite Ivanovichu Paninu. M., 1863.

"Sobstvennoruchnye ukazy i pis'ma imperatritsy Ekateriny Velikoi," ed. D. V. Tsvetaev, *Zhurnal Ministerstva iustitsii*, 1915, no. 10:182–218.

Sochineniia Imperatritsy Ekateriny II na osnovanii podlinnykh rukopisei i s ob-"iasnitel'nymi primechaniiami, ed. A. N. Pypin, vols. 1–5, 7–12, Spb., 1901–1907.

Voltaire and Catherine the Great: Selected Correspondence, ed. and tr. A. Lentin. Cambridge, 1974.

Zapiski imperatritsy Ekateriny Vtoroi. Spb., 1907.

II. Other Primary Sources

Anon., *Authentic Memoirs of the Life and Reign of Catherine II, Empress of All the Russias, Collected from Authentic MS's, Translations, etc. of the King of Sweden, Right Hon. Lord Mountmorres, Lord Malmesbury, M. de Volney, and Other Indisputable Authorities*, 2nd ed. London, 1797.

Arkhiv gosudarstvennogo soveta, vol. 1, pts. 1–2: *Sovet v tsarstvovanie imperatritsy Ekateriny II-i*. Spb., 1869.

Arkhiv kniazia Vorontsova, ed. P. Bartenev, 40 vols. M., 1870–1895.

Bantysh-Kamenskii, N. N. "Moskovskiia pis'ma v poslednie gody Ekaterininskago tsarstvovaniia ot N. N. Bantysh-Kamenskago k kniaziu A. B. Kurakinu," *RA*, 1876, bk. 3:257–284, 387–413.

Betskoi, I. I. "Pis'ma I. I. Betskago k imperatritse Ekaterine Vtoroi," *RS*, 1896, vol. 88:382–420.

Bezborodko, A. A. "Pis'ma A. A. Bezborodka k grafu P. A. Rumiantsovu, 1777–1793," ed. P. M. Maikov, *Starina i novizna*, 1900, bk. 3:160–313.

Bielfeld, Jacob Friedrich von. *Institutions politiques*. 2 vols. The Hague, 1760.

Bobrinskoi, A. G. "Dnevnik grafa Bobrinskago vedennyi v kadetskom korpuse i vo vremia puteshestviia po Rossii i za granitseiu," *RA*, 1877, bk. 3:116–165.

Buckinghamshire, Earl of. *The Despatches and Correspondence of John, Second Earl of Buckinghamshire, Ambassador to the Court of Catherine II of Russia, 1762–1765*, ed. A. D. Collyer, 2 vols. London, 1900–1902.

Corberon, Marie-Daniel Bourrée, Chevalier de. *Un diplomat Français à la Court de Catharine II 1775–1780, Journal intime*, ed. L. H. Labande, 2 vols. Paris, 1904.

Dashkova, E. R. *The Memoirs of Princess Dashkov*, ed. and tr. Kyril Fitzlyon. London, 1958.

Dimsdale, Thomas. *Tracts on Inoculation, Written and Published at St. Petersburg in the Year 1768.* London, 1781.

Esterhazy, Valentin Ladislas. *Nouvelles lettres du cte Valentin Ladislas Esterhazy à sa femme 1792–1795,* ed. Ernest Daudet. Paris, 1909.

Favier, J.-L. "Zapiski Fav'e," ed. F. A. Bychkov, *IV,* 1887, vol. 29:384–405.

Garnovskii, M. "Zapiski Mikhaila Garnovskago, 1786–1790," *RS,* 1876, vol. 15: 9–38, 237–265, 471–499, 687–718; vol. 16:1–31, 207–238, 399–440.

Gribovskii, A. M. "Vospominaniia i dnevniki Adriana Moiseevicha Gribovskago," *RA,* 1899, bk. 1:1–166.

Harris, James. *Diaries and Correspondence of James Harris, First Earl of Malmesbury,* ed. Third Earl of Malmesbury, 4 vols. London, 1844.

Iakubovskii, I. A. *Karlik favorita: Istoriia zhizni Ivana Andreevicha Iakubovskago, Karlika svetleishego kniazia Platona Aleksandrovicha Zubova, pisannaia im samim,* ed. V. P. Zubov. Munich, 1968.

Justi, Johann Heinrich Gottlieb von. *Die Grundfeste zu der Macht und Glückseligkeit der Staaten.* 2 vols. Königsberg and Leipzig, 1760–61.

Ligne, Prince de. *Lettres du Prince de Ligne à la Marquise de Coigny pendant l'année 1787,* ed., M. de Lescure. Paris, 1886.

Lubianovskii, F. P. "Vospominaniia Fedora Petrovicha Lubianovskago," *RA,* 1872, bk. 10:98–185, 449–533.

Macartney, George. *An Account of Russia in 1767.* London, 1768.

Masson, Charles Francois Philibert. *Secret Memoirs of the Court of Petersburg . . . ,* 2 vols. London, 1800.

Ministerstvo imperatorskago dvora. *Kamer-fur'erskii tseremonial'nyi zhurnal,* 1762–1796. Spb., 1853–1896.

Novikov, N. I. *Izbrannye sochineniia,* ed. G. P. Makogonenko. M.-L., 1951.

Osmnadtsatyi vek, ed. P. I. Bartenev, 4 vols. M., 1868–69.

Parkinson, John, *A Tour of Russia, Siberia, and the Crimea, 1792–1794,* ed. William Collier. London, 1971.

Polnoe sobranie zakonov rossiiskoi imperii. 1st series, 46 vols. Spb., 1830.

Poniatowski, Stanislas August. *Memoirs du roi Stanislas-Auguste Poniatowski,* ed. A. S. Lappo-Danilevskii, S. M. Goriainov and S. F. Platonov. 2 vols. Spb., 1914–1924.

Poroshin, S. A. *Semena Poroshina zapiski, sluzhashchiia k istorii Ego Imperatorskago Vysochestva blagovernago gosudaria tsesarevicha i velikago kniazia Pavla Petrovicha naslednika prestolu Rossiiskago.* Spb., 1844.

Radishchev, A. N. *A Journey from St. Petersburg to Moscow,* tr. Leo Wiener, ed. Roderick Page Thaler. Cambridge, Mass., 1958.

Richardson, William. *Anecdotes of the Russian Empire.* London, 1784; repr. London, 1968.

Rostopchin, F. V. "Rostopchinskie pis'ma," *RA,* 1887, bk. 2:149–185.

Ruhlière, Claude Carloman de. *A History or Anecdotes of the Revolution in Russia.* London, 1797; repr. N.Y., 1970.

Sbornik imperatorskogo russkogo istoricheskogo obshchestva, 148 vols. Spb., 1867–1916.

Sbornik starinnykh bumag, khraniashchikhsia v Muzee P. I. Shchukina, 10 vols. M., 1896–1901.

Ségur, Count de. *Memoirs and Recollections of Count Segur, Ambassador from France to the Courts of Russia and Prussia,* etc., *Written by Himself.* 3 vols. London, 1825–1827.

Senatskii arkhiv, 15 vols. Spb., 1888–1913.

Shcherbatov, M. M. *On the Corruption of Morals in Russia,* ed. and tr. A. Lentin. Cambridge, 1969.

Shchukinskii sbornik, 9 vols. M., 1902–1910.

Stedingk, Curt Bogislaus Christophe, Comte de. *Un Ambassadeur de Suède à la Court de Catharine II; Feld-Maréchal Comte de Stedingk: Choix de dépêches diplomatiques, Rapports secrets et lettres particulières de 1790 à 1796,* ed. La Comtesse Brevern de la Gardie, 2 vols. Stockholm, 1919.

Tolchenov, I. A. *Zhurnal ili zapiska zhizni i prikliucheniia Ivana Alekseevicha Tolchenova,* ed. N. I. Pavlenko. M., 1974.

Weikard, Melchior Adam. "Iz zapisok doktora Veikarta," *RA,* 1886, bk. 3: 229–268.

Zavadovskii, P. V. "Pis'ma grafa P. V. Zavadovskago k fel'dmarshalu grafu P. A. Rumiantsovu," ed. P. M. Maikov, *Starina i novizna,* 1901, bk. 4:223–382.

III. Unpublished Dissertations

Afferica, Joan M. "The Political and Social Thought of Prince M. M. Shcherbatov (1733–1790)," Harvard, 1966.

Allen, Robert V. "The Great Legislative Commission of Catherine II of 1767," Yale, 1950.

Daniel, Wallace L. "Russian Attitudes toward Modernization: The Merchant-Nobility Conflict in the Legislative Commission, 1767–1774," North Carolina, 1973.

Givens, Robert D. "Servitors or Seigneurs: The Nobility and the Eighteenth Century Russian State," California/Berkeley, 1975.

Griffiths, David M. "Russian Court Politics and the Question of an Expansionist Foreign Policy under Catherine II, 1762–1783," Cornell, 1967.

Hartley, Janet M. "The Implementation of the Laws relating to Local Administration, 1775–1796, with Special Reference to the Guberniya of Saint Petersburg," London, 1980.

Hopkins, William H. "The Development of 'Pornographic' Literature in Eighteenth- and Early Nineteenth-Century Russia," Indiana, 1977.

Kamendrowsky, Victor. "State and Economy in Catherinian Russia: The Dismantling of the Mercantile System of Peter the Great," North Carolina, 1982.

Kenney, James J., Jr. "The Vorontsov Party in Russian Politics, 1785–1803: An Examination of the Influence of an Aristocratic Family at the Court of St. Petersburg in an Age of Revolution," Yale, 1975.

Kohut, Zenon E. "The Abolition of Ukrainian Autonomy (1762–1786): A Case Study of the Integration of a nonRussian Area into the Empire," Pennsylvania, 1975.

Leonard, Carol S. "A Study of the Reign of Peter III of Russia," Indiana, 1976.

Misunias, Romuald J. "Russia and Sweden, 1772–1778," Yale, 1972.

Munro, George E. "The Development of St. Petersburg as an Urban Center during the Reign of Catherine II (1762–1796)," North Carolina, 1973.

Pavlova-Sil'vanskaia, N. P. " 'Uchrezhdenie o guberniiakh' 1775 goda i ego klassovaia sushchnost'," Moscow State University, 1964.

Permenter, Hannelore R. "The Personality and Cultural Interests of Empress Catherine II as Revealed in Her Correspondence with Friedrich Melchior Grimm," Texas/Austin, 1969.

Petschauer, Peter. "The Education and Development of an Enlightened Absolutist: The Youth of Catherine the Great, 1729–1762," New York University, 1969.

Rasmussen, Karen M. "Catherine II and Peter I: The Idea of a Just Monarch: The Evolution of an Attitude in Catharinian Russia," California/Berkeley, 1973.

Von Herzen, Michael A. "Nikolai Ivanovich Novikov: The St. Petersburg Years," California/Berkeley, 1975.

Weinbaum, Alexandra T. "N. I. Novikov (1744–1818): An Interpretation of His Career and Ideas," Columbia, 1975.

IV. Secondary Works

Alden, John R. *Stephen Sayre: American Revolutionary Adventurer.* Baton Rouge, 1983.

Alexander, John T. *Autocratic Politics in a National Crisis: The Imperial Russian Government and Pugachev's Revolt, 1773–1775.* Bloomington, 1969.

———. *Bubonic Plague in Early Modern Russia: Public Health and Urban Disaster.* Baltimore, 1980.

———. "Catherine II, Bubonic Plague, and the Problem of Industry in Moscow," *AHR,* 1974, vol. 79:637–671.

———. "Catherine the Great and Public Health," *Journal of the History of Medicine and Allied Sciences,* 1981, vol. 36:185–204.

———. *Emperor of the Cossacks: Pugachev and the Frontier Jacquerie of 1773–1775.* Lawrence, 1973.

———. "Nakaz of Catherine the Great," *MERSH,* 1981, vol. 24:45–49.

———. "St. Petersburg and Moscow in Early Urban Policy," *Journal of Urban History,* 1982, vol. 8:145–169.

———. "Tarakanova, Princess," *MERSH,* 1984, vol. 38:173–177.

Anisimov, E. V. *Rossiia v seredine XVIII veka: bor'ba za nasledie Petra.* M. 1986.

Anon., *Konchina imperatritsy Ekateriny Vtoryia: Istoricheskoe i statisticheskoe kratkoe nachertanie o nei, i o Rossii v Eia tsarstvovanie.* M., 1801.

Asprey, Robert B. *Frederick the Great: The Magnificent Enigma.* N.Y., 1986.

Atkins, Muriel. *Russia and Iran, 1780–1828.* Minneapolis, 1980.

Bain, R. Nisbet. *Peter III, Emperor of Russia.* London, 1902; repr. N.Y., 1971.

Barsukov, Aleksandr. *Razskazy iz russkoi istorii XVIII veka.* Spb., 1885.

Bartlett, Roger P. "Catherine II, Voltaire and Henry IV of France," *SGECRN,* 1981, no. 9:41–50.

———. *Human Capital: The Settlement of Foreigners in Russia, 1762–1804.* Cambridge, 1979.

———. "I. E. and the Free Economic Society's Essay Competition," *SGECRN,* 1980, no. 8:58–67.

Barton, H. Arnold. *Scandinavia in the Revolutionary Era, 1760–1815.* Minneapolis, 1986.

Batalden, Stephen K. *Catherine II's Greek Prelate: Eugenios Voulgaris in Russia 1771–1806.* N.Y., 1982.

Beskrovnyi, L. G. *Russkaia armiia i flot v XVIII veke.* M., 1958.

Bil'basov, V. A. *Istoricheskiia monografiia,* 5 vols. Spb., 1901.

———. *Istoriia Ekateriny Vtoroi,* 3rd ed., vols. 1–2, vol. 12, pts. 1–2. Berlin, 1900.

———. "Pokhody Ekateriny II po Volge i Dnepru," *RS,* 1896, vol. 88:423–445.

———. "Vysylka iz Rossii printsa Viurtembergskago Fridrikha," *RS,* 1892, vol. 73:459–468.

Blackwell, William L. "Citizen Genet and the Revolution in Russia," *French Historical Studies,* 1963, vol. 3:72–92.

Bogoliubov, V. *N. I. Novikov i ego vremia.* M., 1916.

Bolkhovitinov, Nikolai N. *The Beginnings of Russian-American Relations 1775–1815,* tr. Elena Levin. Cambridge, Mass., 1975.

Brikner, A. G. "Ekateriny II i frantsuzskaia revoliutsiia," *IV,* 1895, vol. 61:411–420.

————. "Ekaterina II v perepiske s doktorom Tsimmermannom 1784–1791," *RS,* 1887, vol. 54: 271–294, 591–612.

————. *Istoriia Ekateriny Vtoroi.* Spb., 1885.

————. "Puteshestvie Ekateriny II v Krym," *IV,* 1885, vol. 21:5–23, 242–264, 444–509.

————. "Puteshestvie imperatritsy Ekateriny II v Mogilev v 1780 godu," *Russkii vestnik,* 1881, vol. 155, no. 8:459–509; no. 9: 311–367.

————. "Puteshestvie imperatritsy Ekateriny II v Vyshnii Volochek i Moskvu v 1785 godu," *IV,* 1881, vol. 6:681–702.

————. "Zel'mira: Epizod iz istorii tsarstvovaniia imperatritsy Ekateriny II," *IV,* 1890, vol. 41:277–303, 551–572.

[Castéra, Jean-Henri]. *The Life of Catharine II, Empress of Russia,* enlarged tr. [William Tooke], 3 vols. London, 1798.

Chechulin, N. D. "Chetyre goda zhizni Ekateriny II, 1755–1758: Ekaterina i Poniatovskii," *Russkii istoricheskii zhurnal,* 1922, bk. 8:151–177.

Chumikov, A. A. "Gustav IV-i i velikaia kniazhna Aleksandra Pavlovna," *RS,* 1887, bk. 1:59–98.

Cross, A. G. *"By the Banks of the Thames": Russians in Eighteenth Century Britain.* Newtonville, Mass., 1980.

————. " 'O thou, great monarch of a powr'ful reign!': English Bards and Russian Tsars," *OSP,* 1982, vol. 15:80–94.

————. "Richard Paton and the Battle of Chesme," *SGECRN,* 1986, no. 14: 31–37.

————. "The Duchess of Kingston in Russia," *History Today,* 1977, vol. 27: 390–395.

Dashkevich, N. *Literaturnyia izobrazheniia imperatritsy Ekateriny II-i i eia tsarstvovaniia.* Kiev, 1898.

Davis, Curtis Carroll. *The King's Chevalier: A Biography of Lewis Littlepage.* Indianapolis, 1961.

Drizen, N. V. "Gustav IV i velikaia kniazhna Aleksandra Pavlovna, 1794–1796 gg.," *RS,* 1896, vol. 88:193–207.

Dukes, Paul. *Catherine the Great and the Russian Nobility: A Study Based on the Materials of the Legislative Commission of 1767.* Cambridge, 1967.

Dzhedzhula, K. E. *Rossiia i velikaia frantsuzskaia burzhuaznaia revoliutsiia kontsa XVIII veka.* Kiev, 1972.

Dzhincharadze, V. Z. "Iz istorii tainoi ekspeditsii pri Senate (1762–1801)," *Uchenye zapiski Novgorodskii gos. ped. inst,* 1957, vol. 2, fasc. 2, istoriko-fil. fak., 83–118.

Eidel'man, N. Ia. *Gertsen protiv samoderzhaviia.* 2nd ed. M., 1984.

————. *Gran' vekov.* M., 1982.

Esipov, G. "Amazonskaia rota pri Ekaterine II," *IV,* 1886, vol. 23:71–75.

Filippov, A. N. "K voprosu o pervoistochnikakh Zhalovannoi Gramoty dvoriantsvu 21 aprelia 1785 g.," *Izvestiia Akademii nauk SSSR,* 1926, vol. 20: 423–443, 479–498.

Firsov, N. N. *Petr III i Ekaterina II: Pervye gody eia tsarstvovaniia: Opyt kharakteristiki*. Petrograd, M., 1915.

Fisher, Alan W. *The Russian Annexation of the Crimea, 1772–1783*. Cambridge, 1970.

Fox, Frank. "Negotiating with the Russians: Ambassador Segur's Mission to Saint-Petersburg, 1784–1789," *French Historical Studies*, 1971, vol. 7:47–71.

Ganzen, P. "Russkii kniazheskii dvor v gorode Gorsense, 1780–1807 gg.," *Vestnik Evropy*, 1901, vol. 211:5–37, 625–655.

Gip, Bernard. *The Passions and Lechery of Catherine the Great*. London, 1971.

Golder, Frank. *John Paul Jones in Russia*. Garden City, N.Y., 1927.

Golombievskii, A. A. *Biografiia kniazia G. G. Orlova*. M., 1904.

Griffiths, David M. "Castéra-Tooke: The First Western Biographer(s) of Catherine II," *SGECRN*, 1982, no. 10:50–62.

———. "The Rise and Fall of the Northern System: Court Politics in the First Half of Catherine II's Reign," *CSS*, 1970, vol. 4:547–569.

Grigor'ev, V. "Zertsalo upravy blagochiniia," *Russkii istoricheskii zhurnal*, 1917, bk. 3–4:73–103.

Grot, Ia. K. "Ekaterina II i Gustav III," *Sbornik otdeleniia russkago iazyka i slovesnosti imperatorskoi Akademii nauk*, 1877, vol. 18:1–115.

———. "Ekaterina II v perepiske s Grimmom," *Sbornik otdeleniia russkago iazyka i slovesnosti imperatorskoi Akademii nauk*, 1879, vol. 20:1–130; 1881, vol. 21:1–300; 1884, vol. 23:1–339.

Hartley, Janet. "Town Government in Saint Petersburg Guberniya after the Charter to the Towns of 1785," *SEER*, 1984, vol. 62:66–84.

Hassell, James E. "Catherine II and Procurator General Vjazemskij," *JGO*, 1976, vol. 24:23–30.

Hittle, J. Michael. *The Service City: State and Townsmen in Russia, 1600–1800*. Cambridge, Mass., 1979.

Hopkins, Donald R. *Princes and Peasants: Smallpox in History*. Chicago, 1983.

Jones, Robert E. *The Emancipation of the Russian Nobility, 1762–1785*. Princeton, 1973.

———. *Provincial Development in Russia: Catherine II and Jakob Sievers*. New Brunswick, 1984.

Jones, W. Gareth. *Nikolay Novikov: Enlightener of Russia*. Cambridge, 1984.

Kaganovich, A. L. *"Mednyi vsadnik": Istoriia sozdaniia monumenta*. L., 1975.

Kahan, Arcadius. *The Plough, the Hammer, and the Knout: An Economic History of Eighteenth Century Russia*. Chicago, 1985.

Kamendrowsky, Victor, and Griffiths, David M. "The Fate of the Trading Nobility Controversy in Russia: A Chapter in the Relationship between Catherine II and the Russian Nobility," *JGO*, 1978, vol. 26:198–221.

Kaplan, Herbert H. *The First Partition of Poland*. N.Y., 1962.

———. *Russia and the Outbreak of the Seven Years' War*. Berkeley and Los Angeles, 1968.

Kobeko, D. F. "Imperatritsa Ekaterina Alekseevna, pis'ma eia k komendantu Tsigleru (1786–1787 gg.)," *RS*, 1892, vol. 73:267–270.

Kornilovich O. E. "Zapiski Imperatritsy Ekateriny II," *Zhurnal Ministerstva narodnago prosveshcheniia*, 1912, vol. 37:37–74.

Larivière, Charles de. *Catharine II et la Revolution Française*. Paris, 1895.

LeDonne, John P. "Appointments to the Russian Senate," *CMRS*, 1975, vol. 16: 27–56.

————. *Ruling Russia: Politics and Administration in the Age of Absolutism, 1762–1796*. Princeton, 1984.

Likhotkin, G. A. *Sil'ven Mareshal i "Zaveshchanie Ekateriny II"* (*k istorii odnoi literaturnoi mistifikatsii*). L., 1974.

Longworth, Philip. *The Art of Victory: The Life and Achievements of Field Marshal Suvorov* (*1729–1800*). N.Y., 1965.

Lord, Robert H. *The Second Partition of Poland*. Cambridge, Mass., 1915.

Madariaga, Isabel de. "Autocracy and Sovereignty," *CASS*, 1982, vol. 16:369–387.

————. *Britain, Russia, and the Armed Neutrality of 1780: Sir James Harris's Mission to St. Petersburg during the American Revolution*. New Haven, 1962.

————. "Catherine II and Montesquieu between Prince M. M. Schcherbatov and Denis Diderot," in *L'Eta dei lumi settecento europeo in honore di Franco Venturi*. Naples, 1985, vol. 2: 611–650.

————. "Catherine and the *Philosophes*," in A. G. Cross, ed., *Russia and the West in the Eighteenth Century*, Newtonville, Mass., 1983, 30–52.

————. *Russia in the Age of Catherine the Great*. New Haven, 1981.

————. "The Secret Austro-Russian Treaty of 1781," *SEER*, 1959, vol. 38:114–145.

Marcum, James W. "Catherine II and the French Revolution," *Canadian Slavonic Papers*, 1974, vol. 16:189–202.

Marker, Gary. *Publishing, Printing, and the Origins of Intellectual Life in Russia, 1700–1800*. Princeton, 1985.

McArthur, Gilbert H. "Catherine II and the Masonic Circle of N. T. Novikov," *CSS*, 1970, vol. 4:529–546.

Morison, Samuel Eliot. *John Paul Jones: A Sailor's Biography*. Boston, 1959.

Myl'nikov, A. S. *Legenda o russkom printse*. L., 1987.

Orlov, A. S. *Volneniia na Urale v seredine XVIII veka*. M., 1979.

Ovchinnikov, R. V. *Manifesty i ukazy E. I. Pugacheva*. M., 1980.

Panchenko, A. M., " 'Potemkinskie derevni' kak kul'turnyi mif," *XVIII vek*, 1983, vol. 14:93–104.

Papmehl, K. A. *Freedom of Expression in Eighteenth Century Russia*. The Hague, 1971.

Polovtsoff, Alexander. *The Favourites of Catherine the Great*. London, 1947.

Raeff, Marc, ed. *Catherine the Great: A Profile*. N.Y., 1972.

————. "The Domestic Policies of Peter III and His Overthrow," *AHR*, 1970, vol. 75:1289–1310.

————. "The Empress and the Vinerian Professor: Catherine II's Projects of Government Reforms and Blackstone's *Commentaries*," *OSP*, 1974, vol. 7:18–41.

————. *Origins of the Russian Intelligentsia: The Eighteenth-Century Nobility*. N.Y., 1966.

————. *The Well-Ordered Police State: Social and Institutional Change in the Germanies and Russia, 1600–1800*. New Haven, 1983.

Ransel, David L. *The Politics of Catherinian Russia: The Panin Party*. New Haven, 1975.

Roider, Karl A., Jr. *Austria's Eastern Question, 1700–1790*. Princeton, 1982.

Shchepkin, E. N. *Russko-avstriiskii soiuz vo vremia semiletnei voiny 1746–1758 gg*. Spb., 1902.

Shil'der, N. K. *Imperator Pavel pervyi*. Spb., 1901.

————. "Konchina Ekateriny II i votsarenie Pavla I," *RS*, 1896, vol. 88:472–480.

Shtrange, M. M. *Russkoe obshchestvo i frantsuzskaia revoliutsiia 1789–1794 gg*. M., 1956.

Shumigorskii, E. S. *Ekaterina Ivanovna Nelidova, 1758–1839*. Spb., 1898.
———. *Imperatritsa Mariia Feodorovna (1759–1828)*. Spb., 1892.
Sivkov, K. V. "Podpol'naia politicheskaia literatura v Rossii v poslednei treti XVIII v.," *Istoricheskie zapiski*, 1946, vol. 19:63–101.
———. "Samozvanchestvo v Rossii v poslednei treti XVIII v.," *Istoricheskie zapiski*, 1950, vol. 31:88–135.
Soloveytchik, George. *Potemkin: Soldier, Statesman, Lover and Consort of Catherine of Russia*. N.Y., 1947.
Thaden, Edward C. *Russia's Western Borderlands, 1710–1870*. Princeton, 1984.
Troitskii, S. M. *Finansovaia politika russkogo absoliutizma v XVIII veke*. M., 1966.
———. *Rossiia v XVIII veke*. M., 1982.
Wilson, Arthur M. *Diderot*. N.Y., 1972.

V. Fiction

Auteur, Hillary. *The Courtesans: The Carnal Confessions of Catherine the Great*. N.Y., 1984.
Barkov, I. S. *Utekhi imperatritsy*. Tel Aviv, n.d.
Carnegie, Sacha. *The Banners of Power*. London, 1972.
Ivanov, V. N. *Imperatritsa Fike: istoricheskie povesti*. M., 1968.
Lindner, Albert. *Catharina the Second, A Tragedy in Five Acts*. N.Y., 1868.
Pikul', V. S. *Favorit: roman-khroniki vremen Ekateriny II*. 2 vols. L., 1984–85.
Pistolenko, V. I. *Skazanie o sotnike Timofee Padurove: roman*. M., 1974.
Ravich, N. A. *Dve stolitsy: istoricheskii roman*. M., 1975.
Zapadov, A. V. *Opasnyi dnevnik: istoricheskaia povest'*. M., 1974.

Cast of Characters

Bobrinskoi, Aleksei	Catherine's bastard son
Bruce, Praskov'ia	confidante
Chernyshev, Zakhar	courtier, general, official
Dashkova, Ekaterina	companion and rival
Elizabeth I	Empress of Russia
Frederick II, the Great	King of Prussia
Grimm, Friedrich	confidant and correspondent
Gustavus III	King of Sweden, cousin
Ivan VI, Ivan Antonovich	baby emperor, lifelong prisoner
Johanna Elizabeth	Catherine's mother
Joseph II	Emperor-King of Austria
Maria Theresa	Empress-Queen of Austria
Orlov, Aleksei	conspirator and commander
Orlov, Grigorii	Guardsman, favorite
Panin, Nikita	director of foreign affairs
Paul Petrovich, Paul I	Catherine's son and heir
Peter III, Peter Fedorovich	Catherine's husband
Poniatowski, Stanislas	King of Poland
Potemkin, Grigorii	flamboyant favorite
Pugachev, Emel'ian	rebel cossack
Radishchev, Alexander	nobleman dissident
Rumiantsev, Peter	military hero, field marshal
Sheshkovskii, Stepan	head of secret police
Suvorov, Alexander	military hero, field marshal
Viazemskii, Alexander	supervisor of internal affairs
Zavadovskii, Peter	Ukrainian favorite and official
Zubov, Platon	final favorite

Index